JOURNAL FOR THE STUDY OF THE NEW TESTAMENT
SUPPLEMENT SERIES
90

Executive Editor
Stanley E. Porter

JSOT Press
Sheffield

Rhetoric and the New Testament

Essays from the 1992 Heidelberg Conference

edited by

Stanley E. Porter

and

Thomas H. Olbricht

Journal for the Study of the New Testament
Supplement Series 90

Copyright © 1993 Sheffield Academic Press

Published by JSOT Press
JSOT Press is an imprint of
Sheffield Academic Press Ltd
343 Fulwood Road
Sheffield S10 3BP
England

Typeset by Sheffield Academic Press
and
Printed on acid-free paper in Great Britain
by Biddles Ltd
Guildford

British Library Cataloguing in Publication Data

Rhetoric and the New Testament: Essays
from the 1992 Heidelberg Conference.—
(JSNT Supplement Series, ISSN 0143-5108;
No. 90)
  I. Porter, Stanley E. II. Olbricht,
  Thomas H. III. Series

ISBN 1-85075-449-7

CONTENTS

PART II
RHETORIC AND QUESTIONS OF METHOD

PREFACE

The publishing of Hans Dieter Betz's commentary on Galatians marked the rediscovery of rhetorical analysis of Scripture in America. Ancient rhetoric was rediscovered by English professors before World War I, resulting in a new association of professors specializing in speech, now designated the Speech Communication Association. Once again rhetoric was rediscovered by composition professors after World War II. Some interest in ancient rhetoric continued among classical scholars in America from the nineteenth century. With these developments and those elsewhere, internationally rhetoric has come to the forefront in various disciplines in the past two decades, and a number of associations with rhetoric in the title have been generated.

In biblical studies a special interest in rhetorical analysis developed on the west coast of the USA because of the work and publications of Wilhelm Wuellner, Burton Mack, James Hester, Stanley Porter, Jeffrey Reed, Ronald Hock and myself. Several papers have been presented at regional meetings and a special study group has been created in the Western Regional meetings of the Society of Biblical Literature.

In 1990 it occurred to me that while Americans interested in rhetorical analysis met with some frequency, no international conferences of rhetorical specialists had convened. Eventually with the support of Wuellner and Hester, the decision was made to hold the conference at Pepperdine University's Moore Haus in Heidelberg in July of 1992.

The next task was collecting the names of perspective conferees. We hoped to have more Europeans than Americans. We also hoped for some mix of biblical scholars, speech rhetoricians and classicists. We had in mind a working group of about thirty persons, with a few other attendees permitted. By the time we were ready to send out an announcement of the conference and a call for papers, we had accumulated a list of ninety persons. We were surprised and extremely pleased with the response. Almost every person we hoped might attend responded and indicated an interest. The final result was that more persons committed to attend than we had planned for, so we had to change the format of the conference to accommodate the larger numbers. A South African in a moment of euphoria declared that the conference roster was a veritable who's who of rhetorical scholars.

The conference is now history. The printed essays indicate its vitality and quality. We hope to repeat the conference at least every other year. The next projected conference is slated for South Africa in the summer of 1994. We wish to thank David Davenport, President, William B. Adrian, Provost, and William B. Phillips, Dean of International Programs and Research of Pepperdine University for permissions, encouragement, the facilities in Heidelberg, and miscellaneous expenses and staff support. Special appreciation is in order to Pam Moore, director of Moore Haus, who by her dedication and efficient efforts made our stay there very pleasant. We also need to thank Dr William S. Banowsky who helped us obtain a grant from the corporation of which he is Executive Vice President, National Medical Enterprises. We also are indebted to Dr David Worley for additional funds. Our final indebtedness is to Stanley E. Porter, who proposed that Sheffield Academic Press publish the proceedings.

Thomas H. Olbricht

CONTRIBUTORS

CLAUDIO BASEVI
Professor of New Testament at the University of Navarre, Spain

KLAUS BERGER
Professor of New Testament at the University of Heidelberg, Germany

PIETER J.J. BOTHA
Senior Lecturer in Department of New Testament at UNISA, Pretoria, Republic of South Africa

JUAN CHAPA
Faculty of Theology at the University of Navarre, Spain

C. JOACHIM CLASSEN
Professor of Classics at the University of Göttingen, Germany

JEFFREY A. CRAFTON
Department of Humanities at the College of DuPage, Glen Ellyn, IL, USA

†ANGELICO-SALVATORE DI MARCO
Messina, Italy

DAVID HELLHOLM
Professor of Theology at the University of Oslo, Norway

GLEN HOLLAND
Professor in the Department of Philosophy and Religious Studies at Allegheny College, Meadville, PA, USA

FRANK W. HUGHES
Rector of St Mark's Episcopal Church, Lewistown, PA, USA

B.C. LATEGAN
Professor of New Testament in the University of Stellenbosch, Republic of South Africa

J. IAN H. MCDONALD
Reader in Christian Ethics and New Testament Studies, University of Edinburgh, Scotland

DANIEL MARGUERAT
Professor in Faculty of Theology at the University of Lausanne, Switzerland

JOHN W. MARSHALL
Doctoral student in Department of Religion at Princeton University, Princeton, NJ, USA

JAMES J. MURPHY
Professor of Rhetoric and Communication at the University of California, Davis, USA

THOMAS H. OLBRICHT
Professor of New Testament at Pepperdine University, Malibu, CA, USA

STANLEY E. PORTER
Associate Professor of Religious Studies at Trinity Western University, Langley, BC, Canada

JEFFREY T. REED
Talbot Theological Seminary, Biola University, La Mirada, CA, USA

VERNON K. ROBBINS
Doctoral Student in Department of Biblical Studies, University of Sheffield, England

MARC SCHOENI
Assistant, Faculty of Theology at the University of Lausanne, Switzerland

FOLKER SIEGERT
Professor in the Faculty of Theology at the University of Neuchâtel, Switzerland

JOOP SMIT
Professor of New Testament at the University of Utrecht, the Netherlands

A.H. SNYMAN
Professor of New Testament at the University of the Orange Free State, Bloemenfontein, Republic of South Africa

DENNIS L. STAMPS
Curate of St Mary's Church, Moseley, Birmingham, England

LAURI THURÉN
Clergyman in Turku, Finland

JOHANNES N. VORSTER
Senior Lecturer, Department of New Testament at UNISA, Pretoria, Republic of South Africa

DUANE F. WATSON
Professor of New Testament at Malone College, Canton, OH, USA

WILHELM WUELLNER
Emeritus Professor of New Testament at Pacific School of Religion, Berkeley, CA, USA

ABBREVIATIONS

ANRW	*Aufstieg und Niedergang der römischen Welt*
BBB	Bonner biblische Beiträge
BDF	F. Blass, A. Debrunner and R.W. Funk, *A Greek Grammar of the New Testament*
BETL	Bibliotheca ephemeridum theologicarum lovaniensium
BEvT	Beiträge zur evangelischen Theologie
Bib	*Biblica*
BJRL	*Bulletin of the John Rylands University Library of Manchester*
BSac	*Bibliotheca Sacra*
BTB	*Biblical Theology Bulletin*
BWANT	Beiträge zur Wissenschaft vom Alten und Neuen Testament
BZ	*Biblische Zeitschrift*
CBQ	*Catholic Biblical Quarterly*
ConBNT	Coniectanea biblica, New Testament
EKKNT	Evangelisch-Katholischer Kommentar zum Neuen Testament
ETL	*Ephemerides theologicae lovanienses*
ETR	*Etudes théologiques et religieuses*
EvQ	*Evangelical Quarterly*
ExpTim	*Expository Times*
FFNT	Foundations and Facets: New Testament
FN	*Filología Neotestamentaria*
FRLANT	Forschungen zur Religion und Literatur des Alten und Neuen Testaments
GRBS	*Greek, Roman, and Byzantine Studies*
GTA	Göttinger Theologische Arbeiten
HbAltW	Handbuch der Altertumswissenschaft
HNTC	Harper's NT Commentaries
HTR	*Harvard Theological Review*
HUCA	*Hebrew Union College Annual*
ICC	International Critical Commentary
Int	*Interpretation*
JAAR	*Journal of the American Academy of Religion*
JAC	Jahrbuch für Antike und Christentum
JBL	*Journal of Biblical Literature*
JETS	*Journal of Evangelical Theological Society*
JR	*Journal of Religion*
JSNT	*Journal for the Study of the New Testament*
JSNTSup	*Journal for the Study of the New Testament*, Supplement Series
JSOT	*Journal for the Study of the Old Testament*

JSOTSup	*Journal for the Study of the Old Testament*, Supplement Series
JSPSup	*Journal for the Study of the Pseudepigrapha*, Supplement Series
JTC	*Journal for Theology and the Church*
KEK	H.A.W. Meyer (ed.), Kritisch-exegetischer Kommentar über das Neue Testament
LB	*Linguistica Biblica*
LCL	Loeb Classical Library
LSJ	Liddell–Scott–Jones, *Greek–English Lexicon*
NCB	New Century Bible
Neot	*Neotestamentica*
NICNT	New International Commentary on the New Testament
NIGTC	The New International Greek Testament Commentary
NovT	*Novum Testamentum*
NovTSup	*Novum Testamentum*, Supplements
NTAbh	Neutestamentliche Abhandlungen
NTD	Das Neue Testament Deutsch
NTS	*New Testament Studies*
NTTS	New Testament Tools and Studies
OCD	*Oxford Classical Dictionary*
PG	J. Migne (ed.), *Patrologia graeca*
QJS	*Quarterly Journal of Speech*
RelSRev	*Religious Studies Review*
RivB	*Rivista biblica*
RSR	*Recherches de science religieuse*
SBLDS	SBL Dissertation Series
SBLSP	SBL Seminar Papers
SE	*Studia Evangelica I, II, III* (= TU 73 [1959], 87 [1964], 88 [1964], etc.)
SJOT	*Scandinavian Journal of the Old Testament*
SNT	Studien zum Neuen Testament
SNTSMS	Society for New Testament Studies Monograph Series
SR	*Studies in Religion/Sciences religieuses*
SUNT	Studien zur Umwelt des Neuen Testaments
TDNT	G. Kittel and G. Friedrich (eds.), *Theological Dictionary of the New Testament*
TLZ	*Theologischer Literaturzeitung*
TZ	*Theologische Zeitschrift*
WBC	Word Biblical Commentary
WdF	Wege der Forschung
WUNT	Wissenschaftliche Untersuchungen zum Neuen Testament
WW	*Word and World*
ZNW	*Zeitschrift für die neutestamentliche Wissenschaft*
ZPE	*Zeitschrift für Papyrologie und Epigraphik*
ZTK	*Zeitschrift für Theologie und Kirche*

DEDICATION TO WILHELM WUELLNER

We as colleagues and friends, participants in the 1992 Heidelberg Conference on Rhetorical Analysis of Biblical Documents, dedicate this volume of proceedings to Wilhelm Wuellner.

Professor Wuellner has been more active in the international promotion of rhetorical analysis of Scripture than any other person. While it cannot be said that he has created a school of rhetorical analysis, inasmuch as that implies a specific methodology and agenda, yet in the encouragement and, in certain cases, training of younger scholars, no one has expended more time and energy than Wilhelm. He has published a number of seminal articles, both in rhetorical analysis and on the history and current status of rhetorical developments. More than anyone else, Professor Wuellner has been in contact with scholars in the United States, Canada, Europe, South Africa, Australia, Japan and elsewhere. He has compiled bibliographies of books and articles as well as lists of scholars, and has willingly made them available to others. An international meeting of scholars interested in rhetorical analysis such as the one at Heidelberg, the first of its kind, would not have been possible without the wide ranging contacts of Professor Wuellner. He provided the names and insights concerning those interested in such a conference, especially outside of the United States.

We take great pleasure in honoring and saluting Professor Wilhelm Wuellner with the dedication of this volume.

Wilhelm Wuellner

Wilhelm Wuellner was born on February 21, 1927, in Bochum, Germany. After taking his undergraduate and seminary degrees (BD, 1951) in Germany, he entered the University of Chicago from which he was granted the PhD in 1958. He was married to Flora May Slosson in 1954 and is the father of three daughters. He became a citizen of the United States in 1959.

Before embarking upon an academic career, Professor Wuellner served in various capacities in the church. From 1951–1954 he was vicar in the Westphalian Synod of the Evangelical Church of Germany. In 1958 he was ordained by the Iowa Synod of the then United Lutheran Church, now the Evangelical Lutheran Church of America. From 1958–1960 he served as a part-time campus minister at Grinnell College and mission developer at the Amana Colonies, Iowa, for the Lutheran Board of Home Missions. From 1962–1965 he was a member of the New England committee on college and university ministries of the Lutheran Church of America.

Professor Wuellner has received various honors. From 1952–1953 he was a World Council of Churches Fellow at Chicago Theological Seminary. While working on his PhD in Chicago he was recipient of a Divinity School scholarship. In 1970–1971 he was an ATS Research Fellow, in 1977–1978 he received an NEH Research Fellowship, and in 1984–1985, a Lutheran Brotherhood Research Fellowship.

Professor Wuellner commenced his academic career in 1957 as Assistant Professor at Mission House Theological Seminary, Sheboygan, Wisconsin. From 1958–1960 he was an Assistant Professor at Grinnell College. From 1960–1965 he was Professor of New Testament at Hartford Seminary Foundation. In 1965 he became Professor of New Testament at the Pacific School of Religion, from which position he retired in 1992. He also served from 1969–1982 as Chairman of the Center for Hermeneutical Studies in Modern Culture, for the Graduate Theological Union and the University of California, Berkeley.

Professor Wuellner has been active in a number of professional organizations. He has been a member of the Society of Biblical Literature since 1957. From 1958–1964 he was a member of the National Association of Biblical Instructors, from 1965–1970 of the American Academy of Religion, from 1958–1975 of the American Schools of Oriental Research, from 1960–1974 of the American Association of University Professors, from 1960–1973 of the American Oriental Society, from 1964–1965 of the Society for the Scientific Study of Religion, from 1966–1968 of the Berkeley-Santa Clara Ecumenical Colloquium, and from 1967–1973 of the West Coast Theological Group. He has been a member of the following organizations from the dates indicated: 1960 Catholic Biblical Association of America, 1964 Studiorum Novi Testamenti Societas,

1968 Dölger-Institut für Antike und Christentum, 1969 Center for Hermeneutical Studies, 1973 Institutum Judaicum Delitzschianum, 1979 International Society for the History of Rhetoric, and 1982 North American Patristic Society.

Professor Wuellner wrote his dissertation at the University of Chicago on 'The Word of God and the Church of Christ: The Ecumenical Implications of Biblical Hermeneutics' (University of Chicago, June 1958).

He has published two books, *The Meaning of 'Fishers of Men'* in the New Testament Library series (Philadelphia: Westminster Press, 1967), and *The Surprising Gospel: Intriguing Psychological Insights from the New Testament*, co-authored with Robert C. Leslie (Nashville: Abingdon Press, 1984).

Professor Wuellner also served as editor of *The Protocol of the Colloquy of the Center for Hermeneutical Studies* (Berkeley: Center for Hermeneutical Studies) numbering above fifty colloquies. He has also lectured widely internationally.

BIBLIOGRAPHY OF WILHELM WEULLNER

'Haggadic Homily Genre in I Corinthians 1–3', *JBL* 89 (1970), pp. 199-204.

'The Sociological Implications of I Corinthians 1:26-28 Reconsidered', *Studia Evangelica* VI (ed. E.A. Livingston; TU, 112; Berlin: Akademie Verlag, 1973), pp. 666-72.

'Paul's Rhetoric of Argumentation in Romans: An Alternative to the Donfried–Karris Debate Over Romans', *CBQ* 38 (1976), pp. 330-351. Repr. in K. Donfried (ed.), *The Romans Debate* (Minneapolis: Augsburg, 1977; Peabody, MA: Hendrickson, 2nd edn, 1991).

'Der Jakobusbrief im Licht der Rhetoric und Textpragmatic', *LB* 43 (1978), pp. 5-66.

'Toposforschung und Torahinterpretation bei Paulus und Jesus', *NTS* 24 (1978), pp. 463-83.

'Ursprung und Verwendung der *sophos-, dynatos, -eugenes*-Formal in 1 Kor 1,26', in *Donum Gentilicium: New Testament Studies in Honour of David Daube* (ed. C.K. Barrett, E. Bammel and W.D. Davies; Oxford: Clarendon Press, 1978), pp. 165-84.

'Greek Rhetoric and Pauline Argumentation', in *Early Christian Literature and the Classical Intellectual Tradition: In Honorem Robert M. Grant* (ed. W. Schoedel and R.L. Wilken; Théologie Historique, 53; Paris: Beauchesne, 1979), pp. 177-88.

'Tradition and Interpretation of the "Wise-Powerful-Noble" Triad in 1 Corinthians 1:26', *Studia Evangelica* VII (1982), pp. 557-62.

'Paul as Pastor: The Function of Rhetorical Questions in First Corinthians', in *L'Apôtre Paul: Personalité, style et conception du ministère* (ed. A. Vanhoye; BETL, 73; Leuven: Leuven University Press, 1986), pp. 49-77.

'Stil der Bibel und Lust der Auslegung', in *Stil: Funktionen und Geschichten eines kulturhistorischen Diskurselements* (ed. K.L. Peiffer and H.U. Gumbrecht; stw 633; Frankfurt: Suhrkamp, 1986), pp. 590-602.

'Hermeneutics and Rhetorics', *Scriptura* 3 (1989).

'Where is Rhetorical Criticism Taking Us?', *CBQ* 49 (1987), pp. 448-63.

'The Rhetorical Structure of Luke 12 in its Wider Context', *Neot* 22 (1989), pp. 283-310.

'Is There an Encoded Reader Fallacy?', *Semeia* 48 (1989), pp. 41-54.

'The Argumentative Structure of 1 Thessalonians as Paradoxical Encomium', in *The Thessalonian Correspondence* (ed. R.F. Collins; BETL, 88; Leuven: Leuven University Press, 1990), pp. 117-36.

'The Rhetorical Genre of Jesus' Sermon in Luke 12.1–13.9', in *Persuasive Artistry: Studies in New Testament Rhetoric in Honor of George A. Kennedy* (ed. D.F. Watson; JSNTSup, 50; Sheffield: JSOT Press, 1991), pp. 93-118.

'Rhetorical Criticism: Rhetorical Criticism and its Theory in Culture-Critical Perspective: The Narrative Rhetoric of John 11', in *Text and Interpretation: New Approaches in the Criticism of the New Testament* (ed. P.J. Martin and J.H. Petzer; NTTS, 15; Leiden: Brill, 1991), pp. 171-85.

'Putting Life Back into the Lazarus Story and its Reading: The Narrative Rhetoric of John 11 as the Narration of Faith', *Semeia* 53 (1991), pp. 113-32.

INTRODUCTION: THE HEIDELBERG PAPERS IN PERSPECTIVE

Stanley E. Porter

Rhetoric is not a single thing and neither can it be defined simply. In that sense, the title of this volume should be *Rhetorics* rather than *Rhetoric and the New Testament*. For some rhetoric means the categories used by the ancients, as reflected in the classical orators or in the handbooks on rhetoric, or in some combination of both. For others rhetoric means rhetorical categories developed in subsequent times and places, in particular the categories of the European New Rhetoricians of this century. This collection of essays brings together in one volume the proceedings of a single conference that addressed the topic of rhetoric and the New Testament, in other words, how the study of the New Testament has been, is, and promises to be affected by work done in various kinds and types of rhetoric. So far as the participants were concerned, they seemed to be in agreement that discussing this relationship was a task well worth doing, since there has been much incisive work of late that has applied rhetorical categories to exegesis of the New Testament and more is certain to be forthcoming. After that is agreed upon, however, there is also much diversity of opinion reflected in these papers. Some of the papers take up already developed methodologies and apply them anew to texts from the New Testament. Others explore the usefulness and validity of application of these same rhetorical models. Others are endeavoring to create new models and illustrate how they might be relevant to the exegetical endeavor. And others still are analysing rhetoric in terms of its sociological and cultural implications.

With such a difference in approach and expectation, it might seem surprising that such a relatively coherent collection of papers could emerge. They have been categorized under two useful headings. The first part contains the majority of papers, in which there is application of various rhetorical models to particular New Testament texts. This is not to say that these papers are not concerned with method, because many of them are, but they are also dedicated to sustained analysis of particular passages, and are consequently placed together in roughly New Testament canonical order. The second part contains a smaller number of papers but not papers of any less significance. Here, although texts from the New Testament are often mentioned and even treated in some detail, the focus is more on assessing the relative merits of various methodologies and developing new and different strains of rhetorical criticism.

This introduction is not an attempt to offer a full assessment of this collection either in its whole or in its parts, but merely provides a rough guide to the contents of the volume, perhaps drawing out some features and points of connection that would not otherwise be apparent.

Part I, Rhetoric and New Testament Interpretation, begins with five papers that devote attention to Luke–Acts. Frank Hughes treats the parable of the rich man and Lazarus (Lk. 16.19-31) as declamation, Folker Siegert explores the noteworthy prose rhythmic structure of Luke–Acts especially in comparison to Paul's less rhythmic language in his epistles, J. Ian H. McDonald defines the rhetorical units and situations of two passages, one from Luke (10.25-37) and the other from Acts (10.1–11.18), Daniel Marguerat discusses the concept of silence in dictating the rhetorical appropriateness of the ending to Acts (28.16-31), and James J. Murphy draws upon evidence from Acts (as well as from Paul) in looking at early Christianity as a rhetorical movement waging a persuasive campaign. These papers have in common their analysis of narrative literature, so far not treated as extensively as epistolary literature. Only time will tell whether these applications are seen to be as useful, but each paper here is suggestive regarding the significant rhetorical skills of the author of Luke–Acts. Each essay is designed to illustrate how the biblical author has in some way used the rhetorical techniques available to him to create effective and persuasive prose. A useful sidelight, especially in Siegert's and Murphy's essays, is the selection of several points of comparison and contrast between Luke–Acts and the writings of Paul, thereby placing the concerns of rhetorical criticism alongside those of higher-critical analysis of the New Testament.

In the second group of papers, attention turns to epistolary literature, especially that of Paul. In four separate essays on Romans,

Stanley E. Porter finds no theoretical justification among the ancients for application to the Pauline letters of the species and organization of classical rhetoric, David Hellholm offers a *tour de force* in analysing the entire macro-structure of Romans, outlining its organization and describing its use of amplification, J.N. Vorster describes in detail the various strategies that make Rom. 1.16-17 an effective thematic statement for the book, and Marc Schoeni, relying on his understanding of the sublime, sees how this concept informs analysis of Romans 5 and 9–13. Apart from Hellholm's essay, the authors in this group explore various ways that style is used in creating persuasive epistolary prose, Porter going so far as to argue that this is the only category that can be applied to analysis of Pauline epistles in terms of what the ancients would have understood or condoned. The other authors are not limited by this distinction, but bring to bear a range of ancient and modern categories in their analytic endeavors. The stark contrast between Vorster's analysis of a particular text and Hellholm's treatment of an entire book is suggestive that rhetorical analysis has a comprehensive heuristic value not heretofore fully exploited.

In the next four essays, concerned with the Corinthian correspondence, Dennis L. Stamps re-opens the question of the rhetorical situation by pushing for definition in terms of literary rather than historical context, Joop Smit provides a traditional rhetorical analysis of the organization of 1 Corinthians 12–14 as deliberative rhetoric with ch. 13 as a demonstrative digression, Duane F. Watson performs a similar analysis of 1 Corinthians 15 as deliberative rhetoric, and Glenn Holland discusses the concept of irony in 2 Corinthians 10–13, especially the motif of 'foolishness' as a rhetorical strategy to win over and persuade his audience. It is perhaps a sign of the success of rhetorical criticism in establishing itself in the mainstream of New Testament studies that Smit and Watson can engage in detailed historically-based analyses of these sub-sections of their epistolary texts, although Stamps in his re-definition of rhetorical situation would want to emphasize the literary dimensions of this concept more than do most other rhetorical critics.

In the final group of six essays in this first part, concentrating on the shorter epistles of Galatians and Philippians, C. Joachim Classen offers a trenchant and forceful assessment of rhetorical criticism in New Testament studies, especially as it is found in the work of H.D. Betz on Galatians. He argues for a re-evaluation of the rhetorical categories used, a greater precision in formulating the questions and parameters of the enterprise, and an appreciation of work by such neglected earlier writers as Melanchthon. In discussing Philippians, Jeffrey T. Reed argues from the ancient sources that it cannot be proven that Paul was formally influenced by ancient rhetorical traditions or that there was an 'epistolary-rhetorical' genre, A.H. Snyman focuses on the internal proofs used in Phil. 4.1-20 to assess the persuasive force of this passage in its context, Claudio Basevi and Juan Chapa depart from the usual source criticism of the 'hymn' of Phil. 2.6-11 and explore its rhetorical function within the entire letter, even suggesting that various elements reflect Pauline literary originality, and John W. Marshall invokes the concept of ethos, including authorial persona, to explicate the possible rhetorical effectiveness of Philippians as deliberative rhetoric. In the final essay of this section, Thomas H. Olbricht structures Hebrews around its use of amplification through comparison, a device mirrored in ancient funeral orations. Classen's and Reed's articles, though not arguing from identical perspectives, raise necessary voices of caution in the light of increasing enthusiasm for rhetorical criticism. They point out the necessity of clearly articulating what the agenda is for rhetorical criticism and what counts for evidence in the quest, issues not always clearly defined by other rhetorical critics. The other essays in this section offer conclusions consonant with those of more traditional higher-critical analysis, but draw attention to new evidence and argumentation in the process.

In Part II, Rhetoric and Questions of Method, the authors do not neglect the New Testament but raise questions of a methodological sort. Klaus Berger all-too-briefly illustrates a possible rapprochement between rhetorical criticism and a new and improved version of form criticism. Bernard Lategan uses time and space as concepts to analyse how an author positions himself in relation to his readers, with Galatians as a test case. Pieter J.J. Botha focuses on the orality of pre-modern textual production, discussing such useful concepts as multi-authorship, the role of the amanuensis, and letters as community documents, a highly suggestive treatment of influences on literary production that are difficult to quantify. Jeffrey A. Crafton departs from the normally defined rhetorical categories and invokes Kenneth Burke's concept of texts acting or doing something, in Crafton's analysis compelling readers either to join with the biblical text in creating a symbolic world or to reject it altogether. Vernon K. Robbins provides a challenging historical assessment of the work of Wilhelm Wuellner, the dedicatee of this volume who has done as much as anyone in recent times to promote work in biblical rhetorical criticism. Praising his earlier work, Robbins challenges Wuellner to explore more fully than he has the concept of the diversity of cultural rhetorics at play in a social-rhetorical context. Lauri Thurén argues that a complete and inclusive rhetorical perspective must be invoked to arrive at a reliable picture of New Testament ethics or theology. Angelico-Salvatore Di Marco (who, it is regretted, died in July 1993) extends the concept of chiasm to encompass a myriad of texts and structures. And as a fitting conclusion to the volume, as well as the conference, Wilhelm Wuellner offers a retrospective and prospective analysis of rhetoric as viewed at the end of the twentieth century. On the one hand, he explores the reasons for the traditionally close relation between biblical studies and rhetoric throughout the history of Western Civilization. On the other hand, he calls for a re-assessment of the standards of rhetorical criticism, defining and cultivating a new rhetorical criticism that aids in the transfiguration of society. The essays in this section are by far the most diverse and also the most challenging. It is here that the contributors depart in varying ways and to varying degrees from the norms of rhetorical criticism, at least as it is traditionally and usually understood. It is a virtue and a liability of rhetoric as a concept that it encourages such a diversity of thinking. It makes the concept more difficult to define and hence fights against the kind of meticulous precision that some of the authors in Part I strive for, but it also introduces new concepts and perspectives that even traditional rhetorical critics will need to ponder if for no other reason than to refine their thinking, or, better still, to redefine their categories of analysis and discussion.

The papers in this volume seem to suggest several tentative conclusions regarding the current state of discussion in rhetorical criticism. First, recent work in rhetorical criticism does not seem to have been a short-lived phenomenon that has faded with time. To the contrary, a wide and growing group of scholars continues to work in the field. The Heidelberg conference alone brought scholars from twelve countries and three continents. There is no reason why more countries and more continents cannot be included in this discussion as it continues. Secondly, rhetorical criticism provides a venue for truly interdisciplinary study, as scholars from a variety of disciplines bring their differing perspectives to bear. They bring the parameters of their academic disciplines, their educational backgrounds, their cultural orientations, and their personal preferences. Even though there are various 'schools' emerging from the developing discussion, the communal discussion has a welcome tendency (when all is going as it should be) to force reassessment of one's presuppositions and methods. Thirdly, the major approaches to the concept of rhetoric reveal varying emphases. Some wish to go back to the ancient rhetoricians, and thus anchor the discipline in a definable historical, cultural milieu. Others are advocates of the New Rhetoric, and thus pull the discipline into the present, thinking to prevent it from taking on the stale odor of archaism. And others still are looking to the future, suggesting refinements or enhancements of existing methods or even advocating altogether new methods of approach. Fourthly, when all is said and done, despite a large amount of common interest and even similarity of approach, when it is time to 'do' rhetorical criticism, the field of exploration is as encompassing as an entire movement, such as early Christianity, or as large as an entire book, such as Romans, or as small as one or two verses, such as Rom. 1.16-17. Rhetorical criticism is broad enough and specific enough to handle both extremes and much in between, or at least to seem to be able to do so at this stage in the discussion. Within these parameters, some of the treatments can be seen to be broad-ranging in their orientations, highly suggestive even though not particularly detailed, while others are more intensive, agonizing over the particularities of a given text. Both appear to be necessary at this stage, as a balance is struck between capturing the full persuasive force of a text and assessing the particular means by which this force is established. Fifthly, this collection well illustrates the need and the relevant place for self-criticism in rhetorical studies. Whereas there are many enthusiasts in the discipline arguing for ever-widening expansion of its parameters into almost any conceivable direction there are also several nay-sayers calling for restraint, re-definition, and re-assessment. One or more sides in this debate may ultimately prevail, but, as these pages illustrate, in the meantime all sides are engaged in a necessary discussion regarding the theory and praxis of rhetorical criticism.

PART I

RHETORIC AND NEW TESTAMENT INTERPRETATION

THE PARABLE OF THE RICH MAN AND LAZARUS (LUKE 16.19-31) AND GRAECO-ROMAN RHETORIC

Frank W. Hughes

For a variety of reasons, the parable of the Rich Man and Lazarus which appears at Lk. 16.19-31 has been one of the most difficult parables of the New Testament to interpret using traditional historical criticism. I believe that one of the main reasons for the difficulty in interpreting Lk. 16.19-31 has been New Testament scholarship's general ignorance of, or possibly disdain for, Graeco-Roman rhetoric. After having shown the importance of a particular tradition of Graeco-Roman rhetoric as a key to the composition of this parable, I shall then try to show the importance of a rhetorical view of this parable for the understanding of its function in the more general scheme of Luke–Acts.

An Overview of Scholarship on the Parable

The watershed event in the interpretation of this parable was certainly the long article by Hugo Gressmann published by the Royal Prussian Academy in 1918.[1] Gressmann found stories in Egyptian literature, as well as in rabbinic literature, which were parallels to the parable of the Rich Man and Lazarus. It will be useful to review here in some detail Gressmann's method and conclusions.

Gressmann referred to the New Testament Gospels as *Volksbücher*[2] and explored the historical significance of the existence of Aramaic *Volksbücher* in pre-Christian times, including the possibility of the

---

1. H. Gressmann, 'Vom reichen Mann und armen Lazarus', *Abhandlungen der königlichen Preussischen Akademie der Wissenschaften*, philosophisch-historische Klasse, Jahrgang 1918, Nr. 7 (Berlin: Königliche Akademie der Wissenschaften, 1918).
2. Gressmann, 'Vom reichen Mann', p. 3.

existence of 'Aramaic gospel books',[3] which could be understood in the context of popular literature in this time period. Given the variety of Aramaic popular literature in this era, and as a 'prime example to illustrate the foregoing working hypothesis'[4] of an Aramaic gospel book, Gressmann submitted the parable of the Rich Man and Lazarus. After briefly discussing the issues of the meaning of the naming of Lazarus and the anonymity of the Rich Man in the parable, as well as the provision of names for the Rich Man in the New Testament manuscript tradition,[5] Gressmann went on to hypothesize that the story of the Rich Man and Lazarus was related to other similar stories in Judaism, of which there were in existence 'seven characteristic versions [*Fassungen*]'.[6] Ironically Gressmann argued that, concerning the existence of such popular books, it was not necessary to establish a firm text.[7] Nonetheless, if the same story were in circulation in different forms, it would be appropriate to look on authors of these different versions of the same story as 'nothing other than redactors'.[8] Gressmann went on to show similarities and contacts between Luke 16.19-31 and the apparently parallel passages in the Egyptian, Greek and Jewish sources. Against Adolf Jülicher,[9] Johannes Weiss and others who wished to divide the parable into two halves,[10] Gressmann argued that what seemed to be a 'secondary addition' was the original Christian part of the story. He argued that the first part of the story could not have existed as a story on its own,[11] and that the second part could not be successfully divided from the first part. He referred to the author of the parable of the Rich Man and Lazarus as Jesus.[12]

It should be noted that in Gressmann's procedure, it was primarily the contents of the parable of the Rich Man and Lazarus that were compared for similarities and contrasts to the stories in the other languages. It must be noted that, on the grounds of content alone, there is

3. Gressmann, 'Vom reichen Mann', p. 4.
4. Gressmann, 'Vom reichen Mann', p. 5.
5. Gressmann, 'Vom reichen Mann', pp. 6-8.
6. Gressmann, 'Vom reichen Mann', p. 8.
7. Gressmann, 'Vom reichen Mann', p. 9.
8. Gressmann, 'Vom reichen Mann', p. 9.
9.   A. Jülicher, *Die Gleichnisreden Jesu* (Tübingen: Mohr [Paul Siebeck], 1910; repr. Darmstadt: Wissenschaftliche Buchgesellschaft, 1963), II, pp. 617-41.
10. Gressmann, 'Vom reichen Mann', p. 56.
11. Gressmann, 'Vom reichen Mann', p. 58.
12. Gressmann, 'Vom reichen Mann', p. 56.

a great deal of similarity between the Egyptian folktale copied in Demotic on the back of a Greek document, concerning the fate of a rich man and a poor man in the afterlife, and Lk. 16.19-31.[13] More recently in 1987 Ronald F. Hock argued for not only content but also form-critical parallels to Lk. 16.19-31 in two entertaining stories by Lucian of Samosata, the *Cataplus* and the *Gallus*.[14]

We may well ask here, just what reasons there might be for the similarities between the Egyptian, Jewish and Hellenistic Greek stories. No matter where the story in Luke 16 came from, if the Parable of Lazarus and the Rich Man is dependent on another particular story in circulation at the time, are we limited to oral transmission (as Gressmann proposed as the best possibility) to explain how the older story or stories became the parable of the Rich Man and Lazarus in Luke? Oral transmission certainly remains a possibility, of course, but alongside oral transmission of stories should be considered the concept of *imitatio*, a process whereby older texts are repeated and transformed into new texts.

Imitation and Declamation

The Greek word μίμησις, usually translated into English as 'imitation', was normally rendered by *imitatio* in Latin. The concept of μίμησις is one of the most important ideas in the history of Western literature. It is well known that Aristotle taught that poetry should be the imitation of reality; and Erich Auerbach's still interesting book *Mimesis* traced the phenomenon of literature as the imitation of reality through parts of the Hebrew Bible, Homer and much of subsequent Western literature. Notably, Auerbach concluded in several places that rhetoric had a powerful influence on the prose he analyzed.[15] Generally speaking, Auerbach found that Christianity

13. J.A. Fitzmyer, *The Gospel according to Luke (X-XXIV)* (AB 28a; Garden City, NY: Doubleday, 1985), p. 1126.

14. R.F. Hock, 'Lazarus and Micyllus: Greco-Roman Backgrounds to Luke 16:19-31', *JBL* 106 (1987), pp. 447-63. Not all of Hock's parallels between Lucian and Luke 16 are equally convincing.

15. E. Auerbach, *Mimesis: The Representation of Reality in Western Literature* (Princeton: Princeton University Press, 1953); on rhetorical influences on ancient historiography and on early Christian literature, see especially pp. 40-49. One of the contrasts between Homer and the Hebrew Bible, Auerbach finds, is the latter's

profoundly affected the history of literature by introducing a radical kind of literary realism, to the detriment of the classical ideal of the separation of styles in literature. Using more precise definitions, classicists have produced significant discussions of *imitatio* in Graeco-Roman literature.[16] *Imitatio* may be defined as the use of texts, persons and literary patterns from existing literature[17] in the creation of new literature. Hermann Koller's dissertation[18] argued that the original meaning of the word μίμησις was an artistic or intellectual expression, originally limited to music and dancing, and that the later meaning of 'imitation' was a 'watered down' application of the idea to fields (e.g. painting) where it did not properly belong. Then, Koller argued, the fifth-century Pythagoreans expanded the doctrine into a 'grandiose "Ausdrucks-" or "Ethoslehre", embracing the whole range of emotional, therapeutic (cathartic), and

'claim to absolute authority' (p. 16). 'It is all very different in the Biblical stories. Their aim is not to bewitch the senses, and if nevertheless they produce lively sensory effects, it is only because the moral, religious, and physical phenomena which are their sole concern are made concrete in the sensible matter of life. But their religious intent involves an absolute claim to historical truth' (p. 14).

16. On the phenomenon of *imitatio* in general, see T.L. Brodie, 'Graeco-Roman Imitation of Texts as a Partial Guide to Luke's Use of Sources', in C.H. Talbert (ed.), *Luke–Acts: New Perspectives from the Society of Biblical Literature Seminar* (New York: Crossroad, 1984), pp. 17-46. On *imitatio* in rhetorical schools, see Quintilian, *Institutio oratoria* 10.2, as well as D.L. Clark, *Rhetoric in Greco-Roman Education* (New York: Columbia University Press, 1957), ch. 6. Older works on *imitatio* include H. Koller, *Die Mimesis in der Antike: Nachahmung, Darstellung, Ausdruck* (Bern: Francke, 1954); R. McKeon, 'Literary Criticism and the Concept of Imitation in Antiquity', *Modern Philology* 34 (1936), pp. 1-35; A. Reiff, *Interpretatio, imitatio, aemulatio: Begriff und Vorstellung literarischer Abhängigkeit bei den Römern* (DPhil dissertation, Cologne, 1959; Würzburg: Konrad Triltsch, 1959), which was reviewed by M. Fuhrmann in *Gnomon* 33 (1961), pp. 445-48; A.M. Guillemin, 'L'imitation dans les littératures antiques et en particulière dans la littérature latine', *Revue des Etudes Latines* 2 (1924), pp. 35-57. For an explanation of the creative ways Vergil did *imitatio* of Homer, see G.N. Knauer, *Die Aeneis und Homer: Studien zur poetischen Technik Vergils mit Listen der Homerzitate in der Aeneis* (Hypomnemata, 7; Göttingen: Vandenhoeck & Ruprecht, 2nd edn, 1979). On the use of older traditions in Latin poetry, see G. Williams, *Tradition and Originality in Roman Poetry* (Oxford: Clarendon Press, 1968), esp. pp. 250-357.

17. 'Literature' here is broadly defined to include oral literature as well as written literature.

18. Koller, *Die Mimesis in der Antike*.

educational uses of music'. Then this 'Pythagorean-Damonian doctrine was partly adopted, partly adapted and distorted, by Plato and Aristotle, and provides the necessary background not only for their discussions of μίμησις but for the conception of music which was dominant throughout antiquity'.[19] Hence, if Koller was on the right track, μίμησις had its roots in the creative reinterpretation of reality through art. Gerald F. Else's critical review, from which I have quoted, argued that Koller's understanding of μίμησις was essentially backwards: Else saw μίμησις first as a literary phenomenon, and later the semantic range of the word was expanded to include other creative forms. For the purposes of investigating early Christian literature, however, it is clear that μίμησις/*imitatio* as an important phenomenon in literature (if not many other creative expressions) was certainly in existence by the time of the New Testament.

Quintilian is an excellent source for our knowledge of much of rhetorical instruction in the Hellenistic period. Two of the most revealing chapters of Quintilian's *Institutio oratoria* are chs. 1 and 2 of book 10. The first chapter begins with a long survey of the authors whose works Quintilian taught in his rhetorical school. It would not be too much to say that this chapter is a monument to the way a mid-to-late first-century teacher passed on the traditions of Graeco-Roman literature. The second chapter of book 10 is a long discussion of the reasons to choose certain works to imitate. Buried within the first chapter, however, is a significant interpretation by Quintilian of Cicero's practice of *imitatio*:

> For it seems to me that Cicero, who devoted himself heart and soul to the imitation of the Greeks, succeeded in reproducing the force of Demosthenes, the copious flow of Plato, and the charm of Isocrates. But he did something more than reproduce the best elements in each of these authors by dint of careful study; it was to himself that he owed most of, or rather all his excellences, which spring from the extraordinary fertility of his immortal genius. For he does not, as Pindar says, 'collect the rain from heaven, but wells forth with living water', since Providence at his birth conferred this special privilege upon him, that eloquence should make trial of all her powers in him.[20]

---

19. G.F. Else, '"Imitation" in the Fifth Century', *Classical Philology* 53 (1958), pp. 73-90; quotations are from p. 73.
20. Quintilian 10.1.108-109.

However 'imitation alone', as Quintilian explained later, 'is not sufficient' (*imitatio per se ipsa non sufficit*).[21] What Quintilian meant is that the process of creativity is to be tutored by the examination of older literature but not stifled by it: a person with 'a sluggish nature is only too ready to rest content with the inventions of others'.[22] Cicero also advised reading widely, because 'a full supply of knowledge begets a full supply of words'[23] and only a wide acquaintance with the thoughts and writings of others, along with the universal knowledge given by philosophy, would make the orator best able to plead his cases.

Even a cursory examination of the traditions of Greek and Roman rhetoric shows that *imitatio* had been practiced in various ways both in rhetorical instruction and in the writing of literature. A particular kind of *imitatio* practiced in Greek and Roman rhetorical schools during the early Roman empire was declamation. In such schools, boys and young men were taught how to compose and deliver speeches within the *genera* of epideictic, deliberative and judicial rhetoric. One of the most important parts of education was the making and delivery of speeches on imaginary subjects, or imaginary speeches in the style of well-known orators. This practice was known in Latin as *declamatio* and it had as its approximate Greek equivalent μελέτη.[24] The μελέτη was a complete speech, as opposed to the προγύμνασμα, defined by Russell as 'the earlier stages of instruction in which the pupil was taught to compose what might become elements in the final product—narratives, descriptions, comparisons, *loci communes* and so on'.[25]

A declamation could be either an imaginary deliberative speech (*suasoria*) or an imaginary judicial speech (*controversia*), but was never an epideictic one.[26] The μελέτη was both a 'practical exercise'

21. Quintilian 10.2.4.
22. Quintilian 10.2.4.
23. Cicero, *De oratore* 3.125.
24. D.A. Russell, *Greek Declamation* (Cambridge: Cambridge University Press, 1983), pp. 9-15 *et passim*.
25. Russell, *Greek Declamation*, pp. 10-11; Russell refers here to G.A. Kennedy's section on προγυμνάσματα in *Greek Rhetoric under Christian Emperors* (A History of Rhetoric, 3; Princeton, NJ: Princeton University Press, 1983), pp. 54-73, and to D.L. Clark, *Rhetoric in Greco-Roman Education*.
26. Russell, *Greek Declamation*, p. 10, referring to Menander Rhetor 331.16 in the edition of Spengel.

and also 'imaginative literature',[27] revolving especially around a number of imaginary themes (ὑποθέσεις) which were often used in declamations, including conflicts between figures in mythology. Along with stereotypical characters 'set vaguely in the classical past', declamations also dealt with historical themes and historical characters, so that, as Russell shows, '[s]ometimes the mere addition of names turns them into a sort of rudimentary historical fiction'. Russell argues that a difference between Latin and Greek declamation was the 'greater readiness' in the Latin schools to use contemporary themes, whereas the Greek schools were more apt to use themes from history in both deliberative and judicial declamations.[28] In fact, as Russell shows, rhetorical schools were 'always capable of producing speeches which could pass as genuine classical works'.[29]

Many a legal battle was fought in declamation, especially *controversiae* on the justice or injustice of soldiers asking for certain

27. Russell, *Greek Declamation*, p. 12.
28. Russell, *Greek Declamation*, p. 106.
29. Russell, *Greek Declamation*, p. 111; Russell gives as an example the fact that 'serious historians have taken the *Peri Politeias* ascribed to Herodes Atticus as a work of the late fifth century B.C.', and he describes normative features of deliberative declamation found in this speech as the movement of the argument under the heads of 'necessity' and 'expediency', and several imagined objections are stated and answered (*ibid.*). Of greatest interest for those interested in biblical pseudonymity is Russell's statement, which bears quoting in full: 'Confusion between declamations and genuine speeches existed even in antiquity. Dionysius of Halicarnassus knew that there were speeches in the corpus of the Attic orators which were "foolish and sophistical": the speech of Dinarchus on not surrendering Harpalus to Alexander was an example. Speeches of Pericles were in circulation, but widely known to be false, for he left no written work behind. Most striking of all, there is the surviving speech of Demades, "On the Twelve Years", preserved in the manuscript tradition of the Attic Orators, but rightly regarded as one of the numerous declamatory exercises in which Demades is a speaker. Of course, speeches could be forged for other reasons than for the purposes of the schools; but that a certain number of declamations came to be taken for the genuine article seems certain' (pp. 111-12). Hence, the tradition of Greek declamation, carried forward along with other rhetorical traditions in Latin rhetorical schools, means that there is no necessary connection between the presence of a rhetorical discourse within the literary tradition of a well known orator and its true authorship by that orator. The major reason for this conclusion seems to be the fact that rhetorical school tradition, which was at that time responsible for the production of new speeches by old orators, was also generally responsible for the preservation of old speeches and handbooks.

rewards for victory in battle, along with the legality of fathers disowning their sons.[30] The sources, including Libanius's Greek declamations and pseudo-Quintilian's Latin declamations, show us that a major type of declamation involved the many-faceted conflicts between Rich Man and Poor Man. Although the fine article by Ronald Hock mentions the rhetorical tradition of declamation as a possible parallel to Lk. 16.19-31,[31] Hock went on to suggest parallels between the parable of the Rich Man and Lazarus primarily in the tradition of Cynic philosophical schools, as witnessed in Lucian of Samosata. A more thorough investigation of rhetorical traditions would have indicated the pervasiveness of what could be called a genre of declamations having as their subjects the conflicts (especially the legal conflicts, that is *controversiae*) between Rich Man and Poor Man.

Even a brief investigation of prominent collections of declamations, those ascribed to Quintilian, those of Seneca and those of Libanius, shows that Rich Man/Poor Man declamations occupied an important place. Beginning with the 19 major declamations ascribed to Quintilian, we note that declamations 7, 9, 11 and 13 deal with the legal consequences of conflicts between rich men and poor men.[32] We may then proceed to the so-called minor declamations ascribed to Quintilian, and there out of 145 surviving minor declamations (from an original 388), I identify 13 which deal with legal conflicts between rich men and poor men.[33] We find also among the declamations of Seneca, indeed among what Bonner called 'the remarkably limited scope of their subjects', that *controversiae* included 'the frequent opposition of the rich man and the poor man', with no less than five

---

30. Russell, *Greek Declamation*, pp. 21-39. Libanius's *Declamation* 33 combines the themes when he depicts the miserly father who wishes to disown his soldier son who has asked as his reward only a wreath and not gold; this humorous masterpiece is recounted and analyzed by Russell on pp. 96-102.

31. Hock, 'Lazarus and Micyllus', pp. 456-57.

32. L.A. Sussmann, *The Major Declamations Ascribed to Quintilian: A Translation* (Studien zur klassischen Philologie, 27; Frankfurt am Main: Peter Lang, 1987).

33. See especially the fine edition and commentary by M. Winterbottom, *The Minor Declamations Ascribed to Quintilian* (Texte und Kommentare, 13; Berlin: de Gruyter, 1984). I identify these minor declamations as having the Rich Man versus Poor Man theme: 269, 271, 279, 294, 301, 305, 325, 332, 333, 343, 364, 370, 379.

such *controversiae* in evidence.[34] In the Teubner edition of Richard Foerster, there are 51 declamations of Libanius.[35] Beginning with *Decl.* 25, the declamations in the final two volumes are 'ethological' rather than 'historical'; 'ethological' declamations are those which deal with types of people, rather than those which recreate the supposed speeches of historical persons such as Demosthenes. Of the 27 'ethological' declamations of Libanius, Foerster identified four declamations dealing with conflicts between rich men and poor men.[36] Hence, it is surely not too much to say that the ongoing tradition of declamation, as witnessed in both Greek and Latin rhetorical instruction, included what might be called a genre of declamations dealing with legal conflicts between rich men and poor men. These Rich Man versus Poor Man declamations appear to have been *controversiae* rather than *suasoriae*.

Rhetorical Tradition and Luke 16.19-31

Given the existence of a genre of declamations, and given the dynamism of the rhetorical tradition of declamations as a firm part of rhetorical instruction in both Greek and Latin, and, for that matter, given the multiplicity of parallels which have been identified by Gressmann in Egyptian and Rabbinic tradition, along with the perhaps less tempting parallels in two stories by Lucian of Samosata identified recently by Hock, it would appear that the identification of a single story as the solitary source lying behind Lk. 16.19-31 is both impossible and unnecessary. In fact, the existence of a genre of Rich Man versus Poor Man declamations might very well help to explain the diversity of stories, not only in Greek as identified by Hock, but also in Semitic languages as identified by Gressmann. If indeed a rather well educated writer, like the writer of Luke–Acts, had been assigned

---

34. S.F. Bonner, *Roman Declamation in the Late Republic and Early Empire* (Berkeley: University of California Press, 1949), p. 37. Bonner lists these declamations of Seneca as having as their themes the conflict between Rich Man and Poor Man: *Contr.* 2.1, 5.2, 5.5, 8.6, 10.1.

35. *Libanii Opera*, VI, VII (ed. R. Foerster; Leipzig: Teubner, 1911, 1913; repr. Hildesheim: Georg Olms, 1963).

36. Foerster commented on p. 180 of his vol. 7, 'Sequuntur quattuor declamationes quae contentionem divitis et pauperis argumentum habent'. The four declamations so indicated are *Decl.* 35, 36, 37 and 38.

to make declamations in a genre of Rich Man versus Poor Man when
he was in rhetorical school, and if this writer knew how to confect
speeches within such declamations, so that they would fit the appropriate situations, it would not have been difficult for the author of
Luke–Acts to compose the parable of the Rich Man and Lazarus,
either with no particular source, or with only the skeleton of a source.
The most striking difference between the parable of the Rich Man and
Lazarus and the parallels that have been identified by Gressmann is the
particular kind of legal judgment and resurrection/afterlife situation
that is depicted in Luke 16. Yet given some ability in *ethopoiïa*, which
rhetorical instruction and practice would likely have developed in a
person as well educated as the writer of Luke–Acts, it seems unlikely
that the writer of Luke–Acts would find it difficult to portray the Rich
Man calling to Abraham as 'Father Abraham' (Lk. 16.24, 30; cf.
'Father', 16.27; cf. Abraham calling the Rich Man 'child', 16.25), or
that it would be difficult to bestow on the Poor Man the name of
'Lazarus' (the Greek form of the Hebrew name Eleazar). Given the
extreme familiarity of the writer of Luke–Acts with the Septuagint, it
would appear equally easy for this writer to have made the transition
from an earthly legal sphere to the heavenly one, so that the setting of
our parable depicts the final and irrevocable judgment of God on both
the Rich Man and Lazarus, rather than any human judgment. As
Cicero himself showed, the depiction of suffering (which we find in
the earthly situation of Lazarus as well as the post-judgment situation
of the Rich Man), is a compositional matter which allows for great
creativity on the part of a rhetorician.[37]

Luke 16.19-31 within the Rhetoric of Luke–Acts

Much has been said and written about the ways in which Jews are
portrayed in Luke–Acts.[38] The two recent monographs of
Jack T. Sanders and Joseph B. Tyson agree in their interpretation of
Lk. 16.19-31 as saying that it is those Jews who have misinterpreted
Scripture who are condemned, and that this condemnation is not given

---

37. Cicero, *De inventione* 1.106-109; Cicero here shows sixteen different ways
in which to use the topic of suffering in a rhetorical speech.

38. For recent analyses, see J.T. Sanders, *The Jews in Luke–Acts* (Philadelphia:
Fortress Press, 1987) and J.B. Tyson, *Images of Judaism in Luke–Acts* (Columbia:
University of South Carolina Press, 1992).

to Pharisees alone.[39] It is difficult to disagree with the judgments of Sanders and Tyson that the misinterpretation of Scripture by the Jews (as portrayed in Luke–Acts) is their rejection of the gospel of Jesus, since Luke tells his readers repeatedly that the coming and suffering of Jesus is foretold in Scripture.

It seems to me that what a rhetorical reading of Lk. 16.19-31 can contribute to this discussion of the portrayal of Jews in Luke–Acts is the insight that the parable shows Rich Man as an *exemplum* of the rejection of God's purposes by a Jew who has enjoyed the advantages of wealth. Yet what kind of *exemplum* is Rich Man in this parable? As a wealthy Jewish man with large amounts of leisure time, he has nonetheless not devoted either his wealth or his time to the care of the poor (the concrete *exemplum* of this behavior is his treatment of Lazarus) or indeed the study of Torah and the prophets at either advanced or rudimentary levels. Presumably as the result of Rich Man's neglect of Torah and the prophets, his uncaring attitude and behavior towards Lazarus was shown in graphic detail by the writer of Luke–Acts. The result of the divine judgment of his uncaring attitude was his condemnation to Hades, fire and all. Abraham the patriarch appeared in this story not to make the judgment, but to reinforce both its rightness and its irrevocability. And yet Abraham was not merely an unidentified *angelus interpres* in this story: he is none other than the first patriarch of the Hebrew people, whom Jews rightly call 'Father'. As a part of Abraham's explanation of the judgment of God on Rich Man, Abraham explains the rightness of the judgment in terms of its necessity: Rich Man had the ability to help Lazarus during their earthly lives, yet did not. The condemned and tormented Rich Man almost cavalierly asks Abraham to send poor Lazarus to Hades to cool Rich Man's tongue; Abraham replies that this is impossible. Finally, in the midst of his suffering Rich Man has a burst of piety or at least family solidarity: he asks that Lazarus go back to earthly life and warn Rich Man's five brothers. The reason that this cannot be, Abraham says, is that Rich Man's brothers, like Rich Man himself, had all the opportunity needed to repent, since they all had Moses and the prophets. Abraham's next reply is the punchline of the story: those who are not faithful to Moses and the prophets would not

---

39. Sanders, *Jews in Luke–Acts*, pp. 202-203; Tyson, *Images of Judaism*, p. 73. Fitzmyer (*Gospel according to Luke [X-XXIV]*, p. 1125) understands that Luke 16.19-31 is 'addressed to the Pharisees of v. 14'.

be convinced by one who rose from the dead.

I read the conclusion of the Parable of the Rich Man and Lazarus (Lk. 16.31) as what the earlier form critics called an 'etiological legend'. In other words this parable gives the readers of Luke–Acts that writer's reason why Christian evangelization of Jews fails so miserably in Acts, and perhaps why the Jewish opposition to Jesus is so strong in Luke. The reason that Jews failed to accept Jesus as Messiah, the 'one risen from the dead', the writer of Luke–Acts thinks, is because of their unfaithfulness to the former revelation of God in the Torah and the prophets. Using reader-response criticism, John A. Darr has recently pointed out, in his fine chapter on the characterization of the Pharisees in Luke–Acts, that '[t]he Pharisees see and hear the divine revelation in Jesus and others; indeed they observe it quite carefully', yet 'they consistently fail to recognize it'. Their failure to recognize God's work in the person of Jesus and his apostles is due to the fact that they are 'unrepentant, prideful, lovers of money, complainers, unjust, scoffers, and so forth'.[40] Given their disinterest and rejection of the new revelation of God in Jesus, Luke–Acts then constructs stories which portray *exempla* of Jewish disinterest and rejection of God's revelation, not only of Jesus but even of the revelation of God which as self-respecting Jews they should have embraced. A significant part of the writer of Luke–Acts' mosaic about the Jews' disobedience of God, as exemplified by their callous attitude towards the poor, is surely Lk. 16.19-31. In the book of Acts, this disinterest and especially rejection is played out in the repeated attempts of Paul to evangelize Jews, primarily by beginning his missionary work in each town, whenever possible, with the Synagogue. Their rejection of the gospel then leads to two things: their future judgment and condemnation by God, of which we are reminded in Rich Man's infernal torment, and the impetus and justification of Paul's special apostolate to the Gentiles. The fact that the genre of Rich Man versus Poor Man declamations usually did not give proper names to the persons depicted in the declamations made it all the easier for the writer of Luke–Acts to refrain from giving a name to Rich Man in this parable. Indeed, the lack of a proper name for Rich Man, coupled with the inclusion of the unmistakable identification of Rich Man with Judaism

---

40. J.A. Darr, *On Character Building: The Reader and the Rhetoric of Characterization in Luke–Acts* (Literary Currents in Biblical Interpretation; Louisville: Westminster/John Knox Press, 1992), p. 92.

in this parable, means that the reader is encouraged to think that Rich Man could be not merely any rich person, but in fact any rich Jew. Given the fact that Lk. 16.19-31 fits so well into Luke's programmatic treatment of Judaism and Jews, as found in both Luke and Acts, we may entertain a healthy skepticism as to the need to posit a particular pre-Lukan source to explain Lk. 16.19-31. The positing of a pre-Lukan source behind Lk. 16.19-31 has generally functioned in scholarship as an attempt to connect the parable of the Rich Man and Lazarus with the historical Jesus. If we give up the traditional attempt to connect this profoundly surprising parable with the historical Jesus; or if we no longer have such a connection as part of our own theological agenda in reading and interpreting Luke–Acts, it will be possible for modern interpreters to feel the sharp edges of the texture of this Lukan text. What Luke–Acts said to its intended readers about Judaism and Jews has an unquestionably jarring effect today, especially as we compare the punishment of the fire of Hell that Rich Man experienced with what happened to millions of Jews during the Holocaust of our own century. Nevertheless, if one of rhetorical criticism's goals is to discover the power of persuasive language, it is appropriate to make every attempt to discover the sharp edges of the rhetoric of this extremely interesting parable, for this parable's sharp edges contribute mightily to the power of the rhetoric of Luke–Acts.

MASS COMMUNICATION AND PROSE RHYTHM IN LUKE–ACTS

Folker Siegert

1. Preliminary Remarks on Public Communication in Antiquity

It was mainly through reading Luke's two volumes that Christianity apprehended its origins as a public event. οὐ γάρ ἐστιν ἐν γωνίᾳ πεπραγμένον τοῦτο, 'it has been no hole-and-corner business' (Acts 26.26, trans. J.B. Phillips). This is one of the apologetic claims of our author, bearing a rhythmical close at its end (– ˘ – | – x),[1] like many of the texts which we shall now consider. The contents of the phrase have received a very detailed treatment by Abraham Malherbe.[2] In the present article, I shall add the presentation of an analytical tool which has been almost completely neglected by New Testament scholars. I am speaking of metrical analysis in the classical meaning of the term.[3] By this, I do not mean a semitizing reading of the New Testament which attempts to find—more or less subjectively—parallelisms and would-be 'rhythms' of heavy and light syllables,[4] but the objective

---

1. The stroke | marks off single metres; x stands for the final syllable when it is not measured. I do not repeat here the rules of classical Greek prosody. See, e.g., B. Snell, *Griechische Metrik* (Göttingen, 3rd edn, 1962); for prose in particular: E. Norden, *Die antike Kunstprosa* (2 vols.; 2nd edn, Leipzig, 1909) and reprints, I, pp. 135 ff.; II, pp. 600, 909-50; H. Lausberg, *Handbuch der literarischen Rhetorik* (Munich, 2nd edn, 1973), I, §§ 1006-1051.

2. '"Not in a corner": Early Christian Apologetic in Acts 26:26', *The Second Century* 5 (1985/86), pp. 193-210.

3. On the scarcity of literature on this topic, see Postscript 1.

4. The stage of transition from classical quantitative prosody to that of stress accent took a long time; the NT is placed more at the beginning than at the end. The prosody of stress accent received specific rules not earlier than, for the Latin, in the 3rd cent. (with the poet Commodian) and, for the Greek, in the fourth cent. (with certain hymns by Gregory Nazianzen). In the sixth cent., the *kontakia* of Romanos, probably a native of Syria, introduced a completely Semitic prosody. See *Sancti Romani Melodi cantica* (ed. P. Maas and C.A. Trypanis; Oxford, 1963), pp. xii-xiv.

analysis of the *quantities* such as defined by Greek grammar since Dionysius of Thrace in his chapter περὶ ποδῶν. I am aware of the fact that in New Testament times these quantities were disappearing from the spoken language. It was just for this reason that the learned, especially the orators of the epoch, retained them in their performances. For the Latin of the first century AD, Quintilian tells us (9.4.61): *neque enim loqui possumus nisi syllabis brevibus ac longis.*

In Greek antiquity, mass communication had its rules and customs which were quite different from those of modern times. In those days, mass communication by no means demanded simple wording, as is the case with television; on the contrary, orators and all persons appearing in public (which was nearly the same thing) were required to speak as pretentiously, as awkwardly and as oddly as they could.

The passive language competence of the masses cannot be assessed by the poor proofs of active competence which the Egyptian papyri have left us and from which Adolf Deissmann has drawn his well-known conclusions. The passive competence of populations of imperial times left its marks elsewhere. Norbert Hugedé, in his *Saint Paul et la culture grecque*,[5] states: *Suétone conserve une riche collection de calembours et de jeux de mots populaires, en grec, qui couraient sur le compte des Empereurs. Ces jeux d'esprit étaient évidemment compris d'un vaste public.* In his footnote he quotes not only remarks from ancient literature but also epigraphical material, that is, graffiti.

The samples of public discourses we possess show that to fascinate one's audience, one would endeavour to use a language as different as possible from everyday speech. Read Dio of Prusa, Ælius Aristides and all the other authors presented by Eduard Norden in his *Die antike Kunstprosa*, a book which also gives a literary critique of Jewish works such as *4 Maccabees*.[6] One could add the synagogue sermons *On Jonah* and *On Samson* which have come down to us as a part of the works of Philo of Alexandria. The Greek originals were clearly examples of rhetorical prose: ornate, rhythmic and excessively rich in all sorts of effects.[7]

5. (Geneva, 1966), p. 172 n. 4.
6. I, pp. 416-20.
7. I have published a German version under the title: *Drei hellenistisch-jüdische Predigten: Ps.-Philon, 'Über Jona', 'Über Simson',* I: Übersetzung aus dem Armenischen und sprachliche Erläuterungen (WUNT, 20; Tübingen, 1980); II: Kommentar nebst Beobachtungen zur hellenistischen Vorgeschichte der

It seems that rising Christianity was surrounded, as it were, by the cultural achievements of the religions competing with it. The orators of the epoch were also the panegyrists of the gods. Valentine, the gnostic, wrote his ὁμηλίαι in rhythms.[8] The final hymn of the *Poimandres* (*Corpus Hermeticum* 1.30-31), where we might hear an echo of Jewish synagogal liturgy, also uses prose rhythms. One may add such genuinely Jewish texts as the prologue to the book of Sirach and the most accomplished passages in Philo and Josephus—to cite examples of rhythmical prose only.

The first Christians, it seems, were not well enough equipped to climb the high level of contemporary public communication.[9] The grand style was quite beyond their reach. To be sure, the founding events of Christianity had not happened in a corner, but in Jerusalem, a city of worldwide renown, though rather provincial—*eine welt-bekannte Stadt, aber keine Weltstadt*. It was a city of Semitic culture even if they spoke Greek as their second language. The town was known for its temple but not for cultural institutions. There was no academy and no school of rhetoric (as there might have been at Tiberias, home of Justus of Tiberias, the superior rival of Josephus),[10] and there was no center of philosophy (as there was a center of Epicureanism in Gadara, in the North of Palestine). We must admit, however, the existence of a Greek library in the period of Herod I because Nicholas of Damas, a heathen, wrote the greater part of the 144 books of his *Universal History* in Jerusalem.

Be that as it may, neither Jesus nor his disciples, being fishermen and simple folk from Galilee, were likely to become known for their cultural achievements in the sense in which the term 'Hellenism' was

---

Bibelhermeneutik (WUNT, 61; Tübingen, 1992), pp. 32-33 (generalities) and 176-77 (specimen of a retranslation into Greek).

8. See the fragments preserved by Clement of Alexandria; Norden, *Kunstprosa*, II, pp. 545-47.

9. As to the 'hymns' which have been found in the NT, a comparison with epical or lyrical poetry of the time would be even less favourable. This can still be said, in the 2nd/3rd cent., for the famous hymn φῶς ἱλαρόν: see the text in Rouët de Journel, *Enchiridion patristicum*, 108.

10. See M. Hengel, *The 'Hellenization' of Judaea in the First Century after Christ* (London, 1989), p. 24; on Gadara, p. 20. Tiberias and Alexandria are the two towns which we know possessed synagogues in the form of basilicas supported by two parallel rows of columns (see below), a fact which reminds us of Hellenistic architecture and rhetoric at once.

defined—as a culture that was mainly based on ἑλληνισμός, that is, proficiency in the Greek language.[11]

The image of the first missionary activities of the church as a public performance rather differs from this, that is, Peter speaking in the streets of Jerusalem and in front of the Beautiful Gate of the Temple (Acts 2–3); Paul speaking on the Areopagus and elsewhere (διδάξαι δημοσίᾳ: Acts 16.37; 18.28; 20.20). Let us look more closely at the conditions and the *Sitz im Leben* of public communication in antiquity in order not to misinterpret one of the rare Christian individuals that might have been able to take part in it successfully. I am referring to Luke.

2. *Rules of Public Discourse in Antiquity*

The πρέπον *of the Locality*

The spectacular institution of Speaker's Corner in London's Hyde Park had no counterpart, as far as I know, in the Hellenized cities of antiquity. Either you mixed with all those who were shouting in the streets and in the market-places (which, of course, was exhausting), or else you were fortunate enough to be invited to speak in a place where an audience would gather to listen. In those days, all Hellenistic cities had a theatre. In Palestine, one may presume, there were theatres in the cities near the Mediterranean as in Caesarea. In Jerusalem, a gymnasium which had been instituted under the reign of Antiochus IV (it is mentioned in the books of the Maccabees) had been destroyed for religious reasons, and nothing is known of the importance of the theatre erected by Herod in honour of the Emperor. It is the pious imagination of the Christians of the second and third century which credits the apostles with the audacity to speak in a theatre without having been invited to do so, as is the case in the *Acts of John* (chs. 30–31) where the Proconsul, surprised by such an event, hurries to the theatre to see what is going on. Much more significant is the scene in Acts 3, near the Beautiful Gate, where Peter and John, having changed one of the Temple courts into an auditorium, are arrested by the Temple police. Compare also the noteworthy arguments with which an official of the city of Ephesus manages to dissolve an illegal assembly in the theatre, Acts 19.29-40.

---

11. See H.-I. Marrou, *Histoire de l'éducation dans l'antiquité* (Paris, 1948), p. 145.

In addition to the social conditions of mass communication, we should also consider some physical conditions. Imagine yourself speaking to a thousand people, without a microphone! In any locality, except perhaps a theatre, only well-trained professionals would be able to cope with such a situation.

In classrooms and lecture halls the physical demands were considerably less. It is in such a place that we encounter the Apostle Paul in the book of Acts: the σχολὴ Τυράννου in Acts 19.9. Here again, it was necessary to be invited by the owner of the place or by some authority. The stylistic and physical efforts, however, were not comparable to those demanded in mass communication.

To sum up, there were two aspects in what we have called the πρέπον of the locality. First, well-educated Greeks did not shout their words in just any place. Secondly, if they were invited to speak before an audience who had come to listen, they had to meet strenuous physical requirements, and they had to satisfy refined and snobbish tastes. Paul's adventure on the Areopagus will give us a glimpse of this (see below, p. 55).

The πρέπον *of Voice and Gesture*

It is Quintilian who supplies us with most information on this matter.[12] You had to have a strong, well-trained and flexible voice, and you had to be able to sing and to emphasize your words with appropriate gestures. Jesus sitting in a boat does not fit this rule even if the place was well chosen acoustically. In his case, the typical behaviour of an Israelite sage, which was near to that of a Greek philosopher—calm, serious, being in control of his emotions as well as his gestures—contrasts with that of an orator who would be screaming, gesticulating and enthralling the crowd with the display of his art, his emotions and his strength. Unlike the sage's address to his disciples, which has provided us with so many samples of the oral and literary genre of the *diatribe*, speaking to the masses required diverting, amusing, frightening them by means of *elocutio* and *actio*. This was most highly developed in the so-called 'Asianism', of which we shall soon speak.

---

12. See Lausberg, *Handbuch*, § 258, and his references.

The πρέπον *of Expression and Style*

In general it is the *elocutio* (φράσις) to which the theorists of rhetoric devoted the largest number of chapters in their handbooks. The larger the audience, the more the *stylus grandis* was required. This was not only because of the more or less exceptional character of a mass assembly, but also, I think, because of the sheer requirements of acoustics. Imagine the giant synagogue of Alexandria, termed διπλόστοον because of its five naves divided by two double rows of columns—the Tosephta tells us there was an assistant on its *bima* who would give a signal with a cloth when the assembly should say amen after a prayer or a benediction.[13] Imagine such a basilica, and a preacher speaking with a monotonous voice, even if it was loud, and using a language without images, assonances, rhymes, rhythms, puns and other sorts of intellectual and acoustic effects: no one would listen to him, not even for a quarter of an hour, and no one would understand him.

If we take into account these cultural and physical data, we will no longer be surprised by the apparently overdone and over-loaded style of the synagogue sermons mentioned above, which probably originated in Alexandria. And we will, although not without difficulty, look for traces of mass communication in the New Testament, as well.

It is time now to speak of the so-called 'Asianism' which almost exclusively shapes all of the high literature which has come down to us from the New Testament period. We are dealing with a rhetorical fashion which, appearing in the third century BCE, did not fade until after the second century CE when it gave way to its Atticist opposition. Originating in Asia Minor, this extremely artistic *elocutio*, which seemed exaggerated at least to those who disliked it, had been developed for the needs of mass communication in the growing cities of the Hellenistic world. Its success during these five centuries had moulded the expectations of an ancient audience. The Atticist's opposition, which was of a more-or-less elitist character, was insignificant at first when looked at from a quantitative point of view. Only from the third century CE onwards did it begin to dominate Asianism whose documents gradually fell into oblivion. Other writers such as Plutarch and

---

13. Tosephta, *Suk.* 4.6; quoted in German by H. Strack and P. Billerbeck, *Kommentar zum N.T. aus Talmud und Midrasch*, IV.1 (Munich, 1928), p. 122, *lit. g.* At Tiberias in Palestine there was a copy of this synagogue.

the *auctor de sublimi*, who did not belong to either party, were not orators performing before mass audiences.

Let us now turn to the characteristic features of 'Asianic' eloquence. *Der Kleine Pauly*, in his article 'Asianismus', summarizes them as follows: *Hauptmerkmale...sind Vermeidung der klassischen Periode, Verwendung kurzer, stark rhythmischer Kommata, Wortspiele und Reime sowie sehr gewagte Metaphern.* Eduard Norden, in his two volumes on artistic prose in antiquity, goes into detail on these prose rhythms. They are made up of a sequence or a repeated sequence of mainly long syllables, the so-called *versus Creticus* ($-$ ˘ $-$).[14] At the end of the phrase, it may be apocopated to $-$ ˘ or $-$ (but not $-$ ˘ ˘). This rhythmical pattern belongs to the very 'index fossils' of Asianic prose. It is absent from lyrical poetry as well as from epic, and rather rare in classical and atticist prose, both of which abhorred any rhythmical regularity and any blurring of the demarcation between poetry and prose.[15] It marks, however, the final syllables of any important sentence and especially in final syllables of paragraphs of Asianic prose. See the examples in Quintilian 9.4.63-66, all of which have the structure $-$ ˘ $-$ I $-$ x.

Prose rhythm thus is one of the means for structuring texts which have been labelled 'oral typesetting'.[16] This term is well-chosen since we can, in fact, distinguish the sections occurring in texts like Chariton's love romance (*Callirhoë*) or the *Sachprosa* of Artemidorus's book on dreams (*Onirocriticon*) by noticing the accumulations of 'Cretic' rhythms. The main effect of the *clausulae* in $-$ ˘ $-$ evidently was a slowing down[17] of what de Saussure has termed *la chaîne parlée*, therefore it was a means of emphasis and gravity (δεινότης). In my reading of Greek texts of the first and second centuries I had the impression that every writer who was conscious of himself, that is, every writer addressing himself to an audience as

---

14. Dionysius Thrax, in his short enumeration of metres, calls it ἀμφίμακρος. I have consulted the bilingual edition: *Ars Dionysii grammatici et Armeniaca in eam scholia* (ed. N. Adontz; Petrograd, 1915), p. 44. In Quintilian, see 9.4.107-108; in Lausberg, *Handbuch*, §§ 1007-1021.

15. Lausberg, *Handbuch*, § 981.

16. H. v.D. Parunak, 'Oral Typesetting: Some Uses of Biblical Structure', *Bib* 62 (1981), pp. 153-69.

17. Lausberg, *Handbuch*, § 997: *Bremsprinzip*.

spoilt as was that of the big assemblies in the theatres and basilicas needed to employ these rhythms.

It was at least in the introductory and concluding sections of a book that a writer would make efforts to attract the audience (the readers of an ancient book were an audience, too) by the music of his words. Let us keep in mind that at least until the time of Ambrose of Milan it was common practice to read (or to have read) a book aloud. Professor Botha's contribution to the present volume stresses this fact also for epistolary communication. It is not surprising, then, that rhetorical productions in the strict sense, that is, oral discourses of which we possess the scripts or the stenogrammes, show a high frequency of acoustical and musical effects, higher sometimes than in texts edited as literature.

Add to all these refinements of *elocutio*—the puns on words, the flourishes, the rhymes, the rhythms—an elated voice which is almost chanting the Greek accents (which were, in elaborated language, musical accents and not the stress accent of later and present custom),[18] just add a voice that expresses the difference between a non-accentuated vowel and an acute accent by intervals up to a fifth, and you have the typical sound of public declamation in the time of the apostles.

As this written paper does not allow me to represent this acoustically, I ask you to make an effort in auditory imagination while reading Greek texts. Let us look at some passages in Luke's two-volume work where he speaks of persons talking to an audience.

3. *Examples of Public Oratory in Luke*

Due to their very genre, the *logia*, the apophthegms, the summaries and the compositions of gnomic material which represent *Jesus* speaking are not likely to contain much rhetorical effect. Nowhere do we find a *speech* in the rhetorical definition of the word λόγος. Furthermore, if there are any acoustic effects due to the subtlety of prose rhythms we may safely know that they are the merit of the Greek translation.

Keeping this in mind, consider the beatitudes of the Sermon on the Plain, the first two of which end up in rhythms: ἡ βασιλεῖᾱ Ι τοῦ

18. I may refer you to the first ten or so pages, usually skipped, of any grammar of classical Greek.

Θεοῦ (6.20), and χὅρτᾱσθῆσἕσθε.[19] This fact alone does not prove Lukan intention, as the parallels in Matthew are also rhythmical (by chance?). Verse 24, however, which has no parallel, is altogether 'asianic': Πλὴν οὐᾱι ὑμῖν τοῖς | πλοῦσῖοῖς, | ὅτι ἀπεχετε τὴν πᾰρᾱκλῆσῖν ὑ|μῶν. But Luke does not maintain this principle, being bound, as one might suppose, by a tradition that was already Greek.

One might, therefore, anticipate a higher frequency of rhythmical *clausulae* wherever Luke was free to choose his words, which leads us to the hypothesis that prose rhythms may serve as evidence (not a proof, but a means of evidence) of Lukan formulation. I leave it to others to examine this hypothesis in more detail.

Some other instance might include Lk. 14.24 οὐδεῖς...γεῦσἕτᾱι | μοῦ τοῦ δεῖπνοῦ and 14.33 οὐ δυναται˘εῖναῑ | μοῦ μᾰθῆ|τῆς (without parallel). It is worth noticing that in all these cases the emphases match the contents of the phrase.

The Orator Tertullus
One of the few persons of whom we know that they earned their living as an orator in Palestine is a certain Tertullus mentioned in Acts 24.2-8. Luke does not quote nor even re-create his discourse which would have been too long for his purpose. He only summarizes the *captatio benevolentiae* and some arguments. But even so, he makes his readers hear the typical sound of a public harangue. We may note first the anacoluthic syntax, the ambition of the 'asianic' orators. It seems difficult to accumulate as many twisted constructions in as few phrases as does our orator. Secondly, with one possible exception,[20] there are only rhythmical ends of clauses.

We are now well prepared for a rhetorical analysis of Paul—the Paul we know by his letters as well as the Paul we see through Luke. It will be evident that the more accomplished orator of the two is the

19. A sequence of all long syllables is a very effective rhythm, too. I propose to take the ordinary *Cretici* as an attempt at accumulating, in a periodic way, as many lengths as possible. Mere lengths, then, constitute an extreme. See the case of Jas. 2.18 (see below, p. 54).

20. I am not sure as to τῶν Ναζωραίων αἱρέσεως (v. 5 end), where αἱρέσεως could be pronounced either in four syllables, thus avoiding the rhythm (the semantic contents of the words are pejorative—see below, Postscript 2), or in three syllables, with *crasis* of the two final vowels, which would yield, as the end of the phrase, a series of six long syllables followed by a *Creticus*.

latter. So far, I have not found in Paul's letters much prose rhythm that could be understood as intentional, not even in those passages of 2 Corinthians which are most charged with emotion. Rhythmical *clausulae* like Rom. 13.7 (ending up with 7 lengths), 1 Cor. 4.7 (τι καΰ|χᾱσαῐ[21] ὡς I μῆ λᾰβῶν) and 2 Cor. 2.6 (ὑπο τῶν I πλεῐὄνῶν) are exceptional. (The deutero-Pauline epistles are different.)[22] In Paul, as a rule, a sequence of two short syllables not capable of 'positional' length or of *crasis* prevents any effect of quantitative gravity. From this point of view, we may agree with Paul's claim in the same letter (1 Cor. 2.4; cf. 2 Cor. 11.6), that he is not using words of persuasion and of human eloquence. His eloquence is not that of a professional.

In order to get a contrast we may simply compare Paul's farewell address at Ephesus, Acts 20.19-35. Elsewhere[23] I have compiled a list of the rhythmic *clausulae*, of which only vv. 30 and 33 are absent, due probably to their negative contents (cf. Postscript 2 below).

That we are, in fact, dealing with *Lukan* style may be proven on two levels. First, negatively: a comparison of his text with the authentic Pauline letters shows that Paul did not formulate like this. One could only suppose that in public speaking he did; but then why does he not avail himself of this means in 2 Corinthians which demands so much emotional vigour? In antiquity, letters, too, were acoustic experiences for their addressees.[24] Professor Botha's contribution, already referred to, states this with due emphasis. Secondly, positively: in comparing Luke with himself in the passages which he was free to create as he wanted, we notice that he

21. αι pronounced short because of *crasis* with the following syllable.
22. Attempts at writing rhythmically may be found, e.g., in Eph. 1.3-14 (but frequently it is only a semitizing αὐτοῦ, αὐτῷ which yields just two long syllables at the end of a *kolon*) and Col. 1.14-22 (without v. 23). On the clumsy style of the deutero-Pauline epistles, see Norden, *Kunstprosa*, II, p. 506, n. 2.
23. See Siegert, *Drei hellenistisch-jüdische Predigten*, II, p. 33 (to be corrected for v. 27).
24. In a culture that was much more oral than is ours: see 1 Thess. 5.27; Col. 4.16; Rev. 1.3 (ὁ ἀναγινώσκων καὶ οἱ ἀκούοντες). There was an art of reading a written text to the public, which included even *actio*: Cicero, *De oratore* 3.56 § 213 (referring to Aeschines). The messengers who were charged with transmitting a letter, being its 'anagnosts' as well as its interpreters, did an oral job. It would even seem that some of Paul's messengers were able to read better than Paul spoke: 2 Cor. 10.10.

endeavoured quite consciously to employ rhythms wherever they were required by rhetorical and/or literary convention.[25] Let us consider the two prologues, that of the Gospel and that of the Acts, and look also at the end of Acts. In a graphic rendering of their structures, they read thus:[26]

Lk. 1.1-4

Ἐπειδηπερ πολλοι ἐπεχειρησαν ἀνατᾱξᾱισθαῑ δῑῆ | γῆσιν
        περι των πεπληροφορημενων ἐν ἡμῑν | πρᾱγμᾱτῶν,
        καθως παρεδοσαν... αὐτοπται και ὑπηρεται γενομενοῑ | τοῡ λὄγοῡ,
ἐδὄξἔ κᾱιμοῑ
        παρηκολουθηκοτι ἀνωθεν πασιν ᾱκρῑβῶς
    καθεᾱξῆς σοῑ γρᾱψαῑ,
            κρατιστε Θεοφιλε,[27]
    ἱνα ἐπιγνως περι ὠν κατηχηθης λογῶν τῆν | ᾱσφαλειᾱν.

Acts 1.1-5

Τον μεν πρωτον λογον ἐποῑῆσᾱμῆν
        περι πᾱντῶν,
            ὠ Θεοφιλε,
        ὠν ἡρξατο ὁ Ἰησους ποιειν τε κᾱι δῑδᾱσικειν,
            ἀχρι ἡς ἡμερας ἐντειλαμενος τοις ἀποστολοις δια πν. ἁγιου,
            οὑς ἐξελεξατο,
    ἀνελῆμφθῆ.
            οἱς και παρεστησεν ἑαῡτὄν ζῶντα
                    μετα το παθεᾱιν | αῡτὄν (here the rhythm goes on)
            ἐν | πὄλλὄις τεᾱκιμῆρῑοῑς
        δι' ἡμερων... λεγων περι της βασιλεᾱιᾱς | τοῡ Θεοῡ
    και συναλιζομενος παρῆγιγεᾱιλεᾱν αῡιτὄις
            ἀπο Ἰεροσολυμῶν μῆ χῶρῑζεσθᾱι
            ἀλλα περιμενειν την ἐπαγγελιαν του Πατρος,
                ἡν ἡκουσατε μου,
                ὁτι

25. I leave the question unanswered whether every ἀναγνώστης in a primitive Christian cult was able to reproduce these rhythms.
26. The texts are here reproduced according to their macro-syntactical structure, which perfectly conforms to metrical analysis.
27. This name, which is totally alien to a rhythm of long syllables, seems not to be chosen at will.

Acts 28.28-31 (=end):

Ἰωαννης μεν ἐβαπτισεν ὑδατι,
ὑμεις δε ἐν πν. βαπτισθησεσθε ἁγιῳ·
οὐ μετα πὁλλᾱς ταὐτᾱς | ἡμὲρᾱς.

Γνῶστὸν οὖν | ἔστω²⁸ ὑμῖν
ὅτι τοις ἔθνεσιν ἀπεσταλη τουτο το σῶ|τῆρῐὸν | του θἔοῦ
αὐτοι και ἀκοῦσὸνταῖ.

Ἐπεμεινεν δε διετιαν ὁλην ἐν ἰδιῳ μισθωματι
και ἀπεδεχετο παντας τους εἰσπορευομενοῦς πρὁς αὑτον,
κηρυσσων την βασιλἔιᾱν | του θἔοῦ
και διδασκων τα περι του κυριου Ἰῆ|σοῦ Χρῑστοῦ
μετα πασης παρρησιᾱς ἄκω|λῡτῶς.

If there were any need for evidence of Luke's literary ambitions, here it is. This analysis confirms not only that he aspired to give his two books the appearance of a literary *oeuvre*, but also that he took pains to create the typical sound of a harangue where one of his heroes starts talking in public.[29] This explains well the rhetorical style of the Lukan Paul, not less than that of the Lukan Peter (of whom he knew and even explicitly says that he was an 'uneducated and untrained man', Acts 4.13). I have come across some rhythmic *clausulae* at the beginning of his Pentecost speech (Acts 2.14bα, 15, 16 and, after the citation, v. 22) and in his discourse near the Beautiful Gate: Acts 3.12 (= beginning); vv. 16-19 (emotional passage) and vv. 21-24, 25-26 (= end), the quotation from the Septuagint being an exception. But even there, in some clauses resulting from redactional modification, rhythms appear: ὁσα ἀν λἀλῆ|σῆ πρὁς ὑ|μᾱς (v. 22 end). Each time, we sense Luke's desire to let his reader hear a public speech.[30]

Apart from exceptional passages such as the prologues, the epilogue and the discourses, however, we find in Luke quite a different style.

28. ω is short because of *crasis*.
29. This rule is not without exception, which shows even more the literary skill of Luke: in Acts 7.2-53 he presents Stephen as a naïve, simple-minded speaker of semitizing Septuagint Greek—a conscious naïveté which is refined on more than one level.
30. Stephen's apology (preceding note) may serve as an example to the contrary. There we find such irregularity in the ends of phrases that the few rhythms which might be found prove to be unintentional. As a whole, this text is remarkable for its (intended) lack of any trace of eloquence.

In Acts 20.36, for example, immediately after the farewell address mentioned above, the text falls back into the αὐτοῦ, αὐτοῖς, etc., typical of semitizing Greek. Luke, it seems to me, proves to be a writer conscious of his style, choosing at will the language appropriate to the situation. For the hymns in Luke 1 and 2 it was that of the Septuagint.

Compare to this the historiographer Arrian (first half of the second century), whose lecture notes have preserved the unpretending diatribe of Epictetus: in writing his ᾿Αλεξάνδρου ἀνάβασις, however, he chose Attic Greek (imitating, of course, Xenophon), whereas his *History of India* (᾿Ινδική) is composed in an Ionic dialect evidently inspired by Herodotus, the classical model of ethnography.

This observation, by the way, may warn us against attributing a text to a particular author by means of its 'style'. Learned authors used to have at their disposal more than one register.

4. *Some Contrasts*

To enlarge the basis of this analysis, let me put forward two more samples that will illustrate the rigorous stylistic demands of a public discourse and a literary œuvre in antiquity. One is positive, one negative. This procedure will help us to assess Luke as a writer amid the other authors of the New Testament.

The first example is the Epistle of James. It has long been recognized as being a *diatribe* with considerable rhetorical merit (which automatically denies its authenticity as containing the words of a brother of the Carpenter's Son). Here is some further evidence of this: 2.18-19, the famous negation of the Pauline message of righteousness without works. The heavy and emotional nature of the passage will be sensed by reading it aloud: Δεῑξόν μοῑ τῆν πῑστῑν σοῦ χῶρῑς τῶν ἐργῶν, κᾱγῶ σοῑ δεῑξῶ᾽ἐκ[31] τῶν ἐργῶν μοῦ τῆν πῑστῑν. There are 23 continuous lengths! A Greek writer could not have emphasized his thesis more strongly.[32] In the following verse, 'James' gives a

---

31. Pronounce δείξω᾽κ. In ancient orthography there was no obligation to mark the elisions, not even in some manuscripts of Homer. In the NT, cf. the quotation of Menander in 1 Cor. 15.33.

32. In Paul, cf. the example, already quoted, of Rom. 13.7. On the other hand, a heavy rhythm to which the semantic contents of a phrase do not correspond will create a feeling of awkwardness or mannerism. An example may be found in the

sarcastic answer to one who 'believes that there is one God' (here is what the polemicist reduces Paul's position to): 'That's fine. So do all the devils in hell, and shudder in terror!' (trans. Phillips). In Greek: κᾱλῶς ποῖεῑς· καὶ τα δαιμονια πῐστευοῦσῑν κᾱι φρισσοῦσιν. In this manner he goes on more or less until the end of the chapter. With metrical analysis we have in our hands a means to discover what mattered most to a New Testament author such as Luke or pseudo-James. We now come back to Luke and his representation of Paul. In the book of Acts we find an example of historical sincerity which merits our attention, being a negative example. I am speaking of the famous Speech on the Areopagus (Acts 17.16-33). Luke[33] states that the social prerequisites for a public performance were given (vv. 19-20), adding some words on the audience's expectations: 'All the Athenians, and even foreign visitors to Athens, had an obsession for any novelty and would spend their whole time talking about or listening to anything new' (v. 21; trans. Phillips). The speech itself proves to be a Lukan formulation by its elaborate rhythms. (Only the *copia verborum* of a formal speech could not have been reproduced in the given context.) To my mind, 'Paul' was quite up to the requirements of his audience, which leads us to ask the question: why did his persuasive efforts almost totally fail?

Luke's explanation in v. 32 does not provide us with a key. The topic of resurrection was neither embarrassing to the Athenians (as it was to some in Jerusalem), nor boring, being more or less sanctified by the *Dialogues* of Plato and exemplified by numerous persons of folklore and quasi-mythical tradition.[34] The most natural explanation of the Areopagus failure seems to be that the historical Paul did not

literary frame of the *Acts of John* (vol. II.1, Lipsius–Bonnet), p. 151: ἐπεμψεν εἰς Ι 'Ρωμῆν ποιῆσᾰσθᾱι τῆς Εἰρῆνῆς σκῆνωμα. Recent edition: *CChr*, ser. apocr., II (ed. E. Junod and J.-D. Kaestli), p. 863.

33. I suppose that it is not necessary to create, as author of the Lukan corpus, a person other than the 'Luke' mentioned a few times in the NT. See the critique of critiques in C.-J. Thornton, *Der Zuege des Zeugen: Lukas als Historiker der Paulusreisen* (WUNT, 61; Tübingen, 1991). The case of the epistle of 'James' is very different.

34. Alcestis (known from Euripides' play), Thespesius of Soli (Plutarch, *Mor.*, from 563D onwards), Theseus (Seneca, *Herc. fur.*, act 3 sc. 2) and Menippus (Lucian, *Mort. dial.* and *Necyom.*; Lucian, to be sure, does not take this tradition seriously). Other examples of a more mythical character could be added.

possess the rhetorical training that the masses as well as the cultural élite anticipated.

To some extent Luke had already admitted this in 17.18: 'Some of them remarked, "What is this cock sparrow (ὁ σπερμολόγος οὗτος) trying to say?" Others said, "He seems to be trying to proclaim some more gods to us, and foreign ones at that"'. Reading the Greek text, we discover a thoroughly conceited language using the optative mood with ἄν[35] and the word σπερμολόγος which had become rare, too.[36] This is what Paul did not offer, just as Epictetus did not, one of whose hearers once left his lectures saying: Οὐδὲν ἦν ὁ ᾽Επίκτητος· ἐσολοίκιζε, ἐβαρβάριζε (*Diss.* 3.9.14). In Acts 17, whatever one may think of this chapter, Luke respects the historical facts in reporting the failure of the historical Paul who was not a public orator.

Postscript 1 on the History of Research

Literature on this topic seems not to abound, which is quite an exception in New Testament exegesis. On Mark there are the papers by E.I. Robson[37] and G. Lüderitz.[38] These two articles, it seems to me, make Mark more literary than he is. F. Blass, A. Debrunner and F. Rehkopf[39] are ill advised in citing an opinion which F. Blass uttered in 1902: *nach Rhythmus im NT zu suchen, ist allgemein ein unnützer Zeitvertreib, und was man gefunden hat, ist auch zumeist von solcher Qualität, daß es besser unerwähnt bleibt*. In the present article you may have found some evidence for the contrary. Blass should have known *which* rhythms to look for, and *where*.[40]

---

35. Cf. τί ἄν γένοιτο τοῦτο (Acts 5.24) in the words of a member of the high society of Jerusalem. Luke is imitating, in Greek, an elaborate code.

36. E. Norden, *Agnostos Theos: Untersuchungen zur Formengeschichte religiöser Rede* (Leipzig, 1913), p. 333, applies a wrong perspective in blaming Luke for his crediting the people (*das Volk*) of Athens with Atticism. As regards the sociology of expression and style, Luke was a good observer: it is the spokesmen of Athenian bourgeoisie who endeavour to distinguish themselves from the populace and from obscure individuals such as Paul.

37. 'Rhythm and Intonation in St. Mark i–x', *JTh* 17 (1916), pp. 270-80.

38. 'Rhetorik, Poetik, Kompositionstechnik im Markusevangelium', in H. Cancik (ed.), *Markus-Philologie* (WUNT, 33; Tübingen 1984), pp. 165-203.

39. *Grammatik des neutestamentliche Griechisch* (Göttingen, 15th edn, 1979), § 488, n. 6.

40. On Blass, cf. W. Schmid and G. Stählin, *Geschichte der griechischen Literatur* (HAW, 7,2,2), II, p. 1135 n. 4, and p. 1152 n. 1.

W. Bujard[41] assesses the difficulties of knowing to what extent metrical quantities were respected in everyday speech—a problem not dealt with in this paper since I am speaking of the language of the orators. B. Eckmann, in 'A Quantitative Metrical Analysis of the Philippians Hymn',[42] does not touch our topic: the author is speaking of lyrical metres where a long syllable can be substituted by two short ones, which, in prose not sustained by melody, would almost remove the effect of gravity.[43]

The scarcity of literature on this topic is best explained in a recent publication by Hans Dieter Betz. In his introduction to the first volume of his collected papers,[44] Betz recalls an allotment of domains, by the turn of the century, between Classical Philology and the History of Oriental Religions, Christian theology being associated with the latter. This more or less practical allocation, backed by a variety of motifs, became a kind of dogma. Later on, since the middle of our century, the Hebrew/Aramaic and Coptic finds kept scholars on the move. I may add that an increasing interest in Rabbinic Judaism resulted as a kind of intellectual reaction to the Nazi régime's debasing and even exterminating the Jews in central Europe. All these factors formed an obstacle to an unbiased view of the relationship between Jewish and non-Jewish culture in pre-Rabbinic times.

Summing up the tendencies of recent research, Betz asserts: *Ein Hauptergebnis der neueren Forschung ist die Erkenntnis, daß das Judentum und mit ihm das Urchristentum enger als man vorher annahm mit der griechisch-hellenistischen Kultur verflochten sind* (p. 3). I cannot but emphasize this statement, mainly as regards Luke, 'James' and the Epistle to the Hebrews (with which I have not dealt explicitly).[45]

Ancient Judaism will inevitably profit from this turn of affairs—having been, from pseudo-Aristeas to the Jew *apud Celsum*, a sustained dialogue with contemporary

---

41. *Stilanalytische Untersuchungen zum Kolosserbrief* (Studien zur Umwelt des N.T., 11; Göttingen 1973), pp. 139-44.

42. *NTS* 46 (1979–80), pp. 258-66.

43. An exception may be found in Lausberg, *Handbuch*, § 1016,1: a rule which permits the substitution, considered euphonic, of the last long syllable of the last complete Cretic by two lengths, if there is at least one long syllable that follows. For the purposes of the present article there was no need to take into account such a refinement.

44. H.D. Betz, *Hellenismus und Urchristentum: Gesammelte Aufsätze* (Tübingen, 1990), pp. 1-3.

45. As to Paul, I have tried to place him somewhere in the middle of this scale in my *Argumentation bei Paulus, gezeigt an Röm 9–11* (WUNT, 34; Tübingen, 1985). Paul's indebtedness to Palestinian tradition has been assessed by Martin Hengel in his article 'Der vorchristliche Paulus', in M. Hengel and U. Heckel (eds.), *Paulus und das antike Judentum* (Tübingen, 1991), pp. 177-291. This essay gives a detailed account of what *Greek* culture in Jerusalem was—a quite vigourous but restricted branch of Mediterranean culture.

58   Rhetoric and the New Testament

Hellenism. It was precisely from this encounter of cultures and religions that primitive Christianity became inspired in its effort to establish itself in the Roman world and to raise itself to the level of theology (this term being a Greek one, not a biblical one). Methodically, justice would be done to primitive Christianity in replacing its documents under the solid shelter of Classical Philology.

Postscript 2 on an Overlooked Law of Prose Rhythm

One could suspect an inadvertancy in Acts 20.30a and 33 where, in a context of rhythmic prose, we find the *clausulae* λαλοῦντες διεστραμμένα and οὐδενὸς ἐπεθύμησα. Yet it seems to me that these non-rhythms have been deliberately chosen to emphasize the negative content of the phrase. 'Asianic' eloquence was not a euphony without nuances. It seems that it had a πρέπον for that which is negative. Cf. Artemidorus, *Onirocriticon, prooem.*, p. 1 (Pack), l. 8: διατριβᾶς ἑαυτοῖς πορτιζόμενων; p. 2, l. 11 καὶ διεφθαρμένα διελάθεν(!). Another author of rhythmic prose, Libanius, writes in *Or.* 1, § 3, p. 95 (Martin–Petit), 1.13: ἀλλόθεν; p. 96, 1.8: ἀρχὴν ἀπωλσάμενός, etc.

I do not consider it useful to collect more instances of this; a few minutes' reading would soon provide a selection. Even though I did not find anything relevant in the manuals,[46] I have a strong impression that there was a stylistic law which assigned to negative passages the *avoidance* of a rhythm of long syllables.[47]

---

46. Lausberg (*Handbuch*, §§ 1007-1051) does not take account of semantics. On reading the examples of so-called 'bad' *clausulae* given by Quintilian (9.4.107, end; Lausberg, *Handbuch*, §§ 1028-29 and 1032) we may notice, however, that they are mostly of pejorative content.

47. Thanks are due to Mrs Gremaud, Neuchâtel, and Mrs Marion Salzmann, Kassel, as well as to the staff of Sheffield Academic Press, for correcting my English.

RHETORICAL ISSUE AND RHETORICAL STRATEGY IN LUKE 10.25-37 AND ACTS 10.1–11.18

J. Ian H. McDonald

Introduction

If one is interested in rhetoric as persuasion and in the rhetoric of narrative as well as ethics and praxis, the two passages singled out in the above title present a particularly attractive area of investigation. In both, there is a premium on persuasion, for the issues involve radical change in self-understanding and in socio-religious practice. In both, narrative is used, though in contrasting ways; and not only do the central issues deal with matters of socio-religious ethics but the rhetoric itself is permeated with moral concern. The *dispositio* or arrangement of units is designed to reveal or highlight moral reality: not to brainwash the audience, but to open up the moral—and, indeed, theological—issues so that the audience can see things as they really are and take appropriate action. Not that this is a purely cerebral operation, rational though the argument may be. The rhetoric of suasion has also to do with motivation and affect, with arousing passionate concern for and sensitivity to the issues, and with leading the hearers into a realm of being in which they can both will and do what is right. Rhetoric is therefore organically related to disposition, action and commitment.[1]

A few matters require preliminary comment. At the outset, it is important not only to underline the rhetorical nature of the units themselves but to identify the internal relationship of such units and the rhetorical situations or exigencies to which they relate. Any consideration of basic issue (*stasis* or *status*, to use the traditional terms) involves an awareness of context. While in New Testament studies this

---

1. Cf. C. Perelman and L. Olbrechts-Tyteca, *The New Rhetoric: A Treatise on Argumentation* (Notre Dame, 1969), pp. 59-62.

is often interpreted in socio-historical terms, attention has also to be focused (not least in this article) on the rhetorical situation, for both texts relate to issues of controversy in ancient Jewish and Jewish-Christian circles. We are joining a debate rather than witnessing the inauguration of a new one.

Since a particular feature of both texts is their use of narrative, it is important not to confine our exploration to *narratio* in ancient rhetoric (which might well, in this instance, be misleading) but to invoke the modern discussion of narrative rhetoric in order that a fuller understanding might be obtained of the strategies adopted in the texts. To be sure, while narratives involve the interplay of characters, situations and plot, the narrators—both intra-textual and extra-textual—play an important role in developing rhetorical impact as they bring the hearers to participate in the worlds they create for them. Repetition and emphasis are among the methods directed towards this end.[2]

Finally, it is important in an investigation of this kind to complete the hermeneutical circle by highlighting not only the participation of the 'intended' hearer-interpreters but all interpreters at every stage in the process. The existential question is: how far does this study expose us to the realities of which the texts speak?

Rhetorical Issues

In order to identify the rhetorical issues, two matters must be clarified: the coherence of the rhetorical units in question and the nature of the rhetorical situation or exigency that prompts the utterance and defines the issue.[3]

Rhetorical Units

As G. Kennedy has made clear, rhetorical units—convincing or persuasive sections of text—may be long or short but they must have a

---

2. Cf. G. Genette, *Narrative Discourse: An Essay in Method* (Cornell, 1980); R.W. Funk, *The Poetics of Biblical Narrative* (Sonoma, CA, 1988).

3. The terminology broadly reflects the conventions set out in G. Kennedy, *New Testament Interpretation through Rhetorical Criticism* (Chapel Hill, 1984); for summary statements, cf. B.L. Mack, *Rhetoric in the New Testament* (Philadelphia, 1990), pp. 19-48; J.I.H. McDonald, 'Rhetorical Criticism', in *A Dictionary of Biblical Interpretation* (ed. R. Coggins and J.L. Houlden; London, 1990), pp. 599-600.

recognizable beginning and ending (opening and closing) linked by some action or argument.[4] Units may be combined in various ways, 'as atoms are combined into molecules', in W. Wuellner's apt phrase. The Sermon on the Mount is a good example.[5] Similarly, a shorter unit may be accommodated within a longer one. In the case of Lk. 10.25-37, the parabolic unit (Lk. 10.30-35) is set within the larger rhetorical unit of 10.25-37 and interacts with it. This remains the case even if we emphasize Luke's active role as editor of the material and suspect the use of more than one source. The unit of persuasive argumentation begins with the lawyer's test question to Jesus, and closes with Jesus' command to go and do likewise. The issue relates to the interpretation of Torah, namely, the two great commandments, focusing precisely on the identity of neighbour. In this section of Luke's narrative—part of his extensive account of the journey to Jerusalem (9.51–19.27)—priority issues are raised in relation to discipleship. The story of Martha and Mary (10.38-42), which follows the parable in question, also involves a question put to Jesus and concentrates on 'the one thing needful' (cf. 10.42). The parable itself follows the mission of the seventy (10.1-24) and acquires added punch and piquancy from the fact that the Samaritans have already rejected Jesus (9.53).

It is not difficult to decide on the rhetorical unit in the case of the Cornelius episode. The action starts at 10.1, with the narrative about Cornelius himself, his angelic vision and the divine injunction to send for Simon Peter (cf. 10.1-8); and it continues in connected narrative until Peter recapitulates the whole action (11.4-17) and the appropriate conclusion is drawn by his previously critical audience (11.18). The unit is a prime example of narrative layering, as we shall see below.[6] The exigency which prompts utterance is similar to that considered above in that it concerns the parameters which divide people, even when confronted with the call of Christ, and which are therefore reflected in ecclesiastical practice. As in the parable, the issue is expressed in iconic form: in this case, visions present the substance for interpretation. There is a certain sophistication in the way the interpretation is handled. On the one hand, it relates to *eating* what is

---

4. Kennedy, *New Testament Interpretation*, p. 34; Mack, *Rhetoric*, pp. 21-22.
5. W. Wuellner, 'Where is Rhetorical Criticism Taking Us?', *CBQ* 49 (1987), p. 455.
6. For 'narrative layering', cf. Genette, *Narrative Discourse*, pp. 227-28.

common or unclean (10.13-15; 11.3); on the other hand, it concerns *calling any human being common* or unclean (10.28). This daring rejection of the parameters of purity[7] is enjoined by God (10.34-35), is the outcome of Jesus' ministry (10.43), and is endorsed by the Spirit (10.44-48): three powerful 'proofs'. 'Who was I', asks Peter, 'that I could withstand God?' (11.17). If Peter struggled to accept the divine will, so also did his audience, whose objections were silenced (11.3, 18) and who—rather more willingly than the lawyer—glorified God, who had so surprised them. The issue represents a moment of truth in Hellenistic Christianity, of immense consequence for the Gentile mission. It is a high point of the Acts account of the spread of the Church from Jerusalem to Antioch (1.1–12.25), the latter location being a staging point on the way to Rome and the Gentile world (13.1–28.31).

Rhetorical Situation
The second step is to identify the rhetorical situation, that is, the situation or state of affairs which prompts utterance. This is the all-important first stage in invention, involving the audience which the author presupposes and which the speaker (Jesus, Peter or another) addresses.

No account of the rhetorical situation in Lk. 10.25-37 can overlook the fact that the basic requirements of Torah and the propriety of summative statements such as the 'great commandment' (cf. Deut. 6.5; Lev. 19.18) and the 'golden rule' had become matters of debate and strategy at the interface of Jewish and Hellenistic worlds and within rabbinic Judaism itself. There is the famous story of the divergent responses of R. Shammai and R. Hillel to a request by a Gentile to be taught the whole of the Torah while standing on one leg. Shammai drove him away with the builder's measure he was holding in his hand.[8] Such suggestions detracted from the multifold complexity that was the glory of the Torah. But when the same question was put in similar fashion to R. Hillel, he replied undaunted: 'What is hateful to yourself do not do to anyone else. This is the whole Law. The rest is commentary. Go and learn it.' The difference in strategy probably

7.   On the Jewish purity system and the Gentiles, cf. L.W. Countryman, *Dirt, Greed and Sex* (Philadelphia, 1988), pp. 39-42, 58. There was, in fact, a considerable variation in the degree to which the purity laws were observed by Jewish groups.
8.   Cf. *b. Šab.* 31A.

revolves around the question of how much a Gentile needed to know about Judaism before converting to it and how much could be learned later. The problem arose because of the diffusion of the Jewish communities. In a previous age an intending convert would already have been acculturated through residence in a coherent Jewish community. In changing circumstances a rabbi like Hillel saw the need to establish a degree of common ground between the requirements of Torah and Gentile morality. The negative version of the 'golden rule' served for this purpose, but the subsequent task of studying in depth the meaning of Torah (not least its contemporary interpretation) is no whit diminished.[9]

It may be noted that in the rhetoric of Hellenistic Jewish piety and apologetics, the totality of the requirements of the Torah was regularly characterized in terms of duty to God and one's fellows. Thus Philo commended the wisdom of the synagogue by suggesting that the vast range of rules and principles finds unity in two main heads: duty to God expressed in piety and holiness, and duty to humanity expressed in philanthropy and justice. In the *Testaments of the Twelve Patriarchs*, whose origins and milieu are much discussed, *T. Dan* 5.3 counsels: 'Love the Lord all your life, and one another with a true heart'. *T. Iss.* 5.2 urged, 'Love the Lord and your neighbour, and have compassion on the poor and weak' (cf. also 7.2-7). *T. Benj.* 3.1-5 exhorted the faithful to love the Lord and keep his commandments, following Joseph's good example. In this context, most MSS read at 3.3: 'Fear the Lord and love your neighbour'. *T. Zeb.* 5.1 adds a distinctive touch: 'And now, my children, I bid you to keep the commands of the Lord, and to show mercy to your neighbours, and to have compassion towards all, not towards men only, but also towards beasts'. In rabbinic literature, the *Sifre* on Deut. 32.29 says: 'Take upon you the yoke of the kingdom of heaven' (as one does when reciting the *Shema*), 'excel one another in standing in awe of heaven, and conduct yourselves one toward another in love'. All of these represent the substance of the two-fold commandment, but in general terms and without the sharp focus found in the Gospels.

Whatever the paraenetic or apologetic pressures, the debate was about the interpretation of Torah. In the Hebrew Scriptures, to love

---

9. Cf. M. Hilton and G. Marshall, *The Gospels and Rabbinic Judaism* (London, 1988), pp. 18-20. I have also discussed this material in *Great Commandment and Golden Rule* (Festschrift G.W. Anderson; Sheffield: JSOT Press, 1993).

your neighbour means not taking vengeance nor bearing grudges 'against the sons of your own people', that is, not hating but reasoning with your neighbour (Lev. 19.17). Its expression of social justice enfolds the stranger who comes into the community. 'The stranger who sojourns with you shall be to you as the native among you, and you shall love him as yourself' (19.34). Thus neighbour love is grounded in the total life of the people. It ranges over their world, and includes everyone in it. But their world is relatively static: it is the stranger who, for whatever reason, is mobile and in need of acceptance.

Whatever its wider connotation, the denotation of 'stranger' in the Scriptures was thus delimited. The question, 'Who is my neighbour?', echoes this need for delimitation. As we have suggested, Israel's position was neither as static nor as insulated as it once had been. Among the hearers and readers of Luke's Gospel there might well have been some who agonized over split families and who urgently needed a wider view of 'neighbour'. For Luke, Jesus had already addressed that need. But for some the question had political as well as religious overtones. A radical answer might serve to break down those fences with which the pious had sought to defend and sustain Israel. The hidden agenda for the lawyer as he puts Jesus to the test— that is, challenges him to prove himself a true teacher—is whether Jesus will affirm such delimitation as he believed the ethos and wellbeing of Israel demanded. The rhetorical exigency is to present the issue with such persuasiveness that the hearers were inducted into a realm of meaning in which it was impossible to deny the implications of Torah and Jesus' commentary on it.

In the Cornelius episode, the situation is again one in which the parameters of the people of God are put in question. The boundary between Jews and Gentiles was increasingly occupying the attention of the young churches, who had to face anew the problems of induction which the rabbis had addressed in Judaism. When the rabbis accepted a proselyte, they insisted on circumcision (for males), water baptism (*tevilah*) and instruction. Should Gentile converts to the Christian way be required to follow similar procedures? Cornelius, whose devotion and piety as a God-fearer were acknowledged by Luke and the angel (Acts 10.1-2, 4) but who was marginalised by Jewish purity laws, emerged as the *cause célèbre*, and the story of how the issue was resolved entered Christian paraenesis. The situation pressed hard on

Peter who, in the source of a triple vision, learned to adjust his own attitude and policy. Next, the question arose for Peter in his association with Cornelius's household (10.28-29). By overcoming the traditional demarcation he could affirm the reality of divine impartiality (10.34) and celebrate it as blessed by the Holy Spirit (10.44). This too enters narrative tradition. Finally, the situation is one of outright opposition on the part of 'the circumcision party' at Jerusalem (11.2-3), who have to be persuaded that the new initiatives rightly interpret the will of God. However, Peter's rhetoric induces them to withdraw their objections ('they were silenced') and glorify God (thus tacitly admitting to a change of view).

Rhetorical Issues

To view the texts in terms of rhetorical issues has certain advantages. It focuses on the thrust of each text as communication, and contextualizes it in the story that is being told. It resists the diverting of attention into subsidiary interests, whether historical or literary. Thus we are not primarily concerned with whether Luke has used his prerogative as author or redactor to bring together a parable and a setting which he may not have found in church tradition (source, form and redaction critics are virtually unanimous that the setting is 'secondary'). We are much more concerned with what he has presented to us as text; and if there is a seeming discrepancy between the question raised and the answer given, we must ask what the rhetorical significance of this feature is. Above all, Luke's rhetoric presents the issue as a live one—for the lawyer and for the reader. As latter day readers, what does it mean for us in our situation to 'go and do likewise'? What does it mean for me, as a Christian with my denominational traditions and ties, or as a white 'Caucasian' male, or a moderately successful western academic, to have my comfortable presuppositions challenged, perhaps negated, by this Samaritan's action? The challenge comes precisely as one contemplates one's relationship with the outsider, the member of the other group, those on the other side of the social, economic and religious divide.

The Cornelius story focuses on just such a fundamental religious issue for 'the circumcision party' in particular but also for Jewish Christians in general. They now face a shaking of the foundations, a change in the gravitational field, a reconstruction of their entire symbolic system. Faith in Christ, repentance and baptism in his name are now the requirements binding on all. Even if there is more to be said (for example, about life style), this remains a monumental shift in religious structure; and what Luke is presenting here is not so much a single Caesarean episode in early church history as an issue engendered by the church situation which was of great moment for the future of the church and its mission.

Rhetorical Strategy

The next task is to show the strategy Luke used to attain his rhetorical purpose. I propose to deal in turn with the parable episode and the Cornelius story.

The Parable (Luke 10.25-37)
The arrangement of the material to achieve the speaker's (author's) purpose in communication (*dispositio*) is not to be confused with literary structure, which tends to be a static analysis. Rather, it concerns the build-up of the argument and the development of the rhetorical situation during the discourse. Each situation depicted in the parable affects the next—and affects audience reaction. In the end, the position or concern of the audience has changed. The lawyer is left contemplating (however reluctantly) what would have been unthinkable to him at the outset.

To achieve this outcome, Luke presents the initial discussion with the lawyer as the *exordium* to a deliberation on the meaning of Torah (10.25-28). The issue lies squarely within the field of Judaistic ethics and is deliberative in tone, with perhaps epideictic overtones (the Samaritan and his actions are implicitly praised). The question, 'Who is my neighbour?' (10.29), introduces the topic in interrogative form, while the phrase 'desiring to justify himself' probably suggests a combative ethos rather than resentment. The *definitio* or redefinition of the issue is presented not in judicial argument but in parable, used here as in the prophetic tradition of Israel: that is, as a narrative metaphor, projecting a new reality. This owes much to the Hebrew *mashal*, as in Nathan's parable of the poor man's lamb (2 Sam. 12.1-6).[10] Unlike this *mashal*, however, attention stays fixed on the substance of Jesus' parable: it is not an illustration of passing significance

10. Cf. B. Gerhardsson, 'The Narrative Meshalim in the Synoptic Gospels', *NTS* 34 (1988), pp. 339-63.

but is itself the substance of the new reality. We note that the build-up progressively engages the emotions—the sympathy and expectations—of the audience until the dramatic arrival of the Samaritan. The scene is set dramatically and in lifelike terms, leaving the plight of the anonymous victim complete. The identity of the first two characters is important, as is the fact that they failed to relate to the victim: as often in prophetic discourse, the upholders of the purity laws fail in the moral law.[11] There is the further implication that traditional views of the issue in contemporary Judaism were an inadequate response to the Torah. The Pharisaic position, with which the lawyer might be supposed to be in sympathy, insisted that holiness be expressed in everyday life, hence the trauma created by the arrival of the Samaritan in the parable. As Funk has indicated,[12] the description of what he did is treated in some detail, eliciting approval from the audience in spite of their resentment that such a character should be the hero. There is no need to justify what the Samaritan did, and little point in advancing the procedural objection that a Samaritan would never have acted in this way. In modern terms, we engage with 'the world before the text'. The success of the parable as persuasive utterance rests on the fact that Jesus' hearers have already become immersed in the action and that, in spite of themselves, a world of new possibility is opening before them.

The question, 'Which of these three was neighbour...?' (10.36), introduces the *peroratio* and invites a response to the parabolic narrative as a whole. The final imperative (10.37) translates the original 'naive' enquiries about eternal life and obligation to neighbour into the realm of serious practice.

The rhetoric of this passage relates to Scripture using communities, that is, to communities accustomed to parabolic discourse, and to particular tensions both within these communities and in relation to the outside world. Jesus' own rhetoric appears to have allowed him to develop parabolic presentation to the point at which telling became showing and his hearers encountered the reality which his discourse conveyed: here, the wider significance of the divine requirement of neighbour love.

---

11. The prophet/priest tension is evident in the well known appeals to the priority of justice and mercy in Amos, Isaiah, Micah and other prophets.

12. Cf. Funk, *Poetics*, pp. 184-85.

The Acts Narrative (10.1–11.18)

At first sight, this unit seems to operate simply with the rhetoric of narrative, which—like the rhetoric of fiction—is concerned with 'telling': with *diegesis* rather than *mimesis*.[13] These two categories, however, overlap considerably, and in this unit there is a cumulative argument which persuades to a particular conclusion. To explicate the narrative structure, appeal is made to Genette's study of the rhetoric of narrative and to Funk's more recent work on biblical narrative.[14]

Acts 10.1-7 is a mediated but focused narrative in which the perspective of the hyperdiegetic narrator ('Luke') is apparent, particularly in relation to the piety of Cornelius (10.2) and the authority of the angelic vision, which stimulates further action.[15] Acts 10.9-16 is similarly recounted, the focus being on the thrice presented vision to Peter. Instead of a defocalized narrative, however, the element of *mimesis* (or 'showing') predominates: 'what God has cleansed, you must not call common'. Peter's perplexity at these visionary tidings provides the link to the next narrative segment (10.17-23) in which the narrator points to the prompting of the Spirit and relates Peter's encounter with Cornelius's messengers, thus introducing the element of repetition that characterizes his total presentation. The succeeding segment (10.23b-33) presents the dramatic meeting of Peter with Cornelius and then with the assembled company, the narrative switching to that of direct address (intradiegetic narration). The defocalizing or closure of this segment marks the conclusion or outcome of the narrative sequence: Cornelius says to Peter that the whole company has come together in God's sight 'to hear all that you have been commanded by the Lord'. The rhetorical situation has in fact been clearly delineated in this narrative introduction.

Peter's speech (10.34-43), a prime example of intradiegetic narration, exemplifies deliberative rhetoric in that it relates to a decision that must be taken about action in the immediate future; but it also has epideictic features in that it fosters assent to a central value or stance.

---

13. Cf. Genette, *Narrative Discourse*, pp. 161-211; Funk, *Poetics*, pp. 147-50.

14. The author of Acts is 'hyperdiegetic', i.e., he tells from outwith the action; Cornelius's rehearsal of the event is 'intradiegetic', i.e., told within the narrative; and Peter's relating of Cornelius's account is 'hypodiegetic', i.e., told at one remove within the narrative: cf. Funk, *Poetics*, pp. 154-55.

15. The issue (*status*) in the classical theory of rhetoric had four parts: denial, redefinition, justification and procedural objection.

The *exordium* contains the *thesis*, that 'God is not an accepter of faces' (that is, shows no partiality but respects the pious and righteous in every nation: 10.34-35). Because of the preceding experiences, Peter can take for granted the interest and expectation of the audience and can even assume a measure of knowledge as he enters the recital of Jesus' story: 'you know the word which he sent to Israel...' (10.36). The recital constitutes the *argumentation*, for the narrative is essentially mimetic, 'showing' as well as 'telling'. The argument arises cumulatively from the story: 'good news of peace', 'Lord of all', 'anointed...with the Holy Spirit and with power', 'God was with him', 'God raised him up...', 'judge of the living and the dead'. Thus, against those who would controvert the policy decision in view, the story of Jesus redefines, justifies and lends credibility to the grounds on which the new policy will be based, namely, the clearly perceived will of God in Christ. Here indeed is persuasive speech, culminating in the conclusion in 10.43 (which serves as the *peroratio*, or as much of one as the situation requires): belief in Christ affords forgiveness of sins, and is open to all. In fact, the speech was scarcely completed, for while Peter was still speaking (10.44) the Holy Spirit engulfed the whole company. Peter can therefore bring the meeting to the critical decision: 'Can anyone forbid water for baptizing...?' (10.47). Though it entered the liturgy, this question is rhetorical in function: it deals with procedural objection and thus completes the argumentation.[16] In the circumstances of charismatic excitement, the answer is transparent and Peter commands the baptism of the Gentiles.

But rhetoric, like ethics and liturgy, is a public and community action. In Acts 11.1-18 Peter acknowledges his accountability to 'the apostles and brethren who were in Judea' (11.1). His speech is almost forensic, presenting Peter's reply to the charge of 'the circumcision party' that he consorted with uncircumcised men and ate with them (11.3). In fact it is deliberative, leading to an acceptance by the whole community of the proposition (*thesis*) that God has granted the Gentiles also 'repentance unto life' (11.18). The preliminary discussion obviates the need for an *exordium*. In his *narratio*, Peter recapitulates the account of his vision, the steps by which he came to be in

---

16. Reader and reading have received much attention in modern discussion (e.g., Holub, Iser, Sternberg, Tompkins): cf. *Reader Perspectives in the New Testament* (ed. E.V. McKnight), *Semeia* 48 (1989); M. Davies, 'Reader-Response Criticism', in *A Dictionary of Biblical Interpretation*, pp. 578-80.

Cornelius's house, the message Cornelius had for him, and the coming of the Spirit (this time, 'as I began to speak'). The ethos created is one of sympathy for piety, for the visions that impressed themselves ('three times': 11.10) and for the leading of the Spirit. There is the added witness of the Lord (11.16). The *peroratio* once again takes the form of a question: in view of God's granting of the Spirit to the Gentiles, 'who was I to withstand God?' (11.17). In modern parlance, there is no answer to that. The critics are silenced; the community is persuaded, glorifies God and draws the proper conclusion.

Reader and Text

To focus on exigency and issue enables one to avoid such immersion in critical pursuits—whether historical or literary—that they become ends in themselves and thus divert attention from engagement with the text. It also allows one to take on board the thrust of the text in relation to the social situations it addressed in the past and continues to address in subsequent ages. This is not to be anti-critical: criticism serves to correct distorting assumptions and has a function as commentary. It is to be post-critical: to refuse to be confined within criticism's fly-bottle and to claim the freedom to relate to the text as a whole and hear its word. As Robert Bellah has put it, 'The radical split between knowledge and commitment that exists in our culture and in our universities is not ultimately tenable. Differentiation has gone about as far as it can go. It is time for a new integration.'[17]

The two passages above were selected from Luke–Acts because they seemed to relate to similar exigencies and issues. Their ultimate focus is on a similar concern: the will of God for faithful praxis in the world, particularly in the face of traditional or conventional barriers all the more intractible for having been erected by faith communities

---

17. R.N. Bellah, *Beyond Belief* (New York, 1970), p. 257. This emphasis on participation coheres with the emergence of new cultural paradigms which transcend the post-Enlightenment subject-object divide and are evident in many fields, including science (Einstein, Polanyi), philosophy (Gadamer, Habermas), theology (Torrance, Gunton) and rhetoric (Perelman and Olbrechts-Tyteca, *New Rhetoric*, p. 59); cf. C. Gunton, *Enlightenment and Alienation* (London, 1985). By contrast, Mack's negative conclusions concerning 'the very notion of biblical hermeneutics as an essential grounding and guide for Christian faith and practice' appear somewhat reactionary (p. 102).

themselves in defence of their faith. The first explicitly focuses on the direction to which Torah points in its concern with 'neighbour'. The second concerns the 'cleanness' of the Gentiles and the impartiality of God. Both strike deadly blows at defensive and minimalist interpretations of the will of God: the first with a degree of indirection which provokes further thought about the issue; the second with astonishing directness based on visionary revelation but in line with the community's faith story. Both combine a kind of revolutionary challenge with a curious sort of openness. The direction of our action is clearly indicated; the specific steps are not. We are to act like the Samaritan, but precisely what that may entail is not defined. The revelation of God's impartiality is effected in the community of Cornelius and Peter in terms of the baptism of Gentiles in the name of Jesus Christ, but the vision also related explicitly to eating common or unclean food (cf. Acts 10.10-14), and this remained a highly controversial and divisive issue in the church. The radical possibilities of Luke's rhetoric reflected the ambivalent position of the apostles of the Hellenistic mission, like Peter. Were they indeed to 'live like Gentiles' (Gal. 2.14), at least outside Palestine? Were Jewish Christians to cease living like Jews? What happens when there is a mixed community—as at Antioch? It may be, of course, that Luke's narrative, although evoking an early setting, is in fact directed to a later situation contemporary with Luke's writing. If so, Luke's rhetorical purpose is to present the issue with which apostles had wrestled in the context of the exigencies of his own later time.

The openness of the issue—including rhetorical features such as persuasiveness and argumentation—embraces the modern reader. Like Luke, we do not regard the biblical issues *simply* as issues of long ago but as substantive concerns for today. Modern exigencies include denominational defensiveness (in community practice as well as in theology), or divisiveness (whether of class, creed, sex or race) and the ideologies and practices which go with it (racism, sexism, sectarianism). How are we to live and act in a pluralistic world? These issues are not simple ones, and simple answers read out of the Bible on the basis of a non-contextual literalism will not serve. Authoritarian pronouncements would take the place of proper understanding, which is dependent upon following out the process of persuasion.

Dialogue, discussion and persuasion represent the ethos in which issues may be explored today. Real issues arise out of exigency: that is, they are of existential concern to participants. Much effort, in religious teaching as in education generally, is wasted because the subject matter is 'inert', to use Whitehead's term. In a recent television programme dedicated to enquiring whether the church is 'out of touch', a typical response was, 'I felt the sermons had nothing to do with me'. No exigency was addressed, and therefore no persuasion could be accomplished. By contrast, liberation theology has sprung from the grass roots. The matters discussed are of immediate personal, social and political concern to the hearers. Leaders such as Ernesto Cardinal[18] have demonstrated in practice how the Bible can be related to the discussion of such exigencies so that it can guide, deepen and redirect thinking about the issues. Here is the rhetoric of persuasion, the key to which is interactive engagement with exigency and issue. As in the examples discussed above, the focus is 'What is the Lord's will—here, today, in the exigency?' The rhetoric of the discussion takes us beyond the claims of self, profit, power, and so on: an element of denial or refutation is essential. Then comes the need for redefinition, to which biblical passages can make a direct contribution, for their iconic rather than ideological form enables them to present an alternative picture. The new thinking must be justified by persuasive argument—logos, ethos and pathos all having a part to play. And it should lead to a change in praxis consequent upon transformation in personal and community self-perception.

If our contention is persuasive—and I acknowledge the summary and compressed nature of the argument—then rhetorical criticism is not only a means of appraising ancient texts but also a guide to living communication which uses—or may use—these texts. It has therefore something to offer homiletics and religious education—although it demands that both of them throw off the stultifying straitjackets which convention seems to have placed on them and recover the art of communication and persuasion. It would also demand that such procedures became genuinely interactive and were seen to respond to life concerns: in short, to exigency and issue.[19] Through this interaction, the

---

18. Cf. *Love in Practice: The Gospel in Solentiname* (London, 1977); M. Schwantes, 'Biblical Theology together with the People', in S. Amirtham and J.S. Pobee (eds.), *Theology by the People* (WCC; Geneva, 1986), pp. 43-54.

19. In homiletics, cf. L.E. Keck, 'Toward a Theology of Rhetoric/Preaching', in D.S. Browning (ed.), *Practical Theology* (San Francisco, 1983), pp. 126-47; in education, T.H. Groome and Paulo Freire provide examples.

modern reader is transformed 'by receiving a new mode of being from the text itself'.[20]

Finally, this talk of encountering moral reality underlines the connection between rhetoric and ethics. Quintilian observed that the honourable orator would not allow himself to be compromised in his attempt at persuasion but would always say what is good.[21] Skilful oratory in the hands of an evil person can be a dangerous instrument, as the havoc wrought by demagogues and dictators in ancient and modern worlds amply demonstrates, or as George Orwell showed in *Nineteen Eighty Four*.[22] When one's suasion is directed to discerning the will of God or moral reality, any unethical manipulation of rhetoric will have a distorting effect. Ethics without rhetoric is dumb; rhetoric without ethics is lethal.

20. P. Ricoeur, *Interpretation Theory: Discourse and the Surplus of Meaning* (Fort Worth, 1976), p. 94.

21. Quintilian 2.15, 34; cf. 3.5 and 12.1.

22. Cf. Perelman and Olbrechts-Tyteca, *New Rhetoric*, pp. 51-54.

THE END OF ACTS (28.16-31) AND THE RHETORIC OF SILENCE

Daniel Marguerat

The conclusion of the book of Acts has not made an end of puzzling exegetes. This ending, intervening as it does after the endless expectation of Paul's trial—announced repeatedly (23.11; 25.11-12; 26.32; 27.24), but never under way—disappoints the reader's expectation. One understands why this disappointment has stimulated the exegetes, beginning with the Fathers.

The main difficulty for exegesis does not lie so much in what the ending of Acts says as in what it does not say. Why does Luke maintain silence on the appeal to Caesar, while this represents the avowed motive for Paul's transfer to Rome (28.19)? Why keep mute over the outcome of the trial, whether this was favourable (release of the apostle) or not (death of Paul)? Has Luke kept silent on purpose, or did he have the means to say more?

Historical criticism assigns the premature conclusion of the work to a material cause (Spitta, Zahn) or postulates that Luke's documentation had come to an end (Cadbury, Harnack). Theological criticism looks at the end of Acts as the result of a theological strategy, whether in order to obey a theological agenda (Menoud, Conzelmann) or to spare Roman political power (Haenchen).[1] But in my opinion, theological criticism stops too soon. It persists in thinking that the author of Acts ends his work in this fashion because he must not say more. Just like historical criticism, theological criticism is unable to think through the rhetorical function of an ending that is left deliberately open, that is, that plays deliberately with silence.

I want to sustain the thesis that the ending of Acts is left voluntarily in suspense, thus creating in the reader a feeling of incompletion; and

---

1. A status of research may be found in C.J. Hemer, *The Book of Acts in the Setting of Hellenistic History* (WUNT, 49; Tübingen, 1989), pp. 383-87.

furthermore, that this intended incompleteness proceeds from a rhetoric of silence enacted by the author of Luke–Acts.

The often alleged parallel with another abrupt ending in the New Testament, that of the Gospel of Mark (16.8), is instructive in that regard.[2] For the two cases are actually very different on the very point I am dealing with. The ending of Mark is judged incomplete only by dint of a comparison with Matthew 28 and Luke 24. Conversely, the incompleteness of the ending of Acts appears from elements that are internal to the work: Luke has the apostle Paul announce his death (20.35, 38), and repeats it to the reader in terms that are in consonance with the Passion of Jesus (21.11; cf. Lk. 18.32); the judicial appearance before Caesar is demanded by the apostle (25.11), confirmed by the authorities (25.12; 26.32), sealed by the Lord (27.24) and recalled by Paul in Rome as the purpose of his journey (28.19). From chs. 20–28, the author of Acts methodically constructs an expectation in the reader which he finally fails to satisfy. Inadvertently? Out of forgetfulness? From a shift in strategy? I rather think that Luke in chs. 27–28 organizes a concerted displacement of the reader's expectation which he has methodically built up to that point.

My study will begin with a presentation of the rhetoric of silence in Graeco-Roman literature, and then pay particular attention to Hellenistic historiography. I shall then observe how Luke in Acts 27–28 displaces the reader's expectation, before I interpret the ultimate theological disputation in 28.17-28 , and assess the function of the last scene in 28.30-31. I conclude with a brief summary.

1. *What is a Rhetoric of Silence?*

Was ancient rhetoric interested in the effect of silence? It appears to have been the case. In the treatise *On the Sublime*, Pseudo-Longinus asserts that the first of the five sources of the sublime is nobility of mind (μεγαλοφροσύνη): 'The sublime is the echo of nobility of mind' (9.2). Surprisingly, the example put forward is an instance of silence, namely the appearance in the Nekyia of Ajax who refuses to answer Ulysses' questions. 'Whence even without voice, the naked

2.   I refer the reader first of all to the excellent book by J.L. Magness, *Sense and Absence: Structure and Suspension in the Ending of Mark's Gospel* (SBL Semeia Studies; Atlanta, 1986), pp. 83-85.

idea, of itself, sometimes wins admiration by dint of the sole nobility of mind, just as in the Nekyia the silence of Ajax is great and more sublime than any speech' (9.2). The silence of Ajax functions as a perceptible experience of μεγαλοφροσύνη; as such it expresses nothing, it expresses the absolute.[3] Quintilian is not insensitive either to the rhetorical effect of the unsaid. In book 2 of the *Institutio oratoria*, he elaborates on the virtue of not telling everything:

> In painting, what is attractive is the face as a whole; yet if Apelle has shown an image of Antigonus in profile only, it was in order that the deformity of his gouged eye may be hidden. What then? Are there not in speech some details to be concealed, whether they must not be shown, or whether they cannot be expressed for the sake of dignity? Thus did Timanthes, a native of Cythnos I believe, in the picture that made him win over Colotes of Teos. In the sacrifice of Iphigenia he had painted a sad Calchas, a yet sadder Ulysses, and added to Menelaus the maximum affliction that may be rendered by art; having exhausted all affects, not finding how to render the facial expression of the father fittingly, he veiled his [the father's] head and left it to everyone to figure out with his own mind (*et suo cuique animo dedit aestimandum*) (2.13.12-13).

Quintilian provides an indication of a concerted recourse to something unsaid, with a view to soliciting the imagination of the reader.

Surprisingly, these remarks by Longinus and Quintilian as to the rhetorical effect of silence are in agreement with the comments made on our text by St John Chrysostom in his *Homilies on Acts*. His commentary makes use of terms that a narratologist today would not disown:

> The author [i.e. Luke] conducts his narrative up to this point, and leaves the hearer thirsty so that he fills up the lack by himself through reflection (ὥστε τὸ λοιπὸν ἀφ' ἑαυτοῦ συλλογίζεσθαι). The outsiders [i.e. non-Christian writers] do also likewise; for knowing everything makes one slow and apathetic. But he does this, and does not tell what follows,

3. In his *Life of Apollonius of Tyana*, Philostratus is not far from Longinus when he describes the pious respect with which the disciples of Pythagoras surround the transmission of the words of the master: 'And all the revelations of Pythagoras were considered by his fellows as laws, and they honoured him as though he had been a messenger of Zeus, training themselves to the silence that is fitting before the deity; for they heard many divine and secret revelations, which it would have been difficult to keep to themselves if they had not begun by learning that silence is also a word (καὶ τὸ σιωπᾶν λόγος)' (*Life of Apollonius of Tyana* 1.1).

deeming it superfluous inasmuch as for those who happen to read the Scriptures, they only learn from there to add to discourse. Consider indeed that what follows is absolutely identical with what comes before (*Homily on Acts* 15; *PG* 60, p. 382).

According to Chrysostom, the incomplete ending of Acts: (1) is the effect of a literary strategy well-attested in non-Christian literature; (2) aims at activating the reflection of the reader; (3) requires that it be filled up by extrapolation from the previous narrative.

The first assertion requires verification before one makes a commitment as to the others: by ending a literary work without telling his readers everything, does Luke conform to a pattern of Graeco-Roman literature? One may take note of the fact that John the Gospel writer has done it by having recourse to the literary topos of unspeakable profusion ('Jesus did many other signs before his disciples, which are not written in this book', Jn 20.30).[4] What about the author of Acts? One should ask oneself about the literary conventions that regulated the conclusion of a work in antiquity. A glance at the state of research allows one to conclude that the question has received little attention, whereas studies on the *proemia* abound. One must concede that ancient rhetoricians have expressed themselves much more on the beginning of a work than on its ending.

The classic reference is found in Aristotle (*Poetics* 7.1450b): the end 'is that which is inevitably or, as a rule, the natural result of something else but from which nothing else follows...Well-constructed plots must not therefore begin and end at random, but embody the formulae we have stated.'

J.L. Magness has made a list of ancient works that violate the Aristotelian rule of narrative closure.[5] The *Iliad* and the *Odyssey* rank highest. Both Homeric works end, from the standpoint of the plot, by a quieting down: the *Iliad* closes on the gesture of Achilles giving Hector's corpse back to Priam and on the funeral laments of the Trojans (*Il.* 22.405-515);[6] the *Odyssey* terminates in Ulysses

---

4. This motif is found in Sir. 43.27; 1 Macc. 9.22; Justin, *Apol.* 1.31, 48, 54; Lucian, *Dem.* 67; etc. (numerous examples collected by W. Bauer, *Das Leben Jesu im Zeitalter der neutestamentlichen Apokryphen* [Tübingen, 1909], pp. 364-65).

5. *Sense and Absence*, pp. 55ff. As to the end of Acts, the hypothesis of a literary usage has been voiced by such a subtle precursor as H.J. Cadbury, *The Making of Luke–Acts* (London, 1958), pp. 321-24.

6. The study of the ending of ancient works is made difficult by the frequent

triumphing over the revolt in Ithaca and his return home (*Od.* 23.248-296). Now, these endings are preceded in the body of the work by the announcement of non-narrated developments: the reader is left under the effect of the repeated prediction of the death of Achilles and the fall of Troy; in the *Odyssey,* Tiresias predicts to Ulysses that he will have to leave Ithaca again on a new journey (*Od.* 11.119-37). The identification of this procedure of an open closure is paramount, since Homer in antiquity constitutes the source of all culture and the model for all literature. Not only are other authors going to adopt in turn this pattern of narrative suspension (the most frequently cited example is Virgil's *Aeneid*),[7] but the post-Homeric tradition will see the budding forth of numerous works presented as a sequel of Homer.

Magness, with some exaggeration, draws conclusions as to the frequency of narrative suspension in the ending of ancient works. His observations nevertheless uncover the rhetorical power of a nonnarrated ending, the power of a rhetoric of silence which leads readers to supply the outcome of the story through their own reflection.[8] The reflections of Longinus and Quintilian find their confirmation in the specific case of narrative suspension.

The examples invoked thus far stem nevertheless from the tragic poets and the Hellenistic novel as far as Graeco-Roman literature is concerned. What about historiography, after which Luke–Acts is patterned first and foremost? Two ancient theoreticians of historiography

ignorance of research as to the primitive ending of the work; glossed endings abound. Concerning the *Iliad,* the termination at book 22 is only a likely hypothesis (summary of the discussion in Magness, *Sense and Absence*, pp. 28-30).

7.   The *Aeneid* finishes with the murder of Latin chief Turnus, whom Aeneas finishes off in a burst of anger. This ending is problematic, as underlined by the last verse of Virgil (12.952): *Vitaque cum gemitu fugit indignata sub umbras* ('And life with a groaning fled indignant under the shadows'). Now, one encounters in the body of the narrative (12.808-840), under the guise of an agreement between Jupiter and Juno, a prediction of Aeneas's marriage with princess Lavinia; that union is a portend of the peace concluded with the Latins and the founding of a new race, concretized by the founding of Rome.

8.   My theoretical references for a study of narrative closure in literature are: F. Kermode, *The Sense of an Ending* (London, 1966); *idem, The Genesis of Secrecy: On the Interpretation of Narrative* (Cambridge, MA, 1979); B.H. Smith, *Poetic Closure: A Study of How Poems End* (Chicago, 1968); R. Blau Du Plessis, *Writing beyond the Ending* (Bloomington, 1985); A. Kotin Mortimer, *La clôture narrative* (Paris, 1985).

may provide us with information at this point: Lucian of Samosata and Dionysus of Halicarnassus.

2. *The Rhetoric of Silence in Hellenistic Historiography*

In his treatise *How to Write History,* Lucian decides on how a historian ought to begin and construct his work, not on how he ought to finish it; is it an indication of the freedom left to the author in concluding? On the other hand, Lucian deals with silence in an apology of brevity where he defends the idea that 'if you should skim over small and less necessary items, and speak abundantly on matters of importance, there are indeed many that one should even leave out' (56). If these words plead for freedom and discernment on the part of the historian in the selection of recounted facts, they help us understand why Luke has chosen to say certain things (the non-trivial character of the scene in 28.30-31 will have to retain us); they do not yet indicate why Luke has chosen not to say certain things.

The writings of Dionysius of Halicarnassus, especially his *On Thucydides* and his *Letter to Pompeius,* are more explicit.[9] According to Dionysius: 'The first duty, and perhaps the most necessary one for all historians, is to choose a beautiful subject, pleasant to the readers' (*Ep. ad Pomp.* 3.767). The second duty is to determine 'where to begin' and 'how far one must go' (*Ep. ad Pomp.* 3.769). Herodotus is cited as a model because he begins by indicating the cause of the hostilities between Greeks and Barbarians and 'proceeds until he has shown the punishment and vengeance exercised upon the Barbarians' (*Ep. ad Pomp.* 3.769). Dionysius privileges the return in the conclusion of the theme that constitutes 'the beginning and the end' of history (καὶ ἀρχὴ καὶ τέλος ἐστὶ τῆς ἱστορίας, *Ep. ad Pomp.* 3.767). Thucydides, on the other hand, is a target for criticism. Not only does he fail to begin in the appropriate manner (*De Thuc.* 10.338), starting as he does with the decline of the Greeks, but he does not conduct his work to a suitable end. Even though he has promised to 'expose

9.   For a study of literary criticism in Dionysius of Halicarnassus, I have consulted the following: M. Egger, *Denys d'Halicarnasse. Essai sur la critique littéraire et rhétorique chez les Grecs au siècle d'Auguste* (Paris, 1902); W. Rhys Roberts, *Dionysus of Halicarnassus: The Three Literary Letters* (Cambridge, 1901); S.F. Bonner, *The Literary Treatises of Dionysus of Halicarnassus: A Study in the Development of Critical Method* (Amsterdam, 1969).

everything', he concludes by relating the battle of Cynossema in the twenty-first year of the war:

> It would have been better, having related everything, to end History with the most admirable event and the one that must have been listened to with the most delight: the return of the fugitives from Phyle, which was for the city the beginning of the recovery of freedom (*Ep. ad Pomp.* 3.771).

Quite apart from the bad taste embodied in Dionysius by the presentation of the Greeks in a position of weakness, one should retain his insistence on the thematic inclusion which the beginning and ending of the historiographical work must present.[10] As we have seen above, Acts 28 is not to be faulted on this point.

But what about the works which Dionysius criticizes? We know that Thucydides did not have time to finish the *Peloponnesian War* and botched up the ending; one can sense this from the absence of speeches, which Xenophon already felt as a deficiency.

The *Histories* of Herodotus conclude in Book 9 with a perfectly symbolic event: the defeat of Xerxes' troops at Sestos and the destruction of the bridges over the Hellespont, the very same ones that had allowed Persian troops to invade Greece (9.114-20). After victory, in a gesture that seals the Persian defeat, the Athenians on their return home take away the cables of the bridge in order to consecrate them to their gods (9.121). The author concludes with the reminder of a saying of Cyrus, who had once enjoined the Persians to withdraw into their territory and to renounce invading others in order to preserve their autonomy (9.122).[11] Dionysius of Halicarnassus is right: Herodotus closes on a theme which is fundamental to him, the theme of the limit; the ὕβρις of the Persians who started the war had

---

10. Dionysius reproaches: 'Thucydides has not begun his history where one ought to, and he has not adapted to it the suitable end... by no means the least part of a good arrangement is to begin where there shoul¹ be nothing before, and to end where nothing is left to be desired' (*De Thuc.* 10.830). About Xenophon on the contrary, he appreciates the fact that 'everywhere, he has begun and ended in the most suitable and appropriate manner' (*Ep. ad Pomp.* 4.778).

11. The saying attributed to Cyrus is after all perfectly Greek: 'In soft countries, he said, soft men are usually born; and it does not belong to the same soil to produce admirable fruit and men good for war. The Persians agreed; they withdrew after having surrendered to the opinion expressed by Cyrus; and they chose to be masters even though they lived in an infertile land, rather than being slaves to someone else while cultivating luxuriant plains' (9.122).

consisted precisely in violating the limit in order to demand earth and water from the Greeks. But what Dionysius has not taken notice of is the incompletion of this ending. Herodotus was announcing three woes to the Athenians: Darius, Xerxes, Artaxerxes (6.98). His work ends under the reign of Xerxes; the prediction of the third woe remains like a shadow over the future, as an unfulfilled threat, with the overhanging saying of Cyrus, whose violation is denounced as insanity. The unsaid allows Herodotus to suspend the conflict between (Greek) culture and barbarism on a point of great fragility: the respect of a limit. The prediction of the three woes is a portend that the limit will not hold.

What shall we conclude? The attestation, both in Homer and in that great master of historiography Herodotus, of a narrative suspension in the end position has enough to impress, when one knows the considerable role played by these works in ancient culture. The identification of this rhetoric of silence in poetry, theatre, the Hellenistic novel as well as in historiography leads to the conclusion that it existed as a literary convention, from which the author of Acts may have been able to draw inspiration.[12]

The effect of this convention may be summed up in three points:

1. Narrative suspension is a literary device whereby the author, by failing to bring certain narrative data to their resolution, hinders the closure of the narrative world for the reader (thus Thucydides as read by Dionysius of Halicarnassus).

2. The closure effect must be achieved by the reader, who, in order to satisfy the need for completion, is tempted to finish the story in consonance with its plot (*Odyssey, Aeneid, Herodotus*).

3. The narrative, even without closure, may end up with a scene (*Aeneid, Odyssey*) or a declaration (Herodotus) that functions in the way of a metaphor or a synecdoche and induces the unspoken outcome of the narrative.[13]

---

12. P. Davies has made the observation that the second book of Kings ended with a narrative suspension through the symbolic scene of Yehoiachin's release (25.27-30); he has not been able to show that Luke has drawn direct inspiration from that ending in order to compose Acts 28 ('The Ending of Acts' *ExpTim* 94 [1982–83], pp. 334-35).

13. I borrow here categories from Kermode, *Genesis of Secrecy*, p. 65. W. Iser speaks of the 'blanks' of the text as an indispensable factor in the act of reading;

Let us return to the book of Acts. We have said that it contained two announcements for which the narrative offers no fulfilment: Paul's appeal to Caesar and the testimony to the Risen one 'unto the ends of the earth' (1.8). According to what has just been said, one must ask: does the plot of the book contain indications allowing the reader to bring these announcements to their completion? I shall begin with the appeal to Caesar.

3. *Acts 27–28 and the Displacement of the Reader's Expectation*

Luke has prepared his reader for the judicial appearance of the apostle before the emperor (23.11; 25.11-12; 26.32). The eventful journey to Rome has a delaying effect, which, considering the strategic position of the narrative (a few lines before the end!), must have a specific function as to the reader's expectation. Which function?

Commentators have pointed out how the ambivalence of the vocabulary of rescue (σῴζειν, διασῴζειν, σωτηρία)[14] makes this sea epic into a metaphor of salvation. The Hellenistic novel makes the sea voyage into the classic locus of the identity quest of the hero; here, the quest operates by way of a rescue from the powers of evil. It is also clear that the last two chapters of Acts are organized according to a two-part scheme: the tableau of Acts 27.1–28.10, devoted to the pagans, finds its counterpart in the scene of Acts 28.11-31, devoted to the relation with Judaism. The narrative conclusion of 27.44 ('And thus it happened that all came safely [διασωθῆναι] upon the land') must be read in that perspective: the rescue of the passengers of the ship prefigures the salvation of all the nations of the earth.

Paul plays the leading role in that operation of salvation. His bearing dominates the whole of ch. 27.[15] The divine revelation in

---

meaning arises both from what is said and from the reader's projection on the unsaid, so that the silence of the text is not to be considered as an absence of meaning, but as an invitation to find the missing elements through projection ('Interaction between Text and Reader', in S.R. Suleiman and I. Crosman [eds.], *The Reader in the Text* [Princeton, 1980], pp. 106-119).

14. Acts 27.20, 31, 34, 43, 44.

15. Paul gives navigation advice (27.9-10); he comforts (27.21-26); he denounces the flight of the sailors (27.31); he celebrates a eucharistic meal (27.35); his presence saves the life of the prisoners (27.43). Haenchen concludes the following from the Pauline episodes in Acts 27, which he views as redactional additions: 'Damit gliedert sich Kap. 27 dem letzten Abschnitt des Buches ein, der auch

vv. 23-24 interprets the rescue of the ship as a grace granted to Paul (κεχάρισταί σοι ὁ θεός), instituting the apostle as mediator of the salvation of his 276 fellow passengers. The reader is not ignorant of the fact that Paul is not guilty of the crimes he is accused of by the Jews: Luke has made statements of innocence into a leitmotiv (18.14-15; 20.26; 23.3, 9; 24.12-13; 25.18, 25; 26.31-32). But on the narrative plane, the pagans have yet to receive the certainty of it; for them the fantastic rescue in Acts 27 manifests the intervention of the God who is lord of the waters[16] in favour of his witness; for them providence attests the innocence of Paul.

G.B. Miles and G. Trompf have been able to show that in Greek literature, being protected from the peril of the waves is also a classic motif of the divine protection of the just.[17] Thus for the Jewish reader as well as for the Greek reader, the God of the ocean acquits the apostle in the eyes of the pagan world! Are the above cited authors right when they conclude that recounting Paul's Roman trial became superfluous, since 'Paul was acquitted by a tribunal no less formidable than the divinely controlled ocean itself'?[18] Two observations resist this interpretation.

First, the Malta episode (28.1-10) and the end of the voyage (28.11-16) present a chain of arguments attesting the divine favor toward Paul. (a) The apostle's immunity to the viper's bite leads the βάρβαροι in Malta to abandon the idea that Δίκη was pursuing a criminal (28.4); Paul is therefore innocent. (b) Even more, they regard him as a god (28.6b)—Luke does not care to correct that assessment (contrary to 14.14-18), for the Barbarians are allowed to

---

den gefangenen Paulus als den wahren Mittelpunkt der Handlung zeigt: er, der Gefangene, rettet alle !' (*Die Apostelgeschichte* [KEK; Göttingen, 6th edn, 1968], p. 633).

16. In addition to Old Testament tradition (mainly Jonah and the Psalms), see Lk. 5.4-8; 8.22-25.

17. G.B. Miles and G. Trompf, 'Luke and Antiphon: The Theology of Acts 27–28 in the Light of Pagan Beliefs about Divine Retribution, Pollution, and Shipwreck', *HTR* 69 (1976), pp. 259-67; G. Trompf, 'On Why Luke Declined to Recount the Death of Paul: Acts 27–28 and Beyond', in C.H. Talbert (ed.), *Luke–Acts: New Perspectives from the SBL Seminar* (New York, 1984), pp. 225-39. Their thesis has been refined and enlarged by D. Ladouceur, 'Hellenistic Preconceptions of Shipwreck and Pollution as a Context for Acts 27–28', *HTR* 73 (1980), pp. 435-49.

18. 'Luke and Antiphon', p. 267.

voice in an aberrant form a verdict which is substantially correct![19] (c) The healing of 'all the other' (οἱ λοιποί) inhabitants of the island leads to a profusion of honors showered upon Paul and his companions (28.10). (d) Through the ensign of the Dioscuri (28.11) under which the ship sails, Paul's arrival in Puteoli bears the signature of his innocence: the celestial twins are known to be not only the protectors of seafaring people, but even more so the guardians of truth and the punishers of perjury.[20] To sum up: Paul's innocence crystallizes in a chain of signs adapted to the pagan world, but unfitted for the dialogue with Judaism.

Secondly, it must be noticed that Luke in Acts 28.17-28 does indeed set up a trial situation. But the roles are reversed. Let us look at the first interview (28.17-22). Paul is a prisoner, but he is the one who summons others to his own dwelling (28.17a). The Roman Jewish deputation, which on the narrative plane inherits the role of the accusers, is instituted as the judges before whom Paul pleads his innocence (28.17b-20); these judges—who are impartial since no rumor concerning Paul has reached them (28.21)—ratify Paul's innocence. At the second interview (28.23-28), Paul keeps the initiative, but the issue has changed: the debate is no longer about the apostle's innocence, but about the culpability of the Jews before the gospel (28.23). The audience's split reaction before Paul's preaching is interpreted by the apostle by means of the word of judgment of Isa. 6.9-10 (28.25-27). The role reversal is then completed. The accusers have first turned into judges, and then have become the ones judged. In accordance with the Holy Spirit (28.25), the accused wields the word of judgment: 'The heart of this people has grown thick, they have become hard of hearing with their ears, and they have veiled their

---

19. J. Roloff does not heed this narrative effect when he compares the Malta episode with the one in Lystra (ch. 14) and ascribes to a 'naiv-unreflektierte Paulusverehrung' the lack of a challenge of the Maltans' flawed theology, which regrettably assimilates the apostle with a god (*Die Apostelgeschichte* [NTD, 5; Göttingen, 1981], p. 366). But the narrator is more subtle! He leaves this judgment standing, which the reader knows to be wrong, but which testifies to a contextualized version of the recognition of the apostle's status. Luke is a master of the reconstitution of local color. R.I. Pervo (*Profit with Delight* [Philadelphia, 1987], pp. 70ff.), has well grasped the Lukan taste for exotic colouring.

20. See M. Albert, *Le culte de Castor et Pollux en Italie* (Paris, 1883); Ladouceur, *Hellenistic Preconceptions*, pp. 443-48.

eyes, lest they should see with their eyes, and hear with their ears...'
(28.27).

I have spoken earlier of an expectation of the reader being displaced
by the author. The mechanism appears now more clearly. When Luke
methodically constructs the expectation of Paul's trial, this is not in
order to censor it at the last moment for the sake of political decency.
Luke makes the journey to Rome into a providential manifestation of
Paul's innocence in the eyes of the pagan world, and the Maltese are
going to ratify it with their barbaric naivity (28.1-10). The image of
the apostle arriving in Rome as a distinguished visitor, welcomed by a
Christian delegation (28.15), settled into the liberal status of the
custodia militaris (28.16, 30),[21] receiving crowds of people at home
(28.17, 23, 30)—this glowing image[22] does not aim at sparing
imperial justice, but rather at installing an exchange of roles: the
prisoner reaches the capital of the empire and stays there with the
authority of one who shall not be judged, but shall be the bearer of
judgment. The function of the Acts 27.1–28.16 sequence is to prepare
for this reversal. This does not occur, however, without a paradox:
this man, bearer of a word of judgment, is in chains (28.16b).

All being said and done, why is there no mention of the outcome of
the trial? My opinion is that Luke through that effect of judicial
reversal reinterprets a fact that his readers well remember: the execu-
tion of the apostle in Rome, perhaps at the close of his trial.[23] It is not
enough to invoke the reluctance of the author of Acts to recount the
death of witnesses. If it is true that the rhetoric of silence incites the
reader to close the narrative in consonance with the plot, one understands then with what means Luke has provided his readers in order to
guide them in the completion of the narrative. Death is indeed
announced (20.35, 38; 21.11), but the event is reframed in Acts 27–
28: certainly, in view of his behaviour on the ship, Paul will go to his

---

21. One should consult on this the study by H.W. Tajra, *The Trial of St Paul*
(WUNT, 2.35; Tübingen, 1989), pp. 179-81.

22. Concerning the social image of Paul in Acts, on should read, in addition to
the above cited monograph by Pervo, the dissertation of J.C. Lentz, 'Luke's
Portrayal of St Paul as a Man of High Social Status and Moral Virtue in the
Concluding Chapters of Acts' (PhD Thesis, Edinburgh University, 1988).

23. The hypothesis of the death of Paul in Rome has sufficient support from literary and archaeological data (cf. G. Lüdemann, *Das frühe Christentum nach den
Traditionen der Apostelgeschichte* [Göttingen, 1987], pp. 274-76).

death courageously; but first and foremost, the judgment of the apostle will seal the failure of his mission to Israel, who falls under the word of judgment of Isaiah.

Positively, it is essential for the author of Acts to fasten on the ending (28.30-31) the image of Paul preaching, for upon this remembrance and this activity the world of narration and the world of the reader are, in his view, articulated. We shall also see that the second prediction that was left open in the book of Acts, namely the testimony to the Risen one unto the ἔσχατον τῆς γῆς (1.8), towers above this final summary, in which it finds an anticipated fulfilment, as it were. I shall come to this, but only after having paid attention to the theological disputation in vv. 17-28.

4. *The Ultimate Theological Disputation (28.17-28)*

In accordance with the norm invoked by Dionysius of Halicarnassus (see above § 2), the conclusion of Acts resumes the fundamental theme of the work; it delivers the author's theological diagnosis about the relation between church and synagogue, at the moment when Luke brings Paul's ministry to an end. I have already noted the structure of reversal governing the passage; it is now necessary to observe the outcome of this reversal. To what theological result does the aborted dialogue between Paul and the Roman Jews lead?

As I see it, Luke uses here a two-pronged procedure, as he often does in the crucial passages of his work, and I shall sum up his reading of the event with two terms: opening and acknowledgment of failure.

In the first place, the most surprising observation is that in spite of the hardness of the word of judgment of Isa. 6.9-10, neither Paul's discourse (according to Luke) nor the discourse of the narrator concludes by shutting off Judaism. Luke does not, as in other places, point out the Jewish group as a united front either in hostility (13.45) or in opposition (18.6), but his division between the persuaded and the non-believing ones (28.24), which he calls an a-symphony (ἀσύμφωνοι, 28.25a), cuts through the Jewish group; unity through a recognition of the βασιλεία τοῦ θεοῦ in Jesus is not effected. It makes sense, therefore, to see in the universality of Paul's hospitality (ἀπεδέχετο πάντας, v. 30) an invitation to include Jews (as individuals) among the addressees of Christian preaching.[24]

In the second place, one must point out, as a counter-balance to the opening, that the acknowledgment of failure is laid down with gravity. Over against the a-symphony of the chosen people, the triumphant agreement of Isaiah, Paul and the Holy Spirit is set forth (28.25). The passing of salvation to the pagans, as prompted by Israel's refusal as announced in 13.46 and 18.6, is now sealed by the apostle's last word to Judaism, which is the one and last word (ῥῆμα ἕν, 28.25), and at the same time the last word of Paul in Acts. The apostle takes on and duplicates in the face of Israel the prophet's failure; he borrows the prophet's voice (Paul does not *speak* in vv. 26-27, but he *makes* the prophet *speak*) in order to attest to the continuity of a refusal of God's offer all through the history of salvation. For Luke, the time when any mission was sent to Israel as a people is over.[25]

Nevertheless, Paul's last word is not the narrator's last word. It remains to decipher the sense of the conclusive summary in vv. 30-31.

5. *Paul the Exemplary Pastor (28.30-31)*

Among the typology of narrative closure devices as unfolded above (see § 2), it is the task of the open-ended conclusion to induce the unsaid outcome of the narrative through a scene functioning by way of metaphor or synecdoche. This is undeniably the case of the final scene in vv. 30-31, where it is again noticeable how finely Luke knows how to play with language.

This picture carries a biographical purpose: it closes upon the activity of the hero of Acts; both the aorist ἐνέμεινεν (v. 30a) and the chronological indication διετίαν ὅλην (v. 30a) signal a limitation by

24. One must add to that sign of an opening the rhetorical function of the word of judgment in the Old Testament, as recalled by D. Moessner: 'Isa. 6,9f does not foreclose the future by a condemnation, but forcefully exhorts to an ultimate repentance ('Paul in Acts: Preacher of Eschatological Repentance to Israel', *NTS* 34 [1988], pp. 96-104).

25. R.C. Tannehill postulates that, in the eyes of Luke, the preaching to Israel will proceed without change; he adduces support from the resumption of Jewish evangelization after Paul's resolution to turn to the Gentiles in 13.46 and 18.6 (*The Narrative Unity of Luke–Acts: A Literary Interpretation. 2: The Acts of the Apostles* [Minneapolis, 1990], pp. 350-51). There is a similar trivialization of the conclusive character of Acts 28 in B.J. Koet, *Five Studies of Scripture in Luke–Acts* (SNTA, 14; Leuven, 1989), pp. 119-39.

the narrator of Paul's activity to a two-year duration, beyond which readers should fill up the lack through their own information and through narrative data.[26] At the same time, the picture has a paradigmatic purpose: the effect of duration and exemplarity is obtained through the syntactic construction, that is, an imperfect indicative (ἀπεδέχετο, v. 30b) followed by a chain of participles (κηρύσσων, διδάσκων, v. 31); that construction is typical of the summaries of Acts (2.42, 45-47; 5.16; 8.3; 12.25; 15.35; 18.11; 19.8-10; etc.) that describe the ideal state of the Christian community or mission.

This summary confirms the traits that Luke, since ch. 9, has not ceased to ascribe to that figure which he reveres above all others: Paul as the ideal pastor and the model of the persecuted Christian. In the imperial capital where from now on Christianity shall find its 'home',[27] in that place where the Roman power organizes itself, there he preaches God's kingship. His teaching holds together two quantities that are no longer to be set apart from each other: the βασιλεία τοῦ θεοῦ[28] and the Lord Jesus Christ (v. 31). The apostle in chains testifies with a total freedom of speech (παρρησία), which is the effect of the Spirit, and without hindrance (ἀκωλύτως), which represents a promise for the future. In the shape of an ideal picture of the Pauline past, Luke draws up an agenda for the future.

But to whom does this agenda apply? Who must perpetuate it? For which category of readers is Paul set up as an exemplary pastor? The answer to these questions depends perhaps on a specification of the text which might appear trivial at first sight, which is why exegetes have not devoted a lot of attention to it. In 28.16, Luke specifies that on 'our' arrival in Rome, Paul was allowed to 'stay at his own place (καθ' ἑαυτόν) with the soldier who was guarding him'. A similar

26. This historical deadline is not consonant with the suggestion by M.D. Goulder, for whom Paul's survival through the shipwreck corresponds with the christological death-resurrection scenario; this reading is given no support in Acts 27 (*Type and History in Acts* [London, 1964], pp. 62-63).

27. Luke was certainly not insensitive either to the fact that Hellenistic novels (in the pattern of the *Odyssey*) frequently conclude with the hero's homecoming, or to the fact that coming to Rome represents a climax in the life of great philosophers (see the *Life of Apollonius of Tyana* by Philostrates).

28. βασιλεία τοῦ θεοῦ is a synthetic expression of the content of Paul's preaching (Acts 19.8; 20.25) and of the message of Jesus (Lk. 4.43; 8.1, etc; Acts 1.3).

specification comes back unexpectedly in the final summary: Paul 'dwelt for two whole years at his own expense (ἐν ἰδίῳ μισθώματι)...' (28.30). Whatever the exact sense of the rare term μισθώμα—wages or rent[29]—this notation, in conjunction with the καθ' ἑαυτὸν in v. 16, stresses the missionary's material autonomy. The portrait of the ideal pastor, which included already an indication as to the audience (v. 30b) and a synthetic statement of the message (v. 31), is now completed by a technical datum on the conditions of missionary work.

Luke's interest in the perpetuation of the Pauline tradition of evangelism is here manifest. One may understand then why the work of Luke closes with the picture of the ideal pastor, and why this picture is accompanied by some technical data aimed at those who, with Luke or close to him, were perpetuating the memory of the apostle to the Gentiles through their own involvement. They were thus being associated with the witness to the Risen one 'unto the ends of the earth' (1.8)—an agenda which is ever open-ended, but of which the conclusive summary offers something like an anticipation, and which is waiting to be redrawn in the life of the reader.

6. *Summary*

In order to compose the end of Acts, Luke has drawn inspiration from a convention which is attested in the work of Homer, in Graeco-Roman poetry and in historiography as well (Herodotus), namely, the suspended ending. This rhetoric of silence leads the reader to bring the narrative to its completion. It allows Luke to reinterpret the memory of Paul's death through the reversal of the scheme of the trial (Acts 27–28); it succeeds also in making the conclusive summary (28.30-31) into a portrait of the exemplary pastor, whereby the realization of the missionary agenda of the book of Acts is anticipated.

---

29. With hesitation, C. Spicq decides for 'rent' (*Lexique théologique du Nouveau Testament* [Fribourg, 1991], pp. 1040-41).

Early Christianity as a 'Persuasive Campaign': Evidence from the Acts of the Apostles and the Letters of Paul

James J. Murphy

The very existence of a Conference on Rhetorical Criticism of Biblical Documents would seem to argue that it is once again acceptable to apply the secular lore of rhetoric to a religious phenomenon—in this case to better our understanding of 'The Book' (Latin: *biblia*) which historically has been dominant in the Judaeo-Christian tradition.

I say 'once again' because the issue of human art versus divine inspiration has a Judaeo-Christian history extending at least as far back as the collation of the two accounts of Creation in the book of Genesis. It wracked the minds of Hebrew commentators long before the time of Christ; it impelled Saint Paul to declare that he spoke not with human wisdom; in a major crisis of the fourth century it forced Saint Augustine—he who says in his *Confessions* that he was converted from rhetoric to Christianity—finally to embrace Ciceronian rhetoric for the sake of the Christian message, against the Cyprians and Basils who would spurn any human art as destructive of the spirit; it split Franciscans and Dominicans in the Middle Ages; it agitated the reformers of the Renaissance, their attitudes toward liturgy and rhetoric traceable like some radioactive isotope which also identified their doctrinal positions; the issue remains today not only in bodies like the Methodists and the Society of Friends but even in highly-structured bodies like the Roman Catholic Church with its divisions between the 'traditional' and the 'charismatic'.

This is an important background to keep in mind as we try to assess the 'rhetorical' qualities of the biblical text and the human beings represented in that text. We can easily push ourselves into a dilemma: what can possibly be humanly 'rhetorical' about the early church if it is truly 'divine', but on the other hand what can be left of the 'divine' if we can prove to ourselves that the entire development was the product of a highly-efficient band of skilful organizers? After all, other small groups of determined men have effected enormous social change: for example the Bolshevik Revolution in Russia, and the consequent rise of world-wide Communism, was originally the work of only seventeen men—a far smaller number than that available to the Apostles after the death of Christ.

In this connection, however, George A. Kennedy has made a useful statement justifying the application of rhetoric to the New Testament:

> The writers of the books of the New Testament had a message to convey and sought to persuade an audience to believe it or to believe it more profoundly. As such they are rhetorical, and their methods can be studied by the discipline of rhetoric.[1]

If we are indeed free to examine the 'rhetorical' quality of the New Testament, then it becomes important to consider the types of questions we need to ask.

Most recent rhetorical studies of the New Testament, like those of Kennedy himself, have been microcosmic—that is, they concentrate on what Kennedy calls 'a rhetorical unit',[2] a discourse having an identifiable beginning, middle and end. Such a unit may be as short as five or six verses, or as large as the whole of the Acts of the Apostles. Kennedy's own book, *New Testament Interpretation through Rhetorical Criticism*, devotes six of its eight chapters to analyses of such individual units. The figure of Paul naturally has drawn a large number of such studies, as in F. Forrester Church's article, 'Rhetorical Structure and Design in Paul's Letter to Philemon', or Wilhelm Wuellner's 'Greek Rhetoric and Pauline Argumentation'.[3]

It is worth noting in this connection that in the 1992 Heidelberg conference alone there were ten papers on Paul's letter to the Romans, four on Philippians, three on 1 and 2 Corinthians, and one each on

1. G.A. Kennedy, *New Testament Interpretation through Rhetorical Criticism* (Chapel Hill: University of North Carolina Press, 1984), p. 3. See also A. Wilder, *The Language of the Gospel: Early Christian Rhetoric* (London: SCM Press, 1964) and A. Cameron, *Christianity and the Rhetoric of Empire: The Development of Christian Discourse* (Berkeley: University of California Press, 1991).
2. Kennedy, *New Testament Interpretation*, p. 33.
3. Respectively, *HTR* 61 (1978), pp. 17-33 and *Early Christian Literature and the Classical Intellectual Tradition: In Honorem R. Grant* (ed. W.R. Schoedel and R. Wilken; Berkeley: University of California Press, 1979), pp. 177-88.

Thessalonians, Galatians, and Colossians—20 papers devoted to Paul out of 34 altogether.

These are valuable studies, each contributing to our rhetorical understanding of the New Testament, and each necessary to fill in the details as we work toward filling out a mosaic of comprehension. What I propose, however, is the application of another kind of rhetorical analysis, one that is macroscopic. It is modern, and does not depend on solving such historical questions as whether Paul ever studied Graeco-Roman rhetoric or whether he did in fact write the Epistle to the Hebrews.

The Concept of 'Persuasive Campaign'

It is my thesis that the surviving accounts of the early church, especially the Acts of the Apostles and the several letters attributed to Paul, prove the existence of what is today called in technical rhetorical terms a 'persuasive campaign'.

A persuasive campaign may be defined as a prolonged and organized series of actions (verbal and non-verbal), carried on by a number of people, which is designed and executed to change, maintain, or deter designated beliefs or behaviors in a target audience. In those cases in which the campaigners belong to a dispossessed or powerless class, the term 'agitation' is sometimes used, being defined as 'persistent, long-term advocacy of social change, where resistance to change is also persistent and long-term'.[4]

Modern mass media like television and radio have so closely identified the term 'campaign' entirely with political or electoral activity that we may easily overlook the true theoretical sense of the word. It is a campaign whenever numbers of people use their persuasive powers to attempt to change the minds of those they wish to reach; this can occur in advertising, in community affairs, in fund-raising activities and in any number of 'rhetorical situations' involving groups of people.[5] For example, William Wilberforce was a nineteenth-century campaigner mobilizing people to end the British

---

4. J.W. Bowers and D.J. Ochs, *The Rhetoric of Agitation and Control* (Reading, MA: Addison-Wesley, 1971), p. 3.

5. Kennedy's discussion of this factor (*New Testament Interpretation*, pp. 34-36) is based on L.F. Bitzer's landmark article, 'The Rhetorical Situation', *Philosophy and Rhetoric* 1 (1968), pp. 1-14.

slave trade, just as the American William Lloyd Garrison led his followers in a campaign to end slavery in the United States. A persuasive campaign can be used for many things, from anti-smoking drives to improving literacy among Peruvian Indians. And it can occur in proselytizing members for a new religion.

All the modern students of persuasive campaigns agree that each one includes an identifiable sequence of steps or procedures, identifiable goals and sub-goals, and identifiable methods of achieving those goals. As is so often the case in modern theory-building, however, the writers disagree about what to call these segments. I do not wish to provide an exhaustive survey of these various views, but a few examples may suffice to indicate the type of analysis that a study of a persuasive campaign can offer to us. Keep in mind the Acts of the Apostles and the letters of Paul while considering the following descriptions of such a campaign.

Charles U. Larson declares that a campaign has five stages: identity, in which the campaigners decide on their basic message; legitimacy, in which they demonstrate to others their right to identity; participation, in which the campaigners enlist themselves for the campaign; penetration, in which campaigners insert themselves within the target audience; and finally distribution, in which the campaigners' message is spread as widely as possible.[6]

Herbert W. Simons identifies a different five steps: planning, in which the campaigners plot out their actions; mobilization, akin to Larson's participation stage, in which the campaigners decide who will do what; legitimation, identical to Larson's legitimacy step; promotion, in which the identity of the group is clarified to enhance its credibility; and finally activation, in which all the preceding steps are used to broaden message transmission to the target audience.[7] There are numerous other descriptions in literature of persuasive campaign theory. Bowers and Ochs, for example, see four main steps before confrontation and revolution become necessary to achieve a group's goals—petition of establishment, promulgation of desires, coherence

---

6. C.U. Larson, *Persuasion: Reception and Responsibility* (Belmont, CA: Wadsworth, 1979), esp. ch. 6 ('The Persuasive Campaign or Movement').

7. H.W. Simons, *Persuasion: Understanding, Practice, and Analysis* (Reading, MA: Addison-Wesley, 1976), esp. chs. 12 ('Leading Persuasive Campaigns') and 13 ('Persuasion in Social Conflict').

in the face of opposition, and then polarization between the campaigners and their opponents.[8]

Despite the apparent differences in these various descriptions, however, there is a controlling theme among them. A group wishing to influence others must have a plan which includes a means of self-identification, a means of making that identity valuable to their audience, a willingness to work hard to transmit that message of worthiness, and the capacity to keep new members ('converts') committed to the message once they have accepted it. The rhetoric of the persuasive campaign, in other words, involves much more than single speeches, letters or other individual persuasive acts.

In my judgment the portrait of early Christianity offered in the Acts of the Apostles and the letters of Paul, incomplete though that picture may be, fully justifies us in looking carefully there for the elements of a true persuasive campaign in the technical sense of that term.

Early Christianity as a Persuasive Campaign

If the modern observer describes the Acts of the Apostles in terms of the *process* which Luke recounts, then the elements of the rhetorical campaign stand out quite clearly.

Basically Acts describes a group of Jewish men (and some women) who have come to believe that Christ was the promised messiah, who first proselytize those nearest to them, who then fan outwards from Jerusalem to proselytize others, and who then maintain doctrinal contact with the new converts through letters and visits. Throughout this process both the original believers and the converts successfully confront potentially divisive issues of belief and behavior to maintain a coherent belief structure, which in turn enables them to transmit a well-defined message as the movement expands geographically and numerically.

The twenty surviving 'letters' of Paul, Peter, James and John are an integral part of this process, serving in all cases as coherence devices. That is, they enhance the cohesiveness of the group by clarifying doctrine, resolving internal dissensions in the new *ecclesia*—and, above

---

8. Bowers and Ochs, *Rhetoric of Agitation*, pp. 16-37. For an annotated bibliography of 22 campaign-related books, see *Public Communication Campaigns* (ed. R.E. Rice and C.K. Akin; Newbury Park: Sage, 2nd edn, 1989), pp. 369-72.

all, by reminding their audiences that they now belong to a larger community sharing a common message.

It is important to note at the outset that the persuasive process which Luke describes in Acts is radically different from those of Christ himself that Luke recounts in his Gospel. In Lk. 10.1-20, for instance, Christ sends out 72 in pairs, and when they return they report directly to him. No one else is involved.

It is also important to remember that what Luke recounts is almost by definition only a part of what actually must have occurred. Nevertheless his account is so markedly consistent with modern theories of rhetorical campaigns that it seems safe to take it as a reliable picture of the apostolic campaign as a whole.

One or two examples may serve to identify the basic processes in the early Christian campaign. Typically the penetration stage begins in a large city, where a 'Christian'[9] uses his identity as a Jew to participate in regular synagogue liturgy; once allowed to speak he proclaims the arrival of the messiah in the person of Jesus; argument ensues; he is frequently expelled from the synagogue, but not before converting some to his belief. A new worshipping group (*ecclesia*) is formed. The Christian leaves, but he and others keep in contact with the new 'church' through letters and sometimes through later visits.

It is significant that Luke describes numerous apostles and disciples—not just Paul—taking part in this process. Luke's account includes Peter, of course, but also Philip (8.4), Stephen (6.8), John (8.15), Barnabas (11.21), Silas (15.40), Timothy (15.41), and Apollos (18.24-28). Moreover, there are unnamed others, as in 11.19-26, where Luke says:

> Those who had escaped the persecution that happened because of Stephen travelled as far as Phoenicia and Cyprus and Antioch, but they usually proclaimed the message only to Jews. Some of them, however, who came from Cyprus and Cyrene, went to Antioch where they started preaching to the Greeks, proclaiming the good news of the Lord Jesus to them as well. The Lord helped them, and a great number believed and were converted to the Lord.

9. Luke says (11.27): 'It was at Antioch that the disciples were first called "Christians"'. He also uses the term 'Brothers' and 'Followers of the Way'. Citations are from *The Jerusalem Bible* (ed. A. Jones; Garden City, NY: Doubleday, 1966).

Two examples of this process are described in Acts 17.1-15. First Paul reasoned from Scripture in the synagogue in Thessalonika for three sabbaths, convincing some to join Paul and Silas, but also enraging many of the Jews. Then when Paul and Silas fled from there to Beroea (17.10-15) they repeated the process of visiting the synagogue to recruit new believers; 'Here the Jews were more open-minded', Luke tells us, 'and they welcomed the word more readily'. This was in the summer of the year 50. But the Thessalonians pursued them to Beroea, and Paul had to leave for Athens while Silas and Timothy stayed behind. And it was of course from Athens or Corinth that Paul wrote the first letter that winter to the endangered church at Thessalonika.

There are so many other instances that this penetration process can only be seen as a conscious plan. At Iconium, for example, Luke says that Paul and Barnabas 'went to the Jewish synagogue, as they had at Antioch, and they spoke so effectively that a great many Jews and Greeks became believers' (14.1). The same thing happened at Ephesus (19.8-10).

Moreover, Luke tells us of travellers chancing upon new churches though we have no idea who had proselytized these new groups in the first place. One example occurs on Paul's long voyage to Rome, when he stayed a week with Christians he found at Puteoli on the Gulf of Naples; nor do we know who converted the Romans themselves.[10]

Luke is of course not a rhetorical critic interested in the human processes used in these conversions, but he does recount several instances of the planning that clearly lay behind these events. The so-called Council of Jerusalem (15.5-29), the sending of Barnabas on a follow-up mission to Antioch (11.21), the sending of a clarifying letter to Antioch in the hands of Judas Barsabbas and Silas (15.22-33), the appointment of the Seven by the Twelve (6.17)—these and other events portray a rapidly self-organizing, centralizing authority.[11]

10. It also is not clear just when the Roman conversions occurred. They had certainly occurred by AD 57 when Paul wrote his letter to the Roman Christians, and some scholars suggest that the Jews expelled from Rome by Claudius in 49 or 50 may have brought the message of Jesus back to Rome when they returned shortly after Claudius died. In any case the episode demonstrates that there were many more persuaders working than Luke has space to name in Acts.

11. Not every modern observer has recognized this capacity for self-organization. 'Speaking generally', Johannes Weiss says, 'one cannot exaggerate the looseness

Even Paul's letter to the Romans, whom he had not yet met or visited, displays a concern from the center for stabilizing the doctrinal orthodoxy of the outpost converts.

The overall rhetorical function of this letter and the others is to serve as a coherence device. That is, the letters work to cement the readers (and listeners, for they were often read aloud) into a common-message community. Even Paul's letter to Philemon about the slave Onesimus, ostensibly a matter of individual concern, is treated publicly in the early church.

Some Inferences and Conclusions

If what is suggested here has some validity—that is, that Luke's account in the Acts and the evidence from the letters of Paul collectively reveal the existence of a real persuasive campaign in the early church—then it would seem to follow that we can profitably re-examine each microact in this campaign to determine its rhetorical function with the larger plan.

Kennedy concludes his study of the speeches in Acts with this statement: 'Of the rhetorical features of Acts the most important historically is the way the apostles utilize occasions to preach the gospel'.[12] This may be true in a general sense, but there are scores of other rhetorically important issues in Acts that depend precisely upon their place within the structure of a persuasive campaign. For example, the continuing struggles between Christians, Pharisees, Hellenists and Jewish traditionalists led the Christians to subtly-graded differences in terms used for Jesus—differences based on their audiences, for example preferring the term 'Lord' with pagans instead of the term 'Christ' which would be understandable to a Jewish audience. In no case would they use *basileus* ('king'), especially since one of the accusations against them was that they offered Jesus as a new Emperor. These gradations display a purposeful and widespread sense of audience analysis which does not seem to depend upon the talents of any single individual.[13]

---

and freedom of organizations in the earliest period' (*Earliest Christianity: A History of the Period A.D. 30-150* [New York: Harper & Brothers, 1959], I, p. 48).

12. Kennedy, *New Testament Interpretation*, p. 140.

13. Cameron (*Christianity*, pp. 32-39) argues that 'the subtle and complex productions' of early Christian writers indicate a highly skilled literary sense, and

Another promising line of inquiry might be to investigate the distinction Luke makes between 'preaching' and 'teaching'. Also, Luke is not very clear about the ways in which the Christians first reached the non-Jews, though his account of Paul at the Areopagus (17.16-34) suggests that here again the process was to find any existing forum and use it as a preaching platform.

It is not my intention here to spell out all the directions of inquiry which might be possible. Rather, I propose that we use the paradigm of the rhetorical campaign to look again at the familiar.

Naturally there are some difficulties with this approach. Luke is an ancient historian, and his account is a product of his times. He uses multiple sources. Moreover, he sees the Spirit, not human effort, controlling the conversion process.[14] More than half of Acts is devoted to Paul, of course; whether or not it may be an *apologia* for the apostle now imprisoned in Rome at the time of writing, the methodology ascribed by Luke to Paul is so consistent with that ascribed to others that this imbalance is not by itself a detriment to the studies I propose. Some have termed Acts an idealized statement of what Luke wished had happened, but even in the worst case it seems true that Luke is describing a rhetorical phenomenon recognizable to modern rhetorical theorists. It is a phenomenon unknown to ancient rhetoricans like Aristotle, Cicero, or Luke's contemporary Quintilian.[15] The thrust of ancient Greek and Roman rhetoric (and the schools which supported it) was the preparation of the single orator speaking alone.

It is at least remarkable that this particular messiah's cause could have accomplished so much so rapidly. Given that at least 35 other so-called 'messiahs' appeared during the first Christian century, it is worth wondering at the causes for that success. Was it the effect of miracles?[16] Perhaps at times that may be a cause, according to Luke;

that the concept of early Christianity as a 'popular' movement is misleading.

14. For example 16.6-10 where Luke reports that the Spirit forbade Paul and Silas to preach in Asia; then Paul has a dream in which a Macedonian appeals to Paul to come preach to his people.

15. It is interesting to note that Quintilian is reported to have defended in a court case the Bernice who was with King Agrippa (25.13) when Paul was haled before him in Caesarea.

16. During the thirteenth-century revival of interest in preaching theory, one of the justifications for the effort was that the age of miracles had passed and therefore

yet there are dozens of other conversions reported by Luke which depend on argument of one kind or another, rather than on miracles.

In conclusion, then, let me simply reiterate that it would seem to be a profitable rhetorical inquiry to re-examine Acts and the letters of Paul as aspects of a true persuasive campaign. If only because it was so successful, we are entitled to look into the causes of that success.

the church now had to depend on purely human arts. For an account of this revival, see J.J. Murphy, *Rhetoric in the Middle Ages: A History of Rhetorical Theory from Saint Augustine to the Renaissance* (Berkeley: University of California Press, 1974), pp. 269-356.

The Theoretical Justification for Application of Rhetorical Categories to Pauline Epistolary Literature

Stanley E. Porter

Determining the literary form of Paul's writings—as self-evident as it may at first appear—has been a recurring problem in New Testament scholarship.[1] In recent years Paul's letters have been increasingly viewed under the auspices of categories of ancient rhetoric, such as those described in the ancient rhetorical handbooks. But the result has been a certain amount of tension among scholars, because no model has allowed a completely smooth harmonizing of ancient epistolary and rhetorical categories. Thurén has found at least three major approaches to the dilemma of how the epistles are seen in relation to rhetoric.[2] The first approach, represented by White, Doty and Hübner,[3] holds that rhetorical conventions are of only secondary

1. Modern discussion begins with A. Deissmann (*Light from the Ancient East* [trans. L.R.M. Strachan; repr. Grand Rapids: Baker, 4th edn, 1965 (1910)], pp. 148-49, 224-46; *Bible Studies* [trans. A. Grieve; Edinburgh: T. & T. Clark, 1901], pp. 3-59), who distinguished between 'epistles' (i.e. conscious, artistic prose) and 'letters' (i.e. occasional, individual and non-public texts such as Paul's). One of Deissmann's own examples of a letter from son Theon to his father Theon (P.Oxy. 119), which exhibits features of irony, understatement and sarcasm, undermines his own distinction. As D.E. Aune (*The New Testament in its Literary Environment* [Philadelphia: Westminster Press, 1987], p. 161) indicates, few since Deissmann have put forward typologies of ancient letters.

2. L. Thurén, *The Rhetorical Strategy of 1 Peter: With Special Regard to Ambiguous Expressions* (Åbo: Åbo Akademi, 1990), pp. 57-64. His scheme, though not entirely satisfactory, as will be shown below, illustrates a better perception of the issues than most.

3. E.g. J.L. White, *The Body of the Greek Letter* (SBLDS, 2; Missoula, MT: Scholars Press, 1972); W.G. Doty, *Letters in Primitive Christianity* (Philadelphia: Fortress Press, 1973); *idem*, 'The Classification of Epistolary Literature', *CBQ* 31 (1969), pp. 183-99; H. Hübner, 'Der Galaterbrief und das Verhältnis von antiker

applicability to the epistles, which are genuine examples of letter writing from the Graeco-Roman world. The second, represented by Berger and Kennedy,[4] holds that the documents are essentially

Rhetorik und Epistolographie', *TLZ* 109 (1984), pp. 241-50.
4. E.g. K. Berger, 'Apostelbrief und apostolische Rede: Zum Formular frühchristlichen Briefe', *ZNW* 65 (1974), pp. 190-231; *idem*, 'Hellenistische Gattungen im Neuen Testament', in *ANRW* II. 25.2 (ed. H. Temporini and W. Haase; Berlin: de Gruyter, 1984), pp. 1031-432; *idem, Formgeschichte des Neuen Testaments* (Heidelberg: Quelle & Meyer, 1984), pp. 216-17; G.A. Kennedy, *New Testament Interpretation through Rhetorical Criticism* (Chapel Hill: University of North Carolina Press, 1984), pp. 86-87; and now D.E. Aune, 'Romans as a Logos Protreptikos in the Context of Ancient Religious and Philosophical Propaganda', in *Paulus und antike Judentum* (ed. M. Hengel and U. Heckel; WUNT, 58; Tübingen: Mohr [Paul Siebeck], 1991), pp. 91-124. This position has not gained widespread scholarly acceptance, especially in the light of significant studies that show genuine epistolary features throughout the epistles: e.g. P. Schubert, *Form and Function of the Pauline Thanksgiving* (Berlin: Töpelmann, 1939); *idem*, 'The Form and Function of the Pauline Letters', *JR* 19 (1939), pp. 365-77; T.Y. Mullins, 'Petition as a Literary Form', *NovT* 5 (1962), pp. 46-54; *idem*, 'Disclosure as a Literary Form in the New Testament', *NovT* 7 (1964), pp. 44-50; *idem*, 'Greeting as a New Testament Form', *JBL* 87 (1968), pp. 418-26; *idem*, 'Formulas in the New Testament Epistles', *JBL* 91 (1972), pp. 380-90; J.C. Brunt, 'More on *topos* as a New Testament Form', *JBL* 104 (1985), pp. 495-500; J.T. Sanders, 'The Transition from Opening Epistolary Thanksgiving to Body in the Letters of the Pauline Corpus', *JBL* 81 (1962), pp. 348-62; G.J. Bahr, 'The Subscriptions in the Pauline Letters', *JBL* 87 (1968), pp. 27-41; C.J. Bjerklund, *Parakalô: Form, Funktion und Sinn der parakalô-Sätze in der paulinischen Briefen* (Oslo: Universitetsforlaget, 1967); J.L. White, 'Introductory Formulae in the Body of the Pauline Letter', *JBL* 90 (1971), pp. 91-97; *idem*, 'New Testament Epistolary Literature in the Framework of Ancient Epistolography', in *ANRW* 25.2, pp. 1730-56; *idem, Light from Ancient Letters* (Foundations and Facets; Philadelphia: Fortress Press, 1986); *idem*, 'Ancient Greek Letters', in *Greco-Roman Literature and the New Testament: Selected Forms and Genres* (ed. D.E. Aune; SBLSBS, 21; Atlanta: Scholars Press, 1988), pp. 85-105; P.T. O'Brien, *Introductory Thanksgivings in the Letters of Paul* (NovTSup, 49; Leiden: Brill, 1977); J.H. Roberts, 'Pauline Transitions to the Letter Body', in A. Vanhoye (ed.), *L'Apôtre Paul: Personnalité, style et conception du ministère* (BETL, 73; Leuven: Leuven University Press, 1986), pp. 93-99; L.L. Belleville, 'Continuity or Discontinuity: A Fresh Look at 1 Corinthians in the Light of First-Century Epistolary Forms and Conventions', *EvQ* 59 (1987), pp. 15-37; *idem, Reflections of Glory: Paul's Polemical Use of the Moses–Doxa Tradition in 2 Corinthians 3.12-18* (JSNTSup, 52; Sheffield: JSOT Press, 1991), pp. 104-35; G.W. Hansen, *Abraham in Galatians: Epistolary and Rhetorical Contexts* (JSNTSup, 29; Sheffield: JSOT Press, 1989), pp. 21-54;

speeches, almost incidentally with epistolary openings and closings attached. Some, most notably Betz,[5] have combined these two proposals in various ways, trying to maintain the integrity of the epistolary features but in the light of rhetorical features as well. And the third approach, represented by Johanson and Thurén,[6] holds that epistolary and rhetorical categories apply to different levels of examination, and hence are compatible because they answer different sets of questions.

The approach of Betz has perhaps exerted the greatest force on discussion of the Pauline letters regarding the relation of epistolary and rhetorical categories. In his commentary on Galatians, Betz provides a detailed analysis of the letter according to its rhetorical species and organization. He has been so influential that one of the newest subgenres of commentary writing is the rhetorical analysis of a Pauline epistle.[7] It is not uncommon to find the following progression of

L. Alexander, 'Hellenistic Letter-Forms and the Structure of Philippians', *JSNT* 37 (1989), pp. 87-101; L.A. Jervis, *The Purpose of Romans: A Comparative Letter Structure Investigation* (JSNTSup, 55; Sheffield: JSOT Press, 1991).

5. E.g. H.D. Betz, *Galatians: A Commentary on Paul's Letter to the Churches in Galatia* (Hermeneia; Philadelphia: Fortress Press, 1979); *idem*, 'The Literary Composition and Function of Paul's Letter to the Galatians', *NTS* 21 (1974–75), pp. 353-79; *idem*, *2 Corinthians 8 and 9: A Commentary on Two Administrative Letters of the Apostle Paul* (Hermeneia; Philadelphia: Fortress Press, 1985); cf. *idem, Der Apostel Paulus und die sokratische Tradition: Eine exegetische Untersuchung zu seiner 'Apologie' 2 Kor 10–13* (Tübingen: Mohr [Paul Siebeck], 1972). See also L. Hartman, 'On Reading Others' Letters', in *Christians among Jews and Gentiles* (Festschrift K. Stendahl; ed. W.E. Nickelsburg and G.W. MacRae; Philadelphia: Fortress Press, 1986), pp. 137-46.

6. E.g. B.C. Johanson, *To All the Brethren: A Text-Linguistic and Rhetorical Approach to 1 Thessalonians* (ConBNT, 16; Uppsala: Almqvist and Wiksell, 1987), pp. 61-63. See also F. Schnider and W. Stenger, *Studien zum neutestamentlichen Briefformular* (NTTS, 11; Leiden: Brill, 1987); M. Bünker, *Briefformular und rhetorische Disposition im 1. Korintherbrief* (Göttingen: Vandenhoeck & Ruprecht, 1984).

7. See, e.g., the following works: Hansen, *Abraham in Galatians*, esp. pp. 55-71; R. Jewett, 'Romans as an Ambassadorial Letter', *Int* 36 (1982), pp. 5-20; *idem*, *The Thessalonian Correspondence: Pauline Rhetoric and Millenarian Piety* (FFNT; Philadelphia: Fortress Press, 1986), esp. pp. 63-87; *idem*, 'Following the Argument of Romans', in K.P. Donfried (ed.), *The Romans Debate* (Peabody, MA: Hendrickson, 2nd edn, 1991), pp. 265-77; *idem, Romans* (Hermeneia; Minneapolis: Augsburg–Fortress, forthcoming) (for which I have seen sample sections); F.W. Hughes, *Early Christian Rhetoric and 2 Thessalonians* (JSNTSup, 30; Sheffield: JSOT Press, 1989); R.N. Longenecker, *Galatians* (WBC, 41; Dallas:

thought in the introductory material of commentaries and other works. The supposition is made that the so-called species (as part of invention or *inventio*) and/or the organization (arrangement, *dispositio* or *taxis*), besides the style (ornamentation, *elocutio* or *lexis*), of ancient rhetorical practice can be applied to analysis of a Pauline letter. This is frequently supported either by appeal to the 'successful' work of Betz or, more recently, by appeal to the work of Kennedy. (The appeal to Kennedy comes about perhaps because of some of the negative critical reception of Betz and because of the more general statements of Kennedy.) Authors nuance their treatments of these categories, but then usually concentrate upon determining the species of discourse and suggesting a suitable outline of its organization, while

Word Books, 1990); C.A. Wanamaker, *The Epistles to the Thessalonians: A Commentary on the Greek Text* (NIGTC; Grand Rapids: Eerdmans, 1990); B.H. Brinsmead, *Galatians: Dialogical Response to Opponents* (SBLDS, 65; Atlanta: Scholars Press, 1982); N. Elliott, *The Rhetoric of Romans: Argumentative Constraint and Strategy and Paul's Dialogue with Judaism* (JSNTSup, 45: Sheffield: JSOT Press, 1990). See also W. Wuellner, 'Paul's Rhetoric of Argumentation in Romans: An Alternative to the Donfried–Karris Debate over Romans', in Donfried (ed.), *The Romans Debate*, pp. 128-46; *idem*, 'Greek Rhetoric and Pauline Argumentation', in *Early Christian Literature and the Classical Intellectual Tradition* (Festschrift R.M. Grant; ed. W.R. Schoedel and R.L. Wilken; Paris: Beauchesne, 1979), pp. 177-88; F.F. Church, 'Rhetorical Structure and Design in Paul's Letter to Philemon', *HTR* 71 (1978), pp. 17-33; J.D. Hester, 'The Rhetorical Structure of Galatians 1:11–2:14', *JBL* 103 (1984), pp. 223-32; *idem*, 'The Use and Influence of Rhetoric in Galatians 2:1-14', *TZ* 42 (1986), pp. 386-408; B. Standaert, 'La rhétorique ancienne dans Saint Paul', in Vanhoye (ed.), *L'Apôtre Paul*, pp. 78-92; L.R. Donelson, *Pseudepigraphy and Ethical Argument in the Pastoral Epistles* (Tübingen: Mohr [Paul Siebeck], 1986), pp. 67-113; C. Forbes, 'Comparison, Self-Praise and Irony: Paul's Boasting and the Conventions of Hellenistic Rhetoric', *NTS* 32 (1986), pp. 1-30; D.F. Watson, 'A Rhetorical Analysis of Philippians and its Implications for the Unity Question', *NovT* 30 (1988), pp. 57-88; T.H. Olbricht, 'An Aristotelian Rhetorical Analysis of 1 Thessalonians', in *Greeks, Romans and Christians: Essays in Honor of A.J. Malherbe* (ed. D. Balch, E. Ferguson and W. Meeks; Minneapolis: Fortress Press, 1990), pp. 216-37; M.M. Mitchell, *Paul and the Rhetoric of Reconciliation* (Hermeneutische Untersuchungen zur Theologie, 28; Tübingen: Mohr [Paul Siebeck], 1991); and F.W. Hughes, 'The Rhetoric of Reconciliation: 2 Corinthians 1.1–2.13 and 7.5–8.24', pp. 246-61; J.D. Hester, 'Placing the Blame: The Presence of Epideictic in Galatians 1 and 2', pp. 281-307; and C.J. Martin, 'The Rhetorical Function of Commercial Language in Paul's Letter to Philemon (Verse 18)', pp. 321-37, all in D.F. Watson (ed.), *Persuasive Artistry* (Festschrift G.A. Kennedy; JSNTSup, 50; Sheffield: JSOT Press, 1991).

neglecting style almost entirely (or at least placing it a distant third in importance).

The limitations of Betz's treatment of Galatians are at least two, and they have been sufficiently chronicled to warrant only brief mention here. The first is his dependence upon the supposed genre of the 'apologetic letter', purportedly found in such works as Plato's *Epistle* 7, as well as Isocrates' *Antidosis*, Demosthenes' *De Corona*, Cicero's *Brutus* and Libanius's *Oratio* 1. Betz himself admits that the 'subsequent history of the genre is difficult to trace since most of the pertinent literature did not survive'.[8] In fact, the literature he cites is hardly germane, as many have pointed out.[9] Secondly, his organizational analysis especially with regard to chs. 5 and 6, in which he must invent a category not found in any of the classical rhetorical handbooks (*exhortatio*), as well as his inadequate treatment of chs. 3 and 4, shows that it is tenuous to rely upon his analysis of the book of Galatians as the basis for subsequent analysis of any epistle in its entirety.[10]

The use of Kennedy is equally problematic. In Longenecker's commentary on Galatians, there is much significant and useful discussion. But at one point, he says the following:

> And it should not be surprising that a Jew of Tarsus, who trained under Gamaliel at Jerusalem, became a convert to the rising messianic movement called Chrisianity, took leadership in the extension of that gospel among gentiles, and wrote pastorally to converts in Asia Minor, would use in Galatians many literary and rhetorical conventions then current in the Greco-Roman world. 'Even if', as G.A. Kennedy observes, 'he had not studied in a Greek school, there were many handbooks of rhetoric in common circulation which he could have seen. He and the evangelists as well would, indeed, have been hard put to escape an awareness of rhetoric as practiced in the culture around them for the rhetorical theory of the schools found its immediate application in almost every form of oral and written communication' (*New Testament Interpretation through Rhetorical*

---

8. Betz, *Galatians*, p. 15.
9. See esp. Longenecker, *Galatians*, pp. ciii-civ.
10. See, e.g., Hansen, *Abraham in Galatians*, pp. 58-71; Kennedy, *New Testament Interpretation*, pp. 145-46; J. Smit, 'The Letter to Galatians: A Deliberative Speech', *NTS* 35 (1989), pp. 1-26; Longenecker, *Galatians*, pp. cix-cxiii; C.J. Classen, 'Paulus und die antike Rhetorik', *ZNW* 82 (1991), esp. pp. 8-15, 29-33; and the following reviews: W.A. Meeks in *JBL* 100 (1981), p. 306; D. Aune in *RelSRev* 7 (1981), pp. 323-28.

Criticism, 10). The forms of classical rhetoric were 'in the air', and Paul seems to have used them almost unconsciously for his own purposes— much as he used the rules of Greek grammar.[11]

Longenecker, in citing Kennedy, seems to be saying, first, that Paul would have known the contents of the rhetorical handbooks and that he would have had some sort of precedent for use of them in his own writing (that is forms of classical rhetoric were simply 'in the air'), and, secondly, that this, in some way justifies current analysis of the Pauline epistles according to these categories. There may well be elements of ancient rhetoric to be found in Paul or other letter writers of the time, even young Theon. But it is difficult to establish what and how much Paul could have known on a conscious or formal basis.[12] More to the point is the fact that contemporary scholars like Longenecker use the categories of ancient rhetoric not in terms of their original use to guide in the creation of rhetoric but as tools for the analysis of discourse.

An instructive statement is found in Wanamaker's introduction to his commentary on Thessalonians:

> According to ancient rhetorical theory going back to Aristotle there were three genres of rhetoric: judicial rhetoric, deliberative rhetoric, and demonstrative or epideictic rhetoric. These designations originally were applied to types of public oratory, but as Kennedy (*New Testament Interpretation*, 19) points out, they have applicability to any form of discourse.[13]

Kennedy's book at page 19 suggests that the following quotation may have been in Wanamaker's mind: 'Although these categories specifically refer to the circumstances of classical civic oratory [that is, the species of rhetoric], they are in fact applicable to all discourse'.

---

11. Longenecker, *Galatians*, pp. cxii-cxiii. The passage regarding rhetoric being 'in the air' paraphrases Kennedy's further remarks. This passage of Kennedy is cited to similar purpose in Thurén, *Rhetorical Strategy*, p. 49; Hansen, *Abraham in Galatians*, p. 55.

12. This is called into question by J.T. Reed, 'Using Ancient Rhetorical Categories to Interpret Paul's Letters: A Question of Genre', pp. 292ff. in this volume. Classen ('Paul und die antike Rhetorik', p. 31) makes the provocative observation that 'praxis precedes theory', meaning that Paul's performance does not necessarily indicate that there was a theoretical basis for it.

13. Wanamaker, *Epistles to the Thessalonians*, p. 46. This passage of Kennedy is cited to similar purpose in Thurén, *Rhetorical Strategy*, p. 51.

He then describes briefly the three species. This is the extent of Kennedy's 'argument': the simple assertion that the categories of classical oratory are applicable to all discourse, with no reference to any ancient sources or precedents for their analytical use.

These quotations suffice to raise several important definitional questions. When the term 'rhetoric' is used by these and other writers, to what are they referring? 'Rhetoric' is apparently used in at least two senses. Kennedy is not untypical in his use of the term. At the beginning of his book, Kennedy defines 'rhetoric' as 'that quality in discourse by which a speaker or writer seeks to accomplish his purposes'.[14] Modern authors frequently begin by discussing rhetoric in terms of 'persuasion and argumentation', 'rhetorical situation' and 'rhetorical units'.[15] In these instances scholars are referring to what might well be called 'universal rhetoric'. There is usefulness for such a category, a conception found at least as early as Aristotle (*Rhetoric* 1.2) and widely employed in the analytical works of a number of modern 'rhetorical critics'. What these modern analysts are doing might well be called 'synchronic rhetorical analysis',[16] in other words, analysis of all types of communication to appreciate any and all techniques used to promote the art of persuasion. This apparently is the kind of rhetorical strategy promoted and described by Perelman and Olbrechts-Tyteca, within the confines of the Western intellectual tradition.[17] Kennedy seems to have this in mind as well when he says,

---

14. Kennedy, *New Testament Interpretation*, p. 3. He speaks of 'rhetorical criticism' as taking 'the text as we have it, whether the work of a single author or the product of editing, and look[ing] at it from the point of view of the author's or editor's intent, the unified results, and how it would be perceived by an audience of near contemporaries' (p. 4). See also J.N. Vorster, 'Toward an Interactional Model for the Analysis of Letters', *Neot* 24.2 (1990), esp. pp. 118-25.

15. See, e.g., B.L. Mack, *Rhetoric and the New Testament* (Philadelphia: Fortress Press, 1990), pp. 19-22.

16. The term is used in Longenecker, *Galatians*, p. cix (cf. pp. cxiv-cxix), who refers to the article by M. Kessler, 'A Methodological Setting for Rhetorical Criticism', *Semitics* 4 (1974), pp. 22-36. Longenecker gets a bit confused over what constitutes synchronic rhetorical analysis when he actually performs it, relying upon the classical categories of invention.

17. C. Perelman and L. Olbrechts-Tyteca, *The New Rhetoric: A Treatise on Argumentation* (trans. J. Wilkinson and P. Weaver; Notre Dame, IN: University of Notre Dame Press, 1969 [1958]); C. Perelman, *The New Rhetoric and the Humanities: Essays on Rhetoric and its Application* (Dordrecht: Reidel, 1979); *idem*,

Though rhetoric is colored by the traditions and conventions of the society
in which it is applied, it is also a universal phenomenon which is conditioned by basic workings of the human mind and heart and by the nature
of all human society... It is perfectly possible to utilize the categories of
Aristotelian rhetoric to study speech in China, India, Africa... [18]

But why would one want to limit oneself to Aristotelian rhetoric, or
to any other rhetorical model or strategy?

One need not confine one-
self to any particular model, because the claim being made is that
rhetoric is a universal category, one not necessarily confined to the
specific set of techniques that developed in the Graeco-Roman world.
Even though 'rhetoric' is frequently used in a universal sense, the categories that are quite often applied in analysis are the specific ones
found in the ancient rhetorical handbooks (or on the basis of supposedly parallel texts), in other words, the three species of discourse and
the categories of organization.[19] Thus, even though many scholars

The Realm of Rhetoric (trans. W. Kluback; Notre Dame, IN: University of Notre
Dame Press, 1982); E. Black, *Rhetorical Criticism* (New York: Macmillan, 1965);
W. Brandt, *The Rhetoric of Argumentation* (New York: Bobbs-Merrill, 1970). See
also W. Wuellner, 'Where is Rhetorical Criticism Taking Us?', *CBQ* 49 (1987),
pp. 448-63; *idem*, 'Paul as Pastor: The Function of Rhetorical Questions in First
Corinthians', in Vanhoye (ed.), *L'Apôtre Paul*, pp. 49-77; *idem*, 'Hermeneutics and
Rhetorics', *Scriptura* 3 (1989); J. Zmijewski, *Der Stil der paulinische 'Narrenrede':
Analyse der Sprachgestaltung in 2 Kor 11,1–12,10 als Beitrag zur Methodik von
Stiluntersuchungen neutestamentlicher Texte* (BBB, 52; Cologne: Peter Hanstein,
1978); F. Siegert, *Argumentation bei Paulus gezeigt an Römer 9–11* (WUNT, 34;
Tübingen: Mohr [Paul Siebeck], 1985); A.H. Snyman, 'Style and Meaning in
Romans 8:31-39', *Neot* 18 (1984), pp. 94-103; *idem*, 'On Studying the Figures
(schemata) in the New Testament', *Bib* 69 (1988), pp. 93-107; A.H. Snyman and
J.v.W. Cronje, 'Toward a New Classification of the Figures (ΣXHMATA) in the
Greek New Testament', *NTS* 32 (1986), pp. 113-21; N.R. Petersen, *Rediscovering
Paul: Philemon and the Sociology of Paul's Narrative World* (Philadelphia: Fortress
Press, 1985), esp. pp. 43-88; Jewett, *The Thessalonian Correspondence*, pp. 64-67;
Johanson, *To All the Brethren*, p. 34; A.B. du Toit, 'Persuasion in Romans 1.1-17',
BZ 33 (1989), pp. 192-209; P.E. Koptak, 'Rhetorical Identification in Paul's
Autobiographical Narrative: Galatians 1.13–2.14', *JSNT* 40 (1990), pp. 97-113;
S.E. Porter, 'Romans 13.1-7 as Pauline Political Rhetoric', *FN* 3 (1990), pp. 115-
39; Hester, 'Placing the Blame', pp. 282-85; S.M. Pogoloff, 'Isocrates and
Contemporary Hermeneutics', in Watson (ed.), *Persuasive Artistry*, pp. 338-62;
Classen, 'Paulus und die antike Rhetorik', pp. 1-6.

    18. Kennedy, *New Testament Interpretation*, p. 10.
    19. E.g. Wuellner, 'Paul's Rhetoric of Argumentation', pp. 128-32 and 133-46;
Mack, *Rhetoric and the New Testament*, pp. 19-24 and 25-48. See also

begin by recognizing that 'rhetoric' may well be a universal category to describe how humans in a given linguistic situation try to persuade others, they nevertheless perform what might be called 'diachronic rhetorical criticism',[20] in other words, they confine themselves to the categories of rhetoric from the ancient Graeco-Roman world. This progression is a non sequitur.

It may be true that the ancient Greek rhetoricians conceptualized and elucidated their theories more clearly than any other cultural expression of the categories of rhetoric; it simply does not follow that analysis must follow the patterns established by them. Other schemes may be equally productive for analytic purposes. It also begs the question of whether there is any precedent in the ancient world for such analysis.

Thus, there is the need for a second distinction, that is, that when rhetorical analysis occurs there is reference to particular 'rhetorical features' to describe the effect of the discourse. In other words, 'universal rhetoric' is always embodied in various features of 'formal rhetoric'. Within the larger category of (for the sake of argument) a posited universal rhetoric, there are various formal means by which 'the art of persuasion' can be carried out, many if not most of them culture specific. Since each culture is different, the set of features may well be different, as will be the names given to the categories. One notices almost immediately, however, that three of the broad categories of formal rhetoric from the Graeco-Roman world are often referred to in analyses of New Testament texts. These are especially the species of discourse and categories of organization, and less frequently the elements of style, three categories discussed—although in varying ways and to varying degrees—by the ancient rhetorical handbooks.[21] This raises the necessary question regarding what theoretical justification there is for employing these categories, as opposed to other perhaps more contemporary schemes, or even other aspects of Graeco-Roman rhetoric. Many if not most of the stylistic features (especially figures of speech) were common to many forms of

E.P.J. Corbett, *Classical Rhetoric for the Modern Student* (New York: Oxford University Press, 3rd edn, 1990).

20. The term is from Longenecker, *Galatians*, p. cix.

21. Several of the categories of the handbooks are neglected, including memory (*memoria*) and delivery (*pronuntiatio*), probably because they do not have ready application to letters.

literature, and were readily drawn upon in analysis.[22] But application
of the species and categories of arrangement, formal terms describing
categories specifically originating with oratory, is not the same kind
of task. Kennedy, Betz and a host of others suggest that the application
of these formal categories from classical rhetoric to analysis of
ancient letters was something that the ancients themselves were
familiar with and would recognize. This leads to the need for a
further distinction.

In the study of literary genres, such as epistles and orations, there is
always the tension between application of categories familiar to the
ancients themselves and application of categories devised and applied
by modern critics.[23] Sometimes there may be significant overlap in the
categories, but often there is not. For example, the 'novel' is a modern
literary genre describing a kind of Western literature that grew up
with the development of the middle class. However, the term 'novel' is
frequently applied to some ancient prose narrative. One can apply
such a category, but one must realize that the category of 'novel' was
not one the ancients were applying to their literary creations.
Furthermore, the ancients made several distinctions regarding the
'lives' of ancient figures, not all of which modern interpreters would
feel comfortable calling 'biography' because of the high fictive element. Thus Thurén's description of what scholars are doing in the
interplay of epistolary and rhetorical categories is a modern conceptual framework (only his first category—studying the epistles as
letters—would have been recognizable by the ancients; see below).
That is acceptable, so long as one recognizes what one is doing.

The support by Betz and Kennedy for their positions, however,
gives the impression that the ancients themselves would have recognized the kind of analysis being performed by modern interpreters of
the Pauline epistles. There is something inherently satisfactory in
thinking that the kind of analysis being performed has some basis in
the analysis in which the ancients themselves were engaged. But do the

22. See, e.g., R. Bultmann, *Die Stil der paulinische Predigt und die kynisch–
stoische Diatribe* (Göttingen: Vandenhoeck & Ruprecht, 1910). See below.
23. The best essay on this topic is by M. Brett, 'Four or Five Things to do with
Texts: A Taxonomy of Interpretative Interests', in D.J.A. Clines, S.E. Fowl and
S.E. Porter (eds.), *The Bible in Three Dimensions: Essays in Celebration of Forty
Years of Biblical Studies in the University of Sheffield* (JSOTSup, 87; Sheffield:
JSOT Press, 1990), pp. 359-73.

ancients give any credence to such a supposition? How would one go about finding such support? How would one formulate a theoretical justification for analysis of the Pauline epistles by means of the formal categories of ancient rhetoric? The fact that there has been some apparent success in this procedure (for example, in the work of Betz, Jewett, Watson and others) is a proof that this kind of thing can be done from the standpoint of modern interpretation; it is not a proof that the ancients would have had any recognition of this procedure. To find out how the ancients would have viewed such a procedure, one must go to the ancients themselves. Since so much is frequently made of the ancient rhetorical handbooks as sources for the categories of analysis, and since these are programmatic prescriptions about how to use such categories, perhaps the best place to seek a theoretical justification for analysing the Pauline epistles in terms of formal rhetorical categories is within the handbooks themselves.

Malherbe has done scholarship a tremendous service in collating the statements from the rhetorical and literary handbooks that have bearing on epistolary analysis.[24] Unfortunately, Malherbe's statements have been taken somewhat out of context, so that one scholar citing him concludes, 'It is not by accident that the ancient rhetoricians were often occupied with epistolary questions'.[25] Here is what Malherbe actually says: 'Epistolary theory in antiquity belonged to the domain of the rhetoricians, but it was not originally part of their theoretical systems. It is absent from the earliest extant rhetorical handbooks, and it only gradually made its way into the genre.'[26] Again, 'It is thus clear that letter writing was of interest to rhetoricians, but it appears only gradually to have attached itself to their rhetorical systems'.[27] These statements provide no theoretical justification for the kind of systematic analysis being perpetuated in the commentaries, as if determining the species and organization of the epistles (although subject to disagreement over detail) were something the ancients themselves struggled with. But in fact, it appears that Malherbe's own

---

24. A.J. Malherbe, *Ancient Epistolary Theorists* (SBLSBS, 19; Atlanta: Scholars Press, 1988). I have not re-read all of the rhetorical handbooks for this paper, so I rely upon Malherbe's findings (and translations) as the basis for the following comments.

25. Thurén, *Rhetorical Strategy*, pp. 63-64.

26. Malherbe, *Ancient Epistolary Theorists*, p. 2.

27. Malherbe, *Ancient Epistolary Theorists*, p. 3.

statements are open to misunderstanding. The case for the place of letter writing among the rhetoricians is less secure than Malherbe's summary implies.[28]

First, the initial discussion of any significance appears in Demetrius's *On Style* (*De Elocutione*), a manuscript difficult to date, but probably at its earliest written sometime in the first century BCE.[29] Demetrius's comments appear in an excursus. Malherbe is rightly sceptical of Koskenniemi's hypothesis that because Demetrius quotes Artemon, the editor of Aristotle's letters, this theory goes back earlier and is designed to fill a noticeable gap in the rhetoricians' comments on letter writing.[30] Even if he is correct, it draws further attention to the fact that there *is* a noticeable gap in the theoretical literature on the subject, one that only a few paragraphs cannot hope to rectify, since there is no earlier record of any significant comments about letter writing (including Aristotle's *Rhetoric* and the *Rhetoric to Alexander* [*Rhetorica ad Alexandrum*]).

More to the point, however, are Demetrius's statements. First, he says that epistolary 'style' 'should be plain' (223). But this is not all that he says on style. Regarding ellipses, Demetrius says that they are not appropriate to a letter: 'Such breaks cause obscurity in writing, and the gift of imitating conversation is less appropriate to writing than to a speech in debate' (226). 'It is absurd to build up periods, as if you were writing not a letter but a speech for the law courts. And such laboured letter writing is not merely absurd; it does not even obey the laws of friends...' (229). 'If anybody should write of logical

28. The question is immediately raised of how the Pauline epistles relate to the standards established below. It is not the purpose of this paper to determine the success or failure of the Pauline epistles but to discuss the standards by which the ancients might have judged them.

29. The range of dates for this document is from the third century BCE to the first century CE. Malherbe tends toward the earlier date of the first century BCE (*Ancient Epistolary Theorists*, p. 2 and n. 12, following G.M.A. Grube, *A Greek Critic: Demetrius on Style* [Toronto: University of Toronto Press, 1961], pp. 39-56), although Demetrius's standard English translator, W. Rhys Roberts, tends toward the first century CE in his LCL edition (cf. his earlier translation, *Demetrius On Style* [Cambridge: Cambridge University Press, 1902], pp. 49-64, where he suggests the range of 100 BCE to 100 CE).

30. H. Koskenniemi, *Studien zur Idee und Phraseologie des griechischen Briefes bis 400 n. Chr.* (Annales Academiae Scientiarum Fennicae, Series B, 102; Helsinki: Suomalainen Tiedeakatemian, 1956), pp. 24-27.

subtleties or questions of natural history in a letter, he writes indeed, but not a letter. A letter is designed to be the heart's good wishes in brief; it is the exposition of a simple subject in simple terms' (231). '[F]rom the point of view of expression, the letter should be a compound of these two styles, the graceful and the plain. So much with regard to letter writing and the plain style' (235). If anything, there is a *contrast* between letters and orations. Secondly, Demetrius corrects Artemon, who says that 'a letter ought to be written in the same manner as a dialogue' (223). Demetrius believes that 'The letter should be a little more studied than the dialogue, since the latter reproduces an extemporary utterance, while the former is committed to writing and is (in a way) sent as a gift' (224). Demetrius recognizes that there is something inherent in the written nature of the letter that is different from spoken discourse. Thirdly, Demetrius makes a clear distinction between conversation and oratory. After citing Aristotle writing to Antipater, he states, 'A man who conversed in that fashion would seem not to be talking but to be making an oratorical display' (225). Fourthly, Demetrius's recognition of a letter treatise seems to depend on the length of the letter (e.g. Plato and Thucydides) (228).[31] Fifthly, Demetrius recognizes the use of proofs in a letter, when employed in an appropriate manner (233). Thus, Demetrius distinguishes the technique associated with letter writing, in particular in the area of style, from anything oratorical.[32] He does not provide a theoretical basis in his comments for examining letters according to the standards of oratory.

Cicero (first century BCE) has something to say about letters in his own (he was the premier Roman letter writer among a host of letter writers, many of them orators). Even so, it is difficult to trace Cicero's debt to any supposed epistolary theory, since his statements occur incidentally in his letters.[33] But no comments regarding letter

---

31. The standard exposition of this topic is M.L. Stirewalt, Jr, 'The Form and Function of the Greek Letter-Essay', in Donfried (ed.), *The Romans Debate*, pp. 147-71. The status of the 'letter-essay' as a distinct genre is subject to question, as Stirewalt admits.

32. It depends upon what one means by 'theory', but Malherbe is probably optimistic in his assessment of the importance of Demetrius: 'In view of these uncertainties a sober judgment would appear to be that the earliest extensive discussion of epistolary theory dates from the first century BC' (*Ancient Epistolary Theorists*, p. 2).

33. For example, according to Malherbe (*Ancient Epistolary Theorists*, p. 2),

writing appear in any of Cicero's works on rhetoric, including *On the Orator* (*De Oratore*), *Brutus*, and *Orator*. Malherbe says that 'Cicero did know rhetorical prescriptions on letters and was probably familiar with handbooks on lettter writing'.[34] But the difficulty is that, whatever evidence there may be for Cicero knowing the handbooks on letter writing (it seems sparse), this constitutes no evidence for the rhetoricians having a similar concern for analysing letter writing. As in fact Malherbe says, 'to that extent he does show many points of contact with Greek letter theory, but his comments on the types of letters are not the basis for an epistolographic system, nor are they part of such a system'.[35] Thus, even if Cicero's letters (or Paul's) are 'rhetorical' in nature or evidence rhetorical features in their composition, Cicero nowhere gives a theoretical justification for subjecting letters to analysis according to the categories found in the ancient rhetorical handbooks, even with reference to the species and organization. If such were an analytical convention in his day one would have expected discussion—even demanded it—in Cicero.

Seneca (first century CE) shows some awareness of what is appropriate to the letter in distinction to oratory (*Moral Epistles* [*Epistulae Morales*] 75.1-2):

> I prefer that my letters should be just what my conversation would be if you and I were sitting in one another's company... Even if I were arguing a point, I should not stamp my foot, or toss my arms about, or raise my voice; but I should leave that sort of thing to the orator, and should be content to have conveyed my feelings toward you without having either embellished them or lowered their dignity.

Seneca's comments only address matters of situation and delivery, not organization. He shows no knowledge of 'an entire theoretical system' of letter writing, much less that categories from oratory could be applied to their analysis.[36]

Quintilian (first century CE), perhaps the most important theorist so far as the New Testament is concerned, has one passage where he

---

Cicero distinguishes between public and private letters (*Pro Flacco* 16, 37), speaks of a genre of epistle (*Ad Familiares* 4, 13, 1), denounces jocularity in certain letters (*Ad Atticum* 6, 5, 4), and describes a letter as a conversation with a friend (*Ad Atticum* 8, 14, 1) and as mediating a friend's presence (*Ad Familiares* 3, 11, 2).

34. Malherbe, *Ancient Epistolary Theorists*, p. 3.
35. Malherbe, *Ancient Epistolary Theorists*, p. 3.
36. Malherbe, *Ancient Epistolary Theorists*, p. 3.

mentions the style appropriate to a letter, again in distinction to that found in oratory (9.4.19-22). He contrasts the closely welded and woven together style with the looser textured sort found in dialogues and letters. The closely welded style is composed of three elements: the comma, colon and period. Regarding the training of the orator Quintilian recommends a programme of reading (1.8.1-21; 10.1), although in this programme nothing is said of reading letters.

Philostratus of Lemnos (third century CE) wrote in his *On Letters* (*De Epistolis*) to rebuke one Aspasius of Ravenna regarding his style. In doing so, he commends Herodes the Athenian as being the

> best at writing letters although he does, through excessive Atticism and loquacity, in many places depart from the appropriate epistolary style. For the epistolary style must in appearance be more Attic than everyday speech, but more ordinary than Atticism, and it must be composed in accordance with common usage, yet not be at variance with a graceful style.

Although the dating of the treatise and the references to the influences of Atticism place this too late to be of use to analysis of the New Testament letters, it is still worth noting that there is a contrast with ordinary speech, but not a full endorsement of a literary style. And style is the issue at stake.

Finally, Julius Victor (fourth century CE), in an appendix to his *Art of Rhetoric* (*Ars rhetorica*) (§ 27), is the first and only rhetorician to include a discussion of letter writing, after acknowledging that 'Many directives which pertain to oral discourse also apply to letters'. One must notice, however, the kind of 'directives' he cites. In contrasting official and personal letters, he says that official letters deal with a serious subject: 'Characteristic of this type are weighty statements, clarity of diction, and special effort at terse expression as well as all the rules of oratory, with one exception, that we prune away some of its great size and let an appropriate familiar style govern the discourse'. He does not say what all of the rules of oratory are; the only area that he specifies is that of style, where he goes on to say that brevity is the first norm of personal letters. As Malherbe concludes, after recognizing that until Julius Victor the subject of letter writing 'was not part of a system of rhetoric',[37] 'While epistolary style is here, then, part of a rhetorical system, it can nevertheless be argued

---

37. Malherbe, *Ancient Epistolary Theorists*, p. 3.

that its relegation to an appendix shows that it does not properly belong in a discussion of rhetoric'.[38] In fact, even in the two extensive discussions of the proper style of letters—those by Pseudo-Demetrius and Libanius—'while the discussions of letter writing in these manuals are systematic, there is no evidence to indicate that they were part of a rhetorical system'.[39] None of them gives firm indication that rhetorical categories could be used to analyse epistles.

Several points can be drawn from the evidence of the ancients themselves. First, although categories of rhetoric *may* have been 'in the air' so far as writing in the ancient world was concerned, their use in *analysis* of epistles needs further definition. That there were universal rhetorical practices at play in everyday use of language can be granted, since every culture has its rhetorical practices in this sense. It is possible—though difficult to defend—that some rhetorical practices of the orators may have influenced ancient letter writers. That formal rhetorical categories were systematically applied to analysis of epistles, and that there was precedent for this in the literary analyses of the ancient world, are open to serious question. One can be certain from the evidence of the ancient rhetorical handbooks themselves of only one thing: with regard to epistles only matters of style were discussed in any significant way, virtually always with epistles mentioned in contrast to oratory.[40] There is, therefore, little if any theoretical

---

38. Malherbe, *Ancient Epistolary Theorists*, p. 3.

39. Malherbe, *Ancient Epistolary Theorists*, pp. 3-4. Mitchell (*Paul and the Rhetoric of Reconciliation*, pp. 21-23, and n. 5) apparently justifies reading 1 Corinthians as 'deliberative rhetoric' on the basis that the word for 'deliberative' in the orators is found in Pseudo-Demetrius's list of letter types. The problem is that 'deliberative' is one of three species of oration but one of 21 types of letter! The common vocabulary says virtually nothing about any correlation between epistolary and rhetorical theory, and certainly does not provide the kind of foundation needed for analysis of epistles according to ancient rhetorical conventions. S. Stowers (*Letter Writing in Greco-Roman Antiquity* [Philadelphia: Westminster Press, 1986], pp. 51-57) reasons somewhat similarly.

40. Hughes (*Early Christian Rhetoric*, p. 26) concludes his discussion by citing references from the ancient rhetoricians regarding style, but goes on to analyse in terms of the species and organization. He also cites an interesting passage from Cicero, *On the Orator* (2.12 § 49), in which he claims that Cicero has 'one of his rhetorical heroes argue that when official messages, presumably in the form of letters, must be sent to or from the Senate and must be written in an elaborate style, no other *genus* of rhetoric (beyond the traditional three *genera*) is needed, "since the

justification in the ancient handbooks for application of the formal categories of the species and organization of rhetoric to analysis of the Pauline epistles.[41]

Concerning style—the only rhetorical category of sustained concern with regard to epistles in the ancient rhetorical handbooks—its discussion has come under much suspicion by a number of scholars.[42] This probably stems from the fact that many studies of style (or ornamentation) have treated the individual elements in isolation and often as merely ornamental, in other words, as individual literary features that contribute little to the substance or content of a passage, but are included only for aesthetic value.[43] Some scholars have abandoned their use of 'rhetoric' because of such studies. One corrective is to recognize that, so far as the ancients were concerned, stylistic matters were not simply for decorative value but were part of the way in which substance was conveyed, as the few selections from the rhetorical theorists above indicate. As Snyman asks, 'In what way do these devices promote the communication of [the author's] message and how do they contribute to the impact and appeal of his argumentations?'[44] If one wants to consider the epistles as the ancients would have, so far as their explicit relation to rhetoric was concerned, one must analyse

ability acquired by a ready speaker, from the treatment of his other subjects and topics, will not fail him in situations of that description"'. To conclude as Hughes does that Cicero 'argued' that 'it is quite natural for letters written for official purposes to use rhetoric' and that letters belong to one of the three genres of rhetoric goes completely beyond any reasonable interpretation of this passage.

41. It can also be noted that analysis of other forms of literature using categories from ancient rhetoric is not to be found in, for example, Aristotle, Longinus or Horace. Neither is such analysis of the Pauline epistles found by early rhetors such as Augustine.

42. E.g. Thurén, *Rhetorical Strategy*, pp. 47-48; Kennedy, *New Testament Interpretation*, p. 3.

43. Some of the worst offenders in this regard have been the grammars: e.g. BDF, §§ 485-96, on figures of speech and thought; cf. N. Turner, *A Grammar of the Greek New Testament. IV. Style* (Edinburgh: T. & T. Clark, 1976), which is not really a study of style at all. See also C.E.B. Cranfield, *A Critical and Exegetical Commentary on the Epistle to the Romans*, I (ICC; Edinburgh: T. & T. Clark, 1975), p. 26; G.F. Hawthorne, *Philippians* (WBC; Waco: Word Books, 1983), e.g. p. 123; A.B. Spencer, *Paul's Literary Style: A Stylistic and Historical Comparison of 2 Corinthians 11:16–12:13, Romans 8:9-39 and Philippians 3:2–4:13* (Jackson, MS: Evangelical Theological Society, 1984).

44. Snyman, 'Style and Meaning', p. 94.

style. The solution is not to abandon stylistic analysis but to change how study of style is conducted. More must be done to treat the stylistic features, not in isolation but in terms of their coordinated use within an entire passage, or even an entire book. Two recent attempts take such an approach.

The first is found in a recent work by Campbell on Rom. 3.21-26.[45] Although this passage is frequently seen to be at the heart of Paul's message in Romans, it is also seen to be exceptionally difficult.[46] Campbell attempts to solve the structural and conceptual difficulties by arguing for the presence of a number of rhetorical features of the middle style, with perhaps a few features of the grand style.[47] Rom. 3.21-26, according to Campbell, can be broken down into three sections, each utilizing at least one major stylistic rhetorical feature: v. 21 antithesis and paronomasia, vv. 22-25b parenthesis, antithesis and epanaphora, and vv. 25c-26c isocolic reduplication.

Verse 21 is structured around an antithetical statement based on the concept of 'law' and use of νόμος: 'but now, apart from law, righteousness of God is manifest, being born witness to by the law and the prophets'. Although one might hope for better balanced arms to the antithesis, Campbell contends that variation in length would have been more acceptable in the elegant style. The antithetical uses of the term νόμος suggest paronomasia:

45. D.A. Campbell, *The Rhetoric of Righteousness in Romans 3.21-26* (JSNTSup, 65; Sheffield: JSOT Press, 1992), esp. pp. 70-101. See also M. Silva, 'The Pauline Style as Lexical Choice: γινώσκειν and Related Verbs', in D.A. Hagner and M.J. Harris (eds.), *Pauline Studies* (Festschrift F.F. Bruce; Exeter: Paternoster Press, 1980), pp. 184-207; R. Jewett, 'The Rhetorical Function of Numerical Sequences in Romans', in Watson (ed.), *Persuasive Artistry*, pp. 227-45; Classen, 'Paulus und die antike Rhetorik', pp. 9-13.

46. Thus Cranfield (*Romans*, I, p. 199) says that it is 'the centre and heart of the main division to which it belongs', while E. Käsemann (*Commentary on Romans* [trans. G.W. Bromiley; Grand Rapids: Eerdmans, 1980], p. 92) calls the passage 'one of the most difficult and obscure in the whole epistle'.

47. Campbell, *Rhetoric of Righteousness*, pp. 79, 81-82. The rhetoricians seemed to posit three or four styles: plain, middle or elegant and grand style (e.g. Cicero, *Orator* 69), as well as the forcible style (Demetrius, *On Style*). Campbell contends that Paul's use of diatribe resembles Demetrius's forcible style. Since Demetrius is the only one to discuss this category it should be cautiously applied. The characteristics that Campbell uses to describe Paul's style lend themselves most readily to the plain style, as one would expect in a letter.

The theory of paronomasia therefore suggests that, while the word νόμος appears in both flanking phrases in v. 21 and ties them together in a loose antithesis at the level of expression, at the semantic level differing concepts may be operative. The first phrase seems to speak of the fulfilment of the demands of the Mosaic Law by acting in accordance with its prescriptions, that is, by good works... The second phrase speaks conversely of the witness of the Scriptures to this salvation as inspired and authoritative documents.[48]

Verses 22-25b shows instances of parenthesis, antithesis and epanaphora. With the new statement, 'for there is no difference', Campbell sees a shift in the discourse, since it does not complete the opening section and is not tightly aligned with the flow of Paul's argument. This suggests a parenthesis or apostrophe, in which there is a violation of the periodic syntax to introduce a digression or amplification.[49] Verse 23 then explains how 'there is no difference', since Paul 'clearly has not abolished all distinctions between Jew and Gentile in his previous argument'.[50] The use of πᾶς language ties the two parts together: all are without distinction in their sinning and loss of glory. The parenthesis continues with a participial phrase: 'being rightwized freely by his grace'. Even though most commentators see this phrase as resuming the main argument, Campbell sees it as marking the end of the parenthesis by serving as an antithesis to the statement in v. 23 regarding universal sinfulness. The participle in the nominative plural is in agreement with the previous main verb in v. 23. For those who question his breaking the parenthesis at this point, Campbell points to the subsequent use of epanaphora, the parallel use of the three διαν phrases (rather than the first διαν phrase modifying the participle). Epanaphora, the repetition of key words at the beginning of phrases or clauses, is used to link units together. The three διαν phrases are: 'through faith of Jesus Christ...through the redemption in Christ Jesus...through the faith in his blood'. These three phrases thus modify the initial statement, 'righteousness of God is manifest', rather than the immediately preceding participle.

Finally, vv. 25c-26c has two parallel accusative constructions that illustrate isocolic reduplication: 'into (εἰς) a revelation of his

48. Campbell, *Rhetoric of Righteousness*, p. 86.
49. Quintilian 4.3.14-15; 10.6.5.
50. Campbell, *Rhetoric of Righteousness*, p. 88.

righteousness...toward (πρός) a revelation of his righteousness...'
An isocolon occurs when two periods contain the same number of
syllables and thus are balanced rhythmically. One is not meant to
count the syllables, but to appreciate their balanced effect. Reduplication occurs when similar phrasing is used in each colon. The figure
is interrupted, however, by a διαν phrase with the accusative case.
There are several options for understanding this phrase, including
seeing it as parenthetical with reference to the previous διαν phrases,
but if it functions where it is placed, it gives substance to the following reference to 'forgiveness'.

The final infinitival phrase is especially important, in the light of the
significance attached by rhetoricians to closing phrases of periods.[51]
The preposition εἰς echoes the use of the same preposition above and
may form a chiastic structure around πρός. The use of αὐτός echoes
two preceding uses in the isocolic reduplication. There is also
significant vocabulary, including δικ- words and the phrase ἐκ
πίστεως.

In sum, Campbell states,

> our syntactical hypothesis that Paul has inserted a parenthesis into the
> epanaphoric central section of an extended periodic sentence not only
> resolves the immediate problems in vv. 22b-24b [*sic*: 22d-24b], but
> greatly clarifies the entire syntax of Rom. 3.21-26. The section can now
> be seen to constitute a single periodic sentence that is wrapped around an
> inserted remark, with every part of the sentence exhibiting some debt to
> rhetorical syntactical devices...[52]

Whereas Campbell's discussion concerns the level of style in relation to phrasal figures, a second example of stylistic analysis considers
figures of style at the level of the sentence. In a discussion of the pattern of argumentation in Romans 5, I claim that the clearly dialogical
nature of Romans, in particular of chs. 1–4 and 6–8, has been
neglected in ch. 5. Thus, I re-read the chapter in the light of Paul's
use of rhetorical questions to solve structural and conceptual
difficulties.[53] The structural difficulty regards the role of ch. 5 in the

51. E.g. Cicero, *On the Orator* 3.49.192; *idem*, *Orator* 149; Quintilian 9.4.67.
52. Campbell, *Rhetoric of Righteousness*, pp. 99-100.
53. S.E. Porter, 'The Argument of Romans 5: Can a Rhetorical Question Make a
Difference?', *JBL* 110 (1991), pp. 655-77. This article discusses other rhetorical
features as well, for example parallelism, but the rhetorical question is used for illustrative purposes in this paper. See also D.F. Watson, '1 Corinthians 10:23–11:1 in

argument of Romans,[54] and the conceptual difficulty relates to the progression in Paul's thought by means of dialogue from justification to sanctification (to use traditional terms).[55] As a result, I find two significant sets of rhetorical questions that help to solve these difficulties.

In Rom. 5.6-7,[56] the argument of the chapter seems to remain intact even if vv. 6-7 is deleted, although v. 6 seems to anticipate v. 8. This has resulted in several proposals, most of which focus on the set of textual variants in v. 6a regarding connectives. If one seriously considers the faulty repetition of ἔτι, and accepts the (admittedly not well supported) reading εἰς τί γὰρ... ἔτι, sense can be made of the passage (as well as accounting for the other readings).[57] As a result, Paul introduces a hypothetical question into his argument, and thus solves the awkward transition from v. 5 to v. 6. Verse 7, linked by the connective γάρ, is thus part of the question raised by a hypothetical speaker Paul uses in his dialogue. After grounding peace with God in justification by faith and tracing by means of a climax the progress of Christian existence, a question comes to mind: 'for to what purpose did Christ, while we were yet helpless, die then for the ungodly? For hardly for a just person will someone die; for on behalf of a good person perhaps someone might indeed dare to die.'[58] This proposal also solves the perceived theological difficulty of vv. 6-7. It is not that Paul states outright that Christ died for the ungodly, but, as he does elsewhere in the book (e.g. 3.27–4.2; 6.1-3), he posits a possible question that might legitimately be raised in the mind of his audience. The question is related to both the fact that one would die for the ungodly and the possible purpose of this death. Cohesion is thus brought to the chapter's line of argument. In v. 8, Paul responds: 'But

the Light of Greco-Roman Rhetoric: The Role of Rhetorical Questions', *JBL* 108 (1989), pp. 301-18; P.M. McDonald, 'Romans 5.1-11 as a Rhetorical Bridge', *JSNT* 40 (1990), pp. 81-96; M.R. Cosby, 'Paul's Persuasive Language in Romans 5', in Watson (ed.), *Persuasive Artistry*, pp. 209-26.

54. See, e.g., Cranfield, *Romans*, I, pp. 252-54.

55. See, e.g., B.N. Kaye, *The Thought Structure of Romans with Special Reference to Chapter 6* (Austin: Schola, 1979), esp. pp. 14-23.

56. Porter, 'Argument of Romans 5', pp. 665-68.

57. This proposal is found in J.H. Michael, 'A Phenomenon in the Text of Romans', *JTS* 39 (1938), p. 152.

58. The sentiments expressed are very much in keeping with reflection on the virtuous person in Hellenistic thought. See Teles 2.179-82 (ed. O'Neil) (18H).

God established his love toward us in this way, that while we were yet sinners, Chist died for us'. The syntax of v. 8b, which clearly reiterates v. 6, is explained by means of question and answer.

In vv. 13-16, several other structural issues are raised, which are solved by introduction of two rhetorical questions.[59] This is part of an elaborate system of antithetical parallelism, in which the work of Adam and Christ is contrasted from vv. 15-19. In vv. 13 and 14, Paul argues for the existence and relation of sin and death stemming from Adam, the type of the coming one, Christ.[60] After Paul refers to the coming one in v. 14, the issue of transgressions is introduced. Although this coordinates well with the idea that the exemplum with Christ and Adam (an item of invention?)[61] primarily focuses on the sinful behaviour of Adam, the transition is not smooth if vv. 15a and 16a are statements. Verse 15, if it is taken as a statement, is a very badly balanced sentence on account of the negative and the connectives οὕτως καὶ in the first part. A further problem is conceptual. When Paul in vv. 18 or 19 resumes his argument from the elegantly isocolic yet broken construction in v. 12, he essentially reasserts in dogmatic fashion what he has already posited. This indicates that something important occurs in the intervening verses which requires that Paul restate the foundation of his argument. This pattern of repetition is similar to the one that Paul uses with regard to vv. 6-7 and 8 noted above. To alleviate these problems Caragounis suggests that vv. 15a and 16a, with οὐ, are meant to introduce rhetorical questions expecting affirmative answers: 'But does not the free gift operate just like the trespass did?...And is not the free gift transmitted in the same way as sin was transmitted by the one who sinned?' The answer required to each question is 'yes'. Paul then carries forward the interlocutor's suggested contrast between the trespass and free gift.

The use of these two sets of rhetorical questions in Romans 5 serves several purposes. They grammatically and conceptually unite the

59. This proposal comes from C.C. Caragounis, 'Rom 5:15-16 in the Context of 5:12-21: Contrast or Comparison?', *NTS* 31 (1985), pp. 142-48; cf. Porter, 'Argument of Romans 5', pp. 671-74.

60. Cosby ('Paul's Persuasive Language', p. 221) cites this as an instance of *antonomasia*, where a descriptive phrase is substituted for a proper name.

61. On the exemplum, see M.R. Cosby, *The Rhetorical Composition and Function of Hebrews 11: In Light of Example Lists in Antiquity* (Macon, GA: Mercer, 1988).

chapter, against many scholars who divide it between vv. 11 and 12. The similar patterns of intervening question followed by resumption of the argument not only unify the entire chapter but help place ch. 5 within the dialogical flow of Romans 1–8. Conceptually, the questions establish unity between Paul's discussion in vv. 1-11 regarding the work of Christ, which begins with justification (chs. 3–4) and is summarized as reconciliation, and his understanding of reconciliation through the work of Christ as overcoming at every point the alienation caused by Adam (vv. 12-21) and as leading to sanctification (chs. 6–8).

In conclusion, this paper has been concerned with matters of definition and method as they relate to epistolary and rhetorical theory. In the light of the ambiguity regarding the epistolographic character of the Pauline letters, many scholars have turned to what has been called 'rhetorical criticism'. I have argued that one must be precise when one uses the term 'rhetoric' to describe an interpretative analysis. I have shown that there is a necessity for differentiating the term 'rhetoric' in its universal sense to describe interpretation using a variety of analytical models (both ancient and modern) from 'rhetoric' in its formal sense to describe particular, culture-specific features used by practitioners of rhetoric. The ancient Graeco-Roman world had such a formal manifestation of rhetoric, which has been applied to analysis of the Pauline epistles. However, the theoretical justification for using the species and organization of ancient Greek rhetoric to analyse the Pauline epistles is not firmly grounded in the theoretical literature (or apparently the practice) of the time. So far as the ancient rhetorical handbooks are concerned with respect to letters, the only significant discussion of epistolary material concerns stylistic matters. The analysis of matters of style in the epistles from an ancient rhetorical perspective would have been recognizable to the ancients, and is worth exploring in future work.

AMPLIFICATIO IN THE MACRO-STRUCTURE OF ROMANS

David Hellholm

Rhetoric wants to reveal *langue*, which is the conventional means of expression of *parole*. *Langue* without *parole* is dead, *parole* without *langue* is inhumane: language, art, social and individual life demonstrate a dialectic interdependence between *langue* and *parole*.

H. Lausberg 1973: 8.

Introduction

The modest purpose of this contribution to the Festschrift for Wilhelm Wuellner is to explore on the basis of the analysis of Romans:

(a) the applicability of *amplificatio* to the macro-structure of a concrete text, whereby other important aspects regarding amplification have to be left aside;

(b) the relationship between *langue*-determined and *parole*-conditioned structures and the interplay between them;[1]

(c) the possibility of integrating rhetorical and text-linguistic analytical procedures.[2]

The basis for such an undertaking is the methodological presupposition concerning the linguistic-rhetorical interaction between practice, theory, and meta-theoretical deliberations on the one hand and their relationship to rules on the other according to the following schema:

---

1. Cf. the deliberations in Hellholm 1991: 136-42 and see the latest discussion of various interpretations of *langue* and *parole* in Heger 1992.

2. On the relationship between ancient rhetoric and text-linguistics, see Junker 1976; Kalverkämper 1981: *passim*; Kalverkäper 1983a and 1983b; and Heinemann and Viehweger 1991: 19-22.

(A.1)	*practice* that relies on rules,
(A.2)	*practice* that deviates from rules,
(B.1)	*theory* that clarifies the rules and their utilization,
(B.2)	*theory* that argues in favour of deviation from conventional rules, and finally
(C)	*meta-theoretical* deliberations concerning which theories are the most adequate and the most consistent,[3] and which rules should apply or not, or be developed or not.

The reason for this differentiation is obvious: practice need not—and may however—reflect theory but is almost always a reflection of rules, whether positively or negatively; theory and rules need not and in fact often do not reflect meta-theoretical deliberations but ought indeed to do so.[4]

Macro-Structural Analysis of Paul's Letter to the Romans

In order to identify the *amplificatio* in the overall composition of Paul's letter to the Romans it is necessary to analyse the compositional structure of that letter. The compositional macro-structure of a text is in all instances hierarchical in nature, that is, the text can be delimited into a hierarchy of sub-texts on different levels, which to a certain extent discloses the deep-structure of the text as a whole.

Rhetorical devices

When analysing a Pauline letter like Romans by means of rhetorical and text-linguistic methods, it is helpful to describe the procedure as thoroughly as space permits and the reader's perseverance allows.

The langue-determined macro-structure of the rhetorical dispositio. The *langue*-determined macro-structure is primarily grounded in structuring principles of a text-*internal* kind.[5]

The first step will be the macro-syntagmatic analysis of the text in its totality, that is, its compositional structure,[6] since neither sentences

3. See, e.g., Gülich and Raible 1977b: 16ff.
4. Rules are, of course, not scientific rules, but of the same kind as grammatical rules: they can and will be changed in due course, or they can be violated purposely, but these violations are in a sense also governed by rules and/or meta-theoretical deliberations.
5. Lausberg 1976: 27 [§ 46.2], 28-32 [§§ 49-63].
6. Hellholm 1980; Hellholm 1986: 33-54; Hellholm 1994b.

nor sub-texts of various degrees 'have per se any function but only obtain their function from a superior totality, for example (with regard to tones) within a melody or, as far as texts are concerned, within a superior unity of meaning',[7] or in other words 'the meaning of the parts is determined by the structure of the whole'.[8] This has lately been emphasized also by Margaret Mitchell, when she in her analysis of 1 Corinthians writes: 'The rhetorical genre and function of each part is determined by the compositional whole and cannot be correctly determined apart from it'.[9]

In order to establish the textual macro-structure or—as some prefer—super-structure,[10] we have in a descending procedure[11] to delimit the text as a whole into sub-texts of different rankings, because as I have stated elsewhere:

> The ranking of sub-texts *per definitionem* leads not only to a sequential order but also, and more importantly, to the establishment of hierarchically and well-defined interrelationships between various sub-texts, that is to say, to understanding, how sub-texts on higher levels function within the next lower rank all the way down to level 0.[12]

When analysing ancient epistolary texts in their entirety our procedure must be conducted in two steps because of the nature of the text-material itself:

(a) It is necessary to separate the prescript and the postscript from the rest of the text and analyse these separately ($^1ST^{1-n}$), since in the case of a letter we have to do with a *sermo absentis ad absentem*;[13]

---

7.   Raible 1979: 69 (my trans.); cf. Hellholm 1986: 37.

8.   Boers 1978: 38.

9.   Mitchell 1991: 16; cf. Kloppenborg 1984: 58: 'A genre conception is that notion of the whole which both controls the production of a literary work in all its individual parts and allows an interpreter to ascertain correctly the sense of each part'.

10.   Van Dijk 1980: 128-59.

11.   See Hellholm 1994b: § 3.6.

12.   Hellholm 1986: 38.

13.   Plett 1975: 17; Malherbe 1992: 285: 'He (sc. Seneca) wishes his letters to be exactly what his conversation would be if he were with Lucilius [epp. 75,1ff.; 40,1]. His letters are only a substitute'; cf. with regard to the relationship between epistolography and rhetoric also Classen 1991; esp., however, Hughes 1989: 47-50, who with reference to Goldstein (1968) refers to Demostenes' *Epistle 1* as a deliberative *rhetorical letter*, and now Malherbe 1992: 283: 'The ancient handbooks which provided instruction in letter-writing came from the schools of rhetoric';

(b) It is further necessary to analyse the remaining text into its μέρη τοῦ λόγου, its *partes orationis* ($^{2}ST^{21-n}$). In a decoding rhetorical process of analysis it is wise to take as our point of departure the *dispositio* of ancient rhetoric.

The *dispositio* is the arrangement or structuration of the main points in a speech or a writing as a whole. It corresponds roughly to our modern dispositions. This part of the ancient rhetoricians' area of activity was the most neglected due to the circumstance that already the *inventio* provided certain principles of order.[14]

The relationship between the *dispositio* and the *inventio* is characterized by H. Lausberg in an illuminating and succinct way, when he points out that 'the *dispositio* is the necessary supplement to the *inventio* that without the *dispositio* would be a phenomenon without relations'.[15] Thus it is clear that the ancient rhetorical *dispositio* corresponds to the modern text-linguistic *syntagma* or even *macro-syntagma*, while the ancient rhetorical *inventio* corresponds to the modern text-linguistic *paradigma*.[16]

Further, the *dispositio* constitutes the predominantly *langue*-determined structure of texts, while—as far as the *macro-syntagma* is concerned—the *inventio* constitutes the *parole*-conditioned structural aspect of texts.[17]

After the entire letter has been delimited into the frame work of the letter, that is, its prescript and its postscript on the one hand and the rest of the letter, that is, its body, on the other, our second step will be to delimit these *sub-texts on grade one* into sub-texts on grade two. This follows from the hierarchical system employed,[18] and this hierarchical system has its roots in ancient rhetoric as we will see.

The delimitation of the first and last sub-text on *grade one*, that is, the prescript and postscript, takes on the following structure:

Malherbe 1992: 283 n. 68: 'According to Theon, Progymnasmata 10 II 115,22 Spengel, letter-writing was one of the exercises in προσωποποιία'; Malherbe 1988: 6-7.

14. See Plett 1975: 16 and Fuhrmann 1984: 78.

15. Lausberg 1973: 244 [§ 445] (my trans.).

16. For the necessity of supplementing paradigmatic analyses with syntagmatic ones, see Hellholm 1986: 33-34 and for the difference between the two approaches, see Hellholm 1980: 84 n. 42 and esp. Hellholm 1991: 151-57; see also Malherbe 1992: 277.

17. Cf., e.g., Lausberg 1976: 28 [§ 49].

18. For the necessity of hierarchical analyses, see Hellholm 1980: 77-80.

(1) The prescript is delimited into (a) superscript, (b) adscript and (c) salutation.[19] These are *langue*-determined conventions in ancient epistolography. When an author deviates from the convention in one way or another, the reader's curiosity is wakened and he starts asking for the reason for the writer's *parole*-conditioned divergence from the rule.

(2) The postscript was not to the same extent conventional and thus *langue*-determined but encompassed nonetheless usually: (a) greeting commissions (ἄσπασαι, ἀσπάσασθε), (b) greeting deliveries (ἀσπάζεται, ἀσπάζονται), (c) greetings from the hands of the author (*eschatocoll*) and (d) concluding wishes for the prosperity of the addressees (ἔρρωσο, ἔρρωσθε).[20]

The delimitation of the middle sub-text on *grade one*, that is, the body of the letter, may approximately have taken on the following rhetorical structure depending upon the genre the author had chosen for his letter as well as upon his abidance with or deviation from the convention for that genre. The *dispositio* of ancient rhetorical handbooks encompasses the following mevrh tou' lovgou or *partes orationis*[21] or, in modern text-linguistic terms, sub-texts,[22] text-sequences[23] or 'Teiltexte'[24] on grade one:

(1) *Exordium/principium/*prooivmion
(2) *Narratio/*διήγησις
(3) *Propositio/partitio/*[25] πρόθεσις
(4) *Probatio/argumentatio/*πίστις (more common: πίστεις)
(5) *Peroratio/conclusio/*ἐπίλογος

19. See, e.g., Conzelmann 1975: 19-24; Vielhauer 1975: 64-66; and most recently Schnider and Stenger 1987: 3-41.
20. See Schnider and Stenger 1987: 108-67.
21. See Lausberg 1973: 148-49 [§ 202]; Lausberg 1976: 25-26 [§ 43]; Martin 1974: 52-60; Fuhrmann 1984: 83-98; esp., however, the excellent charts in Hommel 1965/1990: 2623 and Hommel 1981: 367-69.
22. Gülich and Quasthoff 1985: 174; Hellholm 1990: 110ff. and Hellholm 1994b: § 3.6.2.
23. Hellholm 1986: 47-54 and Johanson 1987: 59ff. *et passim.*
24. So the German term coined by Gülich and Raible 1975 and 1977a and taken over by Hellholm 1980. Regarding the delimitation of texts into sub-texts of various degrees, see the works by Gülich and Raible and Hellholm just referred to.
25. For the difference between *propositio* and *partitio*, see below.

Not every one of these sub-texts was compulsory. The *narratio*[26] and the *propositio*[27] were optional. Aristotle in rejecting other theoreticians' views considered only two to be *necessary*, viz. the πρόθεσις and the πίστεις.[28] By and large, however, the above given structure of the *partes orationis* was conventional,[29] at least as far as the *genus iudiciale* was concerned and the deviation from it was due to special circumstances at the time of composition.[30] What is even more important to realize at this point, however, is that as a consequence of its

26. Cf. Fuhrmann 1984: 86: 'Eine Erzählung... erübrigt sich in einem zweiten Plädoyer... oder wenn es nicht um Tat, sondern um Rechtsfragen geht'. Aristotle, e.g., confines the *narratio* exclusively to the *genus iudiciale* (*Rhet.* 3.13.3). Martin 1974: 79: 'Wie beim Proömium ist auch bei der *narratio* die Frage heftig umstritten worden, ob sie an einem bestimmten Platz für alle Fälle festgebannt und ob sie überhaupt notwendig ist und nicht unterbleiben kann. Für die meisten epideiktischen Reden hat nun Aristoteles [*Rhet.* 3.13 1414a 37-38; 16 1416b 26-27; 1417b 12ff.] schon festgehalten, daß sie keine *narratio* benötigen, weil die Tatsachen als bekannt vorausgesetzt und nur kurz angedeutet werden müssen. Ferner hat die διήγησις nur in der Gerichtsrede ihren Platz und ist auch da in der Rede des Verteidigers geringer als in der des Klägers...'; Hellwig 1973: 159: 'An der διήγησις wird die Ausrichtung auf die Gerichtsrede besonders klar: in der Rats- und der epideiktischen Rede ist sie eigentlich überflüssig, weil die Zuhörer mit den Ereignissen vertraut sind (vgl. Arist. *Rh.* 1414a 38-39; 1416b 26-28; 1417b 13-14).'

27. Cf. Fuhrmann 1984: 89: 'Für den Übergang von der Erzählung zur Beweisführung wissen die Handbücher zwei fakultative Elemente von geringerer Länge und Bedeutung anzugeben: einmal den Exkurs, die παρέκβασις/*egressio*, zum anderen die Ankündigung des Beweisziels, die πρόθεσις/*propositio/partitio*'. See further Martin 1974: 94.

28. Aristotle, *Rhet.* 3.13.1-5.

29. I.e. *langue*-determined as belonging to the *ordo naturalis*; Lausberg 1973: 245 [§ 448]: 'So gilt die den Geboten der *ars* entsprechende Abfolge *exordium-argumentatio-peroratio*... bei manchen Theoretikern als *ordo naturalis* (während die Abweichung von ihr als *ordo artificiosus* bezeichnet wird).' Cf. also Göttert 1991: 38, and see, e.g., Mart. Cap. 30.506: '*naturalis (est ordo)... cum post principium narratio, partitio, proposito, argumentatio, conclusio epilogusque consequitur.*'

30. I.e. *parole*-conditioned as belonging to the *ordo artificialis*; Lausberg 1973: 247 [§ 452]: 'Der *ordo artificialis* oder *ordo artificiosus*... besteht in der durch die Rücksicht auf die *utilitas* bedingten... absichtlich ("kunstvollen") Abweichungen vom *ordo naturalis*, die dem *ordo naturalis* bei Vorliegen besonderer Umstände... vorgezogen wird'; Martin 1974: 216ff.: 'Die Umkehrung des *ordo naturalis* zum *ordo artificiosus* geschieht, wenn es notwendig oder nützlich ist, auf mancherlei Art, am sinnfälligsten in der geänderten tavxi" der Redeteile' (p. 218); cf. also Hellwig 1973: 163-64, 172; Fuhrmann 1984: 83; Breuer 1990: 115.

being neglected,[31] the rhetorical *dispositio* remained one-dimensional, that is, the text could be delimited on one level only by the applicable rules; no hierarchical text-delimitation was provided for by the ancient theoreticians. This means that if one wants to employ a hierarchical multi-level delimitation of texts, one has to go beyond the *dispositio* of ancient rhetoric, but not necessarily beyond ancient rhetoric as such as we will see.

The third step in this macro-structural analysis will be to delimit the sub-texts on *grade two*. Since the first set of sub-texts (that is, the prescript and the postscript) does not indicate any *langue*-determined signs on grade two, I proceed to the second set of sub-texts (that is, the letter body), where on grade two we encounter some partly *langue*-determined, partly *parole*-conditioned, structural indicators for the delimitation of further sub-texts:

The *exordium*/προοίμιον constitutes the introduction to a speech or a writing. Its purpose is to arouse the listener's or reader's attention and sympathy.[32] Usually it consists of three parts, whose order may vary.[33]

(a) *benevolum parare*: to arouse the listener's or reader's goodwill;

(b) *attentum parare*: to arouse the listener's or reader's attention;

(c) *docilem parare*: to arouse the listener's or reader's receptivity by means of a brief summary of what the author wants to communicate.

These parts are from a paradigmatic point of view entirely *langue*-determined, from a syntagmatic point of view they are so only to some extent .

The *narratio*/διήγησις is made up of a report about the events that have taken place and which are of importance for the case. It should be clear (σαφής/*perspicua*), short (σύντομος/*brevis*), and credible (πιθανή/*verisimilis*).[34]

31. See above at n. 14.

32. See Aristotle, *Rhet.* 3.14.7; cf. Sieveke 1980: 294 n. 214; and Betz 1979: 44-46.

33. Lausberg 1973: 152-60 [§§ 269-79]; Martin 1974: 69-70. Depending on the *genera causarum*, one or the other of the functions of the *exordium* may be placed in focus, e.g., 'beim *genus dubium* muß der Redner vor allem auf das Wohlwollen seiner Zuhörer erpicht sein' (Fuhrmann 1984: 85-86.).

34. See Lausberg 1973: 168-85 [§§ 294-334]; Martin 1974: 75-89, esp. 82; Plett 1975: 16; Fuhrmann 1984: 86-89; Betz 1979: 58-62.

Also here the syntagmatic order varies in the ancient handbooks.[35] Out of necessity it is—and out of strategy it should be—subjective: 'the listener must be able to imagine clearly and without contradiction how, according to the description of the orator, the accomplished facts had occured'.[36] No *langue*-determined structural indicators for further text-delimitations are to be found.

The *propositio/partitio/*πρόθεσις often comes in between a possible *narratio* and the argumentative part, the so called *probatio*. This subtext is of a transitory nature bridging the *narratio*- and the *probatio*-sections. The *propositio* can either constitute a part of or even the entire case of the *narratio* or form a separate sub-text in close conjunction with the *narratio*.[37] The *propositio* discloses the *theme of the argumentation*. When a series of *propositiones* follows upon each other, the series is called *partitio*.[38] Thus, the difference between the *propositio* and the *partitio* consists of whether it concerns one point or more.[39]

One characteristic feature of the *propositio* is its *brevitas*, 'which demands that no superfluous word is being used, since the listener should be enthralled only by the facts and the components of the *causa*, not however, by words and means of ornamentation that are situated out side of the facts'.[40] Again no *langue*-determined structural indicators for the delimitation of further sub-texts are provided by the ancient theoreticians.

The *probatio/argumentatio/*πίστις[41] constitutes the central, dominant

35. See Martin 1974: 82.
36. Fuhrmann 1984: 87.
37. See Martin 1974: 92: 'Die *propositio* hat die Aufgabe das ζήτημα klarzulegen und die Hörer auf den kommenden Beweis aufmerksam zu machen... Die *propositio* kann auch unterbleiben, wenn die Sache an sich klar ist und wenn die *quaestio* sich unmittelbar an die *narratio* anschließt'; cf. also the quotation from Fuhrmann above n. 26.
38. See Martin 1974: 92; Lausberg 1973: 189-90 [§§ 346-47].
39. Fuhrmann 1984: 89: 'Die *propositio* umreißt den Streitpunkt...; wenn es sich um mehrere Punkte handelt, dann werden sie in einer *partitio* der Reihe nach vorgeführt'; cf. Lausberg 1973: 189 [§§ 346-47]; Martin 1974: 91-95.
40. Martin 1974: 94.
41. Wörner 1985: 13; esp. Sprute 1982 and Hellholm 1994a: § 2.3.3. The Greeks usually used the plural indicating that normally the *probatio*-section was made up of a series of proofs.

and necessary part of an argumentative text.[42] There has to be at least one argument or better: proof, but normally a series of different kinds of proofs is combined.[43] The various sets of proofs and the various single proofs will be discussed below.

In connection with our discussion of the *partes orationis* there are two specific features that need to be deliberated upon in some detail. The reason for this is that these features normally are not discussed in connection with the μέρη τοῦ λόγου and, further, they are of utmost importance for understanding the macro-structure of Romans.

As far as my analytical description of the hierarchical ranking of sub-texts goes, it takes its departure from the linear text-structure, beginning with the entire text and ideally ending with the smallest *syntagmata*. This means that my analysis represents a syntagmatic approach proceeding in a descending manner from the larger to the smaller units.[44]

As already mentioned, the *dispositio* of ancient rhetoric also represents a syntagmatic relational approach to the encoding as well as to the decoding of speeches or writings. That this is the case is best illustrated by the conventional delimitation of texts into their *partes orationis*/μέρη τοῦ λόγου: *prooimion, narratio, propositio, probatio* and *peroratio*.

(a) When syntagmatically delimiting the *probatio* sub-text into further sub-texts or text-units, we can no longer rely on the *dispositio* of ancient rhetorical handbooks, since their syntagmatic approach started and ended with the already discussed μέρη τοῦ λόγου which were more or less conventional. The reason for this is that the *langue*-determined *dispositio* to a large extent was neglected by the rhetorical theoreticians[45] in spite of the fact that Aristotle placed the τάξις in third place after the εὕρεσις and the λέξις.[46]

If we want to pursue syntagmatic analyses of, for example, Pauline letters further, we are thus forced to go beyond the *dispositio* as it was developed in classical rhetoric. This does not mean, however, that we should or must dispense with ancient rhetoric altogether as we

---

42. Fuhrmann 1984: 89; Lausberg 1973: 190 [§ 348]; Wörner 1985: 16.
43. Lausberg 1973: 190 [§ 349].
44. Cf. Hellholm 1980; 1986; 1990; and 1994b.
45. Cf. Plett 1975: 16; Fuhrmann 1984: 78.
46. Aristotle, *Rhet.* 3.1 1403b 6ff.; cf. Martin 1974: 213; Sieveke 1980: 293 nn. 208-209; and now Kennedy 1991: 216-17, 299-305; see further below n. 61.

continue our macro-syntagmatic analysis. Instead of leaving rhetoric, we should only move into other areas of rhetorical approaches, in particular into the *status*-doctrine of the paradigmatically conceived *inventio*, that is, the systematic theory of determining the specific situation in which the speech is to be delivered.[47]

With the help of the *status*-doctrine developed by Hermagoras of Temnos[48] and consolidated by Hermogenes of Tarsos,[49] we can distinguish between two sets of proofs: (a) the abstract, theoretical and principal treatment of a question, which was called θέσιϚ/*quaestio infinita* or *quaestio generalis*;[50] (b) the concrete, non-theoretical and practical treatment of a question, which is called ὑπόθεσιϚ/*quaestio finita* or *quaestio particularis*.[51]

These two *quaestiones civilis* are not a part of the syntagmatic *dispositio* but rather of the paradigmatic *status*-doctrine of the *inventio*. From a deductive logical point of view[52] the general theoretical questions must obtain their answers before one can give answers to the specific and concrete questions at stake.[53]

47. See Lausberg 1973: 64-85 [§§ 79-138]; Lausberg, 1976: 21-23; Martin 1974: 28-52; Fuhrmann 1984: 99-114; Breuer 1990: 108-109: '"Situation" kann begrifflich gefaßt werden als die Abweichung der Position (Einstellung) des Textherstellers von der Position (Einstellung) der Zielgruppe bzw. Zielperson in bezug auf einen bestimmten Sachverhalt zu einem bestimmten Zeitpunkt' (p. 109).
48. Cf. Kennedy 1963: 303-21; Kennedy 1983: 73-76; Fuhrmann 1984: 99ff.; Barthes 1990: 66-67; Hommel 1965/1990: 2616-17: 'Bei der *Thesis* (*quaestio infinita* oder *generalis*) handelt es sich um die allgemeine Charakterisierung einer Rede zugrunde liegenden Rechtsproblems (...), gewonnen durch Abstraktion aus der Hypothesis (*quaestio finita* oder *specialis*), dem Spezialfall (...)' (*ibid*: 2616).
49. Cf. Kennedy 1972: 619-33; Kennedy 1983: 76-86.
50. Martin 1974: 17ff.; Lausberg 1973: 61-63 [§§ 69-72]; Fuhrmann 1984: 100-101; Baumhauer 1986: 149: 'Eine *thésis* ist, wenn wir M.F. Quintillianus (III 5,5-18) folgen, eine Frage, die ohne Bezug auf bestimmte Personen, eine bestimmte Zeit, einen bestimmten Ort und ähnliches *pro* und *contra* diskutiert werden kann...'
51. Martin 1974: 17ff.; Lausberg 1973: 63-64 [§§ 73-78]; Fuhrmann 1984: 101-102; Baumhauer 1986: 149.
52. The *quaestiones infinitae* are according to Cicero, *De inv.* 1.6.8 actually a part of philosophy and not of rhetoric.
53. Lausberg 1973: 63 [§ 70]: 'wobei auf die Notwendigkeit der Lösung infiniter Quaestio nen als Vorbedingung für die Behandlung finiter Quaestionen hingewiesen wird: Quint. 3,5,13...'; Martin 1974: 18: 'In Wirklichkeit aber sei es [according to St Augustine, *Aug. rhet.* 5-DH] so, daß zuerst über die zweite Frage,

From a *syntagmatic* point of view, however, there is no way of knowing how the two sets of proofs are sequentially arranged, that is, which one precedes the other or if the two sets alternate in a series of proofs. This is simply due to the fact that while the *partes orationis* within the *dispositio* to a preponderant extent were *langue*-determined, the *quaestiones civiles* within the *status*-doctrine of the *inventio* were *parole*-conditioned. Nevertheless, one should notice that 'as amplifying background and as sustenance of the argumentation, the *quaestiones infinitae* are readily inserted before the *quaestiones finitae*'.[54]

As far as the *probatio* sub-text in Romans is concerned, it is quite clear that at least in one respect the first sub-text constitutes the θέσις/*quaestio infinita*, that is, from 1.18–8.39, and that the second sub-text on the same level constitutes the ὑπόθεσις/*quaestio finita*, from 9.1–11.36 (see below pp. 144ff.).[55]

(b) The other delimitation of the structural grouping of the proofs is made up of two sub-texts, viz. (1) the *positive* set of proofs[56] called pivsti" in the Greek and *confirmatio* or *probatio* in the Latin, and (2) the *negative* set of proofs,[57] that is, the *refutatio* of the claims of the

die Thesis, entschieden werden müsse, und dann erst über die erste, die Hypothesis...'

54. Lausberg 1973: 64 [§ 76].

55. This suggestion of mine, which will have to be substantiated in the analysis with the remarks here and in further detail in a forthcoming publication, would explain the much debated question of the role of chs. 9–11. To my knowledge, nobody has suggested this 'rhetorical' solution to the problem of the *compositional structure of Romans*, which I think is due mainly to the fact that the distinction between θέσις and ὑπόθεσις is not a part of the *dispositio*, which is followed more or less slavishly. It is, e.g., characteristic that Betz in his monumental commentaries from 1979 and 1986 confines himself in his compositional analyses of Pauline letters to the rhetorical *dispositio*; he does not, however—and rightly so—confine his analyses to the primarily one-dimensional delimitation of the *dispositio* but when delimiting the texts into further sub-texts no references to rhetoric are given. Whether the syntagmatic delimitation of the *probatio*-section into further sub-texts according to the distinction between *quaestio infinita* and *quaestio finita* is also adequate as far as other Pauline texts are concerned cannot be discussed here.

56. See Lausberg 1976: 29; *idem* 1973: 147-49 [§ 262]: 'Gerne wird die *argumentatio* in *probatio* und *refutatio* aufgeteilt (Quint. 3,9,1-5; Sulp.Vict. 16, p. 322, 8), so daß fünf Teile der Rede herauskommen (Quint. 3,9,1 *partes, ut plurimis auctoribus placuit, quinque sunt*)'.

57. See Martin 1974: 124ff.: 'Alles, was der Gegner vorbringt, die ἀντιθέσεις,

opposition, called ἀνασκευή or λύσις in the Greek and *confutatio* or *refutatio* in the Latin.[58] Also with regard to these sets of proofs, one has to be aware that they were treated foremost paradigmatically as can be seen in modern handbooks, where these concepts mostly are found in the sections addressing the *inventio*.[59] In the ancient handbooks, however, they were discussed with regard to their syntagmatic position as is the case in Hermogenes when he states that some rhetoricians 'put the counter proposition (*antithesis*) before its refutation (*lysis*)', while Demosthenes is inconsistent, since 'at times...he refutes the arguments of his opponent before he offers his own proposals. At other times he introduces his own proposal first', but he 'arranges his material in such a way that it will be most beneficial to his own point of view...'[60] Aristotle, who treats the *refutatio* in the chapter dealing with the *dispositio*[61] within the *probatio*-section, emphasizes the strategic order

fordert die Widerlegung oder Entkräftung durch den Beschuldigten, die λύσις... *refutatio*. Sie ist die eigentliche und Hauptaufgabe des Verteidigers, *pars defensoris tota est posita in refutatione*, sagt Quintilian [inst. 5,13,1-3].' This set of proofs is generally regarded as the more difficult, since it is harder to refute something than to confirm it: see Lausberg 1973: 236 [§ 430]; Martin 1974: 124.

58. Aristotle, *Rhet.* 2.25.

59. Martin 1974: 95 and 124-33. Lausberg 1973: 262 however treats the *refutatio* in connection with the *partes orationis*.

60. Hermogenes, *On Types of Style* [περὶ ἰδεῶν] 238 (trans. Wooten 1987: 16).

61. Sieveke 1980: 279 n. 152: 'Das Ende von Buch II der *Rhetorik* markiert auch den Abschluß des Teils, der in der späteren Rhetoriktheorie als Inventio-Lehre bezeichnet wird. Buch III wendet sich zwei weiteren Komplexen zu: 1. Der λέξις (*elocutio*), dem Stil der sprachlichen Formulierung, der sprachlichen Einkleidung der Argumente. 2. Der τάξις (*dispositio*), der Anordnung der mit der Inventio-Lehre gefundenen und mit Hilfe der Elocutio-Lehre formulierten Argumente (vgl. Cicero, *Orator* 14.43...).' As far as the treatment of *refutatio* in the *dispositio*-doctrine and the difference between paradigmatic and syntagmatic treatments are concerned, see Sieveke 1980: 299 n. 232: 'Nicht recht verständlich ist die Kritik des Quintilian an Aristoteles... (*Inst. Orat.* III 9.5). Vermutlich spielt Quintilian auf *Rhet.* II 25 an, wo sich Aristoteles mit der Topik der Widerlegung befaßt. Daß er die Topik der Widerlegung losgelöst von der der Argumentation behandelt, ist durchaus verständlich; denn hierbei handelt es sich ja um die systematische Untersuchung eines früheren Stadiums des rhetorischen Arbeitsprozesses, um die Inventio-Lehre. Hier aber, bei der Behandlung der Dispositio-Lehre ist die kritische Bemerkung Quintilians unangebracht; denn Aristoteles selbst teilt der πίστις, der Glaubhaft-

of the *confirmatio* and *refutatio* respectively, when he writes:

> The refutation of the opponent (τὰ πρὸς τὸν ἀντίδικον) is not a particular kind of proof; his arguments should be refuted partly by objection, partly by counter-syllogism. In both deliberative and forensic rhetoric he who speaks first should state his own proofs and afterwards meet the arguments of the opponent, refuting (λύοντα) or pulling them to pieces beforehand. If, however, the case for the other side contains a great variety of arguments, begin with these, like Callistratus in the Messenian assembly, when he diminished the arguments likely to be used against him before giving his own proofs. If you speak later, you must first, by means of refutation (λύοντα) and counter-deduction, attempt some answer to your opponent's speaking, especially if his arguments have been well received.[62]

As far as the *probatio* in Romans is concerned it is further obvious that the first sub-text of the θέσις-argumentation makes up a *refutatio/confutatio* or λύσις-section encompassing 1.18–3.20, while the second sub-text of the θέσις-argumentation constitutes a *confirmatio/probatio* or πίστις-section encompassing 3.21–8.39 (beginning with νυνὶ δὲ χωρὶς νόμου δικαιοσύνη θεοῦ πεφανέρωται...δικαιοσύνη δὲ θεοῦ διὰ πίστεως Ἰησοῦ Χριστοῦ εἰς πάντας τοὺς πιστεύοντας) (see below n. 84 and p. 146).

The place of the *peroratio/conclusio/ἐπίλογος* is discussed in ancient rhetorical handbooks,[63] but most rhetoricians placed it after the *probatio*.[64] This uncertainty[65] once again shows the vacillation between the *langue*-determined *dispositio* and the *parole*-conditioned *inventio* even on grade one.[66]

In the *peroratio* one finds first of all a recapitulation (ἀνακεφαλαίωσις) of what has been said so far, especially of what

---

machung, die beiden Funktionen *Argumentation* und *Widerlegung* zu.' Kennedy 1991: 276: 'Aristotle does not regard the refutation as a distinct part of an oration, as did the followers of Theodorus...'

62. Aristotle, *Rhet.* 3.17.14-15 (trans. LCL [Freese]; cf. now the trans. by Kennedy 1991).

63. See Martin 1974: 147-48.

64. Martin 1974: 147-48.

65. Martin 1974: 148: 'Wie für das prooivmion und die διήγησις wurde auch für den ἐπίλογος die Frage erörtert, ob und wo er in der Rede einen Platz erhalten sollte'; Lausberg 1973: 240 [§§ 441-42].

66. See other instances of the same uncertainty mentioned above.

has been argued in the *probatio*-section.[67] The *peroratio*—like the *exordium*—is concerned with obtaining the listeners' good will (*benevolum parare*).[68] Usually in the *peroratio*-section the author takes the opportunity to appeal to the feelings of the audience.[69] In ancient rhetoric one distinguished between two kinds of appeals: the ἦθος and the πάθος. The ἦθος being the softer one showing the firm and just character of the writer/speaker.[70] The ἦθος being the aggressive mode of awakening anger and wrath towards the accused among the audience.[71] Once more we can observe that no *langue*-determined structural indicators for further text-delimitations are given.

The parole-conditioned macro-structure of the rhetorical amplificatio: the four genera amplificationis. The *parole*-conditioned macro- and micro-structure is primarily grounded in structuring principles of a text-*external* kind.[72] *Amplificatio*/αὔξησις[73] constitutes in the words of Heinrich Lausberg 'a gradual climax of that which is given by nature with the help of art', and this climax is conducted in the interest of the *utilitas causae*'.[74] The amplification can be a part of the *inventio* and be applied both to the *intellectual* (*ad faciendam fidem*) and to the *emotional* (*ad commovendum*) argumentation.[75] The amplification can also be achieved by means of the eloquence of the speech as a part of the *elocutio*, e.g. through tropes and figures. Objects of the *amplificatio* are the thoughts or concepts which then have to be expressed in verbal terms in the speech or in the text itself; the formulations of the

67.   Cf. Lausberg 1973: 237-38 [§§ 434-35]; Martin 1974: 150-58.
68.   Fuhrmann 1984: 97; Martin 1974: 148; Plett 1975: 17.
69.   Cf. Lausberg 1973: 238-40 [§§ 436-39]; Martin 1974: 158-66; Fuhrmann 1984: 98.
70.   See Wörner 1981; Wörner 1992: esp. 310ff.; Hellwig 1973: 251-321; Schweinfurth-Walla 1986: 65-79.
71.   See Wörner 1984 and Wörner 1992: esp. 290ff.
72.   Lausberg 1976: 27 [§ 46.1], 33-41 [§§ 64-90].
73.   See now the art. '*Amplificatio*' by Bauer 1992: 445-71.
74.   Lausberg 1976: 35 [§ 71]; Lausberg 1973: 145 [§ 259]; Heinemann and Viehweger 1991: 20: 'Im Zentrum rhetorischer Überlegungen stand stets die Frage nach dem Erreichen eines optimalen kommunikativen Effekts... "ars bene dicendi" (Kunst, etwas gut, d.h. mit Erfolg zu sagen)...'
75.   Cf. Bauer 1992: 445.

amplification can be realized by means of either *verba singula* or *verba coniuncta*.[76]

The four genera amplificationis, all achieved by means of style and content, were: (a) strengthening or amplification of the argument in a narrower sense (*incrementum*; Quintilian 8.4.1-9); (b) comparisons that rise from the less to the greater (*comparatio*; Quintilian 8.4.9-14); (c) reasoning primarily by means of circumstantial evidence (*ratiocinatio*; Quintilian 8.4.15-26); (d) accumulation of words and sentences (*congeries*; Quintilian 8. 4.27-29).[77]

As far as the macro-structural composition is concerned it is important to take into account Quintilian's statement with regard to the *amplificatio* of the *oratio*, that this can be made

> less obviously, but perhaps yet more effectively, by introducing a continuous and unbroken series in which each statement is stronger than the last (*crescit oratio minus aperte, sed nescio an hoc ipso efficacius, cum citra distinctionem in contextu et cursu semper aliquid priore maius insequitur*),

which means that 'each statement is more forcible than that which went before (*singula incrementum habent*)'.[78]

The Compostional Macro-Structure of Romans

The macro-structural composition of Romans given below is not complete; the delimitation of the text is provided only to the extent that it is necessary for our argumentation in this essay.[79]

1ST[1] Epistolary prescript (1.1-7)
1ST[2] Letter corpus (1.8–15.33)
   2ST[21] *Exordium*: Introduction to the corpus of the letter (1.8-15)
      3ST[211] *Captatio benevolentiae* (1.8)
      3ST[212] *Attentum parare* (1.9-10)
      3ST[213] *Docilem parare* (1.11-12)
      3ST[214] *Benevolum parare (ab nostra persona)* (1.13-15)
   2ST[22] *Propositio:* Thematic proposition: the gospel (τὸ εὐαγγέλιον) of the universality of justification by faith (ἀποκαλύπτεται) (1.16-17)

---

76. Lausberg 1976: 37 [§ 75] and 43-44 [§§ 99 and 100].
77. Cf. Lausberg 1973: 221-24 [§§ 401-406]; Martin 1974: 157-58; Bauer 1992: 447.
78. Quintilian 8.4.8 (trans. according to LCL [Butler]).
79. ST stands for Sub-Text. A complete analysis will appear in my *New Testament and Textlinguistics*, II to be published by Mohr (Paul Siebeck), Tübingen.

²ST²³ *Probatio:* First part of the main argument: the predominantly theoretical-theological treatment of the theme (1.18–11.36)

³ST²³¹ *Quaestio infinita/generalis:* the general treatment of the theme: God's dikaiosuvnh for all people through faith in Jesus Christ (1.18–8.39)

⁴ST²³¹¹ *Refutatio/confutatio:* the negative proofs regarding the necessity of God's δικαιοσύνη for Jews as well as for Gentiles due to the power of sin and, as a consequence thereof, the ὀργὴ θεοῦ (1.18–3.20)[80]

    ⁵ST²³¹¹¹   Thesis: Revelation of God's wrath upon all human beings (1.18)

    ⁵ST²³¹¹²   A *first* line of argumentation in favour of the thesis in form of two *accusations* [see Paul's own retrospective formulation in form of a meta-communicative sentence[81] in 3.9: προητιασάμεθα γὰρ Ἰουδαίους τε καὶ "Ελληνας πάντας ὑφ᾿ ἁμαρτίαν εἶναι] related to each other (1.19–2.11).

        [Amplif.³]

      ⁶ST²³¹¹²¹   *First* accusation in two steps: the injustice of the *Gentiles* as reason for the immanent–presentic effect of God's wrath (1.19-32)

      ⁶ST²³¹¹²²   *Second* accusation in two steps: the impenitence of the *Jews* as reason for the transcendent–eschatological effect of God's wrath (2.1-11)

        [Amplif.⁴]

    ⁵ST²³¹¹³   A *second* line of argumentation in favour of the thesis in form of three accusations[82] with regard to the *law* that are related to each other (2.12–3.8)

        [Amplif.³]

---

80. Cf. also the structural analysis in Theißen 1983: 74-82.

81. On meta-communicative sentences, see Gülich and Raible 1977b: 27-28; Hellholm 1980: 80-84; cf. Schlier 1977: 98: 'Προαιτιᾶσθαι ist soviel wie "vorher, früher die Anklage erheben", mit Acc. c. Infin. Das πρό- meint natürlich das, was 1,18–2,29 gesagt war und jetzt summarisch zusammengefaßt wird'; so also Schmithals 1988: 110: 'in V. 9b in einem den bisherigen Inhalt des 1. Hauptteils... ausdrücklich zusammenfassenden Rückblick...'

82. See previous note.

6ST²³¹¹³¹   *First* accusation regarding the *law* concerning all human beings but addressed to the Jews/Judaizers (2.12-24; σύ!)

6ST²³¹¹³²   *Second* accusation regarding *circumcision* concerning all human beings but addressed to the Jews/Judaizers (2.25-29; σύ!)

[Amplif.⁴]

6ST²³¹¹³³   *Third* accusation: a *diatribe dialogue* with a Jewish interlocutor concerning God's covenantal faithfulness vis à vis the unfaithfulness of the Jews (3.1-8)

[Amplif.⁴]

5ST²³¹¹⁴   Conclusion of the *refutatio quaestionis generalis*-section in two parts (3.9-20)[83]

[Amplif.³]

6ST²³¹¹⁴¹   *Part one* as a prerequisite for part two: all human beings are under the Law (3.9-18)

6ST²³¹¹³²   *Part two*: those under the Law are all sinners (3.19-20)

[Amplif.⁴]

4ST²³¹²   *Confirmatio:* the positive proofs regarding the realization (πεφανέρωται) of God's δικαιοσύνη for Jews as well as for Gentiles through faith in Jesus Christ apart from the law (3.21–8.39)[84]

[Amplif.²]

---

83. See Schmithals 1988: 111: 'Indem Paulus in v.9b den Inhalt des 1. Hauptteils seines Lehrschreibens nach Rom ausdrücklich zusammenfaßt, gewinnt er zugleich das Leitmotiv auch der Klimax dieses Hauptteils und einen angemessenen Übergang zu V.10-19'.

84. One should notice that in the *propositio* 2ST²², being the general thesis of the letter, i.e. the gospel (τὸ εὐαγγέλιον) of justification by faith alone (ἐκ πίστεως εἰς πίστιν), the tense is the present (ἐστίν, ἀποκαλύπτεται), while in the opening thesis (5ST²³¹²¹) of the more limited *confirmatio*-section 4ST²³¹² as the positive counterpart of the immediately preceding *refutatio*-section 4ST²³¹¹ (νυνὶ δέ...) the tense is the perfect (πεφανέρωται), which is logical, since here Paul is not referring to the proclamation of the gospel in general but to the Christ event and its result specifically (δικαιοσύνη δὲ θεοῦ διὰ πίστεως Ἰησοῦ Χριστοῦ [v. 22]), which is then being thematized in the following context which is christological (vv. 23-26); consequently, the change in tense is due to the place of the verbs in the structure of the argumentative flow in the letter, i.e. its macro-syntagmatic position; a merely paradigmatic juxtaposition of the different tenses in 1.16-17 and 3.21 cannot explain the change; this also confirms the importance of changes in tense for the delimitation of texts into subtexts.

5ST23121	Thesis in adhesion to the thematic propo-sition in 1.16-17 (3.21-22a)
5ST23122	*First* proof: the revelation of God's δικαιοσύνη in Jesus Christ = *christological* aspect (3.22b-31)
5ST23123	*Second* proof from Scripture: Abraham as an example of faith (4.1-25)
5ST23124	*Third* proof: the revelation of God's δικαιοσύνη in the lives of the believers = *soteriological* aspect (5.1-8.39)
3ST232	*Quaestio finita/particularis*: the special treatment of the theme: God's δικαιοσύνη and Israel's disobedience and unbelief (9.1-11.36)[85] *[Amplif.[1]]*
4ST2321	Prologue: oath assuring Paul's concern about Israel (9.1-5)[86]
4ST2322	Dialogue concerning the freedom of God's universal election of Jews and Gentiles (9.6-33)[87]

85. See the important observation by Hübner that 'bis Kap. 8 einschließlich begegnet der Name Israel in Röm nicht. In Röm 9-11 finden wir jedoch Israel 11mal erwähnt' (1992: 173). In addition one should not neglect the likewise important observation that the asyndetic connection in Romans is *only* to be found here; see Kümmel 1978: 246: 'Die Kapitelreihe ist seltsam unverbunden an den hymnischen Abschluß 8,39 angeschloßen, eine sonst im Römerbrief ausnahmslos vorhandene verbindende Partikel fehlt in 9,1...'; quoted also by Stegemann 1981: 177-78; cf. Meeks 1990: 107: 'The chain of inferential particles (ἄρα νῦν ἄρα οὖν γάρ κτλ) is interrupted for a moment, only to resume immediately in v. 3'; and Siegert 1985: 115 with n. 9a. As the classical philologist Blomqvist in his studies of Greek particles has emphasized anew, the grammar of Greek 'forbids asyndetic justaposition of sentences', which means that 'every sentence must open with a particle that indicates its relationship to the preceding sentence. Omission of the particle is allowed only under clearly defined circumstances' (1981: 59; cf. Blomqvist 1969: 19; Blomqvist 1991: 267 [§ 300: 8 a-d]). The asyndetic connection—in addition to other criteria of form and content—confirms from a text-grammatical point of view the delimitation of the *probatio*-section into a *quaestio finita* and a *quaestio infinita* section precisely at the end of ch. 8 and the beginning of ch. 9. Regarding the 2nd, 3rd and 4th analytical sub-title on level four of 3ST232, see Wagner 1988: 81, 88, 91.

86. On the importance of the Prologue (= 'Vorspann'), see esp. Brandenburger 1985: 5-6.

87. See Siegert 1985: 115 and 141: 'Ausnahmsweise (vergleichbar ist bei Paulus nur Röm 8,31) leitet τί οὖν ἐροῦμεν hier [9.30 –DH] keinen Selbsteinwand ein, der erst überwunden werden müßte, sondern bereits das Resümee' ['de(s) oberen

4ST[2323]	The obstinacy of Israel's rebellion against God (10.1-21)
4ST[2324]	The miracle of Israel's eschatological salvation (11.1-32)
4ST[2325]	Doxology of the wondrous ways of God (11.33-36)

2ST[24] *Exhortatio*: second part of the main argument: the predominantly practical-ethical treatment of the theme (12.1–15.13)
2ST[25] *Peroratio/conclusio*: concluding section (15.14-33)
1ST[3] Epistolary postscript (16.1-23).

Remarks on Paul's Use of Amplification in the Compositional Macro-Structure of Romans

First the analytical results of the analysis given above will be described and then a synthetic conclusion of the analysis and of the analytical commentary will be given as a summary.

Analytical Remarks

On this occasion I can only provide brief and preliminary remarks on the amplification in the linear macro-structure of Paul's letter to the Romans. The analysis given above has shown that Paul all the way from the macro-structure of the composition to the micro-structure of his argumentation carries out a remarkable intensification and specification from the common and general to the specific and particular.[88] In summarizing the results of his utilization of the *amplificatio* in Romans in descending order we gain the following picture:

(1) The common and fundamental figure of amplification is the juxtaposition between *quaestio infinita* and *quaestio finita [Amplif.¹]*.[89] As has been suggested above,[90] the first part of the *probatio* constitutes a *quaestio generalis* dealing with the principal question of the righteousness that God bestows upon all human beings (Jews and Gentiles

---

Kontext(s) ab V. 6' (p. 115) –DH]; thus, vv. 30-33 constitute the ending of 4ST[2322] and not the beginning of 4ST[2323] as is usually assumed by commentators.

88.   Due to lack of space the analysis of Paul's use of amplification in the *confirmatio*, in the *quaestio finita* as well as in the *exhortatio* sections cannot be dealt with here; see above n. 79.

89.   Lausberg 1976: 38 [§ 82]: 'die *quaestiones finitae* sind ja in den entsprechenden *quaestiones infinitae* sozusagen eingebettet'; Lausberg 1973: 225 [§ 408].

90.   See above p. 135 with n. 53.

alike) through their faith in Jesus Christ without the observance of the law (1.18–8.39); only thereafter can Paul in the second part of the *probatio* turn to the concrete question (*quaestio particularis*) of Israel's unbelief (ἀπιστία) and disobedience (ἀπείθεια)[91] (9.1–11.36),[92] which evidently played such a vital part in Paul's controversy with the Jewish synagogue[93] on the one hand and with the Judaizing opposition he is going to encounter in his impending visit to Jerusalem[94] on the other, and which he presumes will infiltrate[95] or already has infiltrated the church in Rome as it had in his churches in the east.[96] In order to deal adequately with the problem of the unbelief and disobedience of God's Israel, Paul is forced first to take on the principal question of how all human beings can be justified before God.[97] If the main theme of Romans is in fact the universality of sin

91.   See Brandenburger 1985: 47 n. 79.
92.   Cf. on the one hand Siegert 1985: 141: 'Es ist ja nicht so, daß hier ein neues Thema eingeführt würde... sondern Paulus hat sein Hauptthema nie vergessen. Er hat nur in 9,1... neu eingesetzt, um sich in einigen Schleifen zu der Reflexionsebene emporzuarbeiten, die mit dem Begriff "Gottesgerechtigkeit aus Glauben" verbunden ist'; on the other Meeks 1990: 108: 'The function of chaps. 9-11 is thus not to continue but to disrupt the smooth assurances of confidence that have capped the whole argument of chaps. 1-8'.
93.   See Schmithals 1988: 338: 'Hinter [9,]6a steht also nichts anders als z.B. in 3,8; 6,1.15; 7,7.13 ein Vorwurf der Synagoge'; Bindemann 1992: 20-45 *et passim*; cf. Brandenburger 1985: 17-18: "V. 6a muß zunächst eine Deutung im unmittelbar zugehörigen Kontext erhalten. Der Einsatz ist disputative...'; 'hier wird ein Vorwurf abgewehrt. Das aber entspricht dem, was bereits von der Gattung her in anderer Weise den Vorspann 9,1-5 prägt: Paulus muß sich mit einer schwurartigen Beteuerung Verdächtigungen vom Halse schaffen'.
94.   See Jervell 1991: 53-64.
95.   I.e. as a result of Paul's missionary activity in general, especially his plans for missionary work in Spain with Rome as the base for his activity there, his forthcoming visit to Rome and possibly already the letter to the Romans itself as suggested by Brandenburger 1985: 7; further Wilckens 1980: 181ff., esp. 199; and Wagner 1988: 84-85.
96.   See Hellholm 1994a: § 3.1.2.3.1.1. with more references; cf. further Rom. 16.17-20a and hereto Lampe 1991: 221: 'The sharp polemic is directed against third persons: against possible heretics not belonging to the Roman church but maybe planning to infiltrate it. Paul may think of his opponents in the east, fearing that they could reach out and influence the Romans' opinion of him.'
97.   Cf. Brandenburger 1985: 8: 'Das veranlassende Problem ist also für Röm 9–11 zwar *spezieller*, aber im Grunde das gleiche wie für den Römerbrief insgesamt...' (italics mine); further Schmithals 1988: 322, 324.

and redemption, then this ought to be reflected not only in the section encompassing the *quaestio infinita* but also in the *quaestio finita* section. That this is the case is confirmed in general through the parallelism between 1.11–4.25 and 5.12-21 on the one hand and 9.1–11.36 on the other and in particular through the parallel statements in 5.18-19 and 11.32, where Paul at the end of the *quaestio finita* section writes: συνέκλεισεν γὰρ ὁ θεὸς τοὺς πάντας εἰς ἀπείθειαν, ἵνα τοὺς πάντας ἐλεήσῃ.[98] The type of amplification utilized here is clearly developed in the interest of the *utilitas causae*.[99]

(2) Another *amplificatio* figure is the heightening from *refutatio* to *confirmatio [Amplif.2]* or the other way around depending on the external situation behind the argumentation, as we have already seen. This kind of amplification has a close affinity with the *comparatio*-figure[100] with its 'outbid-schema'. In Romans we encounter first an unusually extensive *refutatio*-section (1.18–3.20), which then is outbid by an even more extensive *confirmatio*-section (3.21–8.39). Paul here first brings the *refutatio* according to the rule that if 'it is very extensive, it has to be carried out first'.[101]

(3) Still another usual, perhaps the most usual, figure of amplification is the so called *incrementum*, which is constituted by among other things a successive enumeration of 'aggravating (heightening) circumstances'.[102] Aggravating circumstances are found

98. Cf. Schmithals 1988: 324-25; Brandenburger 1985: 34: through the antithetical pairs of opposition 'ist (es) unverkennbar, daß das Anliegen der paulinischen Rechtfertigungsbotschaft zur Sprache kommen soll. Zwar geschieht das weithin nicht in der gewohnten Terminologie. Sie wird vielmehr vertreten durch die Sprache der Schrift, mit der hier theologisch reflektiert und argumentiert wird.'
99. See hereto Brandenburger 1985: *passim*, esp. 6 n. 10: 'Aber das Bemerkenswerte ist doch nicht, daß Paulus in *9,1-5* eine Klage anstimmt; er muß vielmehr *versichern*, daß er *sonst und beständig* Israel in Trauer und Schmerz zugetan ist. Warum ist diese Beteuerung im Brief nach Rom nötig?—das ist die Frage.' Brandenburger answers his own question as far as Romans 9–11 is concerned by stating that Paul 'vor allem positiv darlegen (muß), wie er sich selbst und insbesondere wie sich sein Evangelium und sein apostolisches Wirken zu Israel und zu den es tragenden theologischen Überlieferungen verhält' (Brandenburger 1985: 7); further Schmithals 1988: ad chs. 9–11 *passim*, e.g. 337.
100. Cf. Lausberg 1976: 37-38 [§ 78]; Lausberg 1973: 222-23 [§ 404].
101. Martin 1974: 124; Aristotle, *Rhet.* 3.17 1417b 21ff.
102. Lausberg 1976: 37 [§ 77.4]; Lausberg 1973: 222 [§ 403]; Martin 1974: 157; Quintilian 8.4.8 and 8.6.36.

144   *Rhetoric and the New Testament*

throughout the *refutatio*-section in Rom. 1.18–3.20 *[Amplif.³]*: (a)
First we encounter the intensification from the *thesis* of the ὀργὴ
θεοῦ (1.18) to the first argumentative line dealing with the accusation
against *Gentiles and Jews generally* (1.19–2.11), (b) further to the
next line of argumentation dealing with the question of the Jews' and
the Gentiles' relationship to the *law in particular* (2.12–3.8) and (c)
finally to the *concluding summary* which confirms the accusation
against both Jews and Gentiles (3.9-20).¹⁰³

    (4) Also in the two lines of argumentation within the *refutatio*-
section we find intensifications of the *incrementum*-type *[Amplif.⁴]*:
(a) between the first accusation, viz. the one against the Gentiles (1.19-
32) and the second accusation, viz. the one against the Jews (2.1-11).
This intensification has accurately been commented upon by Günther
Bornkamm: 'the "prophetic" craftiness of this section consists—one
could almost say—in the fact that Paul here can reckon with the
approbation of the Jews...'¹⁰⁴ If in the first section he takes his
starting point in the accusation against the Gentiles, Paul in the second
section turns against the Jews with even more acrimony. It is further
important to notice that Paul in the first section *talks about the
Gentiles,* while in the second section he carries out the intensification
by *addressing the Jews in direct speech* (σύ!). (b) A further example
of this kind of amplification is the threefold gradual development
within the second line of argumentation against the Jews (2.12–3.8):
(i) from the first accusation concerning the *Law generally* (2.12-24),
(ii) to the second accusation concerning the more specific *concept of
circumcision* (2.25-29), (iii) which reaches it peak in the third and last
accusation on account of the *unfaithfulness* of the Jews over against
God; this third and last accusation is furthermore formulated as a
dialogue in diatribe style to heighten the amplificatory strategy of Paul
(3.1-8). (c) A last example is the *ratiocinatio* in the conclusion of the
refutatio: since all are under the law, they are all sinners (3.9-20); this
conclusion then constitutes the presupposition for the following
confirmatio.

    (5) The consistency in his structuring of the *refutatio*-section is
another example of Paul's *utilitas*-directed strategy, in which he
always commences with general accounts and then becomes more and

103. Lausberg 1973: 236 [§ 430]: 'Die *refutatio* bedient sich besonders gern der
amplificatio'; Martin 1974: 156 #10.
    104. Bornkamm 1963: 95.

more precise by means of concretizations, specifications and finally concluding summaries. One example of the *utilitas*-directed strategy, in addition to the ones given already, can be drawn from the *confirmatio*-section, where the *christological* proof (3.22b-31) is kept extremely short, since it is not controversial. Controversial in this section is instead the *soteriological* proof, which encompasses three entire chapters (5.1–8.39).

(6) A last example of amplification figures is the *ratiocinatio,* primarily from *exampla.* Here I can only refer to my analysis of the argumentative structure of Romans 6.[105]

Synthetic Remarks as Summary

In my opinion it cannot be accidental when the text throughout exhibits a series of amplifications on practically all hierarchical levels of the text. Here, in Romans, we clearly encounter a highly conscious and stylistically reflective compositional effort that is operative on the macro- as well as on the micro-structural levels of the text. What we find in this letter is nothing less than a distinct *syntagmata-coniuncta* structure in which both the more *langue*-determined *dispositio* and the more *parole*-conditioned *amplificatio* have been utilized to their utmost limits.[106] What we ultimately encounter in Paul's accomplishment with regard to the compositional macro- and micro-structures of Romans is in fact a dialectical interdependence between *langue* and *parole,* whereby in view of the *utilitas causae*[107] the *parole* as *ordo artificialis* is as important as the *langue* as *ordo naturalis.*[108]

105. Hellholm 1994a.
106. As to the importance of these insights for the question of Paul's education, see Hellholm 1994a and esp. 1989; and cf. the remark by Johanson 1987: 34: 'It is quite within reason to assume that Paul had some degree of competence regarding Greek rhetorical conventions, besides conventions of Greek letter-writing', and Hübner 1992: 169, who first describes Romans as 'ein *rhetorisches Meisterstück theologischer Argumentation*' and then continues, 'nur wer... den Brief als das Werk eines Mannes mit rhetorischer Kompetenz zu verstehen sucht, nur der kann ihm auch theologisch gerecht werden'.
107. See Lausberg 1973: 245 [§ 446]: 'Das Hauptprinzip der *dispositio* ist die *utilitas.* Ihm zu Dienste stehen zwei Ordnungsprinzipien: der *ordo naturalis* (Sulp. Vict. 14; Fortun. 3,1) und der *ordo artificialis* (Fortun. 3,1) oder *ordo artificiosus* (Sulp. Vict. 14)'. Cf. the quotation from Heinemann and Viehweger above in n. 74.
108. See Lausberg 1976: 28 [§ 47,3]: 'Die *dispositio* sorgt jeweils konkret für parteigünstig wirksame Verteilung von *ordo naturalis* und *ordo artificialis (figura)* im

Bibliography

Barthes, R.
1990 'Die alte Rhetorik: Ein Abriß', in J. Kopperschmidt (ed.), *Rhetorik. Erster Band: Rhetorik als Texttheorie* (Darmstadt: Wissenschaftliche Buchgesellschaft): 35-60 (French original: 'L'ancienne rhétorique: Aide-mémoire', in *Communications* 16 [Paris: Editions du Seuil] 1970: 172-223).

Bauer, B.
1992 'Amplificatio', in G. Üding (ed.), *Historisches Wörterbuch der Rhetorik* (Band 1; Darmstadt: Wissenschaftliche Buchgesellschaft): 445-71.

Baumhauer, O.A.
1986 *Die sophistische Rhetorik: Eine Theorie sprachlicher Kommunikation* (Stuttgart: Metzler).

Betz, H.D.
1979 *Galatians* (Hermeneia; Philadelphia: Fortress Press).
1986 *2 Corinthians 8 and 9* (Hermeneia; Philadelphia: Fortress Press).

Bindemann, W.
1992 *Theologie im Dialog: Ein traditionsgeschichtlicher Kommentar zu Römer 1–11* (Leipzig: Evangelische Verlagsanstalt).

Blomqvist, J.
1969 *The Greek Particles in Hellenistic Prose* (Lund: Gleerup).
1981 *On Adversative Coordination in Ancient Greek and as a Universal Linguistic Phenomenon* (AAU. ASLU. NS) 3.2; Stockholm: Almqvist & Wiksell).

Blomqvist, J., and P.O. Jastrup
1991 *Grekisk-græsk grammatik* (København: Akademisk Forlag).

Boers, H.W.
1978 'Sisyphus and his Rock: Concerning Gerd Theissen, Urchristliche Wundergeschichten', in R.W. Funk (ed.), *Early Christian Miracle Stories* (= *Semeia 11*) (Missoula, MT: Scholars Press): 1-48.

Ganzen der Rede, damit einerseits die Glaubwürdigkeit gesichert und andererseits die Langeweile vermieden wird'. Fuhrmann 1984: 78-79; cf. Klauck 1990: 224: 'Den Ausgleich zu finden zwischen den typischen Gattungsmustern und dem individuellen Einzeltext ist eine ständige Aufgabe der literarischen Kritik'; further Classen 1991: 27-28 and Strecker 1992: 91: 'Eine schematisierende Anwendung der rhetorischen Analyse aufgrund der Theorie der rhetorischen Handbücher, wie sie in der Forschung zuweilen vorgenommen wird, wird weder den antiken noch den neutestamentlichen Briefen gerecht. Primäre Bedeutung kommen vielmehr der genuinen Strukturierung und Argumentation des jeweiligen Autors bei der Analyse seines Werkes zu'.

Bornkamm, G.
1963   'Gesetz und Natur (Röm 2,14-16)', in *Studien zu Antike und Urchristentum: Gesammelte Aufsätze Band II* (BEvT, 28; Munich: Kaiser): 93-118.

Brandenburger, E.
1985   'Paulinische Schriftauslegung in der Kontroverse um das Verheißungswort Gottes (Röm 9)', *ZTK* 82: 1-47.

Breuer, D.
1990   'Vorüberlegungen zu einer pragmatischen Textanalyse (1972)', in J. Kopperschmidt (ed.), *Rhetorik. Band I: Rhetorik als Texttheorie* (Darmstadt: Wissenschaftliche Buchgesellschaft): 91-128.

Classen, C.J.
1991   'Paulus und die antike Rhetorik', *ZNW* 82: 1-33.

Conzelmann, H.
1975   *1 Corinthians* (Hermeneia; Philadelphia: Fortress Press).

van Dijk, T.A.
1980   *Textwissenschaft: Eine interdisziplinäre Einführung* (dtv wissenschaft, 4364; Tübingen: Niemeyer).

Fuhrmann, M.
1984   *Die antike Rhetorik* (Artemis Einführungen, 10; Munich: Artemis).

Göttert, K.-H.
1991   *Einführung in die Rhetorik: Grundbegriffe-Geschichte-Rezeption* (Universitäts-taschenbücher, 1599; Munich: Fink).

Goldstein, J.A.
1968   *The Letters of Demosthenes* (New York: Columbia University Press).

Gülich, E., and U.M. Quasthoff
1985   'Narrative Analysis', in T.A. van Dijk (ed.), *Handbook of Discourse Analysis. II. Dimensions of Discourse* (London: Academic Press): 169-97.

Gülich, E., and W. Raible
1975   'Textsorten-Probleme', in H. Moser *et al.* (eds.), *Linguistische Probleme der Textanalyse* (Jahrbuch des Instituts für deutsche Sprache 1973, Sprache der Gegenwart, Band 35; Düsseldorf: Schwamm): 144-97.

1977a   'Überlegungen zu einer makrostrukturellen Textanalyse: J. Thurber, The Lover and His Lass', in T.A. van Dijk and J.S. Petöfi (eds.), *Grammars and Descriptions* (Research in Text Theory, 1; Berlin: de Gruyter): 132-75.

1977b   *Linguistische Textmodelle* (Universitäts-taschenbücher, 130; Munich: Fink).

Heger, K.
1992   'Langue und Parole', in V. Agel and R. Hessky (eds.), *Offene Fragen—offene Antworten in der Sprachgermanistik* (Reihe Germanistische Linguistik, 128; Tübingen: Niemeyer): 1-13.

Heinemann, W., and D. Viehweger
1991   *Textlinguistik: Eine Einführung* (Reihe Germanistische Linguistik, 115; Tübingen: Niemeyer).

Hellholm, D.

1980   *Das Visionenbuch des Hermas als Apokalypse: Formgeschichtliche und texttheoretische Studien zu einer literarischen Gattung. I. Methodologische Vorüberlegungen und makrostrukturelle Textanalyse* (ConBNT, 13.1; Lund: Gleerup).

1986   'The Problem of Apocalyptic Genre and the Apocalypse of John', in A.Y. Collins (ed.), *Early Christian Apocalypticism: Genre and Social Setting* (= *Semeia 36*) (Decatur, GA: Scholars Press): 13-64.

1989   'Paulus fra Tarsos: Til spørsmålet om Paulus' hellenistiske utdannelse', in T. Eide and T. Hägg (eds.), *Dionysos og Apollon: Religion og samfunn i antikkens Hellas* (Skrifter utgitt av Det norske institutt i Athen, 1; Bergen: Universitetet i Bergen, Klassisk institutt): 259-82.

1990   'The Visions He Saw or: To Encode the Future in Writing: An Analysis of the Prologue of John's Apocalyptic Letter', in T.W. Jennings, Jr (ed.), *Text and Logos: The Humanistic Interpretation of the New Testament* (Festschrift H. Boers; Scholars Press Homage Series; Atlanta, GA: Scholars Press): 109-46.

1991   'Methodological Reflections on the Problem of Definition of Generic Texts', in J.J. Collins and J.H. Charlesworth (eds.), *Mysteries and Revelations: Apocalyptic Studies since the Uppsala Colloquium* (JSPSup, 9; Sheffield: JSOT Press): 135-63.

1994a   'Enthymemic Argumentation in Paul: The Case of Romans 6', in T. Engberg-Pedersen (ed.), *Paul in his Hellenistic Context* (Minneapolis: Fortress Press, in press).

1994b   *Lucian's Icaromenippos: A Textlinguistic and Generic Investigation* (Symbolae Osloenses. Fasc. Supplet. XXVIII; Oslo: Norwegian University Press).

Hellwig, A.

1973   *Untersuchungen zur Theorie der Rhetorik bei Platon und Aristoteles* (Hypomnemata, 38; Göttingen: Vandenhoeck & Ruprecht).

Hommel, H.

1965/1990   'Rhetorik', in C. Andrésen (ed.), *Lexikon der Alten Welt* (Munich: Artemis, 2nd edn): 2611-27.

1981   'Griechische Rhetorik und Beredsamkeit', in E. Vogt (ed.), *Neues Handbuch der Literaturwissenschaft. II. Griechische Literatur* (Wiesbaden: Athenaion): 337-76.

Hübner, H.

1992   'Die Rhetorik und die Theologie: Der Römerbrief und die rhetorische Kompetenz des Paulus', in C.J. Classen and H.-J. Müllenbrock (eds.), *Die Macht des Wortes: Aspekte gegenwärtiger Rhetorikforschung* (Ars rhetorica, 4; Marburg: Hitzeroth): 165-79.

Hughes, F.W.

1989   *Early Christian Rhetoric and 2 Thessalonians* (JSNTSup, 30; Sheffield: JSOT Press).

Jervell, J.

1991   'The Letter to Jerusalem', in K.P. Donfried (ed.), *The Romans Debate* (Peabody, MA: Hendrickson, 2nd edn): 53-64.

Johanson, B.C.
1987   *To All the Brethren: A Text-Linguistic and Rhetorical Approach to I Thessalonians* (ConBNT, 16; Stockholm: Almqvist & Wiksell).
Junker, H.
1976   'Rhetorik und Textgrammatik', *Romanische Forschungen* 88: 378-82.
Kalverkämper, H.
1981   *Orientierung zur Textlinguistik* (Linguistische Arbeiten, 100; Tübingen: Niemeyer).
1983a   'Antike Rhetorik und Textlinguistik: Die Wissenschaft vom Text in altehrwürdiger Modernität', in M. Faust (ed.), *Allgemeine Sprachwissenschaft, Sprachtypologie und Textlinguistik* (Festschrift P. Hartmann; Tübingen: Narr): 349-72.
1983b   'Gattungen, Textsorten, Fachsprachen—Textpragmatische Überlegungen zur Klassifikation', in E.W.B. Hess-Lüttich (ed.), *Textproduktion und Textrezeption* (Forum Angewandte Linguistik, 3; Tübingen: Narr): 91-103.
Kennedy, G.A.
1963   *The Art of Persuasion in Greece* (Princeton, NJ: Princeton University Press).
1972   *The Art of Rhetoric in the Roman World 300 B.C.–A.D. 30* (Princeton, NJ: Princeton University Press).
1983   *Greek Rhetoric under Christian Emperors* (Princeton NJ: Princeton University Press).
1991   *Aristotle on Rhetoric: A Theory of Civic Discourse.* Newly translated with Introduction, Notes and Appendixes (New York: Oxford University Press).
Klauck, H.-J.
1990   'Zur rhetorischen Analyse der Johannesbriefe', *ZNW* 81: 205-24.
Kloppenborg, J.S.
1984   'Tradition and Redaction in the Synoptic Sayings Source', *CBQ* 46: 34-62.
Kümmel, W.G.
1978   'Die Probleme von Römer 9–11 in der gegenwärtigen Forschungslage', in *Heilsgeschehen und Geschichte*, II (Marburg: Elwert): 245-60.
Lampe, P.
1991   'The Roman Christians of Romans 16', in K.P. Donfried (ed.), *The Romans Debate* (Peabody, MA: Hendrickson, 2nd edn): 216-30.
Lausberg, H.
1973   *Handbuch der literarischen Rhetorik: Eine Grundlegung der Literaturwissenschaft* (Munich: Hueber, 2nd edn).
1976   *Elemente der literarischen Rhetorik: Eine Einführung für Studierende der klassischen, romanischen, englischen und deutschen Philologie* (Munich: Hueber, 2nd edn).
Malherbe, A.J.
1988   *Ancient Epistolary Theorists* (SBLSBS, 19; Atlanta, GA: Scholars Press 1988).

1992   'Hellenistic Moralists and the New Testament', in W. Haase and
           H. Temporini (eds.), *ANRW* II, 26.1: 267-333.

Martin, J.
1974   *Antike Rhetorik: Technik und Methode* (Handbuch der
           Altertumswissen-schaft, II.3; Munich: Beck.)

Meeks, W.A.
1990   'On Trusting an Unpredictable God: A Hermeneutical Meditation on
           Romans 9–11', in J.T. Carroll, C.H. Cosgrove and E.E. Johnson (eds.),
           Faith and History: Essays in Honor of Paul W. Meyer (Scholars Press
           Homage Series; Atlanta, GA: Scholars Press): 105-24.

Mitchell, M.M.
1991   *Paul and the Rhetoric of Reconciliation: An Exegetical Investigation
           of the Language and Composition of 1 Corinthians* (Hermeneutische
           Untersuchungen zur Theologie, 28; Tübingen: Mohr).

Plett, H.F.
1975   *Einführung in die rhetorische Textanalyse* (Hamburg: Buske, 3rd edn).

Raible, W.
1979   'Zum Textbegriff und zur Textlinguistik', in J.S. Petöfi (ed.), *Text vs
           Sentence: Basic Questions of Text Linguistics*, I First Part (Papers in
           Textlinguistics, 20.1; Hamburg: Buske): 63-73.

1980   'Was sind Gattungen? Eine Antwort aus semiotischer und
           textlinguistischer Sicht', *Poetica* 12: 320-49.

Schlier, H.
1977   *Der Römerbrief* (Herders Theologischr Kommentar, 6; Freiburg:
           Herder).

Schmithals, W.
1988   *Der Römerbrief: Ein Kommentar* (Gütersloh: Gerd Mohn).

Schnider, F., and W. Stenger
1987   *Studien zum neutestamentlichen Briefformular* (NTTS, 11; Leiden:
           Brill).

Schweinfurth-Walla, S.
1986   *Studien zu den rhetorischen Überzeugungsmitteln bei Cicero und
           Aristoteles* (Tübingen: Niemeyer).

Sieveke, F.G.
1980   *Aristoteles Rhetorik: Übersetzt, mit einer Bibliographie, Erläuterungen
           und einem Nachwort* (Universitäts-taschenbücher, 159; Munich: Fink).

Sprute, J.
1982   *Die Enthymemtheorie der aristotelischen Rhetorik* (Abhandlungen der
           Akademie der Wissenschaften in Göttingen; Philologisch-historische
           Klasse 124; Göttingen: Vandenhoeck & Ruprecht).

Stegemann, E.
1981   *Der eine Gott und die eine Menschheit: Israels Erwählung und die
           Erlösung von Juden und Heiden nach dem Römerbrief*
           (Habilitationsschrift, University of Heidelberg).

Strecker, G.
1992   *Literaturgeschichte des Neuen Testaments* (Universitäts-taschenbücher
           1682; Göttingen: Vandenhoeck & Ruprecht).

Theißen, G.
1983   *Psychologische Aspekte paulinischer Theologie* (FRLANT, 131; Göttingen: Vandenhoeck & Ruprecht).

Vielhauer, P.
1975   *Geschichte der urchristlichen Literatur: Einleitung in das Neue Testament: die Apokryphen und die Apostolischen Väter* (Berlin: de Gruyter).

Wagner, G.
1988   'The Future of Israel: Reflections on Romans 9–11', in W.H. Gloer (ed.), *Eschatology and the New Testament* (Festschrift G.R. Beasley-Murray; Peabody, MA: Hendrickson): 77-112.

Wilckens, U.
1980   *Der Brief an die Römer. 2. Teilband: Röm 6–11* (EKKNT, 6.2; Neukirchen–Vluyn: Neukirchener Verlag).

Wörner, M.H.
1981   ' "Pathos" als Überzeugungsmittel in der Rhetorik des Aristoteles', in I. Craemer-Ruegenberg (ed.), *Pathos, Affekt, Gefühl* (Freiburg: Alber): 53-78.
1984   'Selbstpräsentation im "Ethos des Redners"', *Zeitschrift für Sprachwissenschaft* 3: 43-64.
1985   ' "Pistis" und der argumentierende Umgang mit reputablen Meinungen in der Rhetorik des Aristoteles', in J. Kopperschmidt and H. Schanze (eds.), *Argumente—Argumentation: Interdisziplinäre Problemzugänge* (Munich: Fink): 9-17.
1992   *Das Ethische in der Rhetorik des Aristoteles* (Alber-Reihe. Praktische Philosophie, 33; Freiburg: Alber).

Wooten, C.W.
1987   *Hermogenes' On Types of Style* (Chapel Hill, NC: University of North Carolina Press).

STRATEGIES OF PERSUASION IN ROMANS 1.16-17

Johannes N. Vorster

Introduction

I have more than one objective with this essay. First, a methodological objective. I will approach Rom. 1.16-17 from the perspective of an interactional model (cf. also Vorster 1990), rather than confine myself to the categories of classical rhetoric only. The reason for this lies mainly in the wider scope of what modern approaches to communication and interaction have to offer. Violi (1985: 160) has argued that the genre-typical element of a letter is its own communicativeness. This simply means that even though the propositional content of a letter may be zero, such as that of a 'thank you' note, or a little more than zero, such as that from your bank manager, it still communicates. If communicative intent can be distinguished as one of the diagnostic components of the letter genre even though its propositional contents amount to zero, the informative has to be seen in terms of the communicative. Furthermore, if a letter is never without its communicativeness, our concern should be less with what a letter says, than with what a letter intends to do or to achieve. This is even more urgent where our concern is with letters from an ancient world where the dissemination of information was not as important as their effects and what they could accomplish (cf. Tompkins 1980; also Stowers 1986: 15). Although classical rhetoric of course also emphasized the communicative, the analysis of the communicative phenomenon, that is, how communication works, proceeded from the social values of its day. For example, when Aristotle makes us aware of the various audiences of his day, they are first related to the social situations of the courts, the general assembly and the world of praise and blame (cf. *Rhet.* 1.3.1). As we all know, these situations are depicted as directly responsible for the rhetorical genres and also the corresponding rhetorical structures. Since classical rhetorical categories are inextricably linked to the social situation, it can be asked whether these categories do not contribute more to our knowledge of the ancient social world than to our knowledge of how human interaction works. That does not devalue the study of ancient classical rhetoric. It does mean, however, that if we are interested in the interaction of biblical writings, that is, in the way these writings were intended to interact within rhetorical situations, we will have to take cognizance of what is happening in disciplines studying the same phenomenon.

My first objective is to use Rom. 1.16-17, therefore, as an example of how the boundaries of rhetoric can be expanded to include insights from various audience-oriented approaches, such as reception-criticism, conversational analysis, pragmatics and modern rhetoric. Several dangers lurk in such a pragmatic and eclectic approach, such as superficiality, the use of conflicting and inappropriate theories and being 'Jack of all trades, master of none', but the vast amount of information which has become available on human interaction encourages me to explore further possibilities. I plead, therefore, for methodological expansion, rather than exclusion, modification rather than antithesis, in 'Perelmanian' terms, *dissociation* rather than 'disassociation'.

My second objective pertains to Rom. 1.16-17 itself. Rom. 1.16-17 can be seen as a nucleus in which many of the letter's problems and arguments are condensed and anticipated. For that very reason it is commonly held (and rightly so) as the theme of the letter. However, mainly owing to theological and ecclesiastical traditions, the theme of the letter has been restricted to the ideas of 'God's righteousness' and 'justification by faith'. Such an ideational approach not only fails to clarify a large section of the letter (cf. Boers 1981: 1), but it also neglects the various social and interpersonal relationships, thereby treating the text as if it were a source of information on a coherent theological system (cf. also Stendahl 1976). It is exactly of these relationships and their power over the formation of discourse that rhetorical criticism has made us aware.

I will argue then that the theme of the letter has a pragmatic objective. A positive assessment of the good news is made because of the advantages it entails not only for the Jews, but especially for non-Jewish believers. Not only is the theme of the letter used to identify yet again with the implied audience,[1] but it also serves to confirm the adherence of the non-Jewish believer to the good news.

Owing to this two-pronged objective, various problems pertaining to both methodology and the passage itself will have to be left out of consideration. It will not be possible, for example, to present a complete methodological account. Where the need arises, the appropriate technical jargon has been treated by means of a 'footnote'. Aspects such as the rhetorical situation (theoretical and in the letter to the Romans) and the purpose of this letter were also sacrificed in order to pay more attention to strategies within Rom. 1.16-17 itself.

The Theme of the Letter as Transitus

Although the transitional character of Rom. 1.16-17 has often been observed, its description has been in categories distracting attention from the interactional aspects of this section, while simultaneously suggesting the 'ideational'. Two examples must suffice.

The first comes from classical rhetoric. Kennedy (1984: 153) states that the 'proposition is given enthymematic form by the reason adduced in verse 17', thereby suggesting that 1.16-17 could be taken as *propositio*. That it could be a *propositio* can certainly not be directly rejected. However, there are a few aspects which cause problems for 1.16-17 as *propositio*.

First, a *propositio* as a *pars orationis* is usually in some way or the other associated with the statement of facts or, as it is better known, the *narratio*. It either can be the conclusion of a *narratio* or could replace the *narratio* as a compacted and summarizing form of *narratio* (cf. Lausberg 1960: 189). The question is whether either of these forms is valid for the letter to the Romans. Jewett (1986: 284; 1987: 2-3) sidesteps this problem by finding a *narratio* in 1.13-15. However, the past events portrayed in 1.13b and 1.13c portray a hypothetical situation and function to establish an ethical appeal and cannot be described as a *narratio*.

Secondly, is it possible then to find in 1.16-17 a *propositio* as a replacement or compacted form of *narratio*? This seems to be what

---

1. As a reception-critical category the implied audience should be seen as a personified, interpretative construct which functions as an 'inventional tool' in the production of the text. It should not be equated with the 'real-flesh-and-blood' audiences, but is rather the audience as visualized and entextualized by Paul.

Kennedy (1984: 153) has suggested. If that were the case, the *propositio* would be seen here as the more rational form of expression and would approach the enthymeme.

However, although enthymemes usually have to be constructed, the construction of an enthymeme from 1.16-17 is extremely problematic owing to the polysemic character of the terms involved. Furthermore, certain affective aspects will also be lost, such as *litotes* and the *ethos* appeal of these utterances. Finally, making 1.16-17 a *propositio* could create the impression that the discourse coherently corresponds in neatly demarcated sections (cf. Nygren 1949). Dahl (1977: 79), emphasizing the orality component of the text, cautions against precisely demarcated sections and pleads instead for a consideration of the transitional in Paul's 'flow of thought'. It would therefore probably be wiser to see 1.16-17 simply as *transitus*, while acknowledging propositional elements.

The second example comes from epistolography. Roberts (1986a: 197; 1986b: 96, 97, 98; 1988: 85-87) has correctly identified this section as a discrete period, making a transition to the body of the letter. However, the criterion for its identification is the presence of a 'credal statement' and its function is described as the determination of 'the essential core of the argument to be made by the letter' (1986a: 197; 1988: 85). Besides the fact that such a description presupposes a letter consisting of a coherent system of thought, it also diverts attention from the interactional elements.

While I do not wish to devalue the results of classical rhetoric or epistolography, they should be integrated within an interactional approach. In the case of Rom. 1.16-17 the transitional character is also confirmed by the deictic elements in this section.[2] In 1.8-15

---

2.   While not totally denying the transitional character of 1.16-17, it is particularly studies with a thematic intent which are inclined to see 1.16-17 as part of a larger section consisting of 1.16-3.20 (cf. Ruijs 1964: 260-66; Bassler 1982: 123-31). Under the influence of structuralism, recurrent words and phrases, even repetition in stylistic structure, are emphasized. While these aspects undoubtedly should be considered in determining the coherence of a text, functional aspects such as deixis should also play a role. From a rhetorical perspective, Elliott (1990: 108-17) also prefers to read 1.16-32 as a unity, which he describes as the starting point of the argumentation. However, it is exactly the neglect to take the deictic elements seriously which caused him to link 1.16-17 with 1.18-32. According to him, 1.15-18 not only announces Paul's intention to evangelize the Romans, but also begins to do so. Since Romans is addressed to Gentiles, themes which they would recognise from

person-deictics in the form of first and second person pronouns abounded. In 1.16a the first person still functions to orient the audience to the viewpoint of the author, but then he disappears and τὸ εὐαγγέλιον (1.16a) takes over. The article τό functions as a discourse deictic[3] referring the audience to εὐαγγέλιον which has already been introduced in 1.1, 9, 15. It should be noted that in all these cases the encoded author was closely associated with the good news and the same happens in 1.16a. As such 1.16a still links up with the preceding 1.1-15, but where it served to construct his person in 1.1-15, to define his role and justify his right to address them, εὐαγγέλιον is now foregrounded and its purpose is outlined (1.16b). It should be noted that all other deictics function in relationship to τὸ εὐαγγέλιον. Thus the person-deictic θεός (1.16b) functions, first, to qualify the good news and the good news functions as the location in which, secondly, the righteousness of God (1.17a) is manifested. That τὸ εὐαγγέλιον has shifted into focus is also confirmed by the discourse deictic ἐν αὐτῷ (1.17a) which refers back to τὸ εὐαγγέλιον. Furthermore, by means of the social deictics Ἰουδαῖος and Ελλην, the audience has been oriented to a known ethnographical distinction, thereby associating the good news with social relationships.

The quotation from Hab. 2.4 is explicitly marked by καθὼς γέγραπται, thereby referring the implied audience to a corpus of shared knowledge and linking the immediately preceding discourse to that corpus of knowledge. The quotation appropriately rounds off the transition.

Because of the transitional character of 1.16-17 it can, in terms of the discourse, be called the *transitus*.

---

their own beginnings are evoked in 1.16-32. However, the person-deictic αὐτοί clearly has the function to point away from the implied audience. Associating the αὐτοί with the Gentile implied audience at this stage of the rhetorical process would have been communicative suicide.

3. Fillmore (1971: 70) presents various ways in which discourse deictics function in English to 'point' to preceding or following discourse. In Greek the article can fulfill an 'anaphoric' role when it refers back 'to what is known or assumed to be known' (Blaß and Debrunner 1961: 132). That τὸ εὐαγγέλιον is definitely concerned with shared knowledge can also be seen by the omission of any qualifier.

The Role and Function of Litotes *in Romans 1.16*

Although *litotes* is not a frequently used figure of style in the *Corpus Paulinum* and although it is often difficult to establish whether Paul really intended to use *litotes*, Rom. 1.16a can be seen as *litotes* (cf. Vorster 1979: 219-26). *Litotes* is generally acknowledged as a figure of style aimed at reader-engagement.[4] Paul alerts, therefore, his audience to the specific applicability of this utterance concerning the good news to their situation. However, the function of *litotes* is not only to highlight.

Leech (1983: 147) has made some particularly interesting observations concerning *litotes* from a conversational analytic perspective which are very important for our understanding of Paul's use of *litotes* in this context. Comparing *hyperbole* and *litotes*, he describes the latter as 'a salutary tactic…to restore credibility by using descriptions which so obviously fall short of what could be truthfully asserted that they cannot be supposed exaggerated'. It is first used, therefore, to restore credibility. He mentions a further aspect, which should receive our attention. This pertains to the fact that *litotes* can be used to minimize negative connotations. He states (1983: 148): 'litotes is a way of underplaying aspects of meaning which are pragmatically disfavoured'. Besides credibility then, it also functions to provide a positive connotation.[5]

4. According to Perelman and Olbrechts-Tyteca (1969: 292) *litotes* can be seen as a form of the argument of direction, because the readers are led in a certain direction, only to be tugged away in an opposite direction owing to the negation. It could be summarized as a frustration of anticipation. Brandt (1970: 158) describes *litotes* as a 'stance figure, designed to maintain a sympathetic relation between speaker (or writer) and his audience'. Both Lausberg (1960: 304-305) and Leeman and Braet (1987: 105) classify *litotes* as a trope and more specifically as a periphrasis combining both irony and emphasis. The intended meaning of *litotes* can only be understood 'auf Grund der zwischen dem Sprechenden und dem Angesprochenen bestehenden prästabilierten Sympathie' (Lausberg 1960: 305). Conditional for the correct understanding of *litotes* would be: a shared value-system; a shared attitude towards this value-system; the competency to recognise the ironical and appreciate the emphatic.

5. *Litotes* happens when the *maxim of quality* of the conversational principle is exploited. The *maxim of quality* entails adherence to a conversational contribution which must be true. For the *maxim of quality* to be upheld two conditions usually apply. First, do not say what you believe to be false and, secondly, do not say that

If these observations are applied to Paul's use of *litotes* in 1.16a, it means, first, that Paul wants to restore or confirm the credibility of the good news for his implied audience. Secondly, according to his perspective on the situation concerning the relationship between non-Jewish believers and Jews, it could mean that there was probably a need to underplay disfavourable connotations attached to the good news. Both the use of *litotes* and the use of the lexeme ἐπαισχύνεσθαι suggest that the possibility existed of the good news being tainted with shame. It would be fair to assume that the social value-system of the implied audience, pertaining to shame and honour, is thereby activated (cf. Moxnes 1988a: 210; 1988b: 63-64). When Paul uses ἐπαισχύνεσθαι in litotic form and in association with both δύναμις and θεός, he indicates to the implied audience to what extent he is willing to confirm the credibility of the good news. The honour which he assigns to the good news is exceptionally high and would mean that 1.16a could be translated as: 'I am boasting about the good news...' Simultaneously, by using *litotes* Paul underplays or devalues the element of shame; as such the good news is 'distanced' from that which is disfavoured by ancient society.[6] By confirming the credibility of the good news and simultaneously underplaying any disfavourable connotations, Paul identifies with the Gentile implied audience.

A Pragmatic Argument

The question is, however, what entitles Paul to claim such status, so high a degree of honour for the good news? The answer to this

for which you lack adequate evidence (cf. Grice 1975; Brown and Levinson 1978: 100; Levinson 1983: 101). In the case of Rom. 1.16a the utterance obviously falls short of what could truthfully be asserted—Paul is everything but ashamed of the good news. The implied audience would have been able to make this inference since the preceding discourse has already suggested Paul's pride in the good news (cf. 1.1, 15).

    6. Corrigan (1986: 24), who also applies the honour/shame model to interpret 1.16a, overlooks the litotic aspect of ἐπαισχύνεσθαι. The lexeme ἐπαισχύνεσθαι then becomes confrontational. Paul does not care, according to him, that his gospel contradicts the values of honour/shame. Precisely the opposite is the case in the letter to the Romans! In the letter to the Romans it is Paul's concern to provide the good news with status. Another example of Paul's non-confrontational, but rather socially conformable approach can be seen in Rom. 13.1-7 (cf. also Heiligenthal 1983; Moxnes 1988a: 215).

question lies in the causal sentence in its totality and not only in the first part of this sentence (contra Elliott 1990: 111). Not simply God's power, but God's power which liberates not only Jews, but also Gentiles, conveys status on the good news and justifies Paul's appraisal. As such 1.16 can be seen as a *pragmatic argument* (Perelman and Olbrechts-Tyteca 1969: 267-70; Perelman 1982: 82-83). A pragmatic argument is a manifestation of sequential argumentation, in which an event or fact is favourably or disfavourably appraised in terms of its consequences. In this case the good news is extremely favourably appraised (litotic ἐπαισχύνεσθαι)[7] because of its liberating consequences for every believer.[8] What happens in a *pragmatic argument* is that the values associated with the 'end', that is, the consequences, are usually transposed onto the 'means'. The value of the means is relative, therefore, to the value of the end. In the case of 1.16 the 'means' (the good news) is very positively rated in terms of the end (the liberation of not only Jews, but also Greeks). That means that in the case of 1.16 the 'God-empowered' liberation of not only the Jew, but also the Greek, makes the good news worthy of the highest praise. The ultimate objective of the good news, that is, liberation, is then the criterion for its assessment and this ultimate objective is given in pragmatic ethnographical terms. The good news is to the advantage of Jews and Greeks. If the implied audience can be characterized as Gentile, the identification with them again becomes

---

7.   The performative utterance οὐ γὰρ ἐπαισχύνομαι τὸ εὐαγγέλιον (1.16a) can be seen as a *verdictive*. According to Traugott and Pratt (1980: 229) a *verdictive* belongs to a class of illocutionary acts 'that deliver a finding as to value or fact, and thus rate some entity or situation on a scale'. Because this utterance is a *verdictive*, neither a psychological nor a confessional interpretation is viable. For a psychological or a confessional interpretation an *expressive* would have been more appropriate. From a different perspective, Vorster (1979: 211-12, 237) has also rejected the psychological as well as a 'traditions-geschichtliche' interpretation. Paul thus makes an assessment or appraisal of the good news.

8.   An assessment must always be made according to a certain norm or standard. The assessment must take place according to a certain scale on which the entity is rated (Traugott and Pratt 1980: 211-12). In the case of 1.16 the norm is pragmatic, because here the liberating consequence functions as the standard of evaluation. Paul can rank the good news highly because it is a power of God which liberates πᾶς ὁ πιστεύων, Ἰουδαῖος τε πρῶτον καὶ Ἕλλην (every believer, the Jew first, but also the Greek).

very clear. The good news can be highly appreciated, because it is there for their benefit.

It is possible, however, to delineate the relationship between Jew and Greek a little closer and illustrate that the focus indeed lies on the 'Greek', which emphasises Paul's intention to identify with his non-Jewish audience. To divide 'everyone who believes' into two groups, namely the Jews and the Greeks, can only happen from a Jewish perspective (cf. Fraiken 1986: 96; Dunn 1988: 40). That the good news described as a 'power of God' would pertain to the Jews is therefore fairly obvious. As a matter of fact, their priority is confirmed in status and chronology by the adverb πρῶτον (Fraiken 1986: 96; Dunn 1988: 40; Wedderburn 1988: 89; Ziesler 1989: 69). The surprising element from the perspective of the Jews, however, is the inclusion of the 'non-Jews'. As such it is the 'non-Jews' who receive the focus.

This is confirmed when we approach the utterance from a conversational analytic perspective. The *maxim of quantity* has been exploited by the use of πᾶς.[9] In designating the believers as the group to which God's power is applicable, he qualifies them by using πᾶς. By the use of πᾶς he has already made the strongest possible claim with the evidence at hand. Yet, this does not seem sufficient, since the *maxim of quantity* is again exploited by the ethnographical elaboration. The implicature is to maximize agreement with his implied audience, to emphasize the value of the good news for them. Because the good news is in any case appropriate to the Jews, the πᾶς is there specifically to emphasize the inclusion of the non-Jews. Jews and non-Jews do not function on exactly the same level (contra Ziesler 1989: 69). The inclusion of the Jew is presupposed, the inclusion of the Greek is new information. The exploitation of the *maxim of quantity* is therefore not so much to claim universality, as to bring the inclusion of the non-Jews into focus. This then also confirms what Fraiken (1986: 96) asserted, namely that the priority of the Jews 'means not that all are equal, but that the Gentiles have been received within a

---

9.   Exploitation of the *maxim of quantity* means exploiting a conversational principle which requires that the right amount of information be given, not more and not less than the situation requires (cf. Grice 1975; Brown and Levinson 1978: 100; Leech 1983: 8; Levinson 1983: 101). Where either more or less than the required information is given, an implicature has to be made in which case a new set of principles, namely politeness principles, come into operation. The implicature in this case seems to maximize agreement (Leech 1983: 132, 138).

purpose of God initiated among the Jews'.[10]

Paul then confirms the advantages which the good news entails for the non-Jewish implied audience. Although they are very gently reminded of the priority of the Jews, they are now to share the liberating power of the good news with the Jews. It is precisely because of this benefit, this opportunity which is now also available to the Gentiles, that Paul can be exceptionally proud of the good news.

Dissociation in Romans 1.17

How has this opportunity become possible? On what grounds can it be asserted that the liberating power of the good news has now also become the privilege of the Gentiles? The answer to these questions lies in 1.17, because the pragmatic relation between 1.16b and 1.17a can best be described as an explanatory expansion.[11] That means that 1.17a simultaneously explains and expands 1.16b. The explanatory element lies in the explanation why the good news is a 'power of God for everyone who believes'. By means of the discourse deictic ἐν αὐτῷ the good news is portrayed as the process in which the righteousness of God is aligned with πίστις. The element of expansion lies in the generalization which has been made concerning the relationship between righteousness and faith.

Because 1.17a can be described as an explanatory expansion it stands in an indissoluble relationship with 1.16b and because it expands on 1.16b its concern is still the benefit of 'not only the Jew, but also the Gentile'. The generalization is pragmatically caused by a state of affairs in which the good news is assessed as to the advantage of not only the Jews but also the Gentiles. Although it is a generalization, it should not be seen as a general assertion concerning the

10. Instead of 'not only the Jews, but also the Gentiles' for which one actually would have expected the use of οὐ μόνον...ἀλλὰ καί, the phrase could perhaps also be paraphrased as: 'the Jew, obviously yes, but especially the Greek', expressing with the word 'especially' the focus which lies on the Gentiles.

11. Ferrara (1985: 146) indicates that a speech act enters an explanatory relationship with another if it serves as an answer to the question 'why p?' where p refers to the propositional content of the dominant act. The dominant act should be seen in terms of the relationship between two utterances. An expansion must relate to a state of the world that includes the state of the world the dominant act points to. It can make the dominant act either more general or more specific.

righteousness of God, but rather a generalization which explains the newly acquired status of the Gentiles; a generalization which intended to indicate why the good news also benefits the Gentiles; a generalization intended to substantiate the assessment of Paul's good news.

The reason why this explanatory expansion serves as a substantiation for the state of affairs depicted in 1.16b lies in the redefinition of the righteousness of God. Paul can boast of the advantages of the good news for the non-Jews because the righteousness of God has to be redefined.

It is in this respect that Perelman and Olbrechts-Tyteca's notion of *dissociation* comes to mind. According to Perelman and Olbrechts-Tyteca (1969: 413) *dissociation* is concerned with the modification of a concept's structure. Although it assumes the original unity of a concept or system of thought, it is usually prompted by an *incompatibility* and promotes a radical change. It can be visually expressed as a pair consisting of term I and term II, the latter being the criterion for the former. Term I is usually that which is to be disputed and is depicted as the illusionary, the immediate, while term II is depicted as authentic truth.

Although no indication of an *incompatibility*, prompting *dissociation*, is given in 1.16-17, passages like 2.1-5, 17-29 and 10.2-4 suggest that, in Paul's view on the rhetorical situation of this letter, an incompatibility existed in their understanding of God's righteousness.[12] Their absolutistic and nationalistic claims on the righteousness of God gave them a distorted view on their own status and on their relationship with the non-Jews.[13]

It is this incompatible behaviour and attitude of the Jews concerning the righteousness of God which prompted *dissociation* already in the theme of the letter. It is from this 'need', this problem of Jewish misunderstanding, that the theme of the letter emerges.[14] The

12. The identification of *incompatibilities* in these passages has been worked out in more detail in my dissertation, titled 'The Rhetorical Situation of the Letter to the Romans—An Interactional Approach' (unpublished doctoral dissertation, University of Pretoria).

13. Dunn's (1983) 'new perspective on Paul' clearly highlights this aspect. Although he has mainly emphasized Gal. 2.16, he points out that the heart of Jewish misunderstanding lies in an absolutization of 'covenantal nomism'.

14. The problem of Jewish misunderstanding should not be confused with the

selfacclaimed superior position of the Jew has become a cause of offence to the Gentiles of whom the implied audience formed a part. A number of aspects indicate that *dissociation* is indeed at work in 1.16-17. We have already indicated that an *incompatibility* concerning δικαιοσύνη existed within Paul's perspective of Jewish understanding. There is, therefore, a need which must be fulfilled. The type of utterance also has the same implication. As an expansion it generalizes, indicating that some or other fundamental principle is at work; as explanatory it refers us to the propositional content of the preceding speech act and specifically the benefit which the good news entails for the believer—the implied audience is given a reason why the good news is depicted as 'a power of God for the believer' by means of an underlying principle. The good news is thus seen as a process in which a redefinition of the righteousness of God is appropriate. That a *re*-definition of righteousness is in order in this case can be seen first by the fact that the concept as such is assumed to be known, but secondly, also by the use of the lexeme ἀποκαλύπτειν (cf. also Dunn 1988: 48). We have seen that the circle of believers has been divided from a Jewish perspective (1.16); that Jewish perspective has still been retained. The righteousness of God is taken from a Jewish perspective, but is said to have experienced a modification.

conflict-hypothesis. That Paul's concern is not a conflict between Jewish Christians and Gentile Christians in the communities of Rome, but a general problem which he visualises between Jews and Gentiles can be seen in a universalizing tendency. The relationship between Jews and Gentiles is frequently portrayed on a universal level. This can be seen in the use of πᾶς (1.16-17; 3.9, 20, 22; 4.11; 10.4, 11), ἕκαστος (2.6) and ἄνθρωπος (1.18; 2.1, 3, 9, 16; 3.4, 28; 5.12, 18; 9.20). The universal tendency also features when quotations, traditions or allusions from the Old Testament are used to portray the relationship between Jews and Gentiles (cf. the use of Gen. 3 and the Wisdom of Solomon in 1.18-32; the example of Abraham as father of Jews and Gentiles in Rom. 4; the Adam-Christ typology in Rom. 5; the historical origins of Israel in Rom. 9 and the eschatological mutual joy and worship among Jews and Gentiles in the *recapitulatio* (15.7-13). It is then within a salvation-historical and cosmological perspective that the Jews are being portrayed as a misunderstanding nation. If the tension between Jews and Gentiles caused by this misunderstanding of the Jews is indeed a component of the problem of the rhetorical situation, it functions on a general level. What is at stake is probably the gradual, general process of separation between mother- and daughter-movement. Paul portrays the Jewish nation, however, as a misunderstanding nation. By means of this portrayal he identifies with the Gentile implied audience.

The modification of the Jewish understanding of God's righteousness lies in the introduction of faith. Whether we understand the vague ἐκ πίστεως εἰς πίστιν as 'from God's faithfulness to man's faith' or 'faith from beginning to end' or 'on the grounds of faith in view of faith', the point Paul wishes to make is the association of δικαιοσύνη with πίστις. What has to be removed from the notion of δικαιοσύνη is the Jewish over-estimation of the law. It is πίστις within the structure of *dissociation* which functions as the normative factor, the catalyst which accomplishes the modification. As such it functions as term II, which gives a modified dimension to δικαιοσύνη, which in this case functions as term I.

A view of the righteousness of God which is not associated with faith can, therefore, according to Paul, not be a 'true' and legitimate perspective. Faith has to function as the criterion for what can be regarded as a 'true' righteousness (1.17; 3.21-22, 25-26, 27-31; 4.24; 9.30, 33; 10.4, 10-11; 11.20). A perspective on righteousness which makes νόμος the criterion for true or real righteousness is, therefore, false (3.31; 4.13, 14; 9.31-32; 10.3-4). On the other hand, νόμος as such need not be discarded (7.7), but it has to be appreciated from the perspective of faith. Whenever it poses a threat to faith, it should be seen as an over-estimation. The definition of Jew and Gentile is in the same vein. A 'real' Jew is a Jew who believes and not necessarily one who is supported by the law and who has been circumcised (2.17-18, 23, 28; 10.6-13) just as a 'real' Gentile is someone who does not believe. As such an uncircumcised Gentile can be a 'circumcised Jew' (2.26, 29)! The same applies to the example of Abraham. Abraham becomes father of all by virtue of his faith and not because he is a Jew and the first to be circumcised (4.3, 5, 9, 11, 12, 13, 16).

It is possible to multiply examples in which this technique played a role in the letter to the Romans. This is especially so when one considers that various other *dissociations* can be discerned in the letter, which stand in close association with *dissociations* in which faith functions as criterion. It is important, however, to emphasize one remaining aspect concerning *dissociation* in 1.16-17, namely its relationship to the *pragmatic argument* I identified in 1.16.

We have seen that 1.16 can be identified as a *pragmatic argument* and we have seen that 1.17 can be described as an explanatory expansion of this argument. That means that the *pragmatic argument* has been embedded in the technique of *dissociation*. To put it differently:

dissociation has taken place to serve the *pragmatic argument*, that is, to explain and simultaneously to expand the preceding utterance. The *pragmatic argument* assessed the good news for the implied readers and assured them that the good news is honourable. It is honourable, because it is to the benefit of Gentiles specifically. *Dissociation* provides the implied audience with the underlying argument; it can be to the benefit of the Gentiles, because the righteousness of God should be differently interpreted, namely from the perspective of faith. Modifying the righteousness of God, 'dissociating' the link with the law, but 'associating' with faith, the good news gives the Gentiles a position within the circle of the Jews. Righteousness modified, therefore, entails advantages for the Gentiles who believe. Because of *dissociation* the *pragmatic argument* has become possible.

Embedding the *pragmatic argument* into the *dissociative argument* does not entitle an interpretation which makes justification by faith the theme of the letter on the grounds that *dissociation* validates one or other underlying principle. On the contrary, the incompatibilities giving rise to *dissociation* are usually due to a disparity between values and this disparity often originates from a changing value-system. A change in value-system is effected, however, by social groups. This is then clearly also the case in the letter to the Romans. The *dissociation* of the notion δικαιοσύνη is sociologically determined. Even the choice of this concept, which reflects a Jewish perspective on the covenant relationship, confirms Paul's desire to address a sociological problem.

Embedding the pragmatic argument into the dissociative process indicates Paul's concern to assure the implied audience of the value of the good news and specifically its benefits for them. By means of the *dissociation* of the notion δικαιοσύνη, Paul locates the value of the good news for the implied audience within the wider problem of Jew versus Gentile confrontation and integration.

The Quotation

The quotation from Hab. 2.4 functions authoritatively[15] with respect to the implied audience but subordinately in relationship to the preceding utterance. The utterance in 1.17b can, in its relationship to

15. Plett (1986: 304) indicates that this kind of quotation can be called an 'authoritative quotation', because its claim to authority is not doubted, but accepted.

1.17a, best be described as a comment.[16] Ferrara (1985: 147) describes a comment as an utterance in which the speaker expresses his attitude, feeling or opinion concerning another speech act. However, by referring the implied audience to Scripture, the impression is created that the comment is not that of the encoded author, but of Scripture itself. Their mutual symbol of authority affirmatively expresses its opinion on Paul's preceding explanatory expansion. That Scripture functions as mutual symbol of authority indicates yet again Paul's orientation from the value-system of the Jews. As such it functions to sanction Paul's preceding redefinition of righteousness from the Jewish value-system itself.

Although the quotation functions as authoritative confirmation of Paul's redefinition, its value should not be overestimated as has happened in the past (cf. Nygren 1949). It does not function to determine the rest of the letter, but functions in a subordinate role to 1.17a—it serves as an authoritative comment (cf. also Dunn 1988: 46).

Because 1.17b functions as an authoritative comment to the preceding it should be understood in terms of the preceding explanatory expansion. As such, ὁ δίκαιος is qualified by ἐκ πίστεως.[17] Just as in 1.17a, *dissociation* is also put to use in 1.17b. As faith has become the critical norm for the righteousness of God, the righteous person is now determined by 'faith'. Therefore, faith has also here become the critical norm for whoever can be regarded as righteous. The righteous person has been 'dissociated' from his ethnographical safeguarding; faith opens the way to righteousness also for the non-Jew. The righteous person is an honourable man, not because of certain nationalistic 'in-group' identity markers, but because of faith (cf. also Moxnes 1988a: 210).

When ἐκ πίστεως is taken in conjunction with ὁ δίκαιος, the same interaction between *dissociation* and the *pragmatic argument*, which we have seen in 1.16-17a, can again be discerned. Just as in the case of 1.16-17a, the *pragmatic argument* has been embedded in the

16. The close relationship between 1.17a and 1.17b can be seen in the correspondence of ἀποκαλύπτεσθαι with γέγραφθαι (both in the passive); δικαιοσύνη with δίκαιος; ἐκ πίστεως with ἐκ πίστεως.

17. Louw (1976: 85) and Vorster (1979: 234-35) come to a similar conclusion based on the construction of the sentence and on analysis of the immediate structure. One should be careful, however, not to make 'immediate constituent analysis' and formal similarities the only criteria to establish coherence.

dissociative. By means of ζήσεσθαι the implied audience is pointed to future benefits. Because the righteous man is now constituted by faith, he is assured of 'real' life. Seen within the relationship of the Gentile implied audience and Jews, the implied audience is assured that owing to faith, the notion of the righteous person is reconstituted; this redefinition of the righteous person will be to the advantage not only of the Jews, but also of the Gentiles.

To summarise, the quotation reveals exactly the same underlying argumentative structure as Paul's assessment and explanatory expansion. The *pragmatic argument* has been embedded in the technique of *dissociation.* As such, the quotation serves to confirm authoritatively from the perspective of the value-system of the Jews that Gentiles can now also, owing to faith, be righteous.

Conclusion

I have indicated that when rhetoric as interaction becomes the point of departure, the possibility exists that various audience-oriented disciplines can be integrated. Furthermore, when the boundaries of rhetoric are thus expanded, it comes to light that various kinds of strategies function complementarily and should be taken into account. To restrict rhetoric to the argumentative, or to questions and problems concerning rhetorical structure only, ignores the social relationships from which and towards which the argument develops. Reading the letter from the perspective of an interactional model compels us to take cognizance of the conditions of utterance, thereby focusing our attention on the various intrapersonal aspects of each utterance. Even when these conditions of utterance often also prove themselves to be problematic, they still help us to explore 'between the lines' and make us aware of the 'other-than-cognitive' forces which shaped our texts.

Finally, when Rom. 1.16-17 is approached from an interactional perspective, the ideational recedes to the background, while the social relationships shift into focus. Paul's objective is not the introduction of God's righteousness, but rather the positive assessment and confirmation of the good news. The criterion for this assessment lies in the pragmatic advantages it entails for the Gentile implied audience. As such the *transitus* also serves to confirm Paul's positive identification with his audience.

Bibliography

Bassler, J.M.
    1982   *Divine Impartiality: Paul and a Theological Axiom* (SBLDS, 59;
              Chico: Scholars Press).
Blass, F., and A. Debrunner
    1961   *A Greek Grammar of the New Testament and Other Early Christian
              Literature* (Chicago: University of Chicago Press).
Boers, H.
    1981   'The Problem of Jews and Gentiles in the Macro-structure of
              Romans', *Neot* 15: 1-11.
Brandt, W.J.
    1970   *The Rhetoric of Argumentation* (New York: Bobbs-Merrill).
Brown, P., and S. Levinson
    1978   'Universals in Language Usage: Politeness Phenomena', in E. Goody
              (ed.), *Questions and Politeness* (Cambridge: Cambridge University
              Press): 56-289.
Corrigan, G.M.
    1986   'Paul's Shame for the Gospel', *BTB* 16: 23-27.
Dahl, N.A.
    1977   'The Missionary Theology in the Epistle to the Romans', in N.A. Dahl
              (ed.), *Studies in Paul* (Minneapolis: Augsburg): 70-94.
Dunn, J.D.G.
    1983   'The New Perspective on Paul', *BJRL* 65: 95-122.
    1988   *Romans 1–8* (WBC, 38a; Dallas: Word Books).
Elliott, N.
    1990   *The Rhetoric of Romans: Argumentative Constraint and Strategy and
              Paul's Dialogue with Judaism* (JSNTSup, 45; Sheffield: JSOT Press).
Ferrara, A.
    1985   'Pragmatics', in T.A. van Dijk (ed.), *Handbook of Discourse Analysis*
              (London: Academic Press): II, 137-59.
Fillmore, C.J.
    1971   *Santa Cruz Lectures on Deixis* (Bloomington: Indiana Linguistics
              Club).
Fraiken, D.
    1986   'The Rhetorical Function of the Jews in Romans', in P. Richardson
              (ed.), *Anti-Judaism in Early Christianity: Paul and the Gospels*
              (Studies in Christianity and Judaism, 2; Ontario: Wilfrid Laurier
              University Press): I, 91-106.
Grice, H.P.
    1975   'Logic and Conversation', in P. Cole and J.L. Morgan (eds.), *Syntax
              and Semantics: Speech Acts* (New York: Academic Press): III, 41-58.
Heiligenthal, R.
    1983   'Strategien konformer Ethik im Neuen Testament am Beispiel von Rm
              13.1-7', *NTS* 29: 55-61.
Jewett, R.
    1986   'Following the Argument of Romans', *WW* 6: 382-89.

Kennedy, G. A.
1984   *New Testament Interpretation through Rhetorical Criticism* (Chapel Hill: North Carolina Press).
Lausberg, H.
1960   *Handbuch der literarischen Rhetorik* (Munich: Hueber, 2nd edn).
Leech, G.
1983   *The Principles of Pragmatics* (New York: London).
Leeman, A.D., and A.C. Braet
1987   *Klassieke retorica: haar inhoud, functie en betekenis* (Groningen: Wolters Noordhoff).
Levinson, S.C.
1983   *Pragmatics* (Cambridge: Cambridge University Press).
Louw, J.P.
1976   *Semantiek van Nuwe Testamenties Grieks* (Pretoria: University of Pretoria).
Moxnes, H.
1988a   'Honor, Shame, and the Outside World in Paul's Letter to the Romans', in J. Neusner *et al.* (eds.), *The Social World of Formative Christianity and Judaism: Essays in Tribute to Howard Clark Kee* (Philadelphia: Fortress Press): 207-18.
Moxnes, H.
1988b   'Honour and Righteousness in Romans', *JSNT* 32: 61-77.
Nygren, A.
1949   *Commentary on Romans* (Philadelphia: Fortress Press).
Perelman, C., and L. Olbrechts-Tyteca
1969   *The New Rhetoric: A Treatise on Argumentation* (Notre Dame: University of Notre Dame Press).
1982   *The Realm of Rhetoric* (Notre Dame: University of Notre Dame Press).
Plett, H.F.
1986   'The Poetics of Quotation', in *Annales universitatis scientiarum Budapestinensis de Rolando Eötvös nominatae: sectio linguistica*, XVII (Budapest: s n.): 293-313.
Roberts, J.H.
1986a   'Transitional Techniques to the Letter Body in the *Corpus Paulinum*', in J.H. Petzer and P.J. Hartin (eds.), *A South African Perspective on the New Testament* (Leiden: Brill): 187-201.
1986b   'Pauline Transitions to the Letter Body', in A. Vanhoye (ed.), *L'Apôtre Paul: Personnalité, style et conception du ministere* (BEThL, 73: Leuven: Peeters): 93-99.
1986c   The Eschatological Transitions to the Pauline Letter Body', *Neot* 20: 29-35.
1988   'Belydenisuitsprake as Pauliniese briefoorgange', *Hervormde Teologiese Studies* 44.1: 81-97.
Ruijs, R.C.M.
1964   *De struktuur van de Brief aan de Romeinen* (Nijmegen: Dekker & Van de Vegt).
Stendahl, K.
1976   *Paul among Jews and Gentiles* (Philadelphia: Fortress Press).

Stowers, S.K.
1986   *Letter Writing in Greco-Roman Antiquity* (Philadelphia: Westminster Press).

Tompkins, J.P.
1980   *Reader-Response Criticism* (Baltimore: Johns Hopkins University Press).

Traugott, E.C., and M.L. Pratt
1980   *Linguistics* (New York: Harcourt Brace Jovanovich).

Violi, P.
1985   'Letters', in T.A. van Dijk (ed.), *Discourse and Literature* (Amsterdam: John Benjamins): III, 149-68.

Vorster, J.N.
1990   'Toward an Interactional Model for the Analysis of Letters', *Neot* 24.1: 107-30.
1991   'The Rhetorical Situation of the Letter to the Romans—An Interactional Approach' (unpublished doctoral dissertation, University of Pretoria).

Vorster, W.S.
1979   *Aischunomai en stamverwante woorde in die Nuwe Testament* (Pretoria: University of South Africa).

Wedderburn, A.J.M.
1988   *The Reasons for Romans* (Studies of the New Testament and its World; Edinburgh: T. & T. Clark).

Ziesler, J.
1989   *Paul's Letter to the Romans* (London: SCM).

THE HYPERBOLIC SUBLIME
AS A MASTER TROPE IN ROMANS*

Marc Schoeni

Introduction: Theories Of Tropes

Traditionally, two views of tropes have contended for admission in Western intellectual history. The one views tropes as a deviation from ordinary, 'proper' usage. Whether one seeks to enlist the twists and turns of the figural for the purpose of effective argumentation,[1] or whether the 'figures of style' are sought purely for their esthetic effect, one always expects to fall back on a plain, trope-neutral zero degree of meaning.

On the other hand, we have in the West quite a respectable tradition that considers tropes as a pervasive phenomenon, indeed as a hidden determinant of language, meaning and culture. To the latter tradition belong Vico, Nietzsche, and, in our day, Northrop Frye, Kenneth Burke, Hayden White, and, in a different vein, Paul de Man and Harold Bloom. Vico defined four master tropes: metaphor, metonymy, synecdoche and irony. Out of these, taken in historical sequence, he developed a whole meta-narrative of the history of civilization. White has demystified the meta-narrative, but not the synecdochic reduction to those four master tropes.[2]

---

* I am certainly unable to assess truly how much what follows does owe to Wilhelm Wuellner, both as an incredible resource person—the bibliographies he generously circulates among his students and friends have *copia*, and perhaps even sublimity—and as an energizing catalyst for my own reflections. I dedicate to him whatever might be found worthy of being pursued.

1. Thus the Aristotelian tradition. In this vein, the treatment of tropes by Perelman is extensive and often insightful: C. Perelman and L. Olbrechts-Tyteca, *Traité de l'argumentation: La nouvelle rhétorique* (Bruxelles: Editions de l'Université de Bruxelles, 3rd edn, 1976), ch. III.3b = pp. 499-549.

2. See H. White, *Tropics of Discourse: Essays in Cultural Criticism* (Baltimore:

My approach is rather based on an encyclopedic or etcetera principle: no exhaustiveness is possible, but tropes can be singled out for a consideration of their peculiar dynamic, particularly as that dynamic works toward what is called 'the sublime'. Doing so, I use the term 'master trope' in a syntagmatic sense, that is, as a trope that underhandedly determines the rhetorical functionings of any large segment of text. By its twists and turns (etymological sense of *tropos* = trope), a trope both hides and reveals with dazzling light what is at work within language. That revealing moment can only be rendered through another trope, and one must in turn analyze the interpreter's tropes—other interpreters' and one's own.

The paragraphs that follow shall first examine the relation of tropes to the 'sublime' according to 'Longinus', and then analyze segments of the letter of Paul to the Romans in order to underline the wide-scale tropings of hyperbole and its counterparts, litotes and ellipsis, in that text, and their 'sublime' and 'counter-sublime' effects.

Tropes and the Sublime

According to a scholarly consensus,[3] the author of the now famous treatise *On the Sublime* was not the third-century CE orator Cassius Longinus, but some unknown genius flourishing toward the end of the first century. This anonymous writer, who from now on shall be referred to as 'Pseudo-Longinus' or simply 'the Pseudo',[4] may well have been a Hellenistic Jew, if we judge from his well-known reference to the writer of Genesis 1 as 'the lawgiver of the Jews, who is not the man next door' (9.9).[5]

The reception of his treatise strangely mirrors the Pseudo's own stance as an author. Not only does the paradoxical anonymity of a

Johns Hopkins University Press, 1978).

3. See the extensive treatment by D.A. Russell in his edition of *'Longinus': On the Sublime* (Oxford: Clarendon Press, 1964), the Introduction, pp. xxii-xxx.

4. I borrow this designation from M. Deguy, 'Le grand-dire: Pour contribuer à une relecture du pseudo-Longin', in *Du Sublime* (Paris: Belin, 1988), pp. 11-35.

5. The suggestion that the author was at least in close contact with Hellenistic Jewish circles was first made by E. Norden, 'Das Genesiszitat in der Schrift vom Erhabenen', in *Kleine Schriften zum klassischen Altertum* (Berlin: de Gruyter, 1966 [1955]), pp. 286-313. I do go further in hypothesizing that the Anonymous was himself a Jew. Cf. Russell, *'Longinus'*, pp. xxix-xxx.

strong individual writer reflect the veiling-unveiling strategies of the 'sublime', but his fragmenting treatment of quoted sources is matched with a vengeance by the contingencies of the textual transmission, with lacunae totalling no less than one third of what must have been the original treatise. On top of that, history added insult to injury by forgetting *On the Sublime* for fourteen centuries. No known writer even alludes to it for the rest of antiquity and the Middle Ages. But modern times, since the publication of the treatise in 1554 by Robotello in Basel, and especially since its translation into French by Boileau in 1674, have more than made up for past neglect. Indeed, such a cloud of witnesses, with their own sublime anxieties, have made the Pseudo with his belated consciousness into a dignified ancient, either as a model to be imitated (so the literary tradition), or as a canonical text to be expounded and reflected upon—so the philosophical tradition, from Kant to Lyotard through Benjamin and Adorno, not forgetting American literary and rhetorical theory with Kenneth Burke, Harold Bloom, Hayden White.

Now, for a necessarily unfaithful and reductive sketch of the 'sublime' as delineated by our anonymous author: first of all, 'sublime' is not the best of terms since it may be confused with the *genus sublime,* one of the three stylistic modes codified by Roman rhetorical tradition.[6] The category used is itself a trope, a metaphor of verticality: 'the height' (τὸ ὕψος), which is the term contained in the title and translated by 'the sublime', or 'high speech' (ὑψηγορία), or else 'great speech' (μεγαλήγορον). What is denoted by these terms by definition escapes definition. It is, in the words of the late seventeenth-century French writer and mystic Fénelon, a *je ne sais quoi,* an 'I-don't-know-what'. Yet this supra-human 'I-don't-know-what', at once an effect (exteriority) and an affect (interiority), is made perceptible on human terms by sublime discourse.

In fact, the Pseudo assumes that 'it' was once, in a golden age, immediately effective and overwhelming, but we late-comers must account for a progressive loss, an entropy of it. We may still recreate it through a sustained effort at imitation of the Ancients, τῶν ἔμπροσθεν μεγάλων συγγραφέων καὶ ποιητῶν μίμησίς τε καὶ ζήλωσις (13.2). As Walter Benjamin was to emulate him in our own

---

6. Russell (*'Longinus'*, pp. xxx-xlii) insists on the difference between the *effect* called ὕψος and any kind of codified style.

century, the Pseudo dismembers Homer and other ancient texts into citations which he juxtaposes with his own comments in breath-taking catenae.[7] Thus, as something constantly beyond or below, dazzling future or irrecoverable past, this effect and affect is extremely vulnerable. If one is not careful and demanding, the Pseudo says, 'great speech' will slip into grandiloquence, that is, bombast, or into mannerism. This vulnerability also comes from the dependence of the 'sublime' effect-affect on the hearer. This would be no more than a truism, if the whole speaker–hearer relation of 'high speech' were not indeed one of paradox and reversal. It is the paradox of an overpowering of the hearer which turns out to be an empowering of the same hearer. 'Sublime' is not just elevated speech, it is *excess*. As such, it collapses the temporal process of persuasion. This is how I would understand the Pseudo's obvious polemics against Aristotle's rhetoric of persuasion: οὐ γὰρ εἰς πείθω τοὺς ἀκροωμένους ἀλλ' εἰς ἔκστασιν ἄγει τὰ ὑπερφυᾶ πάντη δέ γε σὺν ἐκπλήξει τοῦ πιθανοῦ καὶ τοῦ πρὸς χάριν ἀεὶ κρατεῖ τὸ θαυμάσιον (1.4). Of course, persuasion is not absent from the kind of discourse being celebrated. But persuasion is pre-empted by what the Pseudo calls 'transport' or 'rapture', ἔκστασις, a violent snatching away of the hearer as by a flood. Is ἔκστασις another name for manipulation? At least the hearers have no *control* over their own reception of sublimity; there is a radical heteronomy involved here. But as after-effect, a role reversal may always be expected. We may be sure that a competent hearer (see section 7) will do just what the Pseudo himself does: exchange roles and overpower 'sublime' authors in turn, through rewriting.

All this smacks of recklessness, of *hybris*. Yet it involves patient, careful work. The whole point of the first part of the treatise is that natural genius is not sufficient, one needs *techne*. One might compare this with the protracted rehearsals needed for a lightning-like performance of a Beethoven or Brahms symphony. Measureless excess must be measured through art in order to be made perceptible. A *limit* (the term is Kantian, not Longinian) is involved here, going through the speaker/hearer's own performance and marking him or her as impervious to that which he or she rises up unto.

---

7. See on this N. Hertz, 'Lecture de Longin', *Poétique* 15 (1973), pp. 292-306.

Another category used by the Pseudo is that of 'synthesis' (σύνθεσις, 10.1-3; 39-43). This melting together, whether at sentence or discourse level, involves heterogeneous elements which do not thereby lose their singularity. The example given by the Pseudo is from Sappho, in a poem that graphically paints the feeling of the organic unity of the human body in the very experience of its alienation and disintegration (10.2-3; the organic metaphor is elaborated in 40). This propels us to the element of speed, the collapsing of time indispensable to the synthesis: rather than the immobility of eternity, the extreme mobility which negates time through acceleration.[8]

One important feature of the 'sublime' is the structural necessity of coming down, or coming out of it. As Michel Deguy notes, one never stays 'up there' very long: 'No one stays "up in the air", and the relapse from the sublime is fatal'.[9] The question is not of whether but of how one falls. One may try to maintain 'high speech' through a repetition compulsion and end up with bombast; or one may fall into the trite or ridiculous. But the most appropriate exit from the 'sublime' is the 'counter-sublime',[10] where one is at a temporal remove from sublimity and comes to some insight into its hidden functionings, its tropings. This point leads us to an exploration of tropes and particularly of hyperbole in relation to the 'sublime'.

Far from a reduction of tropes to a few, the Pseudo works on the assumption of a profusion of tropes. He elaborates on nine tropes, the last of which being hyperbole (38). Let us then examine hyperbole according to both the Pseudo and classical rhetoric.[11] According to

8. One area of research would be to explore the possible affinities between the Pseudo and the apocalyptic tradition.

9. *'Nul ne reste "en l'air", et du sublime la rechute est fatale'* ('Le grand-dire', in *Du Sublime* [Paris: Belin, 1988], p. 17).

10. I use the term somewhat differently from H. Bloom (cf. *Anxiety of Influence* [Oxford: Oxford University Press, 1973], ch. 4 = pp. 99-112), if only because the sublime as I try to expound it is not poetic but interpretative; the will-to-power of the truly significant interpreter may be as effectual as that of the strong poet, but the stance is not the same. The Longinian interpreter's counter-sublime does not try to compete with the predecessor through daemonic hyperbole; it rather adopts a low profile, demystifying the predecessor text (or one's own text) through between-the-lines counter-tropings.

11. I rely here on the enlightening study on the subject done by L. Perrin, 'La vérité dans l'exagération: Comment les rhétoriciens voyaient les dessous de l'hyperbole', in *Etudes de Lettres* (Lausanne) 1991, IV, pp. 23-44.

both traditions, hyperbole is a credible exaggeration, evidencing the oxymoronic law of the truthful lie.[12] How is this possible? The classical tradition emphasizes the conscious role of the hearer: sequentially, hyperbole is first perceived as exaggeration, so that the hearer must *scale down* what is said (*en rabattre*), with the end result that one lands somewhere beyond what a non-hyperbolic mode would have expressed, but below what has been literally said.[13] Sublime hyperbole works according to the same principle of overshooting in order to shoot right, but with two important differences. First of all, the temporal collapse of communication makes it so that in order to succeed, hyperbole must force its effect on the hearer in a single blow, not giving the hearer any time to perceive the exaggeration and then scale it down. The best hyperboles are covert (38.3); or to express it better, exaggeration is indeed perceived, but subliminally (otherwise how could one account for its powerful effect?). The other major difference is that the target at which the speaker is aiming is not necessarily below the literal sense of the hyperbolic statement. Sublime hyperbole is a kind of blind shooting upward, which may after all reveal itself to be truth.

In order to be truth, sublime hyperbole does require a scaling down, but separate in time from the hyperbolic moment. Sublime hyperbole can only be *effective* without the downward movement; but then, it cannot be *true* without it. To explain further: the 'sublime' is constituted by this separation, this temporal cleavage between *effect* and *truth*. The effect of sublime hyperbole is a rapture: no time for a controlled reception; no time for hearing plus interpreting. Yet the truth of the hyperbolic sublime depends on how one comes out of it. The time lag of the counter-sublime is the moment of truth of hyperbole. This is to say that the truth of hyperbole is dependent on another trope, a trope of de-sublimation. As the Pseudo emphasizes in the introduction to his treatment of tropes (17), tropes bring about the 'sublime' only as they hide their own functionings, just as the sun's rays cast forth a shadow. How does he know that? Because he himself has gone through the process wherein ascending tropes, which are 'blind' tropes, are taken over by other tropes which demystify the first

12. *On the Sublime* 37.3. Cf. Quintilian, *Institutio oratoria* 8.6.67; P. Fontanier, *Les figures du discours* (Paris: Gallimard, 1977), p. 123.

13. Perrin, 'La vérité dans l'exagération', pp. 26-27. See on this a well-known contemporary of the Pseudo, Quintilian *Institutio oratoria* 8.6.76.

ones; tropes of insight. This preposterous insight will not bring secrets into the full light of day, as if hiddenness were the polar opposite of an objectifying revelation; rather, it will bring to light *that* there is a veiling which is inseparable from the dazzling revelation of the 'sublime'. It may do so through a trope of denial, naming 'it', the 'sublime', while at the same time denying 'it'.[14]

Yet one would misunderstand the Pseudo by remaining on that cognitive plane. One needs not only cognitive insight (through irony), but emotional healing (through humor).[15] No one comes out of sublime rapture unscathed. The Pseudo makes this point at the end of his treatment of hyperbole, when he evokes comic hyperbole and identifies laughter and the comical as the 'resolution and remedy' of sublime hyperbole: ἔστι γάρ, ὡς οὐ διαλείπω λέγων, παντὸς τολμήματος λεκτικοῦ λύσις καὶ πανάκειά τις τὰ ἐγγὺς ἐκστάσεως ἔργα καὶ πάθη (28.5), among which are τὰ κωμικά (next sentence). There are such things as 'neighbor works and passions' to 'rapture': they are not sublime rapture, but there is a secret affinity between them. They provide healing from rapture. The healing trope may be a second hyperbole of a different kind, that is, comic hyperbole (28.5-6), or a comic litotes (litotes is described in 38.6).

The Pseudo's practice in 9.9 evidences both ellipsis and a serious litotes. Serious litotes works just like hyperbole, but in paradoxical fashion, leading up while apparently going down; one might say, shooting up by ricochetting. Let me quote again from that famous passage: ὁ τῶν Ἰουδαίων θεσμοθέτης, οὐχ ὁ τυχὼν ἀνήρ...This is a *low profile hyperbolic sublime* (if I may be forgiven this oxymoron), commingling the sublime and the counter-sublime; renouncing rapturing speed, but still shooting high toward the invisible target, indeed perhaps more effectively so than the Homeric quotations which precede and follow. The Pseudo is saying covertly (or else he would cease being 'the Pseudo'): for a *true* sublime, for a sublime of truth-*and*-power, go to... 'the lawgiver of the Jews'. The Pseudo's ultimate

---

14. M. Deguy concludes his essay by asking: 'La *dénégation* serait inscrite au coeur même du dire?' ('Le grand-dire', p. 34). Cf. what Poe does in the opening paragraphs of 'The Fall of the House of Usher'.

15. I understand irony to be a 'cold' mode, one of distance, working principally on the cognitive level, while humour is a 'warm', empathic mode, emotional as well as cognitive, and enacting an interplay of proximity and distance.

ruse would be in thus signalling, through overstatement and understatement, that the counter-sublime is after all the true sublime—the sublime of the Jews' Bible ?

Let us now try to follow the shuttle between sublime and countersublime, between hyperbole and its healing trope, in the text of Paul's letter to the Romans.

Hyperbole against Analogy: The Workings of the Qal Wachomer in Romans 5

In that large transitional unit,[16] Paul brings to a melting point the enunciative synecdoche reached at the end of ch. 4. After having been carefully differentiated all through chs. 1–4, believing Jews and Gentiles have been coalesced into one first person shifter from 4.16 on.[17] This then becomes a highly exultant *we* in 5.1-11.

The outrageousness of the second statement καὶ καυχώμεθα ἐπ' ἐλπίδι τῆς δόξης τοῦ θεοῦ (5.2) (outrageous in the light of the exclusion of καυχήσις in 3.27, and even more outrageous if it is construed as an exhortation[18]) is enhanced through a paradoxical hyperbole: οὐ μόνον δέ, ἀλλὰ καὶ καυχώμεθα ἐν ταῖς θλίψεσιν (5.3). Let us be *even more* excessive: let us be proud in the midst of untold hardships. This is meant to be carried out as a consistently defiant gesture toward history, shooting at once at God's future, 'the hope of the glory of God'. The sharpness of this original vision is the sublime blow that hits the reader at first, with the force of a performative—a hyperbolic performative. Then comes the mitigating trope, a sorites (5.3b-4) which builds a chain-like, unbreakable rationale for defiance: from θλῖψις through ὑπομονή through δοκιμή and on to ἐλπίς, all is linked, no gaps. The trope mitigates the flash-like speed at

16. On the transitional character of ch. 5, see J.-N. Aletti, *Comment Dieu est-il juste? Clefs pour interpréter l'épître aux Romains* (Paris: Seuil, 1991), pp. 38-49.

17. The use by Paul of the reverse operation to dissociation, i.e. sublation of dissociation through a newfound unity, has been underlined by F. Siegert, *Argumentation bei Paulus gezeigt an Röm 9–11* (Tübingen: Mohr, 1985), pp. 183-84.

18. If the first verb must be read ἔχωμεν, then καυχώμεθα must also be a cohortative subjunctive. There is strong external testimony for that reading, and internally it has the advantage of being a *lectio difficilior*—which is why later Western, Palestinian and Alexandrian manuscripts as well as the overwhelming majority of modern exegetes have rejected it. I owe those textual observations to Professor Etienne Trocmé from Strasbourg.

which the vision of hope was first shouted, but not the semantics of it. No scaling down, just an argumentative slowing down which amounts to a *je persiste et signe*. The key to this paradox of a rationale beyond evidence lies in the term ἐλπίς: continuity is built from the future.[19] After that first slowing down, Paul can expand yet more, explicate the paradoxical hyperbole by naming the love of God 'spilled out' (ἐκκέχυται, metaphor of waste,[20] that is, excess) through the πνεῦμα (5.5). Building a temporal ring, the statement leads back to the past where the πνεῦμα 'was given us'. This ring does not negate time in a seamless, original continuity. On the contrary, the immeasurable gap between past and future is the necessary presupposition of the three hyperboles that follow. For the first time, Christ is named as agent in the hyperbolic excess; indeed, he is now given priority in excess: twice ἀπέθανεν (vv. 6, 8), an irreducible, obdurately singular past event, which is lost by the very act by which it is committed to writing. How shall one repeat within the common language the crucifixion, the abyss of grief? Yet this loss-by-retrieval through repetition is the necessary condition of hope for *us*. The result is one of the strangest hyperboles one has ever encountered—one large wave (5.6-9) made up of three smaller ones (5.6, 7-8, 9). The obscurities of 5.6-8 are well known:[21] the double ἔτι of v. 6, the not so obvious character of the gradation from δικαίου to τοῦ ἀγαθοῦ in v. 7—and yet the middle hyperbole hinges on that!—and the apparent redundancy of v. 6 and v. 8. As to the last point, repetition is needed to build the temporal link between 'Christ' and 'us', God as subject sublating the singularity of the event by the continuity of his love (συνίστησιν in v. 8 is the only main verb in the present tense within the whole pericope). Or conversely, the variation between the two statements, through the temporal aporia in v. 6 (double ἔτι),[22] brings

---

19. Siegert (*Argumentation*, pp. 206-207) emphasizes how Paul's argumentation is more teleological than causal. One must take full stock of the radical temporal dimension this introduces into argumentation.

20. See M.R. Cosby, 'Paul's Persuasive Language in Romans 5', in D.F. Watson (ed.), *Persuasive Artistry: Studies in New Testament Rhetoric in Honor of George A. Kennedy* (Sheffield: JSOT Press, 1991), pp. 209-26 (215).

21. See *pace* W. Schmithals, *Der Römerbrief: Ein Kommentar* (Gütersloh: Mohn, 1988).

22. I am tempted to make this *really* pleonastic, by linking the first ἔτι to Χριστός and the second to κατὰ καιρόν: 'Still Christ, as we were weak, while it was still time, died for ungodly people'. 'Still' is placed proleptically and then held

to the surface the singular, that which resists sublation in Christ's death. Rhythmically, this is a wide, slow wave, so slow that one must curl up within it just the right way, or the wave shall splash through and leave only an impression of fragmentation. But as one curls up and is carried, one is led to the *a fortiori* or קל וחומר (rabbinic argument of 'the light and heavy')[23] conclusion (v. 9), where the weightiness is a matter of future versus present. The argument is from the heavy to the light: as a result of vv. 6-8, δικαιωθέντες νῦν ἐν τῷ αἵματι αὐτοῦ is of course the weighty, to which is compared the now less weighty eschatological future. The only proof of the future is that past which escapes memory and yet is redeemed by God's memory. The *a fortiori* argument is hyperbolic and paradoxical;[24] a guarantee of hope is of course an oxymoron.

A second hyperbolic קל וחומר follows in v. 10.[25] Semantically, it sums up the preceding one (vv. 6-9), with some significant variations, among which is the shift from 'being justified' to 'being reconciled'. Rhythmically, this is a vertiginous speeding up, like a powerful breaker dashing behind the slow, wide wave. The last sentence (v. 11) sounds then like an anticlimax, merely restating what precedes in the pericope, with no past–future tension. So why is it introduced as a yet

off, until it is resumed and linked to κατὰ καιρόν. The sentence is clumsy and hesitant, the paradox of temporality: nervosity and hesitancy both at once; time running out, and yet hesitancy and repetition compulsion in the face of time. This phenomenon will come to an extreme in the stuttering repetitiveness of 7.14-25.

23. Cf. W.S. Towner, 'Hermeneutical Systems of Hillel and the Tannaim: A Fresh Look', *HUCA* 43 (1982), pp. 101-35 (113-16).

24. Which means that it is not the Aristotelian enthymematic *a fortiori* argument, i.e. there is no hidden universal premise (cf. *Ars rhetorica* 1.1363b-1365b, 1367a; there is a more common sense account in 2.1397b); which does not yet prove that it is Hebraic, but there is a strong likelihood that Paul learned it mainly through his Pharisaic teachers. In any case, despite the commonality of the *a fortiori* argument, I would beware of rushing immediately to an aprioristic universalism, as Siegert (*Argumentation*, pp. 190-91) tends to do.

25. The movement of hyperboles requires us to take vv. 6-9 together and v. 10 as a second hyperbole. Verses 6-9 and 10 are of course united as wave is to wave; this is why the semantic closeness of v. 9 and v. 10 does not invalidate what I am saying, but confirms it. This against the rhetoric-of-persuasion analysis of Cosby ('Paul's Persuasive Language in Romans 5', pp. 216-17). As a consequence of his division of the text, Cosby treats vv. 6-8 as a mere antithesis, not seeing its function as a composite premise of the hyperbolic *a fortiori* expressed in v. 9.

higher hyperbole (οὐ μόνον δέ, ἀλλὰ καὶ...)? It is a hyperbole-litotes, both at once. It first sounds like a low-keyed statement, hardly a wave at all. It is furthermore elliptic, with an ambiguous, tense and mood-neutral participle καυχώμενοι (we shall encounter those again in ch. 12). Yet this is the outrageous exhortation of vv. 2-3, albeit deprived now of its performative status. The excess lies in the quiet, obstinate reaffirmation of defiance over against time and history. It is also a synecdochic affirmation of continuity and unification, built upon the previous hyperboles: gathering together of God and Jesus Christ (καυχώμενοι ἐν τῷ θεῷ διὰ τοῦ κυρίου ἡμῶν Ἰησοῦ Χριστοῦ), repetition of the premise of reconciliation presently obtained (δι᾽ οὗ νῦν τὴν καταλλαγὴν ἐλάβομεν). The difference between the topic of justice and the topic of reconciliation lies precisely here: justice discriminates and divides; it acknowledges singularity, in particular the difference of Jew and Gentile. Reconciliation sublates and unites; it must order singularity into a greater whole, and in so doing willy-nilly deny it. This is 'high', hyperbolic synecdoche, answering at the level of the énoncé the synecdoche of the 'we' at the level of énoncia-tion. It is then no accident that, since 4.16, there is no longer a Jew–Gentile distinction in the text.[26]

5.1-11 and 12-21 are linked—and not linked—through διὰ τοῦτο. This strong connecting particle is a syntactical lie. The connections between the two pericopes, deep and numerous as they may be, are not of a linear argumentative type. Verses 12-21 do not follow from vv. 1-11; they rather start over again—and much further back through time—and restate and widen. This may be taken as a flaw 'reducing... rhetorical effectiveness'.[27] But linear argumentation or narration is not all there is to rhetoric. Furthermore, the Pseudo has a lengthy development about the inevitable flaws of a sublime writer (32.8-36). He must either lapse (in the sense of Freudian lapsus) or consciously lie in order to bring out the truth that there is a resistance

---

26. This correlation between the 'we' and the theme of reconciliation is also noted by Cosby ('Paul's Persuasive Language in Romans 5', p. 212).

27. Cosby, 'Paul's Persuasive Language in Romans 5', p. 218. Schmithals (*Der Römerbrief, ad loc.*) has well noted the absence of a linear continuity between 5.1-11 and 5.12-21. He draws the conclusion that vv. 1-11 is an interpolation. Most types of criticism are ill-equipped to deal with textual discontinuities; they must either deny them through synchronic procedures, or domesticate them through diachronic recon-struction of the text.

to a logic of linear development and semantic correspondence. I cannot tell whether Paul's improper διὰ τοῦτο is a lapse or a conscious displacement. In any case, the lines that follow evidence sublime power and not reduced effectiveness.

In those verses, hyperbole reveals its true colors: it interrupts and denies analogy.[28] The analogy is first broken off by a much entangled discussion over whether really 'all sinned' as v. 12d states (vv. 13-14), as there was no law between Adam and Moses. This first parenthesis is linked (through τοῦ μέλλοντος, v. 14c) to an outright denial of the painstakingly built trope of analogy: ἀλλ᾽ οὐχ ὡς... οὕτως καὶ... (v. 15, repeated in v. 16). Paul tropes the hyperbolic greatness of Jesus Christ by playing the second prosopopeic synecdoche—Christ as the 'one human being' linked to 'all' through time and space—against the first (Adam). Only Christ spans the entire space-time, more sublimely than Homer's divine chariots according to the Pseudo (9.5), since they span only space. This synecdochic hyperbole unfolds in two wave-like קל וחומר arguments. They are in a chiastic relation to the two קל וחומר arguments in vv. 6-10: first the faster wave, which here is not quite a breaker, then the wide, slow wave, composite like vv. 6-9. They are from the less weighty to the more weighty, unlike vv. 6-10. The χάρις/χάρισμα cluster is the locus of excess.

The first קל וחומר (v. 15) is a rather weak, purely quantitative hyperbole: if death comes to the many through the one, *how much more so* (πόλλῳ μᾶλλον) has χάρις abounded through the One to the many. What we have is a figuration of plenty, the term χάρις being repeated in two different syntactical constructions as if they were two different things (ἡ **χάρις** τοῦ θεοῦ **καὶ ἡ δωρεὰ ἐν χάριτι** τῇ τοῦ ἑνὸς ἀνθρώπου Ἰησοῦ Χριστοῦ εἰς τοὺς πολλοὺς ἐπερίσσευσεν): a very bizarre instance of polyptoton (see the Pseudo, 23-26) creating a kind of double vision. The next wave is a two-phased movement. First comes a perfectly parallel antithesis, using symploce, i.e. a double rhyme of beginning and ending of the cola

---

28. As seen by Siegert (*Argumentation*, p. 187). I do hold to the traditional reading of the syntax, which sees v. 12 as the premise of a suspended analogy. Two rhetorical critics have recently tried to read v. 12 as a complete analogy, so J.T. Kirby, 'The Syntax of Romans 5.12: A Rhetorical Approach', *NTS* 33 (1987), pp. 283-86; and Cosby, 'Paul's Persuasive Language in Romans 5', pp. 219-21. Even if their reading is correct, this does not affect my point over the denial of analogy by hyperbole, only about the interruption.

(v. 16b); then follows the overwhelming hyperbole of the second חומר קל (v. 17). Here the double vision engendered by polyptoton comes in the lesser term, the one Adam (εἰ γὰρ τῷ τοῦ ἑνὸς παραπτώματι ὁ θάνατος ἐβασίλευσεν διὰ τοῦ ἑνός). The effect of the weightier term comes by a reversal of subject and object: the recipients of τὴν περισσείαν τῆς χάριτος (resumption of the first חומר קל) are the ones who *shall reign in life through the one Jesus Christ* (πολλῷ μᾶλλον οἱ τὴν περισσείαν τῆς χάριτος καὶ τῆς δωρεᾶς τῆς δικαιοσύνης λαμβάνοντες ἐν ζωῇ βασιλεύσουσιν διὰ τοῦ ἑνὸς Ἰησοῦ Χριστοῦ). Through the ever-recurring present of the newly empowered recipients, the one/many synecdoche now spans the abyss between the past and the unforeseeable future. Sublime synthesis, operating by way of a self-defeating analogy, is what makes the past, present and the future foreseeable in its absolute newness. This is why future tense of βασιλεύσουσιν, coming at the end of this series of חומר קל arguments, cannot be overemphasized. The fulness expressed by the synecdochic resumption of all in 'the One Jesus Christ' is exceeded and thrown into radical indeterminacy at the very point of its acme, through the hyperbolic *how much more* passing into the unrepresentable future.

But then, the very excessiveness of the trope forces Paul to operate a brutal scaling down of hyperbole. By a resumptive ἄρα οὖν (v. 18), he flatly returns to the simple analogy which he had so powerfully denied in between. What does ἄρα οὖν resume anyway? If it is v. 12, then this makes the whole hyperbolic development a seemingly harmless parenthesis; if it is the whole preceding development, then ἄρα οὖν can only resume by openly betraying. In any case, the syntax lies so outrageously that the reader cannot fail to see the distortions and be troubled by them. A reader who has indeed been carried to the heights—who has not been left behind by the intricacy of the text—will then receive the analogies in vv. 18-19 as a dreary school exercise, not worthless since it clarifies conceptually the argument about justification and life, but purposefully undershooting at 'it'. The second analogy (v. 19) re-sublimates somewhat by reintroducing the tension between past and future; of course, it mitigates it by establishing a seeming adequation between the two, but it cannot drive it completely into oblivion, especially after what has preceded. No sublime reader can believe that future being-constituted-righteous will be *just as* past being-constituted-sinners. The scene of justification is exceeded, stretched beyond the bounds of a logic of equivalency and retributive justice.[29] A disruptive element comes with the mention of the Torah 'sneaking in' in v. 20 (παρεισῆλθεν; as a reminder, sin had come in openly, εἰσῆλθεν, in v. 12). But Paul uses the Torah's disrupting of his scheme as a fulcrum to re-hyperbolize: νόμος δὲ παρεισῆλθεν, ἵνα **πλεονάσῃ** τὸ παράπτωμα· οὗ δὲ **ἐπλεόνασεν** ἡ ἁμαρτία, **ὑπερεπερίσσευσεν** ἡ χάρις. The repetition of the verb πλεονάζω, already denoting plenty, serves as an antithetical sorites leading up to the excess beyond measure of χάρις, which is more radically demarcated through the change of term: it is not enough to prefix a ὑπερ-, one must prefix it to a different verb, resumptive of the περισσεύω of vv. 15-17. True resumption was not introduced by ἄρα οὖν in v. 18; it comes now in the adversative statement to v. 18.

True, the ἵνα clause following (v. 21) reestablishes the analogy, but the terms resume v. 17, the radical indeterminacy of the coming eschatological life being now fused with justice (δικαιοσύνη). Furthermore, the clause and the hyperbole that has preceded it in v. 20 are programmatic of what is to follow in chs. 6–8: all in all, a hyperbolic *propositio*,[30] a strange commingling of syntactic linearity and semantic denial of linearity and correspondence! So let us now proceed to the next step, a rapid reading of the following chapters in order to look at tropological transformations which can be of great moment in our vision of the sublimity of Romans.

The Displacements of Sublime Synthesis, the Workings of the Counter-Sublime: Reading of Romans 9–13

I skip chs. 6 and 7 for the moment, because the astonishing sublimity of these chapters is not of a hyperbolic nature. Let me just say about ch. 8 that it carries the rhetoric of reconciliation to its ultimate completion in the *peroratio* of 8.31-39. This would appear by all standards to be a fitting ending for the whole discourse.

Yet the text does not end here. Connecting asyndetically, 9.1-5 points to that which has been left out of the synecdochic move of

---

29. See on this a short, simple but absolutely essential article by P. Ricoeur, 'La logique de Jésus: Romains 5', *ETR* 1980, pp. 420-25.

30. J.-N. Aletti has shown how 5.20-21 is a *propositio*, a programmatic statement of what is to follow in chs. 6–8 (*Comment Dieu est-il juste?*, pp. 47-48).

ch. 8; indeed, what is to follow unravels the whole tropological construction of chs. 5–8. A separate entity, a *not-we*, occupies center stage from here to the end of ch. 11: *Israel*. The entire rhetoric of reconciliation is displaced through this strong *dissociation* in Perelman's sense,[31] a reordering of the argumentative structure, forcing the reader to come to terms with the Jew/non-Jew duality at the very center of the eschatological hope of salvation.

Let us skip the whole development until we get to 11.11, the positive reversal of the fate of the λοιποί (11.7b), that is, the Israelites who are expressly *not* part of the Remnant. Paul first reasons on the premise that the Jewish majority's failure to believe was the Gentiles' greatest chance (11.11b) in order to hyperbolize, by way of קל וחומר, a future 'fulness' of Israel which is properly unimaginable (11.12). The second hyperbole (11.15), this time in the form of a rhetorical question (τίς), resumes the eschatological life terminology of 5.6-11: εἰ γὰρ ἀποβολὴ αὐτῶν καταλλαγὴ κόσμου, τίς ἡ πρόσλημψις εἰ μὴ ζωὴ ἐκ νεκρῶν...Only this time, the hyperbolically postulated future concerns Israel, so much that the former *we*, broken up into *I* and *you*, now appears as a counter-sublime: the very preaching of the gospel to the Gentiles (of which the writing of this letter is a part, 1.14-17!) becomes ancillary to the contemplated 'life from the dead' (11.15). Accordingly, the extended metaphor that follows in vv. 16-24 takes a performative turn, a warning to the Gentiles not to be conceited. The קל וחומר argumentative resumption of the metaphor (11.24) is hyperbolical only by way of an implicit suggestion, as one tries to imagine this future 'grafting in' of the λοιποί.

Of what nature are such hyperboles? I suggest that they are neither classical nor simply sublime. They unfold in a constant interplay of the sublime and the counter-sublime. In fact, the whole passage is a midrash, where the extended metaphor (11.16-24) functions as a *mashal*, that is, a heuristic narration serving as a hermeneutical key for the main text.[32] The main texts are, at one end, a conflation of Deut. 29.3 and Isa. 29.10 (cited in 11.8), plus Ps. 69.23-24 (11.9-10), and at the other end, a conflation of Isa. 59.20-21 and 27.9 (11.26-27). The two קל וחומר in 11.12-15 are thus exegetical, as they serve to

31. *Traité de l'argumentation*, ch. III.4 = pp. 550-609; Siegert, *Argumentation*, pp. 182-84.

32. See on this D. Boyarin, *Intertextuality and the Reading of Midrash* (Bloomington: Indiana University Press, 1990), pp. 80-92 and 105-16.

bring out the positive reversal which, according to Paul, is to be implied from the depiction of Israel's failure in the previously quoted texts. The principle of this positive reversal is explained by means of the *mashal*, and then narrated proleptically in the μυστήριον (11.25-27), which closes on the last scriptural quotation. This would explain the continuity of the μυστήριον statement with the preceding argumentation, in spite of the shift to a revelatory stance.[33] There are surprising gaps in that statement, like the ellipsis of the main premise upon which the καὶ οὕτως... conclusion is based, namely the logically inferred but wholly unexpressed end to the πώρωσις. The scriptural proof offers as one of its most yawning gaps the identity of ὁ ῥυόμενος. These gaps call for elaboration by putting the two stories, the gnomic story of the olive tree and the projected eschatological story of the deliverer, in interaction. Paul's counter-sublime invites his Gentile readers, somewhat humorously, to exercise Jewish midrashic sagacity,[34] while telling them, quoting Prov. 3.7, not to be παρ' ἑαυτοῖς φρόνιμοι—at least one clearly understandable intertextual clue!

The argumentative part of the peroration (11.28-32) brings together the reconciliation theme of chs. 5–8 and the Jew/Gentile distinction of chs. 9–11, in the absence of any christological statement—a notable displacement from the peroration of ch. 8. The doxological peroration (11.33-36) is a juxtaposition of biblical (vv. 33-35) and stoical pagan (v. 36) intertextuality, the whole contributing to a hyperbolic sense of the inaccessibility of the 'mystery' just expounded, due to the gap between God's knowledge and the knowledge of him.

On the whole, Paul's postulated Gentile readers must feel slighted and overwhelmed by the play of the sublime and the counter-sublime in Romans 11. Another counter-sublime, in a different, more accessible mode, must come to their aid. This is done in chs. 12–13.

---

33. Siegert, *Argumentation*, p. 172: '*Man kann sich fragen, ob sich ihm das Geheimnis, das er hier mitteilt, nicht aus seiner eigenen Argumentation erschlossen hat*'. May I suggest that this is certainly the case. The midrashic hypothesis may also provide the beginning of an answer to other questions, like the long stretch without an explicit quote (11.11-26), unusual in Rom. 9–11, and the import of the last quotation (p. 173).

34. Cf. Siegert's enlightening fantasy that Gentile readers must have asked those among the Jewish Christians who were most expert in biblical interpretation about the meaning of Paul's scriptural argument (*Argumentation*, p. 173)!

Let me state at the outset that I do agree with such an extreme paste-and-scissors exegete as Walter Schmithals[35] over the fact that chs. 12–15 are, argumentatively speaking, perfectly expendable: the program set forth in the initial *propositio* (1.16) has been fulfilled[36] and the discourse is thematically saturated. The οὖν in 12.1 is a syntactical phantom, connecting with no traceable premise. True, διὰ τῶν οἰκτιρμῶν τοῦ θεοῦ reminds one of the leading topic of the ἔλεος τοῦ θεοῦ in chs. 9–11, but this semantical connection is not elaborated in the parenesis, which rather takes up bits and pieces of chs. 6–8 in a widely transformed context. Christological language is scarce, indeed wholly absent from the opening exhortation (12.1-2); it comes up only three times later on (12.5, 11; 13.14). Any attempt at a christological or a soteriological-ethical ('indicative–imperative') articulation founders on a close reading of the text.[37]

Unlike Schmithals, I do not advocate a diachronic solution. Articulation across a hiatus is a trademark of the linkage of the counter-sublime with the sublime. The need for a parenetical section thus arises out of the dynamics of reading: Paul's postulated Gentile readership must be granted healing from the scorching heights of chs. 9–11, through the empowerment of an easy and yet exhilarating process of interpretive interaction. Contrary to received opinion, there is no dominance here of the imperative force, as was the case in 6.11-23. The tone is set in 12.1-2: an invitation to action and ethical reasoning, all at the same time; such ethical reasoning is an act of cognition to be performed *by the readers*—not by Paul—as a preposterous response to the sublime imperative of grace that has always already moved the baptized as 'free slaves' (ch. 6). Chapters 12 and 13 provide the raw material on which the readers can exercise their transformed νοῦς.

This parenetical material covers 12.9–13.10. I consider vv. 3-8 to be part of the exordium (12.1-8) because of their discursive stance: Paul in those verses establishes the enunciative relation of speaker and hearers, setting up by the same token the mode of the section, which is

---

35. *Römerbrief*, pp. 417-20.

36. This applies whether 1.16-17 is also a *partitio* or not.

37. A detailed reading aided by unselfconscious christological glossings, as practiced by H.D. Betz in his article 'Das Problem der Grundlagen der paulinischen Ethik (Röm 12,1-2)', *ZTK* 85 (1988), pp. 199-218, is not what I would consider a close reading, where all gap-filling must be as selfconscious as possible, and must arise from a willingness to consider the text at its most unsettling and uncanny.

light-footed, partly humorous, partly serious. The basic exhortation in v. 3 is to scale down: λέγω γὰρ διὰ τῆς χάριτος τῆς δοθείσης μοι παντὶ τῷ ὄντι ἐν ὑμῖν **μὴ ὑπερφρονεῖν** παρ' ὃ δεῖ **φρονεῖν** ἀλλὰ **φρονεῖν** εἰς τὸ **σωφρονεῖν**, ἑκάστῳ ὡς ὁ θεὸς ἐμέρισεν μέτρον πίστεως. The μέτρον ('measure') is a recurring term in the Pseudo's dialectic of the sublime. Here, it marks the return to a human, finite measure of understanding; one of *faith*, but of faith as apportioned by God in order to meet each individual's 'human, all too human' capabilities. The way of saying it, though, belies the moderate stance which is demanded of the readers through its immoderate punning on φρονέω. The *énonciation* contradicts the *énoncé*, as with Paul humorously saying: *Faites comme je dis, mais pas comme je fais!* The unfolding of the metaphor of the body (12.4-8) empowers the addressees as reading subjects, by claiming that a similar 'grace' has been 'given' to them as to Paul (12.6, cf 12.3).[38] Such a human complicity between writer and readers is the reason why I view the mode set in v. 3 as one of humor rather than one of irony.

The general parenesis proper (12.9–13.10) is made up of proverbial units of sapiential traditions,[39] including recognizable Jesus traditions, cited anonymously.[40] The grammatical form of the first group of sayings (12.9-21) is that of ambiguous, or I would rather say performatively unmarked participles,[41] making for maximum reader cooperation. Neither statements nor commands per se, they become speech acts only as the reader reformulates them one way or another. There are exceptions,[42] among which the imperative in v. 16c; this scriptural

38. We know this to be a stereotyped phrase that normally applies only to Paul as apostle (1.5; 15.15). 12.6 is the unique exception.

39. See K. Berger's treatment of the gnomic genres in 'Hellenistische Gattungen im Neuen Testament', *ANRW* II.25.2 (Berlin: de Gruyter, 1984), pp. 1049-74. Since then, W.T. Wilson has published his dissertation on this whole topic, *Love without Pretense: Romans 12.9-21 and Hellenistic-Jewish Wisdom Literature* (Tübingen: Mohr, 1991).

40. Clear parallels to me are 12.14 (Lk. 6.28 // Mt. 5.44), 13.7 (Mk 12.17 // Mt. 22.21 // Lk. 20.25) and 13.8-10 (Mk 12.28-31 // Mt. 22.34-30); cf. M. Thompson, *Clothed with Christ: The Example and Teaching of Jesus in Romans 12.1–15.13* (Sheffield: JSOT Press, 1991), pp. 96-105, 111-40.

41. On this phenomenon, see L. Thurén, *The Rhetorical Strategy of 1 Peter with Special Regard to Ambiguous Expressions* (Åbo: Åbo Akademi, 1990), esp. pp. 4-20.

42. Imperatives in vv. 14, 16c, 19b-20 and 21, infinitives in v. 15.

quotation (Prov. 3.7) is doubly thrown into relief as it caps two previous sayings repeating the terms of v. 3 against sublime 'high-mindedness', and as it harks back to the same quote in 11.25; the counter-sublime mode is thus strongly reaffirmed in the middle of the group of sayings. The double saying of v. 15 mirrors *en abyme* how the whole section is to be read: χαίρειν μετὰ χαιρόντων, κλαίειν μετὰ κλαιόντων. Human empathy in laughing and crying, humor and gravity. The shifts cannot be predetermined by any encoded signifying system; they are left open to both empathy and ad hoc reasoning (cf. vv. 1-2); even though there are intratextual clues (reminders of chs. 5–8), the reader's own extratextual situation is invited to play a large role in his or her own elaboration of the parenesis (cf. 15.14).

The framework in which this elaboration is to take place is that of common-sense morality. This is striking in the treatment of the topic of love (ἀγάπη, according to 12.9a and 13.8-10, setting up an inclusion), sublime in 1 Corinthians 13, de-sublimated here in order to bring it into line with common morality. The force of the quotation from the Q tradition about blessing the enemies in v. 14 (one of the exceptional cases where the saying is in the imperative) is mitigated by a string of other sayings in vv. 17-21, not Jesuanic and partly drawn from the Bible, which set forth the common utilitarian wisdom of not fighting back so as to keep the peace and gain a moral victory for oneself. Yet, as if to remind us that this is only a preposterous response to the sublimity of 'staurological'[43] (word-from-the-Cross) beginnings, there is a sudden rushing back of the sublime in the peroration of 13.11-14, in the guise of a tempestuous intrusion of the eschatological future, making time almost into a black hole under the pressure of an infinite acceleration. This 'dynamic sublime' urges one unique and final exhortation, emphatically christological: ἀλλὰ ἐνδύσασθε τὸν κύριον Ἰησοῦν Χριστόν (13.14a). How such an apocalyptical imperative is compatible with the common-sense ethics of the parenesis that it closes is a question that cannot be answered on a conceptual plane. The 'symbolic wisdom' of the one who, without forgetting the absolute indeterminacy of the sublime foundation, also takes part in the building up of all-too-human institutions, can only articulate itself across a hiatus.[44]

43. Term coined by S. Breton, *Le verbe et la croix* (Paris: Desclée, 1981).
44. Both *sagesse symbolique* and *articulation en hiatus* are recurring expressions used by the Belgian phenomenologist M. Richir in his *Du sublime en politique*

Conclusions

I shall articulate my concluding remarks along four lines: rhetoric and the sublime, rhetoric and culture, rhetoric and religion, and rhetoric and theology.

1. We have seen the 'sublime' working from within the rhetoric of communication and subverting it by using its own resources, namely tropes. One could wish some elaboration on the question of the articulation between intratextual grammar, referential tropes and pragmatic performatives, which is still a desideratum;[45] in any case, the intentionality of persuasion is deviated more than once along its course, not through persuasive weakness, but by dint of an excess of persuasive power.

2. Historically, the Pseudo as well as Paul are at the juncture of two worlds, the Jewish and the Hellenistic. From this liminal position, the two are to be viewed neither as part of a universal whole nor as water-tight simples. If there is a cultural synthesis at work, it is 'sublime', that is, it does not annihilate the heterogeneity of its parts. The Jewishness of both the Pseudo and Paul appears especially in the juxtaposition of what I have chosen to call the 'sublime' and the 'counter-sublime', for example, when it follows midrashic interpretive lines as in Romans 11.

3. Whether one looks at Homer or at the 'Most High', the rhetorical 'sublime' undeniably has preferential links with religious discourse. When that which is at work in dazzling hyperbole is preposterously called 'God' and 'Jesus Christ', the namings do not refer to a ground standing wholly beyond language, in ultimate silence, as Kenneth Burke's Augustinian rereading of the sublime has it.[46] Paul's God is never word-less, but his word displaces meaning, so that, as in mystical discourse, *homo rhetoricus* is constantly beside the point. According to the interplay between the sublime and the counter-sublime, one must also modify Kennedy's view of religious discourse

---

(Paris: Payot, 1991). See especially pp. 437-81.

45. On this question, see P. de Man, *Allegories of Reading: Figural Language in Rousseau, Nietzsche, Rilke, and Proust* (New Haven: Yale University Press, 1979), pp. 270-301, esp. 270-77.

46. K. Burke, *A Rhetoric of Motives* (Berkeley: University of California Press, 2nd edn, 1969 [1950]), pp. 298-333.

as non-rational:[47] the counter-sublime, interpretive moment entails a specific rationality, at least in Jewish, but also in Christian, contexts. 4. The articulation of the rhetorical and the theological is not a matter of mere correlation between textual form and external referent. Tropological functionings themselves are that through which reference happens. To elaborate such tropings theologically is to reflect on them from the perspective of faith declaring the uniqueness of God and, in a Christian context, Jesus Christ. In Paul, we see the effect of the synecdochic confession of Christ and of the irretrievable event of the crucifixion to be a radicalization of the sublime moment, since sublimity is traced to a unique source. At the same time, there is no foundational link with daily morality; rather than an 'indicative' being the source of an 'imperative', what we have is an absolutely non-determined 'indicative–imperative' of grace being juxtaposed with an institution bound moral reason and praxis. Such an articulation contrasts with both Luke and Matthew, who carry the logic of hyperbole into the ethical realm in the Sermon on the Mount.[48] For Paul, positive ethics is entirely on the pole of the counter-sublime.[49] With him, we have passed from the messianic hope of the Jesus movement to a non-messianic Christology.[50] The more or less enlightened social conservatism that results may be seen as a deficiency in his ethical thinking. It may also be seen as the mark of a 'symbolic wisdom' that strives to keep sight of both the utterly new moment of beginnings and the all-too-human world of institutions. Provided one poses the problem of the heterogeneity between the two in all its sharpness, Paul certainly does not have the last word on this. But challenging Paul's ethics by recovering the significance of Kingdom of God messianism will not mean an end to the interpretive shuttle in the truth–and–power game. In other words: instead of the modern Western

47. G.A. Kennedy, *New Testament Interpretation through Rhetorical Criticism* (Chapel Hill: University of North Carolina Press, 1984), p. 6.

48. Ricoeur, 'La logique de Jésus'.

49. See D. Marguerat, 'Paul, un génie théologique et ses limites', in *CBFV* 24 (1985), pp. 65-76, esp. 71-76.

50. See on this A. Chester, 'Jewish Messianic Expectations and Mediatorial Figures and Pauline Christology', in M. Hengel and U. Heckel (eds.), *Paulus und das antike Judentum* (Tübingen: Mohr, 1991), pp. 17-89.

adequation model of truth, the sublime presents us with a model of truth by negotiation between the too much and the too little. Or, between the heroic gaze of the angel and the tender laughter of the mother.[51]

---

51. Where is the Father in all this? Well, maybe he is the negotiator himself. Of course, 'father' and 'mother' are not to be confused with gender roles.

RETHINKING THE RHETORICAL SITUATION:
THE ENTEXTUALIZATION OF THE SITUATION IN NEW TESTAMENT EPISTLES*

Dennis L. Stamps

Introduction

The historical situation, the circumstances in which a text is written and to which a text is a response, has traditionally been one of the key determinate factors in interpreting or reading any New Testament text, and especially a New Testament epistle.[1] In recent years as rhetorical criticism has gained popularity, the historical situation or the epistolary occasion has been renamed or reclassified as the 'rhetorical situation'.[2] In the study which follows, the first section will examine and evaluate the concept of the 'rhetorical situation' as it is generally conceived in the practice of rhetorical criticism. In the second section, an alternative or 'rethinking' of the rhetorical situation will be explored. Specifically, this study is interested in the way the text presents a selected, limited and crafted entextualization of the situation. From this perspective, it is suggested that the situation exists as a rhetorical figure which the audience must construct in the process of the situation's progressive presentation in the text. As such, it becomes

*   My appreciation to the Bethune-Baker Fund, University of Cambridge, for their financial assistance in writing and presenting this paper.
    1.   Most standard New Testament introductions discuss the occasion or situation as a necessary introductory matter for a proper exegesis of a New Testament epistle. See C. Tuckett, *Reading the New Testament* (London: SPCK, 1987), p. 55: 'Knowledge about the situation addressed by a writer is also a very important factor in the exegesis of individual texts'.
    2.   For biblical rhetorical criticism, the influential definition of the rhetorical situation is provided in G.A. Kennedy, *New Testament Interpretation through Rhetorical Criticism* (Chapel Hill: University of North Carolina Press, 1984), pp. 34-36.

possible to evaluate the way this textual presentation creates a rhetorical effect through its overall presentation in the letter as a whole and by its use in specific topical discussions or in what one might call the individual rhetorical units of the letter. Finally, in the third section, this alternative perspective on the rhetorical situation, what one might label a literary-rhetorical perspective, will be applied to a New Testament epistle, 1 Corinthians.

1. *Classical Rhetorical Criticism and the Situation*

Recent rhetorical criticism of the New Testament letters has used classical and modern rhetorical theory to develop the concept of the rhetorical situation.[3] There is actually little in practice which separates the concept of the situation in recent rhetorical criticism from the situation as conceived in historical-criticism. At this point, it seems necessary to review the present attempts at defining the 'rhetorical situation' and in turn to offer some evaluation.

Several scholars stand out as key figures in setting the agenda for the discussion: L. Bitzer, G.A. Kennedy, W. Wuellner and E. Schüssler Fiorenza. Bitzer, exploring the theory of rhetoric from the perspective of philosophy and modern communication theory, suggested:

> Rhetorical situation may be defined as a complex of persons, events, objects, and relations presenting an actual or potential exigence which can be completely or partially removed if discourse, introduced into the situation can so constrain human decision or action as to bring about the significant modification of the exigence.[4]

For rhetorical critics, especially biblical rhetorical critics, the insightful point was the introduction of this dynamic interplay between the perceived exigence and the response as a means to affect or modify that exigence.

G.A. Kennedy's now classic handbook on rhetorical criticism, *New*

---

3. The relationship between classical and modern rhetorical theory for the concept of the rhetorical situation is perhaps best spelt out by L. Thurén, *The Rhetorical Strategy of 1 Peter: With Special Regard to Ambiguous Expressions* (Åbo: Åbo Akademi, 1990), pp. 70-75.

4. L. Bitzer, 'The Rhetorical Situation', *Philosophy and Rhetoric* 1 (1968), p. 6. An important response to Bitzer is provided by A. Brinton, 'Situation in the Theory of Rhetoric', *Philosophy and Rhetoric* 14 (1981), pp. 234-48.

Testament Interpretation through Rhetorical Criticism, drew heavily upon Bitzer in defining the concept of the rhetorical situation.[5] It is Kennedy's formulation which has set the pace for most New Testament scholars' understanding of the rhetorical situation.[6] Kennedy translates Bitzer into the traditional language of biblical criticism: 'Once a preliminary determination of the rhetorical unit has been made, the critic should attempt to define the "rhetorical situation" of the unit. This roughly corresponds to the *Sitz im Leben* of form criticism' (p. 34). Putting the concept in this light suggests a primarily historical dimension to the concept. This is brought out more clearly by Kennedy when he adds time and place (p. 35) to Bitzer's list of factors ('persons, events, objects, and relations') which define the exigence. However, in the end, Kennedy's discussion of the rhetorical situation focuses on two aspects, the audience (both the immediate and the universal), and the primary rhetorical problem which the speaker faces (pp. 35, 36).

For Kennedy what distinguishes the rhetorical situation from the traditional historical understanding of the situation is the rhetorical dimension. As he says, 'the response made is conditioned by the situation and in turn has some possibility of affecting the situation or what follows from it' (p. 35). The rhetorical critic, according to Kennedy's definition, seeks to discover the correlation between the inventional topics and the overriding rhetorical problem, or the relationship between what is said and how it is said and why. L. Thurén explains it this way:

> To reconstruct the rhetorical situation corresponds roughly to the speaker's first task in classical rhetoric, the *inventio*. In this phase of producing a speech the author defines the addressees' premises and needs, sets and clarifies his aims with the speech, and chooses adequate and effective material for its presentation.[7]

Kennedy and those who follow his suggested methodology have highlighted a neglected aspect in reconstructing the situation—the dynamic nature between the speaker's construction of text, the rhetorical problem, and the audience. Yet the overriding historical

5.   Kennedy, *New Testament Interpretation*, pp. 34-36.
6.   For example, D.F. Watson, *Invention, Arrangement, and Style: Rhetorical Criticism of Jude and 2 Peter* (Atlanta: Scholars Press, 1988), pp. 8-9.
7.   Thurén, *Rhetorical Strategy*, p. 71.

dimension to Kennedy's understanding of the rhetorical situation is evident in his effort to define the goal of rhetorical criticism in general. Kennedy's rhetorical criticism is rooted in a recovery of 'real' history: 'What we need to do is to try to hear his [Paul's] words as a Greek-speaking audience would have heard them' (p. 10), and a recovery of the historical author: 'The ultimate goal of rhetorical analysis, briefly put, is the discovery of the author's intent and of how that is transmitted through a text to an audience' (p. 12).

Wilhelm Wuellner's attempts at defining the rhetorical situation in response to Kennedy have helped to clarify where the rhetorical situation differs from the historical understanding of the situation: 'The rhetorical situation differs both from the historical situation of a given author and reader and from the generic situation or conventions of the *Sitz im Leben* of forms or genres in one point: the rhetorical critic looks foremost for the premises of a text as appeal or argument'.[8] In a later writing, Wuellner states more fully what he means, at least in relation to Luke's Gospel:

> To inquire into the rhetorical or argumentative situation is to ask what the specific condition or situation there *is* (not *was*, as an historical question) that generates the text as we now have it in Lk. 12.1–13.9…But the historical situation, both inside and outside of the narrative and its sermon, is categorically different from the argumentative situation, the exigency, the 'intentionality', that gives (not *gave*) rise and shape to the text as argument, that is, in its orientation toward convincing/persuading the audience/reader. Distinct from intentionality, but closely related to it, is the concern for the values contained in, and projected by, the text.[9]

Drawing upon linguistics and literary criticism, Wuellner suggests a move away from an historically conditioned perspective of the rhetorical situation to a perspective governed more by the immediate context of the text. What Wuellner seems to be implying is that the rhetorical situation is not defined by the correspondence between the extrinsic factors and the textual strategy, but by the correspondence between the textual form and its argument or its ability to persuade.

8.   W. Wuellner, 'Where is Rhetorical Criticism Taking Us?', *CBQ* 49 (1987), p. 456.

9.   W. Wuellner, 'The Rhetorical Genre of Jesus' Sermon in Luke 12.1–13.9', in D.F. Watson (ed.), *Persuasive Artistry: Studies in New Testament Rhetoric in Honor of George A. Kennedy* (JSNTSup, 50; Sheffield: JSOT Press, 1991), pp. 99-100.

In this sense, the rhetorical situation is more a textual phenomenon than an historical event.

E. Schüssler Fiorenza, complementing yet distinct from Wuellner, utilizes insights from reader-response criticism to specify a four-stage rhetorical critical analysis which distinguishes between three different aspects of the rhetorical situation: (1) the historical argumentative situation, (2) the implied or inscribed rhetorical situation, and (3) the rhetorical interests of contemporary interpretation.[10] Like Wuellner, she also introduces a critical assessment of the values or the politico-theological self-understanding projected by the text as part of the rhetorics of the text.[11] Though Schüssler Fiorenza is critically astute in her theory, in the end her actual application of these precepts to 1 Corinthians ends up being very much a historically conditioned reconstruction of the rhetorical situation.[12]

In terms of evaluation, the agenda set by Kennedy for defining the rhetorical situation remains the controlling perspective for most New Testament rhetorical critics.[13] For Kennedy, and those who follow his conception, the rhetoric of the text hinges on the correspondence of the form and content of the text with the historical or empirical author and audience. It is not surprising then that these rhetorical

10. E. Schüssler Fiorenza, 'Rhetorical Situation and Historical Reconstruction in 1 Corinthians', *NTS* 33 (1987), pp. 396-89.

11. Schüssler Fiorenza, 'Rhetorical Situation', p. 388.

12. Schüssler Fiorenza, 'Rhetorical Situation', pp. 390-400.

13. Thurén (*Rhetorical Strategy*, pp. 70-75) attempts to distinguish his approach from Kennedy's through the use of the literary concepts of implied author and imagined audience, but it is not completely clear how his concepts differ from Kennedy's in the actual critical application to the text. Similar to Kennedy if not dependent on him are B.L. Mack, *Rhetoric and the New Testament* (Guides to Biblical Scholarship; Minneapolis: Fortress Press, 1990), p. 20; J.D. Hester, 'Placing the Blame: The Presence of Epideictic in Galatians 1 and 2', in Watson (ed.), *Persuasive Artistry*, pp. 282-85. The 'Betz' school of rhetorical criticism does not actually use the term, *rhetorical situation*, and in practice uses a historical-critical reconstruction of the occasion; see for a prime example M.M. Mitchell, *Paul and the Rhetoric of Reconciliation: An Exegetical Investigation of the Language of Composition of 1 Corinthians* (Hermeneutische Untersuchungen zur Theologie, 28; Tübingen: Mohr, 1991). I am aware of D. Hellholm's concept of the 'communication situation', but I have not yet read his work, *Das Visionenbuch des Hermas als Apokalypse: Form-geschichtiliche und textteoretische Studien zu einer literarischen Gattung. I. Metodologische Vorüberlegungen und makrostrukturelle Textanalyse* (ConBNT, 13.1; Lund: Gleerup, 1980).

critics primarily analyze the New Testament texts from a largely ancient rhetorical model.[14] In the end, the rhetorical critic engages in a type of 'rhetorical' form criticism, determining the rhetorical problem which precipitated the speaker's choice of the ancient rhetorical form as a means of assessing the function of the rhetorical unit.

For this perspective, the key factors with regard to the situation are the 'actual' audience and the 'actual' rhetorical problem.[15] The speaker/writer must properly conceive of the 'actual' audience in order to select and construct the proper rhetorical response which will convince this audience. In particular, the speaker/writer must grasp the 'actual' rhetorical problem, that crucial issue which must be resolved or overcome, in order to bring the audience to the point of adherence to the writer's perspective.

Most rhetorical-critical interpretations of the situation do differ from the historical-critical understandings in that a greater emphasis is given to the speaker or writer's perspective as a factor in determining the historical audience and problem. The rhetorical critic sees the text as the speaker's understanding of the situation/exigence. Thus, analyzing the speaker's rhetorical construction of the text (the invention, arrangement and style) provides the clues for reconstructing the rhetorical situation.

Traditional rhetorical criticism, especially that espoused by G.A. Kennedy, has provided a valuable alternative and in some sense auxiliary interpretive approach to reconstructing the situation in comparison with historical criticism.[16] But such critical efforts are limited because they work with a specific interpretive goal, the correspondence of a text with the art of ancient rhetoric, and because they utilize an interpretive methodology that is primarily historical in nature to achieve that interpretive goal, classical rhetoric.

---

14. D.L. Stamps ('Rhetorical Criticism and the Rhetoric of New Testament Studies', *Literature and Theology* 6 [1992]) suggests that there are different kinds of rhetorical criticism operative in New Testament criticism.

15. Kennedy, *New Testament Interpretation*, pp. 35-36. Cf. also Watson, *Invention*, pp. 9, 29.

16. The contribution of Kennedy on this point is evaluated in C.C. Black II, 'Keeping up with Recent Studies. XVI. Rhetorical Criticism and Biblical Interpretation', *ExpTim* 100 (1987), pp. 256-57; and J. Lambrecht, 'Rhetorical Criticism and the New Testament', *Bijdragen* 50 (1989), pp. 245-48.

2. *The Entextualization of the Rhetorical Situation*

After having examined and evaluated a number of scholars' understandings of the rhetorical situation, this section will explore and expand some of the ideas about it as suggested or implied in the writings of W. Wuellner and E. Schüssler Fiorenza. In particular, Wuellner implies that the rhetorical situation stems from the premises of a text as appeal or argumentation, or it could be stated that the rhetorical situation exists as a premise of the text contributing to the argumentative or rhetorical nature of the text. Schüssler Fiorenza speaks about the implied or inscribed rhetorical situation in the text. It is these suggestions about the rhetorical situation which provide a way to rethink the concept.

To speak about the inscribed rhetorical situation is to speak about the entextualization of the situation. That is, the rhetorical situation exists as a textual or literary presentation within the text or discourse as a whole. It is possible to think of the rhetorical situation as a literary construct embedded in the text as a rhetorical device or figure which contributes to the overall rhetorical aim or to the argumentation of the text.

While it may be granted that any text, and an ancient New Testament epistle in particular, stems from certain historical and social contingencies which contribute to the rhetorical situation of a text, it is also true that a text presents a selected, limited and crafted entextualization of the situation. The entextualized situation is not the historical situation which generates the text and/or which the text responds to or addresses; rather, at this level, it is that situation embedded in the text and created by the text which contributes to the rhetorical effect of the text.[17] Certainly, for an epistle like

17. This is not to slip into the error of the formalism of the New Criticism which sees any rendering of the text related only to intrinsic textual factors. At this point it is not possible to analyze the complex philosophical relationship between reality or history and its concomitant textual presentation. What is important to recognize is that any textual presentation of a historical reality represents a process which involves interpretation and narrativization that places a distance or gap between the textual presentation and the 'actual' event(s). For a classical treatment of the issue, see H. White, *Tropics of Discourse: Essays in Cultural Criticism* (Baltimore: Johns Hopkins University Press, 1978). The critical pursuit of bridging that 'gap' remains an important part of biblical interpretation, but this study pursues an alternative

1 Corinthians to work, the sender must present the entextualized situation in such a manner that elicits correspondence with some, if not most, of the audience. Yet it is possible that the sender's perspective on the situation and its subsequent literary presentation in the epistle may become a point of debate in the ongoing relationship between the letter parties. Rhetorically speaking, then, the sender constructs and presents his or her view of the situation in the epistolary text which the audience consents to for the sake of the argument. The persuasiveness of the argument of the letter is linked to this literary presentation of the situation. It is this literary-rhetorical perspective which will be the primary focus of this rethinking of the rhetorical situation for New Testament epistles.

It is probably necessary at this point to identify several of the key assumptions about a letter-text which are operative in the discussion at hand. First, letters are a particular kind of discourse defined chiefly by the transmission of a text in written form according to cultural convention.[18] Letters have a primary communication purpose which is usually to convey some sort of information, which may be factual or a request for an action, etc.[19] Secondly, letters, as a particular kind of discourse, conventionally operate to maintain the relationship between the two letter parties.[20] Usually, from this aspect of the letter, one finds in letters allusions to the 'story' of the relationship between the letter parties and possibly some of the circumstances surrounding the particular correspondence. Thirdly, this second aspect of the letter corresponds directly to the entextualized rhetorical situation or the literary-rhetorical situation.

In order to examine the literary-rhetorical situation a procedure for isolating it from the letter-text as a whole will be proposed. C. Perelman's discussion of a rhetorical figure suggests two characteristics as essential to the isolation of a figure from with a text: (1) a discernable structure independent of the content, and (2) a use that is

---

perspective without necessarily denigrating the historical-critical perspective or other critical perspectives which examine the relationship between the text and history.

18. See the interesting analysis by P. Violi, 'Letters', in T.A. van Dijk (ed.), *Discourse and Literature* (Amsterdam: John Benjamins, 1985), pp. 149-67.

19. J.L. White, *Light from Ancient Letters* (Philadelphia: Fortress Press, 1986), pp. 192-93, 198-211.

20. White, *Light from Ancient Letters*, pp. 198-211.

different from the normal manner of expression.[21] The literary-rhetorical presentation of the situation has an analogous relationship to these characteristics. While the inscribed rhetorical situation is embedded within the text as a whole, its structure as a story or narrative, as will be shown, is easily abstracted from the letter message as a whole. And while the language used in relation to the inscribed situation is 'normal', the deictic references to the situation, that is, those references to the relationship between the letter parties and to the circumstances about how the present correspondence came to be, distinguish them from the primary informational discourse in the letter.[22]

The task now is to find a way to isolate the inscribed situation as a rhetorical figure and evaluate its rhetorical function and effect. The work of Norman Petersen provides a model for such a task.[23] In his book, *Rediscovering Paul*, the first third of the book is an attempt to transform Paul's letter to Philemon into a narrative. The transformation of the letter into a narrative is based on the simple premise that letters tell a story.[24] His theory is more extensive than what has been suggested above, simply that embedded in a letter is a story of the relationship between the letter parties; rather his perspective entails the wholesale transformation of the letter's message into a narrative. This enables him to set up the narrative world of a Pauline letter and analyze that narrative world against the social structures and relations operative in the Pauline story.[25]

However, the wholesale transformation of the letter into a narrative reconfigures the textual structure, the form and content, that is, the letter becomes a narrative. As a result the letter in its transformed state takes on a different function: the letter-text as a narrative tells a story; the letter-text as letter conveys a message. In order to preserve the epistolary structure and function of a letter-text, it seems better to suggest that the inscribed situation tells a story and that that story is embedded in an epistle. In this sense, both theories agree that in a

21. C. Perelman and L. Olbrechts-Tyteca, *The New Rhetoric: A Treatise on Argumentation* (trans. J. Wilkinson and P. Weaver; Notre Dame: University of Notre Dame Press, 1969), p. 168.
22. For a discussion of deixis in letters, see Violi, 'Letters', pp. 149-57.
23. N.R. Petersen, *Rediscovering Paul: Philemon and the Sociology of Paul's Narrative World* (Philadelphia: Fortress Press, 1985).
24. Petersen, *Rediscovering Paul*, pp. 1-5.
25. Petersen, *Rediscovering Paul*, pp. 17-32.

letter there is a story of the relationship between sender and recipients.

Petersen has demonstrated that the story a letter tells has many of the components of narrative. The story is a narrative as it is an ordered account of two or more events.[26] The story has a point of view as it represents the sender's (or narrator's) perspective on the relationship between the letter parties.[27] In addition, there is a spatial and temporal stance with regard to the point of view.[28] Temporally, the story is told from the position of the time of writing, so that the events of the situation receive their temporal marking from that point of view: present equals time of writing; past equals before time of writing; future equals after time of writing. Spatially, the letter suggests a marked distance between the narrator and narratee in time and space: the letter is directed to an absent person in another place who will read the letter in a deferred time.

The story a letter tells also has a plot.[29] Through a temporal point of view, it is possible to plot out a sequential arrangement of selected events and situations referred to in the letter and their possible causality, unity and effect. An interesting feature of the plot in the letter's story is the sequence of events. The textual sequence is the narrator's arrangement, which may or may not coincide with a chronological sequence generally operative in most historians' reconstruction of the situation.

Utilizing this understanding of the narrative components operative in the letter's story of the entexualized literary-rhetorical situation, it is possible to begin the process of extracting that story from the letter message. The first task is to identify the references to the actions/events/situations which particularize the relationship between the letter parties embedded in the letter text. The elements of plot and point of view, as mentioned above, enable these kernel statements about the situation to be listed or plotted chronologically from the temporal perspective of the time of writing. This chronological sequence then represents the inscribed spatio-temporal story of the relationship

26. This is very much a minimalist view of narrative; see G. Prince, *A Grammar of Stories* (The Hague: Mouton, 1973).
27. Petersen, *Rediscovering Paul*, pp. 11-13.
28. Petersen, *Rediscovering Paul*, pp. 11-13.
29. Petersen, *Rediscovering Paul*, p. 13.

between the letter parties, as it would be actualized by any reader(s) who seek(s) the 'logical' order.[30]

One means of evaluating the rhetorical function and effect of the inscribed situation is to compare the chronological sequence of the story with the textual sequence, the sequence of references to the situation as they appear in the text. In a sense, the comparison of the chronological sequence with the textual sequence provides possible insight into how the story provides a causal or motivational link between the situation and the letter message or into how the story helps dispose the audience towards the letter purpose/message. From such a comparison one can see how the plot of the story of the relationship between the letter parties assists the letter's message or informational intent and reinforces the statement of the letter purpose. By such a comparison, it is possible to see how the situation or specific events which are part of the situation are inserted in the letter to assist the rhetorical goal of the letter.

Having adapted Petersen's narratological theory for isolating the literary-rhetorical situation or the story of the relationship between the letter parties inscribed in epistles, it remains to apply this theory to an epistle like 1 Corinthians. Such a plot analysis would work from the temporal perspective adopted in the letter itself: the present tense is the time of writing. The point of view spatially and perspectivally would be the speaker's or author's.

For the purpose of this study, it is not possible to go through the entire text of 1 Corinthians in order to set out all the references to the literary-rhetorical situation in textual and chronological order. Such a survey of 1 Corinthians is provided in my forthcoming book, *The Rhetorical Use of the Epistolary Form in 1 Corinthians: The Rhetoric of Power*.[31] In the final section, in order to illustrate the concept of the literary-rhetorical situation, certain topical discussions in 1 Corinthians will be discussed in order to discover how specific references to the entextualized situation rhetorically function to aid the argument or persuasiveness of the discussions.

30. Petersen, *Rediscovering Paul*, pp. 47-48.
31. D.L. Stamps, *The Rhetorical Use of the Epistolary Form in 1 Corinthians: The Rhetoric of Power* (JSNTSup; Sheffield: JSOT Press [forthcoming]).

3. The Rhetorical Effect of the Inscribed Rhetorical Situation within the Topical Discussions of 1 Corinthians

In the letter-text of 1 Corinthians there are numerous topical discussions on religious and ethical issues or matters which have been raised either by the sender or, through communication or contact with the sender, by the letter recipients.[32] By examining the use of the entextualized rhetorical situation in a number of these topical discussions, a pattern of argumentation emerges in which the inscribed rhetorical situation acts as an essential part of the argument in each discussion.

Most of the topical discussions are introduced by reference to the speaker's source of knowledge about the issue: oral reports (1.11; 5.1; 11.18), unattributed specific knowledge about church problems (6.7; 15.2), and probable references to issues raised in the recent letter from the Corinthians (7.1, 25; 8.1; 12.1; 16.1, 12). All in all, this leaves only two, or possibly three, matters which have no apparent attribution to the kind of knowledge the speaker has about the matter under discussion: (1) sexual immorality and prostitutes (6.12-20), (2) the place of women and men in worship (11.2-16), and possibly (3) the rights of an apostle (9.1-27), which is actually a digression within the discussion about idol meat (8.1–11.1). The source and kind of knowledge the speaker has about the issue or problem in the Corinthian church seemingly determines the manner or pattern of argumentation.

In each matter raised in response to an oral report, the concluding instructions are backed up by a reference to the speaker's presence in the community. The problem of divisions or quarrels (1.11–4.16) concludes with a reference to two future events in the relationship between the letter parties. First is Timothy's imminent arrival in Corinth. He arrives with a specific recommendation, 'who is my beloved son and is faithful in the Lord', and with a specific task, 'who will remind you of my ways which are of Christ, just as I am teaching everywhere in every church' (4.17). Second is the sender's impending visit, during which he will investigate the claims of the arrogant ones (4.19). The tone of this forthcoming visit is to be determined by the

32. The classic analysis of 1 Corinthians in terms of topics and their correspondence to the relationship between Paul and the Corinthians is J.C. Hurd, *The Origin of 1 Corinthians* (repr. Macon, GA: Mercer University Press, 1983), pp. 61-94.

addressees' immediate response to what has been instructed: 'What do you wish? That I come to you with a rod or in love with a spirit of meekness?' (4.21). The promise of Timothy's immediate visit (he will also report back to the sender as the sender states later in the letter [16.11]) followed by a promise of a forthcoming visit by the sender himself acts as a forceful enjoinder to adopt the instructions contained in the discussion.

Similarly the discussion of the immoral brother (5.1-13) concludes with a command for a very specific, verifiable future action, 'Expel the wicked man from among you' (5.13b). While no future visit is specifically attached to this matter, the presence of the speaker is still invoked in a curious way:

> For I indeed, being absent in the body, but being present in the spirit, already have judged, as though I were present, the one having done this thing. In the name of the Lord Jesus, when you are assembled with my spirit [present], with the power of our Lord Jesus, hand over this person to Satan... (5.3-5a).

The speaker makes two points about his presence. First, he is present in spirit, and can rightfully act in the community to make a judgment (5.3).[33] Secondly, when the community gathers together in the Lord, he is present with them as they carry out the necessary judgment upon the offender (5.4).[34] In a very curious sense, the speaker argues for immediate action based on his presence in the community through his spirit and the Spirit. Once again, on the basis of an oral report which provides very specific information about the problem, a definite, situation-specific future action is commanded in association with the presence of the speaker.

Another issue brought to light by an oral report, the Corinthians' practice at the Lord's Supper (11.18-34), is also discussed and concluded with a commanded specific action and with reference to the speaker's presence. After giving concrete details of the Corinthians' unacceptable behaviour (11.21), the audience is given specific instruction which could only apply to the Corinthians: 'So then, my brothers, when you come together to eat, wait for one another' (11.33). This is

---

33. This text is problematic to say the least, and I am heavily influenced by G.D. Fee, *The First Epistle to the Corinthians* (NICNT; Grand Rapids: Eerdmans, 1987), pp. 205-206.

34. Fee, *First Epistle to the Corinthians*, p. 204.

enforced by a reference to the speaker's impending future visit, which is not only a personal follow-up to what has been instructed, but also a promise of further instruction on the matter: 'And the remaining matters [in this regard] I will set in order when I come' (11.34b). Both the 'threat' of a visit and the commitment to set the whole matter in order creates an aura of authority which places the speaker over the situation and the audience under that authority.[35]

There are two other issues which are very situation-specific, the matter of the collection (16.1-4), and the query about Apollos's future plans for a visit to Corinth (16.12). Both are designated by the περὶ δέ formula, and thus possible matters which the Corinthians have raised in their letter.[36] Both of these issues by their very nature can only refer to the situation between the letter parties: the Corinthians' role in the collection is a particular act, and the matter of Apollos is dependent upon a prior established relationship. In each brief discussion, not only is the specificity of the issue indicated, but once again, the speaker's particular role in the matter is set forth.

With regard to the collection (16.1-4),[37] the audience is told to do as the other churches do, in this case the Galatian churches, which establishes a liaison of coexistence to enforce the required action.[38] But note the speaker's stated role, a role that is to be played out in this ubiquitous future visit by the speaker: when he comes, he collects the funds, he sends the envoy with letters of introduction and he may accompany the envoy to Jerusalem. The authorial presence is overwhelming in this discussion: διέταξα, ἔλθω, παραγένωμαι, πέμψω. Such weight of authorial presence in such a short discussion acts as a persuasive argument which in effect emphasizes the importance of this matter in the ongoing relationship between the letter parties.

With regard to Apollos, the matter is simple (16.12). He is not coming now, but he will come when he has the opportunity. This

---

35. Commentators discuss a tone of censure in this section without discussing the rhetorical effect of 11.33-34 on the preceding censure, 11.17-32.

36. The use of περὶ δέ does not have to signify a topic suggested in the correspondence from the Corinthians; see M.M. Mitchell, 'Concerning περὶ δέ in 1 Corinthians', *NovT* 31 (1989), pp. 229-56.

37. For a full discussion of the collection, see K. Nickle, *The Collection: A Study in Paul's Strategy* (London: SPCK, 1966).

38. C. Perelman, *The Realm of Rhetoric* (trans. W. Kluback; Notre Dame: University of Notre Dame Press, 1982), pp. 89-101.

represents a future aspect of the inscribed rhetorical situation. This is a part of the story which is exclusively among the Corinthian church, the sender, and Apollos; hence it is very situation-specific. Again, in such a situation-specific context, the authorial presence is overt: 'I strongly encouraged [πολλὰ παρεκάλεσα] him so that he would come to you with the brothers'. The contrasts between Apollos's plans and the sender's become obvious: Paul is coming soon for a long visit; Apollos may come at some indefinite time (ὅταν [whenever]). Paul wishes Apollos to go now; Apollos wishes to wait. The whole issue of the relationship among Paul, Apollos and the Corinthian church remains a vague undertow in the epistle, fueling much historical speculation as to what has occurred.[39] At the level of the text, little information is given; but in what is given, the authorial presence throughout the letter (see specially 3.1-9 plus 4.15-16!), and in this discussion in particular, rhetorically places the prestige of the sender above that of Apollos.

On the other hand, the remaining issues, especially those which are designated by the περὶ δέ formula (except as discussed above), are dealt with by general instruction which could be in common with all the other churches of God (cf. 7.17; 11.16; 14.33).[40] In none of these other issues is the speaker's presence invoked, whether as a present or future event. In two of the issues not introduced by oral reports or by περὶ δέ, but which evidence specific knowledge of the situation at Corinth on the speaker's part, that is, lawsuits (6.7) and some who are denying the resurrection (15.12), there is more apparent direct address than in other discussions. Yet despite the situation-specific references and the direct address, the instructions still have a general nature to them.

In a letter which is one of the most situation-specific in the Pauline corpus, these general instructions in response to apparent questions or queries by the Corinthian congregation seem peculiar. Why is there little if any rehearsal of the Corinthian church practice on these issues? Why is there almost no direct application of the instructions to the Corinthian church life? At the rhetorical level, this lack of directness or specificity creates an interesting effect in two ways.

39. Scholars vary as to whether Paul's relationship with Apollos was cordial or strained: Hurd, *Origin of 1 Corinthians*, pp. 74, 206-207; Mitchell, *Paul*, pp. 177-78, 293.

40. See Mitchell, 'Concerning περὶ δέ', pp. 229-56 and note above.

First, the occasional reminder in a number of these general discussions that what is instructed is in common with the practice of the other churches (cf. 7.17; 11.16; 14.33), combined with the paraenetic nature of the teaching, in effect places the discussion above the particular.[41] Implicitly, the audience is informed by such a stance that there is a general, catholic ruling on the matter which provides uniformity and expects conformity.[42]

Secondly, the lack of particularity creates a distancing of the authorial presence from the Corinthian situation by subsuming it under the 'common' doctrine and practice. By remaining above the fray, the speaker is presented as persuading by the expression of convictions, and thus not engaging with opponents (if there are any) or even answering the specific question(s) posed by the Corinthians. Presenting the argument/discussion in such a way establishes a communion of values and creates a disposition to action. In a sense, this authorial distancing places the speaker above the actual debate or problem in Corinth, and endows his authorial self-presentation with wider significance, and hence greater authority. In summary, the effect created by this general instructive stance both through the implicit conformity invoked and through the authorial distancing is to persuade and dispose the audience towards the letter message.

The conventional ending of the letter-body with a visit *topoi* (16.5-12, 15-18) provides an effective way to reinforce the entire letter contents.[43] This closing presentation of the speaker's future plans creates the same effect as the authorial presence used in other individual topical discussions. As a result of this talk of a final visit, a reference to the future dimension of the inscribed rhetorical situation, all the instructions in the letter are underscored as issues which have implications for the ongoing relationship between the letter parties.[44]

From examining these textual presentations of the individual topical discussion and the way the references to the inscribed rhetorical

---

41. On paraenesis for this study, see D. Aune, *The New Testament in its Literary Environment* (Library of Early Christianity, 8; Philadelphia: Westminster Press, 1987), pp. 191, 194-97.

42. Perelman and Olbrechts-Tyteca, *New Rhetoric*, pp. 321-27.

43. T.Y. Mullins, 'Visit Talk in New Testament Letters', *CBQ* 35 (1973), pp. 350-58.

44. Mitchell, *Paul*, p. 293.

situation function in each, there emerges a regular pattern of argumentation. Most topics are introduced by a reference to oral reports or by use of an epistolary formula like περὶ δέ. Then there follows instruction on the matter, which is either general or particular. Those matters which are explicitly situation-specific are dealt with by reference to a specifically verifiable, anticipated action on the part of the addressee. Further, in each of these situation-specific discussions, the authorial presence, most often a future visit, becomes a primary textual assertion reinforcing the expected action. In matters which are not presented as situation-specific, from the speaker's point of view, a more general instructive stance is adopted without such an overt assertion of authorial presence. This pattern of argumentation is apparently peculiar to 1 Corinthians with respect to the Pauline epistolary tradition.

Conclusion

At issue in this study is the fact that there is a rhetorical figure, the inscribed rhetorical situation, embedded in the letter-text. This figure can be isolated within the letter-text by its deictic nature or its situation specificity with reference to the relationship between the letter parties. The inscribed rhetorical situation is in essence the story of the relationship between the sender and addressees told from the temporal perspective of the time of writing and from the point of view of the sender. The problem in isolating the story is that the references to the story are 'randomly' interspersed throughout the letter-text. Based on the narrative and deictic references they can be isolated from the primary discourse of the letter. Such a procedure reveals a limited, selected, ordered and perspectivally constructed literary-rhetorical situation. The situation as a rhetorical figure creates a rhetorical effect which contributes to the overall rhetoric of the letter.

As one examines the way in which the individual references to the rhetorical situation function within the different topical discussions, the rhetorical effect of the specific references becomes evident. On an individual level, some of the references to the situation contribute to the argumentative goal of each discussion in various ways: argument from the prestige of the speaker, argument for a liaison of coexistence, etc.[45] In each topical discussion, the specificity of the situational references also determines the pattern of argumentation: whether a direct or general instructive stance is adopted, and whether the authorial presence is specifically invoked or distanced.

In terms of the rhetoric of the letter, it is the textual presentation of the inscribed situation which is crucial to the argument of the letter. The rhetoric of the letter operates from the situation as it is constructed and presented in the text. The argument of the letter, then, is a response to the situation which is presented in the text. This is evident in the way in which the topical discussions utilize certain selected aspects of the story as the basis of the argument and the instructions directed to the readers.

In summary, the textual presentation of the rhetorical situation becomes the basis or a premise for the argument of the letter as a whole and for the individual rhetorical units in the letter. But this textual presentation of the rhetorical situation not only acts as a premise, but is rhetorically persuasive in and of itself. Through the textual presentation of the literary-rhetorical situation, the audience and the speaker are conditioned to adhere to the new reality which the text posits. For the sake of the argument, the ideal reader and the implied speaker accept the textual situation as the situation in which the letter operates. In more literary terms, the textuality of the rhetorical situation means that the speaker and audience as literary constructions themselves only meet in the 'world-of-the-text'. One aspect of the world-of-the-text which the text constructs is the rhetorical situation.

45. Perelman, *Realm of Rhetoric*, pp. 81-105.

ARGUMENT AND GENRE OF 1 CORINTHIANS 12–14

Joop Smit

Introduction

Within the first letter of Paul 'to the church of God in Corinth' (1 Cor. 1.2) the discussion on the 'pneumatic phenomena' (τὰ πνευματικά) forms a separate part. Using a standard phrase Paul begins a new subject in 1 Cor. 12.1: 'About the pneumatic phenomena, brothers...' (cf. 1 Cor. 7.1; 8.1; 16.1) and with another standard phrase he closes the discussion on this subject in 14.39: 'So, brothers...' (cf. 11.33; 15.58). In this passage Paul deals, more in particular, with two of the many spiritual gifts, namely glossolalia and prophecy. The prominent presence of these two gifts in 1 Corinthians 12–14 is all the more conspicuous as they are barely mentioned in the remaining part of the letter. Together they are the theme, uniting these three chapters into a separate part.[1]

To my knowledge, the coherence, which 1 Corinthians 12–14 already exhibits at first sight, has never been looked into thoroughly. Of course commentaries and studies provide outlines and dispositions of this passage, but time and again a justification of the disposition presented and of the criteria determining it fails to be given.[2] Therefore the purpose of this study is to look more closely into the

---

1. The substantive γλῶσσα occurs 21 times in 1 Cor. 12–14 and not elsewhere in the letter. The group προφητεία/προφητεύω/προφήτης occurs 20 times in this passage; besides this only προφητεύω occurs twice in 1 Cor. 11.4, 5.

2. A major contribution to the structure of 1 Corinthians has recently been made by M.M. Mitchell, in *Paul and the Rhetoric of Reconciliation: An Exegetical Investigation of the Language and Composition of 1 Corinthians* (Hermeneutische Untersuchungen zur Theologie, 28; Tübingen: Mohr, 1991). Her analysis of 1 Cor. 12–14, however, on pages 157-75, 267-83 offers little help, while the rhetorical disposition of these chapters is strangely neglected.

coherence of these chapters. In particular the course of the argumentation and the genre this discussion belongs to will be examined. By this we tread on almost virgin soil.[3] To explore the coherence of 1 Corinthians 12–14 I shall use classical, Hellenistic rhetoric. *Rhetorica ad Alexandrum* (c. 340 BCE), *De inventione* (c. 85 BCE) and *De partitione oratoria* (c. 45 BCE) written by Cicero, and *Rhetorica ad Herennium* (c. 85 BCE) are particularly helpful in this exploration, because these schoolish handbooks provide a good impression of the rhetoric that was generally practised in Paul's time and surroundings.

Not all parts of Paul's text receive equal attention in what follows. As for 1 Corinthians 13 in particular I shall limit myself to presenting the conclusions I reached and accounted for in earlier publications.[4] As a result this article is divided as follows. It begins with an examination of the framework of Paul's discussion (1 Cor. 12.1-3; 14.37-40) in the light of the rules the rhetorical handbooks issue for *exordium* and *peroratio*. Next an analysis follows of the two rounds of argumentation (1 Cor. 12.4-30; 14.1-33a) by means of the rhetorical theory on the *partitio*. After that the genre of 1 Corinthians 12–14 is defined on the basis of the characteristics the handbooks ascribe to the *genus deliberativum* and the *genus demonstrativum*. This article concludes with a schematic survey of the *dispositio* of 1 Corinthians 12–14.

1. *Exordium and Peroratio: 1 Corinthians 12.1-3; 14.37-40*

a. *Exordium: 1 Corinthians 12.1-3*
The rhetorical handbooks give detailed directions how a speech ought to begin.[5] From their discussion of the *exordium* the following instructions are of interest here. The intention of the *exordium* is to put the audience in the right mood for listening to the remainder of

3. The only exploration of the field so far is B. Standaert, 'Analyse rhétorique des chapitres 12 à 14 de 1 Co', in *Charisma und Agape (1 Ko 12–14)* (ed. L. De Lorenzi; Rome: Abtei St Paul vor den Mauern, 1983), pp. 23-34.
4. On 1 Cor. 12–14 I published earlier: 'De rangorde in de kerk: retorische analyse van 1 Kor. 12', *Tijdschrift voor Theologie* 29 (1989) pp. 325-43; 'The Genre of 1 Corinthians 13 in the Light of Classical Rhetoric', *NovT* 33 (1991), pp. 193-216; 'Two Puzzles: 1 Corinthians 12.31 and 13.3: A Rhetorical Solution', *NTS* 39 (1993), pp. 246-64.
5. Cicero, *De inventione* 1.15.20–19.27; *Rhetorica ad Herennium* 1.3.4–7.11; Quintilian 4.1.

the speech. This objective is brought about by making the listeners benevolent, attentive and receptive.[6] In the *exordium* the audience may be approached in two different ways. The direct and overt approach is called *principium*. The indirect approach, by way of detours and covert terms, is called *insinuatio*.[7] In difficult cases the second way should be taken, for instance when the audience is an alienated and hostile one; equally so when the speaker criticises something highly favoured by his audience.[8] In case of an *insinuatio* the speaker is advised not to mention at the outset the name of the person or subject matter, which offends the public, but to take cover for the moment behind another person or matter favoured by the audience.[9]

To ensure that the public is well-disposed, four items are usually brought forward in the *exordium*: the person of the speaker, of the opponents, of the auditors and the case in hand.[10]

In 1 Corinthians 12–14 Paul clearly intends to call the Corinthians to order in the question of glossolalia.[11] In this, however, two risks are inherent. Presumably the Corinthians are highly enthusiastic about this gift and should Paul criticise it they might easily turn against him. Moreover Paul's authority as an apostle is contested in Corinth, as has already become apparent in the first part of the letter (1 Cor. 1–4). So Paul is faced with a most delicate affair. Accordingly he avoids raising the matter of glossolalia directly and prefers the *insinuatio*, the indirect and cautious approach.[12] Therefore in 1 Cor. 12.1-3, in

6. *De inv.* 1.15.20.

7. *De inv.* 1.15.20.

8. *De inv.* 1.15.21; 1.17.23; *Rhet. ad Her.* 1.3.5.

9. *De inv.* 1.17.24.

10. *De inv.* 1.16.22.

11. Experts are unanimous on this point. G.D. Fee (*The First Epistle to the Corinthians* [NICNT; Grand Rapids: Eerdmans, 1987], p. 571) remarks: 'The problem is almost certainly an abuse of the gift of tongues'. G. Theissen (*Psychologische Aspekte paulinischer Theologie* [FRLANT, 131; Göttingen: Vandenhoeck & Ruprecht, 1983], p. 272) judges: 'Paulus antwortet sehr diplomatisch. Er bringt durchgehend eine hohe Achtung vor den Geistesgaben zum Ausdruck... aber in Wirklichkeit arbeitet er darauf hin, ihre hohe Wertschätzung in Korinth zu korrigieren.'

12. Standaert ('Analyse rhétorique', pp. 30-32) regards 12.1-11 as *exordium* and more specifically as an *insinuatio*.

covert terms, he deals successively with three of the set items that usually comprise an *exordium*.

In v. 1 he introduces the new subject he intends to discuss. For the time being, however, the specific subject, namely glossolalia, remains concealed under the general term 'the pneumatic phenomena'.

In v. 2 Paul criticises the unrestrained enthusiasm of his audience. This criticism is also not directly expressed but, for the time being, remains cloaked under an apparently innocent reminder of the past.

In v. 3 Paul postulates the authority he has as apostle of the Lord Jesus against the glossolalists. Whoever rejects him, rejects Jesus; whoever recognises him, recognises the Lord. For the time being, however, he as an apostle remains hidden behind the name of the Lord Jesus, who sent him.[13] Only at the end, in the *peroratio*, does he lift this incognito and in plain terms demands that the enthusiastic Corinthians recognise the authority to which he himself is entitled as an apostle of the Lord (14.37-38).[14]

b. *Peroratio: 1 Corinthians 14.37-40*
According to the theory of rhetoric, *exordium* and *peroratio*, the beginning and the end of a speech, are related to each other. They both deal with the case itself as well as with the emotions involved.[15] While the *exordium* introduces the subject and makes the audience well-disposed towards listening to the argumentation, the *peroratio* closes the discussion on the subject and exerts pressure on the audience to take the intended decision.

The difference between *exordium* and *peroratio* mainly lies in the tone used. The *exordium* will be more cautious and reserved than the *peroratio*, which offers the speaker the last opportunity for pressing the listeners into the decision wanted.[16]

13. A more ample justification of the unusual interpretation of this vexed verse proposed here may be found in Smit, 'Rangorde', pp. 335-38.
14. While discussing the *genus deliberativum*, Quintilian (3.8.10-13) has some further remarks which are of interest here. In this genre the *exordium* should be brief, the authority of the speaker should receive special attention and the *narratio* may often be omitted as everyone is sufficiently acquainted with the question.
15. For the *peroratio* see Cicero, *De inv.* 1.52.98–56.109; *Rhet. ad Her.* 2.30.47–31.50; Cicero, *Part. orat.* 15–17; Quintilian 6.1.
16. Quintilian 4.1.28-30; 6.1.9-11.

The *peroratio* usually consists of three parts, corresponding to the two-sided task it has to accomplish. *Recapitulatio* or *enumeratio* sums up the main points discussed. *Indignatio* and *conquestio* excite feelings of indignation or commiseration in the listeners.[17] Contrary to the *exordium*, the *peroratio* may sometimes frighten the audience.[18]

In the light of this general description of the *peroratio*, drawn from the rhetorical handbooks, three characteristics of 1 Cor. 14.37-40 are conspicuous.

1. A striking resemblance connects the beginning and the conclusion of Paul's exposition on the pneumatic gifts. Both passages exhibit the same three items in reverse order.
   a. The cause: the pneumatic gifts (12.1)
   b. The auditors: the glossolalists (12.2)
   c. The speaker: the authority of Paul, the apostle (12.3)
      —first negatively (3a)
      —then positively (3b)
   c'. The speaker: the authority of Paul, the apostle (14.37-38)
      —first positively (37)
      —then negatively (38)
   b'. The auditors: the glossolalists (14.39)
   a'. The cause: the pneumatic gifts (14.40)
   Both passages unmistakeably form an *inclusio*. The section of the letter opened in three steps in 12.1-3 is closed in 14.37-40 in the same three steps.

2. The last verses of Paul's discussion on the spiritual gifts give a retrospective view, a summary. The clause 'What I am writing to you' (v. 37) refers to the entire passage, beginning and ending with an appeal to the authority of the Lord Jesus (12.3; 14.37-38). The conclusion, 'So brothers, zealously strive to prophesy and do not prevent speaking in tongues' (v. 39), is a summary of Paul's argumentation in ch. 14 (cf. 14.1, 5). In the exhortation, 'Everything must be done properly and in order' (v. 40), the entire discussion on the spiritual gifts is, once again, summarized. All elements of this final sentence look back to what has gone before. 'Everything' (πάντα) refers more in particular to the

17. *Rhet. ad Her.* 2.30.47.
18. Quintilian 6.1.13.

'pneumatic phenomena' (τὰ πνευματικά) in 1 Cor. 12.1 and 14.1. 'Properly' (εὐσχημόνως) connotes the observation of the legitimate order of precedence in the church as argued in 1 Corinthians 12 (cf. 12.22-26; 13.5). 'In order' (κατὰ τάξιν) particularly refers to the right order in the meetings of the local church as urged in 1 Corinthians 14 (cf. 14.33a).

3. 1 Cor. 14.37-40 and 12.1-3 clearly differ in tone. The conclusion is more overt and urgent than the cautious beginning.

In 14.37-38 Paul overtly posits what he brought forward only in covert terms in 12.3, namely that he as an apostle is invested with the authority of the Lord Jesus. In 14.39 Paul straightforwardly urges that prophecy should take precedence and cautiously suggests that glossolalia should be restrained. This is plain speech compared to the implicit and circuitous way in which he, in 12.2, reproaches his audience with their unrestrained fervour for glossolalic rapture.

In 14.40 Paul demands of his auditors that they behave themselves in a proper and orderly fashion regarding the spiritual gifts. This is put strongly and explicitly compared to the cautious and colourless expression with which he adresses them at the start in 12.1: 'About the pneumatic phenomena, brothers, I do not want you to be ignorant'. The difference in tone between the opening and the conclusion of 1 Corinthians 12–14 is further enhanced by Paul's use of imperatives in 14.37-40 in contrast to the indicatives in 12.1-3. Moreover, the words 'If somebody ignores this, he will be ignored' (14.38) add a threatening touch to the conclusion, whereas politeness predominates in the beginning.

It is evident that 1 Cor. 14.37-40 cannot be formally divided into *recapitulatio*, *indignatio* and *conquestio*, the three parts a *peroratio* normally consists of. It is clear, however, that this passage positively displays the characteristics of the *peroratio* as described in the handbooks and therefore may justly be called by this technical term of rhetoric.[19]

---

19. *Rhet. ad Her.* 2.30.47 explicitly confirms that each separate part of a speech may be concluded by a *peroratio*. Standaert ('Analyse rhétorique', p. 29) also regards 1 Cor. 14.37-40 as a *peroratio* and confirms this in a brief analysis of the text.

2. *Two Rounds of Argumentation: 1 Corinthians 12.4-30 and 14.1-33a*

a. *Partitio*

The rules in the rhetorical handbooks concerning the *partitio* provide an important key to the structure of 1 Corinthians 12–14. Therefore a survey of the instructions the handbooks issue for this part of the speech is presented first.[20]

Purpose. The *partitio* (διαίρεσις, *divisio*) is a brief, systematic survey of the points to be discussed in the ensuing argumentation (*confirmatio*). Such division intends to render the whole speech clear and perspicuous. This effect may be reached in two ways. A speaker may distinctly indicate which point is in dispute, so that the auditors know on what their attention should be fixed. However, a speaker may also sum up all the points he intends to discuss successively, so that the auditors definitely know which road will be taken and at which point the speech will end.[21]

Component Parts. A *partitio* may be composed of one or several of the following three parts:[22]

 a. The speaker defines the points of agreement with the opponents and the point on which opinions remain divided and on which a decision by the listeners is called for.

 b. The speaker enumerates (*enumeratio*) the points which will be discussed. Preferably these ought to be three in number.

 c. The speaker gives a brief elucidation (*expositio*) of the points to be amply discussed in the following argumentation.

Requirements. A *partitio* ought to have three qualities:

 a. Brevity (*brevitas*): the formulation should not comprise more words than strictly necessary and should avoid distracting, stylistic embellishment.

---

20. *De inv.* 1.22.31–23.33; *Rhet. ad Her.* 1.10.17; Quintilian 4.5.1-28.
21. *De inv.* 1.22.31.
22. *Rhet. ad Her.* 1.10.17.

b. Completeness (*absolutio*): all categories to be discussed should be mentioned. Later addition of categories not mentioned in the *partitio* is strictly forbidden.

c. Conciseness (*paucitas generum*): only the principal categories (genera) should be mentioned in the *partitio*. The subcategories (species) ought to be mentioned only later in the argumentation, when the genus in question is discussed. Genus and species should be distinguished carefully and be neither confused nor mixed.

Moreover, throughout the speech the speaker should bear in mind the order stated in the *partitio*, stick to it and terminate the speech as soon as the points enumerated have been dispatched. When all parts of the *partitio* have been dealt with, nothing whatsoever may be added.[23]

b. *The Logical Structure of 1 Corinthians 12.4-30*
It is no accident that Paul continues his discourse after the *exordium* with the word διαίρεσις. What follows is indeed a *partitio*, rendering the entire ensuing section clear and perspicuous.[24] Verses 4-6 contains a brief, complete and carefully arranged enumeration of three categories, which are subsequently elaborated in the same order. The charismata of the Spirit are central in vv. 7-11, the services of the Lord in vv. 12-26 and the workings of God in vv. 27-30.

The conciseness, which the handbooks demand of the *partitio*, may be recognised in the careful manner in which the difference between genus and species is handled. The *partitio* (vv. 4-6) mentions two genera, the 'charismata of the Spirit' and the 'services of the Lord', both, in their turn, species of the genus 'workings of God', who works out all things in all people. The first part (vv. 7-11) enumerates the species of the genus 'charismata of the Spirit'. At the same time it indicates that all these fall under the 'workings of God' (v. 11). The second part (vv. 12-26) visualises the many species of the genus 'services of Christ' as limbs of a body. This part also clearly indicates that they too fall under the 'workings of God' (vv. 18, 24).

---

23. *De inv.* 1.22.32–23.33.

24. Within the rhetorical system the Latin *partitio* and the Greek διαίρεσις are technical terms with exactly the same meaning. See Hermogenes, 'Peri staseon', *Hermogenis Opera* (Rhetores Graeci, VI; ed. H. Rabe; Stuttgart: Teubner, 1985), ch. 1, p. 28.

The conclusion (vv. 27-30) brings the 'services of Christ' and the 'charismata of the Spirit' together as species in one enumeration of the genus 'workings of God' (v. 28). In that enumeration 'services of Christ', the apostolate in the first place, take precedence over 'charismata of the Spirit', of which glossolalia comes last.

c. *The Logical Structure of 1 Corinthians 14.1-33a*

After the excursus (*digressio*) of 1 Cor. 12.31–13.13 a second round of argumentation follows. This also begins with a *partitio* rendering the entire connected section perspicuous. This *partitio* is composed of two parts. First, Paul defines on which points agreement does exist between himself and his opponents and exactly on which point they hold different opinions. They agree on the ambition for love and spiritual gifts, but contrary to his listeners Paul is convinced that among the gifts not glossolalia, but prophecy takes precedence (vv. 1, 5a). Secondly, in this *partitio* Paul briefly elucidates all theses, which he will subsequently argue in the same order. They are three in number. (a) The glossolalist does not speak to people or build up the church-community, a thesis elaborated in vv. 6-19. (b) The prophet positively speaks to people and builds up the church-community, elaborated in vv. 20-25. (c) So, the prophet is greater than the glossolalist, a conclusion elaborated in vv. 26-33a.[25]

It is of interest that this *partitio* also meets the demand for conciseness. Genus and species are here, once again, carefully distinguished. The *partitio* mentions the genus 'spiritual gifts' (πνευματικά) and two species falling under this category: glossolalia and prophecy, the latter taking precedence.

---

25. The prohibition for women to speak during the meetings of the local church (1 Cor. 14.33b-36) is not announced in the *partitio* (14.1-5). Its addition runs counter to the rhetorical rules concerning the completeness of the *partitio*, which guide Paul here. In addition, the conformity in structure between the two argumentations (12.4-30; 14.1-33a) leaves no room for this prohibition. These data strengthen the growing suspicion that 1 Cor. 14.33b-36 was added to Paul's text by a later hand. Therefore it seems justified to leave this passage out of account here. For ample discussion on this question see G. Dautzenberg, *Urchristliche Prophetie* (BWANT, 104; Stuttgart: Kohlhammer, 1975), pp. 257-73; Fee, *Corinthians*, pp. 699-708; B. Witherington, *Women in the Earliest Churches*, III (SNTSMS, 59; Cambridge: Cambridge University Press, 1988), pp. 90-104.

The first part (vv. 6-19) fixes all attention on glossolalia. In the meantime it clearly indicates that this gift is a species of the genus 'spiritual gifts' (v. 6). The second part (vv. 20-25) fixes attention mainly on prophecy.

The conclusion (vv. 26-33a) places glossolalia and prophecy side by side within an enumeration of several species of the genus 'spiritual gifts' (v. 26). At the same time it shows that prophecy ought to be valued more highly than glossolalia.

d. *Similarities and Dissimilarities*

These two rounds of argumentation exhibit a striking conformity. They both consist of a *partitio*, comprising three theses, followed by three parts, each of which elaborates one of the theses. In addition, in both argumentations one part, namely 1 Cor. 12.12-26 and 14.6-19, is more extensive than the other two, which serves to enhance this conformity. These deviant parts are in their turn of almost equal length, they both contain a series of rhetorical questions (12.15-19; 14.6-9) and they make ample use of similes (12.12; 14.7-9, 10-12). This rather rigid similarity is relieved by some variations. Thus each *partitio* has a different form, which is repeated in the subsequent elaboration. The first *partitio* has the form of parallelistic enumeration (12.4-6). This form is also found in the first and third subsections of the elaboration (vv. 7-11, 27-30). The second *partitio* comprises, besides a definition of the points of agreement and of disagreement, a brief elucidation on the theses, which are subsequently argued. This elucidation has the form of antithetic parallelism (14.2-5). Just the same form is found in the second and third subsection of the ensuing exposition (14.20-25, 26-33a). In addition there is some variation in the sequence of the three subsections that both elaborations consist of. The longer section changes from second to first position.

Both rounds of argumentation apply the same reasoning. In order to make comparison possible two terms are presented as species of one genus. Subsequently they are placed side by side within the framework of that common genus and the conclusion is drawn that the one ranks far higher than the other. At the same time this order is vested with divine guarantee. Here are two instances of 'hierarchising'.[26] The first

26. This term is borrowed from Theissen, *Psychologische Aspekte*, p. 292. In regard to 1 Cor. 14 he writes:

conclusion (12.27-30) offers a list of 'workings of God', which comprises both the 'services of the Lord' and the 'charismata of the Spirit'. The ordinals—first, second, third—leave no doubt that a hierarchy is posited here, in which the 'services of Christ', with the apostles in the first place, rank higher than the 'charismata of the Spirit', of which the glossolalists come last.

The second conclusion (14.26-33a) offers a list of 'spiritual gifts', which encompasses both glossolalia and prophecy. They are compared to each other by means of antithetical parallelism. In this the cardinals —one, two, three—play an important role. The comparison clearly shows that the prophet is greater than the glossolalist. For speaking in tongues is incidentally permitted during the meetings of the church with a maximum of two or three speakers at a time and under the strict condition that there should be only one interpreter. Prophesying, however, is an obligatory part of the meetings with a minimum of two or three speakers and without a maximum, for one by one all may prophesy. This order is finally legitimised as the peace of God.[27]

e. *The Position of 1 Corinthians 12.31–13.13*

In the middle of 1 Corinthians 12–14, amidst the two rounds of argumentation, we find the famous passage on love (1 Cor. 12.31–13.13).

> Das Hauptanliegen des Paulus liegt aber darin, durch Argumentation die soziale Verstärkung glossolalen Verhaltens zu reduzieren. Er schlägt dabei zwei Strategien ein: Einmal nimmt er eine eindeutige Hierarchisierung vor. Prophetie ist der Glossolalie überlegen, die Liebe aber übertrifft alle charismatischen Gaben. Damit wird die Glossolalie relativiert, aber auch in die Gemeinde integriert. Der zweite Vorschlag steht damit in Spannung: Er läuft auf die Privatisierung der Glossolalie hinaus. In der Gemeinde ist Glossolalie ohne konstruktiven Wert, mag sie für den Einzelnen auch noch so wertvoll sein (1. Kor 14,4.19). Daher soll sie soweit wie möglich aus dem Gemeindeleben ausgeschlossen werden.

27. It is highly remarkable that the 'hierarchising', coming to the fore so clearly in both conclusions, is not only constantly overlooked, but even expressly denied in the literature dealing with these passages. Fee (*Corinthians*, p. 620 n. 16; p. 693) represents common opinion in remarking on 1 Cor. 12.27-30: 'But the question of "authority structures" is not asked here, and in terms of the argument it is altogether irrelevant', and on 1 Cor. 14.29-31: 'Paul now turns to give similar guidelines for the exercise of the gift of prophecy'. Regarding 12.28-30, Mitchell (*Reconciliation*, pp. 164, 269-70) twice notices that Paul sets out a hierarchical governance structure ordained by God, but she fails to see the consequences of this observation for the structure of this chapter and of the entire passage 1 Cor. 12–14.

Like the surrounding argumentations this passage consists of three parts. In other respects, however, it differs from its surroundings. This passage on love possesses a particular logical structure. Both rounds of argumentation present two different phenomena as species of one and the same genus, thus making comparison possible, and reach the conclusion that the one ranks far higher than the other. The passage on love does not exhibit such reasoning. It simply places the species of one genus, the charismata, over and against a singular and unique reality: love. This antithesis is not argued, but posited without further discussion and elaborated in three steps: contrary to love the gifts are useless (vv. 1-3), contrary to virtuous love the gifts are devoid of virtue (vv. 4-7) and contrary to perfect love the gifts are defective (vv. 8-12).

In accordance with its particular logical structure the passage on love also exhibits a deviant form. In contrast with the surrounding argumentations this passage does not contain a *partitio*, but is framed by two verses (12.31; 13.13) to the effect that love fully throws the gifts into the shade. Within the framework of these verses their thesis is then elaborated in three respects.

The passage on love, not arguing a conclusion but amplifying an antithesis, is thus clearly outlined against its surroundings as a separate unit. Amidst the two arguments 1 Cor. 12.31–13.13 forms an excursus of a different kind. I shall return to this later in this article.

3. *The Rhetorical Genre of 1 Corinthians 12-14*

a. *Genus deliberativum*

Classical rhetoric divides public speaking into three genres: the judicial plea of accusation and defence (γένος δικανικόν, *genus iudiciale*), the ceremonial speech of praise and censure (γένος ἐπιδεικτικόν, *genus demonstrativum*) and the political address of recommendation and dissuasion (γένος συμβουλευτικόν, *genus deliberativum*).[28] The instructions applying to the deliberative genre clarify the nature of 1 Corinthians 12 as well as 14. A survey of the principal characteristics of this genre is now given in order to substantiate this insight. Because the *genus iudiciale* has already driven

---

28. Aristotle, *Rhetoric* 1.3.1358b-1359a; *Rhet. ad Alex.* 1.1421b.7-15; *Rhet. ad Her.* 1.2.2.

both other genres into the background early in the rhetorical tradition these characteristics have to be gathered from several sources.[29]

Subjects. The deliberative genre has its place in councils and parliaments, in which state-affairs are discussed. They include: religious ritual, legislation, the form of the constitution, alliances and treaties with other states, war, peace and finance.[30] *Rhetorica ad Alexandrum* expands on each of these topics. Its elaboration of legislation and the form of the state is of particular interest here. Legislation and the form of the state (πολιτικὴ κατασκευή) should prevent the different parties and classes, who form part of the polis, from being torn apart by dissension and should promote their living together in harmony. In particular, the assignment of offices is a delicate point, which needs to be regulated with great care. Generally speaking the laws should hinder the multitude from plotting against the wealthy for their property and deter those who are part of the government from treating the weaker citizens with insolence.[31]

The Main Argument. Considerations of utility and advantage (τὸ συμφέρον, *utilitas*) mark the deliberative genre. Whereas a certain course of action is recommended for its expediency, another is dissuaded for its causing harm. Other considerations, such as the question of whether a course of action is just or unjust, honourable or shameful, are only subordinate to this. Advantage forms the main argument, everything else is secondary.[32]

Argumentation resting on the criterion of advantage, however, has its limits. When a certain action is impossible, the discussion whether it may be profitable loses all meaning. And when a course is necessary (ἀναγκαῖον, *necesse*) it must take precedence in public policy over all remaining considerations, alike of honour and of profit.[33]

---

29. An amply documented presentation of the characteristics of the deliberative genre can now be found in Mitchell, *Reconciliation*, pp. 20-64. Her conclusion that 1 Corinthians is deliberative rhetoric confirms the findings of the present article and vice versa.

30. *Rhet. ad Alex.* 2.1423a.

31. *Rhet. ad Alex.* 2.1424a-1424b.

32. Aristotle, *Rhet.* 1.3.1358b; *Rhet. ad Her.* 3.2.3; *Part. orat.* 24.83. *Rhet. ad Alex.* 1.1421b deviates on this point.

33. *Part. orat.* 24.83; cf. *Rhet. ad Alex.* 1.1421b; Quintilian 3.8.22-26.

Specific Means. The use of comparison occurs in all rhetorical genres and does not distinguish the *genus deliberativum* from other genres. The comparison, in which the state with its fighting parties is represented as a human body the members of which are quarreling, appears pre-eminently in the political speech. Famous in this respect is the address of M. Agrippa in which he urges the revolting Plebeians by means of this comparison to submit once again to the authority of the Patricians.[34] Among the means the deliberative genre uses to bring the audience to the decision intended, the example (παράδειγμα, *exemplum*) figures prominently. By this is meant citing something said or done in the past, along with the name of the actor. The example enhances the plausibility and vivacity of the discourse. The experience it contains is most suited for inducing the public to agree with the course of action proposed.[35] The use of such examples is nowhere more in order than in the *genus deliberativum*.[36]

b. *The Genre of 1 Corinthians 12*

The first round of argumentation, comprising 1 Cor. 12.4-30, clearly displays the characteristics of the deliberative genre.

In this section Paul deals with the constitution of the church (v. 28), namely at the official-administrative level. He assigns to the different gifts and services their respective position within the hierarchical structure. Thereby he recommends to the Corinthians to acknowledge the precedence of the services, that is to say to obey the apostles, and dissuades them from ranking the charismata first, that is to say from acting high-handedly as glossolalists.

The criterion of utility plays an important part. It is already mentioned in the first line of the argumentation proper (v. 7). Having stated first that the gifts of the Spirit are useful (vv. 7-11), Paul then clearly shows, with the help of the metaphor of the body and its members, that the services of Christ are of divine necessity (vv. 18,

34. T. Livius, *Ab urbe condita* 2.32; Dionysius of Halicarnassus, *Antiquitates Romanae* 6.86; Plutarch, *Coriolanus* 6. Theissen (*Psychologische Aspekte*, pp. 327-29) has an instructive survey of the classical material. He remarks: 'Meist wird die soziale Leib-Metaphorik dazu verwandt, die unvermeidliche Überlegenheit eines der Glieder herauszustellen. Das ist die Pointe bei Menenius Agrippa.' Mitchell (*Reconciliation*, pp. 157-64) gives much material, but misses this point.

35. *Rhet. ad Her.* 4.49.62; cf. *Rhet. ad Alex.* 8; *Part. orat.* 27.96.

36. Quintilian 3.8.36, 66.

22, 24). From this he then draws the conclusion that the necessary services rank higher than the useful gifts (vv. 27-30). An important device Paul employs to enliven his exposition and to enhance its persuasive power is the comparison of the church and its various services with a body and its members. In this manner he not only presents the services as being of natural necessity but also ranks them. With great irony he shows that, of all members, the 'weak, dishonourable, indecent, backward' apostles are the most indispensable.[37]

c. The Genre of 1 Corinthians 14

The second round of argumentation, comprising 1 Cor.14.1-33a, also exhibits the characteristics of the deliberative genre.

In this section Paul deals again with the constitution of the church but this time at the level of the local meeting. He defines the place that should be given to the various spiritual gifts during the meetings. Thereby he recommends to the Corinthians to give ample place to prophecy and dissuades them from indulging unrestrictedly in glossolalia.

The reasoning of this section entirely hinges on the criterion of utility. In the first line of the argumentation proper this is mentioned explicitly (v. 6, cf. vv. 9, 14). In the remainder it constantly figures as 'building up the community'. The prominent part this criterion plays is already apparent in the *partitio* (vv. 1-5). In the same vein Paul thereupon argues first that glossolalia does not build up the community (vv. 6-19) and then positively demonstrates that prophecy actually does (vv. 20-25). From this he draws the conclusion that during the meeting of the community, glossolalia, which does not build up the community, is facultative and only conditionally permitted, while prophecy, which positively builds up the community, forms an obligatory part of it and should receive ample space (vv. 26-33a).

An important device Paul uses in this argumentation to enliven his exposition and to enhance its power of persuasion is the appeal to his

---

37. The similarities with 1 Cor. 4.6-13 clearly show that in 1 Cor. 12.19-26 Paul also criticises the Corinthians' depreciation of the apostles by way of irony. To my knowledge nobody has as yet noticed this irony. It is generally accepted that here Paul literally has the weakest members of the church in mind. Qualifications such as 'indecent parts' and 'backward members', however, betray self-mockery and exaggeration. Here Paul ridicules the disdain in which the glossolalists hold the apostles by grotesquely overdoing it.

own, personal example. The repeated occurrence of the first person singular in vv. 6-19 indicates that all along in this passage Paul holds up his own person as an example to the Corinthians. This example backs up his assertions concerning glossolalia by authority and experience.

d. A Demonstrative Excursus: 1 Corinthians 13

In the handbooks of rhetoric the *genus demonstrativum* (γένος ἐπιδεικτικόν) is only schematically discussed. The reason for this is that public speeches of praise or censure rarely occurred. The attention this genre nevertheless receives is connected with the practice of including demonstrative excurses in judicial pleas and political addresses. In this manner lawyers and politicians readily put to use the particular qualities this genre offers.[38]

Unlike the other genres, in the demonstrative genre not argumentation but presentation holds sway. The speaker does not raise a question for discussion, but purposefully enlarges or reduces a person or cause so as to influence the valuation of the audience in a positive or negative sense. The principal means to this end is style. In this genre style is all-important. Through an artistic feat the speaker endeavours to captivate and please his audience. A frequent use of conspicuous figures of style accordingly distinguishes the demonstrative genre from the other ones.[39] The *genus demonstrativum* only indirectly incites to action. It is particularly suited for impressing ideas and values upon the audience.

These summary remarks on the *genus demonstrativum* suffice to explain the special character of 1 Cor. 12.31–13.13. The occurrence of the verb δείκνυμι in 12.31 is no accident. This is the only time Paul uses this verb.[40] It should be taken as a reference to the γένος

---

38. *Rhet. ad Her.* 3.8.15; Quintilian 3.7.1-4; 4.3.12-15.

39. *Part. orat.* 21.71-72.

40. The verb admittedly occurs in two letters traditionally ascribed to Paul, which are almost certainly not from his hand: 1 Tim. 6.15; Heb. 8.5. Interestingly the vulgate translates δείκνυμι in 1 Cor. 12.31 with *demonstro*. C.R. Holladay ('1 Corinthians 13: Paul as Apostolic Paradigm', in *Greeks, Romans and Christians: Essays in Honor of A.J. Malherbe* [ed. D.L. Balch, E. Ferguson and W.A. Meeks; Minneapolis: Fortress Press, 1990], pp. 80-98 [87-88]) notices the demonstrative force of δείκνυμι, without relating this however to the demonstrative genre: 'If it is used here in the normal NT sense, its demonstrative rather than pedagogical force is focal and should be rendered *show* in the sense of "display", "point out" or

ἐπιδεικτικόν. Through the choice of this verb Paul indicates that he switches from deliberative argumentation to a demonstrative excursus. As already noticed earlier, Paul does not reason in this passage. He simply places charismata and love against each other and in three steps demonstrates how useless, devoid of virtue and defective the gifts are as contrasted to love. This antithesis is posited and amplified, but not argued. Style also distinguishes this passage from the surrounding argumentations. Although in 1 Corinthians 12 and 14 similar figures of style are found, in 1 Corinthians 13 they occur much more frequently. An uninterrupted series of parallelisms, often reinforced by *anaphora* and *epiphora*, numerous repetitions of words and expressions and an extremely polished rhythm of the sentences provide this passage with a special, artistic appearance. Here the presentation receives all attention.[41]

Between the two deliberative argumentations Paul indeed includes 1 Cor. 12.31–13.13 as a demonstrative excursus.[42] In it he posits three negative appraisals of the charismata, which he renders plausible through an attractive presentation. As a matter of fact, in this manner he intends to diminish the high esteem in which the Corinthians hold the charismata, so as to increase their willingness to take the unpleasant steps he demands of them in the preceding and following argumentation.

Dispositio of 1 Corinthians 12–14

Exordium: 12.1-3
   Content
The causa (12.1)
The addressees and the causa (12.2)
The speaker and his authority concerning the causa (12.3)

"demonstrate"... On this showing, what follows in 1 Cor. 13 is less a didactic explanation than it is a paradigmatic exhibition.'

41. A thorough stylistic analysis of 1 Cor. 12.31–13.13 can be found in Smit, 'The Genre of 1 Cor 13', pp. 199-205.

42. Mitchell (*Reconciliation*, pp. 271-77) discusses the genre and composition of 1 Cor. 13 and concludes that only vv. 4-7 belong to the epideictic genre and 'comprise a very brief encomium on love'. The correct principle, that 'the rhetorical unit to be examined should be a compositional unit' (p. 15), should have taught her otherwise.

Form
Insinuatio
Indicativi

I. *Argumentatio*: 12.4-30
A. Partitio: 12.4-6
   Content
   Thesis 1: There are various charismata from the same Spirit (12.4)
   Thesis 2: There are various services from the same Lord (12.5)
   Thesis 3: There are various workings of the same God, to which both charismata and services belong (12.6)
   Form
   Enumeratio, parallelism

B. Confirmatio: 12.7-30
   Thesis 1: 12.7-11
      Content: The various charismata of the Spirit are useful
      Form: Enumeratio, parallelism
   Thesis 2: 12.12-26
      Content: The various services of the Christ are necessary
      Form: Similitudo
           Rhetorical questions (12.15-19)
   Thesis 3: 12.27-30
      Content: So, among the workings of God the services take precedence above the charismata. This order is validated by the authority of God
      Form: Enumeratio, parallelism
           Ordinals

II. *Digressio*: 12.31–13.13
Demonstratio: 12.31—13.13

   Content
   Comparison through antithesis between charismata and love
   Form
   Speech of praise and blame

Propositio: 12.31
   Content: The charismata surpassed by love
   Form: Ironical permissio and hyperbole

Amplificatio: 13.1-12
Part 1: 13.1-3
   Content: Contrary to love the charismata are useless
   Form: Threefold parallelism

Part 2: 13.4-7

> *Content*: Contrary to virtuous love the charismata are devoid of virtue
> *Form*: Two partite chiasm
> > Eightfold and fourfold parallelism

Part 3: 13.8-12

> *Content*: Contrary to perfect love the charismata are defective
> *Form*: Threefold parallelism

Conclusio: 13.13

> *Content*: The charismata surpassed by love
> *Form*: Four cola of three words each, concluded by: love

III. *Argumentatio*: 14.1-33a

A. Partitio: 14.1-5

> *Content*

Points of agreement and disagreement: 14.1

> Zeal for love and the pneumatic gifts, but among the last prophecy takes precedence above glossolalia

Expositio: 14.2-5

Thesis 1: Glossolaly does not build up the church-community (14.2, 4a)
Thesis 2: Prophecy positively builds up the church-community (14.3, 4b)
Thesis 3: So, prophecy takes precedence above glossolalia, unless this is interpreted (14.5)

> *Form*

Antithetical parallelism

B. Confirmatio: 14.6-33a

Thesis 1: 14.6-19

> *Content*: Glossolaly does not build up the community unless it is interpreted
> *Form*: Exemplum
> > Rhetorical questions (14.6-9)

Thesis 2: 14.20-25

> *Content*: Prophecy positively builds up the community
> *Form*: Antithetical parallelism

Thesis 3: 14.26-33a

> *Content*: So, among the pneumatic gifts prophecy takes precedence above glossolalia.
> This order is validated by the authority of God
> *Form*: Antithetical parallelism
> > Cardinals
> > Imperativi

Peroratio: 14.37-40
  Content
The speaker and his authority concerning the causa (14.37-38)
The addressees and the causa (14.39)
The causa (14.40)
  Form
Recapitulatio
Imperativi

Paul's Rhetorical Strategy in 1 Corinthians 15

Duane F. Watson

The rhetoric of 1 Corinthians has captured the attention of several scholars,[1] with ch. 15 having received particular focus.[2] The more notable analyses of ch. 15 from the perspective of Graeco-Roman rhetoric are those of Michael Bünker,[3] Burton Mack,[4] and Margaret Mitchell.[5] Bünker's rhetorical analysis was the first and remains the

---

1. See W. Wuellner, 'Greek Rhetoric and Pauline Argumentation', in *Early Christian Literature and the Classical Intellectual Tradition: In Honorem Robert M. Grant* (ed. W.R. Schoedel and R.L. Wilken; Théologie Historique, 54; Paris: Editions Beauchesne, 1979), pp. 177-88; *idem*, 'Paul as Pastor: The Function of Rhetorical Questions in First Corinthians', in *L'Apôtre Paul: Personnalité, style et conception du ministère* (ed. A. Vanhoye; BETL, 73; Leuven: Leuven University Press, 1986), pp. 49-77; H.D. Betz, 'The Problem of Rhetoric and Theology according to the Apostle Paul', in *L'Apôtre Paul*, esp. pp. 24-39; E. Schüssler Fiorenza, 'Rhetorical Situation and Historical Reconstruction in 1 Corinthians', *NTS* 33 (1987), pp. 386-403; M.M. Mitchell, *Paul and the Rhetoric of Reconciliation* (Hermeneutische Untersuchungen zur Theologie, 28; Tubingen: Mohr [Siebeck], 1991).

2. A brief passing analysis is offered by B. Standaert ('La rhétorique ancienne dans saint Paul', in *L'Apôtre Paul*, pp. 81-82). J.N. Vorster offers an analysis from the perspective of modern rhetoric ('Resurrection Faith in 1 Corinthians 15', *Neot* 23 [1989], pp. 287-307).

Elements of the Cynic-Stoic diatribe appear in ch. 15, but not a full-fledged diatribe. Paul shows the adaptability of diatribal features to rhetorical argument. For further discussion of diatribe in ch. 15, see T. Schmeller, *Paulus und die 'Diatribe': Eine vergleichende Stilinterpretation* (NTAbh NS., 19; Münster: Aschendorff, 1987), ch. 3.

3. *Briefformular und rhetorische Disposition im 1. Korintherbrief* (GTA, 28; Göttingen: Vandenhoeck & Ruprecht, 1983), esp. pp. 59-72.

4. *Rhetoric and the New Testament* (Guides to Biblical Scholarship; Minneapolis: Fortress Press, 1990), pp. 56-59.

5. *Rhetoric of Reconciliation*, pp. 175-77, 283-91.

most detailed. He argues that ch. 15 is judicial rhetoric and proposes the following outline: *exordium* (vv. 1-3a), *narratio* (vv. 3b-11), *argumentatio* I (vv. 12-28), *peroratio* I (vv. 29-34), *argumentatio* II (vv. 35-49), and *peroratio* II (vv. 50-58). Derived independently of Bünker and also heavily dependent upon the rhetorical handbooks, my own outline is quite similar, but I believe the chapter is deliberative rather than judicial rhetoric.

Burton Mack also argues that ch. 15 is deliberative rhetoric. In addition he claims that the chapter is constructed according to a pattern for the elaboration of a complete argument, and offers the following basic outline: *exordium* (vv. 1-2), *narratio* (vv. 3-20), argument (vv. 21-50), and conclusion (vv. 51-58). I agree that the elaboration pattern for a complete argument structures ch. 15, but only two subunits of *confirmatio* within the chapter, not the entire chapter.

Most recently Margaret Mitchell considers vv. 1-57 as a proof within the *probatio* of the letter, and v. 58 as the *peroratio* of the entire letter. Certainly ch. 15 functions as a proof within the *probatio* of 1 Corinthians, but the analysis does not fully utilize Graeco-Roman conventions of invention, arrangement and style to evaluate the argumentation. This neglect results in a diminished capacity to determine the rhetorical features and functions of the chapter.

Length limitations preclude my interaction with the multitude of subpoints in these studies. I will analyze 1 Corinthians 15 according to the Graeco-Roman rhetorical conventions of invention and arrangement, focusing on the neglected factors of *confirmatio* and *refutatio* and their role in deliberative rhetoric. I will emphasize that an ancient pattern for the development of themes and arguments underlies the *confirmatio* portions of the chapter.[6]

---

6.   All quotations of the rhetorical handbooks are from the LCL editions. The abbreviations used for these works are: Aristotle, *The 'Art' of Rhetoric* = *Rhet.*; Aristotle, *Topica* = *Top.*; *Rhetorica ad Alexandrum* = *Rhet. ad Alex.*; Demetrius, *On Style* = *Eloc.*; Cicero, *De Inventione* = *Inv.*; Cicero, *Topica* = *Top.*; Cicero, *De Oratore* = *De Or.*; Cicero, *De Partitiones Oratoriae* = *De Part. Or.*; Cicero, *Orator* = *Or.*; *Rhetorica ad Herennium* = *Rhet. ad Her.* All quotations from 1 Corinthians are taken from the NRSV.

The Rhetorical Situation

The exact nature of the rhetorical situation behind 1 Corinthians 15 has eluded interpreters. A multitude of reconstructions exists, each with many nuances. It is not possible or necessary to review this immense literature in detail, so only a working reconstruction derived from the literature and the rhetorical analysis to follow is provided here.

There seem to be two factions within Paul's audience: (1) some loyal to the apostolic tradition which he preached, but whose degree of loyalty is in doubt (vv. 2, 11), and (2) others who challenge this tradition by denying the bodily resurrection of the dead (vv. 12, 16, 29, 32) a doctrine which the more loyal faction accepts at least in the case of Christ (vv. 1-2, 11, assumed in vv. 12-19). Behind this denial of the bodily resurrection of the dead is the uncertainty of the form such a body would take (v. 35). This rejection may be explained by an overrealized eschatology which affirmed that the resurrection had already occurred in a spiritual sense (cf. 2 Tim. 2.17-18). It may also be explained as the adoption of either a Gnostic or a Hellenistic-Jewish doctrine which replaced resurrection with an a-somatic immortality in which the self is released from the body at death. This allows for the immortality of the soul, but not the resurrection of the body (cf. Acts 17.32). The audience believed in some existence after death, as their baptism on behalf of the dead indicates (v. 29).

The Species of Rhetoric and the Stasis

Chapter 15 contains many features of deliberative rhetoric and is best classified as such.[7] First, the chapter is intended to advise and dissuade

---

7. For further discussion of deliberative rhetoric, see H. Lausberg, *Handbuch der literarischen Rhetorik: Eine Grundlegung der Literaturwissenschaft* (2 vols.; Munich: Hueber, 2nd edn, 1973) I, pp. 123-29, §§ 224-38; J. Martin, *Antike Rhetorik: Technik und Methode* (HbAltW, 2.3; Munich: Beck, 1974), pp. 167-76. The species of rhetoric for 1 Corinthians as a whole has been identified by Wuellner ('Greek Rhetoric and Pauline Argumentation', pp. 184-85) as epideictic, and by G. Kennedy (*New Testament Interpretation through Rhetorical Criticism* [Chapel Hill: University of North Carolina Press, 1984], p. 87) and Mitchell (*Rhetoric of Reconciliation*, pp. 1, 26-64) as deliberative. Bunker (*1. Korintherbriefe*, pp. 48-51) identifies ch. 15 as judicial, but Fiorenza ('Rhetorical Situation', pp. 392-93), Mack

audience members concerning a particular course of action.[8] It dissuades them from inaccurate theological understanding and advises them to reaffirm the tradition they had previously accepted. Secondly, the argumentation is predominantly constructed from example and comparison of examples.[9] These examples are Adam–Christ (vv. 21-22, 46-49) and seeds–flesh (vv. 36-44a). Thirdly, the deliberative *topoi* (sources of argument) of what is necessary, advantageous and honorable and their opposites are found in various forms. These are especially epitomized in the *topos* of 'in vain' which pervades the chapter (vv. 2, 10, 14, 17, 58).[10]

The stasis or basis of the case in deliberative rhetoric is usually quality, because it is concerned with the nature or import of something.[11] However, here the stasis is fact (conjecture), the question being whether something is real or exists.[12] Quintilian says, 'nor does it suffice to restrict deliberative rhetoric to the *basis* of *quality*...For there is often room for conjecture as well' (3.8.4). The stasis of fact is usually concerned with origins, cause–effect, and corollaries.[13] In

(*Rhetoric*, p. 56), and Mitchell (*Rhetoric of Reconciliation*, p. 286) correctly identify the chapter as deliberative.

8. Aristotle *Rhet.* 1.3.1358b.3; *Rhet. ad Alex.* 1.1421b.17ff.; Cicero, *Inv.* 1.5.7; *De Part. Or.* 24–27; *Rhet. ad Her.* 1.2.2; Quintilian 3.4.6, 9; 3.8.1-6; cf. 3.8.67-70.

9. Aristotle, *Rhet.* 1.9.1368a.40; 2.20.1394a.7-8; 3.17.1418a.5; *Rhet. ad Alex.* 32.1438b.29ff.; Quintilian 3.8.34, 66; cf. 5.11.8.

10. Aristotle, *Rhet.* 1.3.1358b.5; 1.4-8; 2.22.1396a.8; *Rhet. ad Alex.* 1.1421b.17-1423a.11; 6.1.1427b.39ff.; Cicero, *Inv.* 2.4.12; 2.51.155-58.176; *De Part. Or.* 24–27; *Top.* 24.91; *Rhet. ad Her.* 3.2.3–5.9; Quintilian 3.4.16; 3.8.1-6, 22-35; cf. Cicero, *De Or.* 2.82.333-36.

11. Quintilian 3.8.4; 7.4.1-3; cf. 3.7.28. For further discussion of stasis, see Lausberg, *Handbuch*, I, pp. 64-85, §§ 79-138; Martin, *Antike Rhetorik*, pp. 28-52.

12. For further discussion of the stasis of fact, see Cicero, *Inv.* 1.8.11; 2.4.14-16.51; *Top.* 21.82; 23.87; *Rhet. ad Her.* 1.11.18; 2.2.3-8.12; Quintilian 3.6.83; 7.2.

13. Cicero, *Top.* 21.82; 23.87; Quintilian 7.2.3, 35-38. Mack (*Rhetoric*, p. 56) also identifies the stasis as fact. Vorster ('Resurrection Faith', pp. 291, 302-303) argues that vv. 1-34 are based on the stasis of quality, and vv. 35-58 on the stasis of fact. However, the arguments from cause and logical consequence, as found in vv. 12-34, are characteristic of the stasis of fact. Fiorenza ('Rhetorical Situation', p. 394) incorrectly identifies the stasis as that of *status translationis* which she defines as 'when the speaker's/writer's *auctoritas* or jurisdiction to address or settle the issue at hand is in doubt and needs to be established'. Paul does not defend his

ch. 15 Paul defends the reality of the resurrection he preached (v. 12) by using the consequences of denying it (vv. 12-19). He explores the origins of that doctrine in Christ's resurrection (vv. 20-28). He defends the bodily form of resurrection he preached (v. 35) by employing the origins of all creation in bodily form (vv. 36-49) and the corollary that our bodies must be transformed to inherit the kingdom (vv. 50-57).

Invention, Arrangement and Style

A detailed rhetorical analysis of 1 Corinthians 15 emphasizing invention and arrangement follows. The conclusion outlines the findings.

The Exordium (vv. 1-2)

Verses 1-2 are an introduction to the new topic of resurrection in ch. 15. They function like the main *exordium*,[14] the initial element of arrangement which strives to obtain the audience's attention, receptivity and goodwill for the address to follow.[15] The functions of an *exordium* were commonly given to any portion of a work as needed, including the argumentation in the *probatio*.[16] In deliberative rhetoric, the *exordium* need be no more than a mere heading, and set forth the rhetor's concern and intention, topics to be discussed and a call for a hearing.[17] Here Paul introduces his subject as the message he had proclaimed to the Corinthians, their reception of it, and the possibility of hearing it in vain.

There are several techniques for gaining audience attention.[18] These include showing that the matter at hand is agreeable to both the rhetor

authority in order to defend a doctrine. Rather he defends a doctrine while assuming his authority.

14. Mitchell (*Rhetoric of Reconciliation*, pp. 194-97) identifies the main *exordium* of 1 Corinthians as 1.4-9.

15. For further discussion of the *exordium*, see Lausberg, *Handbuch*, I, pp. 150-63, §§ 263-88; Martin, *Antike Rhetorik*, pp. 60-75.

16. Aristotle, *Rhet.* 3.14.1415b.8-10; Quintilian 4.1.72-75.

17. Aristotle, *Rhet.* 3.14.1415b.8 (cf. 3.1415b.12); Cicero, *De Part. Or.* 27.97; Quintilian 3.8.6, 10; cf. Cicero, *De Part. Or.* 4.13.

18. Aristotle, *Rhet.* 3.14.1415a.7-1415b.7; *Rhet. ad Alex.* 29.1436b.5ff.; Cicero, *Inv.* 1.16.23; *De Part. Or.* 8.29-30; *Rhet. ad Her.* 1.4.7; Quintilian 4.1.33-34; 10.1.48.

and the audience, demonstrating that the matter pertains to the audience's welfare and the worship of God, and expressing fear and alarm. Paul announces his topic as the proclamation of the gospel which the audience accepted for their welfare—their salvation— before God. In their current situation the gospel could prove to have been accepted in vain, that is, leaving one in the fearful position of having no hope before God.

The *exordium* also briefly indicates the topics which the rhetor will develop in the *confirmatio* (*probatio*) and *refutatio*.[19] A major *topos* of Paul's argumentation in ch. 15 is introduced here: 'in vain'. It is explicitly mentioned in the *exordium* (εἰκῇ—v. 2), *narratio* (κένος— v. 10), *refutatio* (κένος—v. 14; μάταιος—v. 17), and *peroratio* (κένος—v. 58), and is particularly developed in vv. 12-19, 29-34.

The Narratio (vv. 3-11)

The preposition γάρ beginning v. 3 often marks the transition from the *exordium* to the *narratio*.[20] As γάρ indicates, the *narratio* provides the background for what the *exordium* has announced is a concern— here, the message Paul preached. The *narratio* is defined as 'the persuasive exposition of that which either has been done, or is supposed to have been done...' (Quintilian 4.2.31).[21] The *narratio* is delineated by the beginning and ending references to the transmission of the tradition (vv. 3, 11).

The *narratio* of 1 Corinthians has been delimited by Mitchell as 1.11-17 and concerns divisions within the churches.[22] Chapter 15 presents the substance of yet another division: the resurrection. Since the *narratio* can be interspersed throughout a work,[23] vv. 3-11 is best conceived as a *narratio*. Deliberative rhetoric being future oriented does not use a *narratio* unless the narration of past facts facilitates decision-making on future events (Aristotle, *Rhet.* 3.16.1417b.11;

19. Aristotle, *Rhet.* 3.14.1414b.1; Cicero, *De Or.* 2.80.325; Quintilian 4.1.23-27; cf. Cicero, *De Or.* 2.79.320.

20. Cf. Quintilian 4.1.76-79, which recommends that the transition from the *exordium* to *narratio* be obvious.

21. For further discussion of the *narratio*, see Lausberg, *Handbuch*, I, pp. 163-90, §§ 289-347; Martin, *Antike Rhetorik*, pp. 75-89.

22. *Rhetoric of Reconciliation*, pp. 200-202.

23. Aristotle, *Rhet.* 3.16.1417b.11; G. Kennedy, *The Art of Persuasion in Greece* (Princeton: Princeton University Press, 1963), pp. 147, 262.

Cicero, *De Part. Or.* 4.13). The narration of the past facts underlying the traditional moorings of the doctrine of the resurrection facilitates Paul's argumentation about the future resurrection. This understanding provides a viable rhetorical explanation for the seemingly loose connection of the creed (vv. 3b-5) to the argumentation that follows.

One type of non-judicial *narratio* is based on facts (e.g. historical narrative) and persons (e.g. character traits like vicissitudes endured, reversal of fortune, sudden joy, happy outcomes) (*Rhet. ad. Her.* 1.8.13). Verses 3-11 provides historical narrative and character traits of Paul.

The *narratio* begins in vv. 3-5 with judgments or κρίσεις, 'whatever may be regarded as expressing the opinion of nations, peoples, philosophers, distinguished citizens, or illustrious poets' (Quintilian 5.11.36). Judgments include common sayings, popular beliefs and supernatural oracles.[24] Verses 3b-5 is considered to be a creed (popular belief) of the early church. The creed itself is supported by association with divine oracles ('in accordance with the scriptures'—vv. 3, 4) and the proof of eyewitness testimony of Peter and the Twelve (v. 5).[25] Since the exigence concerns doubts about the bodily resurrection of Jesus, Paul supplies the creed with further eyewitness testimony, most of which could still be elicited: 500 Christians, James and all the apostles (vv. 6-7).

The *narratio* continues in vv. 8-11, emphasizing that Paul too is an eyewitness to the resurrection of which he testifies. Central is his description of his trials endured, reversal of fortune, sudden joy and happy outcome (cf. *Rhet. ad Her.* 1.8.13). He has endured being least of the apostles because he persecuted the church, but experienced the reversal of fortune on the Damascus Road with the happy outcome of a hard-working apostleship by God's grace. The *narratio* ends in v. 11 by underscoring the unanimity of Paul's proclamation and that of the apostles, and reminding the Corinthians that they believed this

---

24. Aristotle, *Rhet.* 2.23.1398b-1399a.12; *Rhet. ad Alex.* 1.1422a.25ff.; Cicero, *Inv.* 1.30.48; Quintilian 5.11.36-44; cf. Cicero, *De Part. Or.* 2.6.

25. For further discussion of eyewitness proof and related proofs, see Aristotle, *Rhet.* 1.2.1355b.2; 1.15.1375a.1-2; 1.15.1375b.13-1376a.19; *Rhet. ad Alex.* 7.1428a.22-23; 15; Cicero, *De Or.* 2.27.116; *De Part. Or.* 2.6; 14.48-51; Quintilian 5.7; Lausberg, *Handbuch*, I, pp. 191-93, §§ 351-54; Martin, *Antike Rhetorik*, pp. 97-101.

proclamation of the resurrection of Christ.

Two persistent questions about ch. 15 can now be more fully answered. First, vv. 8-11 is often understood as an apologetic directed to some who degraded Paul's apostleship (cf. 4.1-5, 8-13; 14.36-38), particularly for his weakness (cf. 1.10-17; 2.1-5).[26] However, not ruling out an apologetic intent, the main purpose of this section is more likely to be to increase the credibility of the *narratio* (whose content is the proclamation) by building up the ethos of the person of the messenger. The ethos of the rhetor is particularly crucial in lending credibility to the *narratio* (Cicero, *De Part. Or.* 9.31-32; Quintilian 4.2.125-27) and was considered the most effective means of proof, particularly in deliberative rhetoric.[27] Secondly, in the debate about whether the resurrection appearances prove or do not prove the resurrection of Christ, rhetoric indicates the latter.[28] The *narratio* is not designed to prove, but to provide the basis of proof in the argumentation.

The Confirmatio (Probatio) and Refutatio (vv. 12-57)

Verses 12-57 provides the proof of the resurrection, and contains two interrelated parts. One is the *confirmatio* (*probatio*) which 'is the part of the oration which by marshalling arguments lends credit, authority, and support to our case' (Cicero, *Inv.* 1.24.34). The other is the *refutatio*, where 'arguments are used to impair, disprove, or weaken the confirmation or proof in our opponents' speech' (Cicero, *Inv.* 1.42.78).[29] The proposition(s) of the case can be implicit in the *narratio*[30] and/or be found at the beginning of every proof (Quintilian 4.4.1). The two propositions Paul is refuting are found at the beginning of two units of *refutatio* and *confirmatio*. The first, the proposition of v. 12 (governing vv. 12-34), is 'There is no resurrection of the

---

26. P. von der Osten-Sacken, 'Die Apologie des paulinischen Apostolats in 1 Kor 15.1-11', *ZNW* 64 (1973), pp. 245-62.

27. Aristotle, *Rhet.* 1.2.1356a.4; Quintilian 3.8.12-13; 4.1.7; 5.12.9.

28. For an overview of this issue, see R.J. Sider, 'St. Paul's Understanding of the Nature and Significance of the Resurrection in 1 Corinthians XV 1-19', *NovT* 19 (1977), pp. 124-41; J. Plevnik, *What are they Saying about Paul?* (New York: Paulist, 1986), pp. 28-37.

29. For further discussion of the *confirmatio* (*probatio*)-*refutatio*, see Lausberg, *Handbuch*, I, pp. 190-236, §§ 348-430; Martin, *Antike Rhetorik*, pp. 95-137.

30. Quintilian 3.9.7; 4.2.54, 79, 86; 4.4.1-2; cf. 4.4.9.

dead', and the second, the proposition of v. 35 (governing vv. 35-57), can be paraphrased as: 'Since a corrupted corpse cannot be raised, there is no resurrection'. The propositions of the resurrection of the dead and resurrection in bodily form that Paul is confirming are implicit within the creed of the *narratio* (vv. 3-11).

First Unit of Refutatio and Confirmatio (vv. 12-34).
Paul's implicit proposition throughout this unit is that Christ's bodily resurrection necessitates the Christian's bodily resurrection. This intimate connection is denied or reinterpreted in a non-corporeal sense by the opposition (v. 12; cf. v. 35). Paul reaffirms that the Christian proclamation is founded on the resurrection of Christ as cited in the *narratio* and once accepted by all his audience.

Refutatio (vv. 12-19). The proposition of the opposition that Paul refutes in this unit is expressed in v. 12 as a rhetorical question premised with a reference to the heart of the creed (vv. 3-4): 'Now if Christ is proclaimed as raised from the dead, how can some of you say there is no resurrection of the dead?' In light of vv. 29 and 35, the Corinthians are not denying the resurrection and resurrection life, only its bodily form as if it were the reanimation of a corpse (a position Paul also rejects in vv. 42-50).

With the stasis of fact the most logical method of refutation is to deny the 'fact' put forward by the opposition (Quintilian 7.1.13). Paul's *refutatio* is based upon necessity (*Rhet. ad Alex.* 13.1431a.7ff.). He argues that the doctrine of the resurrection he preached is necessary to make sense of Christian faith and hope. He does not prove that Christ has been raised from the dead, for that is assumed to be accepted by the audience (vv. 1-2, 11, 12), but that Christ's resurrection guarantees the Christian's resurrection.

In his refutation, Paul momentarily agrees with the proposition and then shows that its natural consequences include conclusions the Corinthians are not willing to grant. The opponents' proposition is thus refuted by logical consequence in vv. 13-19.[31] The negative

---

31. Argumentation from consequences is described in Cicero, *Inv.* 1.26.37; 1.28.43; 1.29.45; 2.12.42; *De Part. Or.* 2.7; 16.55; *Top.* 3.11; 4.20; 12.53–14.57; Quintilian 5.8.5; 5.10.75-79. This method is discussed under *confirmatio*, but all forms of *confirmatio* can be used in *refutatio* (Cicero, *Inv.* 1.42.78; Quintilian 5.13.1; cf. Cicero, *De Or.* 2.81.331).

consequences are preaching in vain and believing in vain (vv. 13-14), the former being developed in vv. 15-16, the latter in vv. 17-18, and both together in v. 19. Preaching in vain includes misrepresenting God by testifying to what he did not do—raise Christ from the dead (vv. 15-16). Believing in vain includes continuing in sin (since the resurrection of Christ was needed to abolish the effects of sin, cf. v. 3) and the Christian dead having died in sin (vv. 17-18). The Corinthians are not willing to accept these logical consequences of their proposition because they believe themselves to be forgiven and take the trouble to be baptized for the dead (v. 29). Paul concludes this section in v. 19 with amplification by pathos[32] and recapitulation of consequences (Cicero, *De Part. Or.* 16.55). If the opponents' proposition and its consequences are true, then Christians will die in their sins and have possessed nothing more than earthly life.

Confirmatio (vv. 20-28). Paul's *confirmatio* is constructed according to the ancient pattern for the complete argument (and amplification of a theme).[33] The five elements of a complete argument are given as: *propositio* (the proposition to be proven), *ratio* (the reason establishing the truth of the *propositio*), *confirmatio* (further proof of the *ratio*), *exornatio* (expansion and amplification of the argument), and *conplexio* (a brief conclusion that draws the argument together). Underlying Paul's use of this argumentation scheme is the *topos* of cause and effect[34]—Christ's resurrection is the origin and cause of the Christian's resurrection. With the stasis of fact, origin and cause– effect are investigated (Cicero, *Top.* 21.82; 23.87-88).

Paul's *propositio* is v. 20. It is premised on the creed given in the *narratio*, and is antithetical to the hypothetical 'if Christ has not been raised' of the preceding *refutatio* (vv. 14, 17): 'But in fact Christ has

32. For further discussion of argumentation by pathos, see Aristotle, *Rhet.* 1.2.1356a.3, 5; Cicero, *De Or.* 2.42.178; 2.44.185-87; *Or.* 37.128; Quintilian 6.2.20-24.

33. Complete argument—*Rhet. ad Her.* 2.18.28-29.46; 3.9.16; theme—*Rhet. ad Her.* 4.43.56-44.58. For full discussion of this pattern, see B.L. Mack, 'Anecdotes and Arguments: The Chreia in Antiquity and Early Christianity' (Occasional Papers, 10; Claremont: The Institute for Antiquity and Christianity, Claremont Graduate School, 1987); *Rhetoric and the New Testament*, pp. 41-47; *Patterns of Persuasion in the Gospels* (with V.K. Robbins; Sonoma, CA: Polebridge, 1989), ch. 2.

34. Cicero, *De Or.* 2.40.171; *De Part. Or.* 2.7; *Top.* 3.11; 4.22-23; 15.58–18.67.

been raised from the dead, the first fruits of those who have died'. As the first fruit harvested is a guarantee of the entire harvest, so Christ's resurrection is a guarantee of the Christian's resurrection.

Paul's *propositio* is further confirmed by a *ratio* in vv. 21-22, as indicated by the opening preposition γάρ. The *ratio* is an inductive proof from example,[35] the type being historical example[36] which compares things similar. The comparison is based on the analogy between the examples of Adam and Christ.[37] The *ratio* unpacks the metaphor of first fruits of the *propositio*.

Verses 23-24 is the *confirmatio* which provides further proof for the *ratio* and often expresses the *propositio* in another form.[38] Verse 23 is the reiteration of the *propositio* in other words, and v. 24 is a further proof of the *ratio*. Christ's resurrection assures the Christian's resurrection because it initiates the defeat of all powers, including death.

Verses 25-28 functions as an *exornatio*, further confirmation of the arguments once established, here initiated by γάρ. The *exornatio* elaborates Christ's handing of the kingdom to the Father and the destruction of the powers. A main feature of the *exornatio* is the continued use of πᾶς from v. 24 (a tenfold use in vv. 24-28) to emphasize the all-encompassing nature of God's sovereignty. Typically the *exornatio* is composed of a combination of four elements: simile, *exemplum*, *amplificatio* and *iudicationes* (κρίσις, judgments) (*Rhet. ad Her.* 2.29.46). Judgments and amplification are found here.

Verse 25 is a proposition about Christ deriving from Ps. 110.1, functioning as an *iudicatio* (or judgment), since judgments include supernatural oracles and judgments of gods (see n. 24). Verse 26 is a

35. For discussion of proof from example, see Aristotle *Rhet.* 2.20; *Rhet. ad Alex.* 8; Quintilian 5.11; Lausberg, *Handbuch*, I, pp. 227-35, §§ 410-26; Martin, *Antike Rhetorik*, pp. 119-24.

36. This would be historical example in the perspective of the first century, not necessarily from our perspective. Historical example was most suited to deliberative oratory because, since the future resembles the past, it aids deliberation on the future (Aristotle, *Rhet.* 2.20.1394a.8; Quintilian 5.11.8). For use of historical examples as opposed to those from fables, poets, and judgments, see Aristotle, *Rhet.* 2.20.1393a.2-1393b.4; *Rhet. ad Alex.* 8; Cicero, *Inv.* 1.30.49; Quintilian 5.11.1, 8, 15-16.

37. For analogy as part of inductive argument, see Cicero, *Inv.* 1.29.46-30.47; 1.31.51-33.56; Quintilian 5.11.34-35.

38. It is also called the *pronuntiatum* (*Rhet. ad Her.* 4.43.56).

further refinement of the *iudicatio* clarifying that death is the last enemy to be subjugated. The *iudicatio* of v. 25 is repeated in v. 27a in another form for the sake of amplification by repetition (Cicero, *De Part. Or.* 15.54), quoting Ps 8.6 (LXX 8.7). Christ's enemies can be subjugated and death destroyed because God put all things under Christ's feet.

Verses 27b-28 further amplifies that Christ, once subjugating all powers including death, will hand over the kingdom to God (v. 24). Both v. 27b and v. 28 begin with the phrase ὅταν δέ and say the same thing, the latter being a fuller statement of the former. Together they form amplification by repetition (Cicero, *De Part. Or.* 15.54).

The Peroratio (vv. 29-34). The *peroratio* of the first unit of *refutatio* and *confirmatio* is vv. 29- 34. A *peroratio* can be used at the end of a division of a work and throughout a complicated case, as well as at the conclusion of an entire work.[39] Like the *peroratio* at the conclusion of a work, vv. 29-34 performs the two main functions of recapitulating the main points of the *probatio* and arousing pathos for the case and against the case of the opposition.[40] In deliberative rhetoric recapitulation can take the form of five figures: argument (διαλογισμός), enumeration (ἀπολογισμός), proposal of policy (προαίρεσις), interrogation (ἐπερώτησις), and irony (εἰρωνεία) (*Rhet. ad Alex.* 33.1439b.12ff.).[41] In this recapitulation Paul is using a combination of argument reliant upon interrogation (vv. 29-32a), irony (v. 32b) and proposal of policy (v. 33-34).

Paul begins the *peroratio* with recapitulation from interrogation (vv. 29-32a) using four rhetorical questions which temporarily assume the truth of the opposition proposition (vv. 12-19) and reject the *confirmatio* based on the creed (vv. 20-28). These questions are a form of recapitulation which puts questions to the opponents' weakest point (*Rhet. ad Alex.* 36.1444b.21ff.): their hypocrisy in praxis. The questions are meant to be answered negatively, pointing out that the behavior of both the audience and Paul is at variance with a denial of

---

39. *Rhet. ad Alex.* 20.1433b.30ff.; 21.1434a.30ff.; 22.1434b.11ff.; 36.1444b.21ff.; Quintilian 6.1.8; cf. *Rhet. ad Alex.* 32.1439a.19ff.

40. For full discussion of the *peroratio*, see Lausberg, *Handbuch*, I, pp. 236-40, §§ 431-42; Martin, *Antike Rhetorik*, pp. 147-66.

41. A similar listing is given for recapitulation at the end of a judicial argument (*Rhet. ad Alex.* 20.1433b.29ff.; 36.1444b.31ff.).

the resurrection. It is 'vain' behavior (cf. vv. 2, 10, 14, 17).

This recapitulation is also refutation from logical contradictories,[42] a *topos* of the stasis of fact (Cicero, *Top.* 23.88). Paul demonstrates that the opponents' proposition is contradictory or foolish (Quintilian 5.13.16-17) and inconsistent (Quintilian 5.13.30), not in its logic, but in relation to their own and Paul's behavior. If there is no resurrection of the dead, there is no reason for the opposition to be vicariously baptized for the dead (v. 29) nor for Paul to put himself in life-threatening situations for the sake of a 'vain' gospel message (vv. 30-32a). 'A "contrary" argument is one made against actions performed by the audience...' (Cicero, *Inv.* 1.50.93). A specific form of refutation in deliberative rhetoric is to show that the opponent's proposition is contrary to policy they advocate (*Rhet. ad Alex.* 34.1440a.5ff.; cf. 5.1427b.12ff.).

Recapitulation from interrogation and logical contradictories is followed by recapitulation from irony and logical consequences (v. 32b). Paul gives the more reasonable response to the proposition that there is no resurrection from the dead (cf. v. 12). He begins by citing the proposition (cf. v. 29b) and then a Greek maxim from anti-Epicurean thought. The maxim is the antithesis of dying daily (v. 31) and is a formula for the dissolute life.[43] This is irony, for Paul certainly does not advocate this behavior, but holds it up as an unacceptable consequence to an unacceptable proposition.[44]

Paul ends his *peroratio* with recapitulation from proposal of policy presented as two exhortations (vv. 33-34). Exhortation to morality and virtue was typically part of the *peroratio* (Cicero, *De Part. Or.* 16.56). In the first exhortation Paul advises his audience to veer away from those who deny the resurrection and are thereby morally tainted. He incorporates a maxim found in Menander's *Thais*.[45] In the

42. Refutation from logical contradictories is described in Cicero, *Inv.* 1.30.46; 1.48.89; 1.50.93; *De Part. Or.* 2.7-8; *Top.* 2.11; 3.17; 4.20; 11.47-49; 12.53–14.57; *Rhet. ad Her.* 4.18; Quintilian 5.10.73.

43. G.D. Fee, *The First Epistle to the Corinthians* (NICNT; Grand Rapids: Eerdmans, 1987), p. 772; A.J. Malherbe, 'The Beasts at Ephesus', *JBL* 87 (1968), pp. 76-79.

44. For further discussion of irony, see Lausberg, *Handbuch*, I, pp. 302-3, §§ 582-85; pp. 446-50, §§ 902-904; Martin, *Antike Rhetorik*, pp. 263-64.

45. Fragment 218, Kock. Cited by H. Conzelmann, *1 Corinthians* (Philadelphia: Fortress Press, 1975), p. 278 n. 139; cf. Malherbe, 'Beasts at Ephesus', pp. 77-78.

second Paul tears down his opposition's ethos by implying that those denying the resurrection have arrived at a pagan position like that of the Epicureans (cf. v. 32) (particularly the drunkenness which is to be countered with a 'sober' mind) and have no knowledge of God.

Second Unit of Refutatio and Confirmatio (vv. 35-57).

With the introduction of an interlocutor and a return to refutation, Paul begins a new section of the argument with v. 35. He argues throughout this section that bodily existence (not strictly a material body) is the continuity between present and future existence, that both a continuity and a discontinuity exist between the earthly and heavenly body. Christian resurrection, like the resurrection of Christ, is the transformation of the physical body into a glorified body. Underlying the argumentation is the common *topos* of the lesser-greater (that is *argumentum a minori ad maius*) which the Jews adapted from Hellenistic rhetoric.[46]

Refutatio (vv. 35-44a). The *refutatio* begins in v. 35 with a proposition of the opposition, focusing on the philosophical question behind their denial of the resurrection. The proposition is framed as two rhetorical questions, the latter specifying the former: 'But someone will ask, "How are the dead raised? With what kind of body do they come?"' These questions constitute anticipation, a figure of thought in which the rhetor anticipates and forestalls the objections of opponents.[47] These questions are also personification:[48] 'By this means we display the inner thoughts of our adversaries as though they were talking with themselves (but we shall only carry conviction if we represent them as uttering what they may reasonably be supposed to have had in their minds') (Quintilian 9.2.30; cf. *Rhet. ad Her.* 4.53.66). Both anticipation and personification play a large role in deliberative rhetoric.[49]

---

46. D. Daube, 'Rabbinic Methods of Interpretation and Hellenistic Rhetoric', *HUCA* 22 (1949), pp. 239-64.

47. For further discussion of anticipation, see Lausberg, *Handbuch*, I, pp. 424-25; §§ 854-55; Martin, *Antike Rhetorik*, pp. 277-79.

48. For further discussion of personification, see Lausberg, *Handbuch*, I, pp. 407-13, §§ 820-29; Martin, *Antike Rhetorik*, pp. 291-93.

49. Aristotle, *Rhet.* 3.17.1418b.14; *Rhet. ad Alex.* 34.1440a.24; Quintilian 3.8.49-54.

The proposition underlying the questions can be expressed thus: 'The dead are not raised, for the corpse is not reanimated'.[50] Paul refutes this by denying that the assumptions are credible (Cicero, *Inv.* 1.42.79), that is, their assumption that reanimation of a corpse is the basis of resurrection. Paul will prove that the doctrine of the resurrection body is reasonable (vv. 36-44a), certain (vv. 44b-49), and necessary (vv. 50-57).

In proving the doctrine of the resurrection is reasonable, Paul bases his *refutatio* on an elaborate proof from comparison of two examples (vv. 36-44a). The proof from example is based on analogy and begins with the figure of thought called *exclamatio* in which an exclamation is used to simulate emotion:[51] 'Fool!' In diatribal fashion the proposition of the opposition is immediately dismissed as foolish before the proof is mustered to refute it.

The first example used in the comparison is the growth of seeds (vv. 36-38). God performs a transformation so that each of the seed's two modes of existence has a body suitable to it. By picking up the topics of death and the body from the proposition, the example illustrates the possibility of a resurrection of the dead with a transformed spiritual body.

The second example is the variety of bodies in God's creation which are adapted to their mode of existence (vv. 39-41). First, all animal bodies are listed: humans, animals, birds, and fish (v. 39; cf. Gen. 1.20-30). Then the antithesis of earthly verses heavenly bodies (v. 40) forms a transition from the earthly bodies of v. 39 to the heavenly bodies of v. 41, and anticipates the antithesis between the earthly and heavenly bodies of believers in vv. 45-49. Finally, the heavenly bodies are mentioned under the categories of sun, moon, and stars (v. 41).

These two examples of seeds and bodies are applied to the resurrection of the dead in vv. 42-44a using four antithetical contrasts. This section begins in v. 42 with the application formula οὕτως καί ('so'). Each antithesis is presented in the form 'it is sown...it is raised', the first three pertaining to seeds and the last to bodies. The antitheses

---

50. πῶς (v. 35) often introduces a rhetorical question that calls an assumption into question or rejects it altogether (BAGD, p. 732). Cf. Wuellner ('Paul as Pastor', pp. 58, 66) for the same conclusion.

51. For further discussion of *exclamatio*, see Lausberg, *Handbuch*, I, p. 399, § 809; Martin, *Antike Rhetorik*, p. 282.

stress that God provides transformation from earthly to heavenly existence, and an appropriate body for each.

First Unit of the Confirmatio (vv. 44b-49).[52] Having refuted the proposition denying the reasonableness of the resurrection, Paul must now confirm its certainty. He continues with two proofs, one from judgment (κρίσις) (v. 45) and the other from comparison of examples based on the Adam–Christ analogy (vv. 46-49, cf. vv. 21-22). Paul begins with the proposition in v. 44b: 'If there is a physical body, there is also a spiritual body'. His first proof is a judgment (here an oracle of God) from Gen. 2.7 with adaptations (v. 45). The physical body (ψυκή) and the spiritual body (πνεῦμα) of the proposition of v. 44b are represented in the two archetypical Adams. The physical body comes through the first Adam, and the spiritual body comes through the life-giving activity of the last Adam—the resurrected Christ.

A proof from example follows in vv. 46-49, shifting from Adam and Christ to the two antithetical modes of existence of which they are representative: physical and spiritual. It presents a series of antithetical contrasts within a proof from comparison of examples. The stress in v. 46 on the temporal priority of the physical (ψυχικός) over the spiritual (πνευματικός) may be to refute the Corinthian claim that they are already πνευματικός. Paul indicates that one is ψυχικός until the resurrection, and then πνευματικός. Verse 47 establishes the quality (not origin) of the life Adam and Christ had (earthly–heavenly), using Gen. 2.7 again to pick up the theme of dust. Verses 48-49 applies the comparative example to the Corinthians. Verse 48 uses the language of v. 47 to include Christians as sharing either earthly or, upon resurrection, heavenly existence. Verse 49 repeats v. 48 for amplification, making it more specific and incorporating an exhortation to live like those who will have a πνευνατικός existence (cf. vv. 33-34, 58).

---

52. It is not typical to break the argument between v. 44a and v. 44b. However, vv. 42-44a forms a unit of four antithetical clauses. Verse 44b introduces a conditional which functions as a proposition with a proof from judgment immediately following. Also, at v. 44b the argument shifts from proving that the resurrection body is reasonable to proving it is certain.

Second Unit of the Confirmatio (vv. 50-57). In this second unit of *confirmatio*, Paul argues that the transformation of the body is necessary to enter heavenly existence.[53] As in the *confirmatio* of vv. 20-28, Paul uses the elaboration pattern for the complete argument. He begins in v. 50 with the *propositio* he wishes to prove: 'What I am saying, brothers and sisters, is this: flesh and blood cannot inherit the kingdom of God, nor does the perishable inherit the imperishable'.

The *ratio* which establishes the truth of the *propositio* comprises vv. 51-52. It is presented with a revelatory formula common to apocalyptic literature: 'I will tell you a mystery'. Paul is thus giving a judgment (κρίσις, *iudicatio*) of the subtype of a supernatural oracle. For both the dead and the living at the parousia there will be transformation from one body to another. Verse 52b repeats vv. 51-52a for amplification.

Verse 53 is the *confirmatio*, which corroborates the *ratio*. Here it begins with γάρ indicating that further reasons are being given. It is a paraphrase of the *propositio*, as was common (*Rhet. ad Her.* 4.43.56). It uses the figure of thought called refining to repeat the idea in a different form, here positively for the purpose of amplification.[54]

The *exornatio*, which confirms the argument once it is established, comprises vv. 54-56. As is typical, it is composed of *amplificatio* (vv. 54, 56) and an *iudicatio* (v. 55). For amplification, it first repeats the proposition of vv. 50 and 53 as a future reality (v. 54) and then supports it with an *iudicatio* drawn from Isa. 25.8 and Hos. 13.14 (v. 55, cf. v. 26). It is followed in v. 56 by the figure of speech called *definitio* which 'in brief and clear-cut fashion grasps the characteristic qualities of a thing...' (*Rhet. ad Her.* 4.25.35).[55] Before the argument closes, *definitio* clarifies the nature of death which is conquered by resurrection. The thanksgiving of v. 57 is the *conplexio* or conclusion.

The Peroratio (v. 58)

A shift in ch. 15 is indicated in v. 58 by the conjunction ὥστε ('therefore') and the vocative ἀδελφοί μου ἀγαπητοί ('my beloved'):

53. A new beginning is indicated by the adversative particle δέ and the vocative ἀδελφοί.

54. For more on refining, see *Rhet. ad Her.* 4.42.54-44.58; Lausberg, *Handbuch*, I, pp. 413-19, §§ 830-42.

55. For further discussion of *definitio*, see Lausberg, *Handbuch*, I, p. 385, § 782; Martin, *Antike Rhetorik*, p. 293.

'Therefore, my beloved, be steadfast, immovable, always excelling in the work of the Lord, because you know that in the Lord your labor is not in vain'. This is the *peroratio* or conclusion for all of ch. 15. Like the *peroratio* of an entire work it recapitulates the main points of the argumentation of ch. 15 and arouses emotion. A key *topos* of the chapter—'vain' (κένος)—is recapitulated. A main purpose of the chapter was to encourage the audience to adhere to the message so their faith was not 'in vain' (vv. 2, 10, 14, 17, cf. vv. 29- 34). In light of the resurrection and the continuity of the physical and the spiritual bodies, their faith and Christian walk are not 'vain'. The *peroratio* is short on recapitulation, for deliberative rhetoric seldom needs any (Cicero, *De Part. Or.* 17.59). Important matters, like moral virtues listed here, were commonly the subject of the *peroratio* (Cicero, *De Part. Or.* 16.56). The *peroratio* is a proposal of policy (προαίρεσις) as is common to the *peroratio* of deliberative rhetoric (*Rhet. ad Alex.* 33.1439.12ff.).

In conclusion, Paul uses deliberative rhetoric in this chapter to advise the audience to adhere to the traditional understanding of the bodily resurrection as a necessary course of action. He incorporates a sophisticated use of *confirmatio* and *refutatio*, particularly incorporating the elaboration pattern for a complete argument. Paul's rhetorical strategy can be outlined as follows:

I.   *Exordium* (vv. 1-2)

II. *Narratio* (vv. 3-11)

III. *Confirmatio* (*Probatio*) and *Refutatio* (vv. 12-57)

   A. First Unit of *Refutatio* and *Confirmatio* (vv. 12-34)

      1. *Refutatio* (vv. 12-19)
         a. Proposition of the Opposition (v. 12)
         b. Refutation by Logical Consequences (vv. 13-19)

      2. *Confirmatio* (v. 20-28)
         a. *Propositio* (v. 20)
         b. *Ratio* as Proof from Example (vv. 21-22)
         c. *Confirmatio* (vv. 23-24)
         d. *Exornatio* (vv. 25-28)

      3. *Peroratio* (vv. 29-34)
         a. Recapitulation from Interrogation (vv. 29-32a)
         b. Recapitulation from Irony (v. 32b)
         c. Recapitulation from Proposal of Policy (vv. 33-34)

B. Second Unit of *Refutatio* and *Confirmatio* (vv. 35-57)

    1. *Refutatio* (vv. 35-44a)
        a. Proposition of the Opposition (v. 35)
        b. Refutation by Comparison of Examples (vv. 36-44a)

    2. First Unit of the *Confirmatio* (vv. 44b-49)
        a. Proposition (v. 44b)
        b. Proof from Judgment (v. 45)
        c. Proof from Comparison of Examples (vv. 46-49)

    3. Second Unit of the *Confirmatio* (vv. 50-57)
        a. *Propositio* (v. 50)
        b. *Ratio* (vv. 51-52)
        c. *Confirmatio* (v. 53)
        d. *Exornatio* (vv. 54-56)
        e. *Conclusio* (v. 57)

IV. *Peroratio* (v. 58)

Speaking Like a Fool: Irony in 2 Corinthians 10–13

Glenn Holland

1. *Introduction*

The study of 2 Corinthians 10–13 has quite properly focused precisely on those elements that establish the distinctive tone of these chapters.[1] In 2 Corinthians 10–13 Paul replies to the charges of unnamed opponents and attacks the 'superlative apostles'. Paul seems to harbor some doubts about the Corinthians and expresses reservations about their response to what he writes. These doubts stand in contrast to the 'confidence' and 'pride' he conveys in 2 Corinthians 1–9.[2] Most notably, however, 'here the tone is sharply polemic and passionately apologetic'.[3] Most notable among Paul's rhetorical tools in these chapters is irony, the pretense that what is said 'hides' from the reader the true state of affairs while in fact revealing it.[4] Already by the time of Paul irony was a familiar philosophical and literary device.[5] In the

---

1. V.P. Furnish, *II Corinthians* (AB, 32A; Garden City, NY: Doubleday, 1984), pp. 35-41, 44-54.
2. See the tables provided by A. Plummer, *A Critical and Exegetical Commentary on the Second Epistle of St Paul to the Corinthians* (ICC; Edinburgh: T. & T. Clark, 1915), pp. xxx-xxxi.
3. Furnish, *II Corinthians*, p. 31.
4. Irony is a wide-ranging topic in discussion of both rhetoric and literary criticism. Modern theories are most often based on classical examples; cf. K. Burke, *A Grammar of Motives* (New York: Prentice-Hall, 1945), pp. 511-17; J.A. Dane, *The Critical Mythology of Irony* (Athens: University of Georgia Press, 1991), pp. 15-70; M. Tarozzi Goldsmith, *Nonrepresentational Forms of the Comic: Humor, Irony, and Jokes* (New York: Peter Lang, 1991), pp. 67-154.
5. For irony in Euripidean drama, see H.P. Foley, *Ritual Irony: Poetry and Sacrifice in Euripides* (Ithaca, NY: Cornell University Press, 1985); for irony in Greek philosophy, see C. Jan Swearingen, *Rhetoric and Irony: Western Literacy and Western Lies* (New York: Oxford University Press, 1991), pp. 22-131, and E. Behler, *Irony and the Discourse of Modernity* (Seattle: University of Washington Press, 1990), pp. 73-150.

case of 2 Corinthians 10–13, the use of irony allows Paul to 'speak like a fool' in his own defense, saying things that must be said but which he could not say *in proper persona*.[6] Paul's use of irony is most pronounced in the so-called 'Foolish Discourse' (*Narrenrede*) of 2 Corinthians 11.1–12.10. Studies by Betz,[7] Zmijewski[8] and Forbes,[9] among others, have dealt at length with Paul's style and have drawn particular attention to the irony and the other rhetorical strategies Paul employs in the Foolish Discourse.

My concern, however, is more specifically with Paul's use of the motif of 'foolishness' as a rhetorical strategy. In the guise of the fool, Paul is able both to speak ironically and to draw his readers' attention to the fact that he is doing so.[10] The whole concept of 'speaking like a fool' invites the reader to look past the surface meaning of the text in order to find its deeper, 'true' meaning. The intention of the Foolish Discourse, and 2 Corinthians 10–13 as a whole, is to induce the reader to see things in the correct way, that is, with the spiritual insight proper to the Christian believer rather than 'according to the flesh'.

6.   On the rhetorical problem of self-commendation in the ancient world, see E.A. Judge, 'Paul's Boasting in Relation to Contemporary Professional Practice', *ABR* 16 (1968), pp. 37-50; C. Forbes, 'Comparison, Self-Praise and Irony: Paul's Boasting and the Conventions of Hellenistic Rhetoric', *NTS* 32 (1986), pp. 1-30; and J.T. Fitzgerald, *Cracks in an Earthen Vessel: An Examination of the Catalogues of Hardship in the Corinthian Correspondence* (Atlanta: Scholars Press, 1988), pp. 107-14.

7.   H.D. Betz, *Der Apostel Paulus und die sokratische Tradition* (BZHT; Tübingen: Mohr [Siebeck], 1972), summarized in Betz, *Paul's Apology: II Corinthians 10–13 and the Socratic Tradition* (Protocol of the Second Colloquy, the Center for Hermeneutical Studies in Hellenistic and Modern Culture, 5 December 1970; ed. W. Wuellner; Berkeley: Graduate Theological Union and the University of California, Berkeley).

8.   J. Zmijewski, *Der Stil der paulinische 'Narrenrede': Analyse der Sprachgestaltung in 2 Kor 11.1–12.10 als Beitrag zur Methodik von Stiluntersuchungen neutestamentlicher Texte* (BBB, 52; Cologne: Peter Hanstein, 1978).

9.   Forbes, 'Comparison'.

10.   Many scholars have commented on Paul's 'foolishness' as a legitimate means of self-commendation; see for example Forbes, 'Comparison'; Judge, 'Paul's Boasting'; A.B. Spencer, 'The Wise Fool (and the Foolish Wise): A Study of Irony in Paul', *NovT* 23 (1981), pp. 349-60; C.H. Talbert, *Reading Corinthians: A Literary and Theological Commentary on 1 and 2 Corinthians* (New York: Crossroad, 1987), pp. 111-30.

Paul's use of irony is not limited to the Foolish Discourse, as most scholars realize, but it is in 2 Cor. 11.1–12.10 that this irony is expressed in its most complex form. I will therefore concentrate my attention on Paul's use of irony in his boasting in the Foolish Discourse, and consider the rest of 2 Corinthians 10–13 only to the extent that it throws light on this main topic.

2. *Rules for Boasting: 2 Corinthians 10.1-8*

Even a casual reading of 2 Corinthians 10–13 reveals it as a carefully-composed, integrated composition. The first verse, 10.1, already introduces two key ideas: that perceptions of Paul may change according to circumstances, and that Paul emulates 'the meekness and gentleness of Christ'. The Corinthians perceive Paul as 'demeaned' when he is present, but as 'bold' when he is absent. This is to some extent a function of Paul's own behavior (10.2, 9; 13.1-4), but seems to be primarily a function of the Corinthians' own judgment (10.10-11). Paul's citation of the humility of Christ in this context, as Ragnar Leivestad has demonstrated,[11] refers specifically to Christ's self-humiliation in the Incarnation. There is an implicit parallel between Christ and Paul: Christ's humility in the world was not the whole story about him nor is Paul's humility among the Corinthians the whole story about Paul.

Indeed, Paul's future demeanor among the Corinthians will depend upon the congregation's response to Paul's appeal in the present letter. He hopes he will not have to show 'boldness' and begs his readers to respond to the letter in such a way as to make that unnecessary. But he can act with authority when the Corinthians force him to do so; the 'boldness' he shows in his letters is at his command (10.2). This point is elaborated in an effective series of military metaphors in 10.3-6. Paul emphasizes that the war he wages is itself not *kata sarka* and the means of war are not fleshly (*sarkika*). This is a 'spiritual' war carried on against 'spiritual' enemies: arguments, obstacles to the knowledge of God, thoughts, disobedience and 'strongholds'[12] (10.5-6).

Oddly enough, following Paul's emphasis on that which is not *kata*

11. R. Leivestad, '"The Meekness and Gentleness of Christ" II Cor. X.I', *NTS* 13 (1966), pp. 156-64.

12. These 'strongholds' are themselves spiritual, so Furnish, *II Corinthians*, p. 458.

sarka, he calls upon the Corinthians to 'Look at the things that are in front of you!' (10.7a). Previously when the Corinthians have looked at what was in front of them they came to the conclusion that Paul was 'weak' (*asthenēs*, 10.10b). Paul does not deny the accuracy of that judgment per se, but now demands that the Corinthians recognize his status as a man in Christ (10.7b). Anyone who claims the spiritual insight to insist on his or her own identity as Christ's should also acknowledge (*logizesthō*) that Paul is Christ's as well. Even if Paul appears 'demeaned' *en sarka*, it is possible to recognize his spiritual status if one's perception of 'the flesh' is correct, since he is not one who acts in a worldly fashion (*kata sarka*). The issue is thus 'correct', that is, 'spiritual' perception, the gift of insight into the true nature of things.

In 10.8, Paul establishes rules for the practice of 'boasting' using his own example. Although he may boast too much, 'I shall not be put to shame' (10.8c), because the content of his boast is the authority 'which the Lord gave for building you up and not for destroying you' (10.8b). Paul boasts specifically about what the Lord has enabled him to do within the limits of his apostolic ministry to the Corinthians.

Paul in 10.9-11 essentially reiterates the points already made in 10.1-2, thereby emphasizing the subjective, and thus fallible, nature of the Corinthians' perceptions of Paul. To promote an 'objective' view of his status, in 10.12 Paul rules out any self-commendation by means of comparison with others, thereby eliminating in theory 'a fundamental tool of rhetoric', *sygkrisis*.[13] *Sygkrisis* is the basis for the self-commendation of Paul's opponents, but he rules such comparison to be illegitimate. Insofar as 'they measure themselves by one another' and not according to the norm or standard established by God (10.13), they are 'without understanding' (10.12b).

Scott Hafemann has investigated Paul's rules for proper self-commendation in 2 Cor. 10.12-18.[14] The fundamental criterion for proper boasting comes from a paraphrase of Jer. 9.23-24: 'Let him who boasts, boast in the Lord' (10.17). Paul boasts within 'the limits God has apportioned us, to reach even to you' (10.13b). Boasting 'beyond limit' (10.13a) would be to boast in the work of other missionaries (10.15a), 'boasting of work already done in another's field' (10.16b).

13. Forbes, 'Comparison', p. 3.
14. S. Hafemann, ' "Self-Commendation" and Apostolic Legitimacy in 2 Corinthians: A Pauline Dialectic?', *NTS* 36 (1990), pp. 66-88.

'Boasting in the Lord' is not self-commendation, but receiving the commendation of the Lord, according to the work the Lord has established for a person to do.[15]

For Paul then, boasting about his work in Corinth is 'boasting in the Lord'. Boasting about anything else, including deeds done or ills suffered in the Lord's service, is boasting *kata sarka* (11.17-18).[16] Paul is thus free to 'boast in the Lord' about his work among the Corinthians. By the same token, his opponents can make no boast 'in the Lord', since they have no proper part in the apostolic work in Corinth. They can only boast *kata sarka*.

3. *The Foolish Discourse: Introduction, 2 Corinthians 11.1-15*

It is generally agreed that the Foolish Discourse begins with 11.1. However, it is not at this point that Paul begins 'speaking like a fool'; this happens only after 11.16. In the intervening verses, Paul attempts to provide a justification for his planned 'foolishness'.

His first justification is his 'divine jealousy' for the Corinthians. His jealousy is like the jealousy a father or guardian feels for the well-being and purity of the bride he presents to her husband (11.2). This image introduces the metaphor of Eve and the serpent, often thought of in Paul's time as having involved a sexual seduction.[17] This metaphor characterizes Paul's opponents in Corinth as deceivers, possibly anticipating his later implication that they are 'servants of Satan' (11.15).

Paul's second justification for 'foolishness', 'I think I am not in the least inferior to these superlative apostles' (11.5), reintroduces the idea of comparison which Paul has so far shunned. Initially, however, he indulges in *sygkrisis* only to expose a deficiency: his own lack of skill in speaking (cf. 10.10b). Paul makes a comparison only to be found wanting. But he maintains that this 'failing' is compensated for by a superior virtue, knowledge (11.6a). This 'knowledge', 'the divine gift of spiritual insight',[18] is the very knowledge Paul wishes to promote among his readers. The comparison Paul now 'dares' to

15. Hafemann, "Self-Commendation", pp. 76-80; cf. R. Bultmann, *TDNT* 3, p. 651.

16. Hafemann, "Self-Commendation", p. 84.

17. Furnish, *II Corinthians*, p. 487.

18. Furnish, *II Corinthians*, p. 490.

make has already been made by the Corinthians, particularly in regard to Paul's refusal to accept support from them. The 'superlative apostles' seem to have accepted such support as their due and also to have encouraged the belief that Paul's refusal to do likewise was an indication that he was not a true apostle.[19] Paul attempts to present his rejection of the Corinthians' support in a 'spiritual' light as an act of love (11.11). Paul 'foolishly' identifies his act of love with some sort of sin in an ironic question (11.7). But far from being ashamed of his 'sin', Paul makes it his 'boast' in all of Achaia (11.10). This is a boast 'in the Lord', since it is directly related to Paul's missionary work in Corinth and is thus within the 'limits' assigned to him by God (10.13-16).

Paul in 11.12 suggests an additional motive for his refusal to accept support from the Corinthians: his desire to undermine the claims of his opponents. Paul does this because they 'want an opportunity to be recognized as our equals in what they boast about' (11.12b Furnish). This is the first direct imputation of 'boasting' to the opponents, and it appears in the same context as Paul's earlier hints of their boast in 10.13, 15: Paul's opponents claim equality with him and rights as apostles in Corinth.

Once again the issue is spiritual insight. Properly perceived, the 'superlative apostles' are 'false apostles', 'deceitful workmen' who are leading the Corinthians astray (11.3-4).[20] Indeed, their deceit makes them 'servants of Satan' (11.14-15), since Satan is the master of deception (11.3). Paul's dire prediction, 'Their end shall be according to their works' (11.15b), is not untypical of Paul's attitude towards his vilifiers (cf. Rom. 3.8).

4. *The Foolish Discourse: Speaking as a Fool, 2 Corinthians 11.16-29*

The Foolish Discourse proper begins with a reassertion of Paul's intention to be foolish in 11.16. Paul is no fool but asks to be received as one since this will give him the opportunity to 'boast', that is, boast

19. On this point see D. Georgi, *The Opponents of Paul in Second Corinthians* (Philadelphia: Fortress Press, 1986), pp. 238-42; Furnish, *II Corinthians*, pp. 506-509; Betz, *Der Apostel Paulus*, pp. 100-117.

20. On whether the 'superlative apostles' and the 'false apostles' are to be identified, see Furnish, *II Corinthians*, pp. 48-49, 502-505.

'foolishly'. So far Paul has boasted 'in the Lord', but now he intends
to boast *kata sarka* (11.18). In so doing, he shares the folly of his
opponents: 'Since many boast of worldly things (*kata sarka*) I too will
boast' (11.18). But in self-consciously sharing the worldly perspective
of his opponents, Paul assumes the mask of the fool in respect to more
than just boasting. He in effect surrenders his own ability to see into
the reality of things, his spiritual insight, in order to share his opponents' judgment of things *kata sarka*.

Thus we may expect a reversal. Paul puts on the mask of the fool
and takes on the perspective and the values of his opponents in order
to outshine them, itself a 'foolish' ambition. Paul thus opens himself
up to the sort of error that has characterized the self-commendation of
his opponents and allowed the Corinthians to be led astray. By
repeatedly referring to his soon-to-be-assumed foolishness in 11.1-21a
before actually putting on the fool's mask in 11.21b, Paul warns his
readers to be aware of the 'foolishness' in what he will say once the
mask is on. Everything he says then may be expected to be self-con-
tradictory, worldly, self-congratulatory, boastful. The long excursus
preceding the assumption of the fool's mask is itself 'foolish', since
Paul on the one hand proclaims his intention to be foolish and on the
other postpones the actual 'foolish speaking' in order to exhort his
readers to a less foolish way of perceiving things.

In adopting his opponents' tactic of boasting *kata sarka*, Paul foolishly enters into the *sygkrisis* he disavowed in 10.12, placing himself
on the same level as his opponents and comparing his 'apostolic credentials' to theirs.[21] He does so even though those who boast *kata
sarka* are fools. At the same time, Paul expects to gain a benefit from
classing himself with his opponents and behaving like a fool. When he
does so, he may expect the Corinthians to put up with him (something
their recent criticism of him proves they are not willing to do when
Paul is 'wise'), since they 'suffer fools gladly' (11.19). And why?
Because the Corinthians are 'wise'.

This evaluation of the Corinthians is usually understood to be highly
ironic.[22] But it would appear this is not in fact the case; when the

21. Forbes, 'Comparison', pp. 18-19.
22. Plummer, *2 Corinthians*, p. 315: 'Here, no doubt [the phrase] is ironical... they are content to tolerate the outrageous conduct of his opponents—no doubt
because they are so serenely conscious of their own superiority'; Furnish, *II
Corinthians*, p. 497: 'Paul has referred to the Corinthians as *wise*... only in a highly

Corinthians 'suffer fools gladly' they are in fact exhibiting what was widely recognized as the behavior of the wise person in the face of the tribulation caused by 'fools'. Paul's list of the offenses of his opponents against the Corinthians in 11.20 forms a short *'peristasis* catalogue', a list of the sufferings the Corinthians have endured.[23] As John T. Fitzgerald has demonstrated within the context of Hellenistic philosophy,

> Whether derided as a fool or acknowledged as a sage the ideal philosopher reveals his sagacity in the way he responds to his adversaries. Injury and insult provide the perfect situation for this demonstration, for 'the power of wisdom is better shown by a display of calmness in the midst of provocation' (Sen., *Const.* 4.3).[24]

More particularly, 'the sage typically either ignores an offense due to its lack of internal impact or responds to it derisively with a smile or a laugh' (Seneca, *Const.* 10.4).[25] If the Corinthians had responded in kind to the 'insults' of the 'superlative apostles' they would have indeed been foolish. Fitzgerald quotes Seneca: 'It is a petty and sorry person who will bite back when he is bitten' (*Ira* 2.34.1).[26] As it is, they suffer and thus are 'wise'. If there *is* irony in 11.20, it lies in the fact that the Corinthians have suffered abuse 'wisely' only because they have 'foolishly' misunderstood the situation in which they find themselves.[27] Although 'wise' in their tolerance, they are 'foolish' to provide an occasion for their wisdom to be proven through suffering (cf. 11.4).

Paul is once again ironic in his apology in 11.21, since he is apologizing for *not* having caused suffering for the Corinthians as his opponents have. Paul attributes this 'failing' to the 'weakness' he has

---

ironic sense'; Spencer, 'Wise Fool', p. 358: 'Their wisdom is emphasized and in doing this Paul stretches the extent to which what he says opposes what he means. Rather than being very wise, the Corinthians are very foolish indeed'; C.K. Barrett, *A Commentary on the Second Epistle to the Corinthians* (HNTC; New York: Harper & Row, 2nd edn, 1973) p. 291: 'The mixture of humility and of bitter retaliatory irony is both subtle and striking'.

23. Fitzgerald, *Cracks*, pp. 44-51; R. Hodgson, 'Paul the Apostle and First Century Tribulation Lists', *ZNW* 74 (1983), pp. 59-80.

24. Fitzgerald, *Cracks*, p. 103; on this subject, pp. 64-65, pp. 103-107.

25. Fitzgerald, *Cracks*, p. 104.

26. Fitzgerald, *Cracks*, p. 103.

27. I am indebted for this suggestion to Hans-Georg Sundermann.

formerly exhibited in their presence (10.1, 10b), a weakness which subsequently becomes the subject of Paul's 'foolish' boasting in 11.30–12.10.

The repeated reminders that Paul is speaking *en aphrosunē* and *kata sarka* in 11.16-21 is often taken as an indication of his uneasiness with the tactic.[28] It seems more likely in view of Paul's concern in 2 Corinthians 10–13 with 'seeing things aright' that the repetition is a warning to his readers to discern the foolishness in what follows and thereby gain the correct perspective.

Initially, Paul's foolish boasting again takes the form of *sygkrisis* with his opponents. He does so in 'foolish' violation of his avowal in 10.12 to refrain from comparisons and now speaks in the guise of one of those 'measuring themselves by themselves'. Paul proves himself the equal of his opponents not least in his willingness to boast as they do.

The comparisons of 11.22 are intended to establish equality between Paul and his opponents, specifically in regard to their ethnic identity as Jews. Although Paul claims equality on the basis of three different assertions of Jewish identity, it seems likely that this is an 'exhaustive' assertion of equality on a point that should have been obvious.[29] In 11.23, however, after a further reminder that he is speaking 'utterly foolishly' (*paraphronōn lalō*), Paul asserts not equality with his opponents but superiority to them: he is more of a servant of Christ than they.

To prove this point, Paul again employs a *peristasis* catalogue, now on his own behalf to prove his status as a 'suffering sage'. As noted above, the hardships which a philosopher or a hero endured were commonly believed to be evidence of the truth of his philosophy and his own status as a sage.[30] Although this *peristasis* catalogue has been recognized as such since the work of Weiss and Bultmann,[31] it is

---

28. Cf. Furnish, *II Corinthians*, p. 532; Plummer, *2 Corinthians*, pp. 313, 317-18; Barrett, *2 Corinthians*, p. 271.

29. Thus Barrett, *2 Corinthians*, pp. 293-94; cf. R. Bultmann, *The Second Letter to the Corinthians* (ed. E. Dinkler; trans. R.A. Harrisville; Minneapolis: Augsburg, 1985), pp. 214-15; Plummer, *2 Corinthians*, pp. 319-20. We may compare Paul's claims of Jewish identity in Rom. 11.1b and Phil. 3.5-6; in each case Paul asserts that he is as Jewish as anyone can be.

30. Fitzgerald, *Cracks*, pp. 44-51.

31. Fitzgerald, *Cracks*, pp. 7-31.

widely believed that Paul's use of the *peristasis* catalogue here is 'a ruthless parody of the pretensions of his opponents'.[32] But the *peristasis* catalogue was widely-used and recognized as a form of philosophical polemic, and there is no reason to believe that Paul's opponents would hesitate to make use of this form of self-commendation. As Fitzgerald argues, it is far more likely that Paul's opponents also listed the hardships of their ministry to prove themselves 'ministers of Christ'.[33] That Paul is engaged in comparison on the basis of hardships is demonstrated by his use of comparatives in 11.23c: 'With *far greater* labors, *far more* imprisonments...'[34] Paul demonstrates his superior status by the means already chosen by his opponents: suffering for the sake of the gospel. To the extent that such boasting is not relevant to Paul's mission among the Corinthians, it is boasting *kata sarka*. Indeed, Paul's boasting in 11.23-27 is quite literally 'according to the flesh', since he boasts about his 'fleshly' hardships. It is the *context* of this boast, not the act of boasting itself, that makes this a 'fool's speech'.[35] Paul's concern with numbers in regard to his hardships (11.24-25) also indicates the foolish nature of this sort of boasting 'according to the flesh'. The point is that whatever others had suffered, Paul had also suffered and more. Although the game of boasting 'according to the flesh' is a pointless one, it is nonetheless a game Paul wins hands down.

The *sygkrisis* between Paul and his opponents is concluded with two rhetorical questions which demand a recognition of Paul's equal status with any who claim to be 'servants of Christ' (11.23a). Paul first asks, 'Who is weak and I am not weak?' (11.29a). Following the *peristasis* catalogue of 11.23-28, the most natural way to understand this question is as a claim of equality: 'Who suffers from such things and I do not?'[36] The question, 'Who is offended [*skandalizetai*] and I do not

32. Forbes, 'Comparison', p. 18; see also Bultmann, *Second Letter*, p. 215; Plummer, *2 Corinthians*, p. 322; Judge, 'Paul's Boasting', p. 47; Georgi, *Opponents*, pp. 242-46; Furnish, *II Corinthians*, pp. 535-36.

33. Fitzgerald (*Cracks*, pp. 24-25 and notes) credits this insight to Oda Wischmeyer in *Der hochste Weg* (SNT, 13; Gutersloh: Mohn, 1981); pp. 85-86 so also Talbert, *Reading Corinthians*, p. 122.

34. The comparatives are often discounted, see esp. Plummer, *2 Corinthians*, p. 322.

35. Hafemann, "Self-Commendation", pp. 84-87.

36. Barrett, *2 Corinthians*, pp. 301-302: 'Repeatedly in this and the following paragraphs Paul declares that he is weak, and that it is in his weakness... that the

burn [*puroumai*]?' (11.29b), would also seem to be a claim for equality since *skandalizetai* and *puroumai* in 11.29b stand parallel to *asthenei* and *astheno* in 11.29a.[37] In both cases Paul asks the same question: 'Who is a minister of Christ and I am not?'

5. *The Foolish Discourse: Boasting of Weakness, 2 Corinthians 11.30–12.10*

With 11.30 a new section begins as Paul abandons an explicit *sygkrisis* in favor of demonstrations of his 'weakness'. In 11.30–12.10 the idea of 'the necessity of boasting/boasting of weakness' is repeated at the beginning of each of its three subsections (11.30-33; 12.1-5; 12.6-10). Although there is still an implicit comparison with his opponents, Paul now concentrates on his own 'weakness', an idea already introduced in 11.29a. 'Boasting' about one's weakness is paradoxical; this point is explicitly made in 12.10. But the revelatory function of Paul's weakness is left unexplained until the end of the section, so Paul at first still appears to be speaking 'foolishly'.[38] There is also 'foolishness' in Paul's parody of recognized forms of self-commendation: tales about courage in battle, divine revelations and miraculous cures.[39] Paul allows his readers to regard these exploits first from the 'outside' as foolishness and only in 12.10 provides the key to seeing these same episodes properly from the 'inside'.

The first exploit, Paul's escape from Damascus, follows a solemn oath affirming the truth of what follows. As Judge notes, not only is this exploit a parody of the 'first over the wall' military boast of the *corona muralis*, but the oath preceding it 'may be read as an example of the *horkou schema* or *figura iusiurandi*, a recognized rhetorical

power of Christ is made known. If anyone can call himself weak, I am yet weaker! (...) Paul means that he too knows what it is to be offended as to burn with anger' (p. 302).

37. Barrett, *2 Corinthians*, p. 302.

38. Contra Bultmann, *TDNT* 3, p. 652: 'Glorying in *astheneia* becomes the dominant theme. Hence Paul abandons the motif of comparison, and *aphrosune* is strictly abandoned even though Paul still maintains the role of *aphron*, vv. 11-13.'

39. For these parodistic themes, Betz, *Der Apostel Paulus*, pp. 70-100; I follow Betz in much of what follows. Cf. Judge, 'Paul's Boasting', pp. 47-50, who maintains 'Paul takes his "foolish" boasting with too much anguish for us to assume it was merely a mockery, unless of course the interjections are themselves part of the irony' (p. 47).

ornament'.[40] Commentators are often left at a loss in explaining why Paul includes this incident, but essentially Paul is boasting about his cowardice: 'As God is my witness, when danger threatened I ran away!'

What does not appear to have been recognized, however, is that Paul's escape from Damascus parallels similar escapes by some heroes of the Hebrew Bible: the two spies sent to reconnoitre in Jericho, who escape the city with the help of Rahab in Josh. 2.15, and David, who escapes Saul's soldiers with the help of Michal in 1 Sam. 19.12. Although the parallels are by no means exact, in both cases the ignominious escape of one day led to the victory of another (Josh. 6.1-25; 1 Sam. 23.1-14). Paul's readers thus might suspect that what appeared at first to be a humiliating escape would in fact lead to powerful works on God's behalf.

The second exploit is introduced in words similar to those of 11.30a: 'It is necessary to boast…' (12.1a). But Paul at the same time reminds his reader that boasting is foolish, 'not beneficial' (*ou sumpheron*). This is true even of Paul's boasting 'of the things that show my weakness'. It is foolish because it is not (apparently) boasting 'in the Lord', ironic because Paul is boasting about 'weakness' (as opposed to the 'strength' demonstrated by the *peristasis* catalogues),[41] doubly ironic since these exploits are in themselves absurd, and finally paradoxical insofar as Paul's weakness demonstrates God's power.

'Visions and revelations' also prove 'not beneficial' in 12.2-4. The story is even told 'foolishly' in the context of 'visions and revelations of the Lord' (12.1c); Paul repeats himself needlessly (12.2-3) and, having thus delayed the story, finally reveals that it has no point. The content of the revelation is 'things that cannot be told, which a person may not utter' (12.4).[42] Paul's readers can derive no benefit from this revelation, although presumably that was why the story was told in the first place.[43]

---

40. Judge, 'Paul's Boasting', p. 47; cf. Furnish on the *corona muralis*, *II Corinthians*, p. 542; for the historical situation, see E.A. Knauf, 'Zum Ethnarchen des Aretas 2 Kor 11.32', *ZNW* 74 (1983), pp. 145-47.

41. Fitzgerald, *Cracks*, pp. 59-65, 114-15.

42. Betz, *Der Apostel Paulus*, pp. 89-92.

43. For the setting of the 'revelation' in its religious context, see A.T. Lincoln, '"Paul the Visionary": The Setting and Significance of the Rapture to Paradise in II Corinthians xii.1-10', *NTS* 25 (1979), pp. 204-20; J.D. Tabor, *Things Unutterable:*

Paul here appears to be parodying the idea that 'visions and revelations' can provide verification of apostolic status. Since they confer no benefit on the apostle's congregation (cf. 1 Cor. 14.6-12), they are not a proper object of boasting. Only a fool would bother to talk about such an experience.

The third exploit begins in 12.5 as Paul explains what he is willing to boast about: 'On behalf of this man [the man of 12.2-4] I will boast, but on my own behalf I will not boast, except of my weakness'. Paul 'foolishly' expects his readers not to recognize that he has in fact been boasting on his own behalf when he boasted about 'such a man'. So Paul boasts about his worthless revelation even while claiming he will not boast, 'foolishly' making himself a liar. Paul then adds a highly ironic comment in 12.6a: if he boasts, it is not really 'foolish', since what he says is the truth. The claim that all his boasts are 'no brag, just fact' is of course typical of a boaster and a fool. Far from being a sober assessment of his apostolic credentials, 12.6a represents the very heights of Paul's 'foolishness'.

Having made such an outrageous claim, Paul maintains 'I shall refrain from it [boasting], so that no one may think more of me than he sees in me or hears from me...' (12.6b). Paul of course has *not* refrained from boasting, with the plain purpose of contradicting the Corinthians' assessment of him after seeing and hearing him (cf. 10.1, 10).

Paul's reference to 'the abundance of revelations' in 12.7a is again ironic. A single account of a fourteen-year-old revelation whose contents cannot be communicated hardly qualifies as an 'abundance of revelations'. The irony is intensified by the repetition of the phrase 'that I might not be too elated' in 12.7b and 12.7c. There has so far been little in the Foolish Discourse that might be expected to induce elation in Paul or to lead him to exalt himself (except perhaps 'foolishly').

Betz takes the third exploit, Paul's 'thorn in the flesh' (12.7-9), as a parody of a healing miracle in which a prayer is addressed to a deity and an answer received in a vision or audition.[44] Here, however, the deity's answer is 'No!' The 'thorn in the flesh' is intended to prevent Paul from exalting himself (*uperairōmai*) and to increase his weakness

Paul's Ascent to Paradise in its Greco-Roman, Judaic and Early Christian Contexts (Studies in Judaism; Lanham, MD: University Press of America, 1986).

44. Betz, *Der Apostel Paulus*, pp. 92-93.

to highlight God's power at work in him. But Paul still exalts himself by boasting about the 'abundance of revelations' his 'thorn in the flesh' was supposed to prevent him boasting about (12.2-4, 7). Moreover, Paul also boasts about the 'thorn' itself insofar as it demonstrates God's power is at work in him.[45] Paul writes, 'I will all the more gladly boast of my weakness' (12.9b), even though such boasting is still 'foolish'. At the same time, this boasting allows Paul to make his point: properly understood, the very things that seem to make Paul 'weak' are paradoxically demonstrations of strength, since they allow the 'power of Christ' to rest on him (12.9b).

In 12.10, the point of Paul's foolish enterprise is made clear. What Paul endures, he endures for the sake of Christ, and in so doing proves himself strong in Christ's service. The paradox of strength hidden in apparent weakness is parallel to the *kenosis* of Christ himself. If the Corinthians 'see' and 'hear' Paul in the correct way, they will recognize Christ's power at work in him. The work of the 'false apostles' is all aimed at deception so the Corinthians will look at things in a 'fleshly' way and misperceive Paul as 'of no account'. Paul's work proves his true apostleship, since he helps the Corinthians to use the gift of spiritual insight to see things correctly.

The concluding verses of ch. 12 discuss correct perceptions and the sorrow arising from misperceptions. Once the Corinthians see things in the right way much of what seems 'foolish' in Paul will be understood properly as demonstration of his apostolic status (12.11-13) and his loving concern for them (12.14-21).

6. *Conclusion*

Many scholars have seen a connection between Paul's 'boasting in weakness' in 2 Corinthians 10–13 and other aspects of his theology. Ernst Käsemann, for example, understands Paul's 'boasting in the Lord' as exempting the apostle from judgment by earthly criteria. Paul's arguments in favor of his apostleship, Käsemann maintains, are not really in tension with this idea since they will only be accepted by those with the spiritual insight to appreciate them.[46] I would agree that 'spiritual insight' is necessary if Paul and his opponents are to be

45. Fitzgerald, *Cracks*, pp. 65-87.

46. E. Käsemann, 'Die Legitimität des Apostels: Eine Untersuchung zu II Korinther 10–13', *ZNW* 41 (1942), pp. 33-71.

perceived correctly, a point we have found to be central to 2 Corinthians 10–13. But Paul does not appear to rule out the possibility of 'boasting' in real, objective accomplishments provided they are 'within limits', part of the specific work God has given the apostle to do.[47]

Paul in 2 Corinthians 10–13 is willing to negate himself and denigrate even his apostolic suffering on behalf of the gospel (12.11b). If he sometimes seems to 'boast a little too much of our authority, which the Lord gave for building you up' (10.8), it is because this is the appointed work for which he 'will most gladly spend and be spent for your souls' (12.15). But only the gift of the Spirit allows the Corinthians to understand his motivation; he tells them this time and again (1 Cor. 1.18-25; 2.14-16; 2 Cor. 4.7-12; 5.16-17).

This is why Paul can use irony to such effect in the Foolish Discourse. Irony implies and depends upon the fact that things are not really what they seem. By assuming the mask of the fool, Paul is free to boast, undercut his own boasting, comment on his own foolishness, and by all means bring the Corinthians to see things as they really are. When the Corinthians use their spiritual insight and understand Paul as he really is, they will commend him themselves and there will no longer be any necessity for Paul to boast.

47. Hafemann, "Self-Commendation", pp. 87-88.

St Paul's Epistles and Ancient Greek and Roman Rhetoric

C. Joachim Classen

At the 29th General Meeting of the Studiorum Novi Testamenti Societas at Sigtuna (Sweden) in August 1974, Professor H.D. Betz, a New Testament scholar who was trained in Germany, but teaches in the United States of America, gave a lecture on 'The Literary Composition and Function of Paul's Letter to the Galatians', which seems to have initiated a new era in biblical studies or at least in New Testament studies in the United States and, to a lesser degree, elsewhere. In 1979 Professor Betz published *Galatians: A Commentary on Paul's Letter to the Churches in Galatia*, in which he repeated the claims he had made in his paper and applied the method in detail which he had outlined five years before. And in 1988 a German translation of his commentary appeared in which he reproduced the original text without noticeable changes;[1] only in the introduction Professor Betz seems to show some awareness of the criticism and doubts some reviewers had expressed.[2]

However, on the whole the reaction to the commentary was favourable. Most reviewers concentrated on the designation of the letter to the Galatians as apologetic and welcomed Betz's approach as leading to results which appeared to them not only new, but well founded. Indeed, some hailed Betz's work as marking the beginning of

---

1. H.D. Betz, 'The Literary Composition and Function of Paul's Letter to the Galatians', *NTS* 21 (1975), pp. 353-79; *Galatians: A Commentary on Paul's Letter to the Churches in Galatia* (Philadelphia, 1979, 1984); *Der Galaterbrief: Ein Kommentar zum Brief des Apostels Paulus an die Gemeinden in Galatien* (Munich, 1988); see also *2 Corinthians 8 and 9: A Commentary on Two Administrative Letters of the Apostle Paul* (Philadelphia, 1985).

2. Reviews: J.N. Aletti, *RSR* 69 (1981) pp. 601-602; W.D. Davies, P.W. Meyer and D.E. Aune, *Religious Studies Review* 7 (1981), pp. 304-307; J. Swetnam, *Bib* 62 (1981), pp. 594-97; H. Hübner, *Theologische Literaturzeitung* 109 (1984), pp. 241-50.

a new era in New Testament scholarship. Today, numerous scholars in this field, especially in the United States, try to employ the same method as Betz, and the terms 'rhetorical' and 'rhetoric' frequently figure in the titles of their papers.[3] For the new element which Betz introduced or rather claimed to have introduced into New Testament studies is the use of the categories of ancient Greek and Roman, that is classical, rhetoric and epistolography for the exegesis of St Paul's letters.

This alone would explain and justify the interest of a classicist in this development; not surprisingly, therefore, one of the leading experts in this field, Professor George A. Kennedy, took his stand in his book, *New Testament Interpretation through Rhetorical Criticism*, approving of this type of exegesis in general and applying it to various texts from the New Testament, but modifying the results of Betz with regard to the letter to the Galatians.[4] However, as the enthusiasm for this new instrument for the interpretation of biblical texts is not shared in all quarters and some scholars prefer simply to ignore it or to suspend judgment, while others, clearly, feel uneasy about their uncertainty or even ask for advice or assistance from classicists,[5]

---

3. See e.g. M. Bünker, *Briefformular und rhetorische Disposition im 1. Korintherbrief* (Göttingen, 1984); R. Jewett, *The Thessalonian Correspondence: Pauline Rhetoric and Millenarian Piety* (Philadelphia, 1986), esp. pp. 61-87—and more convincing than his pupil: F.W. Hughes, *Early Christian Rhetoric and 2 Thessalonians* (Sheffield, 1989); more critical and discerning, W.G. Übelacker, *Der Hebräerbrief als Appell. I. Untersuchungen zu exordium, narratio and postscriptum (Hebr 1–2 und 13, 22–25)* (Stockholm, 1989); W. Wuellner's pupil, L. Thurén (see n. 5), and especially B.C. Johanson, *To All the Brethren: A Text-linguistic and Rhetorical Approach to I Thessalonians* (Stockholm, 1987), whose analyses are more convincing as these authors avail themselves also of the insights of modern rhetoric (see also below n. 76). Any recent volume of *JBL, NTS, NovT, TZ* or *ZNW* will furnish examples of articles on biblical 'rhetoric'. Interestingly some scholars seem to remain totally unaffected by this new approach; see e.g. W.S. Schutter, *Hermeneutic and Composition in I Peter* (Tübingen, 1989).

4. G.A. Kennedy, *New Testament Interpretation through Rhetorical Criticism* (Chapel Hill, 1984), pp. 144-152 on Galatians; reviews: e.g. R.M. Fowler, *JBL* 105 (1986), pp. 328-30; V.K. Robbins, *Rhetorica* 3 (1985), pp. 145-49; J.H. Patton, *Quarterly Journal of Speech* 71 (1985), pp. 247-49.

5. This paper grew out of a talk given at the request of the group of Roman Catholic and Protestant Commentators on the New Testament on March 26th, 1990 in Einsiedeln (Switzerland) and published as 'Paulus und die antike Rhetorik', *ZNW* 82 (1991), pp. 1-33. The English version, written afresh, was first presented at the University of Helsinki on May 8th, 1991. I am most grateful to my Finnish hosts

a new assessment seems to be called for.

In his commentary, Professor Betz claims:

> Paul's letter to the Galatians can be analyzed according to Greco-Roman rhetoric and epistolography. This possibility raises the whole question of Paul's relationship to the rhetorical and literary disciplines and culture, a question which has not as yet been adequately discussed,

and he adds in a footnote to the first sentence: 'This fact was apparently not recognized before'.[6] Then, however, he rather oddly gives a couple of references to Luther and Melanchthon as well as J.B. Lighfoot, thus admitting that he did have predecessors. This raises a number of questions:

1. Are rhetoric and epistolography meant to be taken together as one art or discipline or are they regarded as two separate ones, each of them separately being of service to the interpretation of the New Testament?

2. Is Professor Betz referring to the theory of rhetoric and epistolography or to their practical application?

3. What exactly is the aim of applying the ancient categories?
   a. Is it only to demonstrate to what extent St Paul was familiar with them, with rhetoric and/or epistolography, with theory and/or practice (as the second sentence seems to indicate) or,
   b. Is it in order to arrive at a more thorough understanding of the letter(s)?

4. If this is the aim, the question arises whether one should restrict oneself to applying only the categories and insights of ancient rhetoric or one may also employ whatever new aspects have been added since antiquity.

5. If, however, the aim is a more adequate appreciation of St Paul himself, at least three further groups of problems come up:

---

and to Dr L. Thurén for a copy of his *The Rhetorical Stategy of 1 Peter* (Åbo, 1990) and references to other recent publications.

6. *Galatians*, p. 14 (*Galater*, p. 54); more recently Betz seems to have become more aware of his predecessors; see his *2 Corinthians 8 and 9*, p. 129 n. 2 and his 'The Problem of Rhetoric and Theology according to the Apostle Paul', in A. Vanhoye (ed.), *L'Apôtre Paul: Personnalité, style et conception du ministère* (Leuven, 1986), pp. 16-48 (pp. 16-21).

a. When, where and how is St Paul likely to have become familiar with ancient rhetoric and epistolography?
b. Exactly which form or which aspect of rhetoric and epistolography at which phase of their history is meant (provided it is possible to distinguish clearly several phases of the development)?
c. Did he deliberately draw on such knowledge of rhetorical theory and employ its categories consciously or not?

6. Finally, as Professor Betz stresses the novelty of his method, it seems obvious to ask why it was not discovered and used before or, as he mentions Luther, Melanchthon and Lightfoot in a footnote, were they the first and what did they do?

In view of these questions some general observations seem to be called for. When one turns to the categories of rhetoric as tools for a more adequate and thorough appreciation of texts, their general structure and their details, one should not hesitate to use the most developed and sophisticated form, as it will offer more help than any other.[7] For there is no good reason to assume that a text could and should be examined only according to categories known (or possibly known) to the author concerned. For rhetoric provides a system for the interpretation of all texts (as well as of oral utterances and even of other forms of communication), irrespectively of time and circumstances (except, of course, for the fact that some rules of rhetoric immediately concern the external circumstances).[8]

When one turns to the categories of rhetoric in order more fully to appreciate an author, his background and his manner of writing, one should examine what is known about his education and other factors that influenced him. When, however, lack of independent sources renders this impossible and one has nothing but a text or a group of texts, one has to bear in mind that, in any speech or any piece of writing, elements or features occur which we know from handbooks of rhetoric and are inclined to classify and designate accordingly. They

7. On this problem, see W. Wuellner, 'Where is Rhetorical Criticism Taking Us', *CBQ* 49 (1987), pp. 448-63. Some examples are listed above in n. 3 and below in n. 76.

8. See my paper cited above in n. 5 and my contribution 'Die Rhetorik im öffentlichen Leben unserer Zeit', in C.J. Classen and H.-J. Müllenbrock (eds.), *Die Macht des Wortes* (Marburg, 1992), pp. 247-67.

may originate from four sources: from rhetorical theory (and its deliberate application), from a successful imitation of written or spoken practice, from unconscious borrowing from the practice of others or from a natural gift for effective speaking or writing.

In application to St Paul's letters this means that one may collect the external evidence as regards the conditions under which he grew up and the experience of interpreting the Bible which he gained later. I shall not attempt to do this, as I am not competent;[9] but I should like to make two observations:

a. Anyone who could write Greek as effectively as St Paul did, must have read a good deal of works written in Greek and thus imbibed applied rhetoric from others, even if he never heard of any rules of rhetorical theory; thus, even if one could prove that St Paul was not familiar with the rhetorical theory of the Greeks, it can hardly be denied that he knew it in its applied form;

b. Anyone who studied the Old Testament as carefully as St Paul undoubtedly did must have noticed the rhetorical qualities there displayed and must have given some thought to the best way of expressing himself.

In turning to St Paul's letters now, we have to emphasize a point to which Professor Betz does not seem to have paid enough attention, that is, the difference between rhetoric and epistolography. Most ancient handbooks of rhetoric do not deal with letters, and where they do, they are content with a few remarks mostly on matters of style.[10] Manuals on letter-writing on the other hand differ substantially from handbooks on rhetoric:[11] instead of dealing with either the *officia oratoris* or the *partes orationis*, they list a large number of types of

---

9. The literature on St Paul is too vast to be referred to here; see K.H. Schelkle, *Paulus: Leben–Briefe–Theologie* (Darmstadt, 1981) and O. Merk, 'Paulus-Forschung 1936–1983', *Theologische Rundschau* 53 (1988), pp. 1-81; see most recently J. Becker, *Paulus: Der Apostel der Völker* (Tübingen, 1990).

10. See the two best known examples: Pseudo-Demetrius, *De elocutione*, 223-35; C. Iulius Victor, *Ars rhetorica*, pp. 105-106 (Giomini–Celentano).

11. See *Demetrii et Libanii qui feruntur* ΤΥΠΟΙ ΕΠΙΣΤΟΛΙΚΟΙ *et* ΕΠΙΣΤΟΛΙΚΟΙ ΧΑΡΑΚΤΗΡΕΣ, ed. V. Weichert (Leipzig, 1910); for other texts on ancient epistolary theory, see R. Hercher (ed.), *Epistolographi Graeci* (Paris, 1873), pp. 6-13, 14-16 and A.J. Malherbe (ed.), *Ancient Epistolary Theorists* (Atlanta, 1988).

letters and give some advice on stylistic problems. Obviously, a fundamental difference between a speech or even a poem or another type of composition on the one hand and a letter on the other was felt, and while, for example, brevity, clarity or appropriateness is recommended for letters (as for other pieces of writing or speaking),[12] as regards the structure of letters no particular rule or advice seems to be given.

I could now enter upon a detailed examination of Betz's method, the new arguments which he formulates with the aid of rhetorical theory and the insights he thus gains, or I could offer a rhetorical analysis of St Paul's letter to the Galatians or at least some comments on the elements and features the function of which one would explain with the help of rhetorical categories in any work of ancient literature. Instead, I turn to the last question raised above: what use was made of rhetoric for the interpretation of the Bible before 1974? I cannot, of course, deal here with the history of the exegesis of the Bible in general.[13] But even a brief glance at some arbitrarily selected examples shows very quickly that this method is by no means new. It was practised in antiquity and it was not totally neglected in the Middle Ages; it was frequently employed with great skill during the Renaissance, and it has never been forgotten ever since in some quarters, while others preferred to ignore it;[14] and it was revived after the Second World War first by such Old Testament scholars as J. Muilenburg,[15] before

---

12. See the references given by Malherbe, *Ancient Epistolary Theorists*, p. 13; for these qualities in general, see H. Lausberg, *Handbuch der literarischen Rhetorik* (Stuttgart, 1990) and J. Martin, *Antike Rhetoric* (Munich, 1974) s.v. *brevis/ brevitas, dilucidus, decorum*, etc.

13. For the earliest stages, see the bibliography in H. Graf Reventlow, *Epochen der Bibelauslegung. I. Vom Alten Testament bis Origenes* (Munich, 1990), pp. 205-11; for the church fathers: H.J. Sieben, *Exegesis Patrum: Saggio bibliografico sull'exegesi biblica dei Padri della Chiesa* (Rome, 1983); for the Middle Ages cf. H. de Lubac, *Exégèse médiévale I-II* (Paris, 1959, 1964); B. Smalley, *The Study of the Bible in the Middle Ages* (Oxford, 1985 [1941]); for the humanists and the Renaissance, see J.H. Bentley, *Humanists and Holy Writ: New Testament Scholarship in the Renaissance* (Princeton, 1983) and the bibliographical references given by T.J. Wengert, *Philip Melanchthon's Annotationes in Johannem in Relation to its Predecessors and Contemporaries* (Geneva, 1987), pp. 265-73. The large number of special studies cannot be listed here, but see below n. 68.

14. See below p. 279 with n. 43.

15. 'Form Criticism and Beyond', *JBL* 88 (1969), pp. 1-18.

Professor Betz brought it back to New Testament Studies so effectively.

In this long and varied history, few have done more for the study of ancient rhetoric, for its development and its application to the needs and requirements of his own time and for its use for the interpretation of the Bible than Philipp Melanchthon;[16] and yet, few have experienced a more complete neglect later. Betz refers to him in a footnote, but not in the bibliography where Erasmus and Jacques Lefèvre d'Etaples, Luther, Calvin and Bullinger are listed with their commentaries; G.A. Kennedy does not mention him at all.[17] Some modern scholars seem to ignore him, as they disagree with his theological position, others because he wrote in Latin (or an old fashioned type of German).

How does he proceed, how does Melanchthon practise rhetorical criticism? To what extent does he anticipate Professor Betz? What, if anything, can the modern scholar learn from him and his method? It may not be superfluous at this stage to mention the fact that Melanchthon wrote three rhetorical handbooks himself: *De Rhetorica libri tres* (Wittenberg, 1519), *Institutiones Rhetoricae* (Hagenau, 1521), and *Elementa rhetorices libri duo* (Wittenberg, 1531), also three works on dialectic, the art of defining words and objects, or dividing *genera* and of finding and using arguments: *Compendiaria Dialectices* (Leipzig, 1520), *Dialectices libri quatuor* (Hagenau, 1528), and *Erotemata dialectices* (Wittenberg, 1547). More important, of course, is the large number of commentaries on books of the Old and

---

16. His works: C.G. Bretschneider and H.E. Bindseil (eds.), *Philippi Melanchthonis Opera I-XXVIII* (Halle, 1834–1860) with his commentaries on books of the Bible in vol. XIII, cols. 761-1472, XIV and XV (= *Corpus Reformatorum*, vols. 13-15); see also R. Stupperich *et al.* (eds.), *Melanchthons Werke in Auswahl I-VII* (Gütersloh, 1951–1975) and E. Bizer (ed.), *Texte aus der Anfangszeit Melanchthons* (Neukirchen–Vluyn, 1966). Biography: K. Hartfelder, *Philipp Melanchthon als Praeceptor Germaniae* (Berlin, 1889) with detailed lists of Melanchthon's publications and lectures (pp. 577-620 and 555-66); W. Maurer, *Der junge Melanchthon zwischen Humanismus und Reformation I-II* (Göttingen, 1967-1969). Bibliography: W. Hammer, *Die Melanchthonforschung im Wandel der Jahrhunderte I-III* (Gütersloh, 1967–1981).

17. H.D. Betz, *Galatians*, pp. 14 n. 97, 337 (*Galater*, pp. 54 n. 97, 556-57); Kennedy, *New Testament Interpretation*. N. Elliott (*The Rhetoric of Romans* [Sheffield, 1990]), too, grants him no more than a footnote (p. 22 n. 1).

New Testament, which cannot all be listed here.[18] Suffice it to give some information on Melanchthon's earliest works. In 1519, at the age of 22, he wrote his *Theologica Institutio in Epistolam Pauli ad Romanos* with a summary (*summa*); in the following year he edited the epistles to the Romans and the Galatians, in 1521 the first and the second epistles to the Corinthians and again the epistle to the Romans, each with marginal notes. *Annotationes in Epistolas Pauli ad Romanos et Corinthios*, obviously taken during his lectures, were published in Nuremberg in 1522 by Luther without his consent (a German version in Augsburg in 1523), similarly his *Annotationes in Evangelium Matthaei* by others in Basel in 1523 and his *In Evangelium Ioannis Annotationes* in the same year by himself in Basel and elsewhere, which were printed thirteen times in the year of publication. Though the demand was great, Melanchthon was reluctant to regard his work as finished and ready for the printer or the public. Thus it was not until 1529 that he published his *Dispositio orationis in Epistola Pauli ad Romanos* (Hagenau) which was followed by *Commentarii in epistolam Pauli ad Romanos* (Wittenberg, 1532; in revised form: Strasbourg, 1540), and *Epistolae Pauli scriptae ad Romanos, Enarratio* (Wittenberg, 1566) to list only the works on one epistle by St Paul in order to illustrate that Melanchthon returned to the same work again and again. In addition, notes which students took from Melanchthon's early lectures in 1520 and 1521 on the epistles to the Galatians and the Romans have been preserved and printed.[19] What do they contain, what do they teach us?

Though the notes on the epistle to the Galatians are rather elementary, it seems appropriate to characterize them briefly here, as Professor Betz applied his new method in a commentary on this letter. In accordance with the practice in such lectures, as we learn from the lecture notes on Ciceronian speeches from several scholars,[20]

18. See Hartfelder's list (*Philipp Melanchthon* pp. 577-620); not all of them have been reprinted in the *Opera* (see n. 16), but before each text a (nearly) complete list of the various editions is given.

19. In his *Texte aus der Anfangszeit* Bizer prints the 'Artifitium Epistolae Pauli ad Romanos' (pp. 20-30), the 'Exegesis in Epistolam Pauli pros tous Galatas' (pp. 34-27), the 'ΡΑΨΟΔΙΑΙ (*sic*) ΕΝ ΠΑΥΛΟΥ AD ROMANOS' (pp. 45-85) and the 'Theologica Institutio... in Epistolam Pauli ad Romanos' (pp. 90-99).

20. For such notes see e.g. *In omnes M. Tullii Ciceronis orationes, quot quidem extant, doctissimorum virorum enarrationes* (Basel, 1553).

Melanchthon first determines the *genus* to which he thinks the work should be assigned and gives a summary of the content. Rather surprisingly, he regards it as belonging to the *genus didacticum*, a new *genus*, which he himself had added to the traditional canon of three (*iudiciale, demonstrativum, deliberativum*), as we know from his manual of rhetoric in which he explains and justifies this innovation.[21] Clearly, while Melanchthon is thoroughly familiar with the rhetorical tradition, he feels free to modify it and to introduce a new element where he considers it incomplete or inadequate.

The first two verses he characterizes by an unusual but appropriate term (ἐπιγραφή) and a brief description of their content, the third merely by a Latin term, *salutatio*, again not commonly used in handbooks of rhetoric from antiquity, though familiar from contemporary works on epistolography.[22] The section from 1.6 to 2.21 he regards as *exordium*, dominated by the *affectus indignationis*, and he adds approvingly: 'Sicuti alias optima exordia sunt ab affectibus';[23] perhaps he has such precepts in mind as that given by Quintilian in the fourth book of his *Institutio oratoria* (1.33) that the audience may be made attentive by stirring its emotions. Being also aware of Quintilian's warning that such appeals to emotions should be used sparingly in proems (4.1.14), he interprets St Paul's next sentence appreciatively as 'mitigatio...indignationis' (1.7), perhaps because usually *indignatio* is shown with reference to the adversary (in the courts of law), not to the recipient of a letter. Next Melanchthon explains the inferences St Paul draws or the arguments he proposes in the following verses, sometimes expressly stating the *summa*, that is, the matter in question,

21. *Texte*, p. 34; for the new *genus didacticum*, see *De Rhetorica* p. 13; *Institutiones Rhetoricae* f. A II^r (*dialecticum*) and *Elementa Rhetorices* ff. A 8^v–B 1^r (I quote from the 1536 edition). The fourfold division may have been suggested to Melanchthon by the four qualities which Maximus of Tyre expects the philosophically trained orator to display in the four areas of his activity (*or.* 25. 6 p. 306 Hobein).

22. For the *salutatio*, see e.g. Erasmus's 'De conscribendis epistolis' (*Opera Omnia* I 2 [ed. J.-C. Margolin; Amsterdam, 1971], pp. 205-579 [276-95]). Melanchthon's remarks should be set against the rich discussion of his time on the rules of letter-writing; see e.g. J. Rice Henderson, 'Erasmus on the Art of Letter-Writing', in J.J. Murphy (ed.), *Renaissance Eloquence* (Berkeley, 1983), pp. 331-55 (with references to further literature).

23. *Texte*, p. 34: 'As elsewhere the best proems start from passions'.

sometimes pointing to particular parts of an argumentation.[24] On 3.1 (*O stulti Galatae*) he remarks: 'status seu propositio per obiurgationem.'[25] He takes this verse to contain the point at issue, and by adding a little later 'Idque probat esse Argumentis', he marks the beginning of the argumentation (*confirmatio*).[26]

There is no need to give further details of the manner in which Melanchthon comments on the syllogisms or of the terms he employs himself. However, more than once terms occur which are not common in traditional rhetorical theory: *declaratio per similia* (for *locus e similibus*), *inversio* (for a piece of evidence brought forward against one side when turned in favour of that side), *occupation* instead of *anteoccupation*, *parenesis* for *exhortation*.[27]

Thus we see that Melanchthon seems interested in the general structure of the letter and the arguments and he distinguishes introduction, proposition of the subject matter, argumentation and peroration (*epilogus*); he analyses a number of syllogisms and gives labels from the manuals of rhetoric where they seem appropriate, and he adds new ones whenever the traditional system seems defective to him and he feels the need to supplement it. Thereby he assists the reader in understanding the intention of the letter as a whole, the general line of the argumentation and the structure of particular arguments. As in doing so he falls back upon the tools provided by ancient rhetoric, he demonstrates that this system—even after centuries—may render useful service in interpreting such a text as an epistle by St Paul; but as he introduces new categories and new terms also, he indicates, by implication, that he sees no reason why the modern reader or

24. *Texte*, pp. 34-35: on Gal. 2.6: 'Etiam probat alia coniectura: nimirum ita neque cum apud eos essem aliquid ab eis dididici (*sic*); on Gal. 2.11: 'summa: reprehendi Petrum; ideo nihil ab eo didici, sed per revelationem, cui subiungit rationem sue reprehensionis'; on Gal. 2.15: 'summa: Judaei indigent iustificatione; ergo operibus non sunt iustificati'; on Gal. 2.17: 'summa: Si iustificati in Christo Ad huc habemus opus ulteriore iustificatione per opera-ergo Christus est peccati minister'; on Gal. 2.21: 'si per opera iustificantur ergo Christus nihil confert'.

25. 'State of affairs or statement of facts by means of rebuke.'

26. 'And this he proves to be so by means of arguments.'

27. On *declaratio per similia*, see his *De Rhetorica* p. 45, on *inversio ibid.* pp. 100-101 and *Institutiones Rhetoricae* f. B 3ᵛ: 'inversio qua docemus signum, quod contra nos producit, pro nobis facere'; on *occupatio* (instead of *anteoccupatio*), see *Elementa Rhetorices* f. K 1ᵛ; on *parenesis* (παραίνεσις), see what Melanchthon says on *exhortatio*: *De Rhetorica* pp. 34-35, and *Elementa Rhetorices* f. D 8ᵛ.

scholar should limit himself to what tradition has to offer; rather he encourages him to apply rhetoric in its most advanced form or even to develop it further when and where need be. Tempting though it may be at this point to consider the various stages of Melanchthon's work on the epistle to the Romans, a very few remarks will have to suffice. In the *Summa* which he wrote together with the *Theologica Institutio* in 1520,[28] Melanchthon again gives the *status causae*, assigns the work to one of the traditional *genera* (*iudiciale*) and describes the parts, as if he were analysing a Ciceronian speech. Yet again one meets with unexpected features. Melanchthon notes the *inscriptio* at the beginning before the *exordium*, thus implying that it is a letter, not a speech; and he enumerates the *axiomata* of which the *narratio* consists, which thus turns out—at least in his view—to be not an account of events, but a list of the arguments St Paul intends to prove later.[29] Moreover, Melanchthon registers two digressions (2.1-16 and 3.1-9) which he advises the reader not to overlook in the *narratio*, as otherwise he would not grasp the thread of the discussion.[30] As for the rest, he begins with a list of the arguments in ch. 4, points to the *amplificatio* at its end and the *exhortatio* at the beginning of the following chapter, analyses the next section (5.12–7.14) and labels it as *locus didacticus*

28. *Texte*, pp. 97-99, esp. 97: 'Status causae: Iustitia ex fide sine operibus, id est nullum opus potest affectum immutare, sed sola fides impetrat iustitiam, hoc est innovationem nostri. ORATIO est generis iudicialis, habet exordium, narrationem, confirmationem, apte composita.' On *Summa* und *Theologica Institutio*, see W. Maurer, 'Melanchthons Loci communes von 1521 als wissenschaftliche Programmschrift', *Luther-Jahrbuch* 27 (1960), pp. 1-50, esp. 2-6; see also A. Schirmer, *Das Paulusverständnis Melanchthons 1518–1522* (Wiesbaden, 1967).

29. *Texte*, p. 97: 'inscriptio'; p. 98: 'Summa vero Narrationis constat his axiomatis:

1. Gentes habuere legem naturae.
2. Gentes etsi legem naturae habuerint, tamen peccaverunt.
3. Judaei habuerunt legem divinam.
4. Iudaei, etsi legem divinam habuerint, tamen peccaverunt.
5. Omnes itaque peccarunt, id est et gentes et Iudaei, nec sunt adiuti lege, quominus peccarent.
6. Iustitia vero est per Christum, nec ullis comparatur operibus.'

30. *Texte*, p. 98: 'Hanc narrationem Paulus extendit ad caput usque quartum, et miscet ei aliquot digressiones, quas nisi quis observet, non facile putem adsecuturum disputationis filum'.

('quo quid et unde peccatum, gratia et lex sit, docet'[31]) in which he marks a digression again (6.1–7.7), containing a *moralis disputatio*: 'et is locus arbitrii libertatem tollit'[32] he adds, thereby emphasizing his theological concern. After a short summary of the content of 7.14– 8.12, Melanchthon characterizes the rest up to ch. 9 as exhortatory and consolatory, indicates the content of chs. 9, 10 and 11 by very brief remarks and ends with *reliqua moralia sunt* for the last five chapters.[33] Obviously, he is primarily interested in the first chapters of the epistle and the theological problems they raise, in the arguments advanced there and their validity, but not in the structure of the whole or terminological details. He uses both *oratio* and *narratio* in a rather unusual manner, *oratio* although this is a letter (and he is aware of this, as he points to the *inscriptio*), and *narratio*[34] although even he does not suggest that this section performs the function assigned to a *narratio* by tradition. Indeed, in the *Artificium Epistolae Pauli ad Romanos*, another set of lecture notes taken down by a student, the two terms do not occur, while *narratio* is used in the *Annotationes*

---

31. *Texte*, p. 98: 'Confirmatio quae in capite quarto est, argumenta habet sex.

1. Abraham fide iustificatus est, non operibus; igitur nec nos iustificamur nisi fide, nempe fili Abrahae.
2. David dicit beatitudinem per non imputationem peccati esse; ergo non est ex operibus.
3. Abraham iustificatus est ante circumcisionem; ergo iustificatio non est ex operibus.
4. Per legem non est promissio, id est: iustificatio fuit ante legem Mosaicam; ergo iustificatio non est ex legis operibus.
5. Si ex lege haereditas est, id est: si sufficit lex ad iustificationem, frustra est (scripsi pro: et) promissio χριστοῦ, id est: si ex nobis est, non egemus Christo.
6. Lex iram operatur, ergo non conciliat; lex facit odium Dei, ergo non amorem.'

Texte, p. 99: 'locus didacticus': 'by means of which he teaches what and wherefrom sin, grace and law are'.
32. 'And this point eliminates the freedom of decision.'
33. *Texte*, p. 99: 'Reliqua usque ad IX. Cap. adhortatoria sunt et consolationes quaedam. Caput IX. praedestinationem et vocationem gentium continet. Caput X. comparationem iustitiae fidei et iustitiae pharisaicae. Caput XI. adhortationem. Reliqua moralia sunt.'
34. *Texte*, p. 97 as quoted above n. 28.

published in 1522,[35] also, in a different context, in the *Dispositio* of 1529; but in his later works, the two editions of the *Commentarii* of 1532 and 1540 and the *Enarratio* of 1556, Melanchthon seems to do without them.

Though it would be fascinating and rewarding now to enter upon a detailed comparison between Melanchthon's various explanatory works on St Paul's epistle to the Romans, lack of space forbids me to do so. Only a brief remark seems called for on that aspect to which the ancient theory of epistolography paid special attention, all matters of diction and style. They are largely, though not entirely, absent from the works mentioned so far[36]—obviously not because Melanchthon neglected them completely, but because he seems to have excluded them from some types of lectures, not from others, as we also know from different sets of notes published on Ciceronian speeches. On the epistle to the Romans *ΡΑΨΟΔΙΑΙ ΕΝ ΠΑΥΛΟΥ AD ROMANOS* have been preserved and printed[37] which, in addition to an 'Argumentum', give Melanchthon's comments on the meaning of words as well as on points of style, rhetorical figures and the like. Thus we read, for example, 'Est mirabilis quedam Simplicitas in Paulus, coniuncta cum maiestate, Sicut etiam in Homero. Paulus si ineruditus homo fuisset, non potuisset tam ornatum contexere

35. For the *Artifitium* (*sic*) see *Texte*, pp. 20-30; *Annotationes Philippi Melanchthonis in Epistolas Pauli ad Romanos et Corinthios* (Nuremberg, 1522, not reprinted in the *Opera*) f. B2ᵛ; *Epistola S. Pauli ad Titum, iam recens per Iohannem Agricolam Scholijs novis illustrata, ac multis in locis locupletata. Item Dispositio orationis, in Epistola Pauli ad Romanos, in qua totius disputationis series breviter ostenditur. Philippo Melanchthone Authore* (Hagenau, 1530 = *Opera* XV, cols. 443-92) f. I 3ᵛ (= XV, col. 466) at the end of ch. 7, but not on 1.18; for the *Commentarii: Melanchthons Werke* (ed. R. Stupperich, see n. 16) V (Gütersloh, 2nd edn, 1983 [1965]) and for the second edition: *Commentarii in Epistolam Pauli ad Romanos hoc anno MDXL recogniti et locupletati* (Strasbourg, 1540 = *Opera* XV, cols. 495-796); finally: *Epistolae Pauli scriptae ad Romanos, Enarratio edita a Philippo Melanchthone* (Wittenberg, 1556 = *Opera* XV, cols. 797-1052).

36. Cf. *Annotationes* (1522, see n. 35) f. G IIʳ on 8.6: 'quibus quid clarius, quid magis proprie, contra libertatem voluntatis dici potuit' (also with regard to the content); *ibid.* on 8.12: 'Est enim in verbo debitores Emphasis'. For *figurae* see *Dispositio* (1530, see n. 35) f. H 3ᵛ (= XV, col. 457) on ch. 5: 'rhetorica gradatio'; f. G 3ʳ (= XV, col. 447) on ch. 1: 'amplificat ab effectibus, nam impietatis fructus, postea per congeriem recensentur'.

37. *Texte*, pp. 45-85.

exordium, in quo magna verborum Emphasi utitur.'[38] Again I cannot mention further details, except for one remark which seems worth quoting: 'Essemus magni profecto theologi, si proprium scripturae sermonem intelligeremus'.[39]

Anyone who tries to understand the Bible and St Paul's letters in particular will be well advised to study Melanchthon's observations carefully: a few observations concerning the structure of whole works, more on the validity of particular arguments or stylistic devices. I might add that any reader of the works of Hesiod or Aristotle, Cicero, Virgil or Ovid will also benefit greatly from Melanchthon's commentaries on these authors,[40] and there are more which I have not mentioned.

However, as I am concerned here with St Paul's epistles, I should add that Melanchthon was, of course, by no means the only scholar of his time to write commentaries on these letters or other parts of the Bible. Lorenzo Valla seems to have been the first to avail himself of the newly discovered resources from pagan antiquity for the interpretation of the New Testament; but both he and Jacques Lefèvre d'Etaples and Erasmus were primarily interested in the explanation of factual details or textual criticism.[41] Of Melanchthon's

38. *Texte*, p. 50: 'There is some remarkable plainness in Paul (i.e. in Paul's style) combined with dignity, such as also in Homer. If Paul had been an uneducated man, he would not have been able to weave together so richly embellished an exordium, in which he employs great emphasis in his diction.'

39. *Texte*, p. 51: 'We would, indeed, be great theologians if we understood the specific language (idiom) of the Bible'.

40. They are all listed by Hartfelder, *Philipp Melanchthon*.

41. Cf. *Laurentii Vallensis... in Latinam Novi testamenti interpretationem... Adnotationes apprime utiles* (Paris, 1505, written 1453–1457; the earlier version [*Collatio*] was not published until 1970: *Collatio novi testamenti*, ed. by A. Perosa [Florence, 1970]); see Bently, *Humanists and Holy Writ*, pp. 32-69, also on Erasmus, pp. 112-93. *Epistole divi Pauli apostoli cum commentariis preclarissimi viri Jacobi Fabri Stapulensis* (Paris, 1512); cf. on this and his other works G. Bedouelle, *Lefèvre d'etaples et l'intelligence des ecritures* (Geneva, 1976); *Novum Instrumentum omne, diligenter ab Erasmo Rotterodamo recognitum et emendatum* (Basel, 1516) ff. bbb 1^r - bbb 5^v: *Methodus* and after the text, pp. 231-675: *Adnotationes* (often reprinted); *In Epistolam Pauli Apostoli ad Romanos paraphrasis, per Des. Erasmum Roterodamum* (Basel, 1518); *Erasmus' Annotations on the New Testament: Acts–Romans–I and II Corinthians* (ed. A. Reeve and M.A. Screech; Leiden, 1990); cf. E. Rummel, *Erasmus' Annotationes on the New Testament* (Toronto, 1986); also F. Krüger, *Humanistische Evangelienauslegung:*

contemporaries, Luther and Zwingli, Bucer and Brenz, Bullinger and Calvin deserve more than a place in the bibliography;[42] their works offer valuable insights and are worth studying. However, apart from the fact that they cannot all be presented here and discussed at length with their respective methods and merits, it seems fair to say that no one contributed more to the development of rhetorical criticism than Melanchthon. It is all the more surprising that later generations allowed his observations and achievements to be virtually forgotten. Conscientious study of the history of biblical exegesis shows that the application of rhetorical categories never ceased entirely.

In a lecture, 'Histoire de "l'analyse rhétorique" en exégèse biblique', delivered at the seventh congress of the International Society for the History of Rhetoric in Göttingen in 1989 and published in 1990, Father R. Meynet described a number of scholars and their methods from the middle of the eighteenth century to the middle of the twentieth century and added a specimen of his own manner of interpretation which shows that rhetorical analysis is still practised today by Jesuits as it always has been since the foundation of the order.[43] The 'Introductio hermeneutica in Sacros Novi Testamenti Libros', published in Vienna in 1777 by the Benedictine St Hayd, Professor of Greek and New Testament Hermeneutics at Freiburg, shows that members of other orders also practised rhetorical criticism of the Bible; in this case the author pays special attention to tropes and figures of style, but also to the structure of the argumentation.[44]

Before trying to assess the contribution of rhetorical criticism to the understanding of biblical texts or rather the contribution made by individual scholars and of the possibilities as well as the limits of such

Desiderius Erasmus von Rotterdam als Ausleger der Evangelien in seinen Paraphrasen (Tübingen, 1986).

42. Betz, *Galatians*, p. 337 (*Galater*, pp. 556-57) (Luther, Calvin, Bullinger); in the commentary on *2 Corinthians 8 and 9* they do not even figure in the bibliography. For detailed references, see my article cited above (n. 5), pp. 24-25 n. 83; and T.H.L. Parker, *Commentaries on the Epistle to the Romans 1532–1542* (Edinburgh, 1986); particularly important S. Hausammann, *Römerbriefauslegung zwischen Humanismus und Reformation* (Zürich, 1970).

43. 'Histoire de "l'analyse rhétorique" en exégèse biblique', *Rhetorica* 8 (1990), pp. 291-320.

44. Sectio II, Caput VII: 'Tropi et figurae' (pp. 166-259); arguments are analysed in Sectio III: 'Institutiones analytico-hermeneuticae in singulos Novi Testamenti libros speciales' (pp. 282-416).

a procedure in general, I may be permitted briefly to indicate how I think the categories of ancient rhetoric and of ancient literary theory and criticism can be exploited with profit today.

Anyone attempting to understand and appreciate a speech or a written composition will first determine in a very general way the nature of the piece: literary, non-literary or sub-literary, casual or serious, personal or general, with emphasis on content or form, poetry or prose, etc. In the case of a letter it seems advisable to take into consideration (if possible) the following facts: the writer's education and experiences, the education and experience of the addressee(s) (one should remember that a letter may be directed to an individual or a group,[45] but also—in the form of a literary letter—to future generations), the circumstances of the writer, the circumstances of the addressee or again addressees, present or future (circumstances means time, place and events which have just happened or are imminent). Moreover, one should consider the relationship between writer and addressee(s)—personal knowledge, earlier correspondence, views and experiences shared or not shared, opposing views, etc., and, finally, the intention of the writer, whether he wishes to communicate information on actual facts, on events of the past or expected developments in the future, on personal feelings or on general views, or whether he hopes to give advice on encouragement, consolation or warning, or to express praise or disappointment, etc.

After these general reflections I turn to St Paul's epistle to the Galatians.[46] In his first sentence the apostle makes it abundantly clear that he is writing a letter by using a formula by which letters generally were introduced;[47] but he enlarges this formula, and by making additions he draws attention to what he considers important right from the start: οὐκ ἀπ' ἀνθρώπων οὐδὲ δι' ἀνθρώπου, ἀλλὰ διὰ Ἰησοῦ Χριστοῦ καὶ θεοῦ πατρός. One could register a polyptoton here and an antitheton.[48] However, what matters is not these terms,

---

45. In antiquity this means that it will not only be read aloud by an individual, but may be read aloud to a group.

46. There are too many commentaries to be listed here, and I have refrained from consulting them except for general observations on the structure of the letter.

47. Cf. F. Schnider and W. Stenger, *Studien zum neutestamentlichen Briefformular* (Leiden, 1987), pp. 3-25 (with references to earlier literature).

48. On polyptoton and antitheton in general, see Lausberg, *Handbuch*, pp. 325-29 and 389-98; on St Paul, see N. Schneider, *Die rhetorische Eigenart der*

but the function of the figures thus labelled. They are part of the *ornatus*, chosen to give special emphasis to what the writer is saying. As in this case the two figures stress the same point, it gains considerable momentum, especially as the two members of the antitheton each consist of a twofold expression: the first of a polyptoton, the second of the two nouns Ἰησοῦς Χριστός and θεὸς πατήρ, connected by a participle (τοῦ ἐγείραντος αὐτόν[49]) which describes the unique act which God performed for Jesus and at the same time his resurrection, that is, his divinity.

The salutation 'grace and peace', also found elsewhere,[50] is enlarged by reference to God and Jesus Christ; this repetition serves to relegate the apostle, though being the writer of the letter, to the background. It is God the father and Jesus Christ who are acting here, and while in the first sentence (1.1-2) God's activity (with respect to his son) was described by a participle, in a corresponding construction Jesus Christ is characterized now (with respect to mankind)—and this is even further elaborated in a subclause which repeats for the third time θεὸς (καὶ) πατήρ and ἡμῶν now[51] and resorts to another polyptoton (with three members) in order to contrast the present world from which men will be saved (notice the parallel to Christ being resurrected) and God's eternity. Attentive reading reveals that by means of several additions, carefully constructed sentences and equally well-chosen words the apostle most impressively conveys what he wants his readers to feel: that they are being addressed not so much by him, but in the name of God and together with him of Jesus Christ. The scholar familiar with the rules and categories of rhetoric who observes these details—whether he applies technical terms to them or not—cannot but register that an author is at work here who knows to select and present his ideas and to employ the tools of language in the most effective manner possible.

Having thus used the introductory formula of greeting to manifest his own position, the apostle turns to the addressees, first expressing surprise about their change of mind, adding a clarification: It is not

paulinischen Antithese (Tübingen, 1970).

49. 'Paul, an apostle (not of men, neither by man, but by Jesus Christ, and God the Father, who raised him from the dead).'

50. Gal. 1.3-5; cf. Schnider and Stenger, *Studien*, pp. 25-41.

51. '...that he might deliver us from this present evil world, according to the will of God and our Father: To whom be glory for ever and ever. Amen.'

that they have chosen to give preference to another εὐαγγέλιον instead of the one he had preached to them. There is no other, and it is merely some people who confuse them, trying to invert the gospel of Christ, and this he emphasizes with a curse which he repeats, placing it twice at the end of a sentence. Here again one notices the repetition of several words (εὐαγγέλιον twice, forms of εὐαγγελίζεσθαι three times, ἀνάθεμα ἔστω twice),[52] as well as a correction with respect to one of these words (εὐαγγέλιον). Rhetorical theory warns not to appeal to passions in a proem; the theory of epistolography does not give precepts for the parts of a letter. Are we coming to the end of rhetorical criticism, at least when applied to letters? It is certainly advisable at this stage to remember that St Paul is not making a speech, and that rules for speeches and other types of composition cannot be expected always to be easily applicable to letters, especially as ancient theorists seem to have been aware of the very particular nature of letters. It is no less important to remember that exceptional circumstances require exceptional means, both from a speaker and from a writer of letters. Our stylistic observations and the fact that there is no parallel for such an introduction in St Paul's letters warrant the conclusion that he regards the situation as a very unusual one and that he is—at least here—particularly concerned about the true nature of the εὐαγγέλιον Χριστοῦ and the right understanding of his own position. Is he thereby preparing for and pointing to the central issues(s) of this letter?

In the next three verses (1.10-12) St Paul continues to stress his concern for the correct understanding of the message he is preaching by contrasting men and God, pleasing men and serving Christ, a gospel received from men (which his is not) and a gospel revealed by Christ. Again one notices several forms of antitheton, no less than the elaborate expression τὸ εὐαγγέλιον τὸ εὐαγγελισθέν, echoing the repeated forms for verses 1.7-9, and the polyptoton κατὰ

---

52. Gal. 1.6-9: 'I marvel that ye are so soon removed from him that called you into the grace of Christ unto another gospel: Which is not another; but there be some that trouble you, and would pervert the gospel of Christ. But though we, or an angel from heaven, preach any other gospel unto you than that which we have preached unto you, let him be accursed. As we said before, so say I now again, if any other man preach any other gospel unto you than that ye have received, let him be accursed.'

ἄνθρωπον... παρὰ ἀνθρώπου,[53] taking up the same figure from 1.1. Once more the apostle makes the claim by which he opened his letter, a claim concerning himself, but as mouthpiece of God and Christ. When St Paul devotes the following verses to his own past,[54] he indicates that he is still uncertain whether the addressees are willing to accept him, to listen to him, whether the claim he has so far merely stated will be honoured. A long discourse follows in which the apostle gives an account first, briefly, of his zeal in persecuting the Christians and of the revelation of Christ through the grace of God in order that he may preach the gospel and, next, a little more fully, of his journeys and activities in Arabia, Jerusalem (first visit, contact with Cephas), Syria, Cilicia, Judaea and again Jerusalem. Here the tone changes; St Paul no longer simply reports, he explains, he mentions details, he justifies, he emphasizes differences and distinctions, and in the same manner he describes his conflict with St Peter in Antioch, culminating in a direct question which he asked Peter: 'How do you force the gentiles to live the Jewish way of life?' (2.14), before he outlines at some length and with obvious emotions his own position. While at the beginning of his account he prefers a matter-of-fact kind of style—one coloured by a quotation from the prophets (1.15: Isa. 1.5; Isa. 49.11)—and underlines the intention thus indicated by expressly assuring the trustworthiness of his words (1.20), gradually he changes his tone, not only employing again words he had used before in describing his own conversion, his present activity and the revelation as factors behind it,[55] but also resorting to both polemical expressions (2.4, 6) and words with emotional appeal (2.4 ἐλευθερία, 2.5 ἀλήθεια τοῦ εὐαγγελίου)[56] in order to stress his own steadfastness

53. Gal. 1.10-12: 'For do I now persuade men, or God? or do I seek to please men? for if I yet pleased men, I should not be the servant of Christ. But I certify you, brethren, that the gospel which was preached of me is not after man. For I neither received it of man, neither was I taught it, but by the revelation of Jesus Christ.'

54. Gal. 1.13–2.14 or 2.21; experts disagree whether this section ends at 2.14 or should be extended to 2.21, that is, whether the last seven verses are a summary of what he said in Antioch (see Betz, *Galatians*, pp. 113-14 with n. 6 = *Galater*, pp. 212-13 with n. 1). What matters, to my mind, is that St Paul adopts a different style for these verses and uses them to move from the report of his past to the message he wants to preach to the Galatians.

55. 'I persecuted the church of God, and wasted it' (1.13; cf. 1.23); 'that I might preach him/the gospel' (1.16; cf. 1.23; 2.2); 'revelation' (1.12; cf. 1.16; 2.1).

56. Gal. 2.4: 'liberty'; 2.5: 'the truth of the gospel'.

and the reputation he enjoyed with James, Peter and John. For the controversy with Peter he chooses mostly a factual style again, while in the final section emotion gains more and more ground: antitheta, polyptota and suchlike metaphorical figures and paradoxical expressions abound.[57]

Before one determines the function of this section either with the help of a rhetorical classification or on the basis of stylistic observations or otherwise, one should look at the rest of the letter and examine how what has been said so far serves as preparation for the following chapters, how it is related to what follows, if at all. The first words of the next chapter may cause astonishment: St Paul rebukes the Galatians (3.1). However, such a move is not entirely uncommon in letters (or even in speeches), when a particular effect is intended,[58] and this is obviously the case here. After indicating at the beginning that the Galatians had been turned away by certain people from the true gospel (that is, that which he had preached to them), he now addresses them directly in order to lead them back to the right path. Once more, the tone changes. Saint Paul begins with a number of questions to shake them up, to make them consider and reconsider what they are doing, what had been preached to them, what is being offered to them and by whom and from what: works of the law or hearing of faith (3.1-5). The contrast between ἔργα νόμου and ἀκοὴ πίστεως, pointedly repeated,[59] cannot easily be overlooked. This is the subject matter of the following example: Abraham as testimony, but also as someone whose blessing even the gentiles will receive through Jesus Christ (3.6-14). 'Works of the law' and 'faith' continue to dominate the next section, first the example of the last will (3.15-18) to illustrate the validity of God's promises, next the discussion of the Jewish law which had a temporary function until the coming of faith (3.23, that is Christ: 3.24); and to this argument he adds several lines of promise and encouragement to the Galatians, thus emphasizing the immediate relevance for them of the preceding arguments.

57. Antitheta: Gal. 2.15, 16, 20; polyptota: 2.16, 19, 20-21; metaphorical and paradoxical expressions: 2.18, 19, 20.

58. Even the theory knows the 'blaming', 'reproachful', 'censorious', 'vituperative' and 'accusing' type; cf. Pseudo-Demetrius, *Form. epist. praef.,* 3, 4, 6, 9, 17 (pp. 2, 4-6, 9 Weichert).

59. 'Works of the law': 3.2, 10; 'law': 3.10, 11, 12, 13, 18, 19, 21, 23, 24; 'hearing of faith': 3.2; 'faith': 3.7, 8, 9, 11, 12, 14, 22, 23, 24, 25, 26.

In an even more immediate manner St Paul combines promise and argument at the beginning of ch. 4, where he pronounces rather than proves that through Jesus Christ God freed those subjected to the law, applying this both to himself and to the Galatians by using 'we' and 'you';[60] and in the same vein he continues with questions and requests, expressing more than once his great concern for the Galatians. Thus he adds yet another example from the Old Testament to illustrate once more the difference between slavery and freedom, and this is the key-term for a long series of admonitions and warnings, before St Paul ends with an unusually long postscript in his own hand and the blessing.[61]

Space forbids a more detailed account of this letter. The brief analysis and the few remarks on St Paul's style have, I trust, shown what the apostle is aiming at here. Faced with reports on activities of some people who spread some teaching different from his own in Galatia, he seeks first briefly to establish his position as apostle and to draw a clear line between the εὐαγγέλιον he preaches and the message of the others, before he speaks of his past activities, obviously in view of and in response to accusations which had been levelled against them; and only after clearly stating his own views (as he had maintained them even in opposition to Peter), he turns to the relationship between law and faith, the function of the law in the past, the liberation through Christ, and the meaning of both freedom and faith and their vital importance for people's lives.

Anyone attempting to explain this work with the help of ancient, that is, Greek and/or Roman rhetoric and/or epistolography will soon discover that the function of numerous particular features in the area of *elocutio* can be explained in terms of traditional rhetoric, and also numerous arguments can be analysed in this manner (and this was realized centuries ago and never quite forgotten). But he will also find that the structure of the whole differs fundamentally from the 'ideal' structure of the logos of rhetorical theory. The address is followed by what one might call an *exordium*; but its unusual elements must be taken as a warning that what follows is not one of the three traditional types of logos known to rhetorical theory, and indeed neither a judicial nor a deliberative nor a demonstrative type of speech seems

---

60. 'We': 4.3, 5, 6; 'you': 4.6, 8-21.
61. Gal. 6.11-18; see Schnider and Stenger, *Studien*, pp. 135-67, esp. 145-51.

appropriate here, as St Paul is addressing neither a court of law from which he expects a verdict at the end nor an assembly which will pass a resolution, let alone praising an individual.

Indeed, it is not surprising that the categories of rhetoric fail us with respect to the structure of this epistle, because it is an epistle, and they were not made nor meant to fit such kinds of composition. Instead, one should turn to such types of letters as are listed by Pseudo-Demetrius and Pseudo-Libanius. However, whether their numerous types offer much help seems another matter. For even when one decides—not without hesitation—in favour of τύπος νουθετητικός or διδασκαλικός,[62] such a term alone does not really assist us in understanding the letter's intention or any of its details.

However, Professor Betz is more optimistic, as was indicated above, with regard to the application of the categories of ancient rhetoric, and we have to look briefly at his methods and results. Both in his early article and in his commentary on the letter to the Galatians he states that rhetoric and epistolography help to understand St Paul's epistles, and he states that certain sections are to be given particular labels.[63] He does not seem to offer any arguments, even though he himself complains that 'despite an extensive search, I have not been able to find any consideration given to possible criteria and methods for determining such an outline' (of the epistle as often given in commentaries).[64] Moreover, Professor Betz states as his thesis that St Paul's letter to the Galatians is an example of the apologetic letter genre which, as he informs us with reference to several publications of the distinguished ancient historian A. Momigliano, arose in the fourth century BCE and presupposes the 'letter' form, but also the genres of 'autobiography' and 'apologetic speech'. He then shows that, apart from such features which are typical for an epistle as prescript and postscript, the traditional *partes orationis* follow, with first the *exordium* in which the reasons are stated why the letter was written.[65]

---

62. Cf. Pseudo-Demetrius, *Form. epist.* 7 (p. 6 Weichert); Pseudo-Libanius, *Char. epist.* 27, 72 (pp. 18, 29-30, 47-48 Weichert).

63. Betz, 'The Literary Composition', pp. 359-75; *Galatians*, pp. 16-22 *et saepius* (*Galater*, pp. 57-66).

64. Betz, 'The Literary Composition', p. 353.

65. Betz, 'The Literary Composition', pp. 354-62; *Galatians*, pp. 14-15, 44-46 (*Galater*, pp. 54-56, 98-102). I fail to see how Momigliano's works on Greek biography support Betz's thesis; see also below n. 72.

Any piece of writing has a beginning, as does any kind of orderly speech, so that agreements and similarities are to be expected; they cannot be used to prove that St Paul gave the whole letter the structure of a logos. But the rules for *exordia* may, as was shown above, be used to appreciate particular features, especially when the writer does not follow the recommendations of the theory. The section 1.12–2.14 is understood by Professor Betz as *narratio*.[66] Professor G.A. Kennedy has said what needs to be said to show this to be erroneous:[67] the narrative of the first and second chapters of Galatians is 'not an account of facts at issue'. Their real function was seen and explained by an expert on ancient rhetoric more than fifteen centuries ago, by Marius Victorinus who, in summarizing this section, says 'confirmata igitur auctoritate...'[68] The apostle is anxious first of all to establish or reestablish his own authority before discussing any details. Parallels for this can easily be found in speeches delivered in the courts of law,[69] and insofar one can certainly learn a good deal from oratorical practice for the interpretation of epistles.

What about the other parts of this 'apologetic letter'? Professor Betz finds 2.15–21 conforming to the form, function and requirements of the *proposition*; he claims that this passage is a summary of the

66. 'The Literary Composition', pp. 362-67; *Galatians*, pp. 16-18, 57-62 (*Galater*, pp. 58-60 113-28).

67. *New Testament Interpretation*, pp. 144-46. However his view that the epistle to the Galatians belongs to the deliberative genre (p. 145) is not convincing either (even though it has been accepted by J. Smit, 'The Letter of Paul to the Galatians: A Deliberative Speech', *NTS* 35 [1989], pp. 1-26, and F. Vouga, 'Zur rhetorischen Gattung des Galaterbriefes', *ZNW* 79 [1988], pp. 291-92), for the addressees are not called upon to take a decision as a group as, for example, the Athenian assembly or the Roman senate.

68. 'Then, the authority having been confirmed' (the apostle's own and that of the gospel preached by him). *Marii Victorini Afri Commentarii in Epistulas Pauli ad Galatas ad Philippenses ad Ephesios* (ed. A. Locher; Leipzig, 1972), p. 1 = *Marii Victorini Opera. Pars posterior. Opera exegetica* (ed. F. Gori; CSEL, 82, 2; Vienna, 1986), p. 96; on his commentaries, see A. Souter, *The Earliest Latin Commentaries on the Epistles of St. Paul* (Oxford, 1927), pp. 8-38 (also on 'Ambrosiaster': pp. 39-95; Jerome: pp. 96-138; Augustine: pp. 139-204; and Pelagius: pp. 205-30) and W. Erdt, *Marius Victorinus Afer, der erste lateinische Pauluskommentator* (Frankfurt, 1980).

69. Cf. Cicero, *Mur.* 2–10; *Sull.* 3–10, 17–20, 21–29; *Dom.* 3–32, also *Rab. perd.* 10–17; *Sest.* 36–52.

doctrine of justification by faith.[70] Even if one does not regard these
verses as a summary of St Paul's speech at Antioch, they are clearly
formulated in a very personal way in the first person singular or
plural, and this is not the way he talks later in the third and fourth
chapter after turning to the Galatians. The difficulties Professor Betz
has in discovering the traditional pattern of a logos in St Paul's letter
become even more obvious in the second half, as he is forced to add a
long section called 'exhortatio' (5.1–6.10)[71] which has a place in
letters, not in an apologetic logos. This alone should have warned
Professor Betz not to apply too rashly categories to this letter which
were developed for another genre and are, therefore, not applicable,
except for selected aspects and features. The fact that one element of
the traditional ('ideal') structure seems to occur in a composition (or
possibly two) does not warrant the inference that the other parts must
be discoverable there as well or that the composition as a whole conforms to such a pattern. In the epistle to the Galatians the main body is
not concerned with St Paul's defence, and there is no reason,
therefore, to regard it as an 'apologetic letter', even less so, because
the examples Professor Betz cites are quite different and the model of
an 'apologetic letter' as it is found in Pseudo-Demetrius shows no
resemblance either.[72]

This takes us back to the original questions asked at the beginning,
and I shall try now to combine the answers to them with an assessment
of the possibilities and merits of rhetorical criticism of the epistles of
the New Testament, and of its limits and dangers. It has become clear
in the course of this paper, I hope, that rhetoric (oratory) and epistolography were regarded as two different fields in antiquity, and it
seems advisable, therefore, to stay within the elaboration and

70. 'The Literary Composition', pp. 367-68; *Galatians*, pp. 18-19, 113-14
(*Galater*, pp. 60-61, 212-15); on the controversy with regard to this section, see
above n. 54.

71. See 'The Literary Composition', pp. 375-77 (Paraenesis); *Galatians*, pp. 22-
23, 253-311 (*Exhortatio*) (*Galater*, pp. 66-68, 433-528). The corresponding type of
letter is called παραινετική: Pseudo-Libanius, *Char. epist. praef.*, 1; see also
examples: 1, 90, 91 (pp. 14, 15, 21-22, 56-57).

72. 'The Literary Composition', p. 354; *Galatians*, pp. 14-15 (*Galater*, pp. 54-
56). For the 'apologetic letter', see Pseudo-Demetrius, *Form. epist. praef.*, 18
(pp. 2, 9-10 Weichert); see also Pseudo-Libanius, *Char. epist.* 15 (pp. 16-17
Weichert); for some examples, cf. S.K. Stowers, *Letter Writing in Greco-Roman
Antiquity* (Philadelphia, 1986), pp. 167-70.

presentation of their respective theory. The writers of manuals on rhetoric,[73] though aware of the great variety of speeches required by the realities of life, nevertheless did venture to construe a standard structure and content, and, in addition, to allow for flexibility in its application and to give advice on particular forms. Those trying to formulate general rules for the writing of letters, on the other hand, aware of the even greater variety of letters actually written by people, did not propose an ideal structure or perhaps two—at least we have no knowledge of anything like that—they merely listed types together with recommendations for the appropriate style in each case. Thus the theory of epistolography will be of use with regard to matters of style, while the large number of actual letters in their manifoldness will provide material for comparison.[74] The theory of rhetoric, on the other hand, though developed for another area, together with practical oratory will also render service, but again within limits, that is, in the areas of *inventio* (argumentation) and *elocutio* (where there is overlapping with the theory of epistolography). On *dispositio* rhetorical theory may be consulted, but extreme caution is called for, as has been pointed out. Perhaps the most useful aspect which practical oratory can illustrate is that the best orator disguises his knowledge of the theory,[75] that he alters accepted patterns and adjusts them to the

73. Cf. *Aristotelis ars rhetorica* (ed. R. Kassel; Berlin, 1976); *Anaximenis ars rhetorica* (ed. M. Fuhrmann; Leipzig, 1966); *Incerti auctoris de ratione dicendi ad C. Herennium libri IV* (ed. F. Marx; Leipzig, 1923); *M. Tulli Ciceronis rhetorici libri duo* (ed. E. Stroebel; Leipzig, 1915); *M. Tulli Ciceronis de oratore* (ed. K. Kumaniecki; Leipzig, 1969); *M. Tulli Ciceronis orator* (ed. R. Westman; Leipzig, 1980); *M. Fabi Quintiliani institutionis oratoriae libri duodecim I-II* (ed. M. Winterbottom; Oxford, 1970). For the need of flexibility in applying the rules, see e.g. *Auctor ad Herennium* 3.17: 'est autem alia dispositio, quae cum ab ordine artificioso recedendum est, oratoris iudicio ad tempus adcommodatur'.

74. See above n. 11 for the theoretical works. Recently much comparative material has been collected and analysed; see e.g. W.G. Doty, *Letters in Primitive Christianity* (Philadelphia, 1973); J.L. White, *Light from Ancient Letters* (Philadelphia, 1986); Stowers, *Letter Writing*, and the works listed in their bibliographies (White, pp. 221-24; Stowers, pp. 177-79). To my mind it is more promising and fruitful to set St Paul's epistles against the whole range of Hellenistic literature with its variety of genres (see e.g. K. Berger, 'Hellenistische Gattungen im Neuen Testament', in W. Haase [ed.], *Aufstieg und Niedergang der römischen Welt*, II. 25.2 [Berlin, 1984], pp. 1031-432 and 1831-885), and also, of course, against the Jewish (Rabbinic) tradition.

75. On the *dissimulatio artis*, see C. Neumeister, *Grundsätze der forensischen*

particular case and his special intention. Thus not what conforms to the rules, but what seems at variance with them often proves most instructive for interpretation. Correspondingly, in trying to understand a particular composition, one should always look not primarily for what is in accordance with the rules or with general practice, but for the contrary.

Secondly, as the example of Melanchthon has shown, there is no reason why one should restrict oneself to the rhetoric of the ancients in interpreting texts from antiquity, and not avail oneself of the discoveries and achievements of more recent times.[76] As regards the problems raised (thirdly) concerning the person of St Paul himself, his education and the form of rhetoric he may have been familiar with himself, and the question whether he employed the tools of rhetoric deliberately, it is not my intention to deal with them here, as I am not competent. I would merely like to add one or two observations:[77] (a) that St Paul must have read a good deal of Greek literature and thus have come into contact with rhetoric applied, and (b) that he must have been familiar with the Rabbinic tradition of interpreting the Old Testament and thus have been sensitive to the possibilities inherent in language. As regards the stage in the development of rhetoric he may or may not have known, it should be remembered that the essential insights, classifications and rules, once formulated, remained virtually unchanged for centuries. Furthermore one should not forget that the occurrence of rhetorical figures does not allow the inference that an

Rhetorik gezeigt an Gerichtsreden Ciceros (Munich, 1965), pp. 130-55.

76. See W. Wuellner's general considerations (cited above n. 7) and his numerous articles (listed e.g. by L. Thurén, *Rhetorical Strategy*, p. 204). Most successful in applying modern rhetoric: F. Siegert, *Argumentation bei Paulus gezeigt an Röm 9–11* (Tübingen, 1985), also with special emphasis on sociological aspects: V.K. Robbins, *Jesus the Teacher: A Socio-Rhetorical Interpretation of Mark* (Philadelphia, 1984) and even more so: N.R. Petersen, *Rediscovering Paul: Philemon and the Sociology of Paul's Narrative World* (Philadelphia, 1985); see further F. Watson, *Paul, Judaism and the Gentiles: A Sociological Approach* (Cambridge, 1986); misguided on the other hand, J.L. Kinneavy, *Greek Rhetorical Origins of Christian Faith: An Inquiry* (New York, 1987), as the parallels which he points out do not prove what they are supposed to prove.

77. It should not be overlooked that St Paul at least once uses a technical term (2 Cor. 3.1): συστατικαὶ ἐπιστολαί; cf. Pseudo-Demetrius, *Form. epist. praef.*, 2 (pp. 2-3 Weichert); Pseudo-Libanius, *Char. epist., praef.*, 4, 95 (pp. 14, 16, 22, 58 Weichert).

author employed them because he was familiar with a theory. For they recommended themselves in practice long before any theory was ever developed (Quintilian 2. 17.5-9), and they are found in authors who were never exposed to any theory in any form.

However, it does not follow that rhetorical theory cannot render useful service in such cases. Whether a writer or a speaker had knowledge of such a theory or not, or whether he was familiar with literature written under the influence of such a theory, for the interpretation of texts from any period rhetorical theory offers a most useful set of instruments which have to be used, however, with the greatest care possible.[78]

78. This paper is printed here as it was submitted to *Rhetorica* in July 1991 by kind permission of its editor. Since then I have become aware of a number of relevant publications, references to which I might have added; I refrain from doing so in order not to take up even more space, and refer merely to D.F. Watson's two most useful lists, 'The New Testament and Greco-Roman Rhetoric: A Bibliographical Update', *JETS* 31 (1988), pp. 465-72 and 33 (1990), pp. 513-24, copies of which I owe to the author's kindness; see also now G. Strecker, *Literaturgeschichte des Neuen Testaments* (Göttingen, 1992) and the literature listed there (for a copy of this I am also indebted to its writer). Of special importance is M.M. Mitchell, *Paul and the Rhetoric of Reconciliation: An Exegetical Investigation of the Language and Composition of 1 Corinthians* (Tübingen, 1991); she lists (p. 6) five mandates for rhetorical criticism of New Testament texts, of which three seem acceptable to me: '2: Actual speeches and letters from antiquity must be consulted along with the rhetorical handbooks throughout the investigation. 3: The designation of the rhetorical species of a text (as epideictic, deliberative, or forensic) cannot be begged in the analysis... 5: The rhetorical unit to be examined should be a compositional unit, which can be further substantiated by successful rhetorical analysis' (though with regard to the last a great deal of misunderstanding may be found in recent scholarship). The other two I cannot understand: '1: Rhetorical criticism as employed here is an historical undertaking'—but why? Why should one restrict oneself in this way and not use modern rhetorical theory as well; no literary critic would confine himself to the categories of ancient literary criticism. '4: The appropriateness of rhetorical form or genre to content must be demonstrated'—but why? The underlying assumption seems to be that New Testament writers invariably chose the appropriate rhetorical form or genre. That looks like theology to me, not rhetorical criticism.

USING ANCIENT RHETORICAL CATEGORIES TO INTERPRET PAUL'S LETTERS: A QUESTION OF GENRE

Jeffrey T. Reed

Determining the literary form of Paul's writings has not been without its problems. Granted, few scholars would deny that the extant texts from Paul's pen are letters, that is, part of the Graeco-Roman epistolary genre.[1] Nevertheless, consensus ends here, since ancient letters come in various shapes and sizes, making it difficult to place Paul's letters in their precise cultural setting. Some ancient letters are very 'literary' in nature, containing forms and styles representative of very studied writers; some are very 'popular' in form, representing the grammar and style of a less-educated (but not necessarily uneducated) populace. Deissmann's literary classification of Paul's letters is one of the most well-known. His classification of ancient letters may be portrayed as a continuum, on one end being 'epistles' (that is, conscious, artistic prose intended for the public) and on the other end 'letters' (that is, occasional, personal discourse not intended for the public).[2] According to Deissmann, Paul's letters fall on the latter side of the continuum. Since Deissmann, who was heavily influenced by his *religionsgeschichtliche* perspective, scholars have increasingly moved

---

1. The term 'genre', although recognizably loose in meaning, is used here to designate the distinguishable types or categories into which various discourses are grouped according to their form and function.

2. See A. Deissmann, *Light from the Ancient East* (trans. L.R.M. Strachan; repr. Grand Rapids: Baker, 4th edn, 1965), pp. 148-49, 228-30. W.G. Doty ('The Classification of Epistolary Literature', *CBQ* 31 [1969], p. 194) offers a more balanced typology than Deissmann. He states, 'In contrast to his [Deissmann's] exclusion of the "literary" as of no real worth, all the letters with which epistolary research has to do... appear now in a literary context'. He also rightly argues that 'formally and stylistically the "epistle" *is a letter*' (p. 191). One of Deissmann's own examples of a letter (Theon to his father Theon; P.Oxy. 119), which exhibits features of irony and sarcasm, undermines his differentiation of epistle and letter.

toward the other end of the continuum. First, recent sociological studies demonstrate that Paul's missionary activity was not solely directed towards the poor and bereft. Paul likely ministered his gospel across a broad spectrum of the social strata, even among Gentiles educated under a *grammaticus* (in other words, in grammar, rhetoric, dialectic, geometry, arithmetic, astronomy and music).[3] Secondly, scholars recognize the unique position of Paul's letters within the Graeco-Roman epistolary tradition. Paul does not fit tightly into the categories of the epistolary theorists, nor does he always parallel the extant epistles of the trash dumps in Egypt. However, Deissmann's epistolary typology has not been superseded and 'few typologies of Graeco-Roman or early Christian letters have been proposed and none widely adopted'.[4] In recent years Paul's letters have been increasingly viewed under the auspices of classical rhetorical categories, moving along Deissmann's continuum toward the other extreme and perhaps providing a way forward in the discussion. The assumption is that epistolary categories and ancient rhetoric could be and actually were readily merged. As to the possibility of finding rhetorical species (viz. judicial, deliberative and epideictic) in ancient letters, a noted epistolary scholar, Stanley Stowers, avows, 'There are types of letters which belong to each of the three species'.[5] The purpose of this essay is to question whether ancient (that is, classical) rhetorical practices can shed light on Paul's epistles.[6] Although in a less polemical tone, the question posed by Jerome will be considered: 'What has Horace to do

---

3. W.A. Meeks, *The First Urban Christians: The Social World of the Apostle Paul* (New Haven: Yale University Press, 1983), pp. 51-73.

4. D.E. Aune, *The New Testament in its Literary Environment* (Library of Early Christianity, 8; Philadelphia: Westminster Press, 1987), p. 161.

5. S.K. Stowers, *Letter Writing in Greco-Roman Antiquity* (Library of Early Christianity, 5; Philadelphia: Westminster Press, 1986), p. 51.

6. In 1986, Stowers claimed, 'The relationship of the early Christian letters to the larger world of Greco-Roman letter writing, literature, and rhetoric is today a neglected and a pressing question' (*Letter Writing*, p. 18). Some see little or no rhetorical influence on Paul: e.g. J.L. White, *The Body of the Greek Letter* (SBLDS, 2; Missoula, MT: Scholars Press, 1972), and W.G. Doty, *Letters in Primitive Christianity* (Philadelphia: Fortress Press, 1973). Others see an oratorical structure in his letters: e.g. K. Berger, 'Hellenistische Gattungen im Neuen Testament', in *ANRW* II. 25.2 (ed. H. Temporini and W. Haase; Berlin: de Gruyter, 1984), pp. 1031-432, and G.A. Kennedy, *New Testament Interpretation through Rhetorical Criticism* (Chapel Hill: University of North Carolina Press, 1984), p. 86.

with the Psalms, Virgil with the Gospels, *Cicero with the Apostle'* (*Epistulae* 22.29; emphasis mine)? Will ancient rhetoric resolve scholarly debate over the Pauline genre? Did Paul write ancient rhetoric, or at least an epistolary version of it?

Rhetorical Traditions in Epistles

Christians did not accommodate their letter-writing practices to the rhetorical handbooks until the fourth and fifth centuries CE (e.g. in Greek, Basil, Gregory of Nazianzus, and John Chrysostom; in Latin, Ambrose and Augustine).[7] The church fathers of the early second century CE (e.g. Ignatius), although clearly at home with Graeco-Roman traditions, did not employ strict rhetorical categories in their letters as much as the later fathers did. This is traceable perhaps in part to the absence of epistolary discussion in the rhetorical handbooks.[8] The first rhetorician to treat letter writing as part of a rhetorical system was Julius Victor (fourth century CE), one of the Minor Latin Rhetoricians.[9] In spite of this, recent years have seen

---

7. This movement towards Christian rhetorical literature was partly occasioned by the acceptance of Christianity as a legal religion in the fourth century (G.A. Kennedy, *Classical Rhetoric and its Christian and Secular Tradition from Ancient to Modern Times* [Chapel Hill: University of North Carolina Press, 1980], p. 114). However, as early as the later part of the second century CE, the Christian apologetic literature (e.g. Tatian's *Oration to the Greeks*) in the form of pamphlets made use of Greek philosophy and rhetoric (p. 133). One apologetic letter does survive, *The Epistle to Diognetus* (ΕΠΙΣΤΟΛΗ ΠΡΟΣ ΔΙΟΓΝΗΤΟΝ), which is thoroughly rhetorical in style and shows evidence of an *exordium, narratio, probatio, refutatio* (but lacks any other forms because the last two chapters probably belong to a different document). This letter, which only contains an *adscription*, is both anonymous and of an uncertain date (late second century or later) and is perhaps an academic treatise or exercise of a young theologian (K. Lake, *The Apostolic Fathers*, II [Cambridge, MA: Harvard University Press, 1913], pp. 348-49). It hardly parallels Paul's letters, but it does demonstrate the use of rhetoric in an extremely abbreviated form of the epistolary genre.

8. A.J. Malherbe (*Ancient Epistolary Theorists* [SBLSBS, 19; Missoula, MT: Scholars Press, 1988], p. 3) notes that the subject and act of letter writing was not part of the system of ancient rhetoric.

9. See his *Ars Rhetorica* 27 (*De Epistolis*). Julius Victor's incorporation of letter writing into a system of rhetoric is clearly revealed in his opening statement: 'Many directives which pertain to oral discourse also apply to letters'.

Paul's letters undergo thorough investigation for their ancient rhetorical elements. Few would inflexibly argue that Paul did not use argumentation in his letters. But did he employ the categories of the ancient rhetorical handbooks, especially those of his day? That is, when Paul attempted to persuade the recipients of his letters did he form his arguments from the perspective of contemporary rhetorical practices? We know that Paul wrote in the epistolary genre. But did he write under the auspices of an 'epistolary–rhetorical' genre?[10] One approach to this question is to inspect the epistolary theorists for their relationship with the broader rhetorical traditions.[11] In addition, it is worth considering whether the more literary-minded letter writers, such as those involved in oratory, evidence a relationship between epistolary and rhetorical practices. However, before these primary sources are inspected, one further point demands attention.

Although the epistolary elements of Paul's letters have been treated to a far greater extent than the elements of his rhetoric, some question remains as to his precise relationship with both the occasional, commonplace epistles and with the more literary, 'educated' epistles.[12] Such uncertainty is due in part to the flexibility of the letter as a communicative device, providing Paul with a genre easily adaptable to his own purposes. Paul's letters are unique, say many scholars, falling somewhere between the two extremes of the continuum. Consequently,

10. So C.J. Martin ('The Rhetorical Function of Commercial Language in Paul's Letter to Philemon [Verse 18]', in D.F. Watson (ed.), *Persuasive Artistry: Studies in Honor of George A. Kennedy* [JSNTSup, 50; Sheffield: JSOT Press, 1991], p. 325) apparently maintains: 'The Pauline letters nevertheless reflect Paul's familiarity with recognizable epistolary conventions (an opening, body, and closing) and rhetorical techniques reminiscent of oral argumentation'.

11. Although Ἐπιστολιμαῖοι Χαρακτῆρες came much later than Paul (fourth or fifth century CE) the origin of Τύποι Ἐπιστολικοί falls somewhere between 200 BCE and 300 CE, likely before Paul's era (K. Thraede, *Grundzüge griechisch-römische Brieftopik* [Monographien zur klassischen Altertumswissenschaft, 48; Munich: Beck, 1970], p. 26). *De Elocutione* perhaps originated in the third century BCE, but also perhaps falls into Paul's era, setting precedence for the existence of epistolary theory prior to or at least at the same time as Paul.

12. Although 'literary' and 'non-literary' can be falsely used to characterize the various epistolary types, the terms do help to describe the continuum on which various letters fall. Seneca's letters (first century CE), for example, are examples of literary treatises. His *Epistulae Morales* are letters of 'advice' typically dealing with one philosophical topic, and contain only the minimum epistolary elements.

even if there is a strong relationship between epistolary and ancient rhetorical theory, one cannot simply assume that Paul mimicked the epistolary handbooks (or that he was even aware of them) and thus was also dependent upon rhetorical practices. Nevertheless, a theory about Paul's use of rhetoric in his letters still can be legitimately constructed by inspecting both the epistolary theorists and the more literary-minded letter writers. On the one hand, if Paul did follow the basic principles of epistolary theorists or he was familiar with the more literary epistolary traditions, then analyzing the use of rhetoric in these bodies of literature should shed light on the question regarding the likelihood of Paul's use of ancient rhetorical categories. If the epistolary theorists did incorporate rhetorical theory in their typologies and Paul shows awareness of these theorists, then Paul may well have incorporated rhetorical elements into his letters. On the other hand, if Paul did not mimic the epistolary theorists or was ignorant of the highly 'literary' letters, then it becomes more difficult to associate Paul's epistolary genre with the ancient rhetorical genre, since the epistolary theorists provide some of the best evidence for the potential use of ancient rhetoric in the epistolary genre.[13]

With this caveat aside, let me propose a methodology for investigating the justification for using ancient rhetorical categories to interpret Paul's letters. The rhetorical handbooks generally discuss five aspects of rhetorical practice: invention (*inventio*), arrangement (*dispositio*), style (*elocutio*), memory (*memoria*) and delivery (*pronunciatio*). The last two of this group had little, if any, place in letter writing,[14] being irrelevant to the task. The first three, however, perhaps played a role in epistolary theory and practice. In addition, the various 'species' of rhetoric (types of speeches) may have influenced the epistolary traditions. These four categories, in view of their possible application to Paul's letters, are the categories of

---

13. Of course this point does not prove that Paul could not have used ancient rhetoric in his letters. I am merely trying to point out that the epistolary theorists and literary letter writers provide explicit evidence regarding Paul's parallel with the ancient rhetorical genre. If Paul is not dependent upon the epistolary theorists or literary letter writers, then there remains less evidence for showing his dependence upon ancient rhetorical theory.

14. If the letter was read to a gathering of Christians, the speaker may have been concerned with these features of speech. But it is doubtful that Paul the letter writer was.

rhetoric which will be juxtaposed with the broader epistolary traditions.

Rhetorical Types (Species) in Epistles

Genres are function-specific, that is, they develop a customary form and pattern appropriate to the basic function they serve. Ancient oratory—a genre of argumentation[15]—was typically divided into three sub-genres (or *registers*): judicial, deliberative and epideictic.[16] Generally speaking, judicial speech functioned in the courtroom before a jury or judge. Deliberative speech functioned in the political assembly. Epideictic speech functioned in the public arena, frequently at ceremonial occasions. 'Did he do it or not?' was an essential question scrutinized by the judicial speech. 'Is it more beneficial to do this or that?' was the question explored by the deliberative speech. 'Should something be praised or blamed?' was the question discussed by the epideictic speech.[17] Are these three types of speeches found in ancient epistles?

In contrast to the oral, face-to-face context of most ancient rhetoric,[18] the epistolary genre was occasioned by situations where

15. Rhetoric as argumentation, not logic (analytic), is underscored in the classic work of C. Perelman and L. Olbrechts-Tyteca, *The New Rhetoric: A Treatise on Argumentation* (Notre Dame, IN: University of Notre Dame Press, 1969).

16. Although these three types of speeches were often combined and intertwined in the same discourse, the distinct categories were still maintained by the rhetoricians.

17. Although this is a very condensed and simplistic portrayal of rhetorical species, it represents the basic approach many scholars have brought to their analyses of Paul's letters and therefore will be the approach under scrutiny here.

18. Speech was the primary medium of rhetoric (i.e. primary rhetoric; Kennedy, *Classical Rhetoric*, pp. 4-5). Indeed, the word 'rhetoric' means etymologically 'the art of the rhetor,—the speaker's (the public speaker's) art' (W. Rhys Roberts, *Greek Rhetoric and Literary Criticism* [New York: Longmans, 1928], p. 22). Nonetheless, other written mediums were influenced by rhetorical principles: e.g. 'Plutarch's *Lives* and *Moralia*... the commentaries of Philo of Alexandria, the discourses of Dio Chrysostom, and the letters of Seneca' (B. Mack, *Rhetoric and the New Testament* [Minneapolis: Fortress Press, 1990], p. 30). Indeed, Cicero and Seneca note that the letter is speech in the written medium (Cicero, *Epistulae ad Atticum* 8.14.1; 9.10.1; 12.53; Seneca, *Epistulae Morales* 75.1). These are secondary mediums of classical rhetoric, being mostly influenced by stylistic categories (Kennedy, *Classical Rhetoric*, p. 5). Isocrates was the first major orator to reduce his speeches to written form, doing so four centuries prior to Paul. This tendency towards converting speeches to a written medium (*letteraturizzazione*) allows for the possible fusion of

one or more individuals, spatially separated, wished to communicate
with others.[19] Within this cardinal function, the epistolary genre was
used in various ways and appeared in multifarious forms.[20] Writing to
C. Scribonius Curio in 53 BCE, Cicero identifies this essential function
of letters:

> That there are many kinds of letters you are well aware; there is one kind,
> however, about which there can be no mistake—for indeed letter writing
> was invented just in order that we might inform those at a distance if there
> were anything which it was important for them or for ourselves that they
> should know (*Ad Familiares* 2.4).

Cicero goes on to speak of letters which are 'intimate and humorous'
and letters which are 'austere and serious'.[21] He also distinguishes

the epistolary and rhetorical genres.

19. Cf. the epistolary categorizations of G.J. Bahr, 'The Subscriptions in the
Pauline Letters', *JBL* 87 (1968), p. 27; Doty, 'Classification of Epistolary
Literature', p. 198; and J.L. White, 'The Greek Documentary Letter Tradition Third
Century B.C.E. to Third Century C.E', *Semeia* 22 (1981), p. 91. Aside from this
fundamental function, the letter was used for a host of other purposes (e.g. there
were letters of friendship, family letters, letters of praise and blame, letters of recommendation, letters of petition, and official letters). Cf. Cicero, *Epistulae ad Familiares*
15.21.4, who reveals the epistolary genre's adaptability: 'You see, I have one way of
writing what I think will be read by those only to whom I address my letter, and
another way of writing what I think will be read by many'. This flexibility, however,
did not ensure classical rhetoric a place in the epistolary genre.

20. Gregory of Nazianzus exemplifies this well, giving advice on the subject of
letter writing sent in the form of a letter (*Epistula* 51.8). In addition, many of the literary letters of Horace display his poetic skill (and even resemble his *Satires*); others
are directed toward a more practical function (*Letters* 1.8). Cf. the poetic *Heroides* by
Ovid and the poetic *Silvae* by Statius, both of which are framed by epistolary forms.
This flexibility of the genre, however, also makes it difficult to categorize Paul's letters, since the epistolary genre tends to avoid strict categorization. See, for example,
the three quite distinct typologies proposed for Romans: ambassadorial letter
(R. Jewett, 'Romans as an Ambassadorial Letter', *Int* 36 [1982], pp. 5-20); letter-
essay (M L. Stirewalt, Jr, 'The Form and Function of the Greek Letter-Essay', in
K.P. Donfried [ed.], *The Romans Debate* [Minneapolis: Augsburg, 2nd edn, 1977],
pp. 175-206); and protreptic (Stowers, *Letter Writing*, pp. 112-14, 128; and the
more thorough account of D.E. Aune, 'Romans as a Logos Protreptikos', in *The
Romans Debate*, pp. 278-96).

21. Cicero's typology is less than helpful for this study, since in his definition of
a letter he conflates one function of the genre (i.e. to inform) with the primary
function of the genre (i.e. the need to bridge the spatial gap between people). In his

between public and private letters (*Pro Flacco* 37). Other ancient authors attempted to categorize the various types of letters. The epistolary handbook falsely attributed to Demetrius of Phalerum, Τύποι Ἐπιστολικοί, details twenty-one types of letters. In addition, the epistolary handbook falsely attributed to Libanius (another edition is attributed to Proclus), Ἐπιστολιμαῖοι Χαρακτῆρες, delineates forty-one types of letters. Each type serves different, although at times overlapping, functions. Philostratus (*De Epistulis* 2.257.29-258.28 [third century CE]), although clearly providing a restricted list, mentions letters which grant something or make a petition, which agree or disagree with some issue, which attack someone or defend the writer (judicial?), and which simply express love. Cicero distinguishes between informative letters, domestic letters, letters of commendation, letters of solace, and letters promising assistance (*Epistulae ad Familiares* 2.4.1; 4.13.1; 5.5.1). This short list of ancient typologies reveals the futility of any modern attempt to construct a typology of letters. The ancient typologies were practical, that is, they served the needs of professional letter writers as well as those casual letter writers who dared to conceptualize how they would communicate through the epistolary genre.

The ancient epistolary genre allowed the individual to handle a variety of situations with a variety of types of letters.[22] Therefore, it is no surprise to find types of letters which parallel the three sub-genres of rhetoric. Such parallels do not prove, however, a direct borrowing from rhetorical categories. Rather, the similarities are probably due to common communicative practices in the culture. In other words, argumentation is universal as well as culture-specific, that is, developing from the beliefs and behaviors of individual societies. Groups within the society (lawyers, for example) may have adapted common rhetorical practices to their unique needs, but on the broader schema, judicial, deliberative, and epideictic 'types' of

other two types of letters he speaks of modes in which letters may be written: formal and informal. Many of his own letters in *Epistulae ad Familiares* combine the function of conveying political information about himself and/or the recipient in either a formal or an informal manner.

22. Letters are generally associated with the activities of friendship, client-patron relationships, and the household (Stowers, *Letter Writing*, p. 31). Pseudo-Demetrius (Τύποι Ἐπιστολικοί 22–24) recognizes the flexibility of the epistolary genre and the possibility of future developments in epistolary typologies.

rhetoric, including the letter, would have been used in various Graeco-Roman contexts. But what exactly do the theorists and the letter writers say about the rhetorical types as they pertain to letters?

Nowhere in the theorists is there specific discussion of a judicial letter. Perhaps the 'accusing' (κατηγορικός) letter comes close, but the parallels are again only functional and there is no mention of a courtroom setting.[23] In rebuttal to the 'accusing' letter, the defendant could employ the 'apologetic' (ἀπολογητικός) letter to ward off the indictment of a prosecutor.[24] But the author's example of this type of letter clearly did not replace the courtroom rhetoric. A deliberative type of rhetoric is mentioned in the epistolary theorists. Pseudo-Demetrius speaks of 'advisory' (συμβουλευτικός) letters, which are used to 'impel [someone] to something (προτρέπωμεν ἐπί τι) or dissuade [someone] from something (ἀποτρέπωμεν ἀπό τινος)'.[25] Pseudo-Libanius categorizes the same type of letter as 'paraenetic' (παραινετική). 'The paraenetic type of letter is that in which we impel someone by urging him to pursue something or to avoid something. Paraenesis is divided into two parts: encouragement (προτροπήν) and dissuasion (ἀποτροπήν).'[26] This is, however, one of many types of letters and there is no evidence that the author's terminology directly comes from the rhetorical handbooks. The divergent language suggests otherwise. Once again, the parallel is probably functional. Of the three rhetorical sub-genres, the epideictic type is most at home among the epistolary theorists.[27] Many of

---

23. Pseudo-Demetrius, Τύποι Ἐπιστολικοί 17. Cf. the 'blaming' (μεμπτική) letter in Pseudo-Libanius, Ἐπιστολιμαῖοι Χαρακτῆρες 6; and the 'counter-accusing' (ἀντεγκληματική) letter in Ἐπιστολιμαῖοι Χαρακτῆρες 22. For an example of a letter similar to judicial rhetoric, see Cicero, *Epistulae ad Familiares* 5.2.

24. Pseudo-Demetrius, Τύποι Ἐπιστολικοί 18.

25. Τύποι Ἐπιστολικοί 11.

26. Pseudo-Libanius, Ἐπιστολιμαῖοι Χαρακτῆρες 5. The author does attempt to differentiate the paraenetic from the advisory letter, stating that the latter assumes a counter-argument (i.e. someone who needs to be persuaded) whereas the former does not. Both types of letters, nonetheless, parallel deliberative rhetoric in that they speak of what is beneficial and harmful.

27. Stowers, *Letter Writing*, p. 27. Of the three species of rhetoric, epideictic was most at home in written discourse. 'Epideictic oratory, such as that of Isocrates, was coming more and more to be a pamphlet, not a speech; in theme and occasion it had never been so restricted as the other branches of oratory' (Roberts, *Greek*

Pseudo-Libanius's epistolary types resemble Quintilian's categorization of epideictic rhetoric (Quintilian 3.4.3). But this is perhaps because of the widespread importance of honor and shame in Graeco-Roman culture, in which the 'praise' and 'blame' style characteristic of epideictic rhetoric would have been important to other literary modes as well.

In conclusion, it is fair to surmise that Paul could conceptualize a letter in terms of 'praise or blame' and 'expediency or non-expediency'. Paul's use of epideictic-like and deliberative-like argumentation, however, does not necessarily indicate a direct parallel with the systems of rhetoric found in the rhetorical schools. Furthermore, it is doubtful that a purely judicial letter would come forth from his pen. Of course, he did deal with the question of whether something 'was or was not done' (especially something accused of him), but again this does not necessarily imply usage of judicial categories of the rhetorical handbooks, especially in the sense of courtroom rhetoric. Since the epistolary theorists did not systematize a purely rhetorical typology of letters, the reasonable conclusion can be drawn that Paul probably did not.

Rhetorical Invention in Epistles
Rhetorical invention (*inventio*) concerns the speaker's attempt to select (that is, invent) a subject or thesis as well as the stance taken on the issues. This included the speaker's search for familiar material or topics (τόποι) to make the point. Such topics (both common and special) were often drawn from customary maxims, proverbs, oracles, citations, figures of speech, and stock metaphors, to name a few.

Invention is not unique to the rhetorical handbooks, however. It is a phenomenon of argumentation, literature, and language in general. Thus, as with the 'types' or 'species' of rhetorical speeches discussed above, it should be no surprise that epistolary theorists and letter writers discuss how one should make a point in a letter. Nevertheless, the principle of *inventio*[28] and the use of *topoi*[29] as part of creating a

---

Rhetoric and Literary Criticism, p. 55).

28. Aristotle mentions two kinds of arguments available to the speaker: non-artistic (e.g. witnesses, laws, contracts, tortures, oaths) and artistic (i.e. creating *logos*, *pathos* and *ethos*). *Topoi* aided the speaker in discovering matter for the artistic modes of appeal, and are the primary focus of study in this section.

29. Unfortunately, the essays by D.G. Bradley, 'The *Topos* as a Form in the

thesis and its proofs are not nearly as thoroughly delineated in the theorists as they are in the rhetorical handbooks.

Pseudo-Demetrius (*De Elocutione* 230) notes the existence of topics or 'matter' appropriate only for the letter (πράγματά τινα ἐπιστολικά), citing Aristotle in support of this: 'I have not written to you on this subject, since it was not fitted for a letter' (Fr. 620). He goes on to discuss two types of τόποι: proverbs (παροιμίαι, 232) and logical proofs (ἀποδείξεις, 233).[30] Elsewhere he mentions the inappropriateness of clever types of argumentation (σοφίσματα) in letters: 'If anybody might write a skillful argument (σοφίσματα)[31] or questions of natural history in a letter, he indeed writes, but not a letter' (232). In one of his sample letters, Pseudo-Demetrius (Τύποι 'Επιστολικοί 4) cites the maxim 'know yourself' (τὸ γνῶθι σαυτόν). Gregory of Nazianzus seems to adopt the norm of most letter writers when it comes to the use of *topoi*, avoiding the unadorned (ἀκόσμητα) style 'which allows for no pithy sayings, proverbs or apophthegms, witticisms or enigmas' and warning against 'the undue use of these devices' (*Epistula* 51.5). He also adheres to the use of tropes (but only if done so sparingly and without seriousness) and to the use of antitheses, parisoses and isocola (51.6).[32] Pseudo-Libanius is not as accommodating: 'Mentioning works of history (ἱστοριῶν) and fables (μύθων) will bring charm to letters, as will the use of venerable works (παλαιῶν συγγραμμάτων), well-aimed proverbs (παροιμιῶν εὐστόχων), and philosophers' dogmas (φιλοσόφων δογμάτων), but they are not to be used in an argumentative manner' ('Επιστολιμαῖοι Χαρακτῆρες 50).[33]

Pauline Paraenesis', *JBL* 72 (1953), pp. 238-46, and T.Y. Mullins, 'Topos as a New Testament Form', *JBL* 99 (1980), pp. 541-47, use the term *topos* for a modern formal analysis of the New Testament, rather than an ancient rhetorical one. See the corrective by J.C. Brunt, 'More on *topos* as a New Testament Form', *JBL* 104 (1985), pp. 495-500.

30. Julius Victor (*De Epistolis*) approves of employing a familiar proverb, a text of poetry, or a piece of verse.

31. There is some question whether this term carries the negative sense of 'a sly trick, fallacy, captious argument' or the more positive sense of 'clever device, skillful contrivance' (LSJ, s.v. σόφισμα). In either case the term does denote 'argumentation' in the technical sense, over against the general meaning of the 'style' of a letter.

32. Although Gregory of Nazianzus is discussing 'style' per se, the elements of style he discusses are used as part of *inventio*.

33. Fables and examples from history are also mentioned by the rhetorical

Some letter writers speak of the process of *inventio*. Cicero tells of his difficulty in choosing a topic to write about:

> I have been asking myself for some time past what I had best write to you; but not only does no definite theme suggest itself, but even the conventional style of letter writing does not appeal to me (*Epistulae ad Familiares* 4.13.1).

In a letter to Atticus, Cicero finds himself in a similar dilemma: 'Though now I rest only so long as I am writing to you or reading your letters, still I am in want of subject matter' (*Epistulae ad Atticum* 9.4.1). Cicero realizes that letters need not have one particular subject matter, or any for that matter. Letters written as friendly correspondence reveal this particularly well. 'I have begun to write to you something or other without any definite subject, so that I may have a sort of talk with you' (*Epistulae ad Atticum* 9.10.1). This 'friendly' aspect of the epistolary genre had its own set of *topoi* (cf. Cicero's 'free and easy topics of friendly correspondence' in *Epistulae ad Atticum* 9.4.1). Other possible *topoi* of the epistolary genre include the health wish, prayer formula and the closing greeting.[34] Heikki Koskenniemi identifies three major functions of ancient letters, which perhaps represent 'special *topoi*' for letter writing: maintaining friendship (*philophronesis*), bridging the spatial gap through the sender's presence (*parusia*), and, most relevant to the point made here, carrying on a dialog with the recipient (*homilia*).[35] Regarding *parusia* he states,

> The most important task of the letter was to bring about a feeling of physical togetherness during a period of spatial separation, i.e. to turn ἀπουσία into παρουσία.[36]

---

handbooks in the lists of proofs available to the rhetor. Such discussions of *topoi* appropriate for letters also fall under the rubric of 'style' treated below.

34. These are likely 'special topics', not 'common' ones, being especially applicable to the epistolary genre.

35. H. Koskenniemi, *Studien zur Idee und Phraseologie des griechischen Briefes bis 400 n. Chr.* (Annales Academiae Scientarium Fennicae; Helsinki: Akateeminen Kirjakauppa, 1956), pp. 35-46.

36. 'Es wird nämlich als die wichtigste Aufgabe des Briefes angesehen, eine Form eben dieses Zusammenlebens während einer Zeit räumlicher Trennung darzustellen, d.h. die ἀπουσία zur παρουσία machen' (Koskenniemi, *Studien*, p. 38).

In summary, the epistolary theorists stressed the importance of carefully selecting the topic of one's letter based on the type of letter to be written (cf. Julius Victor, *De Epistolis*). That is, they show concern for how one 'invents'[37] or composes a letter. This concern at least functionally parallels *inventio* in the rhetorical handbooks—viz. the speaker's sensitivity to what he or she should say and how it should be said. The discussions and sample letters provided by the epistolary theorists serve as a type of 'special *topoi*' which could be used by the professional letter writers to invent their own letters. Letter writers, nonetheless, were not confined by rhetorical theory, often failing to invent specific subject matter and neglecting the use of uniquely rhetorical *topoi*.

Rhetorical Arrangement in Epistles

After selecting the type of speech to be delivered, and 'inventing' the subject matter, the rhetor would often proceed to arrange the material into the best possible order. Often the speaker was guided by a predefined outline, which typically contained four points: *exordium* (introduction); *narratio* (the statement of the case under discussion); *confirmatio* (proof of the case); and *conclusio* or *peroratio* (conclusion).[38] This aspect of rhetorical theory, labeled 'arrangement' (*dispositio*), is increasingly being applied to Paul's letters. And yet, the epistolary theorists apparently say nothing about arranging letters after the fashion of the rhetoricians. What they do say, instead, conforms to the standard pattern of letter writing. In part, the reason epistolary theorists do not prescribe rhetorical arrangements to epistolary structures is due to the formulaic traditions long established in letter writing. Therefore, before suggesting any parallels between epistolary structure and rhetorical arrangement, a discussion of epistolary structure is in order.

37. The author of Ἐπιστολιμαῖοι Χαρακτῆρες is familiar with the rhetorical concept of *inventio*, and even uses the Greek term (εὕρεσιν) in his example of a letter of 'inquiry'. There, however, the term is not used in reference to letter writing, but to another form of discourse. This is important in that it shows the author's familiarity with rhetorical theory, and yet demonstrates that he did not use such terminology when describing how to compose letters.

38. To these categories, some Latin rhetoricians (e.g. the author of *Rhetorica ad Herennium*) add the *divisio* (outline of the steps in the argument), which follows the *narratio*, and the *confutatio* (refutation of the opposing arguments), which follows the *confirmatio*.

There are three standard conventions found in the large majority of letters: opening, body and closing.[39] These terms are best understood as spatial locations in the letter which are commonly filled by epistolary formulas. The body, for example, could be filled with a petition, a marriage contract, or a recommendation. The opening could include (among other things) a health wish, greeting and/or thanksgiving formula.[40] The obligatory elements of the opening include the superscription (that is from whom the letter is sent; e.g. Ἀντῶνις Λόγγος) and the adscription (that is, to whom the letter is sent; e.g. τῇ μητρί). Apart from these formulas, other elements used in the opening are discretionary.[41] Even the commonly employed salutation (e.g. χαίρειν) is frequently omitted from the opening, especially in formal contexts (e.g. petitions, complaints).[42] With respect to the

39. This categorization is not solely a modern one. The ancients also recognized that certain elements belonged in certain positions of the letter. For example, Seneca recalls the traditional use of the health wish: 'The old Romans had a custom which survived even into my lifetime. They would add to the opening words of a letter: "If you are well, it is well; I also am well"' (*Epistulae Morales* 16).

40. Although some scholars treat the thanksgiving as part of the body (see e.g. T.Y. Mullins, 'Formulas in New Testament Epistles', *JBL* 91 [1972], p. 381), here it is treated as part of the epistolary opening. Most would admit that it at least serves as a transition from the opening to the body.

41. Two types of letters—'Questions to the Oracle' and 'Letters of Invitation'— often omit the superscription and/or adscription 'since the correspondence was usually local and delivered to the door by a messenger' (J.L. White, 'Epistolary Formulas and Cliches in Greek Papyrus Letters', *SBLSP* 2 [1978], p. 294); see e.g. the invitation in P.Oxy. 1484 (second or third century CE): ἐρωτᾷ σε Ἀπολλώνιος δειπνῆσαι; and the question to the oracle in P.Fay. 133 (58 CE): Σοκωννωκυννῖ Θεῶι μεγαλομαγάλωι. In these cases, the lack of the superscription and/or adscription does not negate the obligatory nature of the formulas; rather, the written formulas would be replaced by oral ones in order to fulfill the obligatory function of identifying the communicants (cf. C.-H. Kim, 'The Payrus Invitation', *JBL* 94 [1975], p. 397). See also, for example, P.Grenf. 1.45 and P.Good. 5, where it has been suggested that the names of the addressees are omitted because the letters are attempts at bribery. Nevertheless, omission of the addressee and recipient is rare, and White ('Epistolary Formulas and Cliches', p. 294) rightly notes that 'it can be demonstrated in almost every instance, however, that these anomalous forms are the result of the letter being either a first draft or copy'. Cf. P.Oxy. 1111; P.Oxy. 1113; P.Petrie 3.46.

42. Examples of letters omitting the greeting include: P.Oxy. 1188 (13 CE); P.Ryl. 166 (26 CE); P.Ryl. 167 (39 CE); P.Ryl. 171 (56–57 CE); P.Oxy. 260 (59 CE); P.Hamb. 5 (89 CE).

body, a host of epistolary materials could fill this slot. Nevertheless, the slot had to be filled.[43] The common epistolary closing of the letter (e.g. ἔρρωσο) is not obligatory, being frequently absent from letters, especially official and business letters (and many literary letters).[44] Most letters, however, contain some element(s) which signal(s) the end of the communication (e.g. closing greetings).

John L. White provides a helpful functional definition of these three sequences in ancient letters. In the opening and closing, 'the keeping-in-touch aspect of letter writing (maintenance of contact), which reveals the general character of the correspondents' relationship toward each other, comes to expression'.[45] In the body, stock phrases express the circumstances which motivated the message of the letter. The bulk of the body however, varies according to the epistolary skills and needs of the particular author. Another way of looking at the opening, body, and closing is that the opening establishes who the participants of communication are and the nature of their current relationship, the body advances the information or requests/commands which the sender wants to communicate, and the closing signals the conclusion or the 'wrap up', so to speak, of the communicative process. Combined, these epistolary functions correspond to the three 'chief operative factors' in the rhetorical speech, viz. speaker, speech, and audience.[46]

Typically, when categories of rhetorical arrangement are applied to Paul's letters, the epistolary opening corresponds to the *exordium*, the body contains at least the *narratio* and *confirmatio* (sometimes other elements), and the epistolary closing corresponds to the *conclusio*. But

---

43. Although White ('Documentary Letter Tradition', p. 92) notes that 'the only epistolary element which cannot be omitted from a letter is the opening', this is only the case for formulaic elements, not for the spatial locations in the letter. Even 'family letters', which White claims 'often have no specific body', have some communicative elements that fill the typical location of the body. In other words, there are no letters that simply have a prescript. Instead, every letter contains some communicative elements after the prescript. However, what fills this region of the body varies, although some patterns exist (e.g. petitions, letters of commendation).

44. F.X.J. Exler, *The Form of the Ancient Greek Letter of the Epistolary Papyri (3rd c. B.C.–3rd c. A.D.): A Study in Greek Epistolography* (repr. Chicago: Ares, 1976), pp. 69, 71.

45. White, *Ancient Letters*, p. 219.

46. Kennedy, *Classical Rhetoric*, p. 21.

the question remains: do the epistolary theorists assign such categories to letters?

In Τύποι 'Επιστολικοί, the author first describes the method by which he has constructed his work. He has set out to describe the various 'styles' (better translated 'class, kind, species') of letters and what distinguishes each style from the other.[47] He then provides a sample of each type, demonstrating how each kind is *arranged* (τῆς ἑκάστου γένους τάξεως). Although his term for 'arrangement' parallels that of the rhetorical handbooks (τάξις, Lat. *dispositio*), the twenty-one letters exemplified in this epistolary handbook are not arranged according to ancient rhetorical categories. They are unmistakeably epistolary categories, hence the name of his work, Τύποι 'Επιστολικοί (epistolary types). Regarding epistolary openings and closings, even Julius Victor, who advocates the use of rhetorical rules in letters (specifically, 'official' letters), maintains that 'the openings and conclusions of letters...should be written according to customary practice' (*De Epistolis* 8–9). He espouses no theory of using the *exordium* and *conclusio* in these parts of the letter.

Certain functional parallels, nevertheless, do exist between the epistolary theorists and letter writers and the customary rhetorical arrangement. In the same way that epistolary openings function to expose the general nature of the relationship between the sender and the recipient (be it positive or negative), so also the *exordium* serves to generate a positive relationship of trust and compliance between the speaker and listener, that is, to build *ethos*. The same may be said of the epistolary closing and the *conclusio*. One type of letter particularly lended itself to creating *ethos*, the friendly type (φιλικός).[48] The epistolary body, which communicated the message(s) of the sender, least parallels the rhetorical categories of, for example, *narratio*, *propositio*, *probatio* and *confirmatio*. However, because the epistolary body was open to various mediums of communication, one must at least concede the possibility of finding a rhetorical arrangement here.

In summary, the three standard epistolary components (opening,

---

47. Cicero is apparently familiar with the various classifications of letters, specifically mentioning a 'letter of exhortation' he had formerly written (*Epistulae ad Familiares* 4.9.1).

48. Pseudo-Demetrius, Τύποι 'Επιστολικοί 1. *Ethos* was not limited to the opening or closing of friendly letters, however. See Cicero's letters, which are replete with language of friendship.

body, closing) share some similarity with the four principal patterns of rhetorical arrangement (*exordium, narratio, confirmatio, conclusio*). But the similarity is functional, not formal. In other words, there is no necessary connection between the basic theory of epistolary structure and the technical teachings about rhetorical arrangement. The similarities may be explained in light of the modern linguistic realization that language is often pragmatically used in different genres to do similar things.[49] More importantly, the epistolary theorists and letter writers say nothing explicit about structuring letters according to a rhetorical arrangement.

Rhetorical Style in Epistles

Rhetoricians' concern for style (λέξις, *elocutio*) was also a concern for the epistolary theorists.[50] This primarily involved questions of grammar, syntax and choice of words. Clarity, figures of speech, metaphors, periodic and continuous syntax, and citations, to name a few, were also discussed under the rubric of style. The epistolary theorists were aware of rhetorical practices and even debated the use of distinctively rhetorical styles in letters.[51] Indeed, the epistolary theorists and letter writers show signs of rhetorical influence mostly in the area of style. For example, although royal letters are largely 'uninfluenced by the rhetorical schools',[52] some letters do exhibit

49. Cf. A.B. du Toit ('Persuasion in Romans 1.1-17', *BZ* 33 [1989], p. 193) who notes that speech-act theory has revealed the use of persuasion in a wide variety of texts. He goes on to argue that 'to force Romans into a rhetorical scheme or to speculate whether this letter belongs to the epideictic or any other rhetorical genre would be methodologically unacceptable'.

50. In Τύποι 'Επιστολικοί, the author sets out to describe the various 'styles' (better translated 'class, kind, species') of letters and what distinguishes each style from the other. This is not to be confused with 'style' as it is being treated here. The former refers to the generic types of letters (i.e. macro-structures), whereas rhetorical and epistolary style, as discussed here, refers to how smaller linguistic elements (i.e. micro-structures) were composed.

51. See also the discussion of rhetorical invention above.

52. C. Bradford Welles, *Royal Correspondence in the Hellenistic Period: A Study in Greek Epigraphy* (repr. Chicago: Ares, 1974), p. 42. Welles goes on to state, 'This neglect of rhetoric is in general characteristic of the royal letters, not only of the purely administrative notes but also of texts of a more "diplomatic" character' (p. 46). This is especially notable since Τύποι 'Επιστολικοί was written as a guide for state secretaries, some of whom apparently did not read it as a work on the

features of style characteristic of them (e.g. antitheses, triads, homoeoteleuton, chiasmus, litotes).[53] Many of the imaginary letters[54] also employ stylistic features found in ancient literary and rhetorical practices. For example, Alciphron (dubbed 'The Rhetor') composed imaginary letters purportedly written by fishermen, farmers, prostitutes and freeloaders. In several of these the real author cites and borrows from other literature (especially from classical authors). The letters attributed to Aelian (entitled ἐκ τῶν Αἰλιανοῦ ἀγροικικῶν ἐπιστολῶν) also echo the voices of the classical era (e.g. Homer, Hesiod, Aristophanes, Demosthenes, and Menander). Aelian is quite aware of his elevated literary style, as is ironically revealed in the following citation from one of his imaginary letters:

> So then do not be contemptuous of farmers; for in them too is wisdom of a sort—not elaborately expressed in speech nor decking itself out with forceful rhetoric, but conspicuous by its silence and confessing its virtue through its very life. If these written words addressed to you are too clever for the country to supply, do not marvel; for we are not Libyan nor Lydian, but Athenian farmers (*Letter* 20).

However, perhaps Fronto is the best model of a letter writer who labored over style, even devoting entire letters to the subject (e.g. letter to Marcus Aurelius, LCL, I, pp. 3-13) while still employing common epistolary conventions (e.g. my lady greets you).[55]

One of the most important discussions of epistolary style is the treatise attributed to Demetrius of Phalerum, *De Elocutione* (Περὶ Ἑρμηνείας), which discusses the 'style' ('expression') appropriate to letter writing. It is partially dependent upon the third book of Aristotle's *Rhetoric* and probably also on Theophrastus's lost work Περὶ λέξεως. The author advocates writing letters according to the 'plain' (ἰσχνότητος) style, which is one of the three kinds or

rhetorical technique of letter writing.

53. See the letters in Welles, *Royal Correspondence*: Ptolemy II to Miletus (14), Antiochus II to Erythrae (15), Seleucus II to Miletus (22), Ziaelas of Bithynia to Cos (25), Ptolemy IV to a provincial governor (30).

54. Imaginary letters resemble little the purposes and practices of most Graeco-Roman letter writing. They are clearly 'literary' in tone and substance. Cf. the love letters of Philostratus (Ἐπιστολαὶ Ἐρωτικαί), which lack all of the common epistolary elements.

55. Fronto, a notable rhetorician of early second century CE, praises the epistolary technique of Cicero (letter to Aurelius Caesar, LCL, I, p. 119).

'characters' of styles (the grand, middle, and plain).[56] However, this kind of style lacks 'ornament and oratorical device',[57] suggesting again that epistolary and rhetorical techniques were not readily conflated. Pseudo-Demetrius also maintains that epistolary style should be flexible and thus, 'it is absurd to build up periods, as if you were writing not a letter but a speech (δίκην) for the law courts' (229). Similarly, Gregory of Nazianzus warns against the abuse of an overly rhetorical style, without excluding its use in letters (*Epistula* 51.5-7).

Although the length of letters was variously debated,[58] 'clarity' (σαφήνεια; a virtue of style) in letter writing was esteemed by many (Gregory of Nazianzus, *Epistula* 51.4; Pseudo-Libanius, Ἐπιστολιμαῖοι Χαρακτῆρες 48–49, quoting Philostratus of Lemnos). Along these lines, Julius Victor juxtaposes a fundamental difference between oratorical style and epistolary style:

> When there is no need to hide anything from others, avoid obscurity more painstakingly in letters than you do in speeches and conversation. For although you can ask someone who is speaking unclearly to elucidate his point, it is impossible to do so in correspondence when the other is absent (*De Epistolis* 19-21).

Although much more could be said about epistolary style (e.g. use of asyndeton, novel expressions, direct address, compliments and jesting), the standard principle of epistolary style seems to be that there was no strictly endorsed stylistic theory. However, letter writers and theorists do seem to agree that letters should be written with the most appropriate style for the context (e.g. Cicero, *Epistulae ad Familiares* 15.21). And this generally involved a style characteristic of dialogue (Cicero, *Epistulae ad Familiares* 7.32.3; 9.21.1; Seneca,

56. See *Rhetorica ad Herennium* 4.11-16. These three kinds of style represent only one theory on the subject. The other theory, developed by Dionysius of Halicarnassus and later continued by Hermogenes, combines various qualities and virtues of style (e.g. clarity, grandeur, beauty, vigor, ethos, verity and gravity) into a more complex scheme (Kennedy, *Classical Rhetoric*, p. 104). Both theories seem to have influenced epistolary theory.

57. Roberts, *Greek Rhetoric and Literary Criticism*, p. 68. Roberts also notes that 'Demetrius never uses the word "rhetoric", and that when he refers to "rhetoricians" there is sometimes a shade of irony or contempt' (p. 68).

58. In support of concise letters see Pseudo-Demetrius, *De Elocutione* 228; in opposition to overly concise letters see Pseudo-Libanius, Ἐπιστολιμαῖοι Χαρακτῆρες 50.

Epistulae Morales 75.1; Pseudo-Demetrius, *De Elocutione* 223), that is, a style conducive to bridging the spatial gap between the sender and the recipient and to establishing a face-to-face atmosphere. Seneca speaks of a friendly, not artificial, setting in which he writes letters: 'I prefer that my letters should be just what my conversation would be if you and I were sitting in one another's company or taking walks together—spontaneous and easy; for my letters have nothing strained or artificial about them' (*Epistulae Morales* 75.1-2).[59]

Letter writers and epistolary theorists, to be sure, recognized the importance of style. This included the recognition that the effectiveness of one's persuasiveness hinged on one's style. For example, Gregory of Nazianzus avows: 'As to clarity (σαφηνείας), everyone knows that one should avoid prose-like (λογοειδές) style so far as possible, and rather incline towards the conversational (λαλικόν)' (*Epistula* 51.4). His basis for this assertion follows:

> Stated briefly, the best and most beautiful letter is written so that it is persuasive to both the educated and uneducated, appearing to the former as written on the popular level and to the latter as above that level, and being immediately understandable.

Two features of epistolary style most parallel rhetorical discussions: clarity and appropriateness for the situation. However, the letter writers and theorists (even those well versed in rhetoric) still differentiate between the epistolary and rhetorical styles.[60] There is no systematic employment of a uniquely rhetorical style in letter writing. Cicero makes this clear in a letter penned to L. Papirius Paetus:

> How do I strike you in my letters? Don't I seem to talk to you in the language of common folk? For I don't always adopt the same style. What similarity is there between a letter, and a speech in court or at a public meeting? Why even in law-cases I am not in the habit of dealing with all of them in the same style (*Epistulae ad Familiares* 9.21.1).

Summary

The above survey of Graeco-Roman epistolary theorists and letter writers reveals both similarities and differences between epistolary

---

59. Contrast Pliny the Younger's letters, which tend to be prose exercises on various subjects, many of which were directed to a public audience (*Letters* 1.1).

60. Quintilian (9.4.19-22), a first century CE rhetorical theorist, also sets the epistolary style apart from the rhetorical. His esteemed *Institutio Oratoria*, interestingly enough, is prefaced by a terse letter to Trypho.

traditions and rhetorical practices. On the one hand, rhetoric is clearly found in letters (see especially Fronto, Pliny, Seneca, Jerome⁶¹). This would be expected especially in letters (e.g. novelistic letters) written as rhetorical exercises that mimic the speeches of celebrated historical persons.⁶² An unknown author unmistakeably displays the presence of rhetoric in letters, writing under the name of the greatest Athenian orator Demosthenes.⁶³ One of the clearest examples of a mixture of the epistolary and rhetorical genres is the first letter to Ammaeus by Dionysius of Halicarnassus—a lengthy argument advocating that Demosthenes did not learn the rules of rhetoric from Aristotle.⁶⁴ In his categorization of the five characters of rational discourse (οἱ τοῦ λόγου χαρακτῆρες), Apollonius of Tyana (letter 19; first century CE) includes the philosopher (φιλόσοφος), historian (ἱστορικός), advocate (δικανικός), writer of epistles (ἐπιστολικός), and commentator (ὑπομνηματικός). Although Apollonius says nothing about the letter writer's use of the rhetor's rules of discourse, he acknowledges the letter writer's concern for argumentation (that is, rational proofs). Cicero divulges the potential persuasiveness of letters when he writes,

> Though my cousin C. Marcellus... not only *advised* me but *urged* me with prayers and entreaties as well, he failed to *convince* me, until your letter definitely *persuaded* me to follow your *advice* and his, in preference to any other (*Epistulae ad Familiares* 4.9.1; italics mine).

Cicero also tells of letters he received from an individual who wrote 'in much the same tone as the public speeches he is said to have made at Narbo' (*Epistulae ad Familiares* 10.33.2).⁶⁵ However, the mere fact

61. See his drawn-out panegyric of the life of virginity (*Letters* 22).
62. Aune, *Literary Environment*, p. 168.
63. Letters 1-4 are some of the best examples of speeches in the epistolary form. The prescripts take the form ΔΗΜΟΣΘΕΝΗΣ ΤΗΙ ΒΟΥΛΗΙ ΚΑΙ ΤΩΙ ΔΗΜΩΙ ΧΑΙΡΕΙΝ ('Demosthenes to the Council and Assembly, greetings'), setting the stage for the epistolary body where Demosthenes attempts to persuade his audience on a particular subject. However, letters 5-6 (one to Heracleodorus and the other to the Council and Assembly) are quite brief and resemble more the attempt at interpersonal dialogue characteristic of ancient letters. Plutarch, *Lives* 20; Quintilian 10.1.107; and Cicero, *Brutus* 121, *Orator* 15, were aware of and likely influenced by Demosthenes' letters.
64. Cf. also his second letter to Ammaeus and his letter to Gnaeus Pompeius.
65. Cf. *Epistulae ad Familiares* 8.16.3; 11.28.8. Plutarch (*Themistocles* 28.1-2)

that he mentions this type of epistolary practice points to its uncustomary nature. Not until Julius Victor, approximately three centuries after Paul, do we see a treatment of letter writing in a rhetorical handbook (*De Epistolis*).[66] On the other hand, the epistolary theorists and letter writers omit several rhetorical categories from discussion. At times they even dissuade the writer from using rhetorical methods. Gregory of Nazianzus, who does not shy away from using rhetoric in epistles, advises against abusing rhetorical devices in letters:

> When the birds were disputing about who should be king, and they came together, each adorned in his own way, the greatest adornment of the eagle was that he did not think that he was beautiful. It is this unadorned quality, which is as close to nature as possible, that must especially be preserved in letters (*Epistula* 51.7).

Seneca as well attempts to distance the letter writer from the orator, without denying the applicability of argumentation to letters:

> Even if I were arguing a point, I should not stamp my foot, or toss my arms about, or raise my voice; but I should leave that sort of thing to the orator, and should be content to have conveyed my feelings toward you without having either embellished them or lowered their dignity (*Epistulae Morales* 75.1-2).[67]

Of course, Paul may have been a lone-ranger of ancient epistolary practices, going off on his own to employ fully the categories of ancient rhetoric in his letters. This is the methodological difficulty of paralleling Paul, or any person, with his or her cultural background. Although Paul skillfully adapted epistolary tradition, when doing so he stayed within the bounds of its categories. And these epistolary traditions apparently make limited use of technical rhetorical categories, even though several letters were written by rhetoricians. In several cases rhetorical technique is altogether avoided. In other cases it is clearly implemented. The question of Paul's literary genre will continue to be debated. But if Paul did use argumentation[68] in his

---

and Diodorus Siculus (11.56.8) felt free to convert a letter of Themistocles recorded in Thucydides (1.137.4) into a speech.

66. Even here, Julius Victor only suggests that rhetorical rules be applied to 'official' (*negotiales*) letters, i.e. letters which are official and serious in nature.

67. In another letter Seneca mentions his preference for philosophy over speech-making (*Epistulae Morales* 14.11).

68. I prefer the term 'argumentation' when speaking in terms of Pauline rhetoric.

letters, and he apparently did, it is doubtful that he addressed his assemblies with the precise rhetoric of the lawyer, or the exact speech of the politician, or the identical style of the public orator.[69] The greatest danger when categorizing Paul's writings is the propensity to prescribe a single typology to an entire letter. Just as the author of Ἐπιστολιμαῖοι Χαρακτῆρες speaks of a 'mixed' (μικτή) type of letter,[70] Paul also enmeshed various forms of epistolary and rhetorical traditions into his letters. To describe, not prescribe (according to ancient rhetorical theory), Paul's argumentative strategy seems to be the safest methodological approach when classifying his letters. One must be wary of doing in genre studies of Paul's letters what James Barr rightly accused scholars of doing in lexical studies of the Bible, viz. 'illegitimate totality transfer'. Just as we should not transfer all the various meanings of a word onto its use in a particular context, so also a complete system of rhetoric should not be imposed *tout de suite* upon our understanding of Paul's distinctive use of the epistolary genre.

Rhetoric in Paul: A Case Study in Philippians

Philippians is striking in view of the lack of rhetorical analysis performed on it. Perhaps this is partly occasioned by several scholars' estimation that Philippians is a composite letter, composed of two or even three different letters. However, Duane Watson argues that, in keeping with Paul's use of rhetorical conventions in his other letters, Philippians exemplifies a rhetorical structure which affirms its unity.[71] An underlying assumption is that Philippians parallels Paul's supposedly confirmed use of ancient rhetoric in his other *Hauptbriefe*. At the culmination of his argument Watson asserts,

The word implies 'a speaker's attempt to persuade a listener', without implying that Paul necessarily employed the rhetorical categories of the technical handbooks.

69. Whereas Seneca's letters contain only minimal epistolary forms, Paul's letters contain several epistolary forms (e.g. superscription, adscription, salutation, thanksgiving, prayer, travelogue, disclosure formula, recommendation, and closing greeting).

70. Pseudo-Libanius, Ἐπιστολιμαῖοι Χαρακτῆρες 45. Cf. P.Bologna 5; 7.6-27 (third or fourth century CE).

71. 'A Rhetorical Analysis of Philippians and its Implications for the Unity Question', *NovT* 30 (1988), pp. 57-88. Pages from this article are cited in the body of the text.

> It may be argued that since Paul utilized the rhetorical conventions of the Graeco-Roman world in his other genuine letters, since the present form of Philippians conforms well to those conventions, and since the proposed interpolations and evidence given for interpolation can be explained by rhetorical convention, than [*sic*] the integrity of Philippians is best assumed (p. 88).

The bulk of Watson's work attempts to divulge the precise rhetorical conventions in the letter, with extensive citation of ancient rhetorical theory. The thoroughness of his work is laudable, and he presents a strong argument in favor of the unity of Philippians by tracing the flow of argument in the text. Nevertheless, in view of the above discussion, his systematic application of rhetorical categories to Philippians is methodologically suspect.[72] Many of his rhetorical explanations of Philippians can be explained from an epistolary perspective (as well as a linguistic one).[73]

Under the subheading *The Species of Rhetoric, the Question, and the Stasis*, Watson categorizes Philippians as deliberative rhetoric, 'intended to advise or dissuade its audience regarding a particular course of action' (p. 59).[74] He admits, nevertheless, that 2.19-30 is

---

72. Watson's rhetorical reading of Philippians is too expansive to offer a complete critique here. Only major sections will be treated. However, other remarks could be directed at his theory of the stasis and rhetorical situation in the letter to the Philippians. For example, Watson claims that the rhetorical question debated in Philippians is 'What is a manner of life worthy of the gospel?' (1.27-30). This is so conceptually broad, however, that it could be applied to any of Paul's letters with apparent success. Indeed, why categorize it as a rhetorical question per se, and not an epistolary theme or topic addressed in the letter? For analysis of the thematic structure of Philippians, without recourse to ancient rhetorical categories, see D.E. Garland, 'The Composition and Unity of Philippians: Some Neglected Literary Factors', *NovT* 27 (1985), pp. 141-73, and R. Russell, 'Pauline Letter Structure in Philippians', *JETS* 25 (1982), pp. 295-306. Cf. the study by R.C. Swift, 'The Theme and Structure of Philippians', *BSac* 141 (1984), pp. 234-54, which is largely an epistolary-literary analysis, but with only one weak comment on the presence of a possible *narratio* in ch. 1 (p. 241).

73. For a comparative analysis of Philippians with 'family letters', see L. Alexander, 'Hellenistic Letter-Forms and the Structure of Philippians', *JSNT* 37 (1989), pp. 87-101. Her work is significant in that it attempts to describe the epistolary body of Philippians, not only the opening and closing.

74. However, see Kennedy, *New Testament Interpretation through Rhetorical Criticism*, p. 77, who classifies Philippians as epideictic rhetoric. That scholars have hardly come to a consensus on the species of any of Paul's letters raises serious

epideictic, which 'lends itself to any attempt to advise and dissuade' (p. 60). The issue is not whether Philippians exhibits features of advice, dissuasion, praise or blame (which it certainly does), but whether such features should be categorized as evidence of Paul's use of ancient rhetorical formulas. We have seen above that epistolary theorists describe types of letters which advise, dissuade, commend and blame. Why not describe Paul's discourses according to epistolary categories, without appealing to the terms of the rhetorical handbooks? Furthermore, Watson's emphasis upon the rhetorical genre of Philippians neglects a primary function of the epistolary genre: the communication of information between spatially separated individuals (*Verbindungsbrief*). For example, Paul's correspondence with the churches at Philippi likely involved several transactions between the two (see e.g. 1.12; 2.26; 4.10). The Philippians would write a letter or send a messenger, and Paul would respond. Part of his response served to inform and to answer questions raised by the recipients' previous correspondence. To overemphasize the rhetorical function of such a response may read more into the communication than is there.

Under the subheading *The Exordium*, Watson classifies Phil. 1.3-26 as an *exordium* with three main functions: 'to obtain audience attention, receptivity, and goodwill' (p. 62). The epistolary thanksgiving and the prayer in Philippians perhaps perform these functions, but that does not suggest that they formally represent an *exordium*. For example, Watson notes that when Paul thanks, rejoices over, and prays for the Philippians he does so to increase goodwill (p. 61). Why not attribute this function to Paul's use of the epistolary thanksgiving and his adaptation of epistolary prayers? For example, the prescript and adscription were commonly expanded so as to reveal the quality of the relationship between the sender and recipient. If there is a functional similarity between the epistolary thanksgivings and prayers of the letter writer and the *exordia* of the rhetor, one cannot conclude that all epistolary thanksgivings and prayers are *exordia*.[75] Watson also

questions about the helpfulness of applying rhetorical species to Paul.

75. In contrast, several thanksgivings direct the reader's attention to the sender's praise of the gods more than beg for the receptivity of the reader: see e.g. BGU 2.423 (second century CE) in which a soldier gives thanks to Serapis (τῷ κυρίῳ Σεράπιδι) for preserving (ἔσωσε) him through a dangerous sea journey. Also note the letter dictated by a Jew who, surprisingly, gives thanks to the gods: CPJ 1.4 (257 BCE) πολλὴ χάρις τοῖς θεοῖς.

remarks, 'Goodwill is obtained by concentrating upon the facts of the case and the persons involved, including the rhetor, the audience, and the opposition' (p. 62). Paul persuades his audience in this manner, however, not only in ch. 1 but throughout the letter, singing praises of his audience (2.25-30 [Epaphroditus—part of the Philippian community]; 4.3, 10, 14) and himself (2.17; 3.4-11, 17-18; 4.11-12, 15-18) as well as chiding certain opponents (ch. 3). Accordingly, one might query: where does the *exordium* in Philippians begin and where does it end? Paul's argumentative style apparently evades strict categorization. Watson even suggests that the epistolary prescript in Philippians (1.1-2) 'functions much like the *exordium*' (p. 65), pointing to elements like the greeting formula, the *topos* of servanthood, and the reference of bishops and deacons (who may have been part of the ecclesiastical problems at Philippi). Watson surely reads more into the text than may be justifiably maintained (although it is interesting to note that he only suggests a 'functional' parallel). Aside from 1 Thessalonians, Philippians has a quite brief Pauline prescript, lacking the epistolary expansions characteristic of Romans, Galatians and 1 Corinthians. Thus Paul probably gave little thought to the persuasive function of his prescript here, rather employing it in light of its typical epistolary function—viz. to introduce the main participants of the communication.[76] Finally, it is interesting to note that Watson subsumes thanksgiving/prayer (1.3-11) and disclosure and travelogue formulas (1.12-26)—and perhaps the prescript (1.1-2)—under the subheading of *exordium*. However, the epistolary prescript and thanksgiving alone may perform the function of the *exordium*, establishing receptivity and introducing the theme(s)[77] of the discourse. Hence the disclosure formula appears somewhat awkward

76. Perhaps the only conscious thought Paul gave to his prescript was the omission of his official title ἀπόστολος, which may signal his desire to address the Philippians as a friend, not a superior, and thus to secure their favor (cf. J.B. Lightfoot, *St Paul's Epistle to the Philippians* [repr. Lynn, MA: Hendrickson, 1981], p. 81). This should not be over-emphasized, since Paul's tone in 3.1–4.3 warns against reading Philippians simply as a friendly, non-authoritative letter (R. Jewett, 'Conflicting Movements in the Early Church as Reflected in Philippians', *NovT* 12 [1970], pp. 372-76).

77. Watson locates the introduction of the letter's main theme in the prayer formula (1.9-11). He does not clarify, however, the relationship between the prayer formula and the supposed *narratio* in 1.27-30.

in Watson's scheme (although elements of *pathos* are evident),[78] but he is forced to take it as part of the *exordium* since the *narratio* (according to Watson) does not begin until 1.27.

The next major rhetorical unit, according to Watson, is the *narratio* in Phil. 1.27-30—an exhortation to a way of life (p. 66). It is 'the proposition that Paul will develop in the remainder of the rhetoric'. Paul attempts to persuade his audience to live an honorable life, exhorting them *to let their manner of life be worthy of the gospel*.[79] Two criticisms may be directed against this rhetorical reading. First, epistles, not just rhetorical discourses, may contain themes (which is essentially what Watson is describing). There is no apparent reason why one could not designate 1.27-30 as the *theme* of Paul's letter, without recourse to rhetorical terminology. Secondly, the precise nature of Paul's supposed *narratio* is unclear. Watson claims,

> Paul's initial exhortation to 'let your manner of life be worthy of the gospel' is repeated in different form as 'stand firm in one spirit, with one mind striving side by side for the faith of the gospel, and not frightened in anything by your opponents' (p. 67).

However, the second form ('stand firm...') is not merely a 'different form', but serves to narrow the meaning of the first form ('let your manner...')—a hyponym (στήκετε) of its superordinant term (πολιτεύεσθε).[80] It represents one of many ways the believer may live his or her life worthy of the gospel. Indeed, the first form is so conceptually broad in meaning that it could legitimately be the theme of any of Paul's letters, making it difficult to envision how it is unique to Paul's letter here. Thus the second imperative (and its adjoining

---

78. Watson claims that the 'matter of an opposing gospel' (p. 62), which serves to obtain the audience's goodwill, appears in vv. 15-18. However, Paul makes it clear that his opponent's gospel is not what opposes him (for Paul recognizes it as the true gospel), but those who proclaim it 'not from pure motives'. Furthermore, these opponents are not the same ones faced by the Philippians and thus would be less relevant to the case at hand. Paul's concern is not with the opponents, but with the continued propagation of the gospel message.

79. In contrast, Alexander ('The Structure of Philippians', p. 95) maintains that 'the point introduced in v. 12 should be taken as part of the central "business" of the letter'. Her reasons include Paul's use of the disclosure formula in v. 12, which frequently introduced the subject matter of ancient letters.

80. Cf. W. Schenk, *Die Philipperbriefe des Paulus* (Stuttgart: Kohlhammer, 1984), pp. 165-66.

participial clauses) is the main thrust of Paul's *narratio*, and must be set against the rest of the letter to see if it is as thematic as Watson claims. The second form is difficult to picture behind the entirety of Paul's rhetoric in Philippians, raising doubts as to its categorization here as part of the *narratio*. *Unity*, which is integral to the second form, is not a significant topic in 2.19–3.21. Similarly, *opponents* are a major topic only in ch. 3 (besides the reference in ch. 1 which, however, occurs before 1.27-30). Phil. 1.27-30 does indeed reflect themes treated in the letter. It does not, however, represent *the* theme of the letter. More probably, there is no one theme in Philippians; instead, Paul's discourse moves from topic to topic, with recognizable cohesive ties between micro-structures but no one overarching rhetorical macro-structure.

The next major rhetorical unit is the *probatio* (2.1–3.21), which follows the *narratio*. 'Here Paul seeks, through the mustering of arguments and examples, to persuade his audience to "live a life worthy of the gospel"' (p. 67). Watson divides the *probatio* into three sections (2.1-11; 2.12-18; 3.1-21), each developing and building upon Paul's larger rhetorical scheme. The same criticism directed at Watson's analysis of the *narratio* applies here. If one defines Paul's rhetorical theme as 'living worthy of the gospel', the remaining discourse would likely fit into such a scheme. In other words, it is difficult to disprove Watson's analysis of the *probatio* based on his broadly defined *narratio*. Phil. 2.1–3.21 partially does serve to prove the supposed *narratio*. But is persuasion the primary function of 2.1–3.21? Regarding this question, Watson's rhetorical categorization of this section as the *probatio* is open to question. His analysis of smaller persuasive units (the use of example, comparison, amplification, for example) is helpful, but some of his grammatical analysis is suspect. For example, the inferential conjunction ὥστε in 2.12 (cf. 4.1) suggests that 2.12-18 flows out of and is dependent on the exemplum of Christ in 2.6-11. Hence it does not by itself embody the second development of Paul's proposition. The life modeled by Christ leads into Paul's exhortation 'to work out your salvation with fear and trembling'. In other words, in view of Christ's example, Paul draws a conclusion. Separating 2.12-18 into its own 'distinct' unit breaks as well as skews the flow of the discourse. This raises questions regarding another of Watson's claims regarding the supposed *probatio*: 'As is often the case, the proposition is reiterated at the beginning of each development' (p. 67). This supposedly occurs in 2.12-13. But if 2.12 is better understood as an exhortation based on the statements of 2.1-11 (as is suggested by the conjunctive ὥστε), then 2.12 is not 'at the beginning' of a rhetorical development as Watson claims (cf. 4.1).[81] More problematic is Watson's handling of 2.19-30—Paul's epistolary commendation of Timothy and Epaphroditus.[82] His categorization of this section as a *digressio*[83] underplays its clear epistolary structure and is difficult to fit into Paul's supposed larger rhetorical purpose. Watson admits that in these sections Paul seeks to inform the Philippians of his future plans for correspondence. But then he sets this epistolary feature aside, highlighting rhetorical elements in the passage. Robert Funk has rightly demonstrated that Paul's epistolary travelogues serve to persuade the audience to obey his directives.[84] Phil. 2.19-30, however, is more than a travelogue seeking compliance from the audience. It contains forms and functions found in epistolary recommendations. Paul praises both Timothy and Epaphroditus, endeavoring to ensure their acceptance by the Philippians. Such persuasive rhetoric is characteristic of a *culture* based on honor and shame. It is not limited to the rhetoric of the professional orators. Furthermore, it is a rhetoric directed at the Philippian audience, but primarily for the sake of Timothy and Epaphroditus, not for the sake

81. Watson strangely links 4.1 with 4.2ff. (pp. 76-77), failing to explain the use of ὥστε as a connective and Paul's shift from speaking to the Philippian community as a group in 4.1 and then addressing them as individuals in 4.2ff. The command to stand firm in the lord (4.1) fits better with the foregone discussion of opponents (3.2-21) than it does with the ensuing exhortation for unity (esp. 4.2-3).

82. Family letters frequently detail the movements of intermediaries (P.Oxy. 1481.8-9; Sel.Pap. 1.112.21-22; P.Mich. 8.466.5-8, 12-17, 35-37; P.Mich. 8.490.5-6). As in Philippians, they show little concern for the placement of such information—a characteristic of informal communication (*Verbindungsbrief*).

83. Quoting Quintilian 4.3.14, Watson notes that the *digressio* is 'the handling of some theme, which must however have some bearing on the case, in a passage that involves digression from the logical order of our speech' (p. 71). It should be noted that *digressio* did not necessarily represent a digression in the argument (Kennedy, *Classical Rhetoric*, p. 94).

84. R.W. Funk, 'The Apostolic Parousia: Form and Significance', in W.R. Farmer, C.F.D. Moule and R.R. Niebuhr (eds.), *Christian History and Interpretation: Studies Presented to John Knox* (Cambridge: Cambridge University Press, 1967), pp. 249-69. Cf. Cicero, *Epistulae ad Familiares* 10.23.7: 'I pray that I may soon be at your side, and so be permitted, by the dutiful discharge of my obligations to you, to enhance the pleasure you take in doing kindnesses to me'.

of Paul's larger rhetorical strategy in his letter. Finally, with regard to the *probatio*, Watson's treatment of Phil. 3.1-21 is helpful overall, especially revealing Paul's use of comparison and contrast (two of the 'common topics' described in the rhetorical handbooks) which point his audience to the 'better' of two ways of life. However, Watson again cites numerous supposed parallels between Paul's style and the categories of the rhetoricians, implying Paul's unmistakeable dependence upon them. In response to this methodology, one might again remark that applying labels to functionally similar language does not prove that there is a formal relationship. The *koine* language itself contained linguistic elements that allowed for comparison and contrast in discourse, without the aid of the rhetorical handbooks.

Finally, Watson categorizes nearly all of the remaining discourse in Philippians as a *peroratio* (4.1-20). This rhetorical section serves a twofold purpose: recapitulation (*repetitio*, 4.1-9) and emotional appeal (*adfectus*, 4.10-20) (p. 76). Regarding the supposed *repetitio*, although Paul does touch upon themes in 4.1-9 which occur throughout the letter (especially 4.1-4), 4.5-9 contains several elements new to Paul's discussion: for example, 'let your gentleness[85] be known to all', 'the Lord is near', 'do not be anxious', 'make your requests known to God in your prayers with all thankfulness',[86] and 'the peace of God'. The virtues listed in v. 8 are also new to the discourse. Furthermore, the specific nature of Paul's exhortation in v. 3 suggests that Paul is not recapitulating past arguments, but continuing to advance new information. Regarding the supposed *adfectus*, according to rhetorical strategy, it should appeal to the emotions of the audience. In part this section does just that. Paul begins in v. 10 by lauding the Philippians for assisting him in the work of the gospel (see also vv. 10, 14-16, 18). However, Watson admits that Paul's *adfectus* is 'only a veiled attempt to elicit pathos' (p. 78). Paul makes it clear that he could

85. Watson (p. 77) translates ἐπιεικές with 'forebearance', claiming that the term summarizes several concepts in 1.27-30 (στήκω, συναθλέω, ἀγών). The word is probably better understood in its typical sense of 'gentleness, graciousness, equitability'. It is often used with reference to persons known for their fairness and equity to others (cf. P.T. O'Brien, *Commentary on Philippians* [NIGTC; Grand Rapids: Eerdmans, 1991], p. 487). Cf. 1 Tim. 3.3; Tit. 3.2; Jas 3.17; 1 Pet. 2.18.

86. 'Thanksgiving, joy, rejoicing' is a subject found throughout Philippians; but it is not the main point of the clause here, as its grammaticalization in a prepositional phrase suggests.

manage without the Philippians: 'I have learned to be self-sufficient in all circumstances' (v. 11).[87] Paul is apparently more concerned about preserving his own reputation than with the rhetorical effect of his statements upon the audience. Indeed, he seems to be breaking with conventional rhetorical practice in the *peroratio*.

Conclusion

Many rhetorical analyses of Paul's letters are difficult to criticize, in that they often accurately describe persuasive functions of the text. However, one should criticize any unjustified application of ancient rhetorical categories to describe Paul's letters. The recent interest in the rhetorical form of Paul's letters has produced a snow-ball effect, in which all of Paul's writings supposedly comprise full-blown rhetorical treatises. I am not denying argumentative elements in Paul's letters. I am, however, advocating methodological prudence. *Functional* similarities between Paul's argumentative style and the rhetorical handbooks do not prove a *formal* relationship between them.[88] In 1928, the distinguished classical scholar, W. Rhys Roberts, wrote of Paul's rhetorical style:

> It is well thus briefly to remind ourselves that, among the early Christians, there were many writers, including St. Paul himself, who knew and appreciated ancient Greek literature, though concerning themselves little with formal rhetoric and literary criticism.

One might agree with Roberts's general statement, but it would be shortsighted to assert that there is no trace of ancient rhetoric in Paul's letters.[89] No literary genre, including that of the epistle, exists in isolation. Genres exist in an intertextual system, each genre containing features common to other genres.[90] However, the larger

87. Such claims would have been striking in a context where reciprocity was valued and expected.

88. This does not render the rhetorical handbooks useless for reading Paul. Both ancient and modern theories are important heuristic devices for analyzing Paul's world; yet neither is infallible in the hands of modern scholars.

89. The sizeable length of Paul's letters (aside from Philemon) suggests some relationship with the 'literary' letters. In addition, the argumentative *functions* served by *pathos* and *ethos* occur frequently in letters (see e.g. Cicero, *Epistulae ad Familiares* 1.4.3; 1.5.4), including Paul's.

90. For example, the Christian homily seems to have been influenced by Stoic

evidence from the letter writers and epistolary theorists suggests that Paul probably did not incorporate a *system* of ancient rhetoric into the epistolary genre. Reading Paul from the perspective of ancient rhetorical categories can prove beneficial. Similarly, modern literary and sociological analyses surely shed light on Paul's literary strategy and his world view. Nevertheless, Paul did not compose his letters according to the principles of modern literary criticism nor did he conceptualize his world according to the categories of modern sociology. And just because ancient rhetorical categories are 'ancient', one cannot conclude that Paul fused the epistolary and rhetorical genres. Perhaps Paul was familiar with some of the rhetorical conventions of his day. Perhaps he did implement some of these in his use of the epistolary genre. But to claim that all or most of his writings are undeniable examples of the classical rhetorical genre is, as argued above, methodologically dubious.[91] And even worse, this perhaps skews Paul's usage of the epistolary genre. To quote a more recent scholar,

> Early Christian letters tend to resist rigid classification, either in terms of the three main types of oratory or in terms of the many categories listed by the epistolary theorists... Attempts to classify one or another of Paul's

and Cynic forms of diatribe (Kennedy, *Classical Rhetoric*, p. 126).

91. J.R. Levinson ('Did the Spirit Inspire Rhetoric? An Exploration of George Kennedy's Definition of Early Christian Rhetoric', in Watson [ed.], *Persuasive Artistry*, pp. 25-40) has usefully traced Kennedy's developing thought regarding a definition of early Christian rhetoric. Early on, Kennedy maintained that early Christian rhetoric was based on 'grace, authority, and proclamation rather than the modes of persuasion of Aristotelian rhetoric known as *ethos*, *pathos*, and *logos*' (p. 26). Later Kennedy espoused that some early Christians utilized classical rhetorical persuasion and others developed a 'radical' Christian rhetoric originating from the wisdom of the Spirit. Levinson, although agreeing that a radical Christian rhetoric existed (one which paralleled early Jewish thought about the Spirit), contends that Mark 13 and 1 Corinthians 1–2—Kennedy's proof texts—do not support such a view (although I doubt that they say nothing about the nature of New Testament rhetoric). He maintains, for example, that Paul was 'a masterful proponent of rhetoric' (p. 40). Levinson does not clarify, however, the exact nature of Paul's rhetoric, only stating that 'the true rhetoric to which Paul adheres is the studied rhetoric of the sage who pores over ancient wisdom and turns of phrase, and who is renowned for instructive and persuasive speech'. This is hardly a precise statement about Paul's use of classical rhetorical categories.

letters as either *judicial* or *deliberative* or *epideictic* (or one of their sub-types) run the risk of imposing external categories on Paul and thereby obscuring the real purpose and structure of his letters.[92]

A verdict concerning a definition of the Pauline genre is far from final. However, in view of the above analysis, some conclusions may be reached regarding the justification of using ancient rhetorical categories to interpret Paul's letters. Regarding the stasis of fact (*an sit*), Paul probably did not employ a system of ancient rhetoric to compose his letters. Regarding the stasis of definition (*quid sit*), although Paul's letters have an undeniable argumentative function, rough functional parallels with classical rhetorical categories do not necessarily imply formal equivalents. Each supposed parallel requires explicit formal and functional definition.[93] Regarding the stasis of quality (*quale sit*), if rhetorical elements do appear in Paul's letters, one must allow for the possibility that Paul's usage may be functionally related to, but not formally (and consciously) based upon, the ancient rhetorical practices.

92. Aune, *Literary Environment*, p. 203.

93. Part of the problem here depends on which system of ancient rhetorical theory one uses to describe argumentation in a text. Does one inspect Paul's possible use of ancient rhetorical categories in an eclectic way or only on the basis of the rhetorical categories of his day?

PERSUASION IN PHILIPPIANS 4.1-20

A.H. Snyman

1. *Introduction*

In recent years rhetorical criticism within New Testament scholarship has developed from epistolographical studies which were mainly concerned with the conventional structure of a letter. This can be seen in the attempts of prominent rhetorical critics to prove relationships between various parts of a text. It started with the pioneering work of H.D. Betz: his article in *NTS* 21 (1975: 353-79) and especially his 1979 commentary. The tendency was followed by Brinsmead (1982: 57-87), Hester (1984, 1986), Hübner (1984), Jewett (1986), Berchman (1987), Hall (1987) and others.

That arrangement of material is an important part of the rhetorical process cannot be denied. In any handbook on classical rhetorical theory, *dispositio* is described as the second stage in the act of composing a speech (Lausberg 1960: 241-47; Corbett 1965: 273-383; Brandt 1970: 49-69). The other parts, however—especially *inventio* and *elocutio*—are at least as important as *dispositio* and should not be neglected in any rhetorical analysis. In fact, *inventio* can be regarded as the most important phase in classical rhetoric. No sensible *dispositio* or *elocutio* is possible without *inventio* (Botha 1991: 175).

Part of the *inventio* phase is the discovery of the so-called proofs, either external (the evidence of witnesses or of documents, for example), or internal (which the author himself invents). According to Aristotle there are only three modes of artistic (internal) proof: ethos (the credibility that the author is able to establish in his writing, that is, his authority), logos (the logical argument found in the discourse, especially inductive and deductive reasoning) and pathos (the emotional reactions of the audience) (Kennedy 1984: 14-16). Although they constitute only one aspect of the first stage in the rhetorical process, one has the impression that Kennedy regards the ways in which these three categories are used as the main concern of rhetorical criticism. This impression is confirmed by the application of his proposal for rhetorical criticism to various New Testament passages (1984: 39-156), as well as by his own remark in the last chapter of his book: 'The Bible speaks through ethos, logos and pathos, and to understand these is the concern of rhetorical analysis' (1984: 159).

In this article, then, the focus will be on the modes of internal proof employed in Phil. 4.1-20, thereby addressing questions such as: what is the persuasive force of this section within its broader textual context? And how does it persuade? The subject will be dealt with as follows.

Since Phil. 4.1-20 forms the conclusion of the letter (Watson 1988: 76-79), I first want to make some comments on the functions of a peroration. This will be followed by a description of three important categories under *inventio*, namely the exigence which Paul seeks to counter in the letter, its rhetorical genre and its stasis. The next step in the rhetorical process is *dispositio*, in which the relation between Phil. 4.1-20 and the letter as a whole is determined. Some remarks on the style of the passage (*elocutio*) will be made as part of the main aim of the article, which is an exposition of the ways in which ethos, logos and pathos are employed in Phil. 4.1-20.

2. *The Functions of a Peroration*

Greek and Latin rhetoricians used certain significant terms to describe the conclusion. The most common Greek term was *epilogos*, which means 'something said in addition'. Latin used the word *peroratio*, which suggested a rounding off of one's plea (Corbett 1965: 302). According to Lausberg (1960: 236) it has two functions: *Gedächtnis-auffrischung und Affektbeeinflüssung* (to refresh the memory and to elicit an affective response). The first is accomplished by a review of the main topics discussed (*enumeratio* or *anakephalaiosis*), the second by arousing the emotions of the audience to take action or to make judgment (Kennedy 1984: 48). For Kennedy (1984: 10-11) these two functions are universal, as is the case with all the categories and functions described in Greek and Latin handbooks on rhetoric.

The peroration usually stands in the final position in the discourse. It is the part that is left with the readers, the part that is meant to linger on in their minds. Accordingly, this is the part where an author tends to display his stylistic eloquence and emotional intensity (Corbett 1965: 303). A discourse may even have several minor perorations, each one being intended to round off an important subsection of the whole, for instance at the end of a *digressio* (Lausberg 1960: 240). Paul often signals the end of a major section by inserting such a per-orative conclusion. Examples are Rom. 4.23-25, 8.31-39 and 11.33-36. Unlike the peroration at the end of the whole letter, it seems as if perorations at the conclusion of smaller units may omit one of the functions described above. Rom. 8.31-39, for example, lacks a reca-pitulation of the main points discussed in Romans 5–8 and only con-centrates on emotional appeals (Snyman 1988: 228). If this impression of Paul's usage of perorations is correct, it offers a good example of the way in which he—as an eclectic writer—used rhetorical means to achieve the results and effects he desired.

3. *On Inventio and Dispositio in Philippians*

Inventio

Watson (1988: 58-60) gave a sound and responsible exposition of the rhetorical situation, the genre and the stasis of Philippians.

The *exigence* which Paul seeks to counter in the letter is the appear-ance of a rival gospel in Philippi. This gospel may be attributed to Judaizing Christians, who espouse the observance of circumcision (3.2), food laws (3.19) and salvation based upon good works (3.2-11, 19). Their influence is increasing, creating tensions in the community, pride in the works of the law and confusion as to the correct approach to faith (Watson 1988: 59). Because the exigence will remain, Paul is warning his readers to be aware of their continued influence. Moreover, he is confident that the Philippians will do what he exhorts them to do. The letter clearly indicates that his authority is by no means threatened by the Judaizers. On the contrary: he relies primar-ily upon his own ethos to prove the validity of his exhortations (see below).

As to the three species of rhetoric, Watson classifies Philippians as deliberative, because

(i)   its intention is to advise and dissuade its audience
         about a particular course of action;
(ii)   this course is to be observed immediately and is to
         characterize their future activity as well;

(iii)   the letter as a whole concerns itself with what is to the
              advantage or disadvantage of the audience; and
(iv)   the deliberation in the *probatio* is constituted by example
              and comparison of example (1988: 59-60).

Most important for our purpose is the *stasis* of the letter. The need or
the exigence of a situation concretizes in the *questio* or the question of
the situation. The question dominates the rhetorical situation and thus
determines its *stasis* (Vorster 1991: 54). Of the four types of *staseis*
identified in classical rhetoric, Watson (1988: 60) is convinced that
Philippians is an example of the *status qualitatis*. This type of *stasis*
means there is a need to indicate that a certain line of action would be
the correct one to follow. The question to which Philippians is the
response can be phrased as: 'what is a manner of life worthy of the
gospel?' The emphasis is on the quality of the deed, the characteristics
of a life worthy of the gospel.

Dispositio

The following exposition of the *dispositio* of the letter, proposed by
Watson (1988), is important for determining the position and function
of Phil. 4.1-20 in the letter as a whole:

> *Exordium* (1.3-26)
> *Narratio/Propositio* (1.27-30)
> *Probatio* (2.1–3.21) (The *probatio* is subdivided into three distinct
> sections, namely 2.1-11, 2.12-18 and 3.1-21.)
> *Peroratio* (4.1-20)

The basic proposition of the letter is stated in 1.27: to live a life
worthy of the gospel. It is reiterated at the beginning of two sections
of the *probatio*, namely 2.1-4 and 2.12-13, as well as in the first part
of the *peroratio* (4.1-9). In the second part of the peroration (4.10-
20), Paul seeks to elicit pathos in order to increase the Philippians'
adherence to the exhortations in 4.1-9. Watson (1988: 77-78) thus
divides the peroration into two distinct sections: the *repetitio* (4.1-9)
and the *adfectus* (4.10-20). To this division of the peroration I want to
return below.

Brandt (1970: 51) has indicated that the beginning and the end of a
letter or discourse have the function of defining or stating the
problem, that is, what the letter is all about. One of the main functions
of the *peroratio* is the *recapitulatio*, which functions to refresh the
memory of the readers. Watson (1988: 77) convincingly links the first

part of the *peroratio* to the *propositio* and other main themes in the letter:

> The admonition in 4.1 'to stand firm' (*stekete*) corresponds
> to the proposition in 1.27 'so that... I will hear
> that you are standing firm...' (*stekete*).

> In 4.2-3 the admonition to Euodia and Syntyche 'to agree
> as sisters in the Lord' (*to auto phronein*) is reiterated
> from 1.27 'standing firm with one common purpose' (*mia
> psuchei*).

> The phrase in 4.3 'worked hard with me to spread the gospel'
> (*en toi euangelioi sunethlesan*) corresponds to 'fighting
> together for the faith of the gospel' (*sunathlountes tei
> pistei tou euangeliou*) in 1.27, as well as to 2.22 'how he
> (Timothy) and I... have worked together for the sake of the
> gospel' and 2.25 'Epaphroditus who has worked and fought by
> my side'.

> The theme of joy/rejoicing in 1.4, 2.2, 2.17,18, 3.1, etc.,
> recurs in the admonition of 4.4, while the admonition to
> forbearance (*epieikes*) in 4.5 summarizes several terms in
> 1.17-30 such as 'standing firm' (*stekō*), 'striving'
> (*sunathleō*) and 'struggling' (*agōn*).

> As a whole, 4.5-7 'reiterates the proposition of 1.27-28 that
> forbearance and striving for the gospel are necessary
> because they are a witness in light of the parousia, and
> that the Philippians need not fear or be anxious because God
> is with them' (Watson 1988: 77).

> Finally Watson links the virtue list in 4.8-9 to the topos
> of purity (*hagnos*) in 2.15, while the exhortation in 4.9,
> namely to imitate Paul and use his life as an example,
> recapitulates the thought of 3.2-17.

In the next section I want to expand somewhat on Watson's convincing analysis, and to suggest refinements on two points. My first problem with his otherwise excellent proposal is that he does not regard the thanksgiving in 1.5 or the reference to Epaphroditus in 2.25-30 as part of the *recapitulatio*. Thanksgiving does, however, occur in Phil. 4.10-20, which is not part of Watson's *recapitulatio* (4.1-9). I accept that Phil. 4.10-20 is also a reiteration of an important theme in the letter (thanksgiving) and that the *recapitulatio* should not be restricted to 4.1-9 alone.

The second problem has to do with pathos (*adfectus*) as a mode of persuasion in the peroration. According to Watson, the function of Phil. 4.10-20 is to create pathos, which the classical rhetoricians regard as a distinct part of the *peroratio*. As a distinct part, pathos is divided into two sections, designated as *indignatio* and *conquestio* (Watson 1988: 78). This classical division creates a problem for Watson, because he finds that *indignatio* is absent from 4.10-20. I hope to prove that pathos is a mode of persuasion throughout the peroration, as is the case with logos and ethos. One should not restrict recapitulation to one section of the peroration only, as if recapitulation on the one hand and pathos on the other constitute separate and watertight sections. Granted that the purpose of his article is to prove that Philippians (as it stands) is a single rhetorical unit and can be analysed as an integrated whole (1988: 58), I venture to suggest that Watson's analysis of the peroration is an example of forcing New Testament material into categories of classical rhetoric. He could have proved his point just as well without the rigid use of these categories from the classical *peroratio*.

4. *Modes of Persuasion in Philippians 4.1-20*

Ethos
(a) According to Watson (1988: 64-65), the example of Paul's life as described in 1.12-26 serves as a basis for his exhortation in 4.9: 'Put into practice what you learnt and received from me, both from my words and from my actions'. His life provides the Philippians with a good example of a life worthy of the gospel in spite of opposition, which is the *propositio* of the letter as a whole (1.27-30). The exhortation of Paul to his readers to imitate himself is a persuasive factor in the peroratio. It is a clear-cut example of Perelman's *argumentum ad vericundiam*:

> The influence of the person on the manner in which his acts are received is exercised through the medium of prestige, which is the quality that leads others to imitate his acts... People imitate his behaviour and adopt his opinions. From this comes the importance of the argument from authority, where the prestige of a person or a group is used to gain acceptance of a thesis (1982: 94).

(b) Another way in which a person is constructed or ethos created is by referring to what happened in the past (Vorster 1991: 185). In

Phil. 4.10-20 (especially 14-18) Paul thanks the Philippians for their support when he left Macedonia to fulfill his role of preaching the Good News (4.15), as well as when he was working in Thessalonica (4.16). The intention of these geographical designations is not to provide exact historical or geographical information (cf. the explicit 'You Philippians know very well that...' in 4.15), but to indicate that his role has been fulfilled. He has carried out the task to which God called him. The gifts of the Philippians, which Epaphroditus brought him, were therefore not only gifts to him in person; they were 'like a sweetsmelling offering to God, a sacrifice which is acceptable and pleasing to him' (4.18). The Philippians helped him to carry out his God-given task; by giving to him, they were giving to God himself. They, the Philippians, played a part in his role as apostle.

The interrelationship of a divine plan, geographical spheres of work and the Philippians' support in the past which define Paul's role, are all elements in the construction of his person (Vorster 1991: 201). Various actions in the past, interpreted within a metaphysical system, contributed to the creation of a certain image of Paul. In this way he substantiates his right to exhort them to live a life worthy of the gospel.

Logos

(a) There is a single example of an *enthymeme* in the peroration, namely in 4.3. This is to be expected, since inductive and deductive reasoning are normally not a feature of perorations. Except in a tightly reasoned argument, speakers or writers usually do not employ all the parts of an *enthymeme* or logical syllogism, namely a major premise, a minor premise and a conclusion. One of the parts is generally assumed or suppressed. The word 'for' (*gar* or *hoti*) is usually the indication of an *enthymeme* (Kennedy 1984: 16-17).

The TEV's translation of Phil. 4.3 reads: 'And you, too, my faithful partner, I want you to help these women [Euodia and Syntyche]; for they have worked hard with me to spread the gospel'. With all the elements spelled out, the logical syllogism behind this verse reads as follows:

Major premise: People who further the gospel must be helped.
Minor premise: Euodia and Syntyche further the gospel.
Conclusion: Euodia and Syntyche must be helped.

The conclusion is formed by deleting the phrases common to both major and minor premises (Botha 1991: 219). The basis of acceptance of the major premise here is once again Paul's person, his ethos.

(b) By the hypotactic constructions in 4.8-9 Paul is effectively guiding his readers towards what he wants them to admit: 'Finally, brothers, whatever is true, whatever is noble, whatever is right, whatever is pure, whatever is lovely, whatever is admirable—if anything is excellent or praiseworthy—think about such things (*tauta logizesthe*). Whatever you have learned or received or heard from me, or seen in me, put it into practice (*tauta prassete*).' Perelman and Olbrechts-Tyteca (1969: 158) describe the hypotactic construction as

> the argumentative construction par excellence...Hypotaxis creates frameworks, constitutes the adoption of a position. It controls the reader, forces him to see particular relationships...and takes its inspiration from well-constructed legal reasoning.

(c) The following stylistic devices are used to further the logical coherence in parts of the peroration, thereby contributing to its persuasive force:

> The repetition of the same logical relation (cause–effect) between 4.2-7 and 4.8-9, by which the link between the two passages is strengthened:
>
> 4.2-6   List of exhortations   (Cause)
> 4.7   God's peace will be with you (Effect)
> 4.8   List of exhortations   (Cause)
> 4.9   God's peace will be with you (Effect)

> The virtue list in 4.8-9 exhibits *epanaphora* (with *hosa*), *asyndeton* and amplification by accumulation, thereby making the virtues seem more numerous (Watson 1988: 77). *Epanaphora*, as the repetition of the same lexical unit, has a cohesive effect.

> 4.11-12 has the structure of generic statements, followed by a series of specifications. The first generic statement is at the end of v. 11: 'I have learnt to be satisfied with what I have'. Then two specifications follow at the beginning of v. 12: 'I know what it is to be in need (*oida kai tapeinousthai*). And I know what it is to have plenty (*oida kai perisseuein*).' These two specifications have the same syntactic structure and the same number of syllables, thereby forming an *isocolon*. One is not merely to count the syllables of an *isocolon*, but to appreciate their balanced effect. The *isocolon* here might serve to underline the fact that Paul is satisfied with whatever he has. He is content, irrespective of lack or abundance.

A second generic statement follows, namely: 'I have learnt the secret of being content in any and every situation' (4.12), with four specifications at the end of the verse. All four of them have the same syntactic structure (*kai* plus infinitive). The function of this structure is to link the four specifications.

Careful analysis might well reveal more stylistic devices, but those listed above are adequate to make the point that sentences and phrases are structured in such a way that they play a role in persuading the readers to admit what the author wants them to admit. The various parallelisms (syntactic and semantic) establish patterns, which further the logical coherence of the discourse. These patterns, as well as certain well-known figures of speech, thus become functional devices of persuasion: they tie verses and pericopes together, and serve to underline the semantic content of what is said.

Pathos

(a) Identification with the implied readers is the first important way of creating pathos in Phil. 4.1-20. That Paul identifies with his readers here is evident from the following:

He addresses them as 'my brothers' (*adelphoi mou*) and 'my joy and crown' (*chara kai stephanos mou*) in 4.1.

The strong bond between author and implied readers is also indicated by the use of various 'in-group' identity markers such as 'brothers' (*adelphoi*), 'beloved' (*agapetoi*) and 'you whom I long for' (*epipothetoi*) in 4.1. This in-group consciousness is strengthened by reference to the other churches, who did not share with Paul his profits and losses 4.15. The Philippians were the only church to help him in his need.

The notion of identification by means of cooperation is suggested by the frequent use of the prefix *sun-* in 4.3: 'yoke-fellow' (*suzuge*), 'who have contended at my side' (*sunethlesan*) and 'fellow-workers' (*sunergoi*). This cooperation implies the sharing of a mutual faith, the confirmation of their mutual value-system. Against the Judaizers, who regard the observation of Jewish laws as a manner of life worthy of the gospel, Paul and his readers agree that such a life should be characterized by values such as love, fellowship, mutual concern, and a single-minded purpose to live for the gospel, all in reliance upon the righteousness of Christ (Watson 1988: 60).

Paul's identification with his readers in a common struggle is portrayed by metaphors borrowed from an athletic contest or fighting in a war (Loh and Nida 1977: 126-27 on *sunethlesan*). These metaphors impart reality to the discourse, and Brandt (1970: 224) is of the opinion that this—in itself—is a significant means of creating pathos:

> The first [way to make a pathetic appeal] is to lower the level of abstraction of one's discourse. Feeling originates in experience, and the more concrete writing is, the closer it is to experience, the more feeling is implicit in it... The tropes that appear at the end of major sections are designed to elicit from the reader a full human response to the point made by making its implications sensuous.

Paul and the implied readers thus belong to the same 'in-group'. By his identification with them he not only secures their goodwill, but also confirms their mutual faith.

(b) The goodwill of the readers is also obtained by showing in what honourable esteem they are held. He addresses them as his 'joy and crown' (*chara kai stephanos mou*). The term *stephanos* 'refers to the crown awarded to a victor in Greek athletic games, or to the wreath placed on the head of a guest at a feast. It is a symbol of victory, pride, happiness and honor' (Loh and Nida 1977: 124).

(c) Giving an account of their acts in the past and thanking them for their support (4.10-20) also serve to gain the goodwill of the readers. When this is ensured, Paul can more convincingly encourage the readers to stand firm in the Lord, to live a life worthy of the gospel in spite of opposition.

(d) The future-orientated nature of the promises in 4.7 ('and the peace of God, which transcends all understanding, will guard your hearts and minds in Christ Jesus'), 4.9 ('And the God of peace will be with you') and 4.19 ('And my God will meet all your needs according to his glorious riches in Christ Jesus') also serve to create pathos. These promises are part of the deliberative nature of the peroration. Pathos inheres in the readers, and its commonest form in the New Testament 'is the promise of eternal life or the threat of damnation' (Kennedy 1984: 15). The reader wants to feel that there is some worthiness in him, something which will be rewarded in future. The content of what is said may thus in itself arouse emotion with the readers.

To summarize, the questions posed at the beginning were: what is the persuasive force of Phil. 4.1-20 within its broader textual context? And how does it persuade? In answering these questions one must, of course, remember that the modes discussed are not distinct categories in the process of speaking or reading. As such they are also simultaneously at work in the act of persuasion. While one is actually performing an analysis of a discourse, however, it is academically convenient—and sound—to distinguish the terms as was done above.

As to the first question, Watson has argued convincingly that 4.1-9 is a recapitulation of the main themes in the letter, in compliance with the major function of any peroration. I am convinced, however, that 4.10-20 also recapitulates an important topos in Philippians, namely thanksgiving, referred to in 1.5 and 2.25-30. In an attempt to answer the second question, the three modes of persuasion were studied and illustrated. It was found that all three are at work throughout the peroration. Paul constructs his person in such a way that it substantiates his right to exhort the readers to live a life worthy of the gospel. Logical argumentation, including functional stylistic devices, is used as a means of persuasion in for example 4.3, 8-9 and 11-12. And pathos is created by an identification between Paul and his readers, by obtaining their goodwill in various ways, and by the future-orientated nature of the promises in 4.7, 9 and 19.

Considering his use of ethos, logos and pathos in 4.1-20, it is clear that Paul succeeds in persuading his readers to adhere to his exhortations as a way to meet the exigence facing them.

5. Conclusion

Classical rhetoric with all its categories can be of help in understanding any written document, provided that it is not followed rigidly but rather used as a frame of reference for empirical study. This is the way in which the rhetorical categories have been used in this article. The various stages in the rhetorical process and the three modes of persuasion are universal concepts, as Kennedy argued so convincingly in the first chapter of his book (1984: 10-11). This being the case, classical rhetorical theory must be employed as 'a fountainhead of insight, rather than as a controlled stream' (Olbricht 1990: 33). In analysing any document, we need to draw upon whatever conventions and later rhetorical insights may be of help—provided that we do not force any rhetorical system upon a text; the more so, since a uniform or unified system of classical rhetoric has never existed, despite the efforts of many modern studies of classical rhetoric to present such a system: 'The existence of the rhetorical handbooks notwithstanding, it is well to remember that ancient rhetoric, in its rules as well as the manifestations of those rules, was extremely fluid' (Kraftchick 1990: 61; see also Wuellner 1991: 171 and Botha 1991: 167).

By using rhetorical categories in this way, the student of the New Testament is able to appreciate the practical and powerful aspects of the text he is privileged to study.

Bibliography

Berchman, R.M.
    1987   'Galatians (1.1-5): Paul and Greco-Roman Rhetoric', in J. Neusner and E.S. Frerichs (eds.), *New Perspectives on Ancient Judaism* (New York: University Press of America): 1-15.

Betz, H.D.
    1975   'The Literary Composition and Function of Paul's Letter to the Galatians', *NTS* 21: 353-79.
    1979   *Galatians: A Commentary on Paul's Letter to the Churches in Galatia* (Philadelphia: Fortress Press).

Botha, J.
    1991   'Reading Romans 13: Aspects of the Ethics of Interpretation in a Controversial Text (unpublished DTh dissertation, University of Stellenbosch).

Brandt, W.J.
    1970   *The Rhetoric of Argumentation* (New York: Bobbs-Merrill).

Brinsmead, B.H.
    1982   *Galatians—A Dialogical Response to Opponents* (SBLDS, 65; Chico, CA: Scholars Press).

Corbett, E.P.J.
    1965   *Classical Rhetoric for the Modern Student* (New York: Oxford University Press).

Hall, R.G.
    1987   'The Rhetorical Outline for Galatians: A Reconsideration', *JBL* 106: 277-87.

Hester, J.D.
    1984   'The Rhetorical Structure of Galatians 1.11–2.14', *JBL* 103: 223-33.
    1986   'The Use and Influence of Rhetoric in Galatians 2.1-14', *TZ* 42: 386-408.

Hübner, H.
    1984   'Der Galaterbrief und das Verhaltnis von antiker Rhetorik und Epistolographie', *TLZ* 109: 241-50.

Jewett, R.
    1986   'Following the Argument of Romans', *WW* 6: 381-89.

Kennedy, G.A.
    1984   *New Testament Interpretation through Rhetorical Criticism* (Chapel Hill: University of North Carolina Press).

Kraftchick, S.J.
1990   'Why Do the Rhetoricians Rage?' in T.W. Jennings (ed.), *Text and Logos: The Humanistic Interpretation of the New Testament* (Atlanta: Scholars Press): 55-79.

Lausberg, H.
1960   *Handbuch der literarischen Rhetorik* (Munich: Heuber).

Loh, I.J., and E.A. Nida
1977   *A Translator's Handbook on Paul's Letter to the Philippians* (Helps for Translators; New York: United Bible Societies).

Olbricht, T.H.
1990   'An Aristotelian Rhetorical Analysis of 1 Thessalonians', in D.L. Balch, E. Ferguson and W. Meeks (eds.), *Greeks, Romans, and Christians: Essays in Honor of Abraham J. Malherbe* (Minneapolis: Fortress Press, 1990): 216-36.

Perelman, C.
1982   *The Realm of Rhetoric* (Notre Dame: University of Notre Dame Press).

Perelman, C., and L. Olbrechts-Tyteca
1969   *The New Rhetoric: A Treatise on Argumentation* (Notre Dame: University of Notre Dame Press).

Snyman, A.H.
1988   'Style and the Rhetorical Situation of Romans 8.31-39', *NTS* 34: 218-31.

Vorster, J.N.
1991   'The Rhetorical Situation of the Letter to the Romans—An Interactional Approach' (unpublished DD dissertation, University of Pretoria).

Watson, D.F.
1988   'A Rhetorical Analysis of Philippians and its Implications for the Unity Question', *NovT* 30: 57-88.

Wuellner, W.
1991   'Rhetorical Criticism and its Theory in Culture-Critical Perspective: The Narrative Rhetoric of John 11', in P.J. Hartin and J.H. Petzer (eds.), *Text and Interpretation: New Approaches in the Criticism of the New Testament* (NTTS, 12; Leiden: Brill): 171-86.

PHILIPPIANS 2.6-11: THE RHETORICAL FUNCTION OF A PAULINE 'HYMN'

Claudio Basevi and Juan Chapa

The rhetorical analysis of a text should seek to determine its rhetorical units.[1] This task is essential when studying long books with varied content, but a delimitation of units can also be employed to discern smaller rhetorical units within a text. The extent of a rhetorical unit may vary from a few verses (a command, for example) to larger combinations of smaller units.[2]

> It is important to discern these smaller units, too, since all of them may have their own rhetorical situation, which affect the interpretation of the text... The conception of a rhetorical unit differs from that of a literary unit inasmuch as it is identified not only by textual markers but also by its interactive function, by which is meant its effect on the implied receiver (and even on the implied author).[3]

It is necessary to determine the arrangement of the material, or *dispositio* of the text, to see how a particular unit interacts within it. On some occasions a particular unit may reveal a great deal about the intention of the author and about his relation with the audience.

Phil. 2.6-11 has traditionally been accepted as a literary unit. The extensive literature on the text is well known and it is usual to begin a study on this 'pericope' by quoting much of this bibliography.[4] It is

---

1. G.A. Kennedy, *New Testament Interpretation through Rhetorical Criticism* (Chapel Hill, NC, 1984), pp. 33-34.
2. W. Wuellner, 'Where is Rhetorical Criticism Taking Us?', *CBQ* 49 (1987), p. 455.
3. L. Thurén, *The Rhetorical Strategy of 1 Peter* (Åbo: Åbo Press, 1990), pp. 69-70.
4. The bibliography on Phil. 2.6-11 is extremely abundant, although it is mainly concerned with the conceptual and theological elements of the text. For a general view up to 1965 it is fundamental to see R.P. Martin, *Carmen Christi: Philippians*

surprising, however, that little has been written concerning the specific function of this text within the letter. These verses have commonly been considered part of a text prior to the letter—a hymn or poem inserted there by Paul—and this may have contributed, unconsciously, to an undervaluing of their function in relation to the rest of the letter, considering them as a mere appendage to the main body. This paper seeks to throw light on the rhetorical function that 2.6-11 plays within the general rhetoric of the letter to the Philippians. The first questions we should ask are what sort of a unit these verses are and what their rhetorical situation may be.

I

We must prefix this treatment with an important statement. We accept the text *prout extat*. The interpolations that some scholars, Lohmeyer

---

ii.5-11 in Recent Interpretation and in the Setting of Early Christian Worship (SNTSMS, 4; Cambridge, 1967). On more recent bibliography, see T. Yai-Chow Wong, 'The Problem of Pre-Existence in Philippians 2, 6-11', *ETL* 62 (1986), pp. 267-82, esp. n. 1 with the bibliography there. From 1986 see: L.D. Hurst, 'Re-Enter the Pre-Existent Christ in Philippians 2, 5-11?', *NTS* 32 (1986), pp. 449-57; N.T. Wright, '"Harpagmos" and the Meaning of Philippians 2:5-11', *JTS* 37 (1986), pp. 321-52; H. Binder, 'Erwägungen zu Phil 2, 6-7b', *ZNW* 78 (1987), pp. 230-43; M. Rissi, 'Der Christushymnus in Phil 2, 6-11', *ANRW*, II.25.4, pp. 3314-26; C.A. Wanamaker, 'Philippians 2, 6-11: Son of God or Adamic Christology?', *NTS* 33 (1987), pp. 179-83; J.A. Fitzmyer, 'The Aramaic Background of Philippians 2:6-11', *CBQ* 50 (1988), pp. 470-83; J.C. O'Neil, 'Hoover on "Harpagmos" Reviewed, with a Modest Proposal Concerning Philippians 2:6', *HTR* 81 (1988), pp. 445-49; F. Rousseau, 'Une disposition des versets de Philippiens 2, 5-11', *SR* 17 (1988), pp. 191-98; U.B. Müller, 'Der Christushymnus Phil 2:6-11', *ZNW* 79 (1988), pp. 17-44. From a philological point of view, see also: R. Deichgräber, *Gotteshymnus und Christushymnus in der frühen Christenheit* (SUNT, 5; Göttingen, 1967), pp. 118-33; C.H. Hunzinger, 'Zur Struktur der Christus-Hymnen in Phil 2 und 1. Petr 3', in E. Lohse, C. Burchard and B. Schaller (eds.), *Der Ruf Jesu und die Antwort der Gemeinde: Exegetische Untersuchungen J. Jeremias zum 70. Geburtstag* (Göttingen, 1970), pp. 142-56; F. Manns, 'Un hymne judéo-chrétien: Philippiens 2, 6-11', in *Essais sur le Judéo-Christianisme* (Jerusalem, 1977), pp. 11-42; B. Eckmann, 'A Quantitative Metrical Analysis of the Philippians Hymn', *NTS* 26 (1980), pp. 258-66; E. Lupieri, 'La morte di croce: Contributi per un'analisi di Fil. 2, 6-11', *RivB* 27 (1979), pp. 271-311; S. Vidal García, 'Flp 2, 6-11: su lugar teológico', *Quaere Paulum, Homenaje a L. Turrado* (Salamanca, 1981), pp. 149-61.

and Jeremias among others, think are present in the actual text should be taken as simple indemonstrable hypotheses. As M. Hooker points out,

it is perhaps dangerous to assume too readily that we can tell from the structure which words belong to an original 'hymn' and which are Paul's own comments. If we are dealing with rhythmic prose this kind of analysis does not allow us to make such a distinction. If it *is* a 'poem' or 'hymn'—then I must analyze the material accordingly, and demonstrate that it is possible to set the passage out as it stands in a poetic form, without making any excisions.[5]

Since 1923 it has been commonly accepted that, from a literary point of view, the unit is a 'hymn', and nowadays it is normally admitted that this text should be called a 'hymn' or 'poem'. There have always been discordant voices which have not fully accepted this text as a hymn but they have hardly been taken seriously. Modern Bibles print it in the form of a hymn, dividing it into verses and stanzas, as Lietzmann first did.[6] There are two main currents of interpretation. That the text was a pre-Pauline Christian-Jewish hymn, perhaps in Aramaic or Hebrew, which Paul quoted in his letter, is an interpretation largely developed by Lohmeyer[7] and Jeremias.[8] The Hellenistic origin of the hymn was maintained by Käsemann who viewed the hymn, inserted in the letter and similar to the one in Colossians, as indicative of an incipient pagan-Christian liturgy.[9] There is little agreement on the question of its origin and we will not enter directly into the discussion. Yet we consider that the term 'hymn' is at least ambiguous. It presupposes an approach to the text which, although seemingly irrelevant, is still the source of frequent misunderstandings

5. M. Hooker, 'Philippians 2:6-11', in E.E. Ellis and E. Grässer (eds.), *Jesus und Paulus: Festschrift W.G. Kümmel* (Göttingen: 1975), p. 158.

6. H. Lietzmann, *Mess und Herrenmahl* (Bonn, 1926), p. 155.

7. E. Lohmeyer, *Kyrios Jesus: Eine Untersuchung zu Phil 2, 5-11* (Sitzungsberichte der Heidelberger Akademie der Wissenschaft, Phil.-hist. Kl., Jahr. 1927-8, 4 Abh; Heidelberg, 1928).

8. J. Jeremias, 'Zur Gedankenführung in den paulinischen Briefen', in *Studia Paulina in honorem Johannis de Zwaan, Septuagenarii* (ed. J.W. Sevenster and W.C. van Unnik; Haarlem, 1953), pp. 152-54 and 'Zu Phil II-7: EAYTON EKENΩΣEN', *NovT* 6 (1963), pp. 182-88.

9. E. Käsemann, 'Kritische Analyse van Phil 2, 5-11', *ZTK* 47 (1950), pp. 313-60 (*Exegetische Versuche und Besinnungen*, I [Göttingen, 1960], pp. 51-95; 'A Critical Analysis of Phil 2.5-11', *JTC* 5 [1968], pp. 45-88).

and debates.[10] We believe the term 'hymn' may be misleading since it might incline us, almost unintentionally, to think that this was a pre-existent text, prior to Paul and quoted by him in his letter, or, in the best of cases, a translation made by Paul of a psalm or other liturgical song of Semitic origin and inserted by him in the text. We prefer to try establishing some basic points of reference previous to any such interpretation. The basis from which we undertake this is rhythm and verse, so essential to any poetical text. A study of the rhythm of these verses can at least help to establish some limits to this confusion and varied understanding of the text.

What is clear and universally accepted is that Phil 2.6-11 has a rhythmical structure.[11] It is not so generally noted, or at least not very often recalled, that it does not have a fixed metrical structure, as other classical Greek hymns have. Sappho's hymn to Aphrodite, Cleanthes' hymn to Zeus, Apollo's paeans, and Greek Christian hymns, for example, show a rigorous metre. There is no proper classical Greek hymn without metre, as is asserted in the traditional definition of hymn as 'any metrical address to a god, originally sung'.[12] Our 'hymn' has poetry in the large sense but not the *metron* of the classical Greek hymns. These present, moreover, an important literary feature. The rhetorical structure of a Greek hymn is well defined in well disposed parts,[13] something which does not occur in Phil. 2.6-11.[14]

---

10. Cf. C. Basevi, 'Estudio literario del himno cristológico de la Epístola a los Filipenses (Phil 2, 6-11)', *Helmántica* (forthcoming).

11. This was first underlined by J. Weiss in 1899 (*TLZ* 9 [1899], p. 263) and confirmed by A. Deissmann (*Paulus* [Tübingen, 1911], p. 113).

12. OCD, s.v. 'Hymn'.

13. Cf. W.H. Race, 'Aspects of Rhetoric and Form in Greek Hymns', *GRBS* 23 (1981), p. 12. The author studies the rhetorical demands on the hymnist: (i) finding the ἀρχή; (ii) establishing χάρις; (iii) elements of request. He maintains that there is a close connection between the rhetorical intention of the hymnist to create a hymn which will please the god and the formal expression of that intention (p. 14).

14. If we were to compare it with a literary form of Greek origin it would be better to relate it to the genre of prose hymns to gods, which is mainly developed from Imperial times onwards. As important witnesses we have the prose hymns of Aelius Aristides and the directions of rhetoricians, like Alexander Numeniu and Menander Rhetor, for the writing of these encomia. Quintilian, whom these authors generally follow, had already dealt with praising of the gods in prose, but he did not call these productions hymns (Quintilian 3.7.7). However, rhetoricians such as Aelius Theon and Alexander disagree on this point when they assert that encomia of

The alternative hypothesis suggested by Lohmeyer, followed by many others (for example, Jeremias, Fitzmyer, and Manns) and now widely accepted, that Phil. 2.6-11 was originally a Hebraic or Aramaic Christian-Jewish hymn, translated perhaps by Paul himself, is also arguable. This hypothesis is based mainly on the abundant lexical and conceptual semitisms and biblical references present in the text. Paul would be quoting a Semitic text with a certain degree of flexibility in adapting it to the Greek language. We think, however, that this interpretation does not provide a satisfactory solution in respect of the important element of Greek rhythm. The presence of Greek rhythmical clauses at the end of the sentences and the strong rhythmical structure of the text makes it very implausible to regard this text as a translation.[15] A comparison with Greek translations of Hebrew poetry, such as the Psalms or the Songs of the Servant, shows that the translators tried to keep the Hebrew rhythm in the Greek text but only managed to reproduce it in an imperfect way. A Greek version of the Old Testament clearly manifests that its translators were unable to translate and reproduce identically the poetry of an original Hebrew text.[16] Thus, the well-defined rhythm of Phil. 2.6-11 proves that it cannot be a literal translation of a Hebrew or Aramaic text. Rather it points to a new composition or, if pre-existing, one modified with great freedom. This does not mean that the author was not inspired by a Semitic text and the rhythm of Semitic poetry.[17] What

the gods should be called hymns (rules for 'praises of a god' are given in Alexander Numeniu 3.4-6 [Spengel] and Theon, *Progymnasmat* 2.109 [Spengel]). In any case, whether hymns or encomia, they too had a clear rhetorical structure, different from that of Phil 2.6-11. Cf. A. Boulanger, *Aelius Aristides: La sophistique dans la province d'Asia au II siècle de notre ère* (Paris 1923), pp. 300-17, esp. pp. 309-10.

15. For further details on this question, cf. Basevi, 'Estudio literario'.

16. The Greek text of Philippians shows a structure of stress accent very similar to the Hebrew one (4+4+4 or 3+3+3 or 4+2+4), whereas translations show a much more diffuse structure (for example 5+7+8 or the like). We should bear in mind that in St Paul's time the stress accent had no relevance at all (only from the fourth century CE did it start to develop a phonological role). On this question, see for instance L. Alonso-Schökel, *Estudios de poètica hebrea* (Barcelona, 1963); *idem*, 'La poèsie hèbraique', *DBS* VIII, pp. 47-90; W.G.E. Watson, *Classical Biblical Poetry* (Sheffield, 1984).

17. For the possible sources of inspiration which scholars dispute, cf. A. Feuillet, *Christologie paulinienne et tradition biblique* (Tournai, 1973). The author mentions six possible literary sources. Four are taken from the Old Testament: Adamic

we would like to emphasize is that it is very difficult to determine to what extent this inspiration affected Paul's text. Since we have no traces or extant vestiges of Christian-Jewish primitive literature of the hymn kind,[18] we prefer, taking a less speculative path, to think that Paul limited himself to the evocation of some Old Testament themes, such as those present, for instance, in the Songs of the Servant and in some of the Psalms related to the righteous man who is persecuted. Unless something new comes to light and gives stronger support to one of the previous hypotheses, one should accept the limitations imposed by the text and accept it as it is.

Let us summarize at this point the basic principles of our understanding of the text. We believe that Phil. 2.6-11 is a praise (or encomium) of Christ, which cannot be considered a hymn, at least in the classical Greek sense of the term; it has neither in Greek nor in the supposed Semitic substratum any proper metrical structure; it fits perfectly within the lexical and rhetorical framework of Philippians (making it difficult to defend the notion of literal quotation by Paul of a previous text); its structure suggests a strong poetical prose, written by someone who knows Greek very well, sprinkled with both lexical and conceptual semitisms. The text thus should therefore be regarded as a homogeneous and original mixture of Greek and biblical elements. Its sources do not seem to be Greek but biblical and a Gnostic derivation should therefore be rejected.[19] Whatever sources the author used they have been elaborated upon and employed in a free and original way. All in all, we think that the strong peculiarity of the text, its relations with the Old Testament, its profound christology, its use of Greek and its coherence with the rest of the letter, are elements supportive of Pauline literary originality.[20] We are, to be sure, aware of the lack of agreement on these questions, but we think it necessary

Christology, Eternal Wisdom, Songs of the Servant, passages of kenosis-exaltation (Job), and two of them extra-biblical in relation to the cult of the heroes and the Hellenistic-Oriental myth of the heavenly man of Gnostic origin.

18. In this sense F. Manns's suppositions lack support on this sort of literature (cf. Manns, 'Un hymne judéo-chrétien', pp. 11-42).

19. J. Jervell (*Imago Dei: Gen. I, 26f. im Spätjudentum, in der Gnosis und in der paulinischen Briefen* [FRLANT, 63; Göttingen, 1960], pp. 227-31), following similar ideas expressed by other authors (Käsemann, Bornkamm and Bultmann), has supposed the existence of a proto-Gnostic hymn, with Jewish influence, which Paul would be quoting.

20. Basevi, 'Estudio literario'.

at least to face some of the limits mentioned above and avoid drawing hurried conclusions. A rhetorical study of the letter and its units may help to discover these limits.

II

In order to establish some rhetorical characteristics of the text, it may be useful to consider the effect that the letter might have produced on the audience when read or heard. Whether it was prose or verse is not an irrelevant question. In this sense rhythm plays a significant role. The text in the letter shows many of the characteristics of rhythmical prose, which supports the view that it is a piece closer to poetical prose than verse.[21] Robbins's rhetorical study of the pericope also supports this interpretation.[22] He concludes his study by saying that what he has attempted to show is that Phil. 2.6-11

> could have been written according to the principles of classical rhetoric, since it conforms to all the principles of periodic structure set forth by the classical authors themselves. This plus the fact that the text was transmitted in Greek for a Greek reading public in an age when Greek influence was all pervasive provides a reasonable presumption that it was so composed. This presumption is strengthened by the further fact that an application of rhetorical principles to the text reveals... a coherent, logical and

21. On Greek prose, cf. E. Norden, *La prosa d'arte antica: Dal VI secolo all'età della rinascenza* (Rome, 1988) (updated Italian translation of *Die antike Kunstprosa*, 1913); *idem, Agnostos Theos: Untersuchungen zur Formengeschichte religiöser Rede* (Berlin, 1913), esp. Λέξις εἰρόμενη (pp. 367-79) and for the style of the hymns: pp. 168-76, 250-63, 385-87; A.W. DeGroot, *A Handbook of Antique Prose Rhythm: History of Greek Prose-Metre* (Groningen, 1919); *idem, La prose métrique des anciens* (Paris, 1926); J.D. Denniston, *Greek Prose Style* (Oxford, 1952); S. Skimina, *État actuel des études sur le rythme de la prose grecque*, I (Lwów, 1930); *idem, État actuel des études sur le rythme de la prose grecque*, II (Cracovie, 1937).

22. C.J. Robbins, 'Rhetorical Structure of Philippians 2:6-11', *CBQ* 42 (1980), pp. 73-82: 'the arrangement [of the pericope] is also more in conformity with the kind of sentence structure found throughout the more eloquent parts of the NT, such as Hebrews, 1 Peter or the speeches of Acts. It is also more compatible with the over-all style of the rest of Philippians, and specifically with the context in which it is found. On the other hand the short line of Lohmeyer, which have become standard in modern translations that attempt a versification of the passage in Greek to a congregation would find himself breaking step with the surrounding text unless he links the phrases together as we have done here' (p. 81).

symmetrical development of the thought. That the rhetorical structure and
the thought so completely coincide is not, we believe, the result of chance
but the consequence of deliberate composition.[23]

What the author calls 'rhetorical principles' might differ from what
some modern rhetorical critics call them, but it brings us nearer to the
final purpose of this paper. Robbins was thinking mainly of the principles of artistic periodic prose, following the criteria established by
rhetorical theorists such as Demetrius in his *On Style*, or Aristotle in
his *Rhetoric* or Cicero in the *Orator*. In these works their authors
inform us of the norms of composition of the periodic style according
to cola and periods.[24] As a first step, we accept that Phil. 2.6-11 may
have been written according to these norms. This enables us to consider Phil. 2.6-11 not only as a literary unit but also as one which
must not be considered isolated from, or accidental or circumstantial
to, the text, but perfectly inserted in a larger unit: Paul's paraenesis of
chs. 1 and 2. In the following lines we will try to show that the whole
exhortation of the first two chapters of Philippians may be founded
upon and explained by Phil. 2.6-11. Prior to analysis it is necessary
first to study the relation of the text to its context.

We suggest that this pericope is not just a text attached to v. 5,
which, if removed, would leave the same basic meaning. If we ask
why the Philippians should be united to Paul and among themselves,
while they are experiencing trials, the answer is that they share a
common faith in Jesus Christ who was God and died on the cross.
Christ, who receives constant praise throughout the letter, founds and
justifies the exhortation of Paul's words. Käsemann rightly points out
that the kenosis of Christ is not just an admirable example of humility,
but the formal motive of the unity among Christians. He thinks that
v. 5 cannot be separated from v. 6 because they are closely connected. To the Christians of the community of Philippi Paul writes
these words: φρονεῖτε ἐν ὑμῖν...have in yourselves the same thoughts
as Christ Jesus. This in an exhortation to live in themselves and among
themselves what Christ did to save them and to unite himself with all
of them. The text as commonly accepted is therefore an *exemplum*,
but at the same time puts forward the definitive and real cause of that

---

23. Robbins, 'Rhetorical Structure', pp. 81-82.
24. On periodical style, see R. Serrano-Cantarín, *La teoría clásica del estilo per-
iódico* (Pamplona, 1987).

unity. If Christ had not been God and had not died on the cross, Paul's argument would be invalid. For this reason v. 8, θανάτου δὲ σταυροῦ, is fundamental. If it were not there, the ultimate and most important reason for the identification of the suffering Philippians with Christ would also be missing. Phil. 2.6-11 is not only therefore an *exemplum*, but the cause of the exhortation. It plays the role of an argument from authority for the Philippians. If the Philippians have to be united among themselves and with Christ it is because Christ is the foundation of this unity. The praise of Christ, who he was and what he did, had the value of *auctoritas* for the hearers. It has the function of a profession of faith.[25]

To understand the text only as *exemplum* in a paraenetic context might be justified under an interpretation of the letter as belonging to the deliberative genus. This is what Professor Watson shows in his rhetorical study of Philippians.[26] Thus of the *probatio*, the part of a speech in which a speaker strengthens his position with argument, Watson says that vv. 5-11

25. In a community who for the most part were of Roman extraction and not of Jewish origin, the warnings of the Apostle against Judaizers may support this thought. It would surprise such an audience if Paul through the reader/carriers of the letter quoted a Christian-Jewish text or translated a text from the Hebrew or Aramaic as an authoritative argument. The content would also cause them surprise. It would be new and probably rather odd for a Christian community of non-Jewish origin that Paul based his argument on a quotation of a text which dealt with the emptying of Christ to the point of dying on a cross. On the other hand, it is unlikely that a christological thought, such as the one that Phil. 2.6-11 implies, would have developed in a Christian-Jewish community. Phil. 2.6-11, in spite of its numerous semitisms, detaches itself from the theological structural thought of the songs of lamentation and it shows notorious differences in respect to the Songs of the Servant or the hymns to Wisdom and Daniel's messianism, which are the probable intellectual *Vorlage* of the pericope. Thus the text shows a Semitic background, but appears to have been elaborated and developed in a christological sense.

26. In his analysis these verses are thought to be just an *exemplum* within the *probatio* of a deliberative speech. Watson distributes the epistle in the following way: *exordium* (1.3-26); *narratio* (1.27-30); *probatio* (2.1-3.21); the latter is divided into a first development of the Proposition (2.1-11); a second one (2.12-18) with a *digressio* (2.19-23); and a third development of the Proposition (3.1-21); then the *peroratio* (4.1-20) with a *repetitio* (4.1-9) and the *adfectus* (4.10-20) (D.F. Watson, 'A Rhetorical Analysis of Philippians and its Implications for the Unity Question', *NovT* 30 [1988], pp. 57-88).

provide another example of the figure of thought known as exemplification, which here embellishes, adds plausibility, clarifies, and vivifies. The example of Christ gives the Philippians a better understanding of the mind conducive to selfless giving and humble service to others. The wording 'have this mind (φρονέω) among yourselves, which you have in Christ Jesus', in v. 5 makes it clear that vv. 6-11 are to function as an example...As a primitive hymn or confession, vv. 6-11 lend considerable ethos to Paul's exhortation.[27]

From this point of view no special role in the letter is given to our text. It is to be taken only as an example within the general context of exhortation to live according to the gospel. 'The exigence, the problem needing solution, which Paul seeks to counter', Watson comments,

is the appearance of a rival gospel in Philippi, a situation which also besets him in his place of imprisonment...Paul expects the exigence to remain, for he is warning the Philippians to beware of the continued influence of the Judaizers. However, the letter indicates that the Judaizers are not yet firmly entrenched, for Paul's stance is not that of someone finding his authority seriously minimized. He is fully confident that the Philippians are capable of implementing what he exhorts. He makes no effort to prove the validity of his exhortation with rational argument, but rather relies primarily upon his own ethos for such support.[28]

Therefore, in disagreement with Kennedy, who thinks Philippians is largely epideictic,[29] Watson's conclusion is that 'of the three species of rhetoric, Philippians is to be classified as deliberative, for it exhibits the major characteristics of this species'.[30]

27. Watson, 'Rhetorical Analysis', pp. 69-70.
28. Watson, 'Rhetorical Analysis', pp. 58-59.
29. Kennedy, *New Testament Interpretation*, p. 77.
30. 'First it is obviously intended to advise and dissuade its audience regarding a particular course of action. As demonstrated below, this is indicated at the beginning of the central proposition in 1.27-30 by the words, "Only let your life be worthy of the gospel". Secondly, although the usual time referent of deliberative is future and only occasionally present, the time referent in Philippians is predominantly present. However, it is clear that the course of action advised is to be observed immediately or to be continued if already being observed, and is to characterize future activity as well. Thirdly, Philippians concerns itself with the ends of deliberative rhetoric: what is advantageous and harmful, expedient and inexpedient. Finally, the main deliberation in the *probatio* is constituted by example and comparison of example. Epideictic rhetoric is found in the *digressio* in 2.19-30 where Timothy and Epaphroditus receive praise, giving an example of the fact that epideictic lends itself to any attempt to advise and dissuade' (Watson, 'Rhetorical Analysis', pp. 59-60).

If we are to ascertain the rhetorical genus of the letter we must uncover the type of response from the audience that the text is designed to provoke. In general terms we may say that Paul is asking for a *paraklesis* from the Philippians. He will obtain consolation from the Philippians staying faithful to the gospel, as Watson also points out. 'There is only one question behind Paul's rhetoric in Philippians, and thus it is a simple rather than complex case. The question... is: What is a manner of life worthy of the gospel? (1.27-30).'[31] But we are not fully satisfied with the following lines: 'As is typical of deliberative rhetoric, the stasis of the rhetoric which underlies the question is the stasis of quality. The nature of a thing is the primary concern, for the focus is upon the characteristics of a life worthy of the gospel.'[32] We do not deny that Watson's question about the rhetoric behind Philippians is correct. We think, however, that this may not be central. What we understand of Philippians is based on an explanation of the letter as a praise of and exhortation to a Christian community, supported and explained by an encomium of Christ.[33] In other words,

31. Watson, 'Rhetorical Analysis', p. 60.
32. Watson, 'Rhetorical Analysis', p. 60.
33. To illustrate the approach taken we would cite the acceptance by other scholars of Pauline texts as belonging to epideictic speech:

> Thus in my opinion, the application of Graeco-Roman rhetorical precepts to Hellenistic persuasive letters can be done, when allowance is made not only for special characteristics of letters (which oral speeches did not have), but also for the diversity and complexity of rhetorical traditions, by the time of the mid-to-late first century CE... In fact, the strong use of epideictic rhetoric, as over against deliberative and judicial rhetoric, indicates a great deal about the intention of the author in writing the letter. Epideictic rhetoric classically focused on the development of persuasive writing based on values held in common between the rhetor and the audience. Although Paul, like other persuasive writers, was quite capable of using features drawn from all the genera of persuasion, the fact that he did not do so in 1 Thes. would seem to indicate the centrality of the epideictic topic of praise and blame to what Paul was trying to do in this letter. However, instead of praising the beauty of a mountain or of a river or of some other physical object or location (or some dead person, as in funeral orations), Paul chose to modify the genus of rhetoric, so that the recipients of the letter themselves were the object of Paul's praise.'

(F.W. Hughes, 'The Social Situations Implied by Rhetoric', paper submitted to New Testament Texts in their Cultural Environment Seminar, at the 46th General

we suggest that the letter belongs rather to the epideictic speech than to the deliberative one. In our opinion, after the *exordium*[34] the *probatio* is centred on two main topics: union with Christ, and the unity of the Philippians amongst themselves and with Paul. There are three basic thoughts in Paul's argument: the joy of Paul and of the Philippians even in the midst of sufferings; the cause of that joy being union with Christ precisely because of suffering; and the consequence of the union of each one with Christ being the union among all of them. These thoughts however are only possible because of what is said in 2.6-11. The text is not only an *exemplum* but a praise, an encomium of the real cause of Christian unity. Christ is praised because of his nature and because of what he did. If Christ had not been God and had not died, Paul's argument could not be maintained. The supposed hymnical unit is then a praise of Christ, for Paul and amongst themselves. In summary, we believe that Phil. 2.6-11 is a key unit within the letter which by its encomiastic nature suggests that the epistle should be classified as belonging to the species of epideictic rhetoric.

III

One may argue that the epideictic genus does not suit a paraenetic section. Here we join issue in an old debate.[35] An exhortative speech

Meeting of the Studiorum Novi Testamenti Societas, held in Bethel July 29–August 1, pp. 12-13);

> If one takes as basic Aristotle's understanding of rhetoric as '...the faculty of discovering the possible means of persuasion in reference to any subject whatever' (Art. I.ii.2), then the critic must be aware of how the 'possible means of persuasion' were understood and applied by the rhetor. The speaker sought to bring an audience from where they were in relationship to their understanding of an exigence to where he wanted them to be. He adjusted to the audience and adopted the necessary 'means' to their response to his argument. He had great flexibility in selecting topics, figures, and the pattern of argumentation of his discourse' (J.D. Hester, 'Rhetoric in I Thessalonians: A Reaction to Rene Kieffer's Essay', New Testament Texts in their Cultural Environment Seminar, p. 7).

34. With a *transitus* between *exordium* and *narratio* in 1.8-11, what we could call *narratio* ranges from 1.12 to 1.20. The *probatio* would follow it from 1.21 to 2.11.

35. If we look at random to some rhetorical analyses of Pauline works, we find that paraenetic sections are a crux for the commentators. To cite just one example, this can be seen in Smit's critique of Betz (J. Smit, 'The Letter of Paul to the Galatians: A Deliberative Speech', *NTS* 34 [1988], p. 4). Gal 5.1–6.10 is

in principle should be considered as deliberative in so far as exhortation naturally looks to something future, since it seeks to persuade the audience to take some action in the future.[36] This may be instanced by the case of Galatians.[37]

We may object to this rather stereotyped approach by suggesting that, although not necessarily so, deliberative rhetoric normally refers to something future, and that its persuasive advice or dissuasion therefore corresponds properly with paraenetic speech. However, we think that epideictic speech is more natural and more adaptable to any situation which demands exhortation, since it seeks to consolidate or diminish assent to some value, to praise or blame something in the present.[38] If the letter answers to a particular present situation, Paul's

considered by Betz as the paraenesis. Smit writes: 'This part creates, as he himself remarks, a serious problem for this rhetorical analysis. In classical rhetoric an exhortative passage such as this is completely unknown as a separate part of a normal speech'. In the footnote Smit quotes H.D. Betz, 'The Literary Composition and Function of Paul's Letter to the Galatians', *NTS* 21 (1975), p. 375: 'It is rather puzzling to see that paraenesis plays only marginal a role in the ancient rhetorical handbooks, if not in rhetoric itself'. Cf. also n. 9 where he remarks that even Quintilian has no special treatment of the paraenesis.

36. Kennedy, *New Testament Interpretation*, p. 19.

37. 'The basic argument of deliberative oratory is that an action is in the self-interest of the audience... That is the pervasive argument of Galatians... The letter looks to the immediate future, not to judgment of the past, and the question to be decided by the Galatians was not whether Paul had been right in what he had said or done, but what they themselves were going to believe and to do' (Kennedy, *New Testament Interpretation*, p. 146).

38. Here lies one of the complicated problems of the study of Pauline rhetoric: the difficulty of applying later rhetorical patterns, sometimes rather stereotyped, to texts which do not fit a particular Graeco-Roman model. We understand that the problem of exhortation which arises so often in Paul's letters might be viewed as in continuity with the Jewish tradition. Paul's exhortations might fit better with the prophetic tradition of the Old Testament or apocalyptic literature, than with Graeco-Roman exhortation (although he did use the Graeco-Roman tools of persuasion). Only an eschatological understanding of life, external to Paul's own person and authority, could provide a basis for his exhortations. Thus, the exhortation found in his letters follows a basic Graeco-Roman pattern but is rooted in Jewish traditions, and particularly in prophetic and apocalyptic literature. In this sense cf. K.P. Donfried, 'The Theology of 1 Thessalonians as a Reflection of its Purpose', in M.P. Horgan and P.J. Kobelski (eds.), *To Touch the Text: Biblical and Related Studies in Honor of Joseph A. Fitzmyer, S.J.* (New York, 1989), p. 259; see also A.M. Denis, 'L'Apôtre Paul, prophète messianique des Gentils: Etude thématique de

words fit better with the prompt response to an immediate and real occasion or life problem, than with a programme which should be followed by the Philippians in the future. It is obvious, however, that the boundaries between, for instance, the deliberative topic of honour and the standard epideictic topics of praise and blame are quite difficult to isolate.[39] We would like to insist that paraenesis is perfectly compatible with and suited to epideictic rhetoric. In this respect it is also interesting to recall the three rhetorical genera and the respective places to which they are normally ascribed: the judicial plea which belongs to the court-room (*genus iudiciale*), the political speech which has its place in parliament (*genus deliberativum*) and the speech of praise and censure which is used at special occasions (*genus demonstrativum*).[40]

The wide and vague determination of the epideictic speech as the one to be pronounced on 'special occasions' seems to fit better with epistolography in general and with particular audiences (neither political, nor judicial, but composed of relatives and friends as in the case of encomia, epitaphs or other such speeches). However, in recalling the three genra, one might be tempted to think of them as fixed. Thus, apology should be connected to the judicial speech, exhortation (or dissuasion) to deliberative and encomium (or blame) to epideictic. But perhaps we should enquire whether it might not be more natural to think that none of the three speeches had such clear limits and ends. Whatever the species of speech was, it had, or almost had, an implicit or explicit exhortation. It is obvious that if an orator is blaming the audience, it is because something has been done which deserves blame and requires correction. If he praises somebody it is natural to think

---

1 Thes. II, 1-6', *ETL* 33 (1957), pp. 245-318; E. Ellis, 'The Role of the Christian Prophet in Acts', in W.W. Gasque and R.P. Martin (eds.), *Apostolic History and the Gospel* (Exeter, 1970), pp. 55-67. It is not our intention to deal in detail with this question. It is marginal to our study in which we are seeking to ascertain the rhetorical genus of Philippians.

39. Hughes, 'The Social Situations Implied by Rhetoric', p. 12.

40. *Rhet. ad Her.* 1.2.2, for example, defines the three genera in the following way:

> Tria genera sunt causarum quae recipere debet orator: demonstrativum, deliberativum, iudiciale. Demonstrativum est quod tribuitur in alicuius certae personae laudem vel vituperationem. Deliberativum est in consultatione, quo habet in se suasionem et dissuasionem. Iudiiciale est quod positum est in controversia, et quod habet accusationem aut petitionem cum defensione (cf. *De In.* 1.5.7; *Rhet. ad Alex.* 1).

that it is because he is looking to his audience for an imitation of the person praised.

Thus, on the basis of their theory and praxis, we think it is necessary to underline the flexibility of the three genera and of the epideictic genus in particular.[41] For this purpose we would like to emphasize some of the elements. First, the kind of public for whom the genus of speech exists. As has been said, forensic and deliberative speech was addressed to judges and politicians; epideictic to general listeners.[42] We ought to bear this in mind because judicial speech, the most formal and well defined type of speech, was restricted to court. The deliberative speech also had its determined public. During the Hellenistic period and especially once the Romans were rulers of most of the civilized world, the deliberative speech practically disappears. Politics was no longer a matter over which normal citizens of the Empire could have any influence, as it had been when the Greek cities were in their heyday. In Paul's time, certainly, to produce political speeches was not of much relevance to the average Greek-speaking person. This fact, and other cultural and social circumstances, led to an increasing development of epideictic rhetoric. It is not surprising then that the majority of rhetorical opportunities were those appropriate to those 'special occasions' characteristic of epideictic literature and less relevant to political and judicial rhetoric. In any case it is useful to keep in mind that encomiastic literature blossomed a good deal during the Empire. To mention just one example, it is useful to

41. For the development of epideictic speech, see D.A. Russell and N.G. Wilson, *Menander Rhetor* (Oxford, 1981), pp. xiiiff.

42. Thus in the literature of the first two centuries of the Empire, on the other hand, the range is less limited. Of course, our evidence is greater, and the contrast we observe may therefore be illusory. We have, in particular, the voluminous remains of Dio Chrysostom and Lucian (The *lalia* is especially a Lucianic form). Many of Dio's speeches have deliberative themes or philosophical lessons; but both formal epideictic elements and the conscious informality of the *lalia* are ubiquitous. Plutarch too has something to contribute. With these in view, if we ask ourselves in what ways the range of epideictic writing was extended in this period, the answer is to be found in two areas: what Menander calls *laliai*, that is to say informal talks, where spontaneity and variety are admired qualities; and highly emotional funeral or disaster speeches, like Dio Chrysostom's Melankomas, or the monody of Aristides on the Smyrna earthquake' (Russell and Wilson, *Menander Rhetor*, pp. xvii-xviii).

recall that it became a popular exercise to see how one might 'make an encomium' of quite unlikely objects and persons. Such encomia then became the vehicle for literary controversies, often obscure to the modern reader.[43] We should, moreover, remember that something as frequent as paradox in the Pauline words is not far removed from typically epideictic paradoxical praise.

Two other important elements may be usefully borne in mind when considering Philippians as epideictic speech. On the one hand, late epideictic literature in practice was destined to be read:

> Since the object of 'epideictic' is to be read, not merely heard—an interesting distinction, and one widely accepted later (cf. Cic. *De oratore* 2.341: 'Ipsi eim Graeci magis legendi et delectationis aut hominis alicuius ornandi quam utilitatis huius forensis causa de laudationes scriptitaverunt'), it should have the precision of style which writing demands.[44]

On the other, epideictic admits a more poetical treatment of the subjects and is nearer to poetry than the two other genera. Aristotle draws a parallel between the kinds of poetry which have plots and the kinds of oratory which relate events or give advice, and again between a discursive kind of lyric poetry and the oratory of praise and blame.[45]

---

43. Thus Polycrates was famous for his paradoxical praise of the Egyptian tyrant Busiris, of Clytemnestra, of mice and of salt (cf. Russell and Wilson, *Menander Rhetor*, p. xvi).

44. Russell and Wilson, *Menander Rhetor*, pp. xx-xxi.

45. Russell and Wilson, *Menander Rhetor*, p. xxi: 'Menander Rhetor, the author of the best handbook on epideictic speeches, and an important witness of this sort of rhetoric for the previous centuries, makes great use of the poets... In any case, a closer link must always subsist between poetry and epideictic than between poetry and the other branches of oratory'. It is noticeable that the differences between what is permitted to poets and what is permitted to orators are repeatedly emphasized. The background to all this is the use made of poetical texts in all rhetorical schools. Not only did they illustrate figures (the most obvious common ground between grammaticus and rhetor) but they could be exploited even for examples of forms of arguments. Naturally, they were especially useful in epideictic oratory. There was a historical reason for this, in the fact that praise and blame, as we have seen, were originally functions of poetry which prose oratory took over, and that occasions like death or marriage had poetical forms of commemoration associated with them long before the development of anything that could be called literature. There was also a theoretical consideration, even if it is never made explicit in our texts. In forensic and deliberative oratory, speech does a real job in a real situation; poetical versions of

We suggest that these various considerations provide a vantage-point for the understanding of Philippians and other letters where exhortation or paraenesis plays a dominant role. We insist on no strict limitation or even predominant linking of exhortation to deliberative rhetoric. Epideictic speech should not be considered a mere rhetorical exercise. It could be that, but it obviously sought a response from the audience. The exhortation may be implicit or explicit, but it is there. Examples of this are clear in epideictic handbooks. If we take the funeral speech, a typically encomiastic form, we see that exhortation was necessarily linked to it. The consolatory speech had both encomiastic and exhortative parts. There could be no consolation (with praise of the deceased) without exhortation.[46] Even clearer is the case of the exhortative speech to athletes. Its features are described by Pseudo-Dionysius, in his *On Epideictic Speeches* within his *Ars Rhetorica*. It is worth noticing that we are dealing here with something called a *protreptikos* speech, an exhortation to athletes (προτρεπτικὸς ἀθληταῖς) considered by the theorist not to be part of the deliberative but the epideictic genus. (His work includes panegyrics, as well as procedures for marriage, for birthdays, for the bridal-chamber, for addresses, funeral speeches and exhortations to athletes.) In this chapter Pseudo-Dionysius starts by stating: 'We have to consider who the speaker is' (284), which provides a rationale for Paul's description of his situation in Philippians. We also find instructions and examples of what the orator should say like: 'athletes should not despise words because their activity is one of deeds. For speech is appropriate for all purposes, and gives strength for any effort: soldiers need the speech and exhortation of the general of war or battle, and then excel beyond themselves in strength' (285).

such discourses, except perhaps in very early times (as with Solon) or in very spcial circumstances, are merely mimetic; they reproduce the situation in an idealized or generalized form, and are intended not for immediate effect but as permanent literary possessions. In epideictic, on the other hand, the poet and the orator are much more on a level: both may be summoned to commemorate an occasion, both hope to leave behind them something which will endure. (Of course, a deliberative or forensic orator may have the same hope, but, if he has, it is in virtue of some qualities other than those displayed in his immediate effort.)' (Russell and Wilson, *Menander Rhetor*, pp. xxxi-xxxii).

46. J. Chapa, 'Is First Thessalonians a Letter of Consolation?', *NTS* (forthcoming).

> Some should be exhorted by appeals to shame, some by appeals to honour; for those who have many crowns and earlier victories, it would be disgraceful to be defeated by those who have never won, while for the others it would be honourable and unsurpassably glorious to have defeated the victorious and won their glory too through a single crown (290).

'We should then endeavour to demolish the reasons which lead some to become corrupted, by using the topics of disgrace and dishonour' (291). Admonitions against cheating are also worth noting: 'one must also remember past history and produce examples of famous athletes; some because they were undefeated, others because they won many victories, others again because they won few, but notable ones—and all honestly!' (292). We do not consider this chapter the source of St Paul's inspiration, but rather as witness to a tradition of epideictic speech with a paraenetic nature, known to rhetorical theorists, which might also have been known by Paul himself. The fact that Philippians is a letter in which one of the favourite Pauline comparisons between the Christian life and agonistic games is present (3.12–4.1) adds to the attraction of this suggestion and lends support to our opinion that the main features of this letter are epideictic rather than deliberative.

As has been said, epideictic became more appropriately written than read. Philippians as a letter, a written text, matches this characteristic. Secondly epideictic is closer to poetry than are the other two genera. The whole poetical structure of 2.6-11 corresponds to this feature of the genus. Besides, if we take other encomia, we see that the prose in which they are written is of a strongly rhythmical and poetical kind. Plato's prose encomium of Eros in his *Symposium* is a good sample of such poetical prose of an epideictic nature.[47] It has a highly poetical form. There are abundant rhetorical figures, such as alliteration, playing on words, etc. It is a prose in which the alternation of trochaic-spondeeic clauses with those of cretic type gives the text more musicality, more agitation, more colour, as frequently occurs in the prose of Sophistic authors. Plato's encomium has poetry, because the encomium was understood as poetical praise. Moreover, it might be useful to recall that prose hymns had a distinct part in cult in the Roman period and the performance of such speeches in temples or theatres seemed to cause an excitement and intensification of religious

---

47. *Symposium* 194E–197E.

feelings, which made them comparable to emotional sermons.[48]

In conclusion, we propose that Phil. 2.5-11 should be viewed as an encomium of Christ which demands a poetical form and has the function of a profession of faith. This lays the foundations for an exhortation to the afflicted community of Christians in Philippi. Knowing what Christ was and what he did, they would be encouraged to stay faithful to the gospel as well as united to Christ, to Paul and amongst themselves.

48. Cf. E.J. and L. Edelstein, *Asclepius: A Collection and Interpretation of the Testimonies*, II (Baltimore, 1945), pp. 204ff.

PAUL'S ETHICAL APPEAL IN PHILIPPIANS[*]

John W. Marshall

Introduction

When a first-century church received a letter from Paul, it paid attention. Something about Paul's letters made people want to read them, obey them, copy them, preserve them and study them. Paul's letters were effective. They were persuasive.[1] Using Paul's letter to the Philippians as a test case, and classical rhetoric as the guiding theory,[2] this study explores one aspect of the question 'why?'

We believe people more than we believe arguments. We pay attention to 'who' speaks as much as to 'what' they say. I set these alternatives in quotation marks because they are not ultimately separable; classical rhetorical theory, especially Aristotle's presentation of it, provides the insight that brings these alternatives together: the people we listen to are created within speech. Classical rhetorical theory employs the concept of *ethos* (denoting moral character) to understand the role of the speaker in the persuasive power of a speech. I attempt to understand Philippians as a persuasive document by understanding

---

[*] This paper was made possible by the generous support of Wilfrid Laurier University and through the encouragement of Dr Harold Remus, Dr Peter Erb and Dr Wilhelm Wuellner.

1. Without asserting that all of Paul's letters were completely persuasive, the volume in which they were preserved suggests they were quite highly valued. The pseudepigraphic letters also suggest that Paul's name would add persuasive force to a letter.

Looking at Philippians, see *Polycarp* 3.2, 11.3 and especially 9.2, for indications that Paul's letter was a success at Philippi. Collange (1973: 3) also suggests that Paul's letter to the Philippians made a deep and lasting impression.

2. See Aristotle, *Rhetoric* 1.1.1, 1.1.4, 1.2.1, for classical justification of rhetoric as a critical discipline. See also Kennedy 1980: 6; 1984: 10.

who Paul is within that document—that is, by understanding Paul's ethos in Philippians.

The first part of this paper examines, synthesizes and develops classical theory regarding ethos and the deliberative genus. The second part applies the theory to Philippians, examining Paul's identifications, roles, style, as well as the inartistic ethos he brings to the text.

1. *Theory of Ethos*

Though ethos is almost universally praised as an extremely powerful means of persuasion, it has received only cursory treatment in both ancient and modern theories and applications of rhetoric, and what treatment it has received is confused and confusing. In spite of this ill treatment, it has received the highest praise from the most influential theorists.[3] For these reasons, an analysis of ethos is necessary, not so much to solve all the questions or quell the debate, but rather to survey thought on ethos and provide a foundational theory of ethos for this inquiry into Paul's ethical appeal.

Aristotle's statement in *Rhetoric* 1.2.3-4 is the first extant theoretical discussion of ethos as an artistic mode of proof. It is basic to my analysis:

> Now the proofs furnished by the speech are of three kinds. The first depends upon the moral character [ἦθος] of the speaker... The orator persuades by moral character when the speech is delivered in such a manner as to render them worthy of confidence; for we feel confidence in a greater degree and more readily in persons of worth in regard to everything in general, but where there is no certainty and there is room for doubt, our confidence is absolute. But this confidence must be due to the speech itself, not to any preconceived idea of the speaker's character; for it is not the case, as some writers of rhetorical treatises lay down in their 'Art', that the worth of the orator in no way contributes to the orator's powers of persuasion; on the contrary, moral character, so to say, constitutes the most effective means of proof.

Key points of this text are: (1) ethical appeal is most relevant when there is the least certainty; (2) ethical appeal is created solely within the speech; and (3) ethical appeal is the most effective means of appeal. Aristotle develops the practical implications of his theoretical

---

3.   Aristotle, *Rhetoric* 1.2.3-4; Cicero, *De Oratore* 2.42.84; Quintilian 3.8.48; Kennedy 1984: 101; Halloran 1982: 60.

discussion in Book 3 of the *Rhetoric*. Aristotle's theory of ethos represented innovation in a number of areas. He was the first rhetorician to conceptualize ethos as an artistic means of persuasion. He discussed means of persuading through ethos and was the first to connect ethos to parts of the speech other than the proem. His recognition of the indirect nature of persuasion through ethos is also central to any attempt to recognize ethos in a document. Aristotle does his best to hold artistic ethos and moral goodness together, but just as he recognizes that rhetoric can be abused, so we must realize that ethical appeals can be abused.

The confusing nature of the classical treatments of ethos invites some development. Although most classical theorists give practical advice on how to make an ethical appeal, very few discuss how ethos works. In dialogue with the classical theorists, I propose two ideas: first, that identification of the rhetor and the audience is a powerful way to create a positive ethos,[4] and secondly, that ethos exists primarily in the relationship of the rhetor to the audience.[5] Though neither of these ideas is at the forefront of classical treatments of ethos, the beginnings of them can be found in the classical theorists, particularly Aristotle (*Rhetoric* 2.4.2-7; 3.14.7).

On the basis of these proposals, I offer the following definition of artistic ethos:

4.   This idea owes much to Kenneth Burke's discussions of rhetoric. See Burke 1951: 203. See also Hauser 1986: 120, 125.

5.   The second idea reconstellates the relationship of the three appeals (logos, ethos and pathos) to the three elements of the speech (subject, speaker and auditor). Rather than associating each appeal with a specific element, it situates the appeals in the relationships that exist between the elements. The first model, which Kinneavy (1987: 49) extracts from Aristotle, looks like figure 1; figure 2 represents the model I propose.

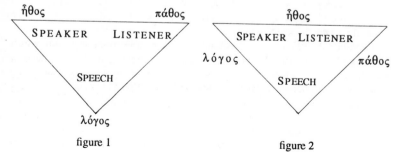

figure 1   figure 2

360 *Rhetoric and the New Testament*

Ethos is the relationship built up within the speech between the rhetor and the auditor which induces the auditor to believe the person speaking. Such a relationship is built up by means of identification between the rhetor and auditor, through participation in the world that exists between them. The persuasive power of this relationship increases as certainty about the subject matter decreases.

This definition maintains the key points isolated above in Aristotle's definition and adds a relational element.[6]

2. *Philippians' Rhetorical and Generic Situation*[7]

According to Bitzer (1968), three elements comprise a rhetorical situation: an exigence, an audience and a constraint. New Testament scholarship has not yet produced a full-length rhetorical-critical commentary of Philippians, and I am unaware of any discussion of its rhetorical situation as such. Looking at the possible exigences for the letter, however, reveals a wide and confusing range of possibilities, none of which holds sway over scholarly opinion.[8] All attempts to

6. Inartistic ethos is the same thing, except that it is brought to the discourse beforehand.

7. Without entering into the debate on whether Philippians is a unified or composite document, I should make clear that this study treats Philippians as a unified letter written by Paul from Rome. See Lightfoot (1953 [1913]), Dibelius (1937), Lohmeyer (1964), Pollard (1967), Jewett (1970), Kümmel (1975), Martin (1976), Garland (1985), and Watson (1988) on the unity of Philippians. See Schmithals (1957), Rahjten (1959), Bornkamm (1962), Beare (1969), Collange (1973), Lohse (1975), Barth (1979), and Perrin/Duling (1982) on the composite nature of Philippians. See Beare (1969) on the Roman provenance. The way in which I construe the exigence of the letter also turns some of the problems that a Roman provenance presents into advantages.

8. The range of ideas, put forth by quite competent scholars, on what prompted Paul to write to the Philippians suggests that it may not be possible to determine positively what prompted him to write.

Jewett (1970: 49) notes that 'Since the early days of historical critical research, exegetes have had difficulty in finding any main theme or line of argument in Philippians'. The following list is just a sample of ideas on what may have prompted Paul to write: Collange: Judaistic Philippian heresy (1973: 13); Koester: Jewish Christian missionaries (1982: 54, 204), perfectionist Gnostics (1982: 34); Martin: unexpected suffering (1.27) and 'Jewish-Christian gnostic emissaries' (3.2) (1976: 125); Lohmeyer: martyrdom (1964: 3-8) Brewer: Imperial cult (1954: 82-83).

In his rhetorical analysis of Philippians, Watson (1988: 58) specifically addresses

isolate a specific problem Paul was trying solve in Philippians depend on a premise which has rarely been questioned: that we can discern exactly what Paul was writing against because Paul himself knew exactly what he was writing against. Considering the unconvincing and contradictory explanations of the exigence, I question whether Paul knew exactly what he was writing against.[9] This means that there can be a difference between the exigence that exists in reality and the exigence that the writer's rhetoric addresses.[10] My reading of Philippians, and of scholarship on Philippians, suggests that Paul had some vague information that there was trouble in the church at Philippi, but very little specific information; to meet this rhetorical challenge, he cast a wide net.[11] Philippians is that wide net, and from it we cannot discern more specific information than Paul had when he wrote.

The implication of this exigence for Paul's choice of appeals is significant. Because Paul does not have all the data on the actual exigence to which he is addressing his letter, his ability to construct arguments through logos is hampered. This is, in Aristotle's terms, a situation 'where there is no certainty and there is room for doubt' (*Rhetoric* 1.2.4), and therefore the power of ethos is greatest. To describe the situation in terms of the communication triangle I have adapted from Aristotle (through Kinneavy 1987), Paul is working in a situation in which the subject-matter (τὰ περὶ ὑμῶν) is vague. Because the subject-matter corner of the triangle is vague, Paul has difficulty constructing appeals based on relationships to the subject matter—that is, he has trouble creating logos, which inheres in the

the question of exigence and asserts that the exigence is 'a rival gospel', but he cannot give any content to this gospel. The simplest explanation for this inability to define the exigence closely—an explanation which the text itself supports—is that Paul was unable to define the exigence closely, that he was writing to a situation where he lacked significant knowledge of the circumstances.

9.   Hawthorne (1983: 122) suggests that Paul might not have had 'full knowledge of the problems they [the Philippians] faced', but does not develop this insight.

10.   Bitzer (1968: 7) acknowledges that the exigence may not be clearly perceived by the rhetor, but does not develop the implications of a difference between the exigence existing and the exigence addressed; nor does he discuss how a rhetor might handle this difference.

11.   Beare (1969: 70) says that Paul seems to be casting about for any basis for appeal. This insight applies to more than the beginning of ch. 2, but Beare does not develop it.

subject matter–rhetor relationship, and also pathos which inheres in the subject matter–audience relationship. Because of Paul's lack of data about the actual exigence, he must rely on ethos, which inheres in his relationship to the Philippians—something of which he has a firm grasp and which is a firm foundation for his appeal.

The general audience that Paul addresses in Philippians was a predominantly Latin-speaking (Collange 1973: 2; Ramsay 1900) Roman colony with very few Jews. Concerning the church at Philippi to which Paul wrote, it is more difficult to obtain information. It seems that the church was ethnically mixed (though no ethnically Jewish names are evident), that it had strong women among its leading figures,[12] and that it was well-disposed towards Paul—his founding of the church and their repeated generosity towards him (1.5; 2.25-30; 4.10-20) attest to this. This latter quality is most important for the rhetorical situation; in writing to a well-disposed audience, Paul did not have to overcome negative attitudes towards himself before starting positive persuasion. Because a positive relationship already exists between the rhetor and the audience, the ground for a strong ethical appeal is already laid.

Though it is unlikely that this list is complete, there are three major identifiable factors which constrain Paul's persuasive efforts in Philippians. Perhaps most basic to Paul's persuasive efforts is his maleness; the rhetorical situation is definitively conditioned by the fact that Paul is a man addressing a congregation from a position of authority. Given the cultural milieu in which the letter to the Philippians exists and its attitudes towards women, the rhetorical situation would have been significantly different (and much more challenging) if the speaker were a woman. Paul's history of interaction with the Philippian church also constrains his rhetoric. Allusions to previous visits to Philippi (1 Cor. 16.5; 2 Cor. 2.13; cf. Acts 20.1, 5), as well as Paul's comments on his relation to the Philippian church within his letter to them, suggest that Paul's audience was, for the most part, well-disposed towards him.

The third major constraint is the letter format within which Paul writes. Though it robs Paul of delivery—one of the most powerful parts of rhetoric (Cicero, *De Oratore* 3.56, 213)—the letter format

---

12. Brewer (1954: 73) suggests that this is an indication of the 'Roman character of the church'. See also Thomas 1971.

also provides a few positive constraints. Though the traditional actual author → implied author → message → implied audience → actual audience chain still operates, the way that these elements are managed and related in a letter increases the power, or at least the potential, of ethos, by fostering the impression that the implied author and the actual author are identical; so too with the implied and actual audience. Ethos lives in this author–auditor relationship and the tightening of the chain increases the power of ethos.[13]

Contrary to Kennedy's view that Philippians is epideictic (1984: 77), I agree with Watson (1988: 59) that the letter is deliberative rhetoric. As the thesis of Philippians (1.27-30) indicates, the letter is concerned with modifying the future conduct of the Philippians—that they should live a life worthy of the gospel, stand firm and unified, and suffer in the same conflict as Paul. Paul devotes space to celebrating qualities (2.1; 4.8 especially), as well as the person of Christ (2.6-11), the Christian community (3.20), and even himself (3.4-11). Although these passages may be characterized as epideictic, their ultimate purpose is deliberative—they celebrate that which the letter as a whole urges the Philippians. This is the type of relationship between the epideictic and deliberative that Quintilian envisions (3.7.29ff.). Given the plain thesis of 1.27-30, it seems that Paul's epideictic passages have a deliberative purpose. Philippians is deliberative for the same reason that the Sermon on the Mount is deliberative (Kennedy 1984: 45): because the rhetor gives advice on the conduct of life.

The situation Paul faces in Philippians, the letter format he employs, and his deliberative purpose[14] converge to bring ethical appeals to the forefront of his persuasive strategy.

3. *Ethos through Identification*

In Philippians, Paul's primary method of building ethos is through identification. Paul builds ethos by casting identifications in two directions: on the one hand, he gains trustworthiness by identifying himself with his audience; on the other, he gains authority by identifying

13. See Demetrius (*On Style*, 277 printed in Malherbe 1988: 19) that the letter emphasizes ethos more than any other written format.

14. It is possible to correlate the deliberative, forensic, and epideictic genera with ethos, logos and pathos, respectively. There is no room here, however, to undertake this investigation.

himself with God and Christ.[15] By identification, I do not mean absolute sameness or synonymy. Although they occur occasionally, proclamations of absolute identity are rare. Paul does not say 'I *am* a Philippian' or 'I *am* Christ'. Instead, identification usually asserts itself in statements of solidarity. Paul identifies himself with God by showing that he is on 'God's team', that he and God are working towards the same ends. Paul identifies himself with the Philippians in the same way. Common interests and goals are the substance of most identification.

Identifications with the audience are found throughout Philippians. As soon as Paul refers to 'our God' in 1.2 he identifies himself with the audience. This identification continues almost constantly through to the greetings Paul brings from the kin and the saints (4.21-22). Though limitations of space make examining every instance of identification with the audience impractical, a few examples may suffice. Paul claims to remember the audience in all of his prayers (1.3-4), to hold them in his heart (1.7), and to be engaged in the same conflict as they (1.30). In ch. 2, Paul calls the Philippians to unities of love and of mind. Though Paul is calling for unity within the congregation, he also calls for unity with himself. Later (2.17b-18), Paul says to his audience: 'rejoice, and I rejoice together with all of you; in the same way, rejoice, and rejoice together with me'. Paul also identifies himself with the audience by identifying with their messenger, calling Epaphroditus 'my brother, fellow worker, fellow soldier, your apostle and servant of my need'. At the end of the letter, Paul emphasizes his unique relation to the Philippian church when he writes in 4.15-16:

> And you know, Philippians, that in the beginning of the gospel, when I came from Macedonia, no church participated with me in the matter of giving and receiving except you only, for even in Thessalonika, once or twice, you sent to me in [my] need.[16]

15. Campbell (1982: 134) articulates most clearly the nature of ethos as a composite of authority and trustworthiness. This notion is also implied by Aristotle (*Rhetoric* 1.8.6) where an example of ethos is composed of competence and goodwill.

16. This is a very clear example of the technique of building ethos through dependence which the *Rhetorica ad Herrenium* (1.5.1) alludes to when it suggests that we can secure the goodwill of the audience, 'by setting forth our disabilities, need, loneliness, and misfortune, and pleading for our hearer's aid, and at the same

These examples are only short glances at a few of the many ways in which Paul builds his ethos by identifying with his audience.[17]

Identifications with God or with Christ are almost as common as identifications with the audience. By identifying with God, Paul builds the authority dimension of his ethos. Again, this begins in 1.1-2, when Paul and Timothy, 'servants of Christ Jesus', bring grace and peace 'from God and from Jesus Christ', and extends through to 4.23 where Paul offers 'the grace of the Lord Jesus Christ'. When Paul asserts that what happens to him is for the advancement of the gospel, he is claiming an identification of himself with God. When Paul exhorts the audience to have among themselves the mind which was in Christ, he implies that he possesses the mind which was in Christ. When Paul speaks of his own religious life and heritage in 3.4-11, he tells a story which parallels the Christ hymn of 2.6-11 and thus identifies himself with Christ.[18] Paul builds identification in this passage by paralleling

---

time showing that we have been unwilling to place our hope in anyone else'. The technique works by forcing the audience to consider its relationship to the rhetor. If there is anything positive in that relationship, the plea of dependence will accent it.

17. It is also instructive to see Paul's identification with the audience in terms of Hellenistic friendship ideals and to see Philippians as a 'friendly' letter. In many places, Paul builds the trustworthiness dimension of his ethos by conforming to those ideals. See White 1990: 201, 207; Stowers 1991; and Marshall 1987: 151-67 on Philippians and friendship; see Aristotle, *Rhetoric* 2.4.2-7 on the ideal picture of friendship; see Stowers 1986: 49ff.; Pseudo-Demetrius, *Epistolary Types* in Malherbe 1988: 31-41; Pseudo-Libanius, *Epistolary Styles* in Malherbe 1988: 67-81 on the 'friendly' letter.

18. Briefly summarized, this hymn is a tale of identification and exaltation: Christ gives up equality with God and takes on the form of a slave—this is an act of identification with humanity. Because of Christ's solidarity with God, he is obedient to the point of death; for this reason God exalts Christ and the identification of Christ and God becomes known to all creation, and a confession of the Lordship of Jesus glorifies God. Paul's digression on himself in 3.4-11 is roughly parallel. Paul has a legitimate claim to identification with God through his Hebrew heritage, but gives it up; this resignation, however, should result in Paul sharing Christ's resurrection. There are a number of verbal correspondences that support this thematic parallel:

- Just as Christ did not 'count' (ἡγήσατο 2.6) equality a thing to be grasped, Paul 'counted' (ἥγημαι, ἡγοῦμαι 3.7, 8) his Hebrew heritage as loss or rubbish.
- Just as Christ 'was found' (εὑρεθείς 2.7) in human form, Paul hopes to 'be found' (εὑρεθῶ 3.9) in Christ.

his own experience with that of Christ.

There are also several places where Paul casts his identification in both directions at once, binding himself simultaneously to his audience and to God. On a number of occasions, Paul makes what can be called double identifications. These are phrases which identify him both with God and with the Philippians. Notable examples are 1.3, 8, 19, 23, 26 and 2.17-18. With double identifications such as these, Paul binds together the authority and trustworthiness he needs for a persuasive ethos.

4. *Ethos through Roles*

The title of this section should not suggest deception. The roles Paul 'plays' are the various ways he tries to present himself and his thoughts to the Philippians. Aristotle (*Rhetoric* 1.2.4) emphasizes that ethos is created within the speech, rather than brought to it. This section examines the questions 'who is the Paul that exists in the text of Philippians?' and 'what roles does he play?' Within the text there is a portrait of Paul and we now examine the function of that portrait in Paul's creation of a persuasive ethos. Successively, Paul portrays himself as slave/envoy (1.1-2), partner (1.3), prisoner for the gospel (1.2-4), mediator (1.15-18), guardian/pedagogue (1.25), commander (2.12), athlete (2.16; 3.14), priest/libation (3.17), father (2.22), super-Jew (3.4-6), beyond-super-Jew (3.7-11), king/victorious athlete (4.1), and worker for the gospel (4.3). It should be clear now that most of the roles Paul takes on in Philippians function to enhance the authority dimension of his ethos. Paul also transforms the image of himself as powerless prisoner into prisoner for the gospel, whose state advances the gospel and emboldens the saints. The authority Paul gains from these roles is an important part of his persuasive ethos.

One role that deserves greater treatment is that of popular philosopher.[19] In three areas, the portrait of Paul that exists in Philippians coincides with the range of what a popular Hellenistic philosopher

---

• Just as Christ abandoned the form (μορφῇ 2.6) of God, taking the form (μορφήν 2.7) of a slave, Paul anticipates 'sharing the form' (συμμορφιζόμενος 3.10) of Christ's death.

Interestingly, Collange (1973: 97) interprets μορφή in terms of identification, saying that it designates 'a most profound and genuine identity'.

19. Malherbe (1986, 1989) deserves most of the credit for this view of Paul.

might be with regard to subject matter, relation to the world, and teaching technique. The list of virtues in 4.8 would easily fit within the preaching of a non-Christian popular philosopher (Beare 1969: 148; Sevenster 1961: 154; Malherbe 1986: 136). Just as the genuine philosopher was free of 'three common vices: pleasure of the body, money, and reputation',[20] Paul claims indifference to bodily pleasure (3.19), financial advantage (4.11-13), and reputation (3.4-12). His use of αὐτάρκης in 4.11 has close affinities to Stoic language (Martin 1976: 162; Collange 1973: 150; Beare 1969: 152; Lightfoot 1953: 163, and others). In his method of teaching, Paul makes use of imitation (3.17)[21] and of the diatribe form[22] to communicate his message and persuade his audience. In depicting himself within the range of what a popular philosopher might be, Paul portrays himself as an authority figure.

5. *Ethos through Style*

Paul's style—diction and composition—emphasizes the ethical appeals he makes by other means. Though ethos is a facet of intention, as Aristotle notes (*Rhetoric* 3.7.6), ethos is revealed in style.

In the realm of diction, Paul frequently uses affectionate language (ἀδελφός, ἀγαπητός, ἐπιπόθητος, etc.)[23] to identify with and ingratiate himself to the audience; he makes quite extensive use of terms prefixed with συν—which bind him to the audience or to God.[24] To similar effect, he chooses many words based on the κοιν-stem.[25] By speaking in the first person plural, Paul claims that he and his audience are one entity.[26] In some cases, the first person plural language may result from Paul importing or modifying catechetical or liturgical materials, but the function of the 'we' language itself is to

---

20. Malherbe draws this summary from Julian, *Oration* 6.200C-201C, printed in Malherbe 1986: 34.

21. See De Boer 1962: 24-29; Kennedy 1984: 31; and Stowers 1986: 39.

22. See Stowers (1981) and Wuellner (1976) for discussions of the diatribe. They do not relate it to Philippians, but several elements of Paul's argumentation in 3.2-17 are consistent with the diatribe form.

23. 1.12; 2.12; 3.1, 13, 17; 4.1 (4x), 8.

24. 1.1, 7, 23 (2x); 2.2, 22, 25 (2x); 3.10, 17, 21; 4.2, 3 (4x), 14, 21.

25. 1.5, 7; 2.1; 3.10; 4.14, 15.

26. 1.2; 3.3, 15, 16, 20 (2x), 21; 4.19.

identify Paul with the audience and thereby increase the trustworthiness dimension of his ethos. Paul's diction emphasizes his close connection and positive relation to the audience. The composition of Paul's sentences often highlights ethical appeals he makes by other means. In 1.8 and 1.21, for example, Paul makes his double identifications especially forceful by casting them in pithy sentences which follow immediately after much longer and more complex sentences. The use of highly mannered rhetorical figures within 3.4-7 gives weight to the super-Jew role. Anaphora makes memorable the virtue lists of 2.1 and 4.8. In Philippians, Paul demonstrates that he has a firm practical grasp of rhetorical figures and that he can employ them effectively to support his appeals.

6. *Ethos through Imported Texts*

Within Philippians, there are a number of passages that may be texts not written by Paul, but incorporated by him into the body of his letter. These are 2.6-11, 3.3, 3.18-21.

One very general effect of including quotations in a letter is to make the writer appear cultured, learned and gracious. Gregory of Nazianzus suggests that a moderate inclusion of 'pithy sayings, proverbs, or apophthegms' is necessary to preserve the charm of a letter (*Epistle* 51.5 in Malherbe 1988: 61). Julius Victor also notes that 'it is very much in form to use a familiar proverb, a line of poetry or a snatch of verse' (*Ars Rhetorica* 27 in Malherbe 1988: 65). By quoting poetic material, Paul builds his ethos by increasing the charm of his letter.

Without examining each text in detail or considering whether the audience knew these texts beforehand, there is a general effect at work when a writer quotes material: the qualities of the material are transferred to the one who quotes it. Aristotle suggests that well-chosen maxims reflect well on the rhetor's character (*Rhetoric* 2.21; 3.17.9). The Christ hymn portrays a figure who is self-sacrificing, identifying, obedient, and, ultimately, authoritative. Paul takes on these positive qualities by quoting the hymn. Later, he develops the relationship between himself and the paradigm of the hymn more explicitly. The catechetical material of 3.2-3 associates Paul with God, Christ and the spirit, and a transcendence of the flesh. Paul receives this ethical capital and it contributes to his authority. In the Commonwealth hymn of

3.18-21, Paul also gains the ethos of the text itself, which, in this case, is identification with Christ, detachment from the world, and identification with ultimate victory over all the world. The effect of quoting these texts is more complex than this summary reveals, but in every case Paul strengthens his ethos by borrowing the power of the text he quotes.

7. Inartistic Ethos

Though Aristotle (*Rhetoric* 1.2.4) disdained inartistic ethos, later theorists recognized its importance. I have not treated it first because I believe, with Aristotle, that ethos constructed within the speech is far more important.

Before looking at Paul's specific relation to the Philippians, it is important to recognize one of the most general features of the relationship: Paul is a man writing to a mixed audience of men and women. Paul's gender is inartistic in that he brings it to the discourse. It is thoroughly necessary to his rhetorical strategy, though it is most likely that he did not see it this way. As a man, Paul could take on roles that a woman could not as plausibly take on. Paul works hard to build authority, but a woman would have to work much harder. Though Paul's maleness was not sufficient to carry his appeal (half the population was male, and yet did not make the same persuasive impact as Paul), it was a necessary inartistic condition for the appeal he constructed.

As I suggested above, Paul's relations with the Philippians were for the most part positive. In 2 Cor. 8.1-5, Paul alludes to the deep poverty of the Macedonian churches, suggesting again that they might feel a bond with him as a fellow member of the working class. During his first visit to Philippi, Paul preached persuasively and performed miracles (according to Acts 16). These acts, which were part of the Philippian church's foundation, would increase the authority dimension of Paul's ethos and be well known by members of the Philippian church even twelve years later.[27]

27. Twelve is approximate. I am using Jewett (1979: appendix), though I have not followed his placement of Philippians within an Ephesian imprisonment in 55 CE.

Though the historicity of miracles is by no means provable, the important possibility is that the account of miracles became part of the Philippians' self-understanding, and therefore part of their image of Paul apart from the discourse.

Another dimension of Paul's first stay in Philippi which affects his inartistic ethical appeal is his imprisonment there. In Acts 16, Paul's imprisonment is a victory for Paul; he performs miracles, his authority is validated, and he stands up to the Roman magistrates. This positive imprisonment in the presence of the Philippians is extremely relevant for Paul's argument in 1.12-14. His prior contact with the Philippians which showed that a bona fide apostle could be imprisoned forms the basis for his justification of his current imprisonment.

Paul's subsequent visits to Philippi are less extensively documented. He passed through Philippi once or twice on his third journey, but we have no account of what took place there. Acts 20.6, however, does not suggest any problems. In fact, the Philippians' enthusiasm for Paul and his mission appears healthy (Rom. 15.26). The last pieces of information about Paul's relation to the Philippians come from within the letter itself. Upon hearing of Paul's imprisonment, the Philippians sent aid to Paul, even though he did not ask for it (4.14-17 and perhaps 2 Cor. 11.9). Later they sent a representative, Epaphroditus, to minister to Paul and continue their service to him (4.18). These things indicate a positive relationship between Paul and the Philippians. A powerful prior ethos, built over a number of visits, and perhaps correspondence, spanning more than a decade, undergirds the ethos which Paul builds within the letter.

Conclusions

When I wrote that we believe people more than we believe arguments, the statement was unsupported. The analyses of this study, however, have given support to the assertion and examples of how 'persona' persuades. Within Philippians, Paul makes extensive and diverse use of identifications with the audience and with God/Christ to build the trustworthiness and authority dimensions of his ethos, respectively. He creates a portrait of himself which casts him in authority roles. And he both builds and maintains his positive ethos through the style with which he writes. He supplements this purely artistic ethos with imported texts and a positive prior ethos undergirds the whole effort.

Aristotle analysed ethos in terms of three qualities: φρόνησις (good sense), εὔνοια (goodwill), and ἀρετή (virtuous excellence). In Philippians, Paul demonstrates all these qualities in himself, and maintains them throughout the discourse. He demonstrates and values good sense (1.7, 15-18; 2.1-2, 5, 14-15; 3.15-16; 4.4-7, 9, 10). He has immense goodwill towards the Philippians (1.1-11, 23-26; 4.10-20). He portrays himself as a model of apostolic excellence (1.12-14, 20; 3.4-11). Paul also fits Cicero's notion of a persuasive ethos. Cicero (*De Oratore* 2.43.184) writes that a character that appears 'upright, stainless, conscientious, modest, and long-suffering under injustice' can be the persuasive element in a case. Paul has all of these qualities in relation to the Philippians and therefore, as Aristotle notes (*Rhetoric* 2.1.5), he will necessarily persuade his audience.

The implication of this understanding of Paul and Philippians is clear: there can be no adequate understanding of Paul's persuasive power which does not incorporate an understanding of his ethos. A study of ethos also provides an additional means of understanding persuasion in an oral context; persuasion does not rely solely on a chain of logical propositions which lead necessarily to a conclusion. If that were the case, a listener whose attention lapsed even slightly could not be persuaded. Instead, a web of associations, roles, and attributions contribute to an impression that the speaker can be trusted. Some of the ethical appeals may miss and others may hit, but a miss does not break a chain. In Philippians, Paul casts a wide net of ethical appeals, and, as far as we can tell, the net is strong enough to carry the audience.

Bibliography

Aristotle
   1926   *The Art of Rhetoric* (trans. J.H. Freese; LCL; Cambridge, MA: Harvard
            University Press).
   1968   *Nichomachean Ethics* (trans. H. Rackham; LCL; Cambridge, MA:
            Harvard University Press).
[Pseudo-] Aristotle
   1957   *Rhetorica ad Alexandrum* (trans. H. Rackham; LCL; Cambridge, MA:
            Harvard University Press).
Augustine of Hippo
   1958   *On Christian Doctrine* (trans. D.W. Robertson; New York: Bobbs-
            Merrill).
Beare, F.W.
   1969   *A Commentary on the Epistle to the Philippians* (BNTC; London:
            Adam & Charles Black, 2nd edn).
Bitzer, L.F.
   1968   'The Rhetorical Situation', *Philosophy and Rhetoric* 1 (1968): 1-14.

Brewer, R.R.
1954   'The Meaning of *POLITEUESTHE* in Philippians 1.27', *JBL* 73: 76-83.

Burke, K.
1951   'Rhetoric—Old and New', *The Journal of General Education* 5: 202-209.
1970   *Language as Symbolic Action* (Berkeley: University of California Press).
1974   *A Rhetoric of Motives* (Berkeley: University of California Press).

Campbell, K.K.
1982   *The Rhetorical Act* (Belmont, CA: Wadsworth).

Cicero
1939   *Brutus* (trans. G.L. Henrikson; LCL; Cambridge, MA: Harvard University Press).
1939   *De Oratore* (trans. H.M. Hubbell; LCL; Cambridge, MA: Harvard University Press).
1949   *De Inventione, De Optimo Oratorium, & Topica* (trans. H.M. Hubbell; LCL; Cambridge, MA: Harvard University Press).

[Pseudo-] Cicero
1954   *Rhetorica ad Herrenium* (trans. H. Caplan; LCL; Cambridge, MA: Harvard University Press).

Collange, J.-F.
1973   *The Epistle of Saint Paul to the Philippians* (trans. A.W. Heathcote;. London: Epworth Press).

Corbett, E.
1971   *Classical Rhetoric for the Modern Student* (New York: Oxford University Press).

De Boer, W.P.
1962   *The Imitation of Paul: An Exegetical Study* (Kampen: Kok).

Demetrius
1965   *On Style* (trans. W. Rhys Roberts; LCL; Cambridge, MA: Harvard University Press).

Garland, D.E.
1985   'The Composition and Unity of Philippians', *NovT* 27: 141-73.

Goodspeed, E.J.
1937   *Introduction to the New Testament* (Chicago: University of Chicago Press).

Halloran, M.S.
1982   'Aristotle's Concept of Ethos, or if not His Somebody Else's', *Rhetoric Review* 1: 58-63.

Hauser, G.A.
1986   *Introduction to Rhetorical Theory* (New York: Harper & Row).

Hock, R.F.
1978   'Paul's Tent-Making and the Problem of his Social Class', *JBL* 97: 555-65.
1979   'The Workshop as a Social Setting for Paul's Missionary Preaching', *CBQ* 41: 436-50.

Isocrates
    1929   *Antidosis* (trans. G. Norlin; LCL; Cambridge, MA: Harvard University Press).

Jewett, R.
    1970   'The Epistolary Thanksgiving and the Integrity of Philippians', *NovT* 12: 40-53.
    1979   *A Chronology of Paul's Life* (Philadelphia: Fortress Press).

Kennedy, G.A.
    1963   *The Art of Persuasion in Greece* (Princeton: Princeton University Press).
    1969   *The Art of Rhetoric in the Roman World 300 B.C.–A.D. 300* (Princeton: Princeton University Press).
    1984   *New Testament Interpretation through Rhetorical Criticism* (Chapel Hill: University of North Carolina Press).

Kinneavy, J.L.
    1987   *Greek Rhetorical Origins of Christian Faith* (New York: Oxford University Press).

Kümmel, W.G.
    1975   *Introduction to the New Testament* (Nashville: Abingdon Press, rev. edn).

Lightfoot, J.B.
    1953   *Saint Paul's Epistle to the Philippians: A Revised Text with Introduction, Notes, and Dissertations* (Grand Rapids: Zondervan).

Lohse, E.
    1975   *Enstehung des Neuen Testaments* (Theologische Wissenschaft, 4; Stuttgart: Kolhammer, 2nd edn).

Lüdemann, G.
    1989   *Early Christianity according to the Tradition in Acts: A Commentary* (trans. J. Bowden; Minneapolis: Fortress Press, 1989).

Lysias
    1943   *Lysias* (trans. W.R.M. Lamb; LCL; Cambridge, MA: Harvard University Press).

Malherbe, A.
    1986   *Moral Exhortation, a Greco-Roman Sourcebook* (Philadelphia: Westminster Press).
    1988   *Ancient Epistolary Theorists* (Atlanta, GA: Scholars Press).
    1989   *Paul and the Popular Philosophers* (Minneapolis: Fortress Press).

Marshall, P.
    1987   *Enmity in Corinth: Social Conventions in Paul's Relations with the Corinthians* (WUNT; Tübingen: Mohr [Paul Siebeck]).

Martin, R.P.
    1976   *Philippians* (NCB; Greenwood, SC: Attic Press).

Murphy, J.J. (ed.)
    1983   *A Synoptic History of Classical Rhetoric* (Davis, CA: Hermagoras Press).

Perelman, C., and L. Olbrechts-Tyteca
    1969   *The New Rhetoric: A Treatise on Argumentation* (trans. J. Wilkinson and P. Weaver; Notre Dame: University of Notre Dame Press).

Perring, N., and D. Duling
    1982   *The New Testament, an Introduction: Proclamation and Parenesis, Myth and History* (New York: Harcourt, Brace, Jovanovich, 2nd edn).

Plato
    1914   *Phaedrus* (trans. H.N. Fowler; LCL; Cambridge, MA: Harvard University Press).

Pollard, T.E.
    1967   'The Integrity of Philippians', *NTS* 13: 57-66.

Quintilian
    1920–22   *Institutio Oratoria* (4 vols.; trans. H.E. Butler; LCL; Cambridge, MA: Harvard University Press).

Rahjten, B.D.
    1959   'Three Letters of Paul to the Philippians', *NTS* 6: 167-73.

Sattler, W.M.
    1947   'Conceptions of *Ethos* in Ancient Rhetoric', *SM* 14: 55-65.

Schmithals, W.
    1957   'Die Irrlehrer des Philipperbriefes', *ZTK* 54: 297-341.

Sevenster, J.N.
    1961   *Paul and Seneca* (NovTSup; Leiden: Brill).

Stowers, S.K.
    1986   *Letter Writing in Greco-Roman Antiquity* (Philadelphia: Westminster Press).
    1991   'Friends and Enemies in the Politics of Heaven: Reading Theology in Philippians', in J. Bassler (ed.), *Pauline Theology* (Minneapolis: Fortress Press).

Thomas, D.W.
    1971   'The Place of Women in the Church at Philippi', *ExpTim* 83: 117-20.

Watson, D.F.
    1988   'A Rhetorical Analysis of Philippians and its Implications for the Unity Problem', *NovT* 30: 57-88.

White, L.
    1990   'Morality between Two Worlds: A Paradigm of Friendship in Philippians', in D.L. Balch, E. Ferguson and W.A. Meeks (eds.), *Greeks, Romans, and Christians: Essays in Honour of Abraham J. Malherbe* (Minneapolis: Fortress Press): 201-15.

Wuellner, W. (ed.)
    1976   *The Diatribe in Ancient Rhetorical Theory: Protocol of the 22nd Colloquy of the Center of Hermeneutical Studies* (Berkeley: Center for Hermeneutical Studies).

HEBREWS AS AMPLIFICATION

Thomas H. Olbricht

The purpose of this article is to reflect upon the rhetorical function in Hebrews of the comparison of Christ with numerous highly respected persons and entities. I conclude that these comparisons are the means of fleshing out the argument, that is, amplification (*auxesis*), in the vocabulary of Aristotle.

In *Rhetoric* 1.9.38-39, Aristotle developed a perspective on amplification in eulogies: 'And you must compare him with illustrious personages, for it affords ground for amplification and is noble, if he can be proved better than men of worth'. The author of Hebrews compared Jesus with such illustrious personages as angels, Moses, Joshua, the Levitical priests and Melchizedek. He also compared the sacrifice of Christ's blood with the respected blood of bulls and goats. He set out to prove that Jesus was superior to these persons of great worth, thereby establishing his higher status.

I will first offer a perspective on the structure of Hebrews. Then I will analyze the comparisons as amplification in the light of funeral oratory of classical Greece and in the early Christian fathers. It is especially in these speeches that such comparisons may be found, for Aristotle declared 'Amplification is most suitable for epideictic speakers' (1.9.40).

The Structure of Hebrews

It is not easy to offer a structure for Hebrews which incorporates all the inherent multiplex rhetorical and theological interests. In his recent landmark commentary Harold W. Attridge wrote:

> Some difficulty in analyzing the structure of Hebrews is due not to the lack of structural indices, but to their overabundance. Hebrews constantly foreshadows themes that receive fuller treatment elsewhere and frequently

provides brief summaries that resume and refocus earlier developments. Any structural scheme captures only a portion of this web of interrelationships and does only partial justice to the complexity of the work.[1]

Even though I think comparisons are crucial in the rhetorical strategy of Hebrews, I agree with Attridge that efforts such as that of Philip Hughes to structure the work according to the comparisons gloss over and skew the basic argument. Hughes proposed as an outline:

I. Christ superior to the prophets (1.1-3)
II. Christ superior to the angels (1.4–2.18)
III. Christ superior to Moses (3.1–4.13)
IV. Christ superior to Aaron (4.14–10.18)
V. Christ superior as the new and living way (10.19–12.29)
VI. Concluding exhortations, requests and greetings (13.1-25)[2]

I have been instructed by Attridge's comments on structure and admire his detailed outline, nevertheless I have been more impressed than he with certain clues provided by the Hebrews writer.[3] It is my judgment that we must first take seriously the author's declaration that Hebrews is a 'word of exhortation' (13.22). In what manner did exhortation inform his argument and arrangement? Some of those to whom the document is addressed have become negligent (10.25) as well as lethargic in regard to increased understanding (5.11). The author is adamant that recovery will come about from in-depth theological reflection upon Christ's achievements as sacrificer and sacrifice: 'Therefore let us go on to perfection, leaving behind the basic teaching about Christ...' (6.1). His strategy, therefore, is to set forth complicated instruction, followed by exhortation, that is, a charge to action. He reveals his basic concerns in 1.2-4 in which he proclaims Jesus as Son, creator, and the very imprint of God's being, the purification for sins, that is, sacrifice, and sitting at the right hand of God as priest forever, that is, sacrificer. I propose therefore as the skeletal arrangement of his strategy the following:

1. H.W. Attridge, *The Epistle to the Hebrews* (Philadelphia: Fortress Press, 1989), pp. 16, 17.
2. See Attridge's comments, pp. 14, 15; P.E. Hughes, *Hebrews, A Commentary on the Epistle to the Hebrews* (Grand Rapids: Eerdmans, 1977), pp. 3, 4.
3. For the detailed outline, see Attridge, *Hebrews*, p. 19.

I. Christ is Son (1.1-14)
   a. Above prophets (1.1-4)
   b. Above angels (1.5-14)
      First Exhortation (2.1-4) Obey his words because of his status
   c. For a time lower than angels, now higher, his brethren included (2.5-18)

II. Christ is superior to Moses (3.1-6)
      Second Exhortation (3.7-4.16) Hold faith firmly because of great high priest

III. Christ as high priest and sacrifice (5.1-10.18)
      [*Third Exhortation* (5.11-6.12) This is an interlude and exhortation for the whole discourse regarding going on to perfection]

      Fourth Exhortation (10.19-39) Be bold, recover commitment, endure

IV. Christ as the pioneer of a better faith complete with fulfilled promises (11.1-40)
      Fifth Exhortation (12.1-13.17) Follow the road of Jesus' suffering

V. Concluding remarks (13.18-25) Glory to Jesus Christ forever

In-depth christological reflection is therefore the path to spiritual renewal, accompanied by encouragement to commitment and action.[4] Several rhetorical agendas are played out in Hebrews, but the chief end is to enhance christological understanding as well as action based upon that newly gained understanding. Comparison is a strategy employed within this larger framework to prove 'that [Christ] is better than men of worth'.

---

4. I am indebted to F.V. Filson, *'Yesterday' A Study of Hebrews in the Light of Chapter 13* (London: SCM Press, 1967), pp. 27-30, for the insights in regard to exhortation. In an impressive study, W.G. Übelacker (*Der Hebräerbrief als Appell* [Stockholm: Almqvist & Wiksell, 1989]) argued that the writer employed the model of deliberative speech. Heb. 1.1-4 is an *exordium*; 1.5-2.18 the *narratio*; with 2.17 as the *propositio*. Heb. 13.22 is the *postscriptum*. While I agree that these items are useful in description, they do not help us understand the rhetorical structure of the body, especially in regard to amplification. I have questioned the usefulness of rigid delineation according to the three genres in 'An Aristotelian Rhetorical Analysis of 1 Thessalonians,' in D.L. Balch, E. Ferguson and W.A. Meeks (eds.), *Greeks, Romans and Christians: Essays in Honor of Abraham J. Malherbe* (Minneapolis: Fortress Press, 1990), pp. 216-36.

The outline provided above is the first level of organization. In the process of reading ancient funeral sermons, however, I have concluded that the work may also in a secondary manner reflect funeral sermon structure. I have been particularly struck with the similarity of the arrangement of Hebrews when compared with the eulogy of Isocrates on Evagoras and Gregory Nazianzus on Basil the Great. Hebrews best conforms to the epideictic genre in its superstructure even though the body of the argument may be conceived as deliberative.

Martin R.P. McGuire proposed that the typical structure of funeral discourses, drawing upon the third century CE work of the Greek rhetorician Menander, was:

I. Exordium

II. Encomium
   a. Family
   b. Birth
   c. Natural endowment
   d. Upbringing
   e. Education
   f. Life and occupation
   g. Achievements
   h. Fortune
   i. Comparison with the great and famous

III. Final Exhortation and Prayer[5]

Employing this pattern, the structure of Hebrews may be set forth as follows:

I. Exordium (1.1-4)

II. Encomium (1.5–13.16)
   a. Family and birth (1.5–3.13)
   b. Endowments, upbringing and education (3.14–6.12)
   c. Life, occupation, achievements, fortune (6.13–10.39)
   d Comparison with the great and famous
      1. Throughout (1.4–12.29)
      2. As a special section (11.1-40)

III. Final Exhortation and Prayer (13.17-25)

---

5. M.R.P. McGuire, 'The Christian Funeral Oration', in *Funeral Orations by Saint Gregory Nazianzus and Saint Ambrose* (trans. L.P. McCauley *et al.*; New York: Fathers of the Church, 1953), p. ix.

A few comments on this proposed structure are in order.[6] One question which has arisen without complete resolution is why the author commences by discussing angels.[7] Isocrates in his oration on Evagoras, composed about 370 BCE, commenced the section on the family of Evagoras with a lengthy discussion of its demi-god backgrounds especially in regard to the Trojan wars and Teucer who settled in Cyprus afterwards.[8] If the Hebrews author had these traditions in mind, he made clear that Jesus descended from God (1.2-3) rather than the demi-gods as in Hellenistic visions of heroes. It is of interest that Isocrates declared Evagoras superior to the demi-gods because his life exhibited greater fortune than theirs (70). The Hebrews writer perhaps commenced with the angel contrast to highlight Jesus' descent from God rather than lesser divine beings (1.5-6). The role of Hebrews 11 is likewise illuminated. The author concludes his catalog of past persons of faith by declaring that 'they did not receive what was promised, since God provided something better so that they would not, apart from us, be made perfect' (11.39-40). Since the action of Christ established the promises, those who believed in him stood above the past heroes of faith. Both Christ and his brothers were superior when compared with great believers of the past. Isocrates had such a section, but much truncated, working through a shorter and less elaborate catalog of Homeric heroes. It is of interest that Gregory Nazianzus in his funeral sermon on Basil the Great followed the structure of the classical Greek funeral sermon, but mixed classical references with biblical ones. His sermon, dated about 380 CE,

---

6. A number of works on classical funeral oratory have been published. These include V. Buchheit, *Untersuchungen zur Theorie des Genos Epideiktikon von Gorgias bis Aristoteles* (Munich: Heuber, 1960); O.C. Crawford, 'Laudatio Funebris', *The Classic Journal* 37 (1941–42), pp. 17-27; M.E. Deutsch, 'Antony's Funeral Speech', *University of California Publications in Classical Philology* 9 (1928), pp. 127-48; W. Kierdorf, *Laudatio Funebris Interpretationen und Untersuchungen zur Entwicklung der römischen Leichenrede* (Meisenheim am Glan: Verlag Anton Hain, 1980); N. Loraux, *The Invention of Athens The Funeral Oration in the Classical City* (trans. A. Sheridan; Cambridge, MA: Harvard University Press, 1986); J. Soffel, *Die Regeln Menanders für die Leichenrede* (Beiträge zur Klassischen Philologie, 57; Meisenheim am Glan: Anton Hain, 1974); J.E. Ziolkowski, *Thucydides and the Tradition of Funeral Speeches at Athens* (New York: Arno Press, 1981).

7. Attridge, *Hebrews*, p. 50.

8. Isocrates, *Evagoras* 12–21.

made reference to classical heroes and gods, but considered the real heroes great men and women of the Scriptures.[9] Toward the end of Gregory's discourse, much like in Hebrews, he compared Basil with a series of biblical heroes: Adam, Enosh, Enoch, Noah, Abraham, Isaac, Jacob, Joseph, Moses, Aaron, Samuel, David, Solomon, Elijah and Elisha, Daniel, the Maccabees, John the Baptist, Peter, Stephen and Paul.[10] The later Christian tradition may have drawn on Hebrews, but as likely drew on Hellenistic funeral oratorical structure, with Hebrews as a Christian model.

In two other ways similarities are striking. In all the funeral orations, obstacles are enumerated which the subject of the eulogy overcame. This is true of the Athenian heroes in the funeral orations of Pericles,[11] Evagoras[12] and Basil (that is, his ancestors)[13] and in Hebrews in respect to Christ, that is, in his suffering (2.9-10; 5.7-10). Likewise, a standard funeral eulogy ended with an exhortation. Isocrates employed the word (*diakeleuō*)[14] as contrasted with (*parakaleō*) of Hebrews (13.22), but both may be translated 'exhortation'. The approach of Isocrates, though not the conception, sounds similar to that of the Hebrews author:

> It is my task, therefore, and that of your other friends, to speak and to write in such fashion as may be likely to incite you to strive eagerly after those things which even now you do in fact desire; and it behoves you not to be negligent, but as at present so in the future to pay heed to yourself and to discipline your mind that you may be worthy of your father and of all your ancestors.[15]

Exhortation to emulate the heroes who have died in the war and to carry on the commitments of Athens is also obvious in the last four sections of Pericles' oration. Hebrews therefore follows the exhortatory purpose with even sharper clarity and magnitude than does the tradition. It would appear therefore that Hebrews in some measure utilized the traditional structure of the funeral oration. Especially, however, it replicates the penchant for comparison and contrast in

---

9. Gregory Nazianzus, 'On Saint Basil' 45–48.
10. Gregory Nazianzus, 'On Saint Basil' 88–94.
11. Thucydides 2.35-46.
12. Isocrates, *Evagoras* 25–27.
13. Gregory Nazianzus 'On Saint Basil' 30–34.
14. Isocrates, *Evagoras* 78–81.
15. Isocrates, *Evagoras* 80.

setting forth the superiority of Christ as the mode of amplification. Whether the borrowing is direct is open to question, but it seems likely. We may wonder about appropriating the structure of a funeral discourse to laud one who did indeed die, but is now alive, seated at the right hand of God (8.1; 12.2). The same essential arrangement, however, was employed to praise those alive.[16] Furthermore, the funeral sermons emphasized the manner in which those who had died continued to live through oncoming generations who emulated their characteristics.

Comparison as Amplification in Hebrews

We turn now to the rhetoric of amplification in Hebrews in regard to showing that Christ is superior to persons and entities. Our author's intent obviously is to highlight the extraordinary achievements of Christ so as to inspire action and endurance. He did this, not so much through straightforward explication, but through showing Christ's superiority to persons venerated by his readers. That he followed this route of argument and amplification likely had to do with the precedents of epideictic and funeral oratory. In fact, he employed comparison far more than the funeral orations of Pericles, Isocrates and Gregory Nazianzus, and Hyperides' oration of 322 BCE over the Athenian dead in the Lamian war. Several such elaborations may be found in Hebrews. I will focus on three: (1) Christ's superiority to angels, (2) to the Levitical priests and sacrifices, and (3) to the past heroes of faith.

(1) Why the author initiated the comparison with angels is problematic. Attridge suggests various possibilities, including that to do so reflects a traditional exaltation schema or a response to certain persons who assimilated the work of Christ to Jewish theories about angels.[17] I have proposed an additional explanation, the analogy from the Hellenistic funeral sermon *topoi*, in respect to establishing divine descent.

Whatever the reason, I am interested in the rhetorical strategy. The larger argument of the author is that though Christ is the exact imprint of God's very being (1.3), in his incarnation he was lower than the angels (2.9), a status reversed and enhanced 'When he had

16. Additional study of the structure of eulogies is appropriate.
17. Attridge, *Hebrews*, pp. 50-53.

made purification for sins...' (1.4). His status as lower defines his being as much as does his prior status and later exaltation. In his incarnation he became one with humanity (2.11) in which in turn he participated in glorification and honor (2.9). The achievement of the one who made purification for sin is unprecedented because of who he is. He is superior to the highest of heavenly beings. He is the very Son of God.

The author employs the means available to him and his readers in establishing Christ's superiority. He chiefly advanced a catena of Old Testament texts. It was only in regard to Christ that God affirmed sonship (1.5-6), angelic worship (1.7), elevation above his companions (1.9), eternity (1.12), and hegemony (1.12), in each case citing the Old Testament. He keyed in on texts employing appellations which affirmed Christ's sonship, the more excellent name he inherited (1.4). The angels in contrast were servants (1.7), especially for the sake of those who are to inherit salvation (1.14). The author's technique was to itemize in short order aggrandized roles for Christ as compared with angels.

Because Christ was superior to angels, believers, on whose behalf he lived and died, also attained a status superior to angels. In Christ's lowered rank he became human in every respect (2.17) and through death made 'a sacrifice of atonement for the sins of the people' (2.17). His action was on behalf of humans, not angels (2.5, 16). The author again authenticated his points through citing the Old Testament: the elevation of humans (2.6-8), and the oneness of Christ with humanity (2.11-13). As yet, evidence establishing Christ as sacrificer and sacrifice on behalf of humankind is only affirmed, not supported (2.17). That awaits future amplification in chs. 7–10. In ch. 2, the stacking effect abates because the explanations overshadow the texts cited. But in ch. 2, as well as in ch. 1, a privileged text, that is, the Old Testament, provided the chief warrant for Christ's superiority.

The power of the text, for the writer, resulted from the exalted role of those whose words appeared in it. He identified the author of the words in each case, mostly God (1.5, 6, 8), in regard to Christ, and in regard to angels (1.7, 13). He also referred to what Jesus said (2.18), but also to 'someone' (2.6), indicating his respect for the force of words in scripture even when the author could not be identified. Apparently for the writer and his readers, first level rhetorical power lay in these specific quoted texts.

While the technique of amplification through comparison is identical with that of the Greek orations, the evidence differs. Pericles in his discourse tells us of the superiority of Athenian culture. He does so by setting out specific attributes which may be empirically verified, such as the government of many, the adherence to laws, provisions for relaxation, homes of good taste, and the use of wealth as a ground of action. Only briefly does he contrast Athens with Sparta, and that in regard to freedom as opposed to discipline (39). Pericles refrained from citing honored texts. In none of the three orations examined did a speaker refer to a statement by a deity. Isocrates on Evagoras mentioned rumors of signs, portents and oracles, and while he did not discount these, he rejected elaborating on them. In fact, he asserted, 'we shall need no Homer to sing our praise nor any other poet whose verses may perhaps delight for the moment...' (41.4). Hyperides likewise cited specific actions to establish Leosthenes' superiority. In the waning section of the speech he held up Leosthenes as superior to the victors at Troy, as well as Harmodius and Aristogiton, heroes from the sixth century BCE (35–40). Isocrates also advanced empirical evidence to tout the superiority of Evagoras.

Neither Hyperides nor Isocrates cited texts. Isocrates mostly asserted the superiority of Evagoras through itemizing such characteristics as courage, wisdom, justice, and noble actions. He employed comparisons in the latter part, referring to Cyrus, Conon, and the heroes of Troy (65–79). Evagoras superseded them all, and even the demi-gods (71). Evagoras loomed larger than Cyrus because almost single handed he recovered his kingdom from the tyrants while Cyrus had several allies. Cyrus was treacherous, killing his maternal grandfather (37–40). Evagoras was superior in action to the respected Athenian Conon and more feared by Cyrus. In Heb. 2.4-18, in contrast, only one empirically observable item was advanced, that Christ tasted death (2.9). Only one accomplishment was paramount, that he died on behalf of his siblings (2.12, 17, 18). His accomplishment was greater than that of other humans because he himself was greater. The writer referred to signs, wonders and various miracles (2.4), parallel to the signs and portents in Evagoras, but he provided no specifics. Hebrews employed far more comparisons, and uniquely cited certain texts containing the very words of God as evidence. The rhetoric is therefore different because it has a different warrant.

(2) In Hebrews 7–10 Christ is set forth as superior in regard to

being a sacrificer and sacrifice. The argument commenced in ch. 5, but since it is broken up by an exhortatory interlude, I shall commence with ch. 7. The writer summed up his argument:

> But when Christ came as a high priest of the good things that have come, then through the greater and perfect tent (not made with hands, that is, not of this creation), he entered once for all into the Holy Place, not with the blood of goats and calves, but with his own blood, thus obtaining eternal redemption (9.11, 12).

His mode of amplification is to declare the superiority of Christ over Old Testament persons and entities. Christ is a superior officiator of sacrifices since he is a priest of the order of Melchizedek. Abraham paid a tenth of his spoil to that priest (7.4) and the Levitical priests are descended from Abraham (7.5). Christ, like Melchizedek, was without priestly precedent since he descended from Judah (7.14). He will be a priest forever since his priesthood is without beginning and end (7.15). The Levitical priests served only brief terms because of death (7.23). Christ is superior to the Levitical priests because they must offer sacrifices daily for their own sins, then those of the people, while Christ offered himself for sin once for all (7.27). In ch. 7, the author worked from Old Testament narratives without the rapid fire quoting found in ch. 1. This metaphorical focus upon Melchizedek and other past heroes was new at least in the eulogies examined, except that Gregory Nazianzus in his own, sometimes different, manner utilized the fathers similarly.

In chs. 8 and 9 the author amplified upon the location of the sacrificer and sacrifice. The sacrifice of Christ is superior because the site is the heavenly temple rather than the earthly one in Jerusalem. He is priest at the right hand of God in the sanctuary which no mortal has set up (8.2). The earthly sanctuary is only a pale reflection (8.5). The covenant of Jesus is therefore a better one since the sanctuary is in heaven as also the priest (8.2; 9.11). The sacrifice itself was offered there (9.12, 23, 24). In giving himself up, Christ was a one time sacrifice, therefore efficacious forever. To make this point, the writer offered a long quotation from Jeremiah (8.8-12). It is clear that in quoting Jeremiah he had in mind the sacrificial change rather than a new Torah, since he repeats the statement from Jeremiah in 10.17, 'I will remember their sins and lawless deeds no more'. His comparisons are not empirical data from experience. Rather they are specifics which come from Scripture. Since the salvific actions of Christ all took place beyond human observation, no empirical reports were possible, only assertions as to the heavenly provenance. Chapter 9 repeats much the same argument except that the comparisons had to do with the details of the temple. The data in regard to the inferior earthly temple, however, were built on observation and Scripture. The argument advanced was that since sin has been taken care of forever, which was never possible with animal sacrifices, the believer no longer has any consciousness of sin (9.14; 10.23).

The power of the comparison in this case derived chiefly from materials regarding the priesthood, the tabernacle, sacrifices and the forgiveness of sin. All the apropos data may be located in the legal materials of the Torah. While comparison was present in the Greek funeral sermons, nothing analogous to Hebrews may be found. In the three funeral sermons examined, no citations are made to ancient materials. References may be found to persons in ancient narratives, especially Homer, but they were miniscule when compared with Hebrews' use of the Old Testament. Even Gregory Nazianzus has no comparisons of this precise character. His discourse on Basil the Great was much longer than the classical ones, thereby providing more space for amplification. He referred to Homeric heroes a number of times, in some cases even citing Homer (29, 30, 33, 36, 42, 46). He also referred to Greek fables and various philosophers (45, 47, 48, 51). But even more than the classical references, though not as much as one might expect, he alluded to several persons and statements in scriptures, occasionally quoting passages, both short and long. While Gregory cited a few cases in which Basil exceeded his contemporaries, as was customary in the Hellenistic eulogies, he mostly employed materials from the Classics and the Scriptures.

(3) The final set of comparisons is in regard to the past heroes of faith found in Hebrews 11 and running into 12. This interesting catalog is somewhat parallel to the discussion of the heroes of Troy in the speeches of Hyperides and Isocrates and appeared in essentially the same position near the end of the discourse.[18] The comparisons,

---

18. I have yet to discover anyone who has compared the structure of Hebrews with the funeral sermon or considered Hebrews 11 in this light. See, for example, J.L. Bailey and L.D. Vander Broek, *Literary Forms in the New Testament: A Handbook* (Louisville: Westminster/John Knox Press, 1992), in comments on Hebrews, pp. 191-95; also L. Wills, 'The Form of the Sermon in Hellenistic Judaism and Early Christianity', *HTR* 77 (1984), pp. 277-99, and C. Black II, 'The

however, were much more detailed in Hebrews. It is of interest that Gregory Nazianzus had such a section in the last part of his sermon on Basil. He included additional biblical persons, but was less expansive than the Hebrews writer on Abraham and Moses. Gregory's comparisons were quick and somewhat pithy, and often analogical. For example, Basil was superior to Noah because Noah was entrusted with the ark and the seeds of a new world were committed to a few bits of wood and preserved amid the waters. Basil escaped a deluge of impiety and made his city an ark of safety, sailing buoyantly over the waters of the heretics, and subsequently restored the whole world (89). The purpose of the comparison in Hebrews 11 and 12 is not so much to show the superiority of Christ, but the status of believers as elevated even above the great heroes of the past (11.39, 40). The venerated attribute of these believers was that they abandoned a secure, familiar status for one unknown.[19] Abraham traveled to a land he had not seen (11.8) and set out to offer Isaac as a sacrifice even though he was about to destroy his own line of descent. Moses turned his back on the royal Egyptian house, for a life in the wilderness (11.27). The people of Israel walked right into the parted sea despite the prospect of drowning (11.29). Even Jesus entered freely into persecution not being sure of the outcome (12.2). Perhaps this is the point rather than because of a later reward, if an alternate translation is accepted 'who, instead of the joy that was set before him, endured the cross'.[20] Believers may be surrounded by a great cloud of past witnesses in their walk with God, but they are to keep their eyes on Jesus who was superior because of the suffering he endured from sinners, even unto death (12.3, 4). Because of their focus on him rather than past heroes, they too became superior to those illustrious persons of faith. Believers should likewise suffer, so that they may enter, not the earthly Jerusalem, but the heavenly one, that is, the city of God

Rhetorical Form of the Hellenistic Jewish and Early Christian Sermon: A Response to Lawrence Wills', *HTR* 81 (1988), pp. 1-18.

19. The common manner of comparing the Hebrews 11 catalog is with example lists of faith, which is not inappropriate. But the more fundamental rhetorical precedent may be the funeral discourse. See M.R. Cosby, *The Rhetorical Composition and Function of Hebrews 11: In Light of Example Lists in Antiquity* (Macon, GA: Mercer University Press, 1988).

20. Attridge admits this as possible, but argues that the NRSV preferred translation is more likely and has major commentator support (*Hebrews*, pp. 356-58).

(12.22). Obviously, the exhortation to step out on faith was amplified through comparison with past heroes who were nevertheless inferior because they did not participate in the promises.

Conclusion

The Hebrews writer, perhaps more than any ancient funeral orator, amplified his argument by comparison. He utilized aspects of the arrangement and strategies of the ancient orations, but he drew heavily from biblical statements, narratives and legal materials. He evinced special recognition of the force of biblical materials in a manner unparalleled in the classical Hellenistic discourses. He employed very little data drawn from his own experience or knowledge of contemporary or past situations. The data of experience, in contrast, were the chief grounds of comparison in the Hellenistic orations. Empirical data were advanced to characterize Christ's inferior predecessors. In Christ's case, the best corroborative evidence was transcendental, that is, from Scripture and projections based upon its alleged intent.

PART II

RHETORIC AND QUESTIONS OF METHOD

RHETORICAL CRITICISM, NEW FORM CRITICISM, AND NEW TESTAMENT HERMENEUTICS

Klaus Berger

General Considerations

In opposition to classical form-criticism, my model of form-criticism[1] departs—although not exclusively—from the literary form of a text, in order to determine the text-type. By this means I try to avoid some of the rather vague text-type definitions given by Bultmann (for example: *Gesetzesworte*). 'Form' means the linguistic and stylistic Gestalt of the text.

Between form and content of a linguistic sign we observe a relationship of interdependence. In other words, formal elements have a semantic function as well. Modern form-criticism is not based on the synoptic question, but on the eidographic problem of the relationship between form and content. In order to describe history we have to depart from the linguistic and stylistic form, because it marks the centre point of communication and is a fairly objective criterion. Therefore forms and genres seem to be the most important bridge between the expectations and the reception of the readers on the one hand, and between the author and the recipients on the other.

For the following reasons, form is a rhetorical element: (a) it is surface-oriented (*Sinnlichkeit*, sensuality), (b) it is to be seen *prima vista*, (c) it is almost always something known and allows easy identification.

If we want to take advantage of rhetoric in establishing genres or text-types we have to look for those elements in a text which have a dominant influence on the effect. That is, those elements which have the greatest power of innovation with regard to the recipients, or, in

---

1. Cf. K. Berger, *Formgeschichte des Neuen Testaments* (Heidelberg, 1984); *Einführung in die Formgeschichte* (UTB, 1444; Tübingen, 1987).

other words, which have the greatest power to 'change' them. This means that we have to ask which of the many conventions determining the text is so dominant that it can be regarded as a criterion for categorization? Or, which features of the text appeal to the interest of the original recipient—according to what we know about ancient rhetoric—in such a way that they allow a classification of the text, opening up the possibility of analogous texts clarifying each other and permitting a view on historical situations? In other words, the text-type is determined by the specific relationship among content, form and effect.

The basic framework of my form-criticism consists therefore of the ancient distinction between symbuleutic, epideictic and dicanic texts, that is: texts intended to activate or admonish the reader (symbuleutic texts), texts intended to impress the reader (epideictic texts) and texts intended to explain a decision (dicanic texts).

With regard to traditional form-criticism we have to depart from the following considerations:

(a) The aspect of origin of a text comprehends all its relationships to the past and to everything that happened before the moment of production. The aspect of effect of a text is the sum total of the elements referring to the achievement of a task or a goal with regard to the recipient or reader. One of the most important elements of these is the text form.

Traditional form-criticism unilaterally deals with the aspect of origin, establishing the wrong alternative between 'individual origin' and 'collective origin'. It is not concerned with the goal-orientedness of a text. Traditional form-criticism considers itself as a palaeontology of texts and regards the text in question (including its form) exclusively as a result of its history. The theological basis of this orientation towards the past is the problem of how to get access to the historical Jesus. In the work of Dibelius and Bultmann, for example, the aspect of tradition has absolute priority. According to these authors, the production of a text can be compared to the process of a translation. Given a new occasion and new recipients, traditions are transferred into a new situation. Traditional form-criticism understood this translation process as a form of more or less equivalent reproduction. It considered the new text as the sum total of all the traditions processed in it, which are reproduced in a more or less equivalent manner, and therefore we should analyse these traditions in order to understand the text.

I would like to suggest another method, analysing the text not in an archaeological but in a teleological fashion. In this case we would have to depart from the hypothesis that a text is intended to achieve an effect that (seen from the production point of view) lies in the future, presupposing that every text is meant to meet the requirements of an intended effect and can be judged according to its success. This means that in this model the freedom of the text producer in his/her specific situation has to be estimated higher than in the equivalent model.

The implied traditions can be considered something like the source text, and the new text is some sort of a target text. Under these conditions we have to assume that the main aim of the text-producer was to meet the requirements of his/her situation. He/she wanted to achieve an effect.

This new perspective leads to a different assessment of the historical dimensions of a text. Now, it is not only the origin of the tradition (asking whether it is with Jesus or a little later, in any case before it was put down in writing) which is of historical interest, especially for form-criticism, but also the function the given text has in the process of the history of early Christianity.

Traditional form-criticism is interested primarily in authenticity and therefore in the 'historia Jesu'. This interest belongs to the domain of the history of traditions (*Traditionsgeschichte*). What is new in my model is the specific question directed at form-criticism as to what was the function which the written text, such as we see it before us, had to fulfil in the history of early Christianity. What kind of effect was it intended to achieve and what does this tell us about the situation? Seen from this point of view, later situations (after Jesus) acquire the status of situations in their own right, and the question whether something is 'secondary' and therefore irrelevant with respect to the decisive problem of authenticity is of minor importance.

Rhetoric is not only concerned with the form of a text, but also with certain aspects of content, such as,

(a) emphatic elements
(b) elements that allow the reader to identify himself with the text
(c) explicit references to the addressees
(d) elements surprising the recipient (*Rezeptionsüberra-schungen*)

(e)   emotional associations that are or may be caused by the text
(f)   the position of a given shorter unit embedded in a composition

To sum up, everything that leads the reader's psyche towards a goal has to be regarded as a rhetorical element. In my opinion, analysing the rhetorical features means to analyse all sorts of psychagogical elements within a given text, including argumentation, which I consider a way on which the reader is guided towards a goal.

Matthew 11.25-30 as an Example

Pure Form-Criticism

According to my starting point in form-criticism I can find within this text the following genres:

(a) Prayer/thanksgiving in 11.25-26.

(b) Self-presentation of the messenger of God in 11.27.

(c) Propaganda: persuasive discourse (*Werberebe*) in 11.28-30.

(d) I consider the combination of self-presentation (v. 27) and the admonition in vv. 28-29 to be a *begründete Mahnrede*, that is: a combination of an epideictic element (self-presentation) and a symbuleutic element (general exhortation). In my opinion it is evident that the goal lies in the symbuleutic element.

(e) Eulogies at the beginning of New Testament letters often function as a part of self-presentation because the self of both the writers and the addressees is mentioned in these cases, for example in 2 Corinthians 1 and in Eph. 1.3.

(f) The combination of thanksgiving in the form of a kind of self-presentation with admonitions occurs in New Testament letters too, for example in Eph. 1.3ff., 16ff./2.1ff. and 1 Pet. 1.3-12/13ff. By comparing these texts with Matthew 11 we learn that the self-presentation by thanksgiving is used as an authorization for the admonitions or exhortations to follow.

Other Rhetorical Aspects of Matthew 11

(a) Emphatic elements:

v. 25 *ehomologoumai soi*

v. 26 *nai o patēr*

v. 28 *deute, pros me*

These elements signal important incisions within the composition of the text.

(b) Elements of self-identification:

The reader is made to believe that he does not belong to the wise men in v. 25 but to the unwise who are presented as the ones who receive revelation.

The reader is made to think that he belongs to those who suffer and carry burdens in v. 28 (*kopiōntes kai pephortismenoi*).

(c) Explicit references to the addressees:

v. 25 Father, Lord of heaven and earth

v. 26 Father

v. 28 all those who are suffering

(d) Elements surprising the recipient (*Rezeptionsüberraschungen*):

The reader expects that some secret or mystery will be disclosed to him. He is guided toward this belief by *tauta* in v. 25 and *panta* in v. 27. But instead of listening to a mystery he only learns about Jesus himself. So the objectivistic utterance about *tauta* and *panta* is followed by speaking about the son and the father in v. 27 and the self-presentation in v. 29. Jesus mentions 'my yoke' and he says: 'because I am *tapeinos kai prays*'. The hidden mystery is substituted by the disclosed son, who is standing before the audience.

So the self of the speaker becomes an important element of human interest.

(e) Emotional associations:

We see that there is no remarkable difference between logical argumentation and the plan of emotional association:

vv. 25-26: The reader is confronted with the paradox of God's choosing and rejecting. He learns that within the sphere of God most things are contrary to what humans usually expect. The author plays on the reader's resentments; he appeals to their inclination of ridiculing so-called scholars and so-called wise men.

In v. 26 the artificial wording is meant to hide the fact that the text deals less with reality than with mere statements.

In v. 27 there is a close intimacy between son and father. The reader has no chance of identifying himself with any person mentioned here. In v. 25 the author has started to radically limit the group of persons at whom God's positive activity is directed. In v. 27 this tendency reaches its climax.

There is then a tension between absolute exclusivity of v. 27 and the openness of Jesus' invitation in v. 28. Everybody can identify himself with the suffering people here. In v. 28 we find suffering and promise. But in v. 29 a condition is mentioned: those who want to obtain the promise must take over Jesus' yoke. So v. 29 appeals to the reader: he cannot have the *anapausis* for his soul without any effort. Contrary to this a new stage of argumentation is reached in v. 30: the condition required in v. 29 is not very hard to fulfil.

After all these rhetorical considerations let us return to the question of form-criticism: the analysis of the rhetorical element has shown the rhetorical aim pursued by the author: he want to make clear that the mystery hidden to the wise men is nothing else but Jesus himself as the example that is put before their eyes by the gospel itself.

I come to the following conclusions: (1) In order to achieve his rhetorical aim the author embeds different genres into his text. We call this a rhetorical strategy. (2) When we find various genres in one textual composition inner coherence is found out by analysis of the rhetorical aim. (3) For the analysis of biblical texts we cannot rely primarily on the old handbooks of classical rhetoric but biblical rhetoric has its own forms and ways.

Hermeneutics

Hermeneutics is based on rhetoric, because application does not merely rely on theoretical comprehension (against Bultmann), but mainly on the pragmatic effect (function).

The starting point of my *Hermeneutik des Neuen Testament* is: we need not suppose anthropological constraints as Bultmann thought nor any eternal truth. There are different situations, and if we want to find an orientation in a given situation we must carefully analyse it and try to find out the *tertium comparationis* between the biblical text and the given situation, that is: the point by which the biblical text can support people in this situation or give them critical guidance.

This has much to do with rhetoric because the *tertium comparationis* between the text and the situation is constituted by the effect that a text or its interpretation can have in the situation.

My hermeneutical model[2] focuses on the interpretation of parables.

2. Cf. K. Berger, *Hermeneutik des Neuen Testaments* (Gütersloh, 1988).

Parables are texts embedded in another context. They have a particular effect on this context by means of a point. In a very similar way a biblical text is transferred today into a new context. In this case, too, the applicant has to look for the point, that is: for the possibilities of effect. These possibilities are verbalized for example in a sermon, whose recipients then have to apply the sermon to their own situation.

So we may ask, for example, whether the *Rezeptionsüberraschung* (the element surprising the recipient)—in our text that the mystery is Jesus himself as a human person—can have its effect still today. Or we may ask whether the play on mystery and disclosure is still valid in a given situation.

TEXTUAL SPACE AS RHETORICAL DEVICE

Bernard Lategan

Introduction

In discussing textual space as rhetorical device, I am fully aware of the risks involved in dealing with biblical material from a rhetorical perspective, as Classen (1991) has pointed out so convincingly. My aim is not to analyse Paul's letter to the Galatians in terms of classical rhetorical conventions. Rather, in the light of recent developments in rhetorical and hermeneutical theory and practice, I am interested in the way Paul uses textual space (in itself a modern concept) in trying to convince his readers.

To my mind, there is no need to impose a rhetorical framework, which was originally designed for speech, on letters by categorizing them as 'speech at a distance' or 'deferred speech'. The specific nature of epistolography should rather be respected for what it is. Written communication with its accompanying feature of the presence/absence of the writer and reader has its own mysteries and fascination and should be studied in its own right. But, in as far as letters have a pragmatic intent, their illocutionary and perlocutionary force have to be taken into account. This provides all the scope for rhetorical analysis of letters in the broader sense of the word. (Cf. *inter alia* Stowers 1986; Doty 1973; Malherbe 1988; Koskenniemi 1956; Wuellner 1989; Petersen 1985; Schnider 1987).

The concept of space has been treated either explicitly or implicitly in a number of ways in studies on social and textual communication. Interesting work has been done on 'social space' (e.g. Bourdieu 1991), a concept developed to describe and explain differences between certain cultures or societies (e.g. Japan, the USA or France). Bordieu himself (1991: 63) distinguishes between social positions (a relational concept), social dispositions (habitus) and specific social positioning, that is, the choices made by social agents in diverse domains like food, sport and politics. (The terms 'right', 'left' and 'center' in political terminology illustrate the important role of space.) In interpersonal communication, the concepts of social distance, of private space and of the protection of this space, are well-known. (Cf. also the work of Schmidt [1991] on texts as structural coupling of cognitive and social systems.)

In theoretical studies on verbal and, more specifically, on textual communication, the term 'textual space' has appeared in a general and fairly vague way. Martin Nystrand (1982) uses it to describe the total area in which communication takes place, and which includes the real writer and reader.

In a penetrating analysis of the letter as the exchange of written dialogue, Patrizia Violi (1985) tries to establish basic criteria which define the letter as a genre. Although she does not use the term 'textual space' as such, she convincingly shows that an essential feature of the letter is the positioning of the writer and reader both 'outside' and 'inside' the text.

She begins by showing that a prominent feature which characterizes letters is the way in which pronouns and space-time deixis are inscribed in the text (1985: 149). (We shall return to the axis of time and space in more detail later when discussing Galatians.) She then proceeds to distinguish between the 'situation of the utterance' and the 'situation of the sentence':

> The former is the situation in which the sentence is produced concretely and in which are contained the categories of space and time and the people who participate in them. The latter, on the other hand, is defined by the elements inscribed within the text itself. On the basis of this distinction, therefore, 'discourse' is defined as those linguistic productions whose description entails reference to the Situation of Utterance, story as those linguistic productions whose description does not (1985: 150-51).

Violi concludes that the letter belongs to discourse, rather than to narrative and that it is a genre in which traces of utterance are *constitutive* of the genre.

The rest of Violi's study is devoted to explaining the referential mechanisms spatially and temporally anchoring the letter sentence to its situation of utterance (1985: 152). Unlike narrative, extratextual references can hardly be concealed in the letter—the salutation, the signature, the reference to the place and date of writing are all indications of the link with the situation of utterance. The interaction between the real and implied author and the real and implied reader is therefore a very prominent feature of the letter.

A very specific aspect of this interaction is the dialectical relationship between the presence/absence of the real/implied author and of the real/implied reader. The letter can contain references to the situation of the writer ('While I am writing this in the early hours of the morning...') or to the situation of the reader ('When you read these lines in the seclusion of your study...'). The letter presupposes an immediacy between writer and reader, indicated by the use of first and second person pronouns, but the very fact of the letter as mediating communication attests to the absence of both writer and reader and to the distance between them. 'In this way, a simultaneous effect of presence and absence is set up where although the narratee is always present in the text, it is a presence which continually alerts us to an "elsewhere"' (Violi 1985: 157). The narratee is therefore ambiguously constituted. On the real communicative axis it refers to a definite empirical addressee, but as soon as the communicative structure becomes inscribed within the text, the empirical subject is distanced to become a textually inscribed addressee.

Violi concludes: 'In fact the communication between Narrator and Narratee is always somehow postponed in the letter and we can refer to the communicative process in the text only by making this gap explicit' (1985: 157).

The aim of this paper is to show how this gap affords the opportunity for rhetorical strategies and how Paul exploits this in the text of Galatians in order to achieve the desired persuasion of his readers.

Textual Space in Galatians

Whereas the attention of Violi is focused on the anchoring of the text of the letter in the situation of utterance and to show how in many ways traces of this situation are inscribed in the text, I would like to take the concept of textual space a step further and to explore its *rhetorical* potential and consequences. I hope to show that textual space plays an important role in the actual process of persuasion, not only in giving evidence of its link with the situation of utterance. In other words, I am interested in the pragmatic consequences of textual space and how it is used by Paul to effect a fundamental change in the thinking and attitude of his readers.

The Argumentative Situation of Galatians

As the argumentative situation of Paul's letter to the Galatians has been at the centre of attention in recent studies and as this has been described more fully elsewhere (cf. *inter alia* Betz 1979; Hübner 1984; Smit 1985; Hester 1986; Lategan 1992), there is no need to provide an extensive discussion of the issue here and of the specific choices underlying the following interpretation. Only a very brief outline of the argumentative situation will be given here to serve as a framework for the subsequent discussion.

Paul is faced with a situation where his erstwhile converts in Galatia have deserted their original position and have adopted what Paul considers to be an aberration of the true gospel. However difficult it may be to come to a full understanding of the nature of this aberration and of the anti-Pauline opposition in Galatia, it is clear that they were very successful on at least one point. They were able to convince the Galatians that they should—in addition to faith in Christ—obey the Torah and adopt the Jewish way of life. Considering the background of most of the Galatians, it is not difficult to understand why the argument was so persuasive. Their conversion to the Christian faith implied a complete reorientation of both their value system and their lifestyle. For Jews this transition was difficult enough, but it did not entail the abandonment of their own tradition—it was rather understood as its continuation and completion. For Gentiles, the break was much more incisive. They found themselves at a double disadvantage—new to the Christian faith, but also unfamiliar with its Jewish roots. As Johnny-come-latelys they were in desperate need of practical advice to guide their day-to-day life in an environment not very sympathetic or supportive of their new convictions. Thus they became easy targets for the proponents of 'another gospel'. For whatever reason, Paul has—at least in their own understanding of the matter—not given them enough practical guidelines to survive as believers under these circumstances. That is why they are so susceptible to the argument of the opponents. Faith in Christ is—also in the opponents' view—essential, but to translate that into action and to make it workable in everyday life, one needs a set of time-tested rules for the practice of this faith. That is exactly what the Jewish way of life can offer—it has stood the test of time, it has guided the Jewish people through the most testing and adverse times of their long history. Not only does it offer a practical guide to the Galatians, but it also provides the means to become part of an age-old tradition, to become fully initiated and accepted by the central leadership in Jerusalem. In view of the psychological needs of new converts, their acceptance into the group, their identity and sense of security after being cut off from their natural environment, this is a very attractive and persuasive argument.

Paul, therefore, faces a formidable task. For him the shift made by the Galatians in adopting the Jewish way of life is a shift away from the gospel to 'another gospel'—which, in his understanding, does not exist. The heart of the gospel is at stake. But to win back his erstwhile converts is no easy task, as they have already abandoned his position for what they consider to be a much more attractive and sensible interpretation of the Christian message.

Time and Space as Rhetorical Devices

Time and space are the two basic dimensions available to an author when creating and shaping a text. Changes along the axis of time and along the axis of space are the fundamental elements which make the development of story and argument possible. In narrative material, the text is essentially constituted by shifts in time and location, forming a sequence of events and changes of scene to create what we call a story.

In argumentative texts, time and space play a different, but equally fundamental role. Here, temporal and spatial shifts are aimed at persuasion. In order to achieve the desired result, time and space are used in a wide variety of ways.

It must be emphasized again that we are dealing here with *textual* time and space, as opposed to real time and space—in the same way that a distinction is made between story time and real time. Of course, textual time and real time may overlap, but as in the case of the real/implied author/reader, we must be very clear that we are dealing with a textual *construct* and that we shall have to analyse argumentative texts from this perspective.

When we turn our attention to the letter of Galatians, which is an argumentative text par excellence, we find that the letter abounds with temporal and spatial markers. For the purposes of this paper, we shall be concentrating on spatial relations. The temporal indicators are a specific feature of Paul's style. He often uses time to differentiate between alternative modes of existence. In the most graphic way, Paul refers to the 'before' and 'after' of his own existence. Gal. 1.13 describes his life ποτε ἐν τῷ 'Ιουδαϊσμῷ and his persecution of the church *before* (ὅτε as temporal marker—1.15) the dramatic event of God's revelation to him which changed his whole life. However, his personal history is indissolubly linked to a much more encompassing and even cosmic history. The πρό of Gal. 3.23 (πρὸ τοῦ δὲ ἐλθεῖν τὴν πίστιν) is a marker of 'universal' time and constitutes the link with 'salvation history'. The classical text for the change in personal existence is certainly 2 Cor. 5.16, where the νῦν marks the transition from non-belief to belief, which results in knowing κατὰ πνεῦμα instead of κατὰ σάρκα. Here again the change on the personal level is immediately understood in the context of a much broader and more supra-individual transition from the ἀρχαῖα that has passed to the καινά of a new situation (2 Cor. 5.17). The text of Galatians abounds with temporal markers of this kind.

Leaving the changes along the axis of time aside for the moment, we concentrate in what follows on changes along the axis of space.

The Function of Spatial Indicators

Spatial indicators function on two levels in the text of Galatians. They are used to identify preferred and non-preferred positions and they are used to effect the shifting of position (which is the essence of rhetoric) through techniques of association and disassociation.

Preferred and Non-Preferred Positions

Parallel to the differences on the temporal axis, where the 'before' and 'after' of coming to faith are marked in many different ways in Pauline texts, run the differences on the spatial axis to indicate *positions* inside and outside faith. The most famous of these is the ἐν χριστῷ formula, which appears prominently in passages like 1.17, 3.14 and 28. The counterpart of this position is on the other hand marked as the existence ἐν νόμῳ or ὑπὸ νόμον (3.11, 23) or ὑπὸ τὰ στοιχεῖα τοῦ κόσμου (4.3).

The preferred existence in faith is expanded by locations on the geographical and genealogical level. The location of Mount Sinai in Arabia (4.25) and its identification with Hagar and slavery, that is, slavery caused by subservience to the law, are all negative allusions to indicate a non-preferred position. The expected counterpart is Mount

Zion, seat of the freeborn descendants of Rebecca. So far, so good. But now comes the unexpected twist. In terms of Paul's experience and dealings with Jerusalem, this location has acquired negative associations for him and became the symbol for the upholding of the Torah. Paul therefore does not shrink from identifying Sinai with (the present) Jerusalem (4.25), giving this whole conglomerate a negative evaluation. He creates as counterpart the Jerusalem 'above' which is indeed the stronghold of the liberated and the mother of us (= believers) all (4.26).

The negative association with the present Jerusalem has its counterpart in 1.17, where Paul illustrates his independence from Jerusalem and the Jerusalem leaders by relating that he did not return to Jerusalem after his conversion, but that he went away (ἀπῆλθον) to Arabia and afterwards even to Damascus. Here Arabia acquires almost a positive connotation.

For our purposes it is important to note that these shifts in position on the geographical level are at the same time closely associated with shifting positions on the genealogical level. This is the other form of textual location which forms an integral part of Paul's rhetorical strategy and which he uses to indicate preferred position. We have already seen how in 4.26 the Jerusalem 'above' is also described as the *mother* of all believers. The family concept or the genealogical metaphor is applied in a number of ways. Most graphic is the history of the two mothers, Sarah and Hagar, and the two sons of Abraham, representing two genealogical lines and symbolizing two covenants, leading to two lines of descent—children of slavery and children liberated from slavery (4.21-30). In a bold move, Abraham is claimed as the father of *all* believers (3.7), liberating him from the restrictive interpretation which made him the exclusivist figurehead of one group.

Staying within the family circle, God is presented as father (1.3), Jesus as son (2.20), while believers become children of God (3.26), adopted sons (4.4), calling God their father (4.6). As children, they also become heirs to God (4.6). The natural terminology for believers amongst themselves is therefore brothers and sisters (1.2; 4.12; 5.31; 6.1).

The social positioning is taken a step further when the identification with Christ leads to specific social consequences (3.28), as we shall presently see.

Shifting Positions

Indicating preferred and non-preferred positions is one thing. To achieve a shift in the right direction is another matter. But that is precisely the point of rhetoric and that is clearly Paul's purpose in his letter to the Galatians. How does he go about ensuring the desired result?

An analysis of his rhetorical strategy reveals at least four facets in this process: by making clear that although textual positions are fixed, shifts by people in more than one direction are possible, by association and disassociation, first with Christ and then with his readers, and, finally, by providing a basis for a new selfunderstanding and a different perspective on reality.

A remarkable feature of the text of Galatians is that although textual positions are fixed and the positive or negative evaluation of these positions does not change, shifts by individuals between these positions are not only possible, but occur quite frequently in all directions. In a self-effacing way—that is not devoid of strong rhetorical intentions— Paul openly admits that at one stage he found himself in a non-preferred position. When he was still ἐν τῷ Ἰουδαϊσμῷ (1.13), he was a persecutor and destroyer of the church. But these reverse shifts can take place also *after* coming to faith. After Peter accepted Paul's approach to the Gentiles in Antioch, he associated with them socially by eating together (2.12). However, the moment James arrived from Jerusalem, he had second thoughts, and distanced himself from his Gentile fellow believers. All the other Jews and even Barnabas were drawn into the same hypocrisy (2.13). But that of course is also the position of the Galatians: after having received the faith with such acclamation, they have now inexplicably gone astray in pursuit of 'another gospel' (1.6). Preferred positions cannot change, but people do. As a dramatic reminder of this possibility, Paul warns the Galatians that should he or even an angel from heaven proclaim a different gospel to them, they should recognize these imposters for what they are and condemn them forthwith (1.8-9)!

If people can change for the worse, they can also change for the better. This is the first premise of Paul's rhetorical strategy and by providing concrete examples to his readers, he makes the possibility for change that much more feasible.

But how does change in actual fact takes place? For Paul, association and disassociation are the key to change. This brings us to the second element of his rhetorical strategy, which he actually employs on two levels: his association with Christ and his association with his readers.

Paul first reminds his readers that his own dramatic change was not self-initiated, but was effected by the closest possible association with Christ and with his death on the cross. Change cannot be achieved on one's own or in isolation—only in solidarity with Christ and with fellow-believers. Being crucified *with* Christ (2.19) is understood by Paul in the most concrete sense. In some way, in terms of corporate solidarity, he was present at the cross. His life consequently is no longer his own—it is in actual fact Christ who lives in him and therefore his life is dedicated to the service of God (2.20-21). Change becomes a reality through this association with the greater power of a living God.

It is this association and this change that Paul so intensely desires for his own readers. In order to make this shift, he develops as part of his rhetorical strategy an *intermediate* form of association with his readers, where association with him becomes the stepping stone— 'Become like me, brothers, as I became like you, I beseech you' (4.12). This leads to a whole process of positioning between Paul and his readers throughout the letter and which takes the form of both association and disassociation. Basically, when Paul is dealing with an undesirable position, he distances himself from the readers, while in a preferred position, he declares his solidarity with them. In this way he hopes to effect the desired change.

In this process, the use of personal pronouns and the terms in which the readers are addressed play a crucial role. In 1.2, Paul sets up a clear distance between himself and his readers. He identifies with the σὺν ἐμοὶ πάντες ἀδελφοί, while the addressees are impersonally described as 'the churches in Galatia'. It is very significant that they are not assigned the status of ἀδελφοί at this stage, while those associated with the writer are. The only acknowledgment of communality is the reference to God as 'our' father (1.3, 4) and the fact that Christ gave himself for 'our' sins (1.4). This sets the pattern for the rest of the letter. Paul keeps his distance from his readers and never calls them 'brothers' until much later in the text. In 1.8 'we or an angel from heaven' are set off against the 'you' of the readers. What common bondage that does exist is acknowledged in an intermediate way, through the acceptance that salvation and freedom are for all.

But this remains to be expressed in an impersonal way, by using the general 'we' when referring to the work of Christ (e.g. 3.13, 22-25)—although the first person can very soon changes again to a 'you' (cf. 3.26 and 28: πάντες γὰρ ὑμεῖς εἷς/ἐστε ἐν χριστῷ Ἰησοῦ).

A very interesting shift takes place in 4.6. The sentence still starts off with the second person form (ἐστε), but then changes to the first person (τὰς καρδίας ἡμῶν) to indicate a lessening of the textual distance between Paul and his readers. This is a prelude of what is to follow in 4.12. In the meantime, the switch is back to the second person when the non-preferred position is spelled out in 4.8-11.

In 4.12 Paul for the first time drops all pretences and states the aim of his letter quite openly: 'Become like me, in the same way I became like you'. The readers are now addressed as 'brothers' and Paul no longer reprimands them—he beseeches them. Even more—he grants that he has not been wronged by them (4.12) and that he has been received like an angel by the Galatians when he first came to them— even like Christ himself (4.14).

At this point the tone changes and Paul consistently addresses his readers as 'brothers' (4.28, 31; 5.11, 13; 6.1, 18). The change is most poignantly expressed in 4.19, where Paul uses the endearing term 'my children' and reveals his deepest feelings towards them—he is in birthpangs till Christ again takes shape in them.

Through a whole process of disassociation and association Paul endeavors to shift his readers. The final element in this process is to provide them with a new selfunderstanding and a new perspective on reality. The different textual positions which Paul elaborates in the letter are in actual fact elements of a 'proposed world' (in Ricoeurian terms) he is suggesting to his readers. He urges them to think of themselves *in terms of* the position they ought to assume—as children in the household of God, as heirs to the promises of Abraham, as one in Christ, as liberated people. As soon as this happens, a range of new possibilities opens up. Believers from the Gentiles no longer have to feel inferior and in a disadvantaged position in comparison to believers from a Jewish background—they can claim Abraham as their father with the same and even fuller right. Being one in Christ suddenly has all kinds of social and political consequences—cultural, social and sexual differences have somehow lost their divisive and destructive force (3.28). One can only be free by thinking and acting as a liberated being (5.1).

Conclusion

The use of textual space and the indication of preferred positions are therefore much more than clever tricks in Paul's rhetorical repertoire. They offer the reader a new selfunderstanding, leading to new attitudes and actions. The very fact of assuming these positions results in a different point of view, leading to a new perspective on reality, setting a series of pragmatic social, ethical and political consequences in motion.

Bibliography

Betz, H.D.
1979   *Galatians* (Philadelphia: Fortress Press).
Bourdieu, P.
1991   'Social Space and Symbolic Space: Introduction to a Japanese Reading of Distinction', *Poetics Today* 12: 627-38.
Classen, C.J.
1991   'Paulus und die antike Rhetorik', *ZNW* 82: 1-33.
Doty, W.G.
1973   *Letters in Primitive Christianity* (Philadelphia: Fortress Press).
Dormeyer, D.
1989   'Die Familie Jesu und der Sohn der Maria im Markusevangelium', in M. Frankemölle and K. Kertelge, (eds.), *Von Christentum zum Jesus: Festschrift für Joachim Gnilka* (Freiburg: Herder): 109-36.
Hester, J.D.
1986   'The Use and Influence of Rhetoric in Galatians', *TZ* 42: 386-408.
Hübner, H.
1984   'Der Galaterbrief und das Verhältnis von antiker Rhetorik und Epistolographie', *TLZ* 109: 241-50.
Koskenniemi, H.
1956   *Studien zur Idee und Phraseologie des griechischen Briefes bis 400 n. Chr.* (Helsinki: Akateeminen Kirjakauppa).
Lategan, B.C.
1992   'The Argumentative Situation of Galatians', *Neot* 26: 257-77.
Malherbe, A.J.
1988   *Ancient Epistolary Theorists* (Missoula, MT: Scholars Press).
Nystrand, M.
1982   'The Structure of Textual Space', in M. Nystrand (ed.), *What Writers Know: Language, Process, and Structure of Written Discourse* (New York: Academic Press): 75-86.
Schmidt, S.J.
1991   'Text Understanding—A Self-Organizing Cognitive Process', *Poetics* 20: 273-301.

Schnider, F., and W. Stenger,
1987   *Studien zum neutestamentlichen Briefformular* (Leiden: Brill).
Stowers, S.K.
1986   *Letter Writing in Greco-Roman Antiquity* (Philadelphia: Westminister
           Press).
Smit, J.
1985   'Paulus, de galaten en het judaïsme: Een narratieve analyze van
           Galaten 1–2', *Tijdschrift voor Theologie* 25: 337-62.
Violi, P.
1985   'Letters', in T.A. van Dijk (ed.), *Discourse and Literature*
           (Amsterdam: John Benjamins): 149-67.
Wuellner, W.
1989   'Hermeneutics and Rhetorics', *Scriptura* 3.

The Verbal Art of the Pauline Letters: Rhetoric, Performance and Presence

Pieter J.J. Botha

Introduction

Communication is the activity that humans engage in to convey meanings, express attitudes and feelings, and seek solutions to problems. *Rhetorical* communication creates a message with verbal and visual symbols/actions to influence an audience which has the ability to change its beliefs and behaviours as a consequence of experiencing the message (or at least, such is the perspective of the creator of the message). The format of these symbols and actions is determined by their socio-cultural context, and their effectiveness can only be described, and consequently understood, within this context. This principle naturally also holds for ancient letters.[1]

It has often been noted that there is an oral aspect to Paul's letters. Hester (1986: 387) describes Paul's style as 'as much oral as it is written. It is as though Paul wrote speeches.'[2] He continues:

1.   This is basically the same point made by Stowers (1986: 16): 'ancient letters will be difficult to understand on their own terms unless we also understand something about the contexts of Greco-Roman society in which the actions were performed and had their meanings'.

2.   Examples can be multiplied: e.g. Funk 1966a: 245 (cited by Hester); Funk 1966b; Lategan 1988: 416; White 1988: 19; Vielhauer 1975: 59; Doty 1973: 75-76; Malherbe 1986: 68. Dahl (1977: 79) draws attention to some of the implications of texts meant to be read aloud. He notes that Greek prose style was in general closer to oral speech than are modern literary products. Kelber (1983: 140-77) has attempted to interpret Paul's theology as orally constituted. Kelber misrepresents orality in Graeco-Roman antiquity, because he underplays the complexities of oral-literate interaction as anthropological phenomena. He separates Paul's (oral) preaching from his (written) letters. It remains an important study, nevertheless. One should add that many studies on Graeco-Roman society also suffer from improper assumptions concerning literacy and education in antiquity.

> If one accepts the notion that Paul's letters are rife with oral expression or style... one had better begin to take seriously the possibility that Paul saw his letters as speeches (Hester 1986: 389).

This study aims to do exactly that: to take the oral aspects of Paul's letters seriously. More than this, this study aspires to promote awareness of orality as a fundamental part of the context of ancient communication and therefore also of ancient rhetoric.

To see the significance of this when it comes to a proper historical understanding of Paul's letters, one need only ask how form, style and structure have been dealt with concerning these writings. *Any* discussion of style, form or rhetorical facets *always* presupposes a larger framework within which these 'formal' aspects make sense. No one would deny that we find certain stylistic characteristics in any text. The problem is what to make of them. These characteristics do not explain themselves; they need to be interpreted, to be related to various communicative strategies, cultural conventions, historical and social phenomena, before they make sense. Any claim that stylistic phenomena per se can guide one to valid interpretation is misleading. Structural phenomena, forms and 'literary' characteristics all presuppose in some way a frame of reference from within which they can be identified for what they presumably are. They can only be interpreted once this larger frame is explicitly brought to bear on the issues. And, what must also be kept in mind is that, in some way or another, *some* sense or idea of a larger framework is in any case at work when we read these ancient letters. The task is to identify the unhistorical and subjective parts of one's 'pre-understanding', so to speak.

Literacy, Visualism and Bias

The very first step needed for a responsible interpretation of ancient communication is to become aware of tacit assumptions. For instance, we must replace our misleading, modern literate view of ancient writing activities with a more responsible view that takes into account their historical, religious, intellectual and psychological situation.

Our literate bias is, however, part of a complex set of interrelated factors, and to understand how easily we can distort ancient rhetoric we need to make a short detour into the difficult terrain of language, culture, communication technology and cognition.

Method and Vision

Few New Testament scholars have considered the possibility that such simple and sensible methods or techniques like delineating a pericope, outlining the structure of a text, drawing syntactic diagrams, making tables, designing comparative charts, or even learning Greek might be biased toward a certain theory of knowledge of which the claims to validity are not beyond questioning.

Notice the way most of us go about the use of ancient languages, as becomes apparent in the metaphors we employ to indicate our methods and results. Most often, our knowledge of the language is pictured as a tool, as a means to elicit information. Somehow, what one seeks is thought to exist separately from language and the activity of speaking. We attempt to *extract*, or *discover*, or even *uncover* the meaning or the thought content. Greek is considered to be the vehicle (or receptacle) of Paul's intent or message. All these images reflect a manipulative use of language derived from visual and spatial conceptualizations.

Our studies abound in charts, diagrams, structural analyses and tables. These phenomena are manifestations of deeply ingrained empirical and positivistic convictions.[3] They rest on a corpuscular, atomic theory of knowledge and information, which is only possible with a prejudice towards visual and spatial conceptualizations. Such a theory encourages quantification and diagrammatic representation so that the ability to 'visualize' someone's meaning (or intent) almost becomes synonymous with understanding it. Following Fabian, we can call this tendency *visualism*: 'The term is to connote a cultural, ideological bias towards vision as the "noblest sense" and towards geometry qua graphic-spatial conceptualization as the most "exact way" of communicating knowledge' (1983: 106). It is important to recognise a paradoxical consequence of visualism, namely that it leads to a (or may be a symptom of) denigration of visual experience. Not only are we 'deaf' to the oral-aural worlds of other, less technologized

---

3.   These developments have a long history in Western philosophical tradition, going back to J. Locke and D. Hume. For the relation between the experience of the primacy of vision and the origins of modern science: Lindberg and Steneck 1972. Though outside their scope of inquiry, we should add that visualism can be traced right back to Plato, *Phaedrus* 250. Graeco-Roman culture is distinctly related to ours; at its closest, however, it is a (very much) younger forebear. On literate bias see McConnell 1986; Botha 1992c.

communication systems, we reduce the symbolic forms of ancient people to 'stuff', to disembodied things.[4]

Another way visualism has a grasp on us is the variety of ways, often in the most simple and seemingly commonsensical recommendations, in which expeditiousness of procedure or notions of speed are involved or emphasized. For instance, notice what is usually *not* asked about Paul's activities: questions about the time Paul needed (wasted!) to get into the situation to deliver a message. Or about the skilful manipulation of social relations needed to have a letter presented in the first place.

There were no letter boxes in antiquity. A letter carrier did not simply deliver the letter. It had to be given to someone; the letter was probably discussed and it was physically handled by various people. Even if a letter was straightforwardly delivered, the receiver had to select the correct time to have it read. Since others were present, there must have been considerable interaction: getting together, waiting for each other; maybe some preparation of the audience. All this is simply ignored in our 'reconstructions'. With regard to the communicative *event*, the important aspects, those making lasting impression, could well have been everything but the letters inscribed on pieces of papyrus.

As an 'object' of knowledge, the communicative event (experience) of Paul and his audiences is processed by us with visual-spatial tools and methods:

> How does *method* deal with the hours of waiting, with maladroitness and gaffes due to confusion or bad timing? Where does it put the frustrations caused by diffidence and intransigence, where the joys of purposeless chatter and conviviality? Often this is written off as the 'human side' of our scientific activity. Method is expected to yield objective knowledge by filtering out experiential 'noise' thought to impinge on the quality of information. But what makes a (reported) sight more objective than a (reported) sound, smell or taste? Our bias for one and against the other is a matter of cultural choice rather than validity (Fabian 1983: 108).

How we read Paul's letters is in fact a reflection of our self-conception. We strive our very best to present visual knowledge: a

---

4. An adaptation of a description of Bauman 1986: 2. Bauman argues that study of oral literature should be done in an integrative spirit, with a performance-centred conception of these traditions as scholars operate within a frame of reference dominated by the canon of elite, modern literary perceptions (Bauman 1986: 1-10).

neatly printed text, with a clearly marked argument, well balanced paragraphs and properly supporting notes. The intention is to present the perfect visual communication.

But what *Paul* did was to engage in dictation. He sent a handwritten, corrected but not without errors,[5] ambiguous, damaged, travel-worn manuscript with someone he trusted, to have that one, or someone else, present his intentions and symbols verbally and bodily to others. What we are looking for is the 'objective argument', the 'line of thought', the 'flow of the argument', which can be represented in spatial lines, diagrammatically, on paper. What we *should* be looking for is an emotional, subjective, playing-up-to-the-audience human being, making meaning present and evoking authority.

Most of Paul's audience probably never even saw the text. The very source of their knowledge about Paul's message, or its content, was never imagined by them to be visible in a non-personal, static way. They did not experience it as knowledge that could be arranged, ordered and easily represented in diagrammatic or tabular form.

This is exactly where the need for studying rhetoric comes to the fore. It is a very important way to discover our biases, and to cope with them. Rhetorical criticism leads us towards the fullness of language, making us attentive to context, symbols and semantics. Even more, it brings us back to language as an experience, not as a mere text.

In line with developments in the philosophy of science, we should recognise that rhetoric belongs to the very essence of science.[6] Meaning and communication is about much more than delineating sources or labelling textual strategies.

Orality in Paul's World
Reading in antiquity was not experienced as a silently scanning, mainly mental activity. It was a performative, vocal, oral-aural happening. The reader literally recited, with vocal and bodily gestures, the text which he (most probably he) usually memorized beforehand.

5.   Quite a few of our text-critical problems must have had their origin in the autographa of Paul himself. An example is the famous ἔχομεν–ἔχωμεν of Rom. 5.1.

6.   The work of Kuhn is well known; see particularly Kuhn 1970: 48, 200-202. Feyerabend (e.g. 1988: 123) likens science to propaganda; within his argument he could as well have used the term rhetoric.

It is to this aspect that reference to the *oral environment* of the Graeco-Roman world draws attention.[7]

We must remind ourselves that the connection between education and literacy, which seems so natural to us, is simply a cultural convention of our own times. In Graeco-Roman societies one could be educated without having the ability to read and write. In fact, being literate (proficient with texts) was not even necessarily connected to oneself writing and reading. Literacy was at the time *not* a social factor in the marketplace.

Writing in antiquity was a technology employed by a small section of a pre-print, pre-literate society:

> It is nevertheless that they [Greek and Roman elites] retained a strong element of orality in their lives... they relied on the spoken word or purposes which in some other cultures have been served by the written word. They frequently dictated letters instead of writing them for themselves; they listened to political news rather than reading it; they attended recitations and performances, or heard slaves reading without having to read literary texts for themselves; and so on (Harris 1989: 36).

Reading, as is well known, was done aloud; it was a vocal, resounding event. Notice the reason for Pliny's concern in his letter to Septicius Clarus:

> I had an easy journey, apart from the fact that some of my people were taken ill in the intense heat. Indeed, my reader Encolpius (the one who is our joy for work or play) found the dust so irritating to his throat that he spat blood, and it will be a sad blow to him and a great loss to me if this makes him unfit for his services to literature when they are his main

---

7.   Achtemeier 1990; Botha 1990, 1992b. Ong (1977: 433) describes the New Testament as 'still exquisitely oral by comparison with texts coming out of latter-day... literacy'. Robbins (1991: 144-45) helpfully distinguishes between oral, scribal, rhetorical and print cultures, describing the environment of the New Testament as characterized by interaction among oral, scribal and rhetorical conditions. Not only did limited literacy exist in antiquity (Carney 1975: 110; Harris 1983; *idem* 1989; Botha 1992a; see also the studies on Roman Egypt by Lewis 1983: 82 and Youtie 1971a, 1971b, 1975a, 1975b with the conclusions relevant to the rest of the Empire), but even the apparent literate facets of the culture must be understood within the context of first-century historical reality: a cultural continuum different from our own. Furthermore, we should beware of ignorance of the complexities of the problems involved. For appraisals of the difficulties and literature see the references in n.9.

recommendation. Who else will read and appreciate my efforts or hold my attention as he does?[8]

The presence of orality in antiquity cannot be doubted. However, orality, it must be emphasized, is about much more than mere talk, or stylistic issues. In a cultural-anthropological sense, orality indicates a whole range of cognitive and social effects and values particular to an orally based communication technology.[9] It might seem superfluous to emphasize these matters—especially in view of the technological changes separating our societies from theirs—but impreciseness and neglect of historical realities permeate discussions of the use of writing in antiquity. This is, of course, partly the effect of our visualist bias; we simply overestimate and overrate textual evidence (cf. also MacMullen 1984: 10-11, 21).

While many scholars have turned to Graeco-Roman rhetoric for help in interpreting Paul's letter (with worthwhile results), the oral, *performative* aspect of ancient communication, and specifically ancient rhetoric, has been neglected. Speech and rhetoric cannot be separated in Hellenistic culture. Their rhetorical principles aimed specifically at the delivery of speech, at oral performance, and, consequently, *also* at creating successful communication through bodily presence.

Paul's Letters, Performance and Presence

Co-Authors and Secretaries

It is generally accepted that Paul made use of a secretary when corresponding (see, *inter alia*, Longenecker 1974). Yet, the impact of this fact seems to be consistently underestimated. As Betz (1979: 313) notices, 'the problem of authorship may be more complicated than we have previously imagined'. Paul usually identifies not only himself but

---

8.   Pliny, *Epistulae* 8.1. See Harris 1989: 225-26; McGuire 1960: 150; Marrou 1984: 196; Saenger 1982: 370-73; Achtemeier 1990: 15-17. Silent reading was possible, of course (Knox 1968, who criticises Balogh 1927 for overestimating the extent of reading aloud), but not practised. 'The heavy reliance of the Roman upper class on readers is familiar, and even for them it is clear that listening, instead of reading for oneself, always seemed natural' (Harris 1989: 226). It has often been remarked that letters bore a kinship to oral messages (e.g. White 1984: 1731).

9.   Finnegan 1988; Zumthor 1990; Olson 1988; Lentz 1989. For an extensive bibliography concerning this and related issues, see Botha 1992c.

also some other persons as author(s) of his epistles.[10]

It can be objected that there is a difference between a co-author and an *amanuensis*. But how do we know the difference? Can we discover the difference between copying, editing and re-writing?

Depending on his skills and the needs of the author, the secretary recorded the dictation syllable-for-syllable or phrase-by-phrase (that is, at the speed of writing) or by means of shorthand, at the speed of normal speech.[11] Or the secretary could be entrusted with the responsibility of writing the letter with incomplete notes. Either because of rapid dictation, or because often only an outline or draft was provided, authors left considerable scope to their secretaries. Invariably, letters contained editing by secretaries. The line between editing and co-authorship is impossible to draw. In fact, within one letter a secretary could play a variety of roles (cf. Roller 1933: 16-23; Bahr 1966: 470-76).

Concerning co-authorship various options present themselves (Prior 1989: 39-50). The authors may have considered the substance of the letter individually, and then gone over the general plan of what they were to compose, or perhaps suggested the style and expression which they had separately chosen while thinking about the message before collaborating towards an agreed content and form.

Now, in 'an age of computers and word processors, one easily forgets that conceiving and writing a text like Galatians or Romans was a long and wearisome procedure' (Hartman 1986: 138), and consequently we tend to underestimate the considerable effort that must have gone into the composition of Paul's letters. These letters were also written by rather sophisticated scribes (men like Timothy, Silas). Yet notice how Sanders draws a quite probable picture of Paul 'writing' to the Galatians:

---

10. Gal. 1.1; 1 and 2 Cor. 1.1; Phil. 1.1; Col. 1.1; Phlm. 1; 1 and 2 Thess. 1.1. Paul is not unique in this (Roller 1933: 153-64; Bahr 1966: 476; Prior 1989: 38). See also Schweizer 1976: 25-26; Bruce 1984: 30. Relevant to understanding the role of co-author/editor/secretary is the phenomenon of scribes: cf. Troll 1990: 115; Lewis 1983: 82; Saldarini 1988: 241-76.

11. Dictation *syllabitim* is self-evident. See, e.g., Seneca, *Epistulae* 40.10; Bahr 1966: 470-71. Dictation *viva voce* supposes shorthand systems and the use of a ταχυγράφος (cf. LSJ); see Seneca, *Epistulae* 40.25; Suetonius, *Divus Titus* 3.2. It was possible for a secretary to record a speech in the Roman senate (Seneca, *Apocolocyntosis* 9.2).

> To read the letter aright, one must read it as one half of a ferocious debate
> and imagine the harassed and distraught apostle pacing and dictating,
> sometimes pleading, sometimes grumbling, but often yelling... (Sanders
> 1991: 54).

Both suggestions, in the light of historical realities, can be correct. Paul's dictation of his letter was, in all probability, also a coaching of the letter carrier and eventual reader. The carrier of the letter would most likely have seen to it that it be read like Paul wanted it to be read.

The implications of co-authorship for understanding Paul's letters are twofold. First, written correspondence was essentially dependent on orality. Whether creating a letter or receiving it, oral-aural aspects were part and parcel of the whole process.

Secondly, we must realize that Paul's letters were not written by him as an individual. It was a complex communal event: some persons combined their efforts to deliberate and 'perform' a letter; there was someone involved in the creation and transportation of it; that same person or someone else finally 'recreated' for others a presentation/ performance of the 'message' intended for sharing.

In the context of an orally oriented culture, composition and performance of 'texts' are aspects of the same process, and the one cannot be understood without reference to the other.[12]

Receiving a Letter

In antiquity the letter carrier was, in a very real sense, the vital link between sender and recipients (cf. McGuire 1960: 148; Aune 1987: 158), and the oral remarks from the carrier were deemed essential to the communication and sometimes even preferred. Cicero often trusted the remarks of those 'who travelled by this route' more than the news in the letters (*Epistulae ad Familiares* 5.4.1; cf. 5.6.1). From Cicero we also learn that there was substantial interaction between letter writer and letter carriers (*Ad Quintum Fratrem* 3.1.23; 3.7.1; *Ad Familiares* 15.17.1-2).

Receiving a letter meant more than acquiring a written document. Usually a message or news was also involved. To communicate effectively by letter in antiquity one faced several difficulties. Consider the problem of

---

12. This is the basic tenet of the oral formulaic theory. References in n. 17.

how to convey information in an organized, understandable way apart from visible indications of such organization. One way... is to have someone deliver the writing who knows what it contains, and what the author intended with it, and have that person give such information. That in fact was frequently done with letters... (Achtemeier 1990: 17).

In the case of Paul's letters we should presume fully-briefed readers carrying and presenting the letters. 'We gain a sense of the importance of his emissaries or letter carriers: they receive authority to convey the letters to expand upon them, and to continue Paul's work' (Doty 1973: 37). How should we picture the recipients of Paul's letters 'reading' these writings?

Technologized print cultures foster rapid reading, in which words are formed chiefly in the imagination and often sketchily... The case was different in the highly oral cultures in which the biblical texts came into being, where reading was less deeply interiorized, that is to say, where reading called for a more conscious effort, was considered a greater achievement, and was less a determinant of psychic structures and personality... In such highly oral cultures, it was not sufficient for the reader simply to imagine the sounds of the words being read. Books in such a culture do not 'contain' something called 'material'. They speak or say words. The written words had to be mouthed aloud, in their full being, restored to and made to live in the oral cavities in which they came into existence (Ong 1977: 437).

Reading in antiquity, especially when it was not private reading, was similar to recitals or to oral delivery.

Rhetoric and Oral Performance

The insight that we should perceive ancient communication as performative communication (performed literature) makes us aware of how one-sidedly we think about rhetoric. The great teachers of rhetoric in antiquity give extensive attention to the presentation (ὑπόκρισις, *actio*) of the rhetorical act. They do so, not simply because the delivery of a speech is important, but because the presentation is fundamentally the essence of rhetorical activity.

Cicero (*De Oratore* 3.56.213–3.61.230) emphasizes that each emotion has its own natural expression in the *actio*. Not only the voice, but the whole body is like a musical instrument, played by the emotions (3.57.216). The full presentation is the 'language of the body' (*sermo corporis*, 3.59.222). Cicero employs a range of citations from Latin plays to discuss the bodily depiction of sympathy, mourning, fear, power, joy or anger. The fact that he (like Quintilian 11.3.57, 181-84) warns against becoming an actor, shows how powerful the impulse towards expressive representation in the voice and body the 'meaning' of a speech was at the time (*De Oratore* 3.56.214, 220).

To Cicero, the face, which he calls an *imago animi*, is a very important part of the body when it comes to relevant gestures. Crucial is the voice, which can be varied endlessly (3.60.224).

Quintilian spends a lengthy chapter on the art of using the voice and gesture (11.3), besides many asides scattered throughout his work. He even includes clothing (*cultus*) of the rhetor, which should be *splendidus et virilus* (11.3.137-149). What is most noteworthy of Quintilian is his concern with appropriateness. The rhetor's activities, gestures, voice should be appropriate to the audience, to the content of the speech and to the theme (11.3.150-188). Quintilian is also very comprehensive: he touches upon every aspect of the rhetorical act, even those gestures preceding the actual speech itself (e.g. 11.3.157).

The point of highlighting this side of ancient rhetoric is to emphasize the performative, dynamic essence of ancient communication. The psycho-physiology of gesture, that is, the connections between memory and bodily motions constituting the oral style (Jousse 1990), must be recognised if we want to understand orally constituted communication. We should not *look* at a text scanning for visual clues or try to 'see' the structure or 'identify' the possible labels for parts of it. We should imagine the experience of participating in the *event* of performing that 'text'.

To reiterate a point made earlier: questions of meaning in orally based communicative events cannot be settled in terms of composition alone. The performance of a text, or its potential performance must be kept in mind.

Paul's dictation of his letters was, in all probability, also a coaching of the letter carriers. The small group of 'Paulinists' worked together to communicate to their followers. They took some care in preparing their letters; some of them transported these letters and delivered them. They probably also participated in the reading and performing of these writings.

Authority and Verbal Presence

Given that oral performance was intrinsic to the Graeco-Roman world, and fundamentally part of communication by letter (particularly complex letters such as the Pauline letters of exhortation and advice) the argument thus far is pressing us towards asking how 'bodily presence' and 'speech' are issues in early Christian letter writing. A performative text only takes on meaning by referring to the instance of its performance, and consequently, because the occasion has been lost, it is true that the intent of the utterance is destabilised. Although we will never be able fully to fathom the various complexities at stake here, we can and should make the attempt. We have considerable and substantial research on ancient letter writing and social values, *and* we can make careful use of anthropological and cultural research, such as orality studies, performance studies and so forth.

Paul's letters are, amongst other things, a means of exercizing power and influence in various communities. This is dependent on the ability to establish presence and authority in a community, and related to the need to have social visibility and prestige. The fact that most of the addressees of Paul's letters would not have read the letters themselves, but would have *listened* to them, leads us to the realization that the presentation (the reading) of the letter itself must have been of concern to Paul and his co-authors.

When referring to the 'contexts' or 'audiences' of many early Christian writings we tend to underestimate the transpersonal identification of reciter and group, the manifestation of collective values that the performance of a 'text' articulates.[13]

The extent to which we have reduced the remains of Paul's communicative events to their (supposed) referential content is particularly clear in the strong scholarly tradition concerning Paul's opponents. In an astounding way, probably completely unrecognisable to Paul and his contemporaries, the identification and localization of his enemies has become the interpretive key to his letters.[14]

13. Introductory discussions in Foley 1977 and Schechner 1988: 193-206.
14. Craffert (1992) shows how anachronistic and ethnocentric assumptions underlie most opponent hypotheses with regard to research on the letter to the Galatians. Adopting a social-scientific approach, he argues that this letter should not be read as a theological struggle but within a situation where Paul's authority and honour were at stake. Paul focused 'on those aspects which, in the eyes of the

But more relevant would be to relate Paul's highly polemical stance and biting denunciations to the oral-aural mindset. In an orally oriented mentality the 'very structure of knowledge had been largely polemic, for the old oral-aural anxieties of a world polarized around persons had been institutionalized by the centering of formal education around dialectic and rhetoric, both arts of verbal strife' (Ong 1967: 236). 'Habits of auditory synthesis charged man's life-world with dynamism and threat...In such a view, polemic becomes a major constituent of actuality, an accepted element of existence of a magnitude no longer appealing to modern technological man' (Ong 1967: 200). Residual oralism reflects a reduction of irrelevant material to virtue–vice polarities. Even commonplace traditions were almost exclusively concerned with virtue and vice (cf. Ong 1967: 202). Virtue and vice polarities are deeply embedded in oral knowledge-storing systems.[15] Paul's caustic remarks and self-boasting claims do not necessarily point to the existence of theological schools. It might even be that Paul's controversy with the 'Jews' is simply an extension of this mentality 'where individuals took for granted that their surroundings were swarming with active, enterprising foes' (Ong 1967: 196). The attempts at identification of the various opponents might be barking up the wrong tree. We might have attempts at in-group self-identification achieved and maintained by feeding on hostilities towards out-groups (cf. Ong 1967: 198).

Marshall (1987a) has drawn attention to the importance of understanding Paul's invective and the issue of his 'inconsistencies' in terms of Greek social and moral standards (1987b: 360), considering the social and cultural dimensions of these activities. He shows that invective had two objectives: to dispose the hearers favourably to the speaker and to shame and humiliate the 'enemy'. 'Using a wide range of rhetorical techniques, popular topics and physionomic traditions, the speaker praised himself as a good person and censured his enemy as an unworthy person...Much of it [invective] was exaggerated or invented' (1987b: 362).

Marshall is surely on the right track. But the argument presented in

Galatians, provided power and secured authority' (Craffert 1992: 238).

15. The considerable role that virtue–vice polarities and lists of virtues and vices play in Graeco-Roman rhetoric (Marshall 1987a: 35-55) is probably due to the residual orality in Graeco-Roman culture. Cicero explicitly defines memory as part of prudence (*De Inventione Rhetorica* 2.53.160).

this paper pushes us beyond questions of reference and truth towards awareness and appreciation of the poetic, experiential function of language use. In performative communication—particularly within an orally based culture—the poetic operation, the breath of voice and the energy of body, is, at the least, as crucial as the utterance's supposed abstraction. There is an 'essence' to it which is more than an 'act'; in Zumthor's graphic phrase, 'a human being takes place, here' (1990: 229). This essence resides in the assumption of responsibility to an audience, and maintaining an audience through communicative skill as such. Enmity, invective, insults, disgrace, humiliation were ways of achieving, maintaining and defending honour and status—which were the real values of antiquity—and the very skill and power with which one displayed these activities determined their value, not the reference, truth, representability outside or unconnected to the speech event itself.

When Aristotle (*Rhetoric* 1.9.28) says that we should use in praise and blame descriptions which closely resemble the person's real qualities because they are identical with them—the cautious man is cold and designing—surely, we should take him seriously. In these, and other rhetorical hints, we notice the use of words to affect certain experiences. At the least, we should recognise that these experiential aims are as important as their possible referents. Powerful speech and authority, given an oral environment, are basically the same thing.[16] 'More: semantically, this society was still largely at the word-magic stage, with words "representing" "real" essences and involving a two-valued, antithetical logic. This makes for insensitivity to relativistic, multidimensional modes of thinking and problem-solving' (Carney 1975: 110).

In fact, orality studies provide us with an interpretive tool to build bridges across the cultural gap between us and the people of antiquity, where, for instance, mere blessings and curses clearly were events of grave magnitude.

Formulas in Paul's Letters

Very much to the point is the role of memory and memorizing. Extensive memorization, which was the dominant characteristic of Graeco-Roman education, is fundamental to an oral-text oriented

16. On the power of words and speech in orally based cultures: Peek 1981; Tambiah 1985.

culture. The dissemination of texts in antiquity relied on recitals and oral performances. Ancient discussions of rhetoric emphasize that all effort concerning the preparation of a speech would be in vain if the speech could not be memorized properly (cf. Leeman and Braet 1987: 118-23).

It is possible to understand the functions of the many formulas and formulaic expressions in Paul's letters as effects of oral rhetoric. The role of formulaic phraseology in communication within an oral environment has been intensively studied[17] and the associative power of memory, and how to exploit this, was well-known in antiquity (e.g. Quintilian 11.2.18-20).

Paul's reliance on formulaic language is not only limited to the conventional epistolary formulas and *topoi*[18] (which is in itself a manifestation of oral dynamics), but extends to a characteristic use of 'summary phrases'. Betz, in his study of Galatians, has listed a number of brief expressions, most of them prepositional phrases: 'All of them are abbreviations of theological doctrines. Their origin is unknown, but they can be most likely explained as coming from the oral transmission of Paul's theology' (Betz 1979: 27-28). This phenomenon is not limited to the letter to the Galatians. The implication of this type of abbreviated expression is twofold.

They clearly are something like condensed reflexive statements. Tannen notes that

> Formulaic expressions [= sayings, cliches, proverbs, and so on, familiar combinations of words, familiar syntactic patterns] function as wholes, as a convenient way to signal knowledge that is already shared. In oral tradition, it is not assumed that the expressions contain meaning in themselves... [but are] the repository of received wisdom (1982: 1-2, 6).

They can also be mnemotechniques: the phrases can be pictured as *loci*, aiding Paul and his co-authors to keep track of an involved argument and to remember a complex speech. They could well have been clues (or opportunities) for the reader to expand and elaborate.

---

17. See, for instance, the immense literature on the oral-formulaic theory: Finnegan 1988: 70-78; Foley 1988; Botha 1991: 307-16.

18. On the various types of stereotyped formulas in Paul's letters: Roller 1933; Mullins 1962, 1968, 1972a, 1972b, 1973, 1980; White 1971, 1978; Lategan 1991.

4. *Concluding Remarks*

This paper takes the insight that orality is an essential aspect of pre-modern communication as a starting point and attempts to situate Pauline epistolography within the context of ancient communicative practices.

To do this attention is first directed to the importance of recognising (and compensating for) our *visualism*, which is related to modern, Western literate bias. On a historical plane, the *oral environment* of the Graeco-Roman world is emphasized. It is argued that the (rather limited) literacy of the time must by understood within the context of first-century reality namely that of a scribal culture.

Many references to Graeco-Roman rhetoric in order to illuminate Pauline letter writing similarly mislead by neglecting the constraints of an orally based culture, and the performative side of classical rhetoric which cannot be separated from bodily presence. Some implications for the writing and reading of letters are discussed: the issue of 'multi'-authorship, the communal experience of letters, the oral performative aspect of letter reading.

Brief discussions of authority and presence as manifested in polemic and formulaic language conclude the paper. Paul, 'writer' of letters, is not a modern scholar, writing theological treatises for modern, literate audiences. Seen within the communication activities of his times, we discover, instead, a small group of early Christians struggling to maintain their identity and defending their views by means of oral presentations.

Bibliography

Achtemeier, P.J.
    1990   '*Omne verbum sonat:* The New Testament and the Oral Environment
                of Late Western Antiquity', *JBL* 109: 3-27.
Aune, D.E.
    1987   *The New Testament in its Literary Environment* (Philadelphia:
                Westminster Press).
Bahr, G.J.
    1966   'Paul and Letter Writing in the First Century', *CBQ* 28: 465-77.
Balogh, E.
    1927   'Voces paginarum: Beiträge zur Geschichte des lauten Lesens und
                Schreibens', *Philologus* 82: 84-109, 202-40.
Bauman, R.
    1986   *Story, Performance, and Event: Contextual Studies of Oral Narrative*
                (Cambridge: Cambridge University Press).

Betz, H.D.
    1979   *Galatians* (Hermeneia; Philadelphia: Fortress Press).
Botha, P.J.J.
    1990   'Mute Manuscripts: Analysing a Neglected Aspect of Ancient Communication', *Theologia Evangelica* 23.3: 35-47.
    1991   'Mark's Story as Oral Traditional Literature: Rethinking the Transmission of Some Traditions about Jesus', *Hervormde teologiese studies* 47: 304-31.
    1992a   'Greco-Roman Literacy as Setting for New Testament Writings', *Neot* 26: 195-225.
    1992b   'Letter Writing and Oral Communication in Antiquity: Suggested Implications for the Interpretation of Paul's Letter to the Galatians', *Scriptura* 42: 17-34.
    1992c   'Oral and Literate Traditions', *Koers* 57.3: 3-22.
Bruce, F.F.
    1984   *The Epistles to the Colossians, to Philemon, and to the Ephesians* (NICNT; Grand Rapids: Eerdmans).
Carney, T.F.
    1975   *The Shape of the Past: Models and Antiquity* (Lawrence: Coronado Press).
Craffert, P.F.
    1992   'A Social-Scientific Key to Paul's Letter to the Galatians: An Alternative to Opponent Hypotheses as a Cypher Key' (unpublished DTh dissertation, UNISA, Pretoria).
Dahl, N.A.
    1977   *Studies in Paul: Theology for the Early Christian Mission* (Minneapolis: Augsburg).
Doty, W.G.
    1973   *Letters in Primitive Christianity* (Philadelphia: Fortress Press).
Fabian, J.
    1983   *Time and the Other: How Anthropology Makes its Object* (New York: Columbia University Press).
Feyerabend, P.
    1988   *Against Method* (London: Verso, 2nd edn).
Finnegan, R.
    1988   *Literacy and Orality: Studies in the Technology of Communication* (Oxford: Basil Blackwell).
Foley, J.M.
    1977   'The Traditional Oral Audience', *Balkan Studies* 18.1: 145-53.
    1988   *The Theory of Oral Composition: History and Methodology* (Bloomington: Indiana University Press).
Funk, R.W.
    1966a   *Language, Hermeneutic, and Word of God: The Problem of Language in the New Testament and Contemporary Theology* (New York: Harper & Row).
    1966b   'Saying and Seeing: Phenomenology of Language and the New Testament', *Journal of Bible and Contemporary Theology* 34: 197-213.

Harris, W.V.
    1983   'Literacy and Epigraphy', *ZPE* 52: 87-11.
    1989   *Ancient Literacy* (Cambridge, MA: Harvard University Press).
Hartman, L.
    1986   'On Reading Others' Letters', *HTR* 79: 137-46.
Hester, J.D.
    1986   'The Use and Influence of Rhetoric in Galatians', *TZ* 42: 386-408.
Jousse, M.
    1990   *The Oral Style* (New York: Garland).
Kelber, W.H.
    1983   *The Oral and the Written Gospel: The Hermeneutics of Speaking and Writing in the Synoptic Tradition, Mark, Paul and Q* (Philadelphia: Fortress Press).
Knox, B.M.W.
    1968   'Silent Reading in Antiquity', *GRBS* 9: 421-35.
Kuhn, T.S.
    1970   *The Structure of Scientific Revolutions* (Chicago: University of Chicago Press, 2nd edn).
Lategan, B.C.
    1988   'Is Paul Defending his Apostleship in Galatians? The Function of Galatians 1.11-12 and 2.19-20 in the Development of Paul's Argument', *NTS* 34: 411-30.
    1991   'Formulas in the Language of Paul: A Study of Prepositional Phrases in Galatians', *Neot* 25: 75-87.
Leeman, A.D., and A.C. Braet
    1987   *Klassieke retorica: haar inhoud, functie en betekenis* (Groningen: Wolter-Noordhoff).
Lentz, T.M.
    1989   *Orality and Literacy in Hellenic Greece* (Carbondale: Southern Illinois University Press).
Lewis, N.
    1983   *Life in Egypt under Roman Rule* (Oxford: Clarendon Press).
Lindberg, D.C., and N.H. Steneck
    1972   'The Sense of Vision and the Origins of Modern Science', in A.G. Debus (ed.), *Science, Medicine and Society in the Renaissance*, I (New York: Science History Publications): 29-45.
Longenecker, R.N.
    1974   'Ancient Amanuenses and the Pauline Epistles', in R.N. Longenecker and M.C. Tenney (eds.), *New Dimensions in New Testament Study* (Grand Rapids: Zondervan): 281-97.
MacMullen, R.
    1984   *Christianizing the Roman Empire (A.D. 100–400)* (New Haven: Yale University Press).
Malherbe, A.J.
    1986   *Moral Exhortation: A Greco-Roman Sourcebook* (Philadelphia: Westminster Press).

Marrou, H.I.
1984   'Education and Rhetoric', in M.I. Finley (ed.), *The Legacy of Greece* (Oxford: Oxford University Press): 185-201.
Marshall P.
1987a   *Enmity in Corinth: Social Conventions in Paul's Relations with the Corinthians* (Tübingen: Mohr).
1987b   'Invective: Paul and his Enemies in Corinth', in E.W. Conrad and E.G. Newing (eds.), *Perspectives on Language and Text* (Winona Lake: Eisenbrauns): 359-73.
McConnell, T.
1986   'Oral Cultures and Literate Research', *Religious Education* 81: 341-55.
McGuire, M.R.P.
1960   'Letters and Letter Carriers in Christian Antiquity', *Classical World* 53.5-6: 148-53, 184-200.
Mullins, T.Y.
1962   'Petition as a Literary Form', *NovT* 5: 46-54.
1968   'Greetings as a New Testament Form', *JBL* 87: 418-26.
1972a   'Disclosure: A Literary Form in the New Testament', *NovT* 7: 44-50.
1972b   'Formulas in New Testament Epistles', *JBL* 91: 380-90.
1973   'Ascription as a Literary Form', *NTS* 19: 194-205.
1980   'Topos as a New Testament Form', *JBL* 90: 541-47.
Olson, D.R.
1988   'Interpreting Texts and Interpreting Nature: The Effects of Literacy on Hermeneutics and Epistemology', in R. Säljö (ed.), *The Written World: Studies in Literate Thought and Action* (Berlin: Springer Verlag): 123-38.
Ong, W.J.
1967   *The Presence of the Word: Some Prolegomena for Cultural and Religious History* (New Haven: Yale University Press).
1977   '*Maranatha*: Death and Life in the Text of the Book', *JAAR* 45: 419-49.
Peek, P.M.
1981   'The Power of Words in African Verbal Art', *Journal of American Folklore* 94: 19-43.
Prior, M.
1989   *Paul the Letter-Writer* (Sheffield: Sheffield Academic Press).
Robbins, V.K.
1991   'Writing As a Rhetorical Act in Plutarch and the Gospels', in D.F. Watson (ed.), *Persuasive Artistry: Studies in New Testament Rhetoric in Honor of George A. Kennedy* (Sheffield: JSOT Press): 142-68.
Roller, O.
1933   *Das Formular der paulinischen Briefe: Ein Beitrag zur Lehre vom antiken Briefe* (Stuttgart: Kohlhammer).
Saenger, P.
1982   'Silent Reading: Its Impact on Late Medieval Script and Society', *Viator* 13: 367-414.

Saldarini, A.J.
1989	*Pharisees, Scribes and Sadducees in Palestinian Society* (Edinburgh: T. & T. Clark).

Sanders, E.P.
1991	*Paul* (Oxford: Oxford University Press).

Schechner, R.E.
1988	*Performance Theory* (New York: Routledge).

Schweizer, E.
1976	*Der Brief an die Kolosser* (Zürich: Benziger Verlag).

Stowers, S.K.
1986	*Letter Writing in Greco-Roman Antiquity* (Philadelphia: Westminster Press).

Tambiah, S.J.
1985	'The Magical Power of Words', in S.J. Tambiah, *Culture, Thought, and Social Action: An Anthropologial Perspective* (Cambridge: Harvard University Press): 17-59.

Tannen, D.
1982	'The Oral/Literature Continuum in Discourse', in D. Tannen (ed.), *Spoken and Written Language: Exploring Orality and Literacy* (Norwood: Ablex): 1-16.

Troll, D.A.
1990	'The Illiterate Mode of Written Communication: The Work of the Medieval Scribe', in R.L. Enos (ed.), *Oral and Written Communication: Historical Approaches* (Newbury Park: Sage Publications): 96-125.

Vielhauer, P.
1975	*Geschichte der urchristlichen Literatur: Einleitung in das Neue Testament, die Apokryphen und die Apostolischen Väter* (Berlin: de Gruyter).

White, J.L.
1971	'Introductory Formulae in the Body of the Pauline Letter', *JBL* 90: 91-97

1978	*Epistolary Formulas and Cliches in Greek Papyrus Letters, SBLSP 1978:* 289-319.

1984	'New Testament Epistolary Literature in the Framework of Ancient Epistolography', *ANRW* 2.25.2: 1730-56.

1986	*Light from Ancient Letters* (Philadelphia: Fortress Press).

Youtie, H.C.
1971a	''Αγράμματος: An Aspect of Greek Society in Egypt', *Harvard Studies in Classical Philology* 75: 160-76.

1971b	'Βραδέως γράφων: Between Literacy and Illiteracy', *GRBS* 12: 239-61.

1975a	'Because they Do Not Know Letters', *ZPE* 19, 101-108.

1975b	''Υπογραφεύς: The Social Impact of Illiteracy in Greco-Roman Egypt', *ZPE* 17: 201-21.

Zumthor, P.
1990	*Oral Poetry: An Introduction* (Minneapolis: University of Minnesota Press).

THE DANCING OF AN ATTITUDE:
BURKEAN RHETORICAL CRITICISM AND THE BIBLICAL INTERPRETER

Jeffrey A. Crafton

The problem of reading the Holy Book—if you have faith that it is the Word of God—is the most difficult problem in the whole field of reading. There have been more books written about how to read Scripture than about all other aspects of the art of reading together. The Word of God is obviously the most difficult writing men can read.

Mortimer J. Adler[1]

Shouldn't we begin by asking ourselves what kinds of terms might best reveal the complexity of the problem?

Kenneth Burke[2]

Introduction: The Problem of Method

The search for productive matches between biblical texts and critical methods is a formidable quest not unfamiliar to the modern exegete. Because of the great variety of approaches available today, many of which scream for attention yet few of which converse with one another, the issue of method is more akin to a problem. Which of the many hermeneutical approaches is most appropriate to the peculiar nature of the Bible and most effective in probing the depth and breadth of its meaning? What 'kinds of terms' should be used for this 'most difficult writing men can read'?

An interpretive method is, quite simply, a set of leading questions which orient readers for an encounter with a text.[3] It directs what to

---

1. *How to Read a Book* (New York: Simon & Schuster, 1940), p. 288.

2. *Dramatism and Development* (Barre, MA: Clark University Press, 1972), p. 72. The juxtaposition of these quotations is borrowed from J. Arthurs, 'Biblical Interpretation through Rhetorical Criticism: Augmenting the Grammatical/Historical Approach' (unpublished PhD dissertation, Purdue University, 1992), ch. 6.

3. Kenneth Burke comments that 'A critic's perspective implicitly selects a set of

look for and why, and where, when and how to look for it.[4] I would suggest, therefore, that the following criteria might be used when deciding whether a method is worth pursuing for a given text: (1) it must be appropriate to the text; (2) it must be methodologically sound; and (3) it should offer rich possibilities for new readings of the text.

Using these criteria, I will test an insightful method which, though having significantly influenced the fields of sociology, anthropology, and literary and rhetorical studies,[5] has had little impact upon biblical criticism—the theory and criticism of Kenneth Burke.[6] I hope by this

questions that the critic considers to be key questions... the point about which the differences in critical schools pivot is not in answers, but in questions... All questions are leading questions.' See 'The Philosophy of Literary Form', in *Philosophy of Literary Form: Studies in Symbolic Action* (Berkeley: University of California Press, 3rd edn, 1973), p. 67. Similarly S.K. Langer claims that 'A question is really an ambiguous proposition; the answer is its determination...the intellectual treatment of any datum, any experience, any subject, is determined by the nature of our questions, and only carried out in the answers.' See *Philosophy in a New Key: A Study in the Symbolism of Reason, Rite, and Art* (Cambridge, MA: Harvard University Press, 3rd edn, 1969), p. 4.

4. Burke, *Philosophy*, p. 68.

5. Harold Bloom, Hayden White, Victor Turner, Clifford Geertz, Paul Ricouer, and Fredric Jameson, to name a few among many, have expressed their indebtedness to Kenneth Burke. Over the past half-century he has been called 'the most important living critic' and 'one of the major minds of the twentieth century' (Wayne Booth), 'unquestionably the most brilliant and suggestive critic now writing in America' (W.H. Auden).

6. There are two apparent reasons for this silence: the preoccupation of most biblical-rhetorical scholars with the application of categories from classical rhetoric, and the idiosyncratic (some say cryptic) nature of Burke's writings. As for the first cause, I can only exhort the scholarly community to recognize that there is more to the rhetorical approach than matching ancient concepts of form, genre and structure to biblical literature. As for the second, Burke responds to this accusation in *Philosophy*, pp. 68, 302-303 by noting that his critical method is no more or less 'intuitive' or 'idiosyncratic' than any other. A slightly more objective response is offered by Marie Hochmuth:

> Kenneth Burke is difficult and often confusing. He cannot be understood by casual reading of his various volumes... Burke is often criticized for 'obscurity' in his writings. The charge may be justified. However, some of the difficulty of comprehension arises from the compactness of his writing, the uniqueness of his organizational patterns, the penetration of his thought, and the breadth of his endeavor.

See 'Kenneth Burke and the New Rhetoric', *QJS* 38 (1962), p. 144. I will attempt in this paper, as I and others have elsewhere, to demonstrate that the benefit of

brief introduction to illustrate the hermeneutical power of Burkean criticism for biblical interpretation.[7]

1. *Is the Burkean Approach Appropriate for Biblical Texts?*

The foundation of Burke's theory and criticism is the idea that texts act. They 'do something' for both writer and reader.[8] They are actions and they are active. Texts name aspects of reality in special ways and entice others to agree with these names. They interpret facets of experience and induce the acceptance of these interpretations. A text is the expression of a perspective or, in Burke's unique language, the 'dancing of an attitude'.[9]

Burkean criticism, therefore, is concerned with how an author uses language to act upon self, community and world. Texts are instruments of change and should be interpreted as such. While most critical methods in use today isolate facets of a text—authorial intention, reception by original or subsequent readers, social and historical influences, ideological connections—Burkean criticism looks for the way in which all of these elements working together manufacture a text's power.[10] Burke would have the critic discover a text's function:

struggling through Burke's writings is worth the cost.

7. Among the few examples of a thorough use of Burkean criticism, see my *The Agency of the Apostle: A Dramatistic Analysis of Paul's Responses to Conflict in 2 Corinthians* (Sheffield: JSOT Press, 1991), and 'Rhetorical Identification in Paul's Letter to the Romans', unpublished paper read at the Pauline Epistles Section of the SBL annual meeting, 1991; P.E. Koptak, 'Rhetorical Identification in Paul's Autobiographical Narrative', *JSNT* 40 (1990), pp. 97-115, and 'Judah in the Biblical Story of Joseph: Rhetoric and Biography in the Light of Kenneth Burke's Theory of Identification' (unpublished PhD dissertation, Northwestern University, 1990).

8. Burke, *Philosophy*, p. 89.

9. *Philosophy*, p. 9.

10. Speaking broadly of the rhetorical approach, M.J. Medhurst in 'Rhetorical Dimensions in Biblical Criticism: Beyond Style and Genre' (*QJS* 77 [1991], p. 216) comments that 'the rhetorical level...almost always makes use of the grammatical and logical levels, but has a goal that transcends those levels'. G.A. Kennedy, in *New Testament Interpretation through Rhetorical Criticism* (Chapel Hill: University of North Carolina Press, 1984), p. 158, has similarly noted of rhetorical criticism that it 'may have an appeal lacking in other modern critical approaches, in that it comes close to explaining what they [the readers] want explained in the text: not its sources, but its power'. It is my argument that the Burkean approach in particular is well-

how an author uses words to create a symbolic orientation to a situation, and how a text invites an audience to participate in this world. The Burkean approach directs the critical eye toward the way literature proposes and promotes alternative visions of reality. That this describes the central purpose of the biblical literature seems clear. According to Eric Auerbach,

> The world of the Scripture is not satisfied with claiming to be a historically true reality—it insists that it is the only real world... The Scripture stories... do not court favor, they do not flatter us... They seek to subject us and if we refuse to be subjected, we are rebels.[11]

Similarly Dale Patrick and Allen Scult have argued that

> The Biblical text, unlike fiction, does not simply ask for a 'willing suspension of disbelief' in order to temporarily inhabit the world the artist has created. Rather, it seeks to persuade its readers to accept the depicted world as their world.[12]

And Meir Sternberg proclaims,

> As persuader, the rhetorician seeks not just to affect but to affect with a view to establishing consensus in the face of possible demur and opposition. Success has only one meaning and one measure to him: bringing the audience's viewpoint into alignment with his own... the biblical storyteller is a persuader in that he wields discourse to shape response and manipulate attitude... his persuasion is not only geared to an ideology but also designed to vindicate and inculcate it.[13]

If the biblical text proposes an alternative vision of the universe and insists upon its acceptance, if it is indeed the 'dancing of an attitude', then to read is to join the dance. To read is to encounter an alternative projection of reality. And in the best of circumstances, to read is to

---

suited to the task of reconciling the fragmentation in biblical hermeneutics by pointing to the symbolic action of texts. That is, it connects internal and external components, author, audience and text to discover what a text does and how it does it. For example, see my article 'Paul's Rhetorical Vision and the Purpose of Romans: Toward a New Understanding', *NovT* 32 (1990), pp. 317-39.

11. *Mimesis: The Representation of Reality in Western Literature* (trans. W. Trask; Garden City: Doubleday, 1953), pp. 14-15.

12. *Rhetoric and Biblical Interpretation* (Sheffield: Almond Press, 1990), p. 19.

13. *The Poetics of Biblical Narrative: Ideological Literature and the Drama of Reading* (Bloomington: Indiana University Press, 1985), p. 482.

cooperate with a text in the creation of a symbolic world,[14] to move away from false visions toward true responses. That this is what the biblical text intends for its readers seems irrefutable. The question of appropriateness must receive a strong affirmative answer.

2. *Is Burkean Criticism Methodologically Sound?*

Although many have acknowledged the brilliance of Burke's ideas and others have borrowed extensively from his writings, few have linked these notions to a coherent or consistent Burkean method.[15] Here I intend to offer such a framework. Because Burke never lays out his entire critical method in a systematic way, what follows is an abbreviated summary gleaned from a variety of sources. This synopsis is presented not as a systematic method which must be followed, but as a pattern of what to look for and how to look for it in a text.

In order to be sound, a critical method must be consistent, coherent, intelligible, and grounded in legitimate theory. As will be demonstrated in the discussion which follows, Burkean criticism satisfies these requirements.

Burke defines works of art as 'strategic' and 'stylized' responses to circumstances, 'the adopting of various strategies for the encompassing of situations'.[16] They are 'strategic' in that they diagnose, order, and interpret some portion of the world. They are 'stylized' in that these strategies are manifest in a form which encourages audience acceptance.

---

14. I believe that this is what Wayne Booth has in mind when he proposes that the principal metaphor of reading should be friendship, or James Boyd White when he describes reading as a relationship, namely, that a text should be approached as a potential partner in the formulation of a world-view. See Booth's *The Company We Keep: An Ethics of Fiction* (Berkeley: University of California Press, 1988), esp. pp. 151-52, 169ff.; and White's *When Words Lose Their Meaning: Constitutions and Reconstitutions of Language, Character, and Community* (Chicago: University of Chicago Press, 1984), esp. pp. 8-19.

15. W.H. Rueckert, in *Kenneth Burke and the Drama of Human Relations* (Berkeley: University of California Press, 2nd edn, 1982), p. xiii, concurs: 'For many people Burke exists in fragments, as the originator of a few stunning ideas and the writer of sporadically brilliant applied criticism. And yet his power comes from, and his real achievement consists in the monolithic dramatistic system he has developed.'

16. *Philosophy*, p. 1.

His critical method, therefore, is designed to disclose the tactics of a work, to discover all the resources of a text and to interpret their individual and corporate significance. He sums up his method in this proposition: 'the main ideal of criticism, as I conceive it, is to use all that is there to use'.[17] Every element within a text is important to the overall effect and must be considered a contribution to the symbolic action of the work.

A Burkean approach begins with the groundwork analysis of a text's use of language, then proceeds to interpret the results of this analysis using various methods which illumine a text's strategy. The following explanation will follow this pattern.

Burkean criticism begins with 'logology', the study of words. It listens closely to recurring words or sounds, the patterns in which they appear, and the rhetorical function these patterns suggest. Certain terms will be featured in a text, and the critic must be attentive to the special placement and meaning given these terms. Verbal selection and arrangement may indicate a great deal about rhetorical strategy.

Building upon this foundation, the critic must observe the ways in which terms are tied into associations and oppositions. Burke variously calls this facet of a text 'dramatic alignment', or 'what goes with what' and 'what vs. what'.[18] The entelechial principle (the drive for perfection, or the impulse to push concepts to their ultimate conclusions) at work in human symbol systems will cause some terms within clusters to be raised to the level of god-terms or devil-terms, that is, they will serve a synecdochic function for the cluster as a whole, or they will stand at the top of the hierarchy of terms and interpret the others within the cluster.[19] Because rhetoric is agonistic, these clusters of terms will be engaged in a struggle with one another. The critic must be aware of the nature of this conflict, the progression toward its resolution, and the god-terms, metaphors and imagery which direct the symbolic battle.

Expanding further, the critic will examine the formal aspects of a text. Burke defines form as

17. *Philosophy*, p. 23.
18. *Philosophy*, pp. 20, 22, 69-89.
19. For an exposition on the significance of such 'ultimate terms' by a follower of Burke, see R.M. Weaver, *The Ethics of Rhetoric* (Chicago: Henry Regnery, 1953), pp. 211-32.

an arousing and fulfillment of desires. A work has form in so far as one part of it leads a reader to anticipate another part, to be gratified by the sequence.[20]

Through form an audience is lured into the symbolic action of a text and guided through it. The reader recognizes patterns within the text, formulates expectations regarding their completion, and is attentive to the progressions which lead toward these goals. Gerard Hauser has summarized the appeal of form in this way:

> This expectation of the future allows us to listen with intelligence and to act with propriety. Once we know where a thought, argument, or theme is headed, we can anticipate what will come next, be alert for evidence and reasoning necessary to make a case, listen with increased critical sensitivity, and evaluate how the thought, argument, or theme fits with the overall pattern of the whole speech.[21]

Burke's interest is not in form as mere structure, but in form as function—as a way for an audience to experience the content of the text, to be engaged by it, and to be transformed from witnesses to participants in the rhetorical event. Through form an audience may experience the 'elation' which results from 'an attitude of collaborative expectancy'.[22]

Burke's concern with rhetorical strategy leads to a fascination with how people deal with life through language, how they attempt to 'encompass' situations. Burke proposes that these ventures may be explored through a 'sociological criticism of literature'.[23] Such a method would develop categories of genre which reveal authors' tactics for handling circumstances, thereby connecting literature to real life:

20. 'Lexicon Rhetoricae', in *Counter-Statement* (Berkeley: University of California Press, 3rd edn, 1968), p. 124. Following this definition (pp. 124-30) Burke lists five main categories of form which the critic may identify: syllogistic progression—step-by-step argument from premise to conclusion; qualitative progression—the process whereby 'the presence of one quality prepares us for the introduction of another'; repetitive form—the 'restatement of the same thing under different guises'; conventional form—'the appeal of form as form'; and minor or incidental form—the various other formal elements which operate at a micro-structural level.

21. *Introduction to Rhetorical Theory* (New York: Harper & Row, 1986), p. 172.

22. K. Burke, *A Rhetoric of Motives* (Berkeley: University of California Press, 1969), pp. 57-58.

23. 'Literature as Equipment for Living', in *Philosophy of Literary Form*, pp. 293-304.

Sociological classification, as herein suggested, would derive its relevance from the fact that it should apply both to works of art and to social situations outside of art.[24]

An author's socialization provides a set of patterns which help to identify strategies and thereby to adjust to situations. These patterns, which Burke calls 'motives', will be manifest in an author's work.[25]

The critic's task is to reconstruct the motivational design of a text. Burke proposes that this may be accomplished with the help of the dramatistic pentad:[26]

Act:	what was done, the character of the symbol use;
Scene:	where the act occurred, the context and conditions of the action;
Agent:	who performed the act, who was responsible for, or engaged in, the symbol use;
Agency:	the means or instrument of the symbolic action;
Purpose:	the end or goal of the act.

These five categories and their interactions (which Burke calls 'ratios') can be used to describe the way in which an author perceives, or induces an audience to perceive, a situation.

The critic must also look for how a text moves an audience from old to new perceptions. Rhetorical discourse urges the reformation of symbolic worlds. It arises out of disorder, either disparity between or disharmony within orientations. Some turmoil needs to be calmed, some order restored, some trouble resolved. False terms which have found a place in a hierarchy must be purged. Through the careful use of terministic clusters, form and the language of motive, an author will specify what must be rejected and what must be accepted. Burke suggests that the paradigm of purification, that is, the movement from pollution through purgation to redemption, is central to the rhetorical process. The critic must discern the way in which an author defines the problem at hand, performs some type of 'kill' whereby the audience is encouraged to become disloyal to a false vision, and proposes

24. *Philosophy*, p. 303.

25. A full exposition of motives is offered in K. Burke, *Permanence and Change: An Anatomy of Purpose* (Berkeley: University of California Press, 3rd rev. edn, 1984), pp. 18-36.

26. This pentad is fully developed in K. Burke, *A Grammar of Motives* (Englewood Cliffs: Prentice-Hall, 1945).

then guides the audience to a solution.[27]

Finally, the critic will reconstruct the way in which a text creates identification. Identification, the ultimate Burkean term for rhetoric, means inducing cooperation from an audience, drawing an audience into one's orientation, encouraging the audience to believe that speaker and hearer should be partners in the formulation of conclusions.[28] When identification occurs, author and audience bridge the separation between their private universes and join in a common perception. An author may create identification at several levels: (1) explicitly connecting the self to the audience through references to one's relationship to them, positive self-presentation, and shared symbols; (2) bonding with the audience more subtly through boundary definitions, insider/outsider symbols, and the purification cycle; and (3) creating an unnoticed 'we' who agree with each other and with the proposed outcome by strategic use of terministic clusters, form, metaphor, entelechy and synecdoche. When identification has occurred, the symbolic action of a text is complete.

3. *Does Burkean Criticism Offer New Readings of Texts?*

Does Burke's approach cause us to read biblical texts differently, or is his unique set of terminology nothing more than new words for old ideas? Does Burkean criticism permit us to see and name things in the text we might otherwise not see and name?

It cannot be doubted that Burke stands solidly within the ancient tradition of rhetorical study. Frequent echoes of that tradition clearly connect his ideas to the classical rhetorical theorists, demonstrating that he is expanding upon, not diverging from, their foundation.

What sets Burke apart, making him the brilliant innovator that he is, is his insight concerning works of art as strategies for the encompassing of situations and his unique manner of discovering those strategies. While he would recognize the importance of classical rhetorical concerns such as integrating authorial intent, textual manifestation, and audience reception into an interpretation, as well as identifying the various elements of form, structure and genre, he would argue that our understanding of these aspects is most lucrative

---

27. The most extensive discussion of this 'rhetoric or rebirth' is found in Rueckert, *Kenneth Burke*, pp. 97ff.

28. *Rhetoric of Motives*, p. 41; *Grammar of Motives*, p. 43.

when they are placed in service to symbolic action. The Burkean approach, therefore, not only points out manifestations of form and content, but it labels them in ways that allow the critic to make sense of them.

Two summaries of Burkean readings will be offered. First, I will demonstrate how cluster and agon analysis might illuminate the argument of Romans by connecting Paul's unique presentation of the law with his broader strategy for encompassing a difficult situation. In the second example, pentad analysis is used to clarify the enigmatic argument of 2 Corinthians.

Romans and Cluster and Agon Analysis

As was noted previously, in rhetorical documents terms will be gathered into mutually-defining clusters. Because rhetoric is agonistic, there will be associations and dichotomies, and a conflict which is (at least partially) resolved through the symbolic action of the text. Certain terms will be assigned a synecdochic (representative) function, and the author will make some symbols into god-terms or devil-terms which engulf others, pushing certain concepts to their ultimate conclusions. By means of this entelechial drive an author is able to make sense of an incomplete or circumstantial experience by extending its ramifications to mythic proportions.

This, I have argued elsewhere,[29] is the essence of Paul's strategy in Romans—to cause members of the audience to view their own situation and Paul's mission entelechially. Their pride and intolerance are theologized into a question of the validity of the divine Word and purpose. The disunity among the Roman house churches is a denial of the gospel which unites all nations. Their potential cooperation with Paul in the Spanish and Judaean projects is a ratification of the divine plan to gather all nations under the Lord. The letter is written to present an image of solidarity among all peoples and to demonstrate the necessity of active participation in this vision.

Paul actualizes this strategy through careful use of terministic clusters. The master cluster contains, among other terms, salvation, life, righteousness/justify, and faith. One or more of these terms is present at all the watershed moments and thematic summaries of Romans; all are introduced in the opening definition of the argument (1.16-17).

29. 'Paul's Rhetorical Vision', pp. 328-39.

This cluster is the standard by which terms are measured, the guide to which the argument turns for direction.

Paul opens his main argument, therefore, with a conflict between clusters which interpret this master group, making it cogent for the audience (1.18–3.20). This initial agon is between the divine design or will, ascription of honor to the Creator, and submission to truth in one association and suppression of truth, reverence for creatures, and the presumption to have all truth or a different truth in its opposition. Within the context of this dichotomy the battle involving faith, works and law is engaged. The lines of demarcation are clearly drawn, the terms carefully placed within each cluster. Added to the positive side are keeping the law, obedience, righteousness, internality, salvation and justification. Thus humble submission to the truth, honoring the Creator's design and will, is tied to faithful obedience and right relationship to God. This is the vision which Paul induces the audience to accept as their own. Added to the opposite side are disobedience, arrogance, boasting, self-certitude, externality, and the devil-terms works, sin and condemnation. This is prideful suppression of truth, dishonoring the Creator's design and will, that which must be purged from the audience's world.

The role which law plays must be carefully observed. The symbolic conflict is not between law and faith, as has commonly been argued, but between faith as representative of the positive cluster and works as representative of the negative. The term 'law' exists in both associations; its valence depends upon which it serves. It is not the source or center of the conflict, merely a player in the larger struggle. Law linked to faith, and to those terms which are in its cluster, verifies God's Word and plan, bringing salvation and unity. Law bound to works and the terms under its service negates the divine purpose, bringing division and intolerance.

Such an ambivalent placement of the term 'law' is enthymematic, forcing the audience to redefine law within their own orientations. They must transform it from a divisive into a cohesive symbol by participating in Paul's symbolic rejection of a false understanding and affirmation of a true vision.

In chs. 1–4 Paul resolves the initial conflict over proper orientation by associating the faith-cluster with justification, the works-cluster with condemnation. 'We' are to accept the law as an operative in the former and reject it in the latter. In chs. 5–8 this conflict is made existential through the struggle between the old and new humanities. Purging occurs as terms associated with the old humanity are linked with death and those of the new humanity with life. Again law exists in both groups; again its valence depends on which it serves. And in chs. 9–11 the conflict between disconnection and connection of Jew and Gentile is resolved with the help of a redefined law. The law as understood through the positive clusters of chs. 1–8 can stand as a cohesive rather than divisive factor. When we last hear of the law (13.8-10) it is to be affirmed and fulfilled by all through love.

Thus a Burkean reading not only describes Paul's use of the law, but it also ties it to Paul's rhetorical strategy to unite the factions in Rome. As the text purges the cluster of negative responses to God's truth and law, it also by associations and oppositions affirms the divine purpose for the nations and the audience's role within it.

2 Corinthians and Pentad Analysis

Upon an initial reading of 2 Corinthians the critic will discover dramatic shifts in mood, style, and argumentation—an eccentric collection of emotional outbursts and theological expositions. A closer 'logological' reading which attends to the selection, placement and grouping of terms reveals some fascinating data. In the long passages of cool logical argumentation (2.14–7.4) Paul selects a vocabulary which emphasizes office over person, corporate over individual identity, his role as conduit, his complete dependence and servitude under God. In sharp contrast, the section of impassioned personal attack and appeal (chs. 10–13) displays a vocabulary emphasizing person over office, individual over corporate identity, his role as leader, his strength and readiness to act. And in the passages appealing for resolution (1.1–2.13; 7.5-16) Paul's language is carefully chosen to exude reconciliation, mediation, consolation and partnership.

While it is difficult if not impossible to account for all of these observations using other hermeneutical methods, an analysis using the dramatistic pentad demonstrates that this apparent mishmash is in fact the implementation of a clever set of rhetorical strategies, each designed to encompass a specific situation. In the first section (2.14–7.4) Paul, faced with declining loyalty, presents his own orientation toward ministry and induces the Corinthians to agree with his definition of leadership. His argument creates a vision of apostleship and offers it for audience perusal. The nature of this vision can be identified in the language of motives as agency: Paul is an instrument of God, a means by which God acts. The contrast between Paul and the rival leadership in Corinth is set in the language of agency versus agent, the conflict between different motive categories presented as a theoretical discussion of contrary perceptions of the apostolic role. Thus Paul's deflection of attention from himself to his purpose, his virtual disappearance into his office, and his abstract argument make sense as essential manifestations of his strategy.

The second section (chs. 10–13) responds to a new situation, and thus activates a new rhetorical plan. A decaying relationship between author and audience demanded more aggressive action from Paul. Here the strategy is to attack opponents and demand obedience. The language of motives, therefore, focuses clearly upon agent; Paul presents himself as actor in order to ridicule the rival apostles and regain the Corinthians' loyalty. As agent Paul is at center stage, the major player. The contrast between Paul and the 'superlative apostles' is set in the language of agent versus counter-agent. It is no longer about perceptions of ministry—now it is personal. Character assassination, personal comparison, and mockery are the rule. Again, Paul's unique vocabulary and style which emphasize personality and individuality are explained by a naming of motives.

And finally, in the third set of passages (1.1–2.13; 7.5-16) Paul's language indicates an attempt to encompass a third situation. Resolution of the prior conflict has occurred; loose ends need to be tied up so that there can be a new beginning. A pentad analysis demonstrates that Paul now selects a motivational grid centered in the co-agent; Paul is partner with God and with the Corinthians. He acts, but only in conjunction or cooperation with others. As in the other portions, the peculiarities of the text are explained through identifying the symbolic action, which in turn is revealed through the categories of motive.

Conclusion: Burkean Criticism and Biblical Interpretation

Rumblings of discontent among scholars over the current fragmentation in biblical hermeneutics and the frustration it causes to students of the Bible are widespread and well-documented. To cite only one of many examples, in a recent article J. Christiaan Beker has written a compelling argument for resolution and redirection in biblical interpretation, citing the 'increasing divorce between theory and praxis', 'narrow specialization' and 'increasing trivialization of the more significant issues in biblical scholarship'.[30]

I and others would argue that a new focus upon the power and purpose of texts would heal these fractures. A rhetorical method should be concerned not only about original or modern settings, the socio-historical circumstances of author and original or subsequent readers, but about the meeting point of author, text and audience. It should consider not only the internal literary and ideological elements which organize a text or the external situation which prompted its production, but how both influence the power of the text to change an audience. While not a hermeneutical saviour,[31] rhetoric can and should serve as an orientation which guides the interpretive endeavor. While not a singular mechanical or definitive system,[32] it can and should be used to integrate the various techniques needed to interpret a text. Rhetorical criticism ought not to be used in the service of historical criticism, but historical criticism in the service of the rhetorical approach.

And I would argue that among rhetorical methods the Burkean approach is especially capable of answering Beker's call. Burke's method is not a 'trivialization' or 'specialization', but a re-orientation which shifts our gaze toward that which is of greatest importance: what a text *does*. Burkean criticism endeavors not to match formal patterns to texts, but to discover a text's own strategy for encompassing a situation, its attempt to create a vision and to induce an audience to accept it as their own. The Burkean critic 'becomes propagandist and craftsman simultaneously' as he or she selects what in the text is most 'important for social reasons',[33] fusing the dichotomy between technical hermeneutics and practical pastoral interests by revealing and regenerating the power of a text to influence both original and modern audiences. And, ultimately, Burkean criticism attempts to bridge the gap between text and reader, thereby allowing modern audiences to join the dance of the text and to discover new visions for their own worlds.

30. 'Integration and Integrity in New Testament Studies', *The Christian Century* 109 (May 13, 1992), pp. 515-17.

31. As noted by Medhurst, 'Rhetorical Dimensions', p. 215.

32. Medhurst, 'Rhetorical Dimensions', pp. 224-25.

33. K. Burke, *Attitudes toward History* (Los Altos, CA: Hermes, 1959), p. 210.

RHETORIC AND CULTURE:
EXPLORING TYPES OF CULTURAL RHETORIC IN A TEXT

Vernon K. Robbins

Introduction

In an article entitled 'Where is Rhetorical Criticism Taking Us?', published in 1987, Wilhelm Wuellner, quoting Perelman and Olbrechts-Tyteca, proposed that rhetorical criticism 'takes us to "the social aspect of language which is an instrument of communication and influence on others"' (Wuellner 1987: 449; cf. Wuellner 1988: 286; Perelman and Olbrechts-Tyteca 1969: 513). As he developed his argument, he cited Sloan's assertion that in rhetorical criticism 'a text must reveal its context', and that 'a text's context means for the rhetorical critic the "attitudinizing convention, precepts that condition (both the writer's *and* the reader's) stance toward experience, knowledge, tradition, language, and other people"' (Wuellner 1987: 450; Sloan 1947: 798-799, 802-803). Then he asserted that '[c]ontext can also come close to being synonymous with what K. Burke and others call the "ideology" of, or in, literature' (Wuellner 1987: 450, citing Burke 1978; Eagleton 1984: 107-24; Hohendahl 1982; Bruss 1982). In the middle of the article, he argues that rhetorical criticism must be identical with 'practical criticism' rather than 'literary criticism', explaining that literary criticism is 'rhetoric restrained' (Wuellner 1987: 453, citing Vickers 1982). Practical criticism, in contrast to literary criticism, is 'rhetoric revalued' (Vickers 1982), 'rhetoric reinvented'. This means that

> texts are read and reread, interpreted and reinterpreted, 'as forms of *activity* inseparable from the wider social relations between writer and readers' (Eagleton 1983: 205-206; 1984: 119, cf. Kennedy 1984: 158-59). Not only do rhetorical devices of disposition and style get studied as means of creating 'certain effects on the reader' (Rhoads and Michie 1982: 35), but the very construct of a theory of rhetorical criticism, compared with past

and present alternative theorizings, can be, indeed should be, examined
'as a practice' (Wuellner 1987: 453, citing Taylor 1983; cf. Mitchell
1985).

At the end of his article, he then asserts that 'rhetorical criticism leads
us away from a traditional message- or content-oriented reading of
Scripture to a reading which generates and strengthens ever-deepening
person, social, and cultural values' (Wuellner 1987: 461). 'The
divided concerns', he concludes, 'are reunited in a new rhetoric which
approaches all literature, including inspired or canonical biblical literature, as *social* discourse' (Wuellner 1987: 462).

I applaud this view of rhetorical analysis, and I have been trying to
work toward a systematic approach that can reach the goals set forth
in this article (Robbins 1991; 1992a: xix-xliv; 1992b; 1992c). The
approach, which is called socio-rhetorical criticism, explores four
arenas of texture in a text: (a) inner texture; (b) intertexture; (c)
social and cultural texture; and (d) ideological texture. My concern in
this paper lies in the third and fourth arenas: social, cultural and ideological texture. Ideological analysis in literary or cultural study is, in
the words of Kavanagh,

> the institutional and/or textual apparatuses that work on the reader's or
> spectator's imaginary conceptions of self and social order in order to call
> or *solicit*... him/her into a specific form of social 'reality' and social
> 'subjectivity' (Kavanagh 1990: 310).

This understanding of ideology is closely related to Kenneth Burke's
assertion that

> Critical and imaginative works are answers to questions posed by the sit-
> uation in which they arose. They are not merely answers, they are *strate-
> gic* answers, *stylized* answers (Burke 1973: 1).

The ideology of a text, then, concerns 'a specific form of social reality
and social subjectivity', and a literary work formulates 'strategic,
stylized answers' in the context of this specific form of social reality
and social subjectivity.

One of the reasons New Testament interpreters have not made more
progress in rhetorical analysis and interpretation of social discourse is
the priority they have given to sociology over anthropology. It is a
mistake for a New Testament interpreter to privilege sociology over
anthropology. Sociology is interested first and foremost in social situations, institutions and structures in which behavior takes place

(Hess, Markson, Stein 1988: 4). Sociology regularly has little or no interest in texts. Anthropology, on the other hand, is interested in the interactive relation of body, mind and culture. As a result, anthropology is highly interested in language, communication and texts. Anthropology has a close relation to sociolinguistics, and it approaches the data of human thought and activity in a manner highly similar to an interpreter's approach to interpretation of a text (Geertz 1973; Fowler 1981, 1986; Malina 1981; Swidler 1986; Patterson 1990; Peacock 1986; Hess, Markson, Stein 1988: 56-58). An ability to analyze and interpret social discourse then will come from an ability to perform exegesis with anthropological insights that will lead us toward insights from sociology.

Wuellner does not move very far toward 'revalued' or 'reinvented' rhetorical practice in his 1987 article that describes where rhetorical criticism is taking us. In the last part of the article, he applies Kennedy's model for analysis of a rhetorical unit to 1 Corinthians 9: (a) defining the rhetorical unit, (b) identifying the rhetorical situation, (c) identifying the rhetorical disposition or arrangement, (d) identifying rhetorical techniques or style, and (e) identifying the synchronic rhetorical function and effect of the whole unit (Wuellner 1987: 455-60). The discussion is brief, and at some points very suggestive. But there are few observations in these six short pages that move significantly beyond Kennedy's approach.

Wuellner's article on 'Paul as Pastor' (1986), which appeared in the previous year, is a different matter. In this article he analyzes the use of codes and shared values in the starting point or premises of arguments and in rhetorical questions (1986: 63-77). His analysis of modalities, argumentative effect, deductive technique, inductive argumentation and dissociation-technique, employing insights especially from Perelman and Olbrechts-Tyteca's *The New Rhetoric*, represents a significant step toward revalued or reinvented rhetoric. The progress in this article looks promising indeed, and Steven Kraftchick recently has used insights from it in a creative manner to reassess the debate about the rhetorical nature of Galatians (Kraftchick 1990). Wuellner made further progress in 'The Rhetorical Structure of Luke 12 in its Wider Context', where he discussed the rhetorical features in: (a) the relationship of the parts of the text, (b) the text's time, place, audience setting, (c) the text's (and reader's) relationship to the real world, and (d) the text's relationship to similar texts

(1988). One of the most instructive aspects of this article is its positioning of rhetorical theory in relation to hermeneutical theory. 'The triumph of hermeneutical theory', he explains, suppressed the rhetorics of texts with a 'theory of extracting "the" meaning (usually restricted to *theological*, occasionally also *ethical*, but rarely any other meanings)' (1988: 305). Rhetorical criticism, in contrast, is designed to explain 'the text's power' (1988: 286), and to explore 'possibilities that are manifestly awakened by the language' (Culler 1982: 247; Wuellner 1988: 287).

The progress Wuellner made in his 1986 and 1988 articles did not reappear, however, in his 1991 essay for the Kennedy Festschrift (Wuellner 1991a). In this essay, a remarkably restrained form of rhetorical analysis appears, a form reminiscent of a 1973 article, to which I will turn in a moment. The restraint appears as Wuellner limits the social and cultural context of Lk. 12.1–13.9 to biblical and Jewish traditions, values and perceived realities. He limits the social and cultural context of the discourse by focusing on 'rhetorical genres', arguing, on the one hand, that significant changes occurred in Hellenistic-Roman society, but that, on the other hand, 'Jewish "preconceptual" and later literary rhetoric, with its Near Eastern origin and Hellenistic influences, was controlled by its own, distinctly Jewish social environments, whether in exile and dispersion, or in *Eretz Yisrael*' (Wuellner 1991a: 116). Here the distinct restraint Wuellner has put on his rhetorical analysis comes from a personal bias toward Christianity's participation in Jewish culture. The salient words are: 'controlled by its own, distinctly Jewish social environments'. The issue here is whether any culture can fully 'control', 'limit', and 'restrain' the thoughts, values, dispositions and actions of its people when that culture exists in the context of another culture.

In order to address this social and cultural issue in rhetorical interpretation, we need a framework for exploring different kinds of cultural rhetoric.[1] Fortunately, anthropologists and sociologists have been hard at work on these matters, and there is significant current

---

1. 'Culture' is meant in the most neutral way possible in this paper. Culture is not being identified simply with 'Greek culture' or 'French culture', so that one presumes from the beginning a position of *Kulturkampf* based on a polarization of 'real culture' versus 'barbarian mentalities'. Culture means 'interaction of body-mind-culture' that goes back millions of years—that which, in Clifford Geertz's terms, makes humans human (Geertz 1973, 1983; cf. Greenblatt 1990).

literature to guide us in this pursuit. As a start in the process, I will introduce four major terms that can be helpful for analysis and interpretation of cultural rhetorics: (a) dominant culture rhetoric, (b) subculture rhetoric, (c) contraculture rhetoric, and (d) counterculture rhetoric. We will start with dominant culture rhetoric and subculture rhetoric together.

Dominant Culture Rhetoric and Subculture Rhetoric

A dominant culture is a system of attitudes, values, dispositions and norms supported by social structures vested with power to impose itself on people in a significantly bounded territorial region. Subcultures, in turn, are

> wholistic entities which affect all of life over a long span of time. '[The term subculture] stands[s] for the cultural patterns of a subsociety which contains both sexes, all ages, and family groups, and which parallels the larger society in that it provides for a network of groups and institutions extending throughout the individual's entire life cycle' (Roberts 1978: 112, quoting Gordon 1970: 155).

An ethnic subculture is a particular kind of subculture. It has origins in a language different from the languages in the dominant culture, and it attempts to preserve and perpetuate an 'old system' in a dominant cultural system in which it now exists, either because a significant number of people from this ethnic culture have moved into a new cultural environment or because a new cultural system is now imposing itself on it.

One major question will be if our texts view Jewish culture as a dominant culture or as a subculture in a dominant Hellenistic-Roman culture. Many current interpreters of New Testament texts proceed as though all of early Christianity were embedded in, and surrounded and protected by, Jewish culture. From this point of view, Christianity had no significant relation to Hellenistic-Roman culture. This approach appears to presuppose that Jewish culture was either a dominant culture in competition with Hellenistic-Roman culture or such a significantly developed subculture that Christianity could live in it so fully that any relation it had to Hellenistic-Roman culture was strictly through features that filtered through Jewish culture and were purified by that filtering process. The presuppositions underlying such a culture-purifying process surely are informed more by a 'revelational ideology' than by an adequate analysis of the language, concepts,

desires, goals and content articulated by New Testament texts.
Wuellner's early article on 1 Cor. 1.26-28 (1973) proceeds as
though the rhetoric in this text has a significant relation to only one
other culture, namely, Jewish culture. He argues that the interrogative
style of Paul in the passage has a 'striking parallel' in the Babylonian
Talmud (*b. Nid.* 69b-70b; Wuellner 1973: 667-69). Moreover, the
language of wisdom, power and well-born comes from Scripture and
is nurtured in post-biblical Judaism. Only time prevents him from
elaborating the data that exist in *b. Sanh.* 101a, *Midr. Num. R.* 22 and
its parallels in the *Tanchuma* homilies, and the fourfold pattern in
Pirke Aboth 41, *Sayings of R. Nathan* 23, and Philo's *de Virtutibus*.
'Much more needs to be done by exegetes in the field of post-biblical
Judaism and early Christianity', he says, 'in further efforts of identifying the tradition of the three gifts of God to mankind' (Wuellner
1973: 670-72). He does not suggest at any point that additional work
should be done in Hellenistic-Roman literature to identify the relation
of σόφος, δύνατος, εὐγενής, even though Johannes Munck had found
two of the three words together 'in traditions concerning sophists and
Atticists' (Wuellner 1973: 671). Wuellner uses a strategy of dissociation of the language, form and rhetoric of the passage from
Hellenistic-Roman culture to associate it fully with biblical-Jewish
culture. The underlying premise is that Paul's language, thought, and
action are thoroughly subcultural Jewish rhetoric. Any relation this
language and thought has to Hellenistic-Roman culture comes through
Jewish culture. In this early article, then, Wuellner interpreted
1 Cor. 1.26-28 through a method of 'restrained rhetoric' which dissociated Paul's language and thought from Hellenistic-Roman culture.[2]

To facilitate this exploration of cultural rhetorics, it will be helpful
to bring another interpreter into the conversation, namely Burton
L. Mack. In *A Myth of Innocence* he describes five different kinds of
cultural rhetoric in early Christianity, and comparison of some of his
discussions with Wuellner's will open new possibilities for us. Similar
to Wuellner's description of subcultural rhetoric in 1 Cor. 1.26-28,
Mack describes subcultural rhetoric in the miracle chains in Mark
4–8. In these stories

> Jesus, the founder and leader of the new movement, is like Moses (as
> leader) and like Elijah (as restorer). Likeness is not identity, however. The

---

2.   Unfortunately, Gail O'Day perpetuates these limitations in a more recent
study (O'Day 1990).

difference between Jesus and his prototypes is as great as the difference between the new congregation and the old. The Jesus movement is fully conscious of its novelty. Those without any claim to membership in Israel are nevertheless included. It is not really 'Israel' that is being renewed or restored. Jesus does not stand in the office of Moses as a 'new Moses'. He does not perform a prophetic critique of Jewish institutions from within as a call to repentance or reform. He marches under his own banner without polemic, effecting those changes in people that had to be made if the new congregation was to form. Jesus is the founder of the new society, and the set of stories is its myth of origins (Mack 1988: 223).

This is subculture rhetoric and not counterculture rhetoric, which we will consider below, since

The stories do not contain a hint of institutional conflict. There is no sense of hostility against representatives of the 'old' Israel. The set of stories marks the differences between the new congregation and traditional views of Israel, not as apology or polemic, but merely as definitional. The idea of ritual purity is used, for instance, to make a positive point about the distinctiveness of the new group that is not based on such prerequisite, not to counter charges of illegitimacy or raise the question of conflict between Jesus' authority and the authority of the law. The choice to imagine what was happening on the model of the Exodus story was natural, given the Galilean climate. The model was taken from the epic and haggadic readings of the scriptures, perhaps even at the level of local lore, not from the conceptualized model of Israel as a temple state based on cultic law. The exodus, that is, was not at first understood to be an exodus from Judaism (Mack 1988: 224).

With these descriptions Mack, like Wuellner, locates a portion of a New Testament text subculturally in Jewish culture. Also like Wuellner, Mack does not raise the issue of the relation of the miracle chains in Mark 4–8 to Hellenistic-Roman culture, even though Paul Achtemeier's delineation and interpretation of them had an eye on 'secular Hellenistic sources' as well as models in the Old Testament and Hellenistic Judaism (Achtemeier 1970: 291; 1972: 200-202). In truth, Mack does not seem to suppress the relation of the rhetoric in the miracle chains to Hellenistic-Roman culture 'intentionally', as Wuellner does in his 1973 article. Rather, Mack's suppression of the relation occurs 'by default'—an absence of description—which, even though it is characteristic for a large number of New Testament interpreters, is not customary for Mack.

Mack's discussion of the parables in Mark 4 represents a distinctive breakthrough in New Testament interpretation as it explicitly describes the relation of the rhetoric in the text both to Jewish culture and to Hellenistic-Roman culture. On the one hand,

> The imageries of the field, sowing, seeds, miscarriage, and harvest are standard metaphors for God's dealing with Israel in Jewish apocalyptic, wisdom, and prophetic literatures. Depending on the context, the use of such imagery would automatically have suggested a statement of theological import about Israel's destiny... Since the parable [of the sower] only works when the listener is concerned about the fate of the seeds, and since the fate of the seeds is calculated to heighten that concern by image.y of loss through destruction, the most plausible reference is not directly to the history of Israel, but to the early history of the Jesus movements. The parable makes good sense about the kingdom of God Jesus announced, but only in retrospect upon some adverse history of its failed attempts to take root (Mack 1988: 155).

For Mack, then, the parable of the sower exhibits subcultural Jewish rhetoric. The rhetoric refers to failure and rejection, but it does not move to a rejection of Jewish tradition. The rhetoric is embedded in Jewish apocalyptic *topoi* and tradition, and it builds willingly upon it. But the rhetoric in the parables also has a relation to Hellenistic-Roman culture:

> Ears acquainted with Hellenistic culture to any degree at all would immediately have recalled the stock image for offering instruction with a view to the inculcation of Hellenistic culture (Mack 1988: 159).

Mack cites four texts from Hellenistic-Roman literature, and I quote them here to show the amazing relation of Mark 4 to them (Mack 1988: 159-60; Mack and Robbins 1989: 156):

> The views of our teachers are as it were seeds. Learning from childhood is analogous to the seeds falling betimes upon the prepared ground (Hippocrates, *Law* III).

> As is the seed that is ploughed into the ground, so must one expect the harvest to be, and similarly when good education is ploughed into your persons, its effect lives and burgeons throughout their lives, and neither rain nor drought can destroy it (Antiphon, fr. 60 in Diels, *Vorsokratiker*).

> Words should be scattered like seed; no matter how small the seed may be, if it once has found favorable ground, it unfolds its strength and from an insignificant thing spreads to its greatest growth (Seneca, *Epistles* 38.2).

> If you wish to argue that the mind requires cultivation, you would use a
> comparison drawn from the soil, which if neglected produced thorns and
> thickets, but if cultivated will bear fruit (Quintilian, *Institutio oratoria*
> 5.11.24).

The parables in Mark 4, then, exhibit both subcultural Jewish rhetoric
and subcultural Hellenistic-Roman rhetoric. There is no open animos-
ity to either culture. Rather, self-definition emerges in a subcultural
posture both to Jewish and Hellenistic-Roman culture. The strategy of
analysis Mack uses does not shut off one or the other culture in
Mediterranean society but plumbs the depths of both to position the
rhetoric in the texts he interprets. Mack proceeds with Mark 4, then,
in a manner that exhibits 'rhetoric revalued' rather than 'rhetoric
restrained', a procedure that he did not attain in his interpretation of
the miracle chains in Mark 4–8 and that Wuellner did not achieve in
his interpretation of 1 Cor. 1.26-28. Nevertheless, these analyses by
Wuellner and Mack bring three kinds of subcultural rhetoric in early
Christianity into view. While further description of these subcultural
rhetorics would be informative, this will have to be left for another
context. For the matter under discussion, it is more important to move
to another kind of rhetoric, namely, contraculture rhetoric.

Contraculture Rhetoric

Further discussion of early Christian tradition by Burton Mack has
raised the issue of the relation of Cynic rhetoric to rhetoric in the
early Jesus movement, and with this discussion contraculture (notice:
contra- not *counter*culture rhetoric, which will be discussed below) in
early Christianity comes into view. A contraculture is a 'short-lived,
counter-dependent cultural deviance' (Roberts 1978: 124). It is 'a
groupculture rather than a subculture'. Contracultures are 'groups
that do not involve more than one generation, which do not elaborate
a set of institutions that allow the group to be relatively autonomous
and self-sufficient, and which do not sustain an individual over
an entire life span' (Roberts 1978: 113). A contraculture is primarily
a reaction-formation response to a dominant culture or subculture.
One can predict the behavior and values in it if one knows the values
of the society or subsociety to which it is reacting, since the values are
simply inverted (Roberts 1978: 123-24; Yinger 1960: 629; Stark
1967: 141, 153; Ellens 1971). In a contraculture, then, the members
have 'more negative than positive ideas in common' (Roberts 1978:
124, citing Bouvard 1975: 119).

In its early stages, Cynic tradition appears to have been a contra-culture in Hellenistic society. Especially the rhetoric associated with Diogenes exhibits the nature of contraculture rhetoric: it does not articulate an extensive ideology; it specializes in 'inverting' whatever remark an interlocutor makes. Mack sees contraculture rhetoric in Jesus' speech in early stages of the gospel tradition and in the earliest stage of the Q tradition. This rhetoric is systematically 'domesticated' by early Christian rhetoric, and I will address this in a moment. Contraculture rhetoric does not present a network of rationales to support its alternative behavior; it prefers the shock that deliberate abandonment of conventional attitudes, values, mores and dispositions produces. First, some of Mack's words about the Cynics; then one of his comments about Jesus:

> The sayings of the Cynics sprang from a frequently unexpressed system of thought that was highly rationalized and firmly in place. They also knew, along with others in the Socratic tradition of popular philosophy, about *nomos* (law), *physis* (nature), wisdom, virtue, *paideia* (culture, education), authority, and especially about the difference between kings on the one hand and tyrants on the other. They stood on the edges of society reminding conventional folk of their foolishness. The only pro-gram they had to suggest was to join them in their unconventional way of life. But the wellspring for the entire venture was a preoccupation with the question of society and its foundation.
>
> Cynics were best known for their pointed remarks and behavior. A game seems to have been played with them by those daring enough to tackle it. Cynics seem to have delighted in the game, seeking occasions to set it up to their advantage. Finding themselves in a tight situation where accommodation to conventional expectations would seem to make sense or be the easiest thing to do, the Cynic would accept the challenge of exposing the absurdity of the expectations (Mack 1988: 67-68).

With these comments, Mack describes a particular kind of contracul-tural rhetoric in Mediterranean society. On the one hand, the rhetoric is embedded in dominant Hellenistic culture, fully informed about it, articulate in it, and dependent on it. On the other hand, the goal of the rhetoric was not to argue a particular point of view but to overturn other people's remarks. What Cynics would share in common, then, was the 'overturning' of other people's arguments (a negative tactic) rather than a positive system of thought. As it began, then, the Cynic tradition was a contraculture, which is a group culture, dependent upon and reactive to dominant Hellenistic culture.

Mack sees dimensions of this kind of rhetoric in speech attributed to Jesus in the earliest stages of the gospel tradition:

> Jesus' use of parables, aphorisms, and clever rejoinders is very similar to the Cynics' way with words. Many of his themes are familiar Cynic themes and his style of social criticism, diffident and vague, also agrees with the typical Cynic stance (Mack 1988: 68).

This kind of rhetoric also exists, according to John Kloppenborg, in a stage of the Q tradition. As he compares it with Cynic traditions, he concludes:

> The idiom of Q is controlled not by a philosophic notion of freedom, but by a historical and soteriological schema of God's constant invitation of Israel to repent, and by the expectation of the imminent manifestation of the kingdom—an event which calls forth a radical response in its adherents, and which produces conflict and polarization in the world... Q...does not appear to hold out much hope for the repentance and salvation of 'this generation'. All that awaits is judgement (Kloppenborg 1987: 324).

The implication of these statements is a dual cultural relationship both for Jesus and for a sector of the Jesus movement in its earliest stages: a relation not only to Jewish culture but also to Cynic Hellenistic-Roman culture. These comments by Mack and Kloppenborg suggest a contracultural relation of Jesus and a sector of early Christianity to Jewish culture. In turn, the comments imply some kind of relation to Cynic culture. This raises three issues. First, if the rhetoric of Jesus and at least one sector of early Christianity had a contracultural relation to Jewish culture, their thought, speech and action were deeply embedded in Jewish culture and dependent on it. Their particular relation to Jewish culture would have been an 'inversion' of key aspects of patterns of thought and behavior in Jewish culture. Secondly, it will be important to describe the kind of Jewish culture in which Jesus and this sector of early Christianity were located. Is the Jewish culture a dominant culture that competes with dominant Hellenistic-Roman culture, a strong Jewish subculture embedded in dominant Hellenistic-Roman culture, or a Jewish subculture in a dominant or subcultural Jewish culture (like Pharisaic Judaism would have been prior to 70 CE)? In other words, the kind of Jewish culture in which contracultural thought, speech and action are generated will be important for understanding and interpreting them. Thirdly, if the rhetoric of Jesus and a sector of early Christianity had a subcultural

relation to Cynic culture during the first century, the issue is the
particular kind of Cynic culture. While the Cynic rhetoric of
Diogenes probably was contraculture rhetoric, Cynic culture by the
first century had become a more established 'system of thought' and
'way of life' (Malherbe 1977). To describe this social and cultural
phenomenon, the term 'counterculture' rather than 'contraculture' is
needed. Turning to a discussion of counterculture rhetoric, then, I
entertain the possibility that the Jewish contracultural nature of the
rhetoric of Jesus and a sector of the early Jesus movement had a
subcultural relation to the rhetoric of Hellenistic-Roman Cynic
counterculture. This relation can be properly described only after we
understand the nature of a counterculture and its rhetoric.

Counterculture Rhetoric

A 1978 article by Keith Roberts can guide us especially well in
analyzing counterculture rhetoric. A counterculture, he suggests,
arises from a dominant culture and/or subculture and is 'concerned
with the rejection of *explicit* and *mutable* characteristics of the culture
from which it arises' (Roberts 1978: 114). The term, therefore, is best
reserved for intra-cultural phenomena; 'counterculturalists are cultural *heretics* trying to forge a new future, not *aliens* trying to preserve their old culture (real or imagined)' (Roberts 1978: 121).
Countercultures are 'alternative minicultures which make provisions
for both sexes and a wide range of groups, which are capable of
influencing people over their entire life span, and which develop
appropriate institutions to sustain the group in relative self-
sufficiency' (at least 25 years) (Roberts 1978: 113). A counterculture
is 'interested in creating a better society, but not by legislative reform
or by violent opposition to the dominant culture'. The theory of
reform is to provide an alternative, and to 'hope that the dominant
society will "see the light" and adopt a more "humanistic" way of life'.
In other words, 'social reform is not a preoccupation' of a
counterculture (Roberts 1978: 121). Its constituents

> are quite content to live their lives and let the dominant society go on with
> their 'madness'. Yet an underlying theme is the *hope* of voluntary reform
> by the dominant society in accord with this new model of 'the good life'.
> Hence, one would expect a fully developed counterculture to have a *con-
> structive* image of a better way of life. In short, the term counterculture
> might best be reserved for groups which are not just a reaction formation

to the dominant society, but which have a supporting ideology that allows them to have a relatively self-sufficient system of action (Roberts 1978: 121).

The value conflict of a counterculture with the dominant society 'must be one which is central, uncompromising, and wrenching to the fabric of the culture. The concept of counterculture also implies a differentiation *between* the two cultures which is more distinct than the areas of *overlap*' (Roberts 1978: 121). There is, then, a 'fundamental difference between a counterculture and a subculture'. A subculture 'finds ways of affirming the national culture and the fundamental value orientation of the dominant society'; 'a counterculture rejects the norms and values which unite the dominant culture' (Roberts 1978: 112-13). There is also a fundamental difference between a counterculture and a contraculture. A contraculture is a short-lived groupculture. If it does not develop into a different kind of culture, it disappears through absorption or discontinuation. A counterculture, in contrast, may continue for generations.

In Wuellner's article entitled 'Paul as Pastor' (1986), he describe a significant countercultural dimension in Paul's thought. The key passage is as follows:

> I disagree with Meeks' formulation, according to which Paul was working for 'the transformation of the multiplicity of individuals into a unity' (Meeks 1983: 159). Certainly, that was one component. But, in the light of our study of the functions of rhetorical questions in 1 Cor, we must add: Paul works also for the transformation of the multiplicity of different social and ethnic/cultural value systems into a unity. It is a new social order, an *imperium* or βασιλεία whose ideology, though different from the imperial norms of Rome and zealotic Jewish nationalism, was yet compatible with 'the hope of Israel', the kingdom of God (Wuellner 1986: 73).

Wuellner's reference to 'the transformation of the multiplicity of different social and ethnic/cultural value systems into a unity' and 'a new social order [which is]... different from the imperial norms of Rome' evokes a countercultural relation of the thought, speech and action in 1 Corinthians to Hellenistic-Roman culture. He elaborates this point of view by agreeing with E.A. Judge's claim that 'three cultural systems were profoundly affected by Paul's critical use of rhetorical conventions': (1) the culture of higher education, by promoting a new kind of community education for adults; (2) the social patronage system, by refusing to accept gifts and benefactions; and (3) the system of self-esteem or boasting, by deliberately tearing down the structure of privilege with which his followers wished to surround him' (Wuellner 1986: 76-77). This additional analysis by Wuellner represents movement toward 'revalued rhetorical analysis' when it does not suppress the presence of Hellenistic-Roman culture like the earlier article on 1 Cor. 1.26-28 did (Wuellner 1973). The comment brings Hellenistic-Roman culture into view as a contributor to the cultural environment of early Christianity. This does not mean that Wuellner changes his mind about the subcultural relation to Jewish culture. Rather, in his view 1 Corinthians contains subcultural Jewish rhetoric that functions as countercultural Hellenistic-Roman rhetoric. For him, Paul's view is 'compatible with "the hope of Israel", the kingdom of God' as it 'profoundly affects' three Hellenistic-Roman systems. Whether Wuellner's view is right or not, the visibility of the bi-cultural nature of the rhetoric, rather than an implication of thorough embeddedness in Jewish dominant culture or subculture, is a significant advance over the analysis in 1973.

If we return now to Mack's work, we find a discussion of counter-culture rhetoric in his analysis of the pronouncement stories in the Gospel of Mark, and his analysis once again explores the bi-cultural nature of the rhetoric. In Mack's words,

> Approximately two-thirds of the pronouncement stories in Mark are set as conflictual situations between Jesus and Jewish leaders. In many of the settings a place has been made both for the disciples and the Pharisees. The questions are sometimes addressed to the disciples about Jesus, sometimes to Jesus about the disciples, but always about issues that divide the synagogue reform movement from the synagogue. One has to assume that the chreiai were elaborated by a group whose social history merged for a time with that of the synagogue and eventually brought it into conflict with proponents of Pharisaic Judaism (Mack 1988: 195).
>
> The issues up for debate... break unevenly into two classes. The larger class pertains to the constitution of the group, its unconventional behavior, and the question of codes by which to judge obligation... But they all share one thing in common: charge and countercharge about social identity. The Jesus people have not accepted Pharisaic codes of obligation, ritual purity, and halakha. The problem centers in the constitution of the Jesus group as mixed, and the behavior of the Jesus people as unclean (from a Pharisaic point of view)... The members of the Jesus movement rejected the Pharisaic critique, but they did take it seriously because they believed that they had some place in the Jewish scheme of things.

Mostly... the pronouncement stories reveal a posture of adamant affirmation of their own way of doing things in the face of Pharisaic criticism (Mack 1988: 195-96).

In the pronouncement stories, then, there is countercultural Jewish rhetoric, rather than subcultural Jewish rhetoric. In the pronouncement stories, early Christians are emphasizing 'their own way of doing things' in a manner that exhibits value conflict that is 'central, uncompromising, and wrenching to the fabric of the culture' (Roberts 1978: 121). This counterculture rhetoric has a significant relation to Jewish culture, because 'they believed that they had some place in the Jewish scheme of things'. But this place, in the end, is like 'new wine in new wineskins' (Mk 2.22).

In the spirit of a revalued rather than restrained rhetoric, Mack does not stop his analysis here. There is, he observes, an 'exceptionally odd' dimension in the rhetoric:

> Jesus becomes his own authority. Everything is attributed to Jesus: chreia, rationale, supporting arguments, and even the authoritative pronouncements (Mack 1988: 199).

His exploration of this kind of rhetoric in Mediterranean society leads him to Hellenistic-Roman Cynic tradition:

> The weird effect for Hellenistic ears would have been the image of a Cynic sage preoccupied with proving his wisdom authoritative. The circle closes. There is no point of leverage outside the sayings of Jesus to qualify or sustain the argumentation and its conclusion. Jesus' authority is absolute, derived from his own Cynic wisdom, and proven by his own pronouncements upon it (Mack 1988: 199).

The rhetoric in the pronouncement stories, then, reveals a dual cultural relationship. It is countercultural Jewish rhetoric that stands in some kind of relation to Cynic rhetoric. What is that relation? As indicated above, Cynic rhetoric had moved beyond its initial contracultural stage to a countercultural movement by the first century. This would mean that the rhetoric in the pronouncement stories would have some kind of relation to eastern Mediterranean Cynic counterculture. We should not too quickly consider it to be a subcultural relation. Perhaps this early Christian counterculture itself functions as a counterculture to a well-developed eastern Mediterranean Cynic counterculture. If the account of Jesus' instructions to the twelve in Mk 6.7-13 is part of the cultural environment of the pronouncement stories, the definition of the disciples 'over against' practices by Cynics could exhibit a countercultural relation to Cynic counterculture as well as to subcultural Pharisaic Judaism. This would not be surprising for a counterculture, since a counterculture is grounded in 'alternative behavior' for which it has its own rationales.

Before this discussion comes to a conclusion, one issue has been postponed until now: the relation of contraculture rhetoric in the thought, speech, and action of Jesus and an early sector of the Jesus movement to eastern Mediterranean Cynic counterculture. The descriptions by Mack and Kloppenborg imply a deep embeddedness of this early Christian contraculture rhetoric in Jewish culture. This means that this 'contraculture' style, experience and life was dependent on Jewish culture. Its relation to Cynic culture must, of necessity then, be other than contracultural, since it is Jewish culture it inverts in its embedded and dependent location. The short-lived contraculture Mack and Kloppenborg describe could be either subcultural or countercultural to Hellenistic-Roman Cynic counterculture, and the likelihood at the earliest stage would be subcultural. In other words, much as Jewish culture functioned as a subculture of dominant Hellenistic-Roman culture, so a Cynic contracultural Judaism would function as a subculture in eastern Mediterranean Cynic counterculture. Within time, this subcultural Cynic Judaism became a countercultural Cynic Judaism through the rationales it developed in its interaction with subcultural Pharisaic Judaism. If this seems complex, it is no more complex than cultural relationships that exist today, and it is exactly the kind of complexity we should expect in the syncretistic, eclectic cultural environment of the Hellenistic-Roman world during the first century CE. The implication would be that this early sector of the Jesus movement would use some of the *topoi* and rationales that some of the members of the Cynic counterculture use in their speech and action. These *topoi* and rationales, however, would be adapted in the manner in which a subculture adapts the norms of a dominant culture. This is precisely the kind of data scholars have found in various strata of the synoptic tradition (Mack 1988: 69 n. 11). In the earliest stage, a contracultural figure (Jesus) and a contracultural sector of the Jesus movement would have had a subcultural relation to a Hellenistic-Roman counterculture. As time went on, the subcultural relation provided rhetorical resources to use as they developed countercultural rhetoric over against Pharisaic culture, which itself was a subculture in Jewish culture. As the Jesus contraculture developed countercultural rationales, it distinguished itself not only from the Pharisaic subculture but from the Hellenistic-Roman Cynic counterculture as well. At this point, the concern is not so much that we have the description precisely right, but that we see how a finely-tuned description would proceed.

Conclusion

In summary, varieties of cultural rhetoric appear in the language in New Testament texts. As a result, the possibility of cultural rhetorical analysis and interpretation of early Christian texts stands before us. Only if we use a form of 'rhetoric revalued' or 'rhetoric reinvented', however, will we meet the task that lies before us. We are poised to make significant advances if we begin to discuss the bi-cultural nature of rhetoric in New Testament texts using a framework of dominant, subcultural, contracultural and countercultural rhetoric. This paper has not attempted to move through these 'cultural' categories to more 'sociological' categories, but the opportunity lies ready at hand (Rohrbaugh 1984, 1987; Robbins 1991; Neyrey 1991). For the moment, this paper issues an invitation to rhetorical critics to engage in forms of practical criticism which explore the cultural nature of the rhetoric in New Testament texts. This will be a revalued and reinvented rhetoric that will lead us forward into regions of analysis we have not yet undertaken.

Bibliography

Achtemeier, P.J.
1970   'Toward the Isolation of Pre-Markan Miracle Catenae', *JBL* 89: 265-91.
1972   'The Origin and Function of the Pre-Marcan Miracle Catenae', *JBL* 91: 198-221.
Bouvard, M.
1975   *The Intentional Community Movement: Building a New Moral World* (Port Washington, NY: Kennikat Press).
Bruss, E.
1982   *Beautiful Theories: The Spectacle of Discourse in Contemporary Criticism* (Baltimore: Johns Hopkins University Press).
Burke, K.
1973   *The Philosophy of Literary Form: Studies in Symbolic Action* (Berkeley: University of California Press, 3rd edn).

1978   'Methodological Repression and/or Strategies of Containment',
              Critical Inquiry 5: 401-16.
Culler, J.
1982   *On Deconstruction: Theory and Criticism after Structuralism* (Ithaca,
              NY: Cornell University Press).
Diels, H. (ed.)
1959   *Die Fragmente der Vorsokratiker* (3 vols.; Berlin: Weidmann, 9th edn).
Eagleton, T.
1983   *Literary Theory: An Introduction* (Minneapolis: University of
              Minnesota Press).
1984   *The Function of Criticism* (London: Verso).
Ellens, G.F.S.
1971   'The Ranting Ranters: Reflections on a Ranting Counter-Culture',
              Church History 40: 91-107.
Fowler, R.
1981   *Literature as Social Discourse* (Bloomington: Indiana University
              Press).
1986   *Linguistic Criticism* (Oxford: Oxford University Press).
Geertz, C.
1973   *The Interpretation of Cultures* (New York: Basic Books).
1983   *Local Knowledge: Further Essays in Interpretive Anthropology* (New
              York: Basic Books).
Gordon, M.M.
1970   'The Subsociety and the Subculture', in D. Arnold (ed.), *Subcultures*
              (Berkeley: Glendessary Press): 150-63.
Greenblatt, S.
1990   'Culture', in Lentricchia and McLaughlin 1990: 225-32.
Hess, B.B., E.W. Markson, and P.J. Stein
1988   *Sociology* (New York: Macmillan, 3rd edn).
Hippocrates
1967   *Works* (trans. W.H.S. Jones; LCL; 4 vols.; Cambridge, MA: Harvard
              University Press; London: Heinemann).
Hohendahl, P.
1982   *The Institution of Criticism* (Ithaca, NY: Cornell University Press).
Kavanagh, J.H.
1990   'Ideology', in Lentricchia and McLaughlin 1990: 306-20.
Kennedy, G.A.
1984   *New Testament Interpretation through Rhetorical Criticism* (Chapel
              Hill Press: University of North Carolina).
Kloppenborg, J.S.
1987   *The Formation of Q* (Philadelphia: Fortress Press).
Kraftchick, S.J.
1990   'Why Do the Rhetoricians Rage?', in T.W. Jennings, Jr (ed.), *Text and
              Logos, The Humanistic Interpretation of the New Testament* (Atlanta:
              Scholars Press).
Lentricchia, F., and T. McLaughlin (eds.)
1990   *Critical Terms for Literary Study* (Chicago: University of Chicago
              Press).

Mack, B.L.
1988   *A Myth of Innocence: Mark and Christian Origins* (Philadelphia: Fortress Press).
Mack, B.L., and V.K. Robbins
1989   *Patterns of Persuasion in the Gospels* (Sonoma, CA: Polebridge Press).
Malherbe, A.J.
1977   *The Cynic Epistles* (SBLSBS, 12; Missoula, MT: Scholars Press).
Malina, B.J.
1981   *The New Testament World: Insights from Cultural Anthropology* (Atlanta: John Knox).
Meeks, W.A.
1983   *The First Urban Christians: The Social World of the Apostle Paul* (New Haven: Yale University Press).
Mitchell, W.J.T. (ed.)
1985   *Against Theory: Literary Studies and the New Pragmatism* (Chicago: University of Chicago Press).
Neyrey, J.H. (ed.)
1991   *The Social World of Luke–Acts: Models for Interpretation* (Peabody, MA: Hendrickson).
O'Day, G.R.
1990   'Jeremiah 9: 22-23 and 1 Corinthians 1: 26-31: A Study in Intertextuality', *JBL* 109: 259-67.
Patterson, L.
1990   'Literary History', in Lentricchia and McLaughlin 1990: 250-62.
Peacock, J.L.
1986   *The Anthropological Lens: Harsh Light, Soft Focus* (Cambridge: Cambridge University Press).
Perelman, C., and L. Olbrechts-Tyteca
1969   *The New Rhetoric: A Treatise on Argumentation* (Notre Dame, IN: University of Notre Dame Press).
Quintilian
1920–22   *The Institutio Oratoria* (trans. H.E. Butler; LCL; 4 vols.; New York: G.P. Putnam's Sons; London: Heinemann).
Rhoads, D., and D. Michie
1982   *Mark as Story* (Philadelphia: Fortress Press).
Robbins, V.K.
1991   'The Social Location of the Implied Author of Luke–Acts', in Neyrey 1991: 305-32.
1992a   *Jesus the Teacher: A Socio-Rhetorical Interpretation of Mark* (Minneapolis: Fortress Press, repr. edn).
1992b   'A Socio-Rhetorical Look at the Work of John Knox on Luke–Acts', in M.C. Parsons and J.B. Tyson (eds.), *Cadbury, Knox, and Talbert: American Contributions to the Study of Acts* (Atlanta: Scholars Press): 91-105.
1992c   'The Reversed Contextualization of Psalm 22 in the Markan Crucifixion: A Socio-Rhetorical Analysis', in F. van Segbroeck *et al.* (eds.), *The Four Gospels 1992: Festschrift Frans Neirynck*, II (BETL, 100; Leuven: Leuven University Press): 1161-83.

Roberts, K.A.
1976   'Religion and the Counter-Culture Phenomenon: Sociological and
           Religious Elements in the Formation of an Intentional Counter-Culture
           Community' (unpublished PhD dissertation, Boston University; Ann
           Arbor: University Mircofilms).
1978   'Toward a Generic Concept of Counter-Culture', *Sociological Focus*
           11: 111-26.

Rohrbaugh, R.
1984   'Methodological Considerations in the Debate over the Social Class
           Status of Early Christians', *JAAR* 52: 519-46.
1987   ' "Social Location of Thought" as a Heuristic Construction in New
           Testament Study', *JSNT* 30: 103-19.

Seneca
1925–43   *Epistles* (trans. R.M. Gummere; LCL; 3 vols.; Cambridge, MA:
           Harvard University Press; London: Heinemann).

Sloan, T.O.
1947   'Rhetoric', in *The New Encyclopaedia Britannica*, XV (15th edn):
           798-805.

Stark, W.
1967   *Sectarian Religion* (New York: Fordham University Press).

Swidler, A.
1986   'Culture in Action: Symbols and Strategies', *American Sociological
           Review* 51: 273-86.

Taylor, C.
1983   *Social Theory as Practice* (Delhi: Oxford University Press).

Vickers, B.
1982   'Introduction', in B.Vickers (ed.), *Rhetoric Revalued* (Medieval and
           Renaissance Texts and Studies, 19; Binghamton, NY: Center for
           Medieval and Renaissance Studies): 13-39.

Wuellner, W.H.
1973   'The Sociological Implications of I Cor 1: 26-28 Reconsidered', *SE* 6
           (TU, 112): 666-72.
1976a   'Paul's Rhetoric of Argumentation in Romans', *CBQ* 38: 330-51.
1976b   'Methodological Considerations Concerning the Rhetorical Genre of
           First Corinthians', SBL Pacific Coast Regional Paul Seminar Paper,
           March 26.
1978   'Der Jakobusbrief im Licht der Rhetorik und Textpragmatik', *LB* 43:
           5-66.
1979   'Greek Rhetoric and Pauline Argumentation', in W.R. Schoedel and
           R.L. Wilken (eds.), *Early Christian Literature and the Classical
           Intellectual Tradition* (Festschrift R.M. Grant; Paris: Beauchesne):
           177-88.
1986   'Paul as Pastor: The Function of Rhetorical Questions in First
           Corinthians', in A. Vanhoye (ed.), *L'Apôtre Paul: Personalité, style et
           conception du ministère* (BETL, 73; Leuven: Leuven University Press):
           49-77.
1987   'Where is Rhetorical Criticism Taking Us?', *CBQ* 49: 448-63.

| | 1988 'The Rhetorical Structure of Luke 12 in its Wider Context', *Neot* 22: 283-310. |

1988 'The Rhetorical Structure of Luke 12 in its Wider Context', *Neot* 22: 283-310.

1991a 'The Rhetorical Genre of Jesus' Sermon in Luke 12.1–13.9', in D.F. Watson (ed.), *Persuasive Artistry: Studies in New Testament Rhetoric in Honor of George A. Kennedy* (JSNTSup, 50; Sheffield: JSOT Press): 93-118.

1991b 'Rhetorical Criticism: Rhetorical Criticism and its Theory in Culture-Critical Perspective: The Narrative Rhetoric of John 11', in P.J. Martin, and J.H. Petzer (eds.), *Text and Interpretation: New Approaches in the Criticism of the New Testament* (NTTS, 15; Leiden: Brill): 171-85.

Yinger, J.M.

1960 'Contraculture and Subculture', *American Sociological Review* 25: 625-35.

1982 *Countercultures: The Promise and the Peril of a World Turned Upside Down* (New York: Free Press).

ON STUDYING ETHICAL ARGUMENTATION AND PERSUASION
IN THE NEW TESTAMENT

Lauri Thurén

Introduction

Revolutionary approaches are accepted among biblical scholars with great hesitation: does this method really help us to a deeper understanding of the text, or is it only a fascinating system which produces little new knowledge? As representatives of rhetorical criticism we should take this challenge seriously, and provide our colleagues with results which are both convincing and useful. In my opinion, one such advantage of rhetoric lies in its capacity to avoid many pitfalls of conventional methods in seeking ideological patterns.

I maintain that in order to obtain a reliable, authentic picture of ethics or theology inherent in New Testament texts, a rhetorical perspective is necessary. Special attention should be paid to the analysis of argumentation, which has to be distinguished from persuasion and general rhetoric. I shall present some approaches in this rapidly growing field, and finally offer practical suggestions for studying ethical argumentation and persuasion.

1. *Ideological Studies Require Rhetoric*

Exegetical attempts to describe theological ideas or ethics tend to suffer from negligence of one basic fact: the scholar wants to find general concepts or doctrines in New Testament texts, but the biblical author never intended to give a neutral, balanced presentation of his ideology.[1] The epistles especially were written in specific situations,

---

1.   Not even Romans, in which Paul has been said to describe his theology, can be counted as such a presentation (against already Melanchthon, *Loci communes* 2.1.7; A. Nygren, *Pauli brev till Romarna* [Stockholm, 1944]; O. Kuss, *Paulus*

and usually to specific audiences, for the purpose of influencing the recipients in a particular manner. Knowledge of the historical situation and of the literary genre is required,[2] but does not suffice for their understanding. Since the author's goal has been to change or modify the addressees' attitudes and behaviour, he could not give an unbiased picture of his thoughts. Instead he has emphasized, even exaggerated, certain aspects. Thus the main goal to a great extent governs the way in which different themes and ideas are presented.

In Paul's letters we have traces of how his search for rhetorical effectiveness led to misunderstanding from the beginning, when the addressees' expectations and the author's intentions did not coincide.[3] Such cases may serve as warnings for modern scholars against too fast, too shallow comprehension and description of the author's thoughts. If we simply focus on some conceptions in a text and then systematize them into a 'theology' or 'ethics', the result is easily dominated by some prejudice, viz. our own ideological patterns.[4]

When the goal is to reconstruct any ideological or theological systems or patterns, these must be considered in their contexts—not only their historical, but especially their argumentative contexts. Two issues are of great importance.

First, we have to discover the type of situation in which the argumentation is intended to function, viz. the rhetorical situation(s). Here even the best historical information is not enough, since we do not know whether the author shared our knowledge. Further, the situation is not static, since what the author says in the beginning is aimed at adjusting the recipients' thoughts so that they can be addressed in the

[Regensburg, 1971], p. 163). This rather common opinion, however, does not mean that Paul did not have a theology.

2. See W.G. Doty, *Letters in Primitive Christianity* (Philadelphia, 1977), pp. 37-38.

3. See, e.g., 1 Cor. 5.9-13. See also the unexpected structure in Rom. 6.3-4, which tries to avoid a misunderstanding of a well-balanced idea: Eph. 2.5-6 may contain an earlier form of the thought. A third piece of evidence is found in 2 Pet. 3.16.

4. Thus J.T. Sanders, preoccupied with the idea of 1 Peter as an example of a 'horrible' ideological degeneration of Paulinism, has great difficulties with the actual text, and has to conclude that the effect of the text is 'the opposite of what the author really intended' (J.T. Sanders, *Ethics in the New Testament* [London, 1986], pp. 84-85).

next part of the text in a different way.[5] We must also be aware of the functions of the stylistic devices.[6] Negligence of these aspects will easily distort any description of the author's theology.

Secondly, we have to identify the statements and ideas, including central implicit thoughts, and clarify their relations in the text. These tasks cannot be carried out by traditional means either. Normal argumentation differs to a great extent from demonstration—people simply do not follow the rules of formal logic in their reasoning, not even scholars.[7] There are also many implicit premises and rules which are not observed in a formal study of a discourse. This basic recognition of the inadequacy of classical formal logic in studying practical reasoning has given impetus to new theories on argumentation, which attempt a more adequate analysis of practical reasoning.

Only after these two steps is it possible to make a quantum leap and search for models or general patterns of thought beyond the text. This in turn may lead to a description of ideological constructions, which are manifested in different ways in the actual text. To characterize, for example, the ethics of the New Testament is a still larger task: several texts have to be treated in the way described above before any sound comparison between them can be made.

In this article I shall concentrate on the second issue: the analysis of the structure of argumentation and persuasion.

2. *Argumentation is not Identical with Persuasion*

Since the terms 'argumentation', 'persuasion', 'convince' and 'motivation' are used in various ways, they need first to be specified.

5.   E.g., the description of the addressees' persistence in 1 Pet. 1.6-9 does not correspond to the exhortation to be persistent in the rest of the text. Ancient rhetoric studied these questions in the *dispositio*. See L. Thurén, *The Rhetorical Strategy of 1 Peter* (Åbo, 1990), pp. 75-77.

6.   E.g., according to Nissilä (*Das Hohepriestermotiv im Hebräerbrief* [Helsinki, 1979], pp. 254-55) Heb. 10.26-31 (οὐκέτι περὶ ἁμαρτιῶν ἀπολείπεται θυσία...) functions as a *deinosis*. With a static reading of the text, which ignores the rhetorical situation, the passage is misinterpreted (if Nissilä's interpretation is correct).

7.   Even scientific reasoning can usually be considered as argumentation, not merely logical demonstration (see H.W. Simons, *The Rhetorical Turn* [Chicago, 1990]. The term 'argumentation' means, in short, activity aimed at an audience in order to obtain their support or disapproval of an opinion. See below.

Like rhetoric, persuasion is not a value-free term.[8] It is often used as meaning an activity, which aims at an uncritical acceptance of something, whereas argumentation and the verb 'convince' are seen as challenges to critical interaction.[9]

Kant separates the words 'persuade' and 'convince' by using the terms 'subjective' and 'objective';[10] Perelman sees the difference in the implied 'particular' and 'universal' audiences.[11] In practice both distinctions have proven to be rather arbitrary.[12]

Brooks and Warren claim that persuasion is aimed at assent, namely assent to the will of the persuader, while argumentation pertains to the search for the truth.[13] Thereby they inaccurately equate argumentation with logical demonstration, since, contrary to demonstration, argumentation always also seeks the adherence of an audience. Thus, it would be better to say that argumentation is aimed at assent to the *opinion* of the speaker, whereas persuasion seeks to assent to his *will*.

The relationship becomes complicated when we notice that some forms of persuasion have little to do with even implicit argumentation,[14] and not all argumentation tries to persuade.[15] It would

8. Cf. already H.W. Simons, *Persuasion* (Reading, 1976), pp. 26-27.

9. See, e.g., F. Siegert, *Argumentation bei Paulus* (Tübingen, 1985), pp. 21-22; cf. also C. Perelman and L. Olbrechts-Tyteca, *The New Rhetoric* (Notre Dame, 1969), p. 111 and my criticism of them (Thurén, *Rhetorical Strategy*, p. 54).

10. Kant, *Critique of Pure Reason* (New York, 1961), pp. 645-46. It is somewhat difficult to discuss German terminology, since 'überreden' has a clearer 'negative' connotation than 'persuade'. Cf. Siegert, *Argumentation*, p. 22.

11. Perelman and Olbrechts-Tyteca, *New Rhetoric*, pp. 28-31, 33-35; C. Perelman, *The Realm of Rhetoric* (Notre Dame, 1982), pp. 17-18.

12. Against Kant, see Perelman, *Realm*, pp. 34-35. For criticism of the 'universal audience', see e.g. F.H. van Eemeren, R. Grootendorst and T. Kruiger, *Handbook of Argumentation Theory* (Dordrecht, 1987), pp. 217-18; for clarifications, see J.L. Golden, 'The Universal Audience Revisited', in *Practical Reasoning in Human Affairs* (ed. J.L. Golden and J.J. Pilotta; Dordrecht, 1986).

13. Cf. C. Brooks and R.P. Warren, *Modern Rhetoric* (San Diego, 1979), p. 109.

14. Cf., e.g., the persuasive force of repetition. For rules of persuadability, see D. Alexandrova, 'Rhetoric and the Theory of Argumentation', in *Argumentation: Perspectives and Approaches* (ed. F.H. van Eemeren *et al.*; Dordrecht, 1987), p. 271.

15. J.W. Meiland, 'Argument as Inquiry and Argument as Persuasion', *Argumentation* 1 (1987), pp. 185-96; K. Zappel, 'Argumentation and Literary Texts', in *Argumentation: Analysis and Practices* (ed. F.H. van Eemeren *et al.*,

be simple to say that persuasion may include reasoning, while argumentation is built exclusively on reasoning.[16] But since even argumentation seeks the assent of the audience, contrary to demonstration, it builds also on many social and situational factors. Thus even such a line remains obscure.

Instead of these suggestions one should focus on the rhetorical[17] functions of the words, since these come close to their everyday use: argumentation aims at changing or modifying the audience's thoughts, while the goal of persuasion is action.[18]

When the author is exhorting the recipients, he at least on some level aims to impel them to act according to the exhortation. To that end, a command itself is hardly enough, nor are good arguments, but the recipients must also be persuaded so that the audience will change or modify its behaviour.

In order to persuade, the author usually needs to give reasons for the change; to give such reasons and to justify them so that the recipient's opinions are affected is called argumentation. But an argumentation may have as its goal and result only that the recipient sees something as valid (in Latin, *persuadere* + Acc. cum inf.). It becomes persuasion if the goal is also to create in the recipient a volition to act in some way (in Latin *persuadere* + *ut*-clause).[19] Thus, according to Wallace, 'persuasion...has a connotation of an "ought", as

Dordrecht, 1987), p. 219.

16. Thus Brooks and Warren, *Modern Rhetoric*, p. 125.

17. Rhetoric is often rephrased as the study of persuasion. My definition of persuasion, however, lets me discern a rhetorical aspect also in such argumentation, which does not point toward action. It is more correct to say that both the argumentative and the persuasive aspects belong to the rhetorical perspective of a text.

18. Cf. Simons' use of the words 'persuasion' (*Persuasion*, p. 137). Van Eemeren's view on the 'normal' use of the words is slightly different (van Eemeren, *et al.*, *Handbook*, p. 217): 'convince' is used for creating understanding, persuading for moving to a course of action. This view equates argumentation with communication, although these two have different goals. The aim of communication is understanding, while the goal or argumentation is an opinion. See also below.

19. K.E. Georges, *Ausführliches Lateinisch-Deutsches Handwörterbuch* (ed. H. Georges; Hannover, 8th edn, 1918), s.v. This distinction differs from Siegert's way of understanding the two meanings of *persuadere* (Siegert, *Argumentation*, pp. 21-22).

opposed to the "is" of expository discourse', by which he means argumentation.[20]

To sum up, it seems meaningful to use the words 'argumentation' and 'persuasion' on two levels, which do not totally overlap. The substantive 'argumentation' and the verb 'convince' mean activity aimed at gaining the audience's assent to the author's theses and opinions. The word 'persuasion' is used for the process of gaining the audience's volitional, often also intellectual, assent to the speaker's will. Finally, 'motivation' refers to the content level of that process. The speaker may (but need not) use argumentation in order to persuade the listener to obey him so that the latter becomes motivated to do something.

The distinctions may be illustrated by Austin's speech-act-theory[21] as developed by Searle.[22] My presentation is based on a modification by van Eemeren and Grootendorst,[23] but I also include an important distinction between cognitive and volitional effects, viz. conviction and persuasion.

Dimension of activity	Subdimension	Speech Act	Inherent effect	Consecutive effect
Demonstrative		Locution	Perceive	Perception
Communicative	Cognitive	Illocution	Understand	Knowledge
Interactive		Perlocution	Accept	
	a) Cognitive	a) Argumentation	a) Conviction	a) Opinion
	b) Volitional	b) Persuasion	b) Motivation	b) Action

When studying ethical persuasion, viz. how exhortations are motivated, it is not enough to understand how the author obtains assent to

20. W.A. Wallace, '*Atitia*: Causal Reasoning in Composition and Rhetoric', in J.D. Moss (ed.), *Rhetoric and Praxis* (Washington, DC, 1986), p. 121.

21. J.L. Austin, *How to Do Things with Words* (Oxford, 2nd edn, 1976).

22. J.R. Searle, *Speech Acts* (Cambridge, 2nd edn, 1970). Searle criticizes Austin for studying verbs instead of acts, and himself attempts to classify different types of illocutionary act.

23. F.H. van Eemeren and R. Grootendorst, *Speech Acts in Argumentative Discussions* (Dordrecht, 1984), pp. 23-25. In order to apply the theory for argumentation analysis they focus on the interactive aspect of speech acts. This aspect is disregarded by Searle, who concentrates on the communicative aspect.

his thesis, but we must also focus on how he attempts to create such volitional impact, that the addressees will act according to his will. Therefore, it is necessary to add the volitional, emotional aspect to the argumentation analysis, that is, to ask what kind of emotions the author attempts to produce in order to elicit assent to his admonition. The volitional aspect is often decisive for the interpretation. For example, the argumentation 'John is sleeping, don't wake him up!' can appeal to opposite implicit motivating ideas: pity or love for John, or fear of an angry John, viz. love for oneself. When studying the grounds for ethics, such differences are of great importance. However, without an adequate and controllable method for analysing the structure of argumentation, the analysis remains arbitrary.

To sum up, when analysing persuasion, we need beside the basic rhetorical procedures a method of analysing the structure of argumentation, which focuses on the volitional aspect.

3. *Theories of Argumentation*

Introduction

In exegetical research, the position of the analysis of argumentation resembles that of its mother branch, rhetorical criticism. The scholars who are stimulated by development in non-theological research are becoming aware of the long neglected aspects in the text. Consequently, a central problem of rhetorical criticism involves also argumentation analysis: to what degree were rhetoric and the art of argumentation bound to the surrounding culture?

If rhetorical conventions in the New Testament are seen mainly as historical phenomena, ancient principles and terminology are the best means for the analysis. However, a close identification of ancient techniques is meaningful only if we can reasonably assume that the authors had learnt those techniques by name at school.[24]

---

24. See Thurén, *Rhetorical Strategy*, pp. 47-52. Rhetoric is always partly bound to the current culture, but Miller notices that already the social contexts of classical ancient rhetoric and biblical rhetoric were rather different (J.H. Miller, 'Is There an Ethics of Reading?', in J. Phelan (ed.), *Reading Narrative, Form, Ethics, Ideology* [Columbus, 1989]). Consequently I have theoretical doubts about Mitchell's remarkable rhetorical analysis of 1 Corinthians, which claims to be historical (M.M. Mitchell, *Paul and the Rhetoric of Reconciliation* [Tübingen, 1991], esp. pp. 6-11); therefore only ancient concepts are used, and the system is based on

According to the alternative, rhetorical features in the New Testament are seen as general human communication, and should be analysed with the best means available, whether ancient or modern. When the goal is to understand the text, not to identify historical features in it, this perspective is feasible. I have difficulties in following the critique, according to which ancient texts cannot be studied with modern concepts, since they are too new. For example, we use Blass-Debrunner rather than the grammar of Apollonius Dyscolus.

In general rhetoric, the choice between the alternative depends on the goal pursued, and the combination is often advisable. When analysing argumentation, the situation may be different.

Ancient Theories

Ancient rhetoric, dialectic and logic are widely seen as the most important predecessors of modern theories of argumentation.[25] The main sources are Greek authors, especially Aristotle, whereas Romans were mostly interested in practical rhetoric.

Particularly the recognition of the relevance of the audience and situation for argumentation and the interactive dimension of ancient theories, for example, the effect of the audience's feedback on the author's presentation,[26] have been important for the development of modern theories of argumentation.

However, just as general rhetoric degenerated step by step into a study of stylistics and of some technical devices,[27] the analysis of argumentation also suffered from a similar development: it was

ancient texts. Non-theological specialists in classical rhetoric or modern rhetoric have a much broader view of rhetorical criticism than exegetes on the 'Betzian' line. See, e.g., C.J. Classen, 'Ars Rhetorica', *Rhetorica* 6 (1988); B. Vickers, *In Defense of Rhetoric* (Oxford, 1988); H. Geissner, 'Rhetorical Communication as Argument', in F.H. van Eemeren *et al.*, *Argumentation: Across the Lines of Discipline* (Dordrecht, 1987), p. 111; J.W. Wenzel, 'The Rhetorical Perspective on Argument', in *Argumentation: Across the Lines*, with an ironical comment on exegetes on p. 103.

25. Van Eemeren *et al.* provide us with an illustrative presentation of the ancient development of argumentation theory (*Handbook*, pp. 55-78; see also Wenzel 'Rhetorical Perspective', pp. 101-102).

26. A. Braet, 'The Classical Doctrine of *Status* and the Rhetorical Theory of Argumentation', *Philosophy and Rhetoric*, 20 (1987), pp. 79-93. This fact is not fully recognized by van Eemeren *et al.*, *Handbook*.

27. Perelman, *Realm*, 4; L. Thurén, 'Vad är retorisk kritik?' *Teologinen Aikakauskirja* 1 (1991), pp. 41-42.

reduced to dialectic and formal logic, which consequently diminished its relevance to the study of ordinary texts, including the Bible.[28]

In connection with the recent revival of rhetorical studies in exegetical research, some attempts have been made to analyse argumentation in the Bible using ancient rhetoric. In 1976 W. Viertel employed exclusively ancient questions and terminology. However, as Siegert rightly observes, such a theoretical basis is very narrow.[29] Another wide effort to analyse argumentation in the New Testament was made by L.R. Donelson.[30] He claims that the use of modern patterns, such as theories of language, in analysing and criticizing ancient documents necessarily leads to misreading.[31] Without any further discussion Aristotle's (and some other ancient authors') works are seen as the only basis for analysing ancient texts.[32] The result is a distorted picture of the theology in the Pastorals.

An interesting statement reveals the trouble with concentrating exclusively on ancient conceptions: 'The peculiar method of argumentation found in the Pastorals could help us understand the logic and style of modern political and ethical debate...Aristotle's *Rhetoric* would provide fruitful categories from which to begin such a discussion.'[33] Donelson is on the right track, but he is only inventing some more powder. From the late fifties there has been a whole 'independent philosophical discipline'[34] doing exactly what he suggests, namely the modern theories of argumentation.

Modern Theories

Within the past few decades, more studies have been published in the field of argumentation analysis than in some hundred years before.[35]

---

28. J.D. Moss, 'The Revival of Practical Reasoning', in Moss (ed.), *Rhetoric and Praxis*, p. 7; cf. Siegert, *Argumentation*, pp. 5-8.

29. Siegert, *Argumentation*, p. 51; W. Viertel, 'The Hermeneutics of Paul' (Waco, 1976 [unpublished]).

30. L.R. Donelson, *Pseudepigraphy and Ethical Argument in the Pastoral Epistles* (Tübingen, 1986).

31. Donelson, *Pseudepigraphy*, p. 3.

32. Donelson, *Pseudepigraphy*, p. 3.

33. Donelson, *Pseudepigraphy*, pp. 4, 288-94.

34. U. Berk, *Konstruktive Argumentationstheorie* (Stuttgart, 1979), p. 190.

35. See, e.g., van Eemeren *et al.*, *Handbook*, pp. 108-13. For the history of argumentation theory, see J.R. Cox and C.A. Willard, 'Introduction: The Field of Argumentation', in *Advances in Argumentation Theory and Research* (ed. J.R. Cox

It is reasonable to assume that this rapidly developing new branch can also contribute to the study of biblical texts.

In 1958 two important treatises were published: *The Uses of Argument*[36] by S.E. Toulmin, and *La nouvelle rhétorique* by C. Perelman and L. Olbrechts-Tyteca.[37] They both share the basic theoretical view that ordinary argumentation cannot be adequately analysed with traditional, logical methods, since there is a quantum leap from logical demonstration to practical reasoning.[38] Not only the logical structure of the explicit argumentation, but especially the function of the arguments in the argumentative situation are crucial for understanding and evaluating the argumentation. The non-verbal aspects of the argumentation are at least as important as the verbal ones.[39] This shift from formal logic to argumentation analysis corresponds to the 'rhetorical turn' in general philosophy.[40]

Both Perelman and Toulmin have been influential in the development of theories and models for analysing argumentation, and many scholars still take one of them as their theoretical or practical basis.

Perelman's theory of argumentation has later been explained and clarified in many articles and books.[41] Its importance has not been limited only to launching a worldwide interest in argumentation; it has also contributed to the renewed interest in rhetoric in general, as a fresh philosophical perspective, even among biblical scholars.

However, severe criticism has been levelled against Perelman's distinction between logic as a formal, and argumentation as a rhetorical

and C.A. Willard; Carbondale, 1982), pp. xiii-xxv. For the current discussion, see, e.g., issues of *Argumentation* I–III and papers of the conferences in Amsterdam in 1986 (*Argumentation: Perspectives and Approaches*; *Argumentation: Analysis and Practices* and *Argumentation: Across the Lines*).

36. S.E. Toulmin, *The Uses of Argument* (Cambridge, 1958).

37. Cited in this article according to the English translation, *The New Rhetoric*.

38. Toulmin, *Uses*, pp. 1-10; Perelman and Olbrechts-Tyteca, *New Rhetoric*, pp. 1-14. For more on the relation between argumentation and formal logic, see several articles in *Argumentation* 3.1 (1989).

39. Cf. Siegert, *Argumentation*, 91.

40. R. Barilli, *Rhetoric* (Minneapolis, 1989); Simons, *Rhetorical Turn*. See also Simons, *Persuasion*, p. 32; J.W. Fisher, 'The Rhetorical View on Argumentation: Exploring a Paradigm', *Argumentation* 1, pp. 73-88, Thurén, *Rhetorical Strategy*, pp. 41-42.

41. See van Eemeren *et al.*, *Handbook*, pp. 293-94.

aspect of reasoning.[42] This reproach can be traced back to the basic gap between rhetoric and logic, which however has narrowed in recent years.[43]

A more crucial objection concerns the application of Perelman's theory as a 'new rhetoric'. Despite the rhetorical features, it deals only with cognitive argumentation, not persuasion. Ethos, pathos and most other volitional factors are to a great extent ignored by Perelman.[44]

In my opinion, Perelman's book is useful in two ways. (a) The general view on argumentation yields a sound basis for studying any human reasoning. (b) Perelman's practical application (which is not the only way of using his theories) often provides more adequate classification of the types of argumentation than the traditional terms.

Compared with Perelman, Toulmin's theory of argumentation is rather unsophisticated,[45] but his practical model for analysing is more popular than is Perelman's.[46] To my knowledge it has not yet been applied to exegesis.

---

42. U. Berk, *Konstruktive Argumentationstheorie* (Stuttgart-Bad Canstadt, 1979), p. 198; van Eemeren *et al.*, *Handbook*, pp. 220, 255-59.

43. It is rather commonly accepted that rhetoric can offer an important perspective to argumentation: see, e.g., J.M. Makau, 'Review of "Rhetoric and Praxis"', *Rhetorica* (1987), p. 194.

44. Perelman even considers persuasion to be a fallacy in argumentation (*New Rhetoric*, p. 111; see L. Huth, 'Argumentationstheorie und Textanalyse', *Deutschunterricht* 27.6 [1975]). Psychological factors are disregarded (van Eemeren *et al.*, *Handbook*, p. 215). Mitchell (*Rhetoric*, p. 7 n. 19) rightly states that Perelman's 'New Rhetoric' is more concerned with argumentation than with rhetoric as a whole.

45. See H. Wohlrapp, 'Toulmin's Theory and the Dynamics of Argumentation', in *Argumentation: Perspectives and Approaches*, p. 327; van Eemeren *et al.*, *Handbook*, pp. 199-207. Their view, however, ignores Toulmin's later modification of the theory (S.E. Toulmin, R. Rieke, A. Janik, *An Introduction to Reasoning* [New York, 2nd edn, 1984; London, 1st edn, 1978]). Similarly to the case with Perelman, the main criticism is aimed at Toulmin's 'rhetorical' view of argumentation.

46. See van Eemeren *et al.*, *Handbook*, pp. 292-93; and e.g. D. Ehninger and W. Brockriede, *Decision by Debate* (New York, 1966); W.L. Benoit and J.J. Lindsey, 'Argument Fields and Forms of Argument in Natural Language', *Argumentation: Analysis and Practices*; W.R. Fisher, 'Technical Logic, Rhetorical Logic, and Narrative Rationality', *Argumentation* 1, (1987), pp. 3-21, 15; J.W. Wenzel, 'The Rhetorical View of Argumentation: Exploring a Paradigm', *Argumentation* 1 (1987), pp. 79-80; Wohlrapp, 'Toulmin's Theory'.

Toulmin's treatise is mainly concerned with analysing the internal functions of argumentation.[47] According to him, each argumentation consists of certain elements, which are identified on the basis of their function.[48] They help us to describe the structure of any argumentation.

The usefulness of Toulmin's model does not consist only in its capacity to clarify arguments and their interrelations,[49] but in its consideration of the open-endedness of argumentation.[50] This means that, behind the assent of every element in the argumentation scheme, there are new, usually implicit chains of argumentation which justify that element.[51]

Toulmin, however, does not take into account the finality[52] or the rhetorical dynamics of argumentation, that is, the changing rhetorical situations. Further, his model gives us no direct means for validating the argumentation; it only provides a possibility of doing so by explaining the structure of argumentation.

Toulmin's model is useful for analysing argumentation, when its narrow limits are fully recognized. In most cases it has to be enhanced with other components, which however should not be confused with the model; such additional steps should be taken clearly after and before that analysis.

After Perelman and Toulmin, several different approaches for analysing argumentation have been presented.

The development in modern logic, rhetoric,[53] structuralism, text-linguistics,[54] etc., has provided scholars with new tools for analysis,[55]

---

47. Characterization by Zappel, 'Argumentation', 217.
48. For a short introduction, see e.g. K.-H. Göttert, *Argumentation* (Tübingen, 1978), pp. 28-29. For more detailed information, see Toulmin *et al.*, *Introduction*, pp. 29-77 and van Eemeren *et al.*, *Handbook*, pp. 174-80.
49. Cf. van Eemeren *et al.*, *Introduction*, p. 203.
50. Wenzel ('Rhetorical Perspective', pp. 106-107) quotes M. Scriven's metaphor: 'Arguments are like icebergs'.
51. Toulmin *et al.*, *Introduction*, pp. 73-77.
52. Zappel, 'Argumentation', p. 217.
53. In a rhetorical approach, J. Kopperschmidt ('Argumentationstheoretische Anfragen an die Rhetorik', *Zeitschrift für Literaturwissenschaft und Linguistik* 43/44 [1981], pp. 52-53) argues that the persuasive force of argumentation is more important than its theoretical functioning, and focuses on the totality of the argumentation instead of separate arguments.
54. E.g., R. Wonneberger, 'Ansätze zu einer textlinguistischen Beschreibung der

although no theory has been generally accepted. Usually the scholars from different fields deal with similar phenomena, but use different conceptions and language. Siegert illustratively reviews some branches which are important for analysing argumentation,[56] van Eemeren *et al.* present and evaluate different major theories of argumentation[57] and the current stage of argumentation theory.[58] One of the most useful approaches is the application of Austin's and Searle's speech-act theory. Although not originally designed for analysing argumentation, it has been successfully used for some types of analysis.[59]

The appearance of *Argumentation*, a journal for studies in argumentation, is one sign of the increasing interest in this field. Recent international conferences have shown the plurality of methods, but also that interdisciplinary collaboration is required in order to achieve better understanding of practical reasoning. Although some scholars still believe in a 'normative theory of argumentation',[60] it has at least become evident that no single method can be preeminent,[61] but that the central interests of the analysis influence the choice of the method.

A principal disagreement exists in the question of the basic nature of argumentation. Perelman, Toulmin and the research influenced by them share, despite the differences, a common rhetorical view of argumentation: no argument is valid as such—it must be assessed with regard to its audience. Contrary to this line, the research which is more directly influenced by formal logic indicates that the validity of

Argumentation bei Paulus', *Textlinguistik und Semantik* (ed. W. Meid and K. Heller; Innsbruck, 1976).

55. E.g., Zappel ('Argumentation', pp. 222-23) operates with a literary theory, wanting to 'systematize textual knowledge and to rationalize the modes of its processing'. First, discursive factors, their semantic qualifications and contextual isotopics are identified, then the information is conceptualized, modulated and finally organized.

56. Siegert, *Argumentation*, pp. 85-107.

57. Van Eemeren *et al., Handbook*, pp. 108-61.

58. Van Eemeren *et al., Handbook*, pp. 260-72. Concerning their evaluation it has to be noted that it lies on a thesis of the priority of directly judging the soundness of argumentation. Thus, they cannot evaluate theories which are designed for other purposes.

59. Huth, 'Argumentationstheorie'; van Eemeren and Grootendorst, *Speech Act.*

60. Van Eemeren *et al., Handbook*, p. 269.

61. See Wenzel, 'Rhetorical View', p. 73. Cf. also Cox and Willard, 'Field', p. xiv.

argumentation must be objectively assessed.

To sum up, it cannot be stated which one of the several modern ways of analysing argumentation is in itself the best. The choice of the tool has to depend on the task and the purpose. Toulmin's system serves as a viable basis for finding ideological structures beyond actual argumentation, if it is equipped with a proper modern rhetorical frame of reference.

4. *Toward a Model for Discovering Ideological Structures*

In this article I have stressed the need for a rhetorical perspective and an analysis of argumentative structures, when studying specific motifs or larger ideological entities, such as the ethics or the theology of an author. Finally I will ask how the quantum leap from the rhetorical to the ideological level can be made.

The first stage consists of clarifying how the argumentation and persuasion are designed to function on the text level.[62] To that end, we must begin by identifying the explicit expressions used in argumentation, which aims at motivating the exhortations in the text. This is a problematic point in the models of modern analysis of argumentation, and with a text, which is both culturally and linguistically foreign to the analyst, such an identification is difficult. Thus, a careful semantic analysis is needed. It should begin with a definition of the logical relations, which can occur between an exhortation and its motivation. Then these relations should be identified in the text. In a case study with 1 Peter, this task has proven to be an Achilles' heel of modern exegesis.[63]

After recognizing the explicit material, the argumentation in the text can be analysed with help of modern theories and with Toulmin's model, emphasizing the role of rhetorical situations, devices and strategy. By taking into account the volitional perspective and emotive factors, the persuasive and motivation aspect can be brought into focus. When the text has been scrutinized in this way, we can see how the expressions used in the persuasive argumentation are connected to each other, that is, we can find convincing and persuasive *structures* attached to different exhortations in various rhetorical situations in the text.

---

62. With 'text level' I signify a counterpart to the ideological level behind the text.
63. See below.

When the specific functions of the expressions used in persuasive argumentation in the text are known, they can be classified according to their content into more general *motifs* and *topoi*. This means a shift in the analysis from a textual level to an ideological level behind the text.

Identification of the functions and interrelations of the *topoi* yields to a general picture of their structure even in larger sections in the text. By the end of the process, we may state something universal about the function of each motif in the whole text.

Thus, by starting from small textual units and proceeding to more general levels and to larger units, we may discover whether there is enough consistency in the persuasive argument, and the use of different motifs, to allow description of its qualities. A corresponding approach may be used in any attempt to describe 'theologies' behind a New Testament paraenetic text.

In my large analysis of the motivation of paraenesis in 1 Peter according to the principles presented above, many mistakes in the earlier research were revealed. The study resulted, as I hope, in a new and more balanced picture of the letter.

RHETORIC AND HERMENEUTIC—ON A RHETORICAL PATTERN: CHIASMUS AND CIRCULARITY

†Angelico-Salvatore Di Marco

If I am not wrong, in present exegetical biblical research, the linguistic-rhetorical pattern of *chiasmus, circularity,* or *circular structure,* is one of the most identified and analysed. Between 1975 and 1979, *Der Chiasmus in der Bibel* was published by me in four sections in *Linguistica Biblica* (Bonn); then in 1980 it was issued in Italian in a single book. In 1981 at Hildesheim, Professor J.W. Welch, in collaboration with other scholars, edited *Chiasmus in Antiquity,* which contains much on chiasmus in the Bible.

It seems evident from some scholarly studies that not all biblical scholars are aware of how diffuse this pattern is in the Bible, and some seem even *annoyed* by this increase of analysis of chiasmus. We are warned that there is no use finding rhetorical patterns in Paul, if we do not show that in these, as in the chiastic or other models that some scholars insist on exhuming, there is any advantage to the interpretation (Aletti 1990: 4).

Another matter under discussion is *terminology,* and it is regretted because chiasmus, for instance, should be defined as only one thing (a-b-x-b-a, or, a-b-b-a) and not another. The lack of unanimity in terminology is not an isolated case; it occurs often in every discipline. Indeed in rhetoric, scholars do not agree how to name a phenomenon, something that the old rhetoricians have already managed. It seems, however, that even if the name of the phenomenon diverges, the figure is the same, as we can see in the singularity of formalization (a-b-b-a, etc.). We can see this when the same scholar employs, for the same item, different terminologies (concentric structure, chiasmus, etc.). Probably, chiasmus is the label more in use, perhaps because it is simpler.

The problem of terminology has to do perhaps with *ancient rhetoric* (which has such a great influence upon recent rhetoric research), in which chiasmus does not exist. The Greek term χιασμος is present for the first time and without special meaning in the fourth century AD by Pseudo-Hermogenes, *De inventione* 4.3.2. It did not become a term of ancient rhetoric, but was a rhetorical term in the last century (Lausberg 1960: I, 361; II, 893; Kennedy 1984: 28; as it was employed especially in the Italian literature: Riva 1979; Watson 1984: 202). In effect, present scholars of ancient rhetoric, when studying the ancient rhetorical topics, include chiasmus. Perhaps this is because the phenomenon that we call chiasmus was not completely unknown, but was detected with other figures, like *inclusio* (today often recalled when we speak of chiasmus, concentric structures and the like), *anaphora*, *antithesis*, *palistrophes*, *commutatio*, etc.; and perhaps then it was used heedlessly. That is not to deny the importance of terminology, because a lot of work lies in the creation of a proper terminology.

The ascertainment of such stylistic and structural procedures could have meaning in itself as forming a *collective terminology* that can be helpful for further studies. Obviously, all this could be criticized as a questionable preference of a categorizer who is not able to reflect independently. Nevertheless, in biblical science, as in many other disciplines, categorization with regard to different topics has always been useful and perhaps absolutely necessary.

In order also to rectify some statements made perhaps too quickly, it is fair to remark that the great majority of scholars who have noted and studied even a single case of chiasmus in the Bible usually have also recognised the many hermeneutical consequences. For nearly every scholar it is not only a matter of style or form (even if there are spoken or written forms without content), but a true rhetorical-hermeneutical procedure, where precisely the way of expression, the selected form, has a meaning, and is intended as a logical strategy, a way of argumentation, as well as a purely aesthetic ornament, which could be analysed (in addition to the value itself of the aesthetics in spoken language and in literature; chiasmus could enlighten understanding of the *aspectual* nature of Hebrew prose: Eskult 1990).

A first synthesis of such remarks and of the hermeneutical implications of several authors who have had an interest in chiasmus can be found in *Linguistica Biblica* 1979 (1980 in Italian). The remarks of the scholars that are collected there appear so different, exciting and sometimes in contradiciton, that it has been said that they even emphasized the necessity of reopening anew the question of *method*: something that today, after almost twenty years, is becoming a topical subject of urgent interest.

Here I mention only a few issues, such as the question of literary genres, of the composition-coherence of the text, of the authors of the different books of the Bible, of the Semitic-Hellenistic meaning of such procedures, of the many linkages in the extrabiblical arts and sciences, besides obviously the *rules* of the function, discovery and interpretation of chiasmus.

Further hermeneutical reflection on chiasmus should be made regarding the distinction between chiamus-circularity in sentences or short compositions, and great structures in a whole work, which might be entirely structured in a concentric-circular way. It is my impression that both could well reflect the same procedure, a general necessity and tendency that links the beginning and the end of a short or a wide statement, and even a mutual influence between the starting point and the conclusion, so that the beginning requires the end, and the end is entirely in the beginning.

A further field of reflection must be the great problem of the *form-content* relation in the chiasmus; that is, if a circular structure is fixed only lexically, and accordingly may be checked in words or terms that are arranged in this figure of chiasmus, either a circularity of *themes-ideas-contents* could also be present, or the last—the content—is the only true resolutive factor. Obviously either is possible.

In the history of literature, we know of many written (oral also, probably, even though less definable and less studied) attempts to convey in the written form what the word means: for example, the famous *depicted word* (*Parola dipinta*: Pozzi 1981) of the Renaissance, which seems to have many more ancient precedents in Hellenism (already in Simia of Rhodus about 300 BC: Gitay 1986; also in the alphabetic Psalms: Bazak 1984). The outside architecture in the Alexandrine editions of Greek lyrical poetry seems carefully provided; they were arranged according to the metrics and/or content (Recanatini 1991: 563). The Latin poets liked the external arrangement of the traditional poetic works, as in the arrangement of the Odes of Horace, and of the Catullian poetry. So also the late work of Prudentius has an external architecture precisely planned by the author, not only as a container of precise topics, but having in itself a semantic value very important for the best understanding of the text. The twelve hymns of his *Liber Cathemerinon* are arranged mirror-like, so that the first six and the last six are in mirror-like correspondence. The number of lines are also in circular numerical correspondence (Recanatini 1991: with outlines). There is a circular proceeding in the work's architecture, an ideal strophic and thematic circle displaying the geometric figure of the circle, a symbol of perfect balance (Recanatini 1991: 567-68), with the central position of the number three, which suggests that the circle may be more than the representation of the microcosm: one may think of the Trinity, the creating and organizing power of the world, without beginning and without end (Recanatini 1991: 569). This is to say that these hymns had the bent to identify form and content.

The proper *ringcomposition* in Greek literature is already known (cf. Angelico 1968: 81). We can find it for instance in Ovid, *Pont.* 4.16.45-46 (Landolfi 1991: 47); or later in the *Technopaegium* of Ausonius: lines begun and finished with monosyllables, and the monosyllable which finishes the line becomes the initial monosyllable of the following one, and so the verses *cohaerent ita, ut circuli catenarum separati*; the chain is closed because the last monosyllable—*res*—is the same one that begins the composition (Di Giovine 1991: 143-44). A similar structure in the content rather than in the form would concern the whole Scripture for Jerome, *Tract. in Marc.* (p. 328, 15 Morin): *Scriptura enim Sancta haeret sibi tota, et in uno spiritu copulata est: et quasi una catenula est, atque ut circulus in circulum innectitur, etc.*; cf. Augustine, *De Civ. Dei*, 21.4 (p. 520, 3ff. Hoffmann), where he speaks of rings not inside but outside tied thanks to a magnet (Di Giovine 1991).

Varro had remembered that

> *periodus, quae latina interpretatione circuitus vel ambitus vocatur, is est compositio pedum trium vel quattuor vel complurium similium atque ad id rediens unde exordium sumpsit, sicut temporis lustrum... ex variis versibus carmen omne compositum per circuitum quendam ad ordinem suum decurrit* (Semi 1965: 28-29);

and previously Aristotle and the Greek rhetoricians (cf. Robbins 1986: 681; Kurz 1987: 212; perhaps Plato, *Phaedrus* 268D: Standaert 1986: 86-87).

Very interesting for such structures, but not yet clarified, seem to be the references and supports that are detected in *other fields* of human activity. First of all, the same circular-concentric procedures have been detected in recent and ancient extrabiblical literary works (see above—more is omitted because it is an extremely immense field, and perhaps will be dealt with in a separate work). The same circular procedure has been detected in other arts and sciences: architecture, painting, music, medicine, logic: logic, mathematics and ontology are circular (cf. Ceccato 1985; Di Marco 1988: 70-71).

I think that two analyses more closely related to rhetoric and linguistics deserve special mention. First is the theory of *semiosphere* (Lotman 1990). The whole culture is a kind of ontological circularity, where the signs or systems do not work alone and by themselves, but in a semiotic *continuum*. The different texts build a semiotic universe, but they also are built with an opposite procedure. Only the 'entire system' actually makes each significant act real: only the entire cow makes possible the different beefsteaks and not vice versa (Lotman 1990: 289-90). The various semiospheres are in contact at their borders, which have the function of activating the process of the periphery and putting it into the interior, and of translating the outer communication into the inner language of the semiosphere (Lotman 1990: 292-93). The culture builds its own organization and the outer disorganization: the barbarous (Lotman 1990: 293-94). For the semiosphere, the distinction between 'nucleus' and 'periphery' is therefore essential (Lotman 1990: 294-96), with an inner multiplicity, a presupposition for the entirety of the semiosphere. Each part is part and mirror of the entirety, with parallels between the consciousness of each person, the text and the culture (Lotman 1990: 296). There is resemblance and difference between the agents of a new text, with give and take (Lotman 1990: 296-97). Without the semiosphere each language does not function and does not exist at all (Lotman 1990: 298-99). The semiosphere has diachronic depth with a complex system of memory, without which it does not function (Lotman 1990: 299). The different communicative processes also have an invariability, which brings them to resemblance. The invariability is based on the connection between symmetry and asymmetry or disintegration of the whole, and from this rise new structures and new multiplicity: a cyclical existence around the axis of the symmetry. In the diversity and resemblance of the components, the asymmetry is produced by a cause which already has this dissymmetry (the 'Curie-Pasteur' principle). Cf. the identity–difference of the figures in a mirror = the *enantimorphisme*: the differentiation of the unitary, and the unification of the different as the basis of the correlation of the parts (Lotman 1990: 300).

This whole has for Lotman a basis and an explanation precisely in a circular literary procedure, that is the *palindrome*, which changes the formation and the consciosness of a text (Lotman 1990: 300-301). The palindrome was employed in magic and esoterism, as in the Latin palindrome of the satanic verses (like: *in girum imus nocte et consumimur igni*). From the palindrome, incalculable data could be derived in the Chinese language, where the structure is emphasized; in the Russian palindrome the totality of the word stands out (Lotman 1990: 301). It works in molecules and in space (Lotman 1990: 302). It is the 'right-left' principle at the genetic molecular level up to the most complicated processes of information, and builds the basis of the dialogue and of every process of meaning (Lotman 1990: 304). When two cultures meet, they set in motion the mechanisms of resemblance and of differentiation. So 'West-East' are functional asymmetric pairs, structures from right to left and from left to right, according to the crossing of the symmetry-asymmetry of the semiosphere (Lotman 1990: 302; cf. also the *universal mirror-like symmetries* of Gardner 1985; Fossion 1982: 155-56).

Another reflection is *circularity in language*, which is more closely connected with our pattern. It seems that in speaking, if we put together two linguistic elements—words, phrases—a circularity follows, as when the two elements also function in the opposite direction, even if put in one direction.

In the Bible the most apparent instance, and perhaps the most acknowledged by scholars, is the genitive, where for instance, ἀγάπη τοῦ θεοῦ and εὐαγγέλιον τοῦ ᾽Ιησοῦ, etc., are, or may be intended, in a double direction, as a chiasmus: the love of God for us, and our love for God; the gospel which Jesus preaches, and/or where Jesus is preached. That is, a genitive that is both subjective and objective.

It seems that this circular movement occurs even where we do not suspect it, as in sentences like *the sabbath is made for man and not man for the sabbath*, where, in spite of the appearance, it seems that there is an implicit acknowledgment that it is sometimes possible also to say *man is made for the sabbath*, that is, for instance, for the feast, for God, etc. Or, whoever said that *it is not man who speaks, but language*, seems to have asserted just what he seems to deny, that is, that in language it is man who speaks. (We have to think also of the many negatives that are really not negatives, as in the phrase 'does not receive me' of Mk 9.37—'he who receives me *does not receive me*, but him who has sent me'—because without this phrase even what seems to be the opposite does not function, that is, *but him who has sent me*.)

So when we assert something in one direction, perhaps the inverse direction is implicit, a way of *implicit* chiasmus. (Every assertion demands its balanced corrective: cf. Crenshaw 1987; the nature of the great truths could be regarded from a thousand points of view: Lambruschini 1930: 54.) In the Bible we find what we could call a chiasmus *in distance* (cf. Christensen 1985: 186; Welch 1981: 19, 43, 103, 136): in Eph. 1.2-23 it is said that Christ was made head of the whole for *the church who is his body*; in Col. 1.24 it is said that the apostle carries in his flesh the sorrows of Christ for *his body who is the church*; in Acts 2.23 there is the mention of the ἐπαγγελία πνεύματος; and in Gal. 3.14 there is the mention of the πνεῦμα ἐπαγγελίας: so perhaps we are right when thinking that in one assertion there is also the inverse. A chiastic structure is like a single phrase (Van Leuven 1985: 56): every assertion is incomplete without its inverse. (We could think of the 'cibernetic model'—an idea controls another idea: cf. *serva ordinem et ordo servabit te*; or, 'we are the social warrant of the *truth*, and consequently, the truth is the ontological warrant of the system that we have put up': Deconchy 1984.)

These instances introduce us to the many ways in which *circularity of language is asserted*, and it seems to be a linguistic universal, that is, the mutual influence of the different parts of the linguistic assertions so that, for example, the end of a sentence (of a text) is at work already in the beginning (Perlmutter and Soanes 1979: 30-73). Cf. the active-passive sentences 'John has written a book, a book has been written by John'; or Wittgenstein's (and Augustine's!) assertion: 'with words we learn/explain things—with things we learn/explain words'; or the mutual influence of two languages in context, between dialects and national language, between particular languages (sociolects) and common language, etc. (cf. Slama-Cazacu 1984: 73-79, 86, 177, 192-93, 210, 242). It seems that *religious* language is especially a circular structure (Schäeffler 1985: 176): think, for instance, that what we say of God is a qualification of ourselves.

We could remember what is said on language's *iconicity*—that the grammatical structure reflects the meaning; that there is isomorphism with the referent, and, on the other hand, that the observer is also an element of the scene; and that to the principles of linguistics belongs that of symmetry, and there is a cyclical character to the linguistic facts (Haiman 1980; 1985; cf. the entire first fascile of *Zeitschrift für Semiotik* 2 [1980]: 1-138.

Linguistic circularity is apparent in *communication* and *reception* theories, where the message circulates between receiver and sender, and between text and reader. It happens that the sender becomes receiver and the receiver becomes sender (Balz 1978: 117-24). God's Word 'circulates' in an unending exchange between Scriptures and readers, going and coming (Fossion 1982: 55). So, when we speak of the *context* of a word, do not forget that not only are words determined by the context, but that they create the linguistic and historical context (Dyrness 1983: 290; Cazeaux 1983: 89).

Such circularity seems to be something deeper and more essential, when we think that our world has the limits of our language (Wittgenstein), but that our language is dependent on our world; that theory depends on praxis, and praxis on theory (praxis-theory circularity: Forte 1981: 60). Many things are said because they happen, but there are things that happen because they are said. There is a whole circularity between language, thought and reality (cf. Di Marco 1988: 70-71). This becomes apparent in a few instances given here at random.

'There is a double movement from Easter to the life of Jesus and from the life of Jesus to Easter' (Schmidt 1984);

Die Bedeutung der Kanongeschichte und der Kirchengeschichte für die Textgeschichte: that is a title in a chapter of Aland's *Der Text des Neuen Testaments* (1982: 58). In fact, also the inverse is dealt with: the meaning of the text's history for the canon's history and for the church's history (cf. also Güttgemanns 1975);

Die Religion in der Moderne—Die Moderne in der Religion: it is the title of the editorial in *Theologische Literaturzeitung* 110 (1985), and there it is said that the second part (the modern in religion) explains the first. And there is not only *Umstrittenheit der Religion in der Moderne*, but also *Umstrittenheit der Moderne* (Rendtorff 1985: 564);

It is true that St Francis created the Minor Order, it is also true that the Minor Order created St Francis (Nicolosi 1983: 10);

The question of the meaning and the meaning of the questions: that is not
a word play, but the stated intention to proceed with the greatest radicality
in studying the human being, that is, the meaning of human existence: in
itself the question of meaning imposes the question about the meaning of
the question (Alfaro 1985: 387);

The chiasmus in *words* with its play shows a problem that goes further
and reaches reality (Marin 1984: 55); perhaps because linguistics as a
science is the basis of every science (Potebnja 1905)? (Cf. Ivanov 1982:
41).

All these citations could give light to a troublesome objection
against all the chiastic and circular structures which we are finding in
texts; that is, how much these structures are *conscious* to the speaker-
writer. An absolute response doesn't seem so easy. I think that whoever speaks or writes does not do it intentionally, therefore it could be
something *unconscious-implicit* (in speech nothing is mere chance; a
text is both stylistic unconscious elements and conscious factors which
the author knows: Black 1987: 551). In themselves the fundamental
principles of language seem to be innate, inaccessible to the conscious
mind; one cannot teach them to most grown people, and they are
common to every language (Piattelli-Palmarini 1990: 76-77). If what
has been said about the frequency and the quasi-universality of the
circularity between two (linguistic) realities in contact is true, it is
easy to think that it is self-evident that in language obviously emerges
what in language is obvious. And if the speaker is not always
expressly aware, this does not mean that it is not there; rather it could
be more real precisely because it is unconscious. It could be 'a sort of
interior rhyme, typical of a psycho-linguistic process with a
concentric growth' (Ravasi 1981: 37).

We must remember the *dynamic* value of the structure, which is
often neglected: a structure is not understood if it is not taken in its
totality, if we do not arrive at the end. A structure, chiasmus, requests
to go further, to arrive at the end to which it takes the reader (in
Psalm 72, for instance, it is linked to the dynamics of groups: poor,
oppressors, mighty ones: Carrière 1991: 58-59).

The reflection on these rhetorical-hermeneutical facts is probably
(unconsciously!) affected by (and will affect!) the *hermeneutical circle*
(cf. *Sein und Zeit—Zeit und Sein: Die hermeneutische 'Kehre'*:
Güttgemanns 1984: 12-15), an essential one, but also very dangerous:
a *circle* can easily turn *vicious*, even if hermeneutic. That is, there can
be a right and logical hermeneutical circle, and it could be also a

vicious hermeneutical circle (cf. Di Marco 1988: 71-73).

In his *De Schematibus et Tropis*, the Verenable Bede, when speaking about the ways of expression or *tropes* of the Bible, and making a list of them, asserts that in the Bible the preeminent trope is *allegory* (Clausi 1990: 288-99): obviously then the biblical exegesis-hermeneutic was—must be—especially allegorical. From there followed the discovery of innumerable allegories. It could happen that, if one is persuaded that in the Bible there are many instances of circularity-chiasmus, one will find many. It seems however that these structures have a verifiable ground exactly in the text: in it can be checked how much structure there is, and therefore how trustful scholars' analyses are.

Bibliography

Aland, K., and B. Aland
1982   *Der Text des Neuen Testaments* (Stuttgart).
Aletti, J.N.
1990   'La présence d'un modèle rhétorique en Romains', *Bib* 71: 2-24.
Alfaro, J.
1985   'La cuestión del sentido y el sentido de la cuestión', *Gregorianum* 66: 387-403.
Angelico Da Linguaglossa, D.
1968   'Il prologo della lettera ai romani (Rm. 1,1-7): Struttura e significato', *Laurentianum* 8: 73-84.
Balz, H.
1978   *Theologische Model der Kommunikation* (Gütersloh).
Bazak, J.
1984   *Structure and Contents in the Psalms: Geometric Structural Patterns in the Seven Alphabetical Psalms* (Tel Aviv, Hebr.).
Black, D.A.
1987   'A Note on the Structure of Hebrews 12.1-2', *Bib* 68: 543-51.
Bouissac, P., *et al.*
1986   *Iconicity, Essays on the Nature of Culture* (Festschrift T.A. Sebeok; Tübingen, 1986).
Breck, J.
1987   'Biblical Chiasmus: Exploring Structure for Meaning', *BTB* 17: 70-74.
Carrière, J.M.
1991   'Le Ps 72 est-il un psaume messianique?', *Bib* 72: 49-69.
Cazeaux, J.
1983   *L'épée du logos et le soleil de midi* (Lyon).
Ceccato, S.
1985   'Per un modello cibernetico della vita mentale', *Mulino* 34: 674-80.
1984   'Chiastic Awareness and Education in Antiquity', *BTB* 14: 23-27.

Clausi, B.
1990   'Elementi di ermeneutica monastica nel "De Schematibus et Tropis" di Beda', *Orpheus* 11: 277-307.

Crenshaw, J.L.
1987   'Murphy's Axiom: Every Gnomic Saying Needs a Balancing Corrective', in K.G. Hoglund (ed.), *The Listening Heart: Essays in Wisdom and the Psalms* (JSOTSup, 58; Sheffield: JSOT Press): 1-17.

Christensen, D.L.
1985   'Prose and Poetry in the Bible', *ZAW* 97: 179-89.

Deconchy, J.P.
1984   'Vérité et ortodoxie', in M. Michel (ed.), *La théologie à l'épreuve de la vérité* (Cogitatio fidei, 126; Paris): 28.

Di Giovine, C.
1991   'Note al "Technopaegium" di Ausonio', *Orpheus* 12: 143-44.

Di Marco, A.
1975   'Der Chiasmus in der Bibel', *LB* 36: 21-97.
1976a   'Der Chiasmus in der Bibel', *LB* 37: 49-68.
1976b   'Der Chiasmus in der Bibel', *LB* 39: 37-85.
1979   'Der Chiasmus in der Bibel', *LB* 44: 3-70.
1980   *Il chiasmo nella Bibbia* (Ricerche e proposte, 1; Torino).
1988   'Κοινωνια πνευματος (2 Cor 13,13; Flp 2.1) Πνευμα κοινωνιας Circolarità e ambivalenza linguistica e filologica', *FN* 1: 63-75.

Dyrness, W.A.
1983   'Symbolism, Modeling and Theology', in M. Inch and R. Youngblood (eds.), *The Living and Active Word of God: Essays in Honor of S.J. Schultz* (Winona Lake, IN): 283-99.

Eisenhut, W.
1990   *Einführung in die Antike Rhetorik und ihre Geschichte* (Darmstadt, 4th edn).

Eskult, M.
1990   *Studies in Verbal Aspect and Narrative Technique in Biblical Hebrew Prose* (Stockholm).

Forte, B. (ed.)
1981   *Gesù di Nazaret: Storia di Dio, Dio della storia* (Paoline).

Fossion, A.
1982   *Leggere le scritture: Teoria e pratica della letura strutturale* (Torino-Leumann).

Fuerst, N.
1989   *Der Schriftsteller Paulus* (Darmstadt).

Gardner, M.
1985   *L'univers anbidextre: Les miroirs de l'espace-temps* (Paris).

Gitay, Y.
1986   *JBL* 105: 709-10.

Grossberg, D.
1990   *Centripetal and Centrifugal Structures in Biblical Poetry* (Atlanta).

Güttgemanns, E.
  1975   '"Text" und "Geschichte" als Grundkategorien der generativen
          Poetik', in U. Gerber and E. Güttgemanns, *Linguistische Theologie*
          (Bonn): 38-55.
Haiman, J.
  1980   'The Iconicity of Grammar', *Language* 56: 515-37.
Haiman, J. (ed.)
  1985   *Iconicity in Syntax* (Amsterdam).
Ivanov, V.V.
  1982   'Die Linguistik', *Zeitschrift für Semiotik* 4: 41-54.
Kennedy, G.A.
  1984   *New Testament Interpretation through Rhetorical Criticism* (Chapel
          Hill).
Kurz, W.S.
  1987   'Narrative Approaches to Luke–Acts', *Bib* 68: 212.
Lambruschini, R.
  1930   *Scritti di varia filosofia e di religione* (Florence): 54.
Landolfi, L.
  1991   'Manil.Astr. 2,1-48: il catalogo letterario', *Orpheus* 12: 47.
Lausberg, H.
  1960   *Handbuch der literarischen Rhetorik: Eine Grundlegung der
          Literaturwissenschaft*, I–II (Munich).
Lotman, J.M.
  1990   'Über die Semiosphäre', *Zeitschrift für Semiotik* 12: 287-305.
Mack, B.L.
  1990   *Rhetoric and the New Testament* (Minneapolis).
Man, R.E.
  1984   'The Value of Chiasm for New Testament Interpretation', *BSac* 141:
          146-57.
Marin, L.
          'Les discours comme norme de l'institution', in M. Michel (ed.), *La
          théologie à l'épreuve de la vérité* (Cognitatio fidei, 126; Paris): 55-57.
Nicolosi, S.
  1983   *Medioevo francescano* (Rome).
Perlmutter, D.M., and S. Soanes
  1979   *Syntactic Argumentation and the Structure of English* (Berkeley).
Piattelli-Palmarini, M.
  1990   'Seletion Sémantic:Le róle causal du lexique', *Révue de Synthese* 111:
          58-77.
Pozzi, G.
  1981   *La parola dipinta* (Milan).
Ravasi, G.
  1981   *Il libro dei salmi: Commento e attualizzazione*, I (Bologna).
Recanatini, F.
  1991   'Strutture numeriche del "liber Cathemerinon" di Prudenzio',
          Orpheus 12: 563-69.

Rendtorff, T.
1985   'Die Religion in der Moderne—Die Moderne in der religion', *TLZ*
            110: 561-74.
Riva, A.
1979   'La figura del chiasmo in un sonetto di Jacopo da Lentini', *REI* 25:
            145-60.
Robbins, C.J.
1986   'The Composition of Eph 1,3-14', *JBL* 105: 677-87.
Schäeffler, R.
1985   'Neue Aspekte des Sprechens van Gott', in J. Möller (ed.), *Der Streit
            um den Gott der Philosophen* (Düsseldorf).
Schmidt, P.
1984   'The Interpretation of the Resurrection: Historical and Theological
            Truth', *Communio* 11: 75-88.
Semi, F.
1965   *M.Terentius Varro III (Scriptorum romanorum quae extant omnia 41-
            42* (Venetiis).
Slama-Cazacu, T.
1984   *Linguistique appliquée* (Brescia).
Standaert, B.
1986   'La rhétorique ancienne dans Saint Paul', in A. Vanhoye (ed.),
            L'apôtre Paul (Leuven): 86-91.
Van Leuwen, R.C.
1985   'What Comes out of God's Mouth: Theological Wordplay in Deut 8',
            CBQ 47: 55-57.
Watson, D.F.
1988   'The N.T. and Graeco-Roman Rhetoric: A Bibliography', *JETS* 31:
            465-72.
1990   'The N.T. and Graeco-Roman Rhetoric: A Bibliographical Update',
            JETS 33: 513-24.
Watson, W.G.E.
1984   *Classical Hebrew Poetry* (Sheffield).
Welch, J.W. (ed.)
1981   *Chiasmus in Antiquity: Structures, Analyses, Exegesis* (Hildesheim).

BIBLICAL EXEGESIS IN THE LIGHT OF THE HISTORY AND HISTORICITY OF RHETORIC AND THE NATURE OF THE RHETORIC OF RELIGION

Wilhelm Wuellner

Introduction

Certain aspects of biblical interpretation (few for some, for others many) have been perceived as closely related to rhetoric ever since early Christian times. This liaison may well have been generated, or at least sustained, by the role which liberal arts education played in Christian as in Jewish circles of late antiquity and extending into the medieval and Renaissance period.[1] But this liaison, though constitutive

---

1. See J. Koch (ed.), *Artes Liberales: Von der antiken Bildung zur Wissenschaft des Mittelalters* (Studien und Texte zur Geistesgeschichte des Mittelalters, 5; Leiden: Brill, 2nd edn, 1976); and J. Dolch, *Lehrplan des Abendlandes: Zweieinhalb Jahrtauseud seiner Geschichte* (Ratingen: Kastellaun, 3rd edn, 1971; repr. Darmstadt: Wissenschaftliche Buchgesellschaft, 1982).

C.J. Swearingen (*Rhetoric and Irony: Western Literacy and Western Lies* [New York: Oxford University Press, 1991], p. 8) critically examines 'the paradoxical pairing of persistent mistrust of and respect for the powers of rhetoric... and the simultaneous if contradictory placement of [rhetoric, logic, literature] at the center of the forms and methods of education for more than two millennia'.

For late Western antiquity in general, see H.I. Marrou, 'Education and Rhetoric', in M.I. Finley (ed.), *The Legacy of Greece: A New Appraisal* (Oxford: Oxford University Press, 1981); see earlier E. Norden (*Die antike Kunstprosa vom VI. Jahrhundert v. Chr. bis in die Zeit der Renaissance* [Stuttgart: Teubner, 3rd edn, 1958 (1898)], pp. 670-79), on rhetoric's role in education from Plato till Augustine. Other recent studies: B.A. Kimball, *Orators and Philosophers: A History of the Idea of Liberal Education* (New York: Teachers College Press, 1986); H. Kirkby, 'The Scholar and his Public', in M.T. Gibson (ed.), *Boethius, his Life, Thought, and Influence* (Oxford: Oxford University Press, 1981); T.P. Halton, 'Paideia in Transition in the Greco-Roman World: 200–400 A.D.', in W. Haase (ed.), *ANRW* II. 35.1 *Sprache und Literatur* (Berlin: de Gruyter, forthcoming); and J. Dolch, *Lehrplan*, pp. 47-71 and 89-95, on paideia in Hellenistic schools till the first century

of biblical exegesis, has not always been fully acknowledged, let alone fully appreciated.

In the last quarter of the twentieth century we are emerging at long last from an extended eclipse of rhetoric in Western culture, both Jewish and Christian, as well as later secular Western culture. This eclipse has lasted since the beginning of the hegemony of modern scientific exegesis and the rise of historical criticism. With the near volcanic eruption of rhetoric at the center of biblical interpretation in the last quarter of the twentieth century, such re-emergence of rhetoric, as evidenced in this Heidelberg conference, forces us to face a number of crucial issues.

CE. For progymnastic rhetorical training and on the rhetorical nature of culture-transmitting school traditions, see R.F. Hock and E.N. O'Neil, *The Chreia in Ancient Rhetoric. I. The Progymnasmate* (Atlanta: Scholars Press, 1986). See also the contributions in H.-T. Johann (ed.), *Erziehung und Bildung in der heidnischen und christlichen Antike* (WdF, 377; Darmstadt: Wissenschaftliche Buchgesellschaft, 1976).

For early Christianity, see B. Mack and V. Robbins, *Patterns of Persuasion in the Gospels* (Sonoma, CA: Polebridge Press, 1989); F. Young, 'The Rhetorical Schools and their Influence on Patristic Exegesis', in R. Williams (ed.), *The Making of Orthodoxy: Essays in Honour of Henry Chadwick* (Cambridge: Cambridge University Press, 1989), pp. 182-99. U. Neymeyr (*Die christlichen Lehrer im zweiten Jahrhundert: Ihre Lehrtätigkeit, ihr Selbstverständnis und ihre Geschichte* [Vigiliae Christianae Supplements, 4; Leiden: Brill, 1989]) emphasizes the disconti-nuity between second-century developments and those in the first and third centuries respectively. He also highlights the regionally distinct developments (see also below n. 16); compare the five different cultural subgroups in first-century Christianity, as proposed by B.L. Mack, *A Myth of Innocence: Mark and Christian Origins* (Philadelphia: Fortress Press, 1988).

What goes for early Christianity, chronologically and geographically, applies also to pre- and post-70 CE Judaism in the similarities and differences of the liaison between rhetoric and education, whether in the Roman or Babylonian/Persian Dispersion or in Eretz Israel. See M. Hengel, *The 'Hellenization' of Judaea in the First Century after Christ* (Philadelphia: Fortress Press, 1989); and *idem*, 'Der vorchristliche Paulus', in M. Hengel and U. Heckel (eds.), *Paulus und das antike Judentum* (WUNT, 2.58; Tübingen: Mohr, 1991), see esp. pp. 212-39 and 256-65; ET 'The Pre-Christian Paul', in J. Lieu, J. North and T. Rajak (eds.), *The Jews among Pagans and Christians in the Roman Empire* (Longon: Routledge, 1992), pp. 29-52; and W. Wuellner, 'Der vorchristliche Paulus und die Rhetorik', in S. Lauer (ed.), *Before and After 70. Festschrift for Clemens Thoma* (Judacia et Christiana; Bern: P. Lang, 1994 forthcoming). See also the references to P.S. Alexander and G.M. Phillips, below n. 14.

One of the issues is (1) how best to account for the liaison between biblical scholarship or hermeneutics and rhetoric in the history of Western Christian and Jewish scholarship,[2] and (2) how to account for rhetoric's demise in modern times with its consequences for exegesis.

Another issue, even more crucial in its ramifications, is to account for the growing need to warn against the widespread current tendency of simply reestablishing the connections that existed for so many centuries between biblical hermeneutics and classical Western rhetoric. What should motivate current exegetes, interested as many may be in rhetorical criticism, to join forces with students of contemporary rhetoric (1) to learn the lessons to be learned from the history of rhetoric, and (2) to appreciate fully the implications generated by the growing realization of the historicity of the rhetoric of classical and Hellenistic-Roman antiquity?

We will discuss these issues in the sequence just outlined. As the first gathering of students of rhetoric with students of biblical exegesis, this Heidelberg conference of 1992 constitutes a milestone event in itself. It is to be hoped that the contributions to, and the discussions during and after, this conference will bring into focus the agenda that needs urgently to be set and agreed on for a number of critical discernments to be made, and for future developments to be anticipated in this explosive field of study, so rich in assets and so full of old and new liabilities.

For medieval developments, see G.R. Evans, *Old Arts and New Theology: The Beginnings of Theology as an Academic Discipline* (Oxford: Clarendon Press, 1980); K. Dockhorn, 'Rhetorica movet: Protestantischer Humanismus und karolingische Renaissance', in H. Schanze (ed.), *Rhetorik: Beiträge zu ihrer Geschichte in Deutschland vom 16.–20. Jahrhundert* (Frankfurt: Fischer, 1974), pp. 17-42; and A. Grafton and L. Jardine, *From Humanism to the Humanities* (Cambridge, MA: Harvard University Press, 1986).

   For the growing importance of national, cultural, political and religious developments (see also n. 16 below), and for the increasingly troublesome liaison between rhetoric and education, see the incisive survey for the German speaking realms of Europe by E. Ockel, 'Zur rhetorischen Bildung als Indiz gesellschaftlicher Strömungen', in G. Ueding (ed.), *Rhetorik zwischen den Wissenschaften: Geschichte, System, Praxis als Probleme des 'Historischen Wörterbuchs der Rhetorik'* (Tübingen: Niemeyer, 1991), pp. 363-70.

   2.   See K. Eden, 'Hermeneutics and the Ancient Rhetorical Tradition', *Rhetorica* 5 (1987), pp. 59-86, and below n. 18.

Biblical Exegesis in the Light of the History of Rhetoric

For some, perhaps many, of our colleagues the discipline of rhetorical criticism applied to biblical studies is 'a comparative newcomer to the field of biblical studies'.[3] This is true only in the sense that it is relatively new for exegetes to think of rhetoric in critical terms. No longer are we simply assuming that rhetoric, especially in its Hellenistic-Roman forms, whether Aristotelian or Ciceronian, was then (or ever) a uniform and closed 'system' readily to be discerned in the numerous rhetorical handbooks spawned by some presumed normative *Schulrhetorik*—a 'system' which only needs to be recovered, similar to the Renaissance and humanist developments, and then to be applied anew. Instead, we have come to realize that the history of rhetoric has been 'the history of a continuing art undergoing revolutionary changes',[4] and that it is the history of both 'the splendor and misery of rhetoric' in a series of intensifying crises.[5]

The influence of the history of rhetoric on Patristic and early medieval exegesis was characterized by a historian as follows: Boethius's *De differentiis topicis* reflects the legacy of Aristotle; Augustine's *De doctrina IV* the legacy of Plato and Cicero; and Bede's *De schematibus et tropis Sacrae Scripturae* the legacy of 'the sophists' love of language'.[6]

---

3. M. Warner (ed.), *The Bible as Rhetoric: Studies in Biblical Persuasion and Credibility* (Warwick Studies in Philosophy and Literature; London: Routledge, 1989), p. 3.

4. R. McKeon, *Rhetoric: Essays in Invention and Discovery* (ed. M. Backman; Woodbridge, CT: Ox Bow Press, 1987), p. 20.

5. T. Todorov, *Theories of the Symbol* (trans. C. Porter; Ithaca, NY: Cornell University Press, 1982), pp. 60-83; for the related crises in Western literacy, see Swearingen, *Rhetoric and Irony*.

6. See L. Reinsma, 'The Middle Ages', in W.R. Horner (ed.), *Historical Rhetoric: An Annotated Bibliography of Selected Sources in English* (Boston: Hall, 1980), pp. 43-108 (45); on Augustine, see K. Eden, 'The Rhetorical Tradition and Augustinian Hermeneutics in *de doctrina christiana*', *Rhetorica* 9 (1990), pp. 45-63; J. McWilliam (ed.), *Augustine: From Rhetor to Theologian* (Waterloo, Ontario: Wilfrid Laurier University Press, 1991), and Swearingen, *Rhetoric and Irony*, pp. 175-214 on Augustine's critique of the notorious mendacity associated with rhetoric and literature. On regional differences in Christian rhetoric (e.g. Africa, Gaul, and other Roman provinces), see Norden, *Die antike Kunstprosa*, pp. 586-654; see also n. 16.

What was regenerated by the renaissance of classical Western rhetoric, and bequeathed to the sixteenth-century Reformation and Counter-Reformation alike,[7] was a legacy not only of Byzantium (see n. 6), but also of the impact of Moslem culture on both Judaism and Christianity.[8] Biblical exegesis was profoundly affected by three developments in the wake of the renaissance of rhetorical literacy: (1) the rise of a 'new rhetoric' indebted to the vernacular cultures replacing the waning homogeneity of the classical Latin culture of Europe's 'Holy Roman Empire';[9] (2) the rise of print

For the developments in the Byzantine tradition, see R. Browning, 'Rhetoric: Byzantine', in J.R. Strayer (ed.), *Dictionary of the Middle Ages* (New York: Charles Scribner's Sons, 1988), X, pp. 349-51; T. Conley, 'Byzantine Teaching on Figures and Tropes: An Introduction', *Rhetorica* 4 (1986), pp. 335-74; H. Hunger, 'Rhetorik als politischer und gesellschaftlicher Faktor in Byzanz', in Ueding (ed.), *Rhetorik zwischen den Wissenschaften*, pp. 103-107; G. Kustas, *Studies in Byzantine Rhetoric* (Thessaloniki, 1973); H. Maguire, *Art and Eloquence in Byzantium* (Princeton: Princeton University Press, 1981).

7. See G.R. Evans, *The Language and Logic of the Bible: The Road to Reformation* (Cambridge: Cambridge University Press, 1985); K. Meerhoff, *Rhétorique et poétique aux XVIe siècle en France: Du Bellay, Ramus et les autres* (Studies in Medieval and Reformation Thought, 36; Leiden: Brill, 1986); J.J. Jerry (ed.), *Renaissance Eloquence: Studies in the Theory and Practice of Renaissance Rhetoric* (Berkeley: University of California Press, 1983); H.R. Plett, 'Rhetorikgeschichte im Lichte der Rhetorikbibliographie—Am Beispiel der englischen Renaissance', in Ueding (ed.), *Rhetorik zwischen den Wissenschaften*; J.E. Seigel, *Rhetoric and Philosophy in Renaissance Humanism* (Princeton: Princeton University Press, 1968); R. Weiss, 'The Humanist Rediscovery of Rhetoric as Philosophy: Giovano Pontano's AEGIDIUS', *Philosophy and Rhetoric* 13 (1980), pp. 25-42; W. Wuellner, *Hermeneutics and Rhetorics: From 'Truth and Method' to Truth and Power* (Scriptura S3; Journal of the Bible and Theology in Southern Africa; Stellenbosch: Centre for Hermeneutical Studies, 1989), pp. 3-5.

8. On Arab contributions to the Jewish and Christian renaissance of rhetoric, see A. Altmann's study of 1981 cited in n. 13 below. See also A.S. Halkin (ed.), *Moshe ben Yaakov ibn Ezra, KITAB AL-MUHĀDARA WAL-MUDHADARA: Liber Discussionis et Commemorationis [1055-1135 CE]* (Poetica Hebraica; Jerusalem: Mekize Nirdamin, 1975); A. Hamori, 'Rhetoric: Arabic, Hebrew, Persian', in *A Dictionary of the Middle Ages* 10 (1988), p. 348; and T. Todrosi, *Averrois Commentarius in Aristotelis de arte rhetorica libros tres hebraice versus a Todrosis Todrosi Arelatensi* (Leipzig: Goldenthal, 1842). Todrosi also translated into Hebrew Aristotle's *Logic* and *Poetics*.

9. See, e.g., D.K. Shuger, *Sacred Rhetoric: The Christian Grand Style in the English Renaissance* (Princeton: Princeton University Press, 1988); B. Stolt, 'Martin

culture technology;[10] and (3) the Ramist reform of the liberal arts curriculum. Ramism's effect was the institutionalization of the separation of the study of rhetoric's *officium* from the study of rhetoric as *technê*. In early modern times it became the separation of the study of thought or content (in biblical studies: theology, or ethics) from the study of form or feeling (linguistic or literary forms or style, and religious experience).[11] In Protestant developments, as early as the late sixteenth century, this fateful separation in the study of rhetoric led to the largely still unreconciled conflicts between advocates of theological orthodoxy focusing on doctrine elaborated in terms of topics, dialectics, and logic, and advocates of religious experience focusing on what 'moves' the heart (e.g. Pietists, Quakers, etc.).

Mainline modern biblical exegesis, Jewish or Christian, is still largely under the spell of this fateful change in the approach to rhetoric. This change inevitably resulted in what Todorov called 'the end of rhetoric' in the course of the nineteenth century—whether in terms of the history of rhetoric in the European tradition, or in terms of rhetoric's relevance for biblical exegesis.

As an aside on the subject of the importance of the rise of the study of the rhetoric of the European vernacular languages, let me briefly point out two important areas: (1) the contributions made by the Christian Hebraists[12] to an appreciation of the distinctiveness of Jewish

---

Luthers rhetorische Syntax', in G. Ueding (ed.), *Rhetorik zwischen den Wissenschaften*, pp. 207-20. On the beginnings of European vernacular literature, and, with it, interest in vernacular rhetorics, see E.R. Curtius, *Europäische Literatur und Lateinisches Mittelalter* (Bern: Francke, 6th edn, 1976), pp. 387-91.

10. See E.L. Eisenstein, *The Printing Press as an Agent of Change: Communications and Cultural Transformation in Early Modern Europe* (2 vols.; Cambridge: Cambridge University Press, 1979); and H. Schanze, 'Vom Manuskript zum Buch: Zur Problematik der "Neuen Rhetorik" um 1500 in Deutschland', *Rhetorica* 1 (1983), pp. 61-73.

11. See, e.g., W.J. Ong, *Method and the Decay of Dialogue: From the Art of Discourse to the Art of Reason* (Cambridge, MA: Harvard University Press, 1958); for Ong the period from 1550 to 1650 was a time of method gone berserk. For an overview of 'Recent Work on Peter Ramus (1970–1986)', see P. Sharratt's essay in *Rhetorica* 5 (1987), pp. 7-58, and Swearingen's reflections in *Rhetoric and Irony*, pp. 220-34.

12. For an overview, see R. Hallo, 'Christian Hebraists', *Modern Judaism* 3 (1983), pp. 95-116; and W. McKane, *Select Christian Hebraists* (Cambridge:

rhetoric, and (2) the contributions which the study of the rhetoric of vernacular languages made for the distinction between two kinds of rhetoric and two kinds of literacy: cultured versus primitive, school versus market place, scribal versus am-ha'aretz.[13]

The subject of Jewish rhetoric, both biblical and postbiblical, has received some increased attention recently, but still awaits further critical attention by biblical (and other) scholars, Jewish and Christian.[14] At the end of the twentieth century we have barely begun

Cambridge University Press, 1989).

13. Eduard Norden (*Die Antike Kunstprosa* [1909, repr. 1958]) notes in Paul that 'Man is oft frappiert, mitten in Partien, die nur mit der Rhetorik des Herzens in ungefeilter Sprache geschrieben sind, alte Bekannte aus der zünftigen griechischen Kunstprosa anzutreffen' (p. 502). He also takes it as obvious that preachers using the 'einfache Spache des Herzens' were often more effective by these means than many other speakers or writers using 'ihre glänzende Diktion' (p. 535).

14. More familiar are the studies of the rhetoric of the Hebrew Bible, e.g., R.C. Katz, *The Structure of Ancient Arguments: Rhetoric and its Near Eastern Origins* (New York: Shapolsky/Steinmatzky Publishing, 1987); G.A. Kennedy, *Classical Rhetoric and its Christian and Secular Tradition from Ancient to Modern Times* (Durham: University of North Carolina Press, 1980), pp. 120-25 on 'Old Testament Rhetoric'; D. Patrick and A. Scult, *Rhetoric and Biblical Interpretation* (Bible and Literature, 26; Sheffield: Almond Press, 1990); Jesper, Høgenhaven, 'Prophecy and Propaganda: Aspects of Political and Religious Reasoning in Israel and the Ancient Near East', *SJOT* 1 (1989), pp. 125-41.

Less familiar are the few studies available on the history of Jewish rhetoric since the end of the Second Temple period, e.g. A. Altmann, 'ARS RHETORICA as reflected in some Jewish Figures of the Italian Renaissance', in *Essays in Jewish Intellectual History* (Hanover: Brandeis University Press, 1981), pp. 97-118; N. Brüll, 'Zur Geschichte der rhetorischen Literatur bei den Juden', *Ben Chananja* 6 (Szeged, 1863), pp. 486-532; D. Daube, 'Rabbinic Methods of Interpretation and Hellenistic Rhetoric', *HUCA* 22 (1949), pp. 239-64; H.A. Fischel, *Rabbinic Literature and Greco-Roman Philosophy: A Study of Epicurea and Rhetorica in Midrashic Writings* (Studia Post-Biblica, 21; Leiden: Brill, 1973); H.A. Fischel, 'Story and History: Observations on Greco-Roman Rhetoric and Pharisaism', in *Essays in Greco-Roman and Related Talmudic Literature* (New York: Ktav, 1977), pp. 443-72; D.C. Kraemer, 'New Meaning in Ancient Talmudic Texts: A Rhetorical Reading and the Case of Pluralism', *Proceedings of the Rabbinic Assembly* 49 (1988), pp. 201-14; J. Neusner, *Talmudic Thinking: Language, Logic, Law* (Columbia: University of South Carolina Press, 1992); and J. Neuser, *The Bavli's Primary Discourse. Mishnah Commentary: Its Rhetorical Paradigms and their Theological Implications in the Talmud of Babylonia, Tractate MOED QATAN* (South Florida Studies in the History of Judaism, 43; Atlanta: Scholars Press, 1992), with the study of comparative rhetoric.[15] Likewise, only recently has there been any attention paid to rhetoric and its history as regionally, that is, culturally centered,[16] and to rhetoric, in practice as in theory, related to culture-specific gender roles[17] and other manifestations of ideology (e.g. *topoi*, or premises, in argumentation). It is at points like these that rhetorical criticism and ideological criticism converge. These two forms of criticism are like two sides of one coin: distinct but inseparable. Rhetoric is not reducible to sociological or ideological studies, but both are indispensable for rhetoric—also, indeed especially, for the study of the rhetoric of religion.

The subject of the difference between the cultured rhetoric of the academy (whose handbook industry develops in proportion to the centrality of rhetoric in the 'liberal arts' curriculum; see above n. 1) and the popular rhetoric of the marketplace is a topic familiar to

pp. 147-61; and J. Neusner, *The Bavli's Massive Miscellanies: The Problem of Agglutinative Discourse in the Talmud of Babylonia* (South Florida Studies in the History of Judaism, 43; Atlanta: Scholars Press, 1992), pp. 17-48 on the 'fixed rhetorical pattern (governing the Talmud) throughout'; G.M. Phillips, 'The Practice of Rhetoric at the Talmudic Academies', *Speech Monographs* 26 (1959), pp. 37-46; I. Rabinowitz, 'Pre-Modern Jewish Study of Rhetoric: An Introductory Bibliography', *Rhetorica* 3.2 (1985), pp. 137-44; D. Stern, *Parables in Midrash: Narrative and Exegesis in Rabbinic Literature* (Cambridge, MA: Harvard University Press, 1991), see esp. pp. 46-62 on how rhetoric served midrash.

15. The classical study is by R.T. Oliver, *Culture and Communication: The Problem of Penetrating National and Cultural Boundaries* (American Lecture Series, 506; Springfield, IL: Thomas, 1962); it was illustrated by his *Communication and Culture in Ancient India and China* (Syracuse: Syracuse University Press, 1971). For an update, see M. Garrett, 'Asian Challenge', in S.K. Foss, K.A. Foss and R. Trapp (eds.), *Contemporary Perspectives on Rhetoric* (Prospect Heights, IL: Waveland Press, 2nd end, 1991), pp. 295-314.

16. On Slavic and Byzantine 'regionally-centered studies', see the works cited by J.J. Murphy, 'The Historiography of Rhetoric: Challenges and Opportunities', *Rhetorica* 1 (1983), pp. 4-5 nn. 7 and 8. For a critical awareness of regional characteristics in second-century Patristic approaches to education and, with it, to rhetoric, see Neymeyr, *Die christlichen Lehrer*, referred to in n. 1. The regions dealt with are Rome in the West, Alexandria and Carthage in North Africa, and Syria in the East.

17. See G. Lloyd, *The Man of Reason: 'Male' and 'Female' in Western Philosophy* (Minneapolis: University of Minnesota Press, 1984); C. Poyton, *Language and Gender: Making the Difference* (New York: Oxford University Press, 1989); S.C. Jarratt, 'The First Sophists and Feminism: Discourses of the "Other"', *Hypatia* 5 (1990), pp. 27-41, and Swearingen, *Rhetoric and Irony*, pp. 215-54. See also below n. 38 on gender roles.

biblical scholars since at least Overbeck's distinction between *Hochliteratur* and *Kleinliteratur*, or since Deissmann's distinction between epistle and letter. The former is by definition rhetorical (Atticistic or Sophistic), the latter is not; the former belongs to art, the latter does not. This distinction continues to be one of the major obstacles for a re-orientation of rhetorical criticism in contemporary biblical scholarship. So long as biblical scholars remain blind to the reality that there is more rhetoric to be experienced in one hour in the marketplace (or even in the nursery) than in one day in the academy, scholarship devoted to biblical rhetoric will remain in a quandary—in a prison self-made and self-imposed.

I will return to some of these issues raised here, when I discuss the historicity of rhetoric and its importance for biblical scholarship currently being sensitized and committed to the needs of biblical interpretation as a form of cultural criticism. This includes a critique of scholarship's own practices both past and present.

Dockhorn complimented Gadamer for having recognized and reemphasized that, at least in Western tradition, hermeneutics had arisen from rhetoric. Dockhorn also noted approvingly Heidegger's comment that 'the rhetoric of Aristotle [was] the first systematic hermeneutic of everyday life'. Dockhorn's translator referred to Gadamer's and Dockhorn's contributions as the continued study of the 'rhetoric of hermeneutics' with Dockhorn wanting Gadamer to recognize 'the hermeneutics of rhetoric'.[18] What many consider 'the real beginning of scholarly hermeneutics'[19] was the work of a contemporary of Peter Ramus, Matthias Flacius (Vlacich) Illyricus (1520–75) with his *Clavis Scripturae Sacrae seu De Sermone Sacrarum Litterarum plurimas generales Regulas continens* of 1567.[20] Nearly

---

18. See Marvin Brown's translation of Klaus Dockhorn's 1966 review of Gadamer's *Truth and Method*, published in *Philosophy and Rhetoric* 13 (1980), pp. 160-80. For Gadamer's positive response to Dockhorn's review, see 'Rhetorik, Hermeneutik und Ideologiekritik: Metakritische Erörterungen zu "Wahrheit und Methode"', in *Hermeneutik und Ideologiekritik* (Frankfurt: Suhrkamp, 1971), now also in *Kleine Schriften*. I. *Philosophie, Hermeneutik* (Tübingen: Mohr, 2nd edn, 1976), pp. 113-30. See also S. Mailloux's proposal for 'Rhetorical Hermeneutics', *Critical Inquiry* 11 (1985), pp. 620-41.

19. See W.G. Kümmel, *The New Testament: The History of the Investigation of its Problems* (London: SCM; Philadelphia: Fortress Press, 1973), p. 27.

20. For Flacius in context, see D. Shuger, 'Morris Croll, Flacius Illyricus, and the Origin of Anti-Ciceronianism', *Rhetorica* 3 (1985), pp. 269-84.

50% of this voluminous work is pure rhetoric. What Gadamer had to say about Flacius, and what was amplified by Dockhorn, gets echoed by David Tracy when he claims that 'modern hermeneutical discourse analysis...is...only a modern return to, and rethinking of, both ancient rhetoric and earlier hermeneutics'.[21] But with the rapid spread of Ramism—including its early export from Europe overseas!—the history of rhetoric as well as the history of biblical exegesis changed.

The crucial question for any critical assessment of biblical exegesis in the light of the history of rhetoric is not whether the rebirth of rhetoric in late twentieth-century biblical scholarship is real and genuine. Rather, the crucial question is what kind of rhetoric do we witness rising from its ashes like a Phoenix: is it yet another renaissance of rhetoric as a system of 'techniques of argumentation' or style, thus perpetuating the historical process of the cyclical patterns of the *letteraturizzazione* of rhetoric to the point of its reduction to stylistics or poetics? If yes, as it appears in wide circles of contemporary biblical scholarship, such renaissance would only continue rhetoric's much lamented fragmentation, enhanced as it was and is by modern scientism. This makes the history of rhetoric, and with it the history of biblical exegesis what Ricoeur saw as 'an ironic tale of diminishing returns'—a history in which rhetoric was increasingly 'restrained'[22] if not downright irrelevant.

Biblical Exegesis in the Light of the Historicity of Rhetoric

There are four aspects to the examination of the significance of the historicity of rhetoric; a fifth aspect will be examined in the final part of this paper.

To speak of the historicity of rhetoric is to explain what Kennedy means by 'all religious systems are rhetorical', and what he claims to be the appeal of rhetorical criticism over other modern critical

21. *Plurality and Ambiguity: Hermeneutics, Religion, Hope* (San Francisco: Harper & Row, 1987), p. 65.
22. See W.C. Booth, 'Rhetorical Critics Old and New: The Case of Gérard Genette', in L. Lerner (ed.), *Reconstructing Literature* (Oxford: Basil Blackwell, 1983), pp. 124-41; Booth refers to Genette's *Figures of Literary Discourse* (New York: Columbia University Press, 1982), pp. 103-26 on 'Rhetoric Restrained'. Note also the observations of D.L. Stamps in 'Rhetorical Criticism and Rhetoric of New Testament Criticism', *Literature and Theology* 6.3 (1992), pp. 268-79.

approaches due to its coming closer to explaining what readers of the Bible, or for that matter of the Scriptures of other religions, 'want explained in the text: not its sources [nor its aesthetic appeal or propositional contents], but its power'.[23] To say that 'all religious systems are rhetorical' is to say that all religions in their manifestations are 'purposeful'. Even religious poetry can be read and experienced as 'poetry with a purpose',[24] and came to be fully appreciated as 'sacred rhetoric' as distinct from all other rhetorics in Renaissance Europe.[25]

Secondly, to speak of the historicity of rhetoric is made necessary by the realization that the nature of rhetoric, including sacred rhetoric, and given the scope of their respective critical practices and theories, reflects the wider social and cultural situations in which rhetoric was cultivated in its long and checkered history in both Western and non-Western cultures, down to our times.

Thirdly, to speak of the historicity of rhetoric is to challenge the familiar notion, enhanced by the allegations of the ubiquity of rhetoric, that rhetoric, 'though colored by the traditions and conventions of the society in which it is applied...is also a universal phenomenon which is conditioned by basic workings of the human mind and heart and by the nature of all human society'.[26] It also challenges the legacy of 'the whole movement of the New Critics and of their associates [such as I.A. Richards[27] who were] trying to propose a

23. Kennedy, *New Testament Interpretation through Rhetorical Criticism*, p. 158. For a critical appraisal of Kennedy's approach, see J.R. Levison, 'Did the Spirit Inspire Rhetoric? An Exploration of George Kennedy's Definition of Early Christian Rhetoric', in D.F. Watson (ed.), *Persuasive Artistry: Studies in New Testament Rhetoric in Honor of George A. Kennedy* (JSNTSup, 50; Sheffield: JSOT Press, 1991), pp. 25-40.

24. See H. Fisch, *Poetry with a Purpose: Biblical Poetics and Interpretation* (Indiana Studies in Biblical Literature; Bloomington: Indiana University Press, 1988).

25. See D.K. Shuger, *Sacred Rhetoric: The Christian Grand Style in the English Renaissance* (Princeton: Princeton University Press, 1988), and D.S. Cunningham, *Faithful Persuasion: In Aid of a Rhetoric of Christian Theology* (Notre Dame: University of Notre Dame Press, 1990).

26. Kennedy, *New Testament Interpretation through Rhetorical Criticism*, p. 10.

27. I.A. Richards, *The Philosophy of Rhetoric* (New York: Oxford University Press, 1936); see also A.E. Berthoff (ed.), *Richards on Rhetoric: I.A. Richards: Select Essays (1929–1974)* (New York: Oxford University Press, 1990).

global philosophy of rhetoric'.[28] What the historicity of rhetoric seeks to bring and keep in focus is to emphasize a point all too often overlooked by exegetes adopting Kennedy, that 'classical' rhetoric and its legacy consists of a wide diversity of practices and their resulting theories, each 'more or less defined by...values and functions of culture'[29] which are not those of the modern interpreter's own culture.

Finally, to speak of the historicity of rhetoric may appear to be redundant, for the very nature of rhetoric, its rhetoricity, is its historicity. I want to distinguish here between three dimensions of historicity: (1) the uniqueness of any given historical and cultural manifestation; (2) the cultural contests and conflicts, that is, the suasive argumentations within a culture and between cultures; and (3) what J. Hillis Miller calls 'the materiality of reading', as part of what Paul de Man called 'the materiality of history'.[30]

Relating to the first dimension, modern critics point out for instance that classical rhetoric was developed to account for discourse in a different and perhaps simpler social, cultural context.[31] This difference in context applies regardless of whether the discourse in question belongs to the literature sanctioned by the cultural elite, or to the popular literature of the 'illiterates'; to the rhetoric of the marketplace or to the rhetoric of the *paideia* inspired rhetorical handbooks; to oral or literary rhetoric; to the rhetoric of 'the god of Abraham, Isaac, and Jacob' or to the rhetoric of 'the god of the philosophers'.

Relating to the second dimension, the cultural contests and conflicts, the concern for the historicity of rhetoric focuses on what modern rhetorical critics discern in Jewish and early Christian literature as something that *challenged* the prevailing dominance of norms of discourse in their respective societies. Rhetoric in Hellenistic-Roman

28. R. Barilli, *Rhetoric* (trans. G. Menozzi; Theory and History of Literature, 63; Minneapolis: University of Minnesota Press, 1989), p. 114.

29. Kennedy, *New Testament Interpretation through Rhetorical Criticism*, p. 8.

30. J.H. Miller, 'The Triumph of Theory, the Resistance to Reading, and the Question of the Material Base', *Publications of the Modern Language Association* 103 (1987), pp. 281-91; see also his 'Is There an Ethics of Reading?', in J. Phelan (ed.), *Reading Narrative: Form, Ethics, Ideology* (Columbus: Ohio State University Press, 1989), pp. 79-101.

31. See V.K. Robbins, 'Writing as a Rhetorical Act in Plutarch and the Gospels', in Watson (ed.), *Persuasive Artistry*, pp. 142-68. For the changing social and cultural contexts in antiquity itself, from the pre-Platonists till Cicero, see Swearingen, *Rhetoric and Irony*, pp. 22-174.

culture could depend on 'a common value set as criteria for selecting... the means for resolving common problems' confronting society.[32] This was challenged, however, in the cultural contest, if not conflict, between 'Athens and Jerusalem'.[33] The witty quotation, 'In the sermon I have just completed, wherever I said Aristotle, I meant Saint Paul',[34] does not do justice to the historicity of rhetoric discussed here.

The conflict between Athens and Jerusalem arose between classical antiquity and Judaism or Christianity respectively. Or it arose as a clash of indigenous cultures, as in Near Eastern cultures' resistance against Hellenism,[35] resisting the homogenizing forces of cultural, political, racial-ethnic, or gender ideologies. The same conflicts developed even within a given religious tradition, as for instance in the Judaisms and Christianities of the first century CE. The conflict the Rabbinic sages faced or precipitated were ongoing 'controversies for the sake of heaven' which is 'for the truth of Torah'.[36] Likewise, the conflicts Paul faced or precipitated, whether at Antioch, Galatia, Corinth, Jerusalem or Rome, were all a contest over 'the truth of the gospel' or the gospel's true power. What E.A. Judge calls 'a society of

32. So D.P. Cushman and P.K. Tompkins, 'A Theory of Rhetoric for Contemporary Society', *Philosophy and Rhetoric* 13 (1980), pp. 43-67 (51).

33. For a Jewish perspective on this cultural contest, see P.S. Alexander, 'Quid Athenis et Hierosolymis? Rabbinic Midrash and Hermeneutics in the Graeco-Roman World', in P.R. Davies and R.T. White (eds.), *A Tribute to Geza Vermes: Essays on Jewish and Christian Literature and History* (JSOTSup, 100; Sheffield: JSOT Press, 1990), pp. 101-24; for a Christian perspective, see E.G. Weltin, *Athens and Jerusalem: An Interpretive Essay on Christianity and Classical Culture* (Atlanta: Scholars Press, 1988).

34. Attributed to the turn-of-the-century Oxford don W.A. Spooner, and quoted as amotto by George Kennedy at the beginning of his book *New Testament Interpretation through Rhetorical Criticism*, p. 1, and chosen as the title of one of David Jasper's essays in M. Warner (ed.), *The Bible as Rhetoric*.

35. See S.K. Eddy, *The King is Dead: Studies in the Near Eastern Resistance to Hellenism, 333–31 BC* (Lincoln: University of Nebraska Press, 1961).

36. On the controversies between the Jewish sages in the first centuries BCE and CE as 'one of the foremost positive factors in the creation of halakha', and the fact that the significance of the phenomenon of halakhic controversies in rabbinic tradition 'has not been sufficiently emphasized in previous research', see S. Safrai (ed.), *The Literatur of the Sages*. Compendia Rerum Iudaicarum ad Novum Testamentum 3.1: Oral Tora, Halakha, Mishna, Tosefta, Talmud, External Tractates (Maastricht: Van Gorcum; Philadelphia: Fortress Press, 1987), see pp. 168-75.

vigorous talk and argument about behavior and ideas'[37] characterizes first-century CE Jewish and Christian cultures as much as it does late Republican, early Imperial Roman culture. Variations on this theme reappear in the numerous reform and revolutionary movements of medieval and modern Christian, as well as Jewish, traditions.

In its third dimension, the historicity of rhetoric relates to 'the material base', which is 'the name for the whole region of what presumably exists outside language', which includes the 'unexamined ideology of the material base'. For Miller there are four aspects to this material base or the historicity of rhetoric: (1) the material base of the whole biblical canon as a rhetorical unit.[38] (2) The material base of the day-to-day life of those who were, or still are, speaking or writing rhetorically, as well as those who write about rhetoric; this includes 'their social, class, institutional, professional, familial situations'.[39] (3) The material base of 'the substance on which is written'—regardless of whether the focus is on the Bible or on biblical scholarship. Here the concerns range from the chirographic culture of antiquity to the typographic culture of print technology until our current electrographic computer technology. Each in its own way alerts us to rhetoric's life in the persistent shadows of the establishment: the 'literary-industrial complex',[40] with its vested interests, regardless

---

37. E.A. Judge, 'St Paul and Classical Society', *JAC* 15 (1972), pp. 19-36 (32). See also above n. 36 on Safrai's comments on the significance of halakhic controversies in first century CE Judaism.

38. This point would apply also to secular literary canons. For a mandate to engage in cultural criticism of old or new canons, secular or sacred, see J.A. Winders, *Gender, Theory, and the Canon* (Madison: University of Wisconsin Press, 1991).

39. See historian M.A. Noll's 'Review Essay: The Bible in America', *JBL* 106 (1987), pp. 493-509, on 'the Bible as a concern of the academy', and 'the Bible as a standard for competing ideological groups' (p. 496).

Similar concerns are voiced by Evans (*Old Arts and New Theology*) about the sometimes acrimonious tensions between advocates of the monastic *lectio divina* and early academic exegesis; between the *via antiqua* and the *via moderna* at the time of the first European universities challenging the educational hegemony of the monasteries or diocesan centers.

40. For a discussion of some of the issues involved, see M. Heim, 'The Technological Crisis of Rhetoric', *Philosophy and Rhetoric* 21 (1988), pp. 48-59; and M. Poster, *The Mode of Information: Poststructuralisms and Contexts* (Chicago: University of Chicago Press, 1990). On how rhetoric is influenced, both in practice and theory arising from it, by the institutional setting, exemplified by the Catholic

whether the establishment is secular or religious. (4) The material base includes for Miller 'the one time only of each unique act of reading; the here and now of the man or woman with the book in hand...what is...radically inaugural in each act of reading'.[41] This applies equally to the reading of the Bible or of biblical scholarship.

What the study of biblical texts in the light of the historicity of rhetoric ultimately amounts to, and what its implications are, has been identified for me best by J. Hillis Miller when he notes:

> That the opponents of the rhetorical study of [biblical] literature from both sides of the political spectrum continue to misrepresent it as ahistorical and apolitical... indicate[s] the importance of what is in question here... The stakes are enormous... in continuing to think out the implications of a rhetorical study of [biblical] literature for our political and ethical life.[42]

What is at stake in approaching biblical exegesis in the light of the historicity of rhetoric is the task now facing us of defining the liaison between the text (that is, all that is intrinsic to text or discourse) and its context (that is, all that is supposedly extrinsic to the texts); between discourse and reference; between literature and representation; between theory and practice.

Historicity of Rhetoric and the Rhetoric of Religion

Writing and reading literature, secular or sacred, makes the biblical critic face the task of accounting for the power of religious texts, or the text's 'verbal reality'.[43] Miller calls it 'the materiality of history' for which 'a rhetorical analysis of the most vigilant and patient sort is indispensable'.[44] The historicity of rhetoric accounts for the otherwise meaningless statement that 'the rhetorical study of [biblical] literature (or of the "literariness" in any piece of language as soon as it is taken as a text) is the encounter with that thing articulated *within* language which is irreducible by historical, sociological or psychological

Church, see G. Cheney, *Rhetoric in an Organizational Society: Managing Multiple Identities* (Studies in Rhetoric/Communication; Columbia, SC: University of South Carolina Press, 1991).

41. Miller, 'The Triumph of Theory', pp. 288, 289.

42. Miller, 'Is There an Ethics of Reading?', pp. 79-101 (84).

43. Kennedy, *New Testament Interpretation through Rhetorical Criticism*, pp. 158-59.

44. Miller, 'Is There an Ethics of Reading?', p. 81.

methods of interpretation'.[45] It is precisely these three methods, however, that remain the most attractive to conservative and progressive scholars alike, both Jewish and Christian.

I identified the issue of the power of biblical rhetoric, and presumably also the power of rhetorical criticism in biblical scholarship, with their respective quality of being 'purposeful'. If all rhetoric is purposeful, based on its 'invention' or 'intentionality' of convincing and 'moving' its invented audience/reader, what then is distinctive of biblical or sacred rhetoric? Does it make sense to speak of the historicity of rhetoric in connection with the rhetoric of religion? How do the divided worlds of rhetoric and religion get reintegrated to serve, among other tasks, the ever necessary illumination of 'the long night of superstition and the sacred',[46] or the lingering task of overcoming the misleading alternative between 'rhetoric and magic' on the one hand,[47] and 'rhetoric and the irrational' on the other.[48] The association of magic and irrationalism with rhetoric should be of special concern to students of the rhetoric of religion, now more than ever, when the postmodernist 'rage against reason' promotes what Swearingen

---

45. Miller, 'Is There an Ethics of Reading?', p. 81, emphasis added. On p. 82 Miller formulates the same idea in yet another way: 'In order to understand how a certain kind of language would make history happen, it is necessary first to understand what it means to speak of a given text as a texual allegory with a high level of rhetorical complexity'.

The rabbinic sages, as the heirs of the biblical hagiographers, understood this all too well. See S. Handelman, 'Fragments of the Rock: Contemporary Literary Theory and the Study of Rabbinic Texts—A Response to David Stern', *Prooftexts* 5 (1985), pp. 75-95; and J. Faur, *Golden Doves with Silver Dots: Semiotics and Textuality in Rabbinic Tradition* (Jewish Literature and Culture; Bloomington, IN: Indiana University Press, 1985).

46. F. Jameson, *Postmodernism, or The Cultural Logic of Late Capitalism* (Post-Contemporary Interventions; Durham: Duke University Press, 1991), p. 393.

47. See J.O. Ward, 'Magic and Rhetoric from Antiquity to the Renaissance: Some Ruminations', *Rhetorica* 6 (1988), pp. 57-118, and J. de Romilly, *Magic and Rhetoric in Ancient Greece* (Cambridge, MA: Harvard University Press, 1975). For the broader cultural context of equating rhetoric with magic or cunning enchantment, see M. Détienne and J.-P. Vernant, *Cunning-Intelligence in Greek Culture and Society* (trans. J. Lloyd; Atlantic Highlands, NJ: Humanities Press, 1978).

48. See K. Dockhorn, *Macht und Wirkung der Rhetorik* (Bad Homburg: Gehlen, 1968). Related to, but different from, irrationalism is mysticism. See the essays edited by F. Bolgiani, *Mistica e Retorica* (Florene: Olschki, 1977). See also below the discussion on rhetoric and the sublime.

calls 'a reductive and monolithic caricature of rationality'.[49]

Granted that religion, no less and no more than science, is by nature persuasive, and that the study of the rhetoric of religion[50] is a study in persuasiveness and motives indigenous to religion,[51] we must ask: is there a distinct rhetoric of religion? For Kennedy, the rhetoric of religion is recognizable by two characteristics. First, as 'pure sacred language' it is characterized by authorial proclamation which lacks any rational efforts of persuasion.[52] What is conveyed by this proclamation is divine revelation which aims at 'moving' or inducing responses to the will of God, the divine intentionality or purpose, God's own *inventio*. Recipients of divine revelation are 'moved' or affected by God's holiness, or divine love, or any number of attributes associated with manifestations of the divine. Of special interest to biblical exegetes is the relation between rhetoric and the sublime in its sacred as distinct from its secular sense.[53]

Secondly, Burke, Kennedy and others call attention to such other forms of religion's rhetorical nature as the use of myth, that is, the use of 'the analogies between words and the Word which are characteristic of religious discourse',[54] or the use of the arts in ritual, music, painting and the like. The persuasive uses of the arts in religion— comparable to their uses in modern advertisements, that is, in commercial art—are for Kennedy 'a rhetoric of their own to move the mind or the emotions'. What Kennedy points to is the peculiarity of the literary revelation: the paradox of casting into intelligible, that is, both plausible and persuasive words, what is outside of time and space, beyond human imagination, and resisting the idolatry of the 'single sense' of the empiricism of modern science—what William Blake called 'Newton's sleep'.

49. *Rhetoric and Irony*, p. 292 n. 49.

50. Such as K. Burke, *The Rhetoric of Religion: Studies in Logology* (Berkeley: University of California Press, 1961).

51. See K. Burke, *A Grammar of Motives* (Berkeley: University of California Press, 1945).

52. Kennedy, *New Testament Interpretation through Rhetorical Criticism*, p. 6.

53. See P. De Bolla, *The Discourse of the Sublime: Readings in History, Aesthetics, and the Subline* (Oxford: Basil Blackwell, 1989), and L. Poland, 'The Bible and the Rhetorical Sublime', in Warner (ed.), *The Bible as Rhetoric*, pp. 27-47.

54. Kennedy, *New Testament Interpretation through Rhetorical Criticism*, p. 158 with reference to Kenneth Burke.

For Burke it is an oxymoron to speak of literary mysticism or religious, that is, divinely inspired, discourse which claims to express, plausibly and persuasively, what is by nature ineffable.[55] What is being claimed here for a rhetorical criticism of the sublime in literature (religious or otherwise) has also been shown to apply to the experience and interpretation of music which makes audible the inaudible.[56]

Burke's analysis of the 'rhetorical radiance of the "divine"'[57] is concerned with the same issues that engaged Jewish and Christian sages in the pursuit of understanding 'the passion, sublimity, and grandeur of sacred discourse'.[58] Where Kennedy spoke of 'power', Shuger speaks

55. K. Burke, *A Rhetoric of Motives* (Berkeley: University of California Press, 1950), pp. 324-28. On speaking/writing the unspeakable, see S.A. Tyler, *The Unspeakable: Discourse, Dialogue, and Rhetoric in the Postmodern World* (Rhetoric of the Human Sciences; Madison: University of Wisconsin Press, 1987); M. Colomo, *Dai Mistici a Dante: Il linguaggio dell'ineffabilita* (Florence: La Nuova Italia Editricie, 1987); and S. Handelman, *The Slayers of Moses* (Albany: State University of New York Press, 1983). See also Swearingen's reference (*Rhetoric and Irony*, p. 291 n. 27) to the 'inexpressibility topoi' in medieval rhetorics, as noted by E.R. Curtis, *Europäische Literatur und Lateinisches Mittelalter* (Bern: Francke, 6th edn, 1967; ET *European Literature and the Latin Middle Ages* [trans. W.R. Trask; New York: Pantheon Books, 1953]); but our discussion is served not so much by the Unsagbarkeitstopoi (pp. 168-71), but by his excursus on Theologische Kunsttheorie in 17th century Spain (pp. 530-40).

56. See M.E. Bonds, *Wordless Rhetoric: Musical Form and the Metaphor of the Oration* (Cambridge, MA: Harvard University Press, 1991); M.R. Maniates, 'Music and Rhetoric: Faces of Cultural History in the Renaissance and Baroque', *Israel Studies in Musicology* 3 (1983), pp. 44-69; H.H. Unger, *Die Beziehung zwischen Musik und Rhetorik im 16.–18 Jahrhundert* (Würzburg, 1941); and C. Peter, *Rest and Repetition in Music* (trans. A. Stott; Stourbridge, England: Robinswood Press, 1992).

57. Burke, *A Rhetoric of Motives*, pp. 291-333.

58. Shuger, *Sacred Rhetoric*, p. 7. The classic study of the grotesque, the gruesome, dreadful or weird as an integral part of the sublime of the holy, the divine, or the apocalyptic, is by R. Otto, *The Idea of the Holy: An Inquiry into the Non-Rational Factor in the Idea of the Divine and its Relation to the Rational* (trans. J.W. Harvey; London: Oxford University Press, rev. edn, 1925). See also M. Eliade, *The Sacred and the Profane* (trans. W.R. Trask; New York: Harcourt, Brace, Jovanovich, 1959).

R.M. Rilke reflected this post modern perception of the sublime in the opening of his *Duineser Elegien* when he saw the essence of every encounter between the human and the divine to be terrifying (*das Schöne ist nichts/als des Schrecklichen Anfang,*

of 'affective strength' of the Bible's grandeur or sublimity.[59] In articulating the rhetoric of religion, three aspects converge in early modern times into a coherent concept of a 'sacred rhetoric': (1) the usefulness of certain categories of Hellenistic (as distinct from Roman) rhetoric with its 'numinous and sacral cast'; (2) the emphasis on the importance of 'the connection between emotions and...stylistic features in sacred texts; and (3) the pivotal role of the imagination, what the Greeks called *phantasía*, in generating emotions and thought about God, or love and knowledge of God.[60] For an example of how the canons of ancient religious literary style were skillfully, that is, rhetorically, used by biblical authors, the rhetoric of the Fourth Gospel is particularly interesting.[61]

What contemporary rhetorical theory has contributed to the reshaping of rhetorical criticism applied to biblical interpretation is ultimately this: the task of interpreting religious literature theologically, ethically or spiritually is

> no longer restricted to self-conscious questions of validity or eternal verities, but turned to the discovery of interpretations or new combinations within the body of [the rhetorical topics] that constitute [the] common store of 'facts' and 'evidence' [familiar to biblical culture] that will allow

---

den wir noch grade ertrangen, / und wir bewundern es so, weil es gelassen verschmäht, / uns zu zerstören. Ein jeder Engel ist schrecklich).

J. Faur (*Golden Doves with Silver Dots*, 1985, p. xxv) speaks of God as the one who 'functions as the final difference that escapes articulation and identification'.

59. On the role of the sublime in modern psychoanalysis, see N. Hertz, *The End of the Line: Essays on Psychoanalysis and the Sublime* (New York: Columbia University Press, 1985); J. Kristeva, *Powers of Horror: An Essay on Abjection* (trans. L.S. Roudiez; European Perspectives; New York: Columbia University Press, 1982) and J.-F. Lyotard, 'The Sublime and the Avant-Garde', in A. Benjamin (ed.), *The Lyotard Reader* (Oxford: Basil Blackwell, 1989), and his essay 'L'interêt du sublime', in J.-F. Courtine *et al.* (eds.),. *Du Sublime* (Paris: Belin, 1988), pp. 149-77.

60. Shuger, *Sacred Rhetoric*, p. 11.

61. See F. Thielman, 'The Style of the Fourth Gospel and Ancient Literary Critical Concepts of Religious Discourse', in Watson (ed.), *Persuasive Artistry*, pp. 169-83; see also the pioneering study by E. Norden, *Agnostos Theos: Untersuchungen zur Formgeschichte religiöser Rede* (Leipzig, 1913; repr. Darmstadt: Wissenschaftliche Buchgesellschaft, 1956).

[the biblical authors as well as the biblical interpreter] to discover new 'facts' and relations in what gets written...[62]

whether by the biblical author, or by biblical exegetes as rhetorical critics.

Conclusion

Muilenburg and Kennedy, while different in many ways, had one thing in common: both were gifted teachers who inadvertently generated a 'school' of rhetorical criticism of biblical exegesis. For reasons worth contemplating, two other gifted teachers of rhetoric, Walter Jens in Germany and Chaim Perelman in Belgium, while equally effective in generating 'schools' of their own, nevertheless failed to have any impact on European biblical exegesis. For Hillis Miller, however,

> it is in principle impossible to institutionalize [the rhetorical study of literature]... to make it into a 'method' with practical rules and procedures that can be passed on from teacher to student. The study of the rhetoric of literature [whether secular or sacred] is not a 'method' of reading in this sense. As soon as [it] is formalized in this way... it is dead.[63]

For Martin Medhurst,

> the possibilities of coming to know such a complex work of rhetorical and literary artistry as the Bible are infinite, resisting all systems, paradigms, models, or theories. Just when we think we understand, TL (shorthand for 'the Lord' in Burke's logological universe) appears to remind us: 'It's more complicated than that'.[64]

To approach biblical exegesis in the light of the history and historicity of rhetoric, we come to reaffirm what was said a generation ago by Edwin Black in a book which 'dethroned neo-Aristotelian criticism':[65] 'We have not evolved any *system* of rhetorical criticism,

---

62. T. Conley, *Rhetoric in the European Tradition* (White Plains, NY: Longman, 1990), p. 289.

63. Miller, 'Is There an Ethics of Reading?', p. 100.

64. M.J. Medhurst, 'Rhetorical Dimensions in Biblical Criticism: Beyond Style and Genre', *Quarterly Journal of Speech* 72 (1991), pp. 214-26 (225).

65. M.C. Leff and M.O. Procario, 'Rhetorical Theory in Speech Communication', in T.W. Benson (ed.), *Speech Communication in the 20th Century* (Carbondale: Southern Illinois University Press, 1985), pp. 3-27 (15).

but only, at best, an orientation to it...We simply do not know enough yet about rhetorical discourse to place our faith in *systems*, and it is only through imaginative criticism that we are likely to learn more'.[66]

More recently another veteran rhetorical critic, Wayne Booth, put it this way: 'no one to my knowledge has ever developed a fully articulated rhetorical criticism adequate to the "structures of appeal" in works like [the Bible]'.[67] And yet, even if rhetorical theory were to succeed in developing rhetorical criticism as a method, it would remain valid that 'no critical principles can prevent misreading',[68] just as traffic laws and their enforcement cannot prevent bad driving.

Another veteran rhetorical critic, Carl Joachim Classen, observed in his conclusion about the merits of rhetorical criticism for biblical exegesis that the successful or profitable use of any and all aspects of rhetorical theory in its application to biblical criticism depends ultimately on the critical discernment of the interpreter, and her or his relationship to an interpretive community (or to more than one!). This discernment is based on, and gets regenerated by, the interpreter's knowledge, experience, taste or sensitivity.[69]

The verdict is still out on just how successful and profitable the application of rhetorical theory has become in the rebirth of rhetorical criticism in today's practices of biblical interpretation. The biblical exegete has joined with other critical scholars in combatting 'uncompromising and irreducible philosophic [and, we may add,

---

66. E. Black, *Rhetorical Criticism: A Study in Method* (New York: Macmillan, 1965; repr. Madison: University of Wisconsin Press, 1978), p. 177, emphasis added.

67. W.C. Booth, *Critical Understanding: The Powers and Limits of Pluralism* (Chicago: University of Chicago Press, 1979), p. 307. The eight 'structures of appeal' indigenous to fictional literature, as outlined by Booth (pp. 307-14), differ from, as overlap with, the structures of appeal found in religious literature. Whether the similarities in the structures of appeal found in both types of literature are few or many, the danger is to ignore or minimize the remaining difference between religious and fictional, let alone nonfictional literature, but also the remaining difference between the literatures of the different religions.

68. Booth, *Critical Understanding*, p. 277.

69. C.J. Classen, 'Paulus und die antike Rhetorik', *ZNW* 82 (1991), pp. 1-33 (33). For Miller ('The Triumph of Theory', p. 288) the day-to-day life and the 'social, class, institutional, professional, familial situations' of all three parties to interpretation need to be taking seriously and critically: the reader, the interpreter and 'those who are writing the theory'.

dogmatic theological] oppositions presented by all kinds of absolutism [and religious exclusivism]'. Perelman counted among these oppositions the 'dualism of reason and imagination, of knowledge and opinion, of irrefutable self-evidence and deceptive will, of a universally accepted objectivity and an uncommunicable subjectivity, of a reality binding on everybody and values that are purely individual'.[70] A new rhetoric and a new rhetorical criticism are in the process of emerging, and need to be cultivated, not once, nor once and for all, but ever anew, to enable readers of sacred scriptures to let the reading and critical study of those texts do its work: 'transforming society', or in Burke's terms aiming at 'identification through transformation'.

---

70. C. Perelman and L. Olbrechts-Tyteca, *The New Rhetoric: A Treatise on Argumentation* (trans. J. Wilkinson and P. Weaver; Notre Dame: University of Notre Dame Press, 1969), p. 510. See also Swearingen's concluding chapter 'Inscriptions of Self and the Erasure of Truth', in *Rhetoric and Irony*, pp. 215-54.

INDEXES

INDEX OF REFERENCES

OLD TESTAMENT

NEW TESTAMENT

INDEX OF AUTHORS

JOURNAL FOR THE STUDY OF THE NEW TESTAMENT

Supplement Series